THE ROUTLEDGE HISTORY HANDBOOK OF CENTRAL AND EASTERN EUROPE IN THE TWENTIETH CENTURY

Challenges of Modernity offers a broad account of the social and economic history of Central and Eastern Europe in the twentieth century and asks critical questions about the structure and experience of modernity in different contexts and periods.

This volume focuses on central questions such as: How did the various aspects of modernity manifest themselves in the region, and what were their limits? How was the multifaceted transition from a mainly agrarian to an industrial and post-industrial society experienced and perceived by historical subjects? Did Central and Eastern Europe in fact approximate its dream of modernity in the twentieth century despite all the reversals, detours and third-way visions? Structured chronologically and taking a comparative approach, a range of international contributors combine a focus on the overarching problems of the region with a discussion of individual countries and societies, offering the reader a comprehensive, nuanced survey of the social and economic history of this complex region in the recent past.

The first in a four-volume set on Central and Eastern Europe in the twentieth century, it is the go-to resource for those interested in the 'challenges of modernity' faced by this dynamic region.

Włodzimierz Borodziej is Professor of History at Warsaw University, Poland.

Stanislav Holubec is a researcher at the Institute of History of the Czech Academy of Sciences, Prague.

Joachim von Puttkamer is Professor of Eastern European History at the Friedrich Schiller University Jena, Germany and Co-Director of the Imre Kertész Kolleg, Germany.

The Imre Kertész Kolleg at the Friedrich Schiller University in Jena is an institute for the advanced study of the history of Eastern Europe in the twentieth century.

The Kolleg was founded in October 2010 as the ninth Käte Hamburger Kolleg of the German Federal Ministry for Education and Research (BMBF). The directors of the Kolleg are Professor Joachim von Puttkamer and Dr Michal Kopeček. Professor Włodzimierz Borodziej was the Kolleg's co-director from 2010 to 2016 and is now chairman of its advisory board.

THE ROUTLEDGE TWENTIETH CENTURY HISTORY HANDBOOKS

The Routledge History Handbook of Central and Eastern Europe in the Twentieth Century
Volume 1: Challenges of Modernity
Edited by Włodzimierz Borodziej, Stanislav Holubec and Joachim von Puttkamer

The Routledge History Handbook of Central and Eastern Europe in the Twentieth Century
Volume 2: Statehood
Edited by Włodzimierz Borodziej, Sabina Ferhadbegović and Joachim von Puttkamer

For more information about this series, please visit: www.routledge.com/The-Routledge-Twentieth-Century-History-Handbooks/book-series/RHHC20.

THE ROUTLEDGE HISTORY HANDBOOK OF CENTRAL AND EASTERN EUROPE IN THE TWENTIETH CENTURY

Volume 1: Challenges of Modernity

Edited by
Włodzimierz Borodziej, Stanislav Holubec
and Joachim von Puttkamer

LONDON AND NEW YORK

First published 2020
by Routledge
2 Park Square, Milton Park, Abingdon, Oxon OX14 4RN

and by Routledge
52 Vanderbilt Avenue, New York, NY 10017

Routledge is an imprint of the Taylor & Francis Group, an informa business

© 2020 selection and editorial matter, Włodzimierz Borodziej, Stanislav Holubec and Joachim von Puttkamer; individual chapters, the contributors

The right of Włodzimierz Borodziej, Stanislav Holubec and Joachim von Puttkamer to be identified as the authors of the editorial material, and of the authors for their individual chapters, has been asserted in accordance with sections 77 and 78 of the Copyright, Designs and Patents Act 1988.

All rights reserved. No part of this book may be reprinted or reproduced or utilised in any form or by any electronic, mechanical, or other means, now known or hereafter invented, including photocopying and recording, or in any information storage or retrieval system, without permission in writing from the publishers.

Trademark notice: Product or corporate names may be trademarks or registered trademarks, and are used only for identification and explanation without intent to infringe.

British Library Cataloguing-in-Publication Data
A catalogue record for this book is available from the British Library

Library of Congress Cataloging-in-Publication Data
Names: Borodziej, Włodzimierz, editor. | Ferhadbegović, Sabina, editor. | Puttkamer, Joachim von, editor.
Title: The Routledge history handbook of Central and Eastern Europe in the twentieth century / edited by Włodzimierz Borodziej, Sabina Ferhadbegović and Joachim von Puttkamer.
Other titles: Central and Eastern Europe in the twentieth century
Description: New York : Routledge, 2019- | Series: Routledge twentieth century history handbooks | Volume 1 title information from publisher's website. | Includes bibliographical references and index. | Contents: [Volume 1. The Challenges of Modernity] —Volume 2. Statehood —
Identifiers: LCCN 2019049033 (print) | LCCN 2019049034 (ebook) | ISBN 9781138301665 (hardback) | ISBN 9780367822118 (ebook)
Subjects: LCSH: Europe, Central—Politics and government—1989- | Europe, Eastern—Politics and government—1989- | Post-communism—Europe, Central—History—20th century. | Post-communism—Europe, Eastern—History—20th century.
Classification: LCC DAW1051 .R68 2019 (print) | LCC DAW1051 (ebook) | DDC 943.009/04—dc23
LC record available at https://lccn.loc.gov/2019049033
LC ebook record available at https://lccn.loc.gov/2019049034

ISBN: 978-1-138-30164-1 (hbk)
ISBN: 978-0-367-37606-2 (ebk)
ISBN: 978-0-367-51865-3 (set)

Typeset in Bembo
by Swales & Willis, Exeter, Devon, UK

CONTENTS

Series introduction ... vii
    Włodzimierz Borodziej and Joachim von Puttkamer
Acknowledgements ... ix
List of figures ... x
List of tables ... xi
List of maps ... xiv
List of abbreviations ... xv
List of contributors ... xvii
Volume introduction: challenges of modernity ... xx
    Włodzimierz Borodziej, Stanislav Holubec and Joachim von Puttkamer

1. Urban and rural development in Eastern Europe ... 1
    Błażej Brzostek and Ivana Dobrivojević Tomić

2. Social structure, mobility and education ... 64
    Zsombor Bódy and Stanislav Holubec

3. Transport, infrastructure and communication ... 129
    Luminiţa Gatejel and Jerzy Kochanowski

4. Women between the public and private spheres ... 183
    Kateřina Lišková and Stanislav Holubec

5. Population and family ... 235
    Stanislav Holubec and Béla Tomka

6	Economic development *Jerzy Łazor and Bogdan Murgescu*	313
7	Consumption and leisure in twentieth-century Central and Eastern Europe *Béla Tomka*	385

Index   444

SERIES INTRODUCTION

What were the central twentieth-century experiences for Eastern European societies? Depending on whom you ask and depending on which country their thoughts intuitively drift towards, the answer is likely to be quite different. The answer could refer to significant dates, such as the 1939 Molotov-Ribbentrop Pact, the 1956 Hungarian uprising, the Prague Spring of 1968 or the year of Solidarity in 1980–1981. It could also revolve around the experiences in various countries – the Stalinist deportations left deep scars in the Baltic states, as did the wars of the 1990s in former Yugoslavia. The thoughts of a Western European are likely to jump to 1989 and the collapse of communist rule – perhaps also to the disappointed (or at least unlikely) prospects of a unified Europe. Hopefully, he or she might learn something from this volume.

As that Western European will discover, there were particular as well as shared experiences. The volumes presented here focus on both, grouped around what the editors regard as central, overarching themes. To emphasize the experience of *Violence* (vol. 4) is just as obvious as prioritizing the manifold *Challenges of Modernity* (vol. 1) of a region that has often been described – and perceived by its own inhabitants – as the periphery of Europe. The need to address the transformation of *Statehood* (vol. 2) over the course of the century may initially seem less apparent, but it allows for an elucidation of profound changes and phenomena that are otherwise obscured in a discussion of the emergence and emancipation of modern nation-states. *Intellectual Horizons* (vol. 3) reflects the wealth of self-descriptions and self-localizations in and about the region.

What do these volumes offer the reader? Not an encyclopaedia of Central, Eastern and Southeastern Europe in the long twentieth century, but a series of essays written from different perspectives and life experiences. The authors live in Bulgaria, Germany, Canada, Austria, Poland, Romania, Serbia, Czechia, Hungary and the United States. They belong to different generations and milieus and often have vastly different conceptions of historiography and the writing of history. Therein lies – according to the editors – the appeal of these volumes.

The shared goal of these contributions is to tell the story of the 'suburbs' of Europe in the twentieth century; to tell how the story unfolded, how it was perceived within this region and how it can be interpreted today.

The authors were not given any methodological parameters to follow. Some contributions may seem conservative or even old-fashioned; others argue in the spirit of what, in many universities today, is considered mainstream. None of the authors, however, crosses the boundary beyond which they see traditional sources as nothing more than merely conceptual obstacles. If the present volumes provide a new impetus for a collective reflection on Eastern Europe, both in teaching and in research, then much will have been gained.

ACKNOWLEDGEMENTS

The present volume is the result of a collective endeavour and joint reflection on the transformations of Central and Eastern Europe throughout the twentieth century. Thinking through these processes was a highly rewarding undertaking for all those involved, and we hope it will be equally rewarding for the reader. The editors wish to thank all the authors for inspiring discussions during the conceptual phase and the writing process, and for their patience and cooperation during the editing process.

Bringing together international experts for a volume of this scope is in itself a challenge. Many people helped behind the scenes to give the manuscript its final shape. The editors would like to express their deep gratitude to all of them. Mark Adrian Bence translated parts of the chapter *Transport, infrastructure and communication* which was originally written in Polish; Allison Brown translated the parts that were written in German. Dr. Zoltán Cora translated the chapter *Family and demography*, and Attila Török translated *Consumption and leisure in twentieth-century Central and Eastern Europe* from Hungarian. Scotia Gilroy and Jasper Tilbury co-translated parts of the chapter *Urban and rural development in Eastern Europe* from Polish. Tom Lampert translated the chapter *Social structure, mobility and education* from German. We would also like to express our gratitude to Daniela Gruber for straightening out the tables and figures according to the publisher's guidelines and for her keen sense of oversight on important issues that would have otherwise gone unnoticed. Last but not least, Jaime Elizabeth Hyatt has managed the entire editing process with almost inexhaustible patience and cheerfulness. Without her diligent work, the entire undertaking might have fallen apart at several points. The responsibility for any remaining errors and flaws, of course, rests with us.

Finally, we would like to thank the German Federal Ministry of Education and Research for generously providing the project funding which has thus allowed us the unique opportunity to develop each of the four volumes in this series.

FIGURES

6.1	Aggregate Central and Eastern European per capita GDP at PPP, 1890–2010 (1990 Geary–Khamis international dollars)	319
6.2	Year-to-year percentage change in per capita GDP by region (1971–1990)	342
6.3	Oil import prices (1972–1989) (US dollars per barrel)	342
6.4	GDP per capita in Central and Eastern Europe, 1990–2010 (seven countries)	347
6.5	Romanian oil exports and export prices (1920–1938)	351
6.6	Students per 10,000 inhabitants (1950–2000)	357
6.7	HIHD growth and its composition in Central and Eastern Europe (including Russia), 1870–2007	359
6.8	GDP per capita in Central and Eastern Europe and Latin America in relation to Western Europe, 1890–2010 (in %)	379
6.9	HIHD in Central and Eastern Europe and Latin America in relation to Western Europe, 1890–2007	379

TABLES

2.1	Percentage distribution of the labour force according to economic sectors in Central, Eastern and Southeastern European countries in the twentieth century	68
2.2	Urban population in Central and Eastern Europe, 1920–2006 (in %)	74
2.3	Percentage of elites in Central and Eastern Europe, 1993	83
2.4	Distribution of the peasant agrarian population according to farm size in Hungary (including unpropertied groups) in 1935	104
2.5	Distribution of farms according to size in Romania in the late 1930s	104
2.6	Distribution of land according to ownership categories in Poland in 1925/26	104
2.7	Distribution of peasant family farms in Yugoslavia in 1931	105
2.8	Estimated rates of literacy in Central and Eastern Europe, 1900 and 1930 (in %)	113
2.9	University students in Central and Eastern Europe, 1920–2013 (in thousands)	115
3.1	Employment in transportation and freight in socialist countries, 1950–1972 (percentage of the total number of employees)	136
3.2	Length of railway lines in operation, 1950–2000	147
3.3	Structure of loads per type of transport, 1955–2000	148
3.4	Automobiles per 1,000 inhabitants, 1919–2012	158
3.5	Central and Eastern European airlines: loads transported, 1937–2010 (million tonne-kilometres)	166
3.6	Central and Eastern European airlines: passenger transport, 1937–2010 (millions passenger-kilometres)	167
3.7	Central and Eastern European airlines: number of planes, 1970–2000	169
3.8	Telephones per 1,000 inhabitants, 1920–1980	174
4.1	Proportion of female students at universities in Central and Eastern Europe, 1950–2010 (in %)	189

4.2	Female employment rates in Central and Eastern Europe, 1930–2010 (in %)	193
4.3	Labour force participation by gender in Central and Eastern Europe in 1990 and 2006 (in %)	196
4.4	Political positions held by women in Central and Eastern Europe, 1972–1975	201
4.5	Women in politics in Central and Eastern Europe in 2009 (in %)	203
5.1	Population growth in Central and Eastern Europe, 1920–2009 (in %)	242
5.2	Persons aged 0–14 in the population of Central and Eastern Europe, 1920–2000 (in %)	247
5.3	Proportions of the ethnic majority of populations in selected Central and Eastern European countries in 1930 and 2001 (as a percentage of the whole population)	257
5.4	Mean age of women at first marriage in Central and Eastern European countries, 1900–2010 (year)	270
5.5	Female celibacy in Central and Eastern European countries, 1900–2000 (percentage of women never married in the 45–54 age group)	271
5.6	Number of divorces per 10,000 married persons in Central and Eastern European countries, 1930–2000	276
5.7	Ratio of married and unmarried persons among women aged 25–34 in Central and Eastern European countries, 2000–2002	277
5.8	Extramarital births as a percentage of all births in Central and Eastern European countries, 1930–2010	278
5.9	Mean household size in Central and Eastern European countries, 1900–2010 (persons)	282
5.10	Percentage of solitary households among all households in Central and Eastern European countries, 1920–2010	283
5.11	Forms of legal patriarchy in Europe in the early twentieth century	289
5.12	Abortion rates in Central and Eastern European countries, 1960–1996 (induced abortions per 1,000 women aged 15–44)	301
6.1	Per capita GDP at present purchasing power (PPP) (1990 Geary–Khamis international dollars)	318
6.2	Rate of growth of per capita GDP, regional averages, 1870–2001	318
6.3	Central and Eastern European population and economic performance in comparison with Western Europe and the world, 1890–2010	320
6.4	HIHD, Central and Eastern Europe, 1890–2007	321
6.5	GDP per capita of CEE economies in 1890, 1900 and 1913 (1990 international Geary–Khamis dollars)	321
6.6	Growth of exports in CEE economies and European average, 1870–1910; level of exports per capita in 1910	322
6.7	Per capita industrialization levels in CEE (Great Britain in 1900 = 100)	325

6.8	Occupational structure in Central and Eastern European economies, 1910 (in %)	326
6.9	Agricultural productivity in various European countries, 1911–1936 (million calories produced yearly by a male agricultural labourer showing five-year averages around the given year)	329
6.10	Indices of manufacturing output, 1913–1929 (1913 = 100)	330
6.11	GDP per capita in Central and Eastern European economies, 1929–1938	330
6.12	Value of exports per ton in Bulgaria, Poland and Romania, 1929–1934 (1928 = 100)	331
6.13	Indices of GDP per capita in 1913 and the worst year of the Great Depression in each country (1929 = 100)	331
6.14	Export structure in selected countries, 1913–1937 (in %)	333
6.15	Level of industrialization per capita in CEE countries in 1910 and 1937 within their interwar borders (UK = 100)	335
6.16	Agricultural productivity in various European countries, 1948/52–1988/92 (in five-year averages, million calories produced yearly by a male agricultural labourer)	338
6.17	Crude steel production (in million tons)	338
6.18	Industrial output per capita (UK in 1900 = 100)	339
6.19	Per capita GDP at PPP (1990 international Geary–Khamis dollars)	340
6.20	Foreign debts of Central and Eastern European countries (in billion dollars)	343
6.21	Central and Eastern European per capita GDP at PPS in 2000–2014 (EU-28 average = 100)	349
6.22	Pollution in Poland compared with Western European and world averages	353
6.23	Historical Index of Human Development (HIHD)	358
6.24	Percentage of respondents who believe that the legal system will 'uphold [their] contract and property rights in business disputes'	362
6.25	Gross household income using Gini coefficient, 1890–2000	363
6.26	The role of state expenditure in net national product directly before the First World War	363
6.27	Transparency International Corruption Perceptions Index	369

MAPS

3.1   The railway network before 1914   141

ABBREVIATIONS

ACTA – Anti-Counterfeiting Trade Agreement
BAC – British Aircraft Corporation
BBC – British Broadcasting Corporation
CCIF – Consultative Committee for International Telephony
CEE – Central and Eastern Europe
CER – Cifarski elektronski računar/Digital Electronic Computer (Yugoslavia)
CFRNA – Compagnie Franco–Roumaine de Navigation Aérienne/The French-Romanian Company for Air Transport
CITSEE – The Europeanisation of Citizenship in the Successor States of the Former Yugoslavia
ČLS – Československá letecka společnost/Czechoslovak Air Force Company
CMEA/Comecom – Council for Mutual Economic Assistance
ČMLS – Czecho–Moravian airlines
Convair – Consolidated Vultee Aircraft Corporation
COP – Centralny Okręg Przemysłowy/Central Industrial Region of Poland
ČSA – České aerolinie/Czechoslovakian State Airlines
DVS – Direktsiya na vazdushnite saobshtenia/Directorate of Air Communications (Bulgaria)
FDI – Foreign Direct Investment
FIPRESCI – Fédération Internationale de la Presse Cinématographique/International Federation of Film Critics
GATT – General Agreement on Tariffs and Trade
GDP – Gross Domestic Product
GDP/c – Gross Domestic Product per Capita
GDR – German Democratic Republic
GNP – Gross National Product
HDI – Human Development Index
HDZ – Hrvatska Demokratska Zajednica/Croatian Democratic Union
HIHD – Historical Index of Human Development
IATA – International Air Transport Association
IBM – International Business Machines Corporation
ICAO – International Civil Aviation Organization

List of abbreviations

IFIs – International financial institutions
ILGA – International Lesbian, Gay, Bisexual, Trans and Intersex Association
IMF – International Monetary Fund
IPPF – International Planned Parenthood Federation
ITU – International Telecommunication Union
JAT – Jugoslovenski Aerotransport/Yugoslavian Airways
KLM – Koninklijke Luchtvaart Maatschappij/Royal Dutch Airlines
LARES – Liniile Aeriene Române Exploatate de Stat/Romanian State Airlines
LOT – Polskie Linie Lotnicze LOT/LOT Polish Airlines
LTL – Lithuanian litas (currency of Lithuania)
MALÉRT – Magyar Légiforgalmi R. T./Hungarian Airlines
MALÉV – Magyar Légiközlekedési Vállalat/Malév Hungarian Airlines
Maszovlet – Magyar–Szovjet Polgári Légiforgalmi Részvénytársaság/Hungarian–Soviet Joint-Stock Civil Aviation Company
NATO – North Atlantic Treaty Organization
NNP – Net National Product
OECD – Organisation for Economic Co-operation and Development
ÖLAG – Österreichische Luftverkehrs AG/Austrian Airlines
OSJD – Organization for Cooperation between Railways
PGR – Państwowe gospodarstwo rolne/State Agricultural Farm (Poland)
PHARE – Poland and Hungary: Aid for Restructuring of the Economies
PISA – Programme for International Student Assessment
PKP – Polskie Koleje Państwowe/Polish State Railways
PPP – Purchasing Power Parity
PPS – Purchasing Power Standard
SAPARD – Special EU Accession Programme for Agriculture and Rural Development
SARTA – Societatea Anonimă Română de Transporturi Aeriene/The Romanian Air Transport Society
SAS – Scandinavian Airlines
SED – Sozialistische Einheitspartei Deutschlands/Socialist Unity Party of Germany
SHS – The Kingdom of Serbs, Croats and Slovenes
SNNA – Serviciul Național de Navigație Aeriană/The National Air Navigation Service of Romania
TABSO – Transportno-aviatsionno balgaro-savetsko obedinenie/Bulgarian–Soviet Transport Aviation Corporation
TAROM – Transporturile Aeriene Române/Romanian Air Transport
TARS – Transporturi Aeriene Româno–Sovietice/Romanian–Soviet Air Transport
TEM – Trans-European North-South Motorway
TSCS – Trans-Siberian Container Service
UIC – International Union of Railways
UNECE – United Nations Economic Commission for Europe
UNHCR – United Nations High Commissioner for Refugees
USSR – Union of Soviet Socialist Republics
VCR – Video Cassette Recording
WHO – World Health Organization
ZRIPS – Zakona o registraciji istospolne partnerske skupnosti/Law on the Registration of Same-Sex Partnerships (Slovenia)

CONTRIBUTORS

Zsombor Bódy is the author of *Magyarország társadalomtörténete a két világháború között* ('A social history of Hungary in the interwar period', PPKE BTK 2013) as well as two other books on early twentieth-century Hungarian history and a number of articles in such journals as *Social History* and *Genèses*. He is editor of the volume *Háborúból békébe. A magyar társadalom 1918 után* ('From War to Peace: Hungarian Society After 1918', MTA TTI, 2018) and co-editor of *Korall Journal for Social History*. He teaches History and Sociology at Pázmány Péter Catholic University in Budapest.

Włodzimierz Borodziej is Professor of Modern History at Warsaw University. He was Co-Director of the Imre Kertész Kolleg in Jena (2010–2016) and is currently the chairman of the Kolleg's academic advisory board. His books include *The Warsaw Uprising of 1944* (English translation, Univ. of Wisconsin 2006), a seminal twentieth-century history of Poland (*Geschichte Polens im 20. Jahrhundert*, C.H. Beck 2010), and many key studies of Polish and Polish-German history. The two-volume monograph, which he co-authored with Maciej Górny, *Nasza Wojna. Imperia 1912–1916* (WAB 2014) and *Nasza Wojna: Narody 1917–1923* (WAB 2018) has been published in German as *Der Vergessene Weltkrieg: Europas Osten 1912–1923* (wbg Theiss 2018) and offers the most comprehensive account of the First World War in Central and Eastern Europe. An English translation is forthcoming.

Błażej Brzostek is the author of an innovative comparative urban study of Warsaw and Bucharest *Paryże innej Europy* ('Parises of the other Europe', WAB 2015) and a history of food culture in communist Poland *PRL na widelcu* ('People's Poland on a fork', Baobab 2010). He received the prestigious Polityka Prize for his first book, *Za progiem. Codzienność w przestrzeni publicznej Warszawy 1955–1970* ('Across the threshold: Everyday life in public space in Warsaw, 1955–1970', TRIO 2007). He is Assistant Professor of History at Warsaw University.

Ivana Dobrivojević Tomić is the author of *They Never Had It Better? Modernization of Everyday Life in Socialist Yugoslavia* (Museum of Yugoslav History 2014), *Selo i grad. Transformacija agrarnog društva Srbije 1945–1955* ('Village and city: The transformation of agrarian society in Serbia', ISI 2013) and *Državna represija u doba diktature kralja Aleksandra 1929–1935* ('State repression during the dictatorship of King Alexander', ISI 2006). She is a senior research fellow at the Institute of Contemporary History in Belgrade.

Luminița Gatejel recently published an innovative comparative study of consumerist practices under state socialism, *Warten, Hoffen und endlich Fahren. Auto und Sozialismus in der Sowjetunion, in Rumänien und in der DDR 1956–1989/91* ('Waiting, hoping and finally driving: Cars and socialism in the Soviet Union, Romania and the GDR', Campus 2014) and is co-author of *Verkehr in der DDR* ('Traffic in the GDR', with Andreas Becker, Landeszentrale f. polit. Bild. Thüringen 2017) Her current book project explores the life world of commerce between the Hapsburg, Russian and Ottoman Empires in the nineteenth century.

Stanislav Holubec is the author of *Ještě nejsme za vodou: Obrazy druhých a historická paměť v období postkomunistické transformace* ('Not yet out of the woods: Images of others and historical memory after 1989', Scriptorium 2015), co-editor of *From Revolution to Uncertainty: The Year 1990 in Central and Eastern Europe* (Routledge 2019) and has written and edited many other books and articles on communist-era and post-communist Czech history. From October 2010 to September 2016, he was a researcher at the Imre Kertész Kolleg Jena, responsible for the Challenges of Modernity research area. He is currently a researcher at the Department of 20th-Century History at the Institute of History of the Czech Academy of Sciences in Prague.

Jerzy Kochanowski has published widely on nineteenth- and twentieth-century Polish history and Polish–German relations. His most recent publications are the award winning *Rewolucja międzypaździernikowa. Polska 1956–1957* ('An inter-October-Revolution: Poland 1956–1957', Znak 2017) and *Through the Back Door: The Black Market in Poland, 1944–1989* (Peter Lang, 2017). Other books include the high school textbook *Deutschland, Polen und der zweite Weltkrieg* ('Germany, Poland and the Second World War', with Beate Kosmala, Deutsch-Polnisches Jugendwerk 2013) and *People on the Move: Forced Population Movements in Europe in the Second World War and its Aftermath* (with Pertti Ahonen et al., Bloomsbury 2008). From 2013 to 2019, he was Editor-in-Chief of the key journal *Przegląd Historyczny*; he is currently a Professor of History at Warsaw University.

Jerzy Łazor writes on twentieth-century economic history both in Poland and globally, concentrating on capital flows and the consequences of (political) migrations. He has recently published the award-winning *Brama na Bliski Wchód. Polsko-palestyńskie stosunki gospodarcze w okresie międzywojennym* ('A Gateway to the Middle-East: Polish-Palestinian economic relations in the interwar period', IPN 2016) and an edition of the memoirs of Poland's second president, Stanisław Wojciechowski (Muzeum Historii Polski, 2017). He is currently an Assistant Professor at the Warsaw School of Economics and is working on his new book project on the political economy of French capital in interwar Poland.

Kateřina Lišková is Associate Professor in Gender Studies and Sociology at Masaryk University Brno, Czech Republic. Her research is focused on gender, sexuality and the social organization of intimacy, particularly in Central and Eastern Europe. Her papers have recently appeared in such journals as *Sexualities* and *History of the Human Sciences*. Her most recent publication is *Sexual Liberation, Socialist Style: Communist Czechoslovakia and the Science of Desire, 1945–1989* (Cambridge University Press 2018).

List of contributors

Bogdan Murgescu is Director of the Centre for Administrative, Cultural, and Economic Studies and Professor of History at the University of Bucharest. He is the author of *Romania si Europa. Acumularea decalajelor economice 1500–2010* ('Romania and Europe: The accumulation of economic backwardness, 1500–2010', Polirom 2010) and many other books, articles and school textbooks on the history of Romania, the Ottoman empire, Ottoman–Romanian relations and recent historiography. He has held fellowships at the Humboldt University, the University of Pittsburgh and Central European University.

Joachim von Puttkamer is Co-Director of the Imre Kertész Kolleg and Chair of Eastern European History at the Friedrich Schiller University of Jena. He has published widely on the histories of nationalism, state-building and statehood, education, and security apparatuses, as well as on cultures of memory and political thought in the region. He is the author of the survey history *Ostmitteleuropa im 19. und 20. Jahrhundert* ('East Central Europe in the 19th and 20th centuries', Oldenbourg 2010), *1956 – (nieco) inne spojrzenie* ('1956: A somewhat different perspective', co-edited with Jerzy Kochanowski, Neriton 2016) and is co-editor of numerous publications including *From Revolution to Uncertainty: The Year 1990 in Central and Eastern Europe* (Routledge 2019) and *Catastrophe and Utopia: Jewish Intellectuals in Central and Eastern Europe in the 1930s and 1940s* (de Gruyter 2017).

Béla Tomka is Professor at the Department of History, University of Szeged, Hungary. His main research area is twentieth-century social and economic history with an emphasis on international comparisons. He is the author of *A Social History of Twentieth-Century Europe* (Routledge 2013, designated a Choice Outstanding Academic Title by the American Library Association). Tomka has published over 14 books on twentieth-century Hungarian and European social and economic history and is the recipient of numerous awards, grants and international fellowships.

VOLUME INTRODUCTION: CHALLENGES OF MODERNITY

Włodzimierz Borodziej, Stanislav Holubec and Joachim von Puttkamer

Spatial and temporal structures

How does one define a region with no clear-cut geographical borders? In the case of Central and Eastern Europe, a definition that takes into account both geography and history would seem to be most plausible. According to Paul Robert Magocsi, this region is an aggregate of three geographical zones.[1] The first part, the northern zone, covers the central part of the European plain.[2] It is the drainage basin for the rivers that flow into the Baltic Sea (Oder, Vistula, Neman, Daugava) and includes the western half of Ukraine, situated between the Carpathian Mountains and the Dnieper River. Historically, the zone's sheer size and swampy terrain presented obstacles to communication, and its exposure to the east left it vulnerable to invasion. Although culturally divided between Catholicism and Eastern Orthodoxy, the zone has a shared cultural legacy in the Polish-Lithuanian commonwealth.

The second zone, which Magocsi calls the Alpine-Carpathian zone, comprises the Pannonian Basin and the Bohemian Massif, as well as Slovenia, northern Croatia and northern Serbia. This zone roughly coincides with the territory of the former Habsburg Empire. Although Magocsi includes Austria in this zone, we chose not to include it in our analysis, because its history after 1945 differs radically from that of the rest of the region. In some parts of this zone, mountainous terrain and relative remoteness from the coast hindered communication with the outside world.

The third zone, the Balkans or Southeastern Europe, is bordered to the south by the Mediterranean Sea and to the north by the line formed by the Danube, Kupa and Sava rivers, which approximates the northern reach of the Ottoman Empire in the eighteenth and early nineteenth centuries. To a far greater extent than in the Alpine-Carpathian zone, mountains hampered economic development in this zone and, contrary to what modern maps may suggest, isolated its inhabitants from the outside world. The Balkan zone's proximity to Anatolia made it the first target of Ottoman expansion into Europe. However, in some cases the mountains

---

1 Paul Robert Magocsi, *Historical Atlas of East Central Europe* (Seattle: University of Washington Press, 1993).
2 The European plain is a much larger region, which is bordered by the Urals, the Carpathians, the Central European Highlands and the Pyrenees. Attempts by geographers to divide it into a North European and an East European plain reflect political and cultural, rather than geographical divisions.

provided defence against invasion. Thus, the zone's north-western coastline – more or less detached from its hinterlands – was culturally oriented towards the Catholic Mediterranean (Dalmatia). Owing to its geography, Montenegro was the only Balkan state to maintain its independence from the Ottoman Empire, yet it entered the twentieth century as a unique relic of the medieval world. Although Magocsi includes Greece in this zone, we decided to largely omit it from our considerations due to its early independence from the Ottoman Empire and its divergent history after 1945.

The roots of future development in all three zones can be found in their topographies. The geographical features of the first two zones were conducive to the development of agriculture, while the mountainous terrain of the Balkan zone can explain why it has retained its pastoral character. Geography also played a major role in the region's population development. In the early medieval period, the Balkan zone was more populated than the other two zones due to its proximity to the centres of the Roman and Byzantine Empires. However, as agriculture developed in the northern and Alpine-Carpathian zones, their populations eventually surpassed that of the Balkans. In the last 150 years, however, Southeastern Europe has caught up with the other two zones. In contrast to the late eighteenth century, when the combined population of the northern and Alpine-Carpathian zones was about three times that of the Balkans, the ratio is now almost one to one. This can be explained to a large degree by the delayed onset of demographic transition in Southeastern Europe and the greater potential for population growth in that zone.

The history of Central and Eastern Europe as a region with a common fate begins with the collapse of the great empires (Ottoman, Russian, Habsburg and German) and the subsequent creation of nation states. This process started in the Balkan zone, which was the least predisposed to such a development in terms of socio-economic factors, but local elites quickly filled the vacuum created by the disintegrating Ottoman Empire. The process of nation state-building intensified in 1918 and was later boosted by waves of ethnic cleansing from 1939 to 1948; it culminated in the division of Czechoslovakia and the ethnic cleansing that accompanied the dissolution of Yugoslavia from 1991 to 1999.

The region was the target of renewed imperial expansion after 1938, first by Nazi Germany and then by the Soviet Union. The unprecedented suffering of the local population under Nazi and Soviet domination led Timothy Snyder to coin the term, 'Bloodlands'.[3] As a satellite of the Soviet Union, the region became involved in an attempt to build a socialist variant of modernity. After the collapse of the Soviet Union, most of the area was incorporated into Western economic and power structures and tried to adopt capitalist forms of modernity. Based on the region's common history, the timeframe of our analysis approximates a 'long twentieth century', beginning with the disintegration of the great powers and the first attempts to industrialize and urbanize in the 1880s, and finishing with the region's integration into broader European structures and globalization processes in the 1990s and 2000s.

This approach, based as much on structural features as on political caesuras, has more advantages than disadvantages over the more widely known concept of the 'short twentieth century'.[4] While Eric Hobsbawm's 'short century' may be more neatly defined – beginning with the collapse of the great empires at the end of the First World War, and ending succinctly with the collapse of communism – it fails to take into account that many changes, particularly in the social and economic spheres, commenced in the late nineteenth century, as is described in this

---

3 Timothy Snyder, *Bloodlands: Europe Between Hitler and Stalin* (New York: Basic Books, 2010).
4 Eric Hobsbawm, *Age of Extremes: The Short Twentieth Century 1914–1991* (New York: Pantheon, 1995).

volume. Moreover, while marking 1989 as the end of the twentieth century may have been appropriate when Hobsbawm wrote his *Age of Extremes* (1994), in 2016, it would hardly be acceptable to exclude the last quarter of a century considering that the events after 2000, such as accession to the EU or the financial crisis, have shown the notion of an 'end to history', popular in the early 1990s, to be premature.

On terms, or the rejection of normativity

Near the end of the 1990s, perhaps in 1997, a man by the name of Kurt Drawert took a train through Poland. The land was familiar to him; he had grown up in the GDR. He would later write that the subversive intellectual climate of the 1970s had repeatedly led him to seek refuge further east. He now anticipated a journey through time, a renewed encounter with former longings, but one filled with the scents and moods of a youth under socialism. And that it was. The sallow faces, monotone clothing, the lively clamour of voices and the smell of tobacco, sweat and perfume in the cabin between Warsaw and Poznan were indistinguishable from those on the regional train between Halle and Leipzig 30 years hence, were it not for one passenger relentlessly fiddling about on his mobile phone. The Cracow market square awake from its deep slumber, blithe passers-by out on a stroll, a handful of nouveau riche beauties, and then the desolation, poverty and decay at the peripheries. Wide swathes of the country had missed the boat to modernity. But which modernity? As per Drawert's closing thoughts, the past of the East would not in fact link to the present. Indeed, upon the present 'are layered the slides of an expected future of the world.'[5]

This volume focuses on the economic and societal developments of the twentieth century in Central and Eastern Europe. If momentary snapshots like this cannot make do without an invocation of modernity, then it is even more true of the analysis of processes that span an entire century. However, we do owe the reader an explanation of the title.

While 'challenges' might generally be understood, 'modernity' (along with its kin, 'modernization') is amongst the most controversial terms in the social and human sciences. Moreover, modernity has its own tradition – not necessarily linked to research – in individual national cultures and languages, as well as in art and architecture. The term was perhaps most commonly used from the 1950s to the 1980s as the antithesis to 'traditionality'. It harbours the explicit hope of overcoming backwardness and a strong belief in progress, which has deflated significantly over recent decades.

This transatlantic history of the term is not our topic. We understand modernity as a reference point for an utmost value-neutral euphemism for societal transformation. Until 1939, it reflected Western inspiration; after 1945, its patterning developed in Moscow; and in 1989, the West returned to its traditional role as the benchmark of modernity.

The appropriation of patterning models in CEE varied from country to country. One volume is insufficient to document these differences either systematically or exhaustively. Nevertheless, with the aid of examples, the authors attempt to shed light on the specifics in each country. In a narrow sense, the economic history plays a role in this context, insofar as it has a say in these differences, yet falls short of determining them.

As a rule, the authors steer clear of value judgements in the sense of good and evil. Readers can decide for themselves the extent to which morality was a factor in the fundamental

---

5 Kurt Drawert, 'Polen, eine innere Reise', in *Spiegelland. Roman Prosa Material* (Wiesbaden: Luxbooks, 2014), 425–42 (Originally appeared in Frankfurter Rundschau, 28 March 1998).

transformation of worlds that transpired between the start of the twentieth century and the start of the twenty-first. When infant mortality drops from 1 in 10 newborns to 1 in 1,000, average life-expectancy rises from 40 to 70 years, and illiteracy ceases – decades ago – to be a relevant aspect of society, a new phenomenon is upon us. This volume makes tangible this phenomenon's convergence to the norm.

The authors ascribe to various schools. Some consider the recently scorned invocation of backwardness to be a truism, while others shun it. Some prefer to follow the lines of interpretation of traditional social history, while others have interiorized the cultural turn. Common to them all, however, is the conviction that modernity is always bound to time and place, as well as dependent on the status and flow of information.

While this insight into the limited validity of one's own depiction has its roots in the professional self-perception of the historian, who continually contextualizes facts and processes, it may not be inconsequential that these texts were written in the last three years, when all concepts of an end to history – including that of CEE – were pronounced dead.

In this spirit, we believe in presenting a provisional assessment with an open outlook to the future, the validity of which will be tested again and again over the coming decades. Whether 'the slides of an expected future of the world' are perceptible in the disruptions and tensions that Central and Eastern Europe are undergoing – even in this third decade since the fall of communism – is an open question, the answer to which is left to the reader.

1

URBAN AND RURAL DEVELOPMENT IN EASTERN EUROPE

Błażej Brzostek and Ivana Dobrivojević Tomić

In 1908, a group of farmers from a village near Warsaw went on an educational trip financed by a large research foundation, the Józef Mianowski Fund. They travelled from a province of the Romanovs' empire to a province of the Habsburgs' empire, from the former Republic of Poland to the former Czech kingdom. One of the farmers, a certain Teofil Kurczak, published his impressions. A train transported the peasants across the border to Cracow, the historical capital of Poland, where they were received with patriotic warmth and were given accommodation for the night. The next day, with their faces pressed to the train's windows, they observed the landscapes of Moravia. In Kurczak's words:

> We see, as far as the eye can reach, flat crops everywhere, grains are swaying evenly like a wave on the sea ... from border to border, as if perfectly trimmed, they stand in a solid wall that stretches across the entire field. How would our fields – which barely yield anything in the furrows and burn along the ridges – compare to these? They would be like squalor next to affluence! Oh, you poor, backwards Polish peasant! ... The villages we see up close and far away on the horizon are all white with houses built of brick and stone and, as we found out later, roofed with slate. At first we found it difficult to believe that these were villages, just town after town, and as for poor villages or wooden houses, especially those covered in straw – you simply don't see them.

Their impressions intensified during the two-week visit. Kurczak described village schools, the robustness of crops and cattle, the opulence of houses, the democratic relations between people ('they don't kiss women on the hand. Equality is equality'). The name of the Moravian town of Vyškov sounded the same as Wyszków, a town near Warsaw that was well known to Kurczak. But there was a difference:

> In ours it's dirty; foul-smelling sewage flows through the gutters; in the alleys, in the hallways, in the shops and stalls, filth assaults a passer-by's nose like some kind of acid ... and here – there's cleanliness everywhere, sewage flows through underground sewers ... all of the streets are lit with gas lamps; here and there, electric light can

even be seen in the windows ... Houses, some of them a few stories high, with large windows, with very clean hallways, painted ... In a word, the exemplary order of the civilized world can be seen everywhere here, while our towns present such a vision of poverty, slovenliness and mud that only hogs feel content there'.[1]

This 'order of the civilized world' was one of the aspirations taking root, clearly, in the consciousness of various social groups. While the elite considered the Western world as a model for civilization, for the peasant population it was, quite simply, the 'world', which could reveal itself even on a trip from Wyszków to Vyškov. The indicators of civilization were recognized in the quality of the crops, village houses, peasants' clothes and the cobblestones on the streets of towns. This concept also encompassed the character of relations between villages and cities, as well as the extent and character of urban development – reflecting social and economic order, the effectiveness of administration and probably a certain quality of life sometimes measured today by indices such as the World Happiness Report.

There were enough images of overpopulated, impoverished villages and small towns stinking of sewage in the vast areas of Eastern Europe to imagine the 'world' as their opposite. This world built industry, allowing emigrants from villages to earn money for food and impressing newcomers. In 1901, Dimitrie Marinescu, a typesetter from Bucharest, was awed by the factory chimneys he saw in the suburbs of Budapest. Of course, a large city also needed, in addition to chimneys, a rich history and monuments of national culture, aspects that other chimney-endowed cities – Lodz, in the Kingdom of Poland, springs to mind – nonetheless lacked. Budapest, as the capital city of a nation, put great effort into displaying attributes of this kind, with the aim – as Maciej Janowski writes – of diminishing the 'prestige deficit'.[2] In this respect, it achieved the highest status among all of the cities of Eastern Europe. In the eyes of the typesetter Marinescu the city appeared as a 'temple of beauty and civilization'.[3]

The splendour of the kingdom's capital was meant to illuminate the nation. Neighbouring capitals that emerged in the second half of the nineteenth century – Bucharest, Sofia and Belgrade – also constructed public buildings, drew up boulevards and established parks, though with less flair than Budapest, which dared to rival Vienna itself. In the local context, all of these cities could be considered metropolises, though they were not among the world's largest capital cities. At the turn of the twentieth century, the yardstick for being a large city was to have a million inhabitants. London was far beyond all of the others with 4.7 million (6.4 including the suburbs), while Paris had 2.7 million (3.3 with the suburbs). Of the capital cities that dominated the region that interests us, the smallest was Istanbul, which had reached one million inhabitants by 1900. Petersburg had 1.4 million residents (the same as Tokyo and Manchester), Vienna 1.7 million and Berlin 2.7 million (including its suburbs), which ranked it among the five largest cities of the world. At this time, Sofia and Belgrade each had about 70,000 inhabitants, and Bucharest 280,000. Budapest, this 'temple of beauty and civilization', was smaller than Vienna

---

1 Teofil Kurczak, *Pierwsza wycieczka włościan polskich do Czech i na Morawy w r. 1908-ym* [Polish peasants' first journey to Bohemia and Moravia] (Warsaw: Władysław Pepłowski, 1909), 9–10, 90–91.
2 Maciej Janowski, 'Stolica na peryferii: specyfika rozwoju wielkiego miasta w Europie Środkowo-Wschodniej' [The capital on the periphery: characteristic developments of the great cities in East Central Europe], in *Drogi odrębne, drogi wspólne: Problem specyfiki rozwoju historycznego Europy Środkowo-Wschodniej w XIX-XX wieku*, ed. Maciej Janowski (Warsaw: IH PAN, 2014), 368.
3 Dimitrie Marinescu, *Impresiuni de voiaj culese din Austro-Ungaria, Germania, Belgia și Franța* [Travel impressions collected from Austria-Hungary, Germany, Belgium and France] (Bucuresci: Tipografia 'Speranța', 1904), 3.

by one million inhabitants, but its population of 700,000 gave it a metropolitan status in the region. Warsaw was also nearly this size, but it lacked the qualities of a capital city. However, the size alone of the nation's primary city held an important place in people's imaginations. A Polish woman from Galicia wrote in 1911: 'We are a nation that has no worth in the world. We have disappeared ... And yet ... Warsaw ... A certain pride overcomes me when I'm in this city. Immensity, greatness, this language of mine heard everywhere, these hard-working hands of ours, this vast number of us, all together ... The shame which made me hang my head in the face of other nations has vanished'.[4]

Many of the nations of Eastern Europe did not have their own capital city. Some did not really have cities to speak of, with the overwhelming majority of the population living in villages, subject to the economic and political domination of the privileged few, as in the case of the Ruthenians in Galicia and the Slovakians in Upper Hungary. This constituted one of the many complications in relations between the village and the city and influenced the image of urbanity and the development of nationalism. The defining feature of these concepts was often an idealized, post-romantic image of a rural community most fully expressing the 'national spirit', in opposition to the city. Rivalry was very much alive between indigenous concepts, invoking the peasantry and countryside as the embodiment of a healthy society, and modernizing ones in which urbanization held the leading position, particularly in the first half of the twentieth century.

The desire for the 'order of the civilized world' was a profound aspiration of the elite. Villages, at least in terms of health and hygiene, were expected to try to resemble towns, and towns to follow the model of cities. The second half of the twentieth century, marked by the consequences of war, represented the triumph of modernization, both in endeavours to undertake material reconstruction (and restructuring) and in the ideology of so-called communist regimes. The triumph was perhaps superficial, especially against the backdrop of the various transformations that were occurring in Western Europe. The accelerated development that was inscribed in national plans was meant to free the East from economic dependence, primarily through the building of its own industrial base in conjunction with swift urbanization. Would it be, however, 'urbanization without modernization'?[5]

Dominated by the development of heavy industry and marked by constant shortages, a centrally controlled economy was not conducive to the development of the services that constituted an important element of urbanization. It was not able to satisfy the long-term needs of the masses who, in most countries of the region, flowed into cities, nor to fulfil the requirement (exhibited most strongly, perhaps, in Romania and Bulgaria) of effacing the cultural gap between the village and the city. Overpopulation in villages decreased due to increased migration, and poor areas shrank. At the same time, however, villages became based on collectivized farming, which ended in most countries at the beginning of the 1960s. The result was the perpetuation of economic dependence on agriculture and the dominance of cities, the supplying of which became a strategic goal of political leaders. However, in places where collectivization was permanently halted (Poland and Yugoslavia), villages remained areas of private economy in nations geared towards collective ownership. While in Western sociology the established opposition of the concepts of 'city' and 'village' could be challenged (for example, by Manuel Castells in *The Urban Question*, 1982), these concepts seemed to remain as antithetical in Central

---

4 Marcelina Kulikowska, *Z wędrówek po kraju* [From wanderings through the country] (Cracow: Spółka Nakładowa 'Książka', 1911), 132–33.
5 Jan Węgleński, *Urbanizacja bez modernizacji?* [Urbanization without modernization?] (Warsaw: Instytut Socjologii UW, 1992).

and Eastern Europe as before.[6] It is true that traditional folklore had survived in very few of its regions and that radio and television – information carriers that people had not even dreamed of at the beginning of the century – were reaching villages everywhere, serving as an indication of the massification of culture. However, in an economic and psychological sense, the village was still marked with the stigma of being second-rate, dependent on the city and 'backwards'. The road to the city remained a road of liberation, almost like in traditional cultures. On the other hand, cities were often plunged into deep crisis in the 1980s and remained dependent on villages, which supplied cities through unofficial routes with various goods – goods that were attractive in an economy plagued by shortages.

The following text is an attempt to investigate the relationship between the village and the city in Central and Eastern Europe – a relationship informed by both the real socio-economic standards of living and by the collective ideas about them.

We begin by outlining elements of the situation at the beginning of the twentieth century, when traces of feudal structures, scarcely noticeable in large cities, were still present in the provinces. These characterized, to a great extent, the mentalities of the landed gentry and the peasantry, groups tended more towards continuity rather than towards change, although – as shown by the example of Teofil Kurczak – there existed inclinations towards modernization among farmers (although few peasants were able, like Kurczak, to write accounts of their travels). Set against this conservative disposition towards preserving the existing resource of the land, which was often shrinking (in the case of landowners who were in debt and peasants who had to divide their fields), the expansionistic mindset of the middle-class elite contrasted sharply. This elite had already previously conquered the economic and cultural space of the West, as noted by Charles Morazé.[7] The bourgeoisie created a new type of life path, marked by a desire for success. Although the traditional East was expected to differ from the realities of England, France and Germany through its 'lack of a middle class', this group gained leading standard-setting importance there, as well. The beginning of the twentieth century was marked by numerous tensions connected with the aspirations of various social groups. The example of advancement demonstrated by the middle class had an effect on the attitudes of workers and even some peasants, who were distancing themselves from the conservative mindset and turning towards a vision of change for individual and communal fates.

Next, we attempt to depict the various consequences of this movement, into which collective ideas were inserted. It generated, on the one hand, rather paternalistic aspirations among the elite to improve the 'destiny of the common people', whose situation was examined by means of statistical tools, and, on the other hand – radical political programmes with a revolutionary undertone. The clash of projects and aspirations instigated from above and below marked social relations, including relations between the city and the village, during the first half of the twentieth century.

The second half of the century was divided from the first by the dramatic consequences of war and the establishment, usually by means of violence, of a political system that promised a break from the past and the effective elimination of conflicts between the city and the village, defined in terms of class war. Countries espousing the 'people's democracy' led their inhabitants into modernity, as it had been defined until then – into an economy dominated by cities and

---

6 Wanda Patrzałek, *Społeczne i ekonomiczne relacje miasto-wieś w okresie realnego socjalizmu i zmian systemowych w Polsce* [Social and economic relations between city and village during the period of real socialism and the regime change in Poland] (Wrocław: Uniwersytet Wrocławski, 1996), 8–9.

7 Charles Morazé, *Les bourgeois conquérants* (Paris: Editions Complexe, 1957).

industry. After the first, brutal phase (1945–1955), there ensued a certain stability, which created conditions for a generation of young emigrants from villages to achieve real advancement and feelings of social security, which would be recalled with nostalgia after 1989. However, this social revolution was led from above and, although to a great degree it fulfilled the expectations of the masses, it did not allow authentic manifestations of these expectations. What is more, it incapacitated farmers, depriving them, in most of these nations, of the possibility to freely farm the lands and influence prices. It also preserved the village–city dichotomy, which was full of resentment (the city 'taking away' the village's production, the village 'hiding' its earnings from the city, etc.). Andrzej Leder, when analyzing these phenomena (taking Poland as an example) using psychoanalytical concepts, seems to confirm what economists once noticed: alongside what appeared to be a quite sudden modernization, the old post-feudal relations and mental mechanisms were preserved. Leder calls this an 'industrial *folwark*'.[8]

Having been sustained for political reasons despite an increasingly evident crisis, this structure was eliminated after the political transformation of 1989. This elimination process became burdened with interpretations as well and was met with a very critical attitude, in which 'neoliberal reforms' were portrayed as further authoritarian restructuring of the social order from above, depriving a significant segment of society of autonomy. The transformation also signified new changes in relations between the city and the village, and one can regard the entry of the region's nations into the European Union, beginning in 2004, as a kind of closure. This belongs to the 'history of the present time'.

Heritage

Between Tallinn and Tirana, Prague and Chișinău, people settled in areas that were divided both naturally (by mountain ranges and rivers) and as a result of many centuries of political and socio-economic changes. These spheres differed from each other in the density of their populations and urbanization, their ethnic and religious characters, agricultural methods, the dominant building material that was used, and also – at least until the middle of the nineteenth century – their folklore. There were differences between them that were often so fundamental that describing the region as some kind of cohesive whole would have been questionable. How much did the *bordei*, a Wallachian dugout peasant hut, have in common with the impressive house of a Saxon farmer living on the other side of the Carpathian Mountains? Or a *kurna chata* on Polish lands, with wood smoke coming out of a hole in the straw roof, with the brick house of a Moravian farmer? Equally significant differences were present between terrains with vineyards and terrains where vodka was bootlegged from potatoes or rye, or between the isolated regions of swamps and peat bogs, where a natural economy prevailed – Polesia or the delta of the Danube River – and the open, commercially active villages of Silesia. In many cases, it was not necessary to travel 400 kilometres, as Teofil Kurczak did, in order to discover the 'civilized world'. Not many kilometres separated the wooden Kurpie villages on the peripheries of the Polish lands annexed by Russia from the brick-and-stone houses of farmers in Eastern Prussia, who used electric machines and drank coffee. The concept of civilization was not connected solely to the material level of life, however. It had wider implications, important in an era when people were thinking in terms of national categories and searching for ancestral roots in distant history.

---

8 Andrzej Leder, *Prześniona rewolucja. Ćwiczenie z logiki historycznej* [Sleepwalking through a revolution: an exercise in the logic of history] (Warsaw: Krytyka Polityczna, 2014), 192–4.

To the south of the Danube, from Austria to Dobruja, vestiges remained of an ancient settlement, which became increasingly important in the nineteenth century in the international competition for prestige. Nations were eager to combine the modern achievements of civilization with traces of a noble past. While Paris discovered its Lutetia and Vienna invoked Vindobona, Budapest found Aquincum, and Romania exhibited the remains of Tomis in Constanta. The antiquity of urbanization became an essential cultural and political factor, perhaps especially at a time when the current state of development did not correspond with the ambitions of the elite. In Romania in the 1930s, there emerged the idea of reorganizing the urban network, the significant centres of which – named 'municipia' after the Roman model – were meant to be reconstructed, with centrally located market squares surrounded by monumental public buildings.[9] This signified the taming of the spatial chaos that was characteristic of cities that had been under Ottoman rule.

With the exception of some stone-and-brick cities – former Venetian colonies on the coast of the Adriatic – the entire southern part of the region from the Adriatic to the Black Sea had been under the administration or authority of Turkey in modern times. The trajectory of trade routes, locations of fortresses, control of settlement and migration, as well as the characteristics of the empire's system of rule, affected the character of the network of cities and villages. This influence has remained clearly visible in the territory of present-day Hungary. To the west of the former Turkish border, a Central European agricultural model developed, a rather homogeneous network of average-sized towns and small villages; while to the east of the border, the population coalesced in scarcer rural clusters that were substantial in size (also called agricultural towns) and in scattered farms.

A feature of the 'oriental' model of urbanization was the lack of the Western style of municipal law. Towns grew spontaneously through the joining of various neighbourhoods, each containing a cluster of diverse nationalities specializing in specific types of trade or craftsmanship. To a newcomer, these towns looked similar, scarcely differentiated from one another in the chaos of their arrangement, the tangled network of streets and the lack or low number of public buildings.[10] The town of Ruse was described in *The Tongue Set Free* by Elias Canetti, who was born there in 1905, as a town of seven languages, with Turkish and Sephardic Jewish neighbourhoods supplemented by Greeks, Armenians, Romanians, Russians and Bulgarians, mostly coming from villages. Constanta, Braila, Sarajevo and Skopje were similar to Ruse. The 'foreign' character of the towns gave rise to a backlash of chauvinism in the nineteenth century. Mihail Eminescu described Romanian cities as settlements of 'riff-raff from the East and West – Greeks, Jews and Bulgarians', from whom 'our liberals' developed.[11] These liberals were responsible for the abrupt Westernization of the country, most clearly visible in large cities. A similar 'foreignness' of the cities, not only ethnic, but also ethical, was stressed in 1827 by Vuk Stefanović Karadžić:

> There are no members of the Serbian nation but peasants. The small number of Serbs who live in town as traders and craftsmen are called townsmen. They wear Turkish

---

9 This concept was revived under communist rule, when the Roman names Napoca and Drobeta were added to the names Cluj and Turnu-Severin.

10 Alexandra Yerolympos, 'A New City for a New State: City Planning and the Formation of National Identity in the Balkans (1820s–1920s)', *Planning Perspectives* 8 (1993): 233–57, here 236.

11 Kazimierz Jurczak, 'Między akceptacją a odrzuceniem: Kultura rumuńska wobec Wschodu i Zachodu' [Between acceptance and rejection: Romanian culture's views on the East and the West], in *Współcześni historycy Polscy o Rumunii*, ed. Tadeusz Dubicki (Toruń: Adam Marszałek, 2009), 340–61.

costumes and live according to the Turkish way of life; during rebellions and wars they shut themselves up with the Turks in the towns, or run away to Germany with their money; for this reason they are not called Serbs by the people and are despised by them. The Serbs, as peasants, live only from land and livestock.[12]

In this citation, the connection between the city and money seems typical, as well as the connection between money and a lack of national spirit. This foreignness, precisely, was the foundation for the development of prejudices against cities, as well as for all of the justification theories in which the infection of cities by a foreign element was presented as a cause of national economic and political misery.

Similar anti-city attitudes had a solid foundation in most of the cultures of Eastern Europe. Jerzy Jedlicki writes that it was connected to the gentry's aversion to profiteering (identified with trade and banking), cosmopolitanism (appearing as a threat in an era when national sentiments were growing) and the West. The city was a foreign body, existing according to separate rules, morally inferior, causing cultural depravity.[13] Prejudices of this kind also found support in the Romantic imagination and, later, in fears connected to the consequences of industrialization.

A different kind of relationship with the city was inherent in peasant culture. It was characterized by a strong ambivalence. On the one hand, the city was worthy of admiration. Urban houses and people overshadowed everything that was rural. Peasants got lost in the city and became objects of ridicule, although perhaps to a lesser extent in the Balkans than in Central Europe. Connected to this was also a negative image of the city: teeming with fraud and vice, set against the kindness and sincerity of rural people. It was possible, however, to travel to the city and try to emulate the city-dwellers, and either become wiser and richer, or, on the contrary, fall victim to theft or moral decay.[14] Yet, a city-dweller visiting a village played a different role in this *imaginarium*. He was a person with money, welcome as a summer holidaymaker in the villages where the inhabitants had become accustomed to serving the recreational needs of the nearby city, but he was treated in other regions with distrust. There were also those who came to the villages for money: civil servants, for example, were associated with tax collection and inspired fear and hostility. Local authorities – priests, teachers and doctors – had an intermediary position between rural and urban culture, to a certain extent. Female teachers had a distinct position, presenting a different model of femininity, weak in relation to village society, but endowed as well with a certain privilege. A similar role was played by the female ethnographer, the 'city lady' with white hands, accepted by the community.[15] There existed, of course, a disparity between such a newcomer from the 'world' (in general identified with the city) and the more familiar intermediary between the village and the local market, or small town. Small

---

12 Vuk Stefanović Karadžić, in *Danica II* (Vienna, 1827); quoted according to Joel Halpern, 'Farming as a Way of Life: Yugoslav Peasant Attitudes', in *Soviet and East European Agriculture*, ed. Jerry F. Karcz (Berkeley, CA: University of California Press, 1967), 356–81, here 357–8.

13 Jerzy Jedlicki, *Świat zwyrodniały. Lęki i wyroki krytyków nowoczesności* (Warsaw: Wydawnictwo Sic!, 2000), 83–112 [in English: Jerzy Jedlicki, *A Degenerate World*, ed. Elena Rozbicka, trans. Tristan Korecki (Frankfurt a.M.: Peter Lang Verlag der Wissenschaften, 2016)].

14 Nikołaj Pańkow, '"Podróż do miasta" jako motyw tematyczny w ludowych kulturach słowiańskich' ['The journey to the city' as a thematic motif in Slavic folk cultures], in *Miasto i kultura ludowa w dziejach Białorusi, Litwy, Polski i Ukrainy* (Cracow: Międzynarodowe Centrum Kultury, 1996), 29–42.

15 Kazimiera Zawistowicz-Adamska, *Społeczność wiejska: Wspomnienia i materiały z badań terenowych, Zaborów 1937–1938* [Village society: memoirs and field research materials, 1937–1938] (Warsaw: Ludowa Spółdzielnia Wydawnicza, 1958).

towns could not generally provide a person from a village the same opportunities for social advancement that a distant, large city could, but were associated with the circulation of money and with taverns, and also – in many cases – with a foreign ethnic and religious element.

The above-mentioned multi-ethnic urbanization was not a phenomenon that was specific to the Balkans. It emerged in the nineteenth century as a characteristic of Eastern Europe as a whole. Observers have connected it with the weak development of the local 'third state', which, in turn, is assumed to have resulted from the domination of the nobility, which preserved *folwarks*, blocked the movement of rural people and resisted industrialization. The development of cities in the Polish Kingdom was made possible by the actions of the central administration and a protectionist policy, and was facilitated, at least at the beginning, through German immigration (primarily to cities that were important centres of the textile industry) and then Jewish immigration. The city of Lodz developed in this way, where German, Jewish and Polish communities co-existed, albeit with very unequal capital assets. The complicated relations between the social classes and ethnic-religious groups in this city were depicted at the end of the nineteenth century by Władysław Reymont in his novel *The Promised Land*. Another factor that increased the ethnic characteristics of urbanization was the politics of the empires whose vast peripheries constituted the region we are examining. The development of Jewish settlements in the last quarter of the nineteenth century and the proliferation of *shtetls* in the territory of present-day Belarus, Lithuania, Ukraine, Poland, Romania, Moldova and Russia resulted, to a great extent, from the politics of the Russian empire, which established an area for Jewish settlement and forced mass migration. The larger urban centres of these regions had much in common with the above-mentioned 'oriental' cities. In both, various ethnic groups converged, often living quite isolated from each other: Jews, Poles, Belarusians, Russians, Tatars and Roma; and in this case, some groups (such as Belarusians) seemed closer to the rural environment, while others (such as Jews) were closely bound to the urban world.[16]

Both the industrial city and the *shtetl* were nineteenth-century phenomena, when city–village and nation–city relationships had significantly older references. The network of cities in this part of Europe gained its fundamental shape in the late Middle Ages – in the lands of present-day Czech Republic, Slovakia, Poland and Hungary, as well as in Transylvania, under the influence of German law and settlement. A symbol of this influence was Magdeburg, one of the German 'gates to the East' on the Elbe, first a missionary centre, then a model for municipal law. Colonial cities were established on the basis of this law and were given regular networks of streets and a centrally located market square with a town hall, surrounded by walls. These became, to the north-west of the Carpathians, a defining image of urbanity. German colonists were drawn by Czech, Hungarian and Polish dukes and kings to lands that were in need of commercial stimulation, lands that were ravaged by war. A powerful influence on the shaping of towns also came from the Teutonic Order on the Baltic Sea, which developed, from Malbork to Ludza, a civilization of brick castles and fortified towns. The German influences were a consequence of many scattered actions, though German historiography treated them in the nineteenth century as coherent, and even inevitable. This influence subsequently became a factor in the legitimization of the concept of *Mitteleuropa* and, later, of expansion of the Nazi regime. Scholarly research was carried out in order to confirm the legitimacy of this expansion, such as the research conducted by the Institute of German Work in the East beginning in 1940, organized in *Krakau, die alte deutsche Stadt* (Cracow, the old German city).

---

16 A.S. Zamoysky, *Transformatsiya mestechek Sovetskoy Byelorusii 1918–1939* [The transformation of small towns in Soviet Belarus 1918–1939] (Minsk: I.P. Logvinov, 2013), 35–57.

Cracow, in fact, having been only slightly transformed by industrialization, with its late medieval structure still preserved, seemed to correspond to the idealized vision of the city that had formed among German 'folkists' (traditionalists) and had been partially adopted by national socialists. These ideas reflected a cohesive urban community cultivating craftsmanship and trades, protecting itself from cosmopolitan foreignness and harmoniously connected with an agricultural supply network. This was a reaction to the nineteenth-century experience of heavy industrialization, which in the course of only one generation, had changed the landscape of north-western Europe. This type of reaction appeared first in England, where anti-urban movements invoked images of rustic idylls with the slogan 'return to the village'. They evolved towards the designing of new city districts and neighbourhoods in a way that was intended to weaken the contrast between the city and the village, providing inhabitants with the comforts of civilization and simultaneously with contact to nature, which was regarded as an essential condition of physical and moral health.[17] In German territory, however, the developing industrialization was often treated as an imported phenomenon, something 'foreign' which separated people from nature, tangling people up in the cogs of soulless civilization and destroying the national community. This prompted the idealization of the artisans' Burg living in symbiosis with the village, as Oswald Spengler vividly described it shortly before the First World War in his famous work *The Decline of the West*.

Of course, in the region that is the object of our focus, the industrial revolution was a local phenomenon, completely absent in large swathes of territory. As stated by historian Ivan T. Berend, 'the only successful structural modernization' occurred in the Austrian and Czech areas of the Habsburg Monarchy.[18] The mining, chemical, engineering, food and textile industries were the main branches that stimulated the development of urban network in the nineteenth century. Solid transport infrastructure greatly facilitated not only the shipment of raw materials and goods, but also the influx of new labourers. The agricultural landscape was quickly changing, as the small market towns rapidly became industrial centres. Nonetheless, the population growth in towns remained relatively slow. In the period 1830–1890 only the populations of Prague and Pilsen grew significantly, while the majority of other urban settlements remained medium-sized or small.[19] These formed a sustainable network of centres that had been fully developed since the Middle Ages, in successful cooperation with the rural infrastructure. Prague, with 200,000 inhabitants in 1900, was still over three times smaller than Warsaw (100 years earlier they had been of comparable size) and smaller than Lodz, with its 250,000 inhabitants (up from only 250 inhabitants one hundred years earlier). The development of industry in the Polish lands was considerably more rapid, irregular and painful. In the Kingdom of Poland, informally known as Congress Poland (1815–1830), it was political rulers who stimulated industrial investments. Among the towns that were established, there were those that were based on the textile industry – Lodz, Zgierz, Tomaszów, Pabianice and Żyrardów – the development of

---

17 Jeremy Burchardt, *Paradise Lost: Rural Idyll and Social Change in England since 1800* (London: I.B. Tauris, 2002); Carl E. Schorske, 'The Idea of the City in European Thought: Voltaire to Spengler', in *The Historian and the City*, ed. Oscar Handlin and John Burchard (Cambridge, MA: Harvard University Press, 1963), 95–114.

18 Ivan T. Berend, *Decades of Crisis: Central and Eastern Europe Before World War II* (Berkeley, CA: University of California Press, 1998), 21.

19 E.A. Gutkind, *Urban Development in East Central Europe: Poland, Czechoslovakia and Hungary* (New York: The Free Press, 1972), 196; Luda Klusakova, 'Cultural Institutions as Urban Innovations: The Czech Lands, Poland and Eastern Baltic 1750–1900', in *Culture and Society from 1800 to the Present*, eds Malcom Gee, Tim Kirk and Jill Steward (Aldershot: Ashgate, 2003), 85–6.

which was not very strongly connected to local circumstances, but rather focused on processing goods delivered from the Russian empire. Among these centres, Lodz became the most important. The city's construction began in 1820 on a regular plan. At first it was settled by German weavers and earned the nickname 'the Polish Manchester'. Although by about 1900, it was more than four times smaller than the real Manchester; in the local context it was a powerful city, one of the main industrial centres of the Russian empire. It also shared with Manchester the fate of a nineteenth-century industrial city. Its swift growth came at a price: the increase in population was not accompanied by substantial infrastructure development – water supplies became polluted and workers had to cope with low wages and dreadful living conditions.

Such images of spectacular development, inscribing the city into the collective consciousness as a centre of large-scale production, were few in this region. Rather, cities remained places for trade and craftsmanship existing within a limited sphere of possibilities, proffering little hope for particularly profitable business or for the absorption of the overflow of the rural population. This is why these large cities, of which there were few, became a 'promised land' for those who were resourceful and those who were starving. It was a land not as distant as mythical America, which was a destination for emigrants from Galicia and Podlasie, Transylvania and Banat. For many, 'America' became Budapest, with its rapid growth due not only to administrative functions, but also to its role as a centre of industrial production.[20] It was, however, an island of this type of civilization in a region which was generally not associated with industry; the Polish geographer Wacław Nałkowski wrote near the end of the nineteenth century about the 'pastoral-chivalrous aversion of Hungarians towards industry'.[21] Similar stereotypes concerned neighbouring nations, of course excluding Germans and Czechs, whose lands were characterized by the heaviest urbanization and industrial development in this part of Europe. When mention was made of quarries and ore mines in the central area of Polish territory, oil wells, distilleries and salt mines in Eastern Galicia and the large mining area around Ploieşti, it was in order to draw attention to isolated phenomena in the agricultural and impoverished expanse of the East. There were entire regions – in particular, mountainous and swampy landscapes – where not only was there no talk of industry, but none even of wider financial circulation, with the population subsisting largely within a natural economy.

All of this created a situation of 'backwardness'. Admittedly, Spengler's idea of civilization as something which destroys culture was reflected in the intellectual world of Eastern Europe as clearly as the modernist exaltation of machines and urban crowds. The local context was, however, different. It was backwardness, in fact, which fundamental discourses revolved around. It manifested itself in relatively weaker urbanization, in the inadequacy of the city and the machine, in the primitiveness of small towns which were harder to idealize than real Burgs, and of course in rural poverty. It aroused commiseration, but also embarrassment. In Polish journalism at the end of the nineteenth and beginning of the twentieth century, expressions of shame accompanied the 'appearance of the provinces'. Towns in the Russian partition (in this case in the Kielce Governorate) were described as 'shabby', 'foul' and 'tidied up only for the arrival of the *nachalstvo* [bosses]'.[22] An important topic in these lamentations was the increase in towns of

---

20 Gábor Gyáni, *Parlour and Kitchen: Housing and Domestic Culture in Budapest 1870–1940* (Budapest: CEU Press, 2002), 6–8.
21 Wacław Nałkowski, *Zarys geografii powszechnej (rozumowej) II* [The outline of general (comprehensive) geography] (Warsaw: Teodor Paprocki, 1894), 382.
22 Stanisław Wiech, *Miasteczka guberni kieleckiej w latach 1870–1914: Zabudowa-rozwój-społeczeństwo* [The small towns of Kielce gubernia 1870–1914: Buildings–development–society] (Kielce: Kieleckie Towarzystwo Naukowe, 1995), 20, 25.

the number of Jewish people, who had migrated from the East and were allegedly responsible for the towns' degradation. Publicly, it was difficult to directly express another, basic topic concerning foreigners: the responsibility of the Russian administration for the stagnation of small towns in the Kingdom, which lacked town councils. This topic emerged strongly in Polish journalism after Poland regained independence in 1918. The tendency to place blame on foreigners was accompanied by continued feelings of shame about the filth and mud, and a depiction of national aspirations. The provinces, regarded from the perspective of large cities, seemed like an exotic phenomenon, bringing to mind Asia or Africa.[23] Similar themes appeared in interwar journalism in Romania (the foreigners who had degraded the country were, here, the eighteenth-century Phanariote Greeks) and in Serbia ('five hundred years under Turkish rule'). An image of backwardness could be seen in peripheral Sandžak with its dusty little towns, bread baked from oats and millet, windows without glass panes in rural homesteads and its lack of paved roads. Of course, 'backwardness' was defined by the local intelligentsia.[24]

In the 1930s, this became a severe political issue. The authoritarian statist policy that dominated the region, aiming to increase the productiveness of the masses and control agrarian overpopulation, sought to overcome this problem. Using statistics, the basis of economic planning, it aimed to initiate an abrupt change.[25] In this context, swift urbanization seemed like an obvious aim in most countries of the region, although it was not treated as essential. From the point of view of modernizers who held important positions among the nations' elite, the past was a burden, though in official ideology it remained a treasury of symbols that integrated society (and the increasingly marginalized minorities). The authoritarian regimes, which, in the 1930s, disassembled or weakened the democratic institutions of most of the nations in the region, thus attempted to make 'the choice of tradition',[26] reconciling symbolic images of the past and future in the prospect of rebuilding the nation. A similar dilemma was faced by the communists who assumed power after the Second World War. They promised, at first, to solve problems in villages through the emancipation of peasants. Then, in most countries, they took away ownership rights, depriving farmers of economic independence and the power to be involved in political activity while granting, however, the 'common people' wider opportunities than before for advancement, connected with intensive industrialization and the development of cities. The legitimization of these regimes was based for a long time on the mobilization of huge investments, as well as exploiting the possibilities inherent in the nation – this type of idea had been circulating much earlier, supported by statistical data which were meant to show the potential that was being suppressed either by pressure from 'foreigners' or by the egotism of the native elite. Now neither the former elite, deprived of property and influence, nor foreign capital had any role to play in economic development, which depended on full nationalization – in other words, state control. These regimes faced serious problems with symbolic legitimization and attempted to create it by invoking folk traditions, and – with time – traditional nationalism.

---

23 Błażej Brzostek, *Paryże Innej Europy: Warszawa i Bukareszt, XIX i XX wiek* [Parises of the other Europe: Warsaw and Bucharest in the 19th and 20th century] (Warsaw: WAB, 2015), 166.
24 Krzysztof Marcin Zalewski, *Naród, religia, rasa: Muzułmańskie ideologie i ruchy narodowe pogranicza w Południowo-Wschodniej Europie – Przykład Sandżaka nowopazarskiego w XX wieku* [Nation, religion, race: Muslim ideologies and national movements in the borderland of Southeastern Europe – the case of the Sandzhak of Novi Pazar in the 20th century] (Warsaw: Trio, 2010).
25 Adam Leszczyński, *Skok w nowoczesność: Polityka wzrostu w krajach peryferyjnych 1943–1980* [Jumping into modernity: the politics of growth in the countries of the periphery 1943–1980] (Warsaw: Krytyka Polityczna, 2013).
26 Cf. Marcin Kula, *Wybór tradycji* [Opting for tradition] (Warsaw: DiG, 2003).

The village and the city thus found themselves on playing fields connected with historical politics. A relative openness to the world enabling comparison with it to a greater degree – especially with the world of Western Europe, which had experienced its *miracolo economico* and its *trente glorieuses* after the Second World War – must have aroused new tensions that were difficult to resolve. The syndrome of Teofil Kurczak, who knew that he was living outside of the 'order of the civilized world', was one of the factors weakening the significance of the relative successes of the regimes of the 'people's democracy'. It was undoubtedly also an incentive for actions after 1989, which aimed to make the cities and villages of the East resemble their counterparts in the West.

'You settle for the lesser part': villages before 1939

The Moravian villages seen by the peasants from Mazovia seemed like cities to them. This implied, among other things, that the civilizational distance between the city and the village in Moravia was considerably less than in the reality that was familiar to the peasants. In other words, the village co-existed more harmoniously with the city: it was not as overpopulated and was connected to a denser and more regular network of urban centres. In the Czech lands at the beginning of the twentieth century, the rural population represented less than 60 per cent of the total, while in the Polish territory, it was 75 per cent and in the Balkans, over 80 per cent.[27] It was in the latter, in particular, that contrasts between rural and urban were the greatest, although a significant number of the smaller cities would have been regarded by a visitor from the northwest rather as villages. At the end of the nineteenth century, nearly half of the inhabitants of Bulgarian towns did agricultural work.[28] Many towns in the Polish lands would have been difficult to classify: those with a more urban appearance (with a central market square, a regular network of streets, houses built of brick and stone) often lacked city rights (as a result of repressive Russian policies), while those with a rural appearance (dominated by agricultural functions, with a population of a few hundred people) were often formally cities. In Eastern Hungary there existed, in turn, several dozen villages with populations of over 10,000 residents.[29]

In the dominant *imaginarium* that distinguished between urban and rural, status and lifestyle were quite clear. Equally clear remained the economic and cultural superiority of the urban element, in the consciousness of both city residents and villagers.

> You humbly carried dairy products, poultry, eggs and vegetables to the city. City-dwellers, happy that you fulfil your duty, fail to consider that by giving cities the best of what you have, you settle for the lesser part, and that city children are taking nourishing milk away from village children

wrote a Polish author in 1915.[30] Indeed, it was predominantly the city that dictated the sale prices of agricultural products. Cities consumed the best-quality products from villages. Cities

---

27 David Turnock, *The Economy of East Central Europe 1815–1989: Stages of Transformation in a Peripheral Region* (London: Routledge, 2006), 251.
28 Irwin T. Sanders, 'The Social Stratification of the Balkan Town: An Introduction', *Southeastern Europe* 5, no. 2 (1979): 1–10, here 8.
29 Turnock, *The Economy of East Central Europe*, 251.
30 Stefan Jentys, *Miasto a wieś* [The city and the village] (Cracow: Nakładem Autora [edition by the author], 1915), 3–4.

held bureaucratic and police control over villages, which was often particularly troublesome in regions where the administration spoke a different language and was of a different faith than most of the rural population. It was the city that ultimately created the dominant discourses concerning the village.

As Jeremy Burchardt points out, the village was usually described (in England) from two perspectives: first, as a terrain of agricultural production, more or less efficient and mechanized, judged from the point of view of economic interests and work organization; and second, as an area for close contact with nature, relaxation and contemplation.[31] These were constructs that were distinctly urban and had consumer references, although in the second of these perspectives one could detect spiritual virtues of the village and provinces, connected with their idyllic image in the industrial era. Of course, the realities of Eastern European villages remained far removed from those in England, but both perspectives appeared in discourse created by foreigners and by locals. From the productive perspective, villages mainly presented backwardness, poverty in everyday life and images that could have been taken from the 'Merovingian Chronicles' (as a certain Frenchman described the level of civilization in Polish lands[32]). From the idyllic perspective, the village showed its unchanging tradition and even archaism, and the discourse was often spiced with 'orientalism', in this case nostalgia for the picturesque and simple life of remote societies. The meeting of these two perspectives revealed, as in England, a tension between the aspiration for modernity and a desire to preserve the traditional world. The construction of tree-lined residential neighbourhoods, an idea adopted from England, was meant to be a practical solution to this dilemma. Such districts, known as 'gardens' or 'parks', were created in Budapest, Bucharest and Warsaw. The above-mentioned tension was, however, quite extreme in the local context, and was also tinged with a feeling of shame that was surely not known in England to such an extent.

The medieval state of villages was described as embarrassing and was illustrated by evocative statistics. The average lifespan, infant mortality rate, calorific value of meals and incidence of disease – all of these indicated a vast disparity between Eastern and Western Europe, as well as between the village and the city. In Poland, at the beginning of the 1930s, the average lifespan was about 10 years shorter than in Germany – 53 years in cities and 48.7 years in villages.[33] Similar differences between cities and villages were registered in the average body height. Interpretation of this knowledge became a topic of controversy. The blame for this could be placed on the 'ignorance of the peasant', of which Kurczak the farmer was convinced at the beginning of the century, and this was an opinion that was quite typical for the 'enlightened'. The peasantry was in need of education, however futile this challenge was depicted as being. In cities, there prevailed prejudices towards villagers who were seeking work there, and who – as written in the Romanian press – should be sent 'to the plough'.[34] As stated by Maria Todorova, this 'undisguised revulsion with the peasantry' was 'exclusively Romanian and unheard of in the other Balkan discourses'.[35] The blame for the deplorable state of the economy could also be placed, of course, upon foreign violence: the 'Turkish yoke' or the 'Russian invader'. Causes were also sought in the events of local social relations, the long period of serfdom and the ruthless domination of the nobility (who had supposedly, in Poland's case, caused not only the backwardness of villages but also the decline of the state).

---

31 Burchardt, *Paradise Lost*, 2–3.
32 Luc Durtain, *L'autre Europe: Moscou et sa foi* (Paris: Gallimard, 1928), 17, 32.
33 *Mały Rocznik Statystyczny 1939* [Small statistical yearbook, 1939] (Warsaw: GUS, 1939), 51.
34 Brzostek, *Paryże Innej Europy*, 198.
35 Maria Todorova, *Imagining the Balkans* (Oxford: Oxford University Press, 1997), 47.

Answers to the question of whether changes were possible fell predominantly into two fundamental models: modernizing and autochthonous. According to the first, a village could be described as being subject to a transformation coming from the outside, which was inscribed into the paradigm of modernization as a process that (1) was necessary and unavoidable, but (2) too slow locally, and thus (3) required institutional support. This model involved 'following the world'. According to the autochthonous model, villages were seen as (1) being able to influence, as a nationally and morally untainted environment, the social surroundings, and (2) being able to halt modernization of the urban type, which was regarded as a deterioration of the cultural fabric, as well as (3) being able to transform and free themselves from poverty by interacting with centres of power. This model in its purest form was presented by the Legion of Michael the Archangel in Romania. There could be no talk of 'following' – the focus was on revealing to the world the truth that was lurking in the soul of the nation.

The need for change in villages was widely shared, and this resulted from the truly difficult living and farming conditions. The abolishment of serfdom in the nineteenth century allowed the formation of groups of farmers who were capable of supporting themselves independently, but a widespread problem was the 'famine of the earth' and a phenomenon known as 'secondary serfdom'. Well-to-do farmers represented only around 10 per cent of peasantry and the agrarian question became one of the central issues that dominated the political realm in the early twentieth century. Unlike in Western Europe, around 50 per cent of the peasants remained landless. As the industry could not absorb all the impoverished, those landless peasants usually tried to earn a living by working as servants on large estates or as temporary workers wandering from place to place in pursuit of a job. Large estates remained in the possession of the old noble elites. In the Czech lands, 33 per cent of the land was ruled by 0.5 per cent of the landowners; in Hungary, nearly 33 per cent of land belonged to the 0.2 per cent of farms with an acreage of over 600 ha. After the abolishment of serfdom in the Polish Kingdom, one half of the land stayed in the possession of the former *szlachta* (nobility). Romanian peasants were given two thirds of the land, while the boyar class kept one third of the best land and gained even more through the secularization of monastic possessions. Although the median farm size across Austro–Hungary was small, larger and more viable estates existed in Bohemia, Moravia and parts of Hungary. On the other hand, in 1902 farms of less than 5 ha accounted for 80.3 per cent holdings in Galicia, 85.7 per cent in Bukovina and 87.4 per cent in Dalmatia. Peasants in Serbia and in Bulgaria were living in similar conditions. After the end of Ottoman rule, dwarf holdings prevailed – farms of over 247 acres accounted for only 5 per cent of the total land.[36]

Most of the described areas were characterized by a high fertility rate. Whereas in industrialized countries this rate (the annual number of live births per 100 women between the ages of 15 and 49) did not exceed 7, in Poland it was closer to 10, and in the Balkans, it was over 10 (11.4 in Bulgaria in 1936). This strong growth aggravated the effects of agrarian overpopulation, which was estimated at about 50 per cent in Poland, Romania, Bulgaria and Greece in the mid-1930s, while it was 22 per cent in Hungary and 78 per cent in Albania.[37] In the interwar Polish press, the alarming number of 10 million 'superfluous people' was often repeated.

The absence of primogeniture and the consequent equal division of land among all sons resulted in further fragmentation of dwarf properties. Relative overpopulation and underemployment in the countryside were successfully masked by 'controlled' pauperization, which

---

36 Turnock, *The Economy of East Central Europe*, 59–61; Barbara Jelavich, *The History of the Balkans: Twentieth Century*, vol. 2 (Cambridge: Cambridge University Press, 1983), 17.

37 *Mały Rocznik Statystyczny 1939*, 48; Derek H. Aldcroft, *Europe's Third World: The European Periphery in the Interwar Years* (Aldershot: Ashgate, 2006), 7.

hindered the emergence of viable individual farms. The traditional land cultivation and way of life created a vicious circle of poverty most clearly visible in low yields, poor diet and high child mortality. Subsistence agriculture and the self-sufficiency of peasant families could not boost agricultural commerce. Paradoxically, well-off peasants in Serbia preferred to invest in shops, inns and various agricultural buildings rather than in agricultural production for the market. Although the Serbian, Bulgarian and Romanian economy heavily relied on agricultural exports, the governing elites did not do much to alleviate the situation in the countryside. The taxes imposed represented a burden too difficult to bear, and the peasantry often had to take on debt in order to survive. Subsistence farming and low consumption could not provide a stimulus for the development of the industry, while the slow pace of industrialization prevented large-scale migration to cities and any reduction of the agrarian overpopulation.

Land was cultivated almost entirely by hand or with animal-drawn implements. The use of steam-powered machinery was possible only on large estates. Thus, even in the most developed Czech lands, threshing was the only totally mechanized operation. In the Balkan countries, even iron ploughs were a rarity. Agriculture was cereal-based, and fertilizers – both natural and artificial – were seldom used. However, as a result of higher inputs of manpower, a favourable climate and fertile soil, yields per unit of land attained global averages.[38] Such practices as the use of a farm rotation system instead of the old field system, new ploughs, sowing machines, drainage, stabled animal breeding and a paid labour force were a luxurious exception. Estates that employed these methods, situated in Poland, the Baltic countries and Hungary, usually belonged to a few wealthy landowners. The impact of these isolated endeavours was very limited. However, Bohemia was an exception. Strong industrial development there boosted the modernization of agriculture.[39]

Mass movements and peasant revolts before the First World War and revolutionary tensions during the war, as well as the extent of the war's destructive effect on agriculture (particularly in the territories of Serbia, Romania, Poland, Lithuania and Latvia), established a strong background for fundamental reforms. All the more so when farmers obtained voting rights and peasant parties became important participants in the political battle. Land redistribution was expected to alleviate the pressing social problems arising from the existence of a vast number of landless peasants. The demands of the demobilized peasant soldiers could not be ignored, as political elites were well aware that the 'peasantry had borne the brunt of the war ... it deserved to be given its share of the wealth of the nation'.[40] Moreover, the peasantry was becoming a politically active class aware of its inadequate social position, and leaders of agrarian parties were becoming more and more outspoken. Out of fear of upheaval, the political elites of the young parliamentary democracies attempted to win over the peasant's sympathies. Thus, land redistribution and peasant hardships became a crucially important political issue in the interwar period. In Yugoslavia, where several types of landownership existed before unification, the redistribution of the land was interwoven with the dismantling of the remains of the feudal system (Dalmatia, Bosnia, Macedonia). National feelings also played a part, as the majority of large

---

38 Ivan T. Berend, 'Agriculture', in *The Economic History of Eastern Europe 1919–1975*, vol. 1, eds M.C. Kaser and E.A. Radice (Oxford: Clarendon Press, 1985), 149–50.

39 Peter Gunst, 'Agrarian Systems of Central and Eastern Europe', in *The Origins of Backwardness in Eastern Europe: Economics and Politics from the Middle Ages until the Early 20th Century*, ed. Daniel Chirot (Berkeley, CA: University of California Press, 1989), 74–76.

40 Hugh Seton-Watson, *Eastern Europe Between the Wars 1918–1941* (Cambridge: Cambridge University Press, 1945), 79.

estates in parts of Romania (Transylvania, Bessarabia), parts of Poland, Slovakia, Croatia and Vojvodina (northern Serbia) belonged to the foreign aristocratic elites, the former oppressors.[41]

Governments in Yugoslavia and Romania were the first to carry out (radical) land reforms that were announced in December 1918. Despite the widely acknowledged principle that the land belongs to those who till it, agrarian reform in Yugoslavia was a subject of political horse-trading, as the government managed to secure the necessary majority for passing the Vidovdan Constitution (1921) by promising certain agrarian concessions to former Muslim landlords in Bosnia and Macedonia. The economic motives of the reform were almost insignificant, although some tried to argue that not only the political but also the economic stability of the country depended on small properties. The redistribution of the land profoundly changed the old social structure, as, according to estimates, around half a million peasant families received land. Agrarian reform encompassed colonization, as veterans were given compensation for their war service and settled in bordering areas (Kosovo, Macedonia, Vojvodina). Around 1.7 million ha was redistributed, but large estates that belonged to the Serbian Orthodox and Catholic Church were not affected.[42] In Romania, about 6 million hectares were expropriated; of these about 60 per cent were given to 1.4 million peasants. However, the reform had not been completed by the end of the 1930s and thus large estates were not altogether eliminated.[43] In Czechoslovakia, which chronologically followed Yugoslavia and Romania in implementing the reform, 29 per cent of land (4 million ha) was affected by the Confiscation Act. However, 57 per cent of the taken land was eventually returned to its pre-war owners and another 34 per cent excluded from redistribution. Polish land reform was rather modest, since the strength of the ruling landed-class hindered any significant social transformation. Only 2.6 million ha of land (little more than 10 per cent) was redistributed to landless peasants, while 5.4 million ha was given to dwarf holders. However, 'neither were the large estates broken up, nor land fragmentation stopped, nor landlessness removed'.[44] Hungarian land reform was even more moderate: 300,000 ha were expropriated, from which 400,000 families received tiny plots of land. Large estates hardly suffered any significant damage, given the fact that the area held by such farms diminished by only 10 per cent. Moreover, the reform was used to strengthen the social basis of the Horthy regime, since around 100,000 ha was given to former members of the national army. Since Bulgaria already had the most egalitarian land system, radical land reform was neither possible nor necessary. However, the government limited the maximum area of estates to 30 ha (50 in mountain regions). Thus, 6 per cent of the land was expropriated and 173,000 peasants received 133,000 ha.[45]

After the land reform, peasant problems were very much taken off the political agenda. Although small peasant farms were enhanced, and further pauperization stopped for a while, many peasants remained in a semi-agrarian proletarian state. Small-holdings, which in Bulgaria, Yugoslavia and Poland consisted mainly of scattered strips of land, continued to be as unsustainable as before the war. The situation became more complex in the years of the Great

---

41 Berend, 'Agriculture', 153.
42 Jozo Tomasevich, *Peasants, Politics, and Economic Change in Yugoslavia* (Stanford, CA: Stanford University Press, 1955), 350–51; Nikola Gaćeša, *Agrarna reforma i kolonizacija u Jugoslaviji* [Agrarian reform and colonization in Yugoslavia] (Novi Sad: Matica Srspka, 1984), 9; Branko Petranović, *Istorija Jugoslavije* [The history of Yugoslavia], vol. 1 (Belgrade: Nolit, 1989), 63.
43 Jelavich, *The History of the Balkans*, 162; Alice Teichova, 'East-Central and South-East Europe 1919–1939', in *The Cambridge Economic History*, vol. 8, eds Peter Mathias and Sidney Pollard (Cambridge: Cambridge University Press, 2008), 897.
44 Teichova, *East-Central and South-East Europe*, 899–900.
45 Berend, 'Agriculture', 160.

Depression, as wheat prices in 1934 fell to 40 per cent of the pre-crisis level. The peasantry had neither the money nor the know-how to modernize land cultivation and increase yields. Most families needed short-term loans in order to pay taxes and survive. Much-needed money was often borrowed from private creditors who charged tremendous interest rates. For instance, peasants were given loans for grain or food during the winter or spring months by promising that the repayment would be made in at least double the quantity after the harvest, which meant a yearly interest rate of 100 per cent or more.[46] Due to the Depression and 'price scissors', peasant debts became unbearable. During the early 1930s, in order to alleviate the situation in the countryside, the governments of Yugoslavia, Poland, Bulgaria, Hungary and Romania had to intervene by passing regulations that postponed the repayment of loans.

Per capita production for male workers remained low. Yugoslavia did not reach half of the European average, Bulgaria, Poland and Romania stood at 50–60 per cent, Hungary reached 75 per cent, and only Czechoslovakia surpassed the average European level by 14 per cent. In the second half of the 1930s less than 2 kg of fertilizers was used per hectare in Hungary, Poland, Bulgaria, Yugoslavia and Romania, whereas 100–300 kg was being applied in Western Europe. Although Czech and Hungarian agriculture underwent technological modernization, and the Balkan countries imported a lot of agricultural machinery, the basic technical equipment for land cultivation remained scarce. In many districts in the Balkan and Polish countryside the wooden plough was still being used. Many households had no plough at all. Moreover, the abundance of manual labourers depressed wage levels, rendering mechanization too expensive by comparison. Although agrarian production was largely grain-based, overpopulation stimulated highly intensive horticulture and market-gardening, mostly in Hungary, parts of Serbia and Bulgaria. The number of fruit trees in Hungary increased, the levels of tobacco production in Bulgaria and Yugoslavia rose and cultivation of industrial plants became more widespread. Animal husbandry improved, poultry farming became more extensive and peasants became more market-oriented. Moreover, the vast majority of peasants retained 'somewhat of a feudal approach and afforded conditions under which labour may be employed without reference to its marginal productivity'.[47]

The life of the peasants was centred on land cultivation, family and village. Most households were self-sufficient and bought only indispensable goods that could not be produced at home. In Hungarian villages, it was believed that it was more or less regrettable or even shameful if someone had to purchase a commodity that could be produced in their own household. The daily routine of peasants was dictated by the season. During the spring and summer, when fieldwork was abundant, peasants got up before dawn, sometimes at about 2 am. In the fall, after the crops had been harvested, the daily rhythm was more relaxed. All members of the family had their duties: men worked in the fields and took care of the cattle, women were in charge of smaller animals and the household (although in Yugoslav villages they used to work in the fields as well), while children, usually from the age of five, took the cattle to the pastures; grandparents stayed at home and took care of toddlers. Peasant families were patriarchal, but the division of duties on a farm, as well as the assumption of responsibility for them by women during the absence of their husbands (especially seasonal work), created relations between men and women which were more equal than in most families of the working class. Everyone married, including widows, widowers, feeble men and women, since marriage was usually concluded out of interest, not out of affection. The 'marriage for love' model was, after all, a middle-class concept. Families were tight-knit. Peasants relied on their neighbours if their land cultivation

---

46 Tomasevich, *Peasants, Politics and Economic Change*, 656.
47 Berend, 'Agriculture', 184–207.

required extra manpower. Men frequently left the village in order to serve in the army, to find seasonal work or to emigrate overseas.[48]

From the point of view of urban ideas about hygiene, neither peasants' living quarters nor food generally met the lowest expectations, which were gauged in terms of the number of people per room and the number of healthy ingredients in the daily diet. Although the quantity of food consumed was sufficient to supply the minimum number of calories, its variety and quality were inadequate. Daily requirements were satisfied mostly by bread, corn, beans, cabbage, potatoes, onions, radishes, tomatoes and paprika, depending on the region, while meat, fat and sugar were consumed only on holidays. The specific characteristics of rural consumption and the size of the agricultural sector had an influence on the general data concerning consumption, clearly differentiating countries in Western Europe from those in Eastern Europe. The population of Eastern Europe consumed more grains (in the 1930s in Romania, over 200 kg per year per person, in Poland and Czechoslovakia about 130 kg, while in Germany and France, over 100 kg) and less meat or animal products (in 1938 in France and Germany over 50 kg of meat per head, in Czechoslovakia 33 kg, in Poland 26 kg, in Romania 18 kg). Even greater disproportions appeared in the consumption of sugar: in France, Germany and Czechoslovakia about 24 kg per head were consumed, while in Poland 9 kg, and in Romania 5 kg.[49] Meanwhile, the increase in sugar consumption raised hopes of improving children's health, which in Poland assumed the form of a campaign with the slogan 'Sugar Invigorates!'. Children energetically repeated this statement and deemed a piece of bread sprinkled with sugar as the greatest treat (because it was so rare).

Paradoxically, in villages that were far from town, the diet was occasionally somewhat better, since cheese, cream cheese, eggs and poultry were consumed and not sold on the market. Moreover, peasant families had sufficient food during the autumn and winter months, while in the spring they faced shortages, since food supplies from the previous harvest were coming to an end. The irregular diet based mainly on carbohydrates reflected on the health and life expectancy of the population.[50] Tuberculosis, malaria, typhoid and typhus were endemic diseases in the Balkan villages. Poor sanitary conditions, along with a chronic lack of physicians, pharmacies and hospitals in rural areas, even in Czechoslovakia, contributed to the already high rates of infant mortality. This high rate was prevalent primarily in villages. In 1930, the infant mortality rate in Romania was 182.5 per 1,000, in Poland 140 and in Czechoslovakia 109.6, while in France and Germany these rates were about 65.5 and 60 respectively.[51]

The way in which homes were organized in the region from Macedonia to Mazovia was described as extremely chaotic: a peasant family usually lived together in one room (called the 'black room' in the Polish lands), leaving a second ('white') room for representational purposes. The sleeping conditions – considered a criterion for judging the state of a civilization's

---

48 Edit Fel and Tamas Hofer, *Proper Peasants: Traditional Life in a Hungarian Village* (New York: Viking Fund, 1969), 94–141.
49 Ioan Scurtu, *Istoria civilizației românești: Perioada interbelică (1918–1940)* [The history of Romanian civilization: the interwar period (1918–1940)] (Bucharest: Editura Enciclopedică, 2012), 194.
50 Aleksandar Petrović, *Rakovica – socijalno–zdravstvene i higijenske prilike* [Rakovica: social health and hygiene conditions], vol. 1 (Belgrade: Štamparija Centralnog higijenskog zavoda, 1939), 139; Ivana Dobrivojević, *Selo i grad: Transformacija agrarnog društva Srbije 1945–1955* [The transformation of rural society in Serbia 1945–1955] (Belgrade: Institut za savremenu istoriju, 2013), 32.
51 M. Hauner, 'Human Resources', in Kaser and Radice, *The Economic History of Eastern Europe 1919–1975*, vol. 1, 109–47; Bogdan Murgescu, *România și Europa: Acumularea decalajelor economice (1500–2010)* [Romania and Europe: the accumulation of economic disparities (1500–2010)] (Bucharest: Polirom, 2010), 217, 219.

advancement – were atrocious: entire families slept together in one bed (if they had a bed; this piece of furniture was deemed in the Balkans as belonging to an urban lifestyle). Field research was conducted in order to determine the extent of the 'backwardness'. In 1938 in ten districts of Sava Banovina (Croatia), one fourth of all peasant houses had only one room for living and sleeping, and in one third of all households, there were five or more people sharing a single room.[52] It was even worse, of course, if – as in Macedonia, Kosovo and Bosnia – domestic animals were kept in homes. Bourgeois culture, the categories of which became an indication of the civilized way of life, did not allow cohabitation with farm animals (but accepted the presence of domestic pets). For this reason, Czech and Prussian villages, which had been influenced the most by bourgeois culture, were expected to serve as exemplary models. Another indicator also cast them in a favourable light: electricity. In 1938, 73 per cent of inhabitants had electricity in their homes in Czechoslovakia, while in Poland electricity was used in only 4 per cent of villages.[53] Furthermore, during the period of the Great Depression, the earnings of many farmers fell so dramatically that they were no longer able to buy kerosene: the kerosene lamp became an extravagant luxury in some Polish villages.

Both the real difficulties of life and the imagined possibilities of changing their fates led the younger generations of village residents to migrate to cities. This phenomenon occurred on very different scales depending on the region, and was given various, often contradictory, appraisals. The indicators of urbanization were generally very far removed from the averages in industrialized nations (which served as exemplary models): in Bulgaria, Romania and Yugoslavia, the urban population made up one fifth of the overall population during the years of the Great Depression, while in Poland it was under one third, in Hungary slightly over 40 per cent (primarily due to the gargantuan size of the capital city within the diminished country) and only in Czechoslovakia did it amount to nearly half of the population. It thus seemed that villages served as a reservoir of people for the growing cities. In this context, complaints were made about the stagnancy of the rural populations, who were aware of very little beyond the confines of their villages. In Yugoslavia, out of 3.5 million people who were born after the unification, the cities absorbed only 19 per cent, which means that, on average, around 30,000 people moved to urban centres on a yearly basis. On the other hand, this influx was excessive in relation to the opportunities presented by the urban job market. Poland and Romania faced a similar problem. Migrants reinforced the ranks of the urban *lumpenproletariat*, multiplying social problems and burdening the inadequately developed urban infrastructure. During the Great Depression, Yugoslavian authorities tried to limit immigration to cities, particularly to Belgrade.[54]

Generally speaking, a large city seemed like an agglomeration of every possible opportunity, which is why it became bound to villages by long successions of family members and neighbours – in other words, there were local traditions of moving to a specific district of a city where one could be among one's own, making it easier for newcomers to find work and lodging. This preserved the specializations of villages or regions, for example, in jobs connected with clean-

---

52 Tomasevich, *Peasants, Politics, and Economic Change*, 579.
53 Berend, 'Agriculture', 166; Stefan Nowakowski, 'Town Dwellers versus Village Dwellers in Poland', *Journal of Contemporary History*, 4, no. 3, *Urbanism* (1969): 111–22, here 119.
54 Ivana Dobrivojević, 'Changing the Cityscapes: The Ruralization of Yugoslav Towns in Early Socialism', in *Mastery and Lost Illusions: Space and Time in the Modernization of Eastern and Central Europe*, eds Włodzimierz Borodziej, Stanislav Holubec and Joachim von Puttkamer (München: Oldenbourg, 2014) 139–58, here 140; Todor Stojkov, *Opozicija u vreme šestojanuarske diktature (1929–1935)* [Opposition during royal dictatorship (1929–1935)] (Belgrade: Institut za savremenu istoriju, 1969), 27.

ing, domestic service or the caretaking of buildings. It was also conducive to a phenomenon described in American sociology as the establishment of a 'city-village continuum'[55] – in other words, an intermediary territory between a city and a town, connecting the features of both and helping migrants (by establishing one-way migration from the village to the city) to find a footing in the new reality they faced. This continuum had various forms. The most obvious were the vast outskirts of large cities, which externally resembled villages, maintaining substantial backyard farming that was, however, connected with the city's labour market. Some arose through the absorption of villages (the expansion of a city's area), while others persisted beyond the borders of a city, transforming under its influence, while still others had the character of colonies springing up spontaneously in the suburbs. The last of these phenomena had, to a great extent, an illegal character. There also existed official town-planning projects that aimed to facilitate the acclimatization of the incoming work force. All households in workers' colonies in industrially developed Ostrava had a garden with vegetables while some even rented plots and cultivated grain.[56] There was a city–village continuum of another kind which had a completely different character: emigrants from villages settled in densely built, culturally foreign districts of cities, finding either shelter among relatives who had migrated earlier, or work as domestic servants. The courtyards of residential buildings, kitchen stairs, cramped servants' rooms and the tiny flats of building caretakers were spaces where the influence of the village and folklore was very much alive, otherwise so carefully suppressed (or stylized in a certain way) in the middle-class world.

The painful consequences of migrants' alienation appeared in various forms of degradation and pathology, when unlucky life events led emigrants from villages to become beggars or prostitutes. A researcher of the latter phenomenon, Irena Surmacka, wrote in 1939:

> Girls come to Warsaw from all directions, often even travelling on foot from the distant countryside, not possessing any form of education or preparation for work, often even lacking any form of personal identification. Warsaw quite eagerly takes advantage of this supply of fresh bodies from villages, the girls ... quite easily find so-called 'duty', but they just as easily lose it when it turns out that they are unfit for work ... Not all 'good country girls' are talented at adapting to the quick tempo of city life. For a girl who is unable to keep up with the tempo of life here and doesn't meet its demands, there remains either a return home to her village, or a descent into the depths. Girls encounter the second possibility quite often – indeed, every second girl on the street is a former servant.[57]

As proven by the data gathered by Surmacka, this situation was quite typical in large European cities. It also added to the negative image of urbanization, which was thought to destroy or contaminate authentic folk culture – the antithesis of the 'exemplary order of the civilized world'.

---

55 For the concept of the 'city-village continuum' (also known as the 'folk-urban continuum'), see Robert Redfield's *Tepoztlan, A Mexican village: A Study in Folk Life* (Chicago, IL: University of Chicago Press, 1930) and his *The Primitive World and Its Transformations* (Ithaca, NY: Cornell University Press, 1953).

56 Martin Jermelka, 'The Ostrava Industrial Agglomeration in the First Half of the Twentieth Century: Where the Urban Countryside Met the Rural Town', in Borodziej, Holubec and von Puttkamer, *Mastery and Lost Illusions*, 71–98, here 84–5.

57 Irena Surmacka, *Czynniki prostytucji oraz charakterystyka prostytutek: Ankieta zebrana wśród prostytutek warszawskich* [Prostitution factors and the characteristics of prostitutes: a survey among Warsaw prostitutes] (Warsaw: Zarząd Miejski, 1939), 21–2.

The national styles

The order of the civilized world that struck Teofil Kurczak in Vyškov was defined, above all, by a city's conditions. Not necessarily a large city, since small ones could also have carefully cobbled streets and a sewage system. Exemplary models came from above, however, and the imitative relationships which formed between cities in the social life at the turn of the twentieth century were observed by Georg Simmel: even clothing trends seemed to perfectly express the spontaneous desire of the lower levels of society to imitate the higher ones, a spectacle that was most clearly reflected in the world of very large cities.

A wonderful example, inspiring for the Eastern European elite, was the bourgeois metropolis – a carefully arranged 'work-of-art-city', as Donald J. Olsen wrote.[58] Until the mid-nineteenth century, the most magnificent city was London, described (by Frenchmen) as a city of the future. Paris, which adopted London's trends and named its most elegant district *le West End*, created, however – thanks to a brutal campaign by the prefect Haussmann – its own unique style, a style that conquered Europe in the second half of the century. Parisian boulevards, Parisian opera and Parisian railway stations became vivid models. It was difficult to imagine imitating the Eiffel Tower, however, or the panache of the World Fairs in Paris in 1889 and 1900, where it was essential to present oneself. Greece, Romania, Hungary, Serbia and Bosnia-Herzegovina were able to do so, but not the Poles, Czechs, Slovakians, Croatians – they could only be witnesses of this 'great competition of nations'.

The World Fairs influenced the formation of a new mental map of Europe. This map was dominated by a constellation of metropolises that were closer to each other than ever before, joined by railway systems, the telegraph and, in the near future – telephone lines. These connections also encompassed large cities in the eastern part of the continent. The development of the railway was of immense importance here, of course. In 1830, the journey from Paris to Bucharest (by post riders) took one month; by the end of the century, about 60 hours, in a comfortable carriage of the Orient Express. Cities 'coming closer' to each other resulted in an increase in imitative tendencies, as well as efforts to adapt to the needs of newcomers. At the beginning of the twentieth century, a traveller from Paris or Vienna arrived in Budapest, Sofia, Warsaw or Bucharest and went to a hotel that met his expectations of comfort, equipped with running water and a telephone. Outside of the hotel there were sidewalks – made of asphalt (in Bucharest), concrete (in Warsaw) or clinker tiles (in Sofia) – and rows of buildings with at least two storeys, with attractive window displays on the ground floors. All of this was an imitation of the Parisian and Viennese models, as was the entire concept of a city which had to have boulevards, buildings with balconies ornamented with cornices and caryatids, shopping arcades, an impressive theatre, museums, railway stations and trams. Steel constructions and glass ceilings, evidence of engineering and technical artistry, made a particularly striking impression, evident in the construction of enclosed shopping arcades. In Bucharest, which eagerly copied Parisian models, the first such arcade was built in 1859, and the most impressive, *Pasajul Macca-Villacrosse*, 33 years later. In 1903, the Art Nouveau *U Nováků* arcade was inaugurated in Prague. Ten years later in Budapest, there was the eclectic *Párizsi udvar*. The largest structure of this kind in Warsaw, *Galeria Luxenburga*, was built in 1909.

In large cities, Parisian models rivalled Viennese models, although Vienna at the beginning of the twentieth century was already – according to Michael Pollak – becoming

---

58 Donald J. Olsen, *The City as a Work of Art: London, Paris, Vienna* (New Haven, CT: Yale University Press, 1986), 44, 51.

somewhat provincial, in comparison to Berlin.[59] Vienna was a place of ideological confusion in which later generations would seek the causes of the two world wars. This elegant and modern metropolis made a deep impression on a 'country bumpkin' – even the tram traffic, alone. 'How many lines they had! In Cracow, there were only three and all of them moved at a snail's pace.'[60] But even the trams in Cracow were already electric. The tramlines were opened in 1900, barely three years after those of Vienna, at the same time as Iasi and a year before Sofia. Civilizational innovations spread at an impressive speed in this era. Power stations were constructed in small towns that seemed very remote – Uzhhorod (1902), Mukacheve (1903) and Berehove (1908). These innovations merged with traditional life. In Mukacheve, inhabited mostly by Jews – who, during the Sabbath, could not use electricity generated by manual labour in a power plant – the rabbi's secretary turned off the public power system on Friday evenings, but electricity continued to flow from special batteries.[61]

Modernization did not proceed so smoothly everywhere. On the contrary, it aroused a great deal of fear and resistance. In 1894 the Belgrade press wrote that 'electricity is dangerous', that it would 'introduce disorder among citizens' and that people could 'become blind and mute' if they stared at light bulbs for a long time.[62] Electric trams, which ran to Cracow's medieval market square six years later, gave rise to resistance of a different kind. They were seen as threatening the atmosphere of a place where national identity was strongly expressed. Cracow wished to be a 'little Vienna', but at the same time was afraid of losing its unique character.[63] In the absence of a Polish national capital, the city fulfilled the role of a repository of national sacredness. This manifested itself in Cracow precisely because of its relative provincialism, and a conflict that was characteristic of the modern era – a conflict between the introduction of innovation, usually imported from abroad, and the preservation of an imagined community – in this case endowed the city with an essential symbolic mission.

Budapest seemed able to solve this conflict, thanks to the success of its transformation. It entered the international stage and introduced Hungarian cakes, music and art into the European consciousness. It became a metropolis equipped not only with trams, but also with a metro line (1896). This material beautification of the city's centre in the belle époque would, over the course of decades, create the illusion of being in the capital city of a country that was as rich as France or Germany, as one Western visitor observed.[64] Such was the premise of the designers in Budapest who, as Maciej Janowski writes, made use of numerous 'citations from European capitals': concentric and radial boulevards based on Haussmann's urban design; Heroes' Square with a monument in honour of the 1,000th anniversary of Hungary, which was an 'obvious reference to Saint Peter's Square in Rome'; and, above all, the impressive parliament building designed by Imre Steindl, 'bringing to mind, with its riverside location, the parliament building

---

59 Michael Pollak, *Vienne 1900: Une identité blessée* (Paris: Gallimard, 1992).
60 Zbigniew Grabowski, *Śpiew dziewcząt: Opowieść o dzieciństwie* [The girls' song: a childhood tale] (London: Polska Fundacja Kulturalna, 1964), 32–3.
61 Jean Musset, *Les villes de la Russie Subcarpatique (1919–1938): L'effort tchécoslovaque* (Paris: Librairie Droz, 1938), 130.
62 Dubravka Stojanović, 'Between Rivalry, Irrationality and Resistance: The Modernization of Belgrade 1890–1914', in *Races to Modernity: Metropolitan Aspirations in Eastern Europe, 1890–1940*, eds Jan C. Behrends and Martin Kohlrausch (Budapest: CEU, 2014), 162.
63 Nathaniel D. Wood, *Becoming Metropolitan: Urban Selfhood and the Making of Modern Cracow* (DeKalb, IL: Northern Illinois University Press, 2010), 130–34.
64 A. Soulange-Bodin, *À travers la nouvelle Europe: Hier-aujourd'hui* (Paris: Librairie Académique, 1926), 28.

in London designed by Sir Gilbert Scott'. As Janowski states: 'First representative buildings are erected, and only later the city itself – in other words, that which needs to be represented.'[65] Nevertheless, the city undoubtedly existed, and the substance of the multi-storey buildings was very important. Financial policy favoured construction – big tax reductions or total exemptions were given to the building investors. In the second half of the nineteenth century, the population increased threefold (and the number of buildings doubled in the years 1870–1910). On the eve of the First World War, Budapest was one of the ten largest urban centres in Europe. Of course, it did not represent, in any way, the character of smaller Hungarian cities, which the geographer Nałkowski, whom we have already quoted above, described as appearing, at the end of the century, 'with wide, unpaved streets (due to a stone shortage), huge squares and low houses made of sun-baked bricks (due to a fuel shortage), they take up vast areas and look like the camps of people from the Steppes'.[66] This description was not completely up-to-date; it contained a fixed stereotype of Hungarianness. The beautiful capital city was meant to crush this by exhibiting the nation's Western aspirations, although at the same time Hungarians were searching for a national style by turning towards Eastern roots (the Steppes). In any case, life in the vast and multi-ethnic Kingdom of Hungary was not marked by industrial progress, and only to a very minor extent by urbanization. In 1900, just under 17 per cent of the total population of Hungary lived in 149 cities (not including Budapest). Debrecen, the second most populated town, had fewer than 100,000 inhabitants.[67] Kassa (later known as Košice), at the beginning of the twentieth century, was described by Sándor Márai in *Confessions of a Bourgeois* as a one-storey town, with only about a dozen two-storey houses. The city lacked a sewage system but had electricity. It was a town that existed in close contact with the countryside and filled up on market days with peasants 'in felt jackets and sheepskin caps'. The narrator lived in one of the largest houses, which in fact had two storeys (but only in the front), which gave an initial impression of 'a real skyscraper and gained fame throughout the entire county'. It was the first house which

> hadn't been built so that the inhabitants could spend their entire lives, to their very deaths, within its snug shelter … Just residential buildings with tenants. Old aristocratic families would never move into a house like this. And they slightly scorned its occupants, who had been uprooted and had come from some unknown place.[68]

Thus was perceived the clash of values between the 'gentry', in other words the ancient, established type of elite, and the new, uprooted bourgeoisie, who might be seeking new roots, symbolizing here the active material of modernity.

The appearance of modernity in the cities of Southeastern Europe, described as 'oriental', was an even more striking spectacle. Their chaotic spatial structures were 'backwards', in need of drastic reconstruction. Bucharest at the beginning of the twentieth century, with a population of about 300,000 residents, equalled Vienna and Paris in geographical area, but had a population that was many times smaller. There were nearly 35,000 buildings in the city, but only 199

---

65 Janowski, *Stolica na peryferii*, 369.
66 Nałkowski, *Zarys geografii*, 382.
67 Gabor Zovanyi, 'Structural Change in a System of Urban Places: The 20th-century Evolution of Hungary's Urban Settlement Network', *Regional Studies*, 20 (1986): 47–71, here 53.
68 Sándor Márai, *Wyznania patrycjusza* [The confessions of a middle-class man], trans. Teresa Worowska (Warsaw: Czytelnik, 2014), 7–12.

had more than two storeys.[69] From the point of view of Western town-planning criteria, which had been learned by the elite educated in Paris and Vienna, the city also lacked such large-city attributes as straight streets, dense frontage and impressive public buildings. In 1909 the mayor of Belgrade stated that the city was 'without order, not paved with modern cobblestones, full of mud and dust, unregulated, without sewage, ill-equipped with water – in one word, lacking everything that could elevate the city to the status of the cultural city'.[70] The construction of the first modern boulevard in the city, Terazije, was in progress. Belgrade, like Bucharest and Sofia, became enriched by borrowing from large cities in the West. The authorities in Sofia even organized, with this aim, a month-long study trip for the city's urban commission in order to examine achievements of modern planning abroad. The creation of representational spaces, above all boulevards and public buildings, was accompanied by the destruction of the urban fabric. This triggered conflicts, and not only in connection with people being evicted from their homes. When the authorities of Sofia demolished several old churches in the downtown area, angry citizens rose up in protest and ended up clashing with the police.[71]

Costly investments in the centres of large cities reflected national ambitions, but often aggravated social unrest. These two spheres posed crucial questions in this era. The local poor in Prague 'felt alienated from the very urban projects that were designed to make them feel pride in their cultural capital'.[72] In city centres, the elite created surroundings that were suitable for themselves, inspired by the Western world that they knew. The existence in Belgrade of two hundred flats equipped with bathrooms (1907) highlighted rather clearly the limited extent of this social class, as the majority of Belgrade residents were living in cramped one-room apartments with one window and without basic sanitary conditions. The wretched state of these single-storey buildings, the provisional outdoor toilets, the lack of hygienic habits and the dreadful sanitary conditions resulted in rising numbers of persons infected with tuberculosis. Although early twentieth-century Belgrade resembled a 'shantytown', rents there continued to rise steadily. By the last pre-war year families of three of four members paid out one third of their income for rent, which was two to three times more than in Western Europe.[73] With the growth of the populace, cities became increasingly socially segregated. Workers lived in housing that was 'too often overcrowded, dirty, damp and in disrepair'. One ordinary workers' area in Budapest (1911) consisted of 'wooden shacks and one-story rental barracks described by one observer as a line of cells in a prison'.[74] City-dwellers in Balkan capitals grappled with housing shortages as well. Although the population in the decade from 1900 to 1910 increased by one half, housing in residential areas increased only by one third. Thus, over 40 per cent of the population of Sofia and over 30 per cent in Bucharest in 1912 were living in overcrowded flats.[75] Differences

---

69 Frédéric Damé, *Bucureștiul în 1906* [Bucharest in 1906], trans. Lucian Pricop and Sînziana Barangă (Pitești: Paralela 45, 2007), 218, 345–6.
70 Stojanović, *Between Rivalry, Irrationality and Resistance*, 157.
71 Maximilian Hartmuth, 'Negotiating Tradition and Ambition: Comparative Perspectives on "De-Ottomanization" of the Balkan Cityscapes', *Ethnologia Balkanika* 10 (2006): 15–33, here 18; Elitza Stanoeva, 'Sofia', in *Capital Cities in the Aftermath of Empires: Planning in Central and Southeastern Europe*, eds Tanja Damjanović Conley and Emily Gunzburger Makaš (London: Routledge, 2010), 98.
72 Cathleen M. Guistino, 'Prague', in Conley and Makaš, *Capital Cities*, 164.
73 Nataša Mišković, *Bazari i bulevari: Svet života u Beogradu 19. veka* [Bazaars and boulevards: life-worlds in Belgrade in the 19th century] (Belgrade: Muzej grada Beograda, 2012), 312–19, originally published in German as *Basare und Boulevards. Belgrad im 19. Jahrhundert* (Vienna: Böhlau, 2008).
74 A. Lees and L. Hollen Lees, *Cities and the Making of Modern Europe 1750–1914* (Cambridge, MA: Harvard University Press, 2007), 149.
75 John Lampe, 'Modernization and Social Structure: The Case of the Pre-1914 Balkan Capitals', *Southeastern Europe* 5, no. 2 (1979): 11–32, here 21.

between metropolitan-like city centres and their peripheries, which often lacked paving and were dominated by wooden constructions, became more and more pronounced.[76] 'Occasionally one has the impression that a different tribe lives there, a different human race', stated a writer before the Second World War, when describing the outskirts of Warsaw.[77]

In this way, the 'social' clashed with the 'national' – which had no space for various races and demanded solidarity, particularly in the face of foreign domination. In about 1905, social and nationalistic tensions intensified in the cities of Eastern Europe. Anti-Semitism, previously barely noticeable, became visible in Budapest.[78] Warsaw was swept up in the turmoil of revolutionary events in Russia. There were demonstrations in front of the National Theatre in Bucharest to protest the staging of plays in French. A year later, an architectural style known as Neo-Romanian triumphed at a national exhibition in this city. It was one of the national styles that were spreading during this time from the Polish lands all the way to Bulgaria.

National styles were implemented in reconstruction programmes aimed at rebuilding capital cities and in opposition movements against foreign domination. In order to find inspiration, architects, appearing as some of the leading exponents of concepts of identity, sought out models from the past. As Elitza Stanoeva writes, Bulgarian national romanticism was created through a combination of modern building techniques and materials and motifs borrowed from Byzantine and old-Bulgarian architecture.[79] One of the most expressive styles was one that began to spread at the beginning of the century among official (but not only) architecture in Romania. Known as Neo-Romanian, it was created in the 1880s by Ion Mincu, an architect educated in Paris, who wished to give his designs a 'Romanian atmosphere'. Mincu's students sought inspiration among seventeenth and eighteenth-century residences in Wallachia, the monasteries of Moldova and peasant architecture. They tried to synthesize Western (primarily Italian, but also Polish) with Eastern (Byzantine) influences.[80] In turn, Hungarian architects searching for a national style reached back to older, medieval models, and appeared even more intensely interested in the peasant and oriental part of their heritage. In the period 1909–1912, more than 50 primary schools were erected in this style. According to Eva Blau, 'through their conscious imitation of traditional village life' these buildings aimed at embedding a sense of national unity among children and thus creating a new national identity.[81] Unlike Bulgarian, Romanian and Hungarian architects, Polish architects did not have many opportunities to introduce a 'national style' into the official architecture. On the contrary, under Prussian rule, Polish children learned German in schools built in the official neo-Gothic style, which was treated as the hallmark of German cultural cohesion. But in the Russian partition, the neo-Gothic style in turn enabled Poles to acknowledge their Western affiliation within a country

---

76 Friedrich Lenger, *European Cities in the Modern Era, 1850–1914* (Leiden: Brill, 2012), 100.
77 *Myśl Niepodległa* [Independent thought], no. 182, IX (1911): 1240.
78 John Lukacs, *Budapest 1900: A Historical Portrait of a City and Its Culture* (New York: Weidenfeld & Nicolson, 1988), 188–96.
79 Stanoeva, 'Sofia', 101.
80 Carmen Popescu, *Le style national roumain: Construire une Nation à travers l'architecture* (Rennes: Presses Universitaires de Rennes, 2004), 50–55.
81 Eva Blau, *Shaping the Great City: Modern Architecture in Central Europe 1890–1937* (London: Prestel, 2000), 110; János Gerle, 'Historyzm narodowy Jenö Lechnera, czyli specyficzne środkowoeuropejskie podejście do tożsamości narodowej' [Jenö Lechner's national historicism, or the specific Central European approach to national identity], in *Sztuka około 1900 w Europie Środkowej. Centra i prowincje artystyczne*, eds Piotr Krakowski and Jacek Purchla (Cracow: Narodowe Centrum Kultury, 1997), 157.

subject to planned Russification. It was in precisely this style that the towering Cathedral of St. Michael the Archangel and St. Florian the Martyr was built in Warsaw (1901), a counterpoint to the immense Orthodox cathedral on the opposite bank of the Vistula River, which was a symbol of Russian domination. In the Austrian Partition, in turn, where the Polish people had autonomy, the source of a national style gushed forth strongly, inspired by the architecture of Podhalian highlanders. It was used to design mountain huts and holiday homes, as well as residential buildings. After the First World War, when Poland regained its independence, the manor house style, which made reference to rural aristocratic homes, gained major importance and would become the style of school buildings and train stations in the 1920s.

National styles were one of the less dramatic symptoms of processes that, at the beginning of the twentieth century, aimed to explode the framework of culture up until that point, and at the same time, the multinational empires that dominated the central part of the continent. In any case, the consequences of the Second World War imposed this point of view. These consequences, even without taking into consideration the destruction and loss of life, were so arresting that the pre-war years became, in people's minds, an epoch that was very remote, or even completely mythical.

The effects of the collective trauma caused by the brutal political and social changes in the interwar years were clear in statistics concerning suicides. Budapest's leading position on this list (57 suicides per 100,000 people in the mid-1920s) is difficult, of course, to explain primarily by the 'Trianon syndrome' – a longing for the former territory and glory of Hungary, lost in the Treaty of Trianon at the end of the First World War – but it did have a certain significance. Vienna's second position on this list (47 per 100,000) and Berlin's third position (43) could confirm this, since they were the capital cities of countries that had been equally humiliated in defeat. In London, there were only 13 suicides per 100,000 inhabitants, and in Paris 19 – these were obviously capital cities of victorious nations. In Warsaw (30), nostalgia for the former world (when the city had grown rich thanks to Russian markets) resonated alongside hopes inspired by the new world (in which it had become a capital city).[82] It was significant that in this city, 55.4 per cent of suicides in 1930 were committed by women, which was a tendency that was essentially new, explained by an analyst of the time as an expression of a situation in which women 'had become more independent and were competing on the same level as men for a livelihood'. This was assumed to characterize societies that had already experienced women's suffrage and other legal aspects of emancipation, as well as the economic difficulties that forced women to become active in the labour market. In small Polish cities that were more conservative, men continued to dominate.[83]

The distance between small towns and large ones continued to increase. The latter gained international telephone connections in the 1920s, the expansion of cinema and radio, and in the 1930s the development of airline connections and the beginnings of television. In the capital cities of Central and Eastern European nations, civil airports were inaugurated at the beginning of the 1920s, soon becoming the base for national airlines, and in the following decade, they began to serve international flights. Also at this time, airports were moved further away from cities and were given modernist designs. In 1937, it was possible to fly on Air France from Paris to Berlin and Prague in about four hours, to Warsaw (with a stopover in Prague) in seven and a half hours, and to Bucharest in ten hours (with stops in Prague, Vienna, Budapest and

---

82 *Kronika Warszawy* [The chronicle of Warsaw], vols 11–12 (1927): 11.
83 Witold Grzywo-Dąbrowski, *Samobójstwa w Warszawie w r. 1930* [Suicide in Warsaw in 1930] (Warsaw: Czasopismo Sądowo-Lekarskie, 1931), 1–2.

Belgrade). It was possible to fly from Paris to Berlin twice a day, and to Bucharest six times a week in summertime and three times a week in the winter.[84]

A paradox manifested itself, consisting in the unprecedented development of transport and inflow of information, and a simultaneous increase in political and administrative barriers. The former world, now cut through by a network of borders and customs barriers, was recalled by many people with nostalgia. North-eastern Europe had been 'balkanised', as an English observer remarked in the mid-1920s.[85] Of course, this judgement could be recognized as an expression of the imperial mindset, or quite simply the result of irritation at the necessity of having to apply for visas at the diplomatic posts of new, exotic countries. On the other hand, balkanization would indeed become a fact when growing nationalistic feelings and the political manipulations of minorities would make dark clouds appear over the region.

In the mid-1930s, in the area between Greater Berlin (as it was known), with a population of 4.2 million, and Moscow (a city undergoing massive new construction) with a population of 3.6 million, the largest city remained Vienna, with 2 million residents, though it had completely lost its geopolitical influence. Both Berlin and Moscow had become 'hot topics' not only for political, but also ideological and architectural reasons. It was there that the impressive and terrifying 'new' was being forged, an ideal which would spread in various ways to the capital cities of Central Europe. Apart from Prague, which seemed, for a time after the Treaty of Versailles, to be the success story of Europe, these were cities in search of a new identity. The largest among them was Warsaw. It doubled in size between 1900 and 1939, reaching 1.3 million inhabitants, comparable with Rome in terms of population (as well as Cairo and Bombay – the times of African and Asian megacities were still to come).[86] It also had the second-largest urban population of Jews in the world, after New York: about 400,000, mostly Orthodox, living primarily in the northern district. It lacked, however, the proper elegance of a capital city, which was a constant subject of criticism. The case of Budapest, a large capital of a small-sized nation, was precisely the opposite – its grand appearance now seemed to accentuate its lack of real attributes. Budapest, to which masses of migrants were drawn from the former Hungarian provinces, was full of 'phantom pains' from its lost cities, the Hungarian names of which had disappeared from maps. In 1935, Ferenc Fejtö's book *A Sentimental Journey* was published in Budapest – a description of the author's journey from Budapest to Zagreb, being at the same time a journey into the past, to the land of childhood, when these cities were both under the control of one ruling power. This pre-war 'Hungarian' Zagreb came back to life in the author's recollections.

A typical experience of the 1920s and 30s was the new interpretation or the transformation, sometimes radical, of symbolic meanings connected with cities that had changed their national affiliation. New offices and administrative departments appeared within them. The group that had previously dominated was now a minority, treated with suspicion. The Prussian city of Toruń is a good example of this. Before the First World War, it was a wonderful Gothic city that gave the impression of having an entirely German character, although Poles made up quite a large segment of its population – 15,700 in 1910, while there were 24,800 Germans. When Toruń found itself within Poland's borders after the war, its new rulers began a swift Polonization of the city's cultural space, eliminating symbolic elements (such as a plaque in honour of Bismarck) and limiting the use of the German language (which was banned from

---

84 Guy le Roux de Bretagne, *Air-France, Société aérienne subventionnée* (Paris: Librairie Technique et Économique, 1937), 81–82, 125.
85 Alexander MacCallum Scott, *Beyond the Baltic* (London: George H. Doran Company, 1926), 8.
86 *Mały Rocznik Statystyczny 1939*, 39.

written correspondence with the administration in 1922) and the operation of the German education system. In connection with this, there was a mass emigration of Germans who, by 1939, had already become a minority, making up only 3.2 per cent of the city's population, while Toruń itself, thanks to the (encouraged) immigration of Poles and the (less favourably viewed) immigration of Jews, grew to the size of a city with nearly 80,000 people, twice as large as it had been before the First World War. However, the German community maintained a significant position in the city's economy. Five out of eleven large factories were owned by Germans in the mid-1930s, and the German banking and credit sector was strong, supported by branches of Danzig (now Gdansk)-based banks. Meanwhile, after Hitler gained power, local German organizations that had been previously designed chiefly for the cultural preservation of the dwindling community became tools in the political expansion of the Nazi regime, giving rise to many conflicts. The two sides in these conflicts observed each other's actions with growing distrust.[87]

In fact, distrust was a quite typical phenomenon in the new social relations in numerous cities that had changed their national allegiance. A French observer described this experience as follows:

> Let us imagine a Romanian from Bucharest, accustomed to a certain level of comfort and entertainment, who travels as a prefect to one of the small towns of Bessarabia, being a rather large village with low houses stretched out along streets that change into cesspools with merely the tiniest amount of rain and often inhabited by dirty Jews. His situation will not be much more pleasant in a Transylvanian city, where the enemy Hungarian or German element prevails, the latter apparently milder, but retreating into contemptuous isolation.[88]

The cities that had been taken over by Romania – Cluj, Braşov and Sighişoara – were highly esteemed by Romanians due to their level of civilizational development (as Toruń inspired admiration among newcomers from Central and Eastern Poland). But they still remained 'so foreign', lamented the writer Liviu Rebreanu, since they 'were growing like enemy cells within the Romanian nation'.[89] In order, therefore, to give these cities a more 'national' aspect, the Romanian authorities began to build impressive Orthodox churches in their centres, which were meant to eclipse the Protestant churches. At the same time, in the mid-1920s, the Polish authorities tore down the huge Orthodox cathedral in the heart of Warsaw – a souvenir of Russian rule. Similarly, all the monuments in Prague, due to their association with the Habsburgs, were taken down. Dismantled memorials included the Catholic Mary Statue on the Old Town Square, the bronze equestrian statue of the emperor Franz I and the monument to Field Marshall Joseph Radetzky. As in France and England, the idea of creating a tomb of the unknown soldier was adopted – in both Bucharest (1923) and in Warsaw (1925) these were

---

87 Mieczysław Wojciechowski, 'Niemcy w społeczności miejskiej Torunia w okresie międzywojennym (1920–1939)' [Germans in the urban community of Toruń during the interwar period (1920–1939)], in *Wspólnoty lokalne i środowiskowe w miastach i miasteczkach ziem polskich pod zaborami i po odzyskaniu niepodległości*, ed. Maria Nietyksza, (Toruń: Wydawnictwo Uniwersytetu Mikołaja Kopernika, 1998), 191–208.
88 Archives du Ministère des Affaires étrangères (AMAE), Paris, collection Europe 1914–1940: Roumanie, P. 1743891-Z 580/1, 159: Extrait d'un rapport sur la Roumanie par M. E. de Martonne, XI, 1921.
89 Liviu Rebreanu, 'Ardealul, Banatul, Crişana, Maramureşana şi Bucovina' [Transylvania, Banat, Crişana, Maramureş and Bukovina], in Rebreanu, *Opere*, vol. 15, (Bucharest: Minerva, 1991), 345.

monuments in praise of the expansion and revival of the nation. Similar symbols in federal states had a somewhat different significance. In Prague, this type of tomb was part of the large Liberation Monument raised in honour of the Czech and Slovak legionaries (1929–1938), and in Belgrade the Monument to the Unknown Hero, designed by Ivan Meštrović, was built atop Mount Avala (1934–1938). In Budapest, however, the Monument to National Heroes (1929) served rather to mark solemn and bitter recollections of lost greatness.

Although the 1920s were a period of the creation of national monuments and institutions, during this decade, the national aesthetic in architecture and design lost its resonance, and large cities began to be marked by various forms of modernism ranging from purist functionalism to luxurious art deco. This was linked to new inspirations, to a great extent North American, as well as to a fascination with technology, the prevalence of which was greatly lamented by Spenglerian intellectuals. These developing tendencies, in which the construction of cities intensified, were significant. In the 1930s, the construction was facilitated by building concessions introduced during the Great Depression. The syndrome of the elite abandoning densely populated city centres and forming residential colonies on the outskirts of large cities became evident throughout the entire region. Nonetheless, in city centres from Riga to Novi Sad, dreams of American-style skyscrapers were being fulfilled, even though these skyscrapers rarely rose above 40 metres (the Empire State Building in New York was 380 metres tall). The symbols of modernity were the 45-metre Manderla shopping mall in Bratislava (1936), the 52-metre Telephone Palace in Bucharest (1933), the Albania edifice in Belgrade, which was of comparable height (1939), the 60-metre skyscraper Drapacz Chmur in Katowice (1934), the 66-metre Prudential Building in Warsaw (1933) and, finally, the impressive 77-metre Building No. 21 belonging to the Bata firm in Zlín (1938). However, the construction of buildings of this type, particularly in capital cities, aroused not only pride, but also resentment. The costs seemed staggeringly high in a time of economic crisis and the designs too 'cosmopolitan', 'American' or downright 'Jewish' (as the Prudential Building in Warsaw was described in the right-wing press).[90] On the whole, the luxury of the main streets and new houses in the capital cities seemed like an outrage to the provinces – this topic appeared in discussions concerning Budapest, and in the multi-ethnic reality of Yugoslavia the development of Belgrade became an argument that fuelled Croatians' claims that the Serbs were, allegedly, living off them.[91]

Extravagant investments, both those that were carried out and those merely planned (like the vast rebuilding of Bucharest or the idea of the impressive Marshal Piłsudski District in Warsaw) seemed outrageous in light of the basic shortages and shabbiness in other parts of cities. Occasionally this shabbiness resulted from specific town-planning characteristics, especially of cities in Southern Europe. Their huge swathes of single-storey houses, with dense networks of irregular streets, required costly installations. While in Paris, near the end of the 1930s, there were about 900 energy consumers for each kilometre of electricity in the streets, and in Prague 426, in Bucharest there were only 166.[92] This indicated unprofitable calculations in the fields of investment and exploitation, even irrespective of the average incomes of inhabitants. These

---

90 Brzostek, *Paryże Innej Europy*, 215–16.
91 Vera Bacskai, 'The Historical Metropolis in Hungary in the 19th and 20th Century', in *The Historical Metropolis: A Hidden Potential, International Conference 26–29.5.1996*, ed. Jacek Purchla (Cracow: Narodowe Centrum Kultury, 1996), 136; Ivana Dobrivojević, *Drzavna represija u doba diktature kralja Aleksandra 1929–1935* [State repression during the dictatorship of King Aleksander 1929–1935] (Belgrade: Institut za savremenu istoriju, 2006), 32–3.
92 Brzostek, *Paryże Innej Europy*, 130.

low incomes hindered the development of mass construction. A typical aspect was the contrast between very luxurious new residential buildings in the centres of Bucharest or Belgrade and farmsteads on the outskirts, which were built at the homeowners' own expense and with traditional methods (for example, wooden constructions filled with clay). The extent of this social polarization was illustrated in numbers: the rate of infant mortality in a refugee quarter in Sofia was 155 per 1000 in 1940, versus 42 for the centre and 93 for the city as a whole. The death rate among tuberculosis patients was much higher in the Sava Mala slum than in downtown Belgrade, although those two quarters were only two kilometres apart.[93]

The more books and lectures presented on the 'proper, hygienic' home, the more deplorable the real condition of homes seemed by comparison. They were characterized, above all, by a lack of space stemming from inadequate construction and high rental prices in relation to average incomes. The average density of people living in flats in Polish cities at the beginning of the 1930s (about two people per room) was twice as high as the average in Germany. While in Warsaw there were two people per room, in Prague the number was 1.44, Rome 1.37, Berlin 1, Paris 0.95 and London 0.89. In cities with populations of over 20,000, 65 per cent of flats had a maximum of two rooms, and in smaller cities, nearly 90 per cent. In Hungary, three fourths of the populations of provincial towns lived in such flats, and in Budapest 54 per cent (1930).[94] While in Bohemia and Moravia, which had a large urban network, housing developed generally, in Poland and Hungary it improved only in the largest towns. The situation in the Balkans was even bleaker – a relative increase in the number of flats and improvement in their quality occurred only in capital cities.[95]

These data were derived from living conditions, in particular, the quality of flats, which is why similar phenomena led to attempts at developing mass construction through cooperatives and state loans. These attempts, inspired by achievements in Austria and Germany, yielded very limited results, however. Contrary to assumptions, members of the intelligentsia, rather than workers, moved into the small homes constructed by the Warsaw Housing Cooperative in impressive modernistic blocks of flats, since the latter were not able to pay even the relatively low rent prices. Workers' families lived either in nineteenth-century residential buildings which offered them primarily one-room flats with sinks in the corridors and toilets in the yards, or in small houses in the suburbs, often built illegally and taking the form of sheds, the squalor of which was camouflaged in summer by flower and vegetable gardens. Workers also often rented a single room or simply a corner of a room, marked by conflicts with their landlords and ending in the necessity of frequently moving. In large cities, a separate segment of the rental market consisted of furnished rooms, an uncertain haven for single men or sometimes entire families. Lodgings of this type were frequently run by women, which provided an opportunity for humorous portrayals of their often-complex relationships with tenants (such as in the novel *Camere mobilate* by the Romanian writer Damian Stănoiu, 1933). In Warsaw, the way to find furnished rooms, which were often carefully hidden so that the owners could avoid paying taxes, was through personal contacts. The Jewish district was full of lodgings of this kind. Merchants from small towns who did business in the capital city often lived there, but also workers and students, Jews and Christians. Their existence was vividly described in literature: in Zygmunt Uniłowski's *Wspólny pokój* [A Shared Room] (1931) and Jan Dąbrowski's *Miejsce pod*

---

93 Dobrivojević, *Selo i grad*, 45–6; John Lampe, 'Interwar Sofia versus the Nazi-style Garden City: The Struggle over the Muesmann Plan', *Journal of Urban History* 11, no. 1 (1984): 39–62, here 46.
94 *Mały Rocznik Statystyczny 1939*, 61; Teichova, 'East-Central and South-East Europe 1919–1939', 969.
95 E. Ehrich, 'Infrastructure', in Kaser and Radice, *The Economic History of Eastern Europe 1919–1975*, 348.

niebem [A Place Under the Sky] (1938). These were naturalistic portrayals of hopeless stagnation, as the tenants waited either to move once again or die from tuberculosis.

This type of tone was characteristic not only of fashionable literary conventions, but also of wider impressions about social life, particularly housing conditions. The building of the large port town of Gdynia provided rich material: from the villas and comfortable flats of the bureaucratic and industrial elite to the ring of poverty-stricken districts surrounding the city, inhabited by migrants from all over the country who were seeking their fortune in this 'Polish Klondike'.[96] Gdynia was the nation's calling card. Built at record speed and attractively modernistic, it became an economic rival to the Free City of Danzig. It was a perfect response to the myth of the great tempo of building cities and industry that had arisen via news of progress in the USA. In the course of just 15 years (1924–1939), a small fishing village that housed 1,000 people turned into a significant town with more than 120,000 inhabitants, which handled nearly half of Polish foreign trade on the eve of the Second World War.

The realization of a similar dream was visible in the Czech city of Zlín, 'an American city in the middle of Europe', as a Romanian journalist called it in 1936.[97] The city had, at that time, 40,000 residents: 12 years earlier, it had been 10 times smaller. Just as Gdynia grew around the port, Zlín developed around a huge industrial complex – the Bata shoe factory – which employed half of the city's residents. Its owner and the mayor of Zlín, Tomáš Baťa, a sympathizer of the garden city movement, was trying to modernize the town by turning it into a functionalist city. Next to the factory, a city centre was constructed. It consisted of a central green area and public and cultural buildings. Edifices were highly uniform – mostly constructed out of red brick, glass and concrete. The Bata company built three department stores, a hotel, cinema, hospital, school facilities, film studios and a skyscraper. The residential area reflected Baťa's motto: 'work collectively – live individually'. Thus, each worker's family lived in a 'two-story single-family semi-detached house with a yard'.[98]

Achievements of the kind, as witnessed in the Czech city of Zlín, seemed to point towards an urbanized future. It was believed that the construction of specialized industrial centres in poor rural areas could be the cure for many problems: excess labour, the dependence on prosperity in the countryside and the shortages of essential industrial production (felt especially by the army and exporters). The new cities that the Mussolini regime established on the Pontine Marshes, and the industrial development of the Soviet Union, were seen as models of success. In both cases, the decisive factor seemed to be political will imposed by a strong central authority – the opposite of the chaos and fragmentation that were attributed to democracy. Ideas about urbanization were thus often based on authoritarian assumptions. The process had to be orchestrated by the elites – state patronage (often embodied in the person of the dictator, 'the great creator') would give architects and engineers the unfettered freedom to act, and they, in turn, would create a living environment that expressed the vitality of the community within it. This kind of discourse, replete with references to ancient Greece as the ideal of strength and beauty, and averse to bourgeois culture and private property, can be found in the opinions of Romanian and Polish architects at that time, and indeed of Le Corbusier himself.[99]

---

96 Zbigniew Uniłowski, 'Gdynia na co dzień' [1936, everyday Gdynia], in *Brama na świat: Gdynia 1918–1939*, ed. M. Rdesiński (Gdansk: Wydawnictwo Morskie, 1976), 185.
97 'Zlín, un oraş american în mijlocul Europei' [Zlín, an American town in Central Europe], *Gazeta Municipală* (Bucharest) 11 X (1936): 3.
98 E. Blau, *Shaping the Great City*, 69.
99 Cf. Xavier de Jarcy, *Le Corbusier: Un fascisme français* (Paris: Albin Michel, 2015).

The discourse took on an additional meaning in 'backward' territories that required – or so it seemed – a particular intensification of efforts. One expression of this was the construction in central Poland of a huge industrial district with affiliated towns, known by its Polish acronym of 'COP' (Central Industrial Region of Poland), in which the town of Stalowa Wola ('Steel Will': a name in keeping with the style of the era) led the way. 'The bourgeois, worker, and peasant alike/See COP rise in all its might/There a new life buzzes and throbs/Plenty of work, plenty of jobs/No more idleness, poverty, and tears/Today and tomorrow a new home appears.'[100]

What was important for similar projects was the belief that there existed huge untapped reserves of labour in the countryside and huge reserves of raw materials that needed to be exploited – so long as it was not by foreign capital. Associated with this was a tendency to create centralized institutions and vertical management structures oriented towards planning, while in the field of propaganda the emphasis was on discipline, uniform aims and military symbolism. Within this one can discern an attempt by the state apparatus to channel what Ortega y Gasset termed the 'revolt of the masses', in other words, the radicalization of collective expectations under the influence of mass culture. This entailed a negation of liberalism, an intolerance of minorities and a tendency to believe in the quasi-revolutionary destruction of social and economic barriers.

The revolt of the masses was largely diffused in the vortex of war. Here one could cite Jan T. Gross, who emphasizes the continuity between the Second World War and the ensuing Sovietization, which was in fact a continuation of the wartime revolution caused by the collapse of the existing social order.[101] The origins of this phenomenon may be traced back to the Great Depression, which for the masses was a disaster of 'revolutionary' proportions. In turn, the national revolution that started in Germany in 1933 aroused anxiety but also set out a path for its imitators. The latter appeared in most countries of the region. They aimed to redraw boundaries and discriminate against minorities, and later – after the Munich Agreement of 1938 – they realized their vision so effectively that even they were surprised by it. The social order was rocked, not just from the carnage wrought by the war machines, but also by the spontaneous activities of groups and individuals who tried to find a relatively safe haven within the turmoil and often tried to profit from it. The national revolutions were necessarily social revolutions, if only because they entailed the discrimination, expulsion and even annihilation of certain groups of citizens, whose property and workplaces passed into the hands of others.

Urban and rural areas after 1939: 'revolution'

Józef C. was born in 1891 into a large family in the town of Bartschin in Kujawy, a formerly Polish region that for more than a century had belonged to Prussia. His father was a Polish carpenter. At the age of 14, Józef obtained an apprenticeship at a pharmacy in Gnesen, a city known to Poles as their ancient capital – Gniezno. He worked in various pharmacies in that part of Prussia until 1913, when he was conscripted into the military, training as a photographer for the Imperial German Air Service. Germany lost the war, and Józef C. took part in the Wielkopolska Uprising of 1918–19, as a result of which the region became part of the new Polish state. In 1920, he opened his own pharmacy in the town of Leszno and made a

---

100 A fragment of a rhyme printed in Polish school notebooks in the late 1930s.
101 See Jan Tomasz Gross, 'Social Consequences of War: Preliminaries to the Study of Imposition of Communist Regimes in East Central Europe', *East European Politics and Societies* 3, no. 2 (1989): 198–214.

success of it. Nineteen years later, after the German attack on Poland, Leszno became part of Nazi territory and was renamed Lissa. Poles were expelled to the German zone of occupation, the *Generalgouvernement*. After his pharmacy was taken over by a German, Józef C. travelled to Warsaw. There he worked on the black market until the opportunity arose to acquire a pharmacy that the German authorities had confiscated from a Jewish individual; it was situated on Bielańska Street, a good location in the city centre. The previous owner died in the Warsaw Ghetto. Józef C. acted as a *Treuhänder* (trustee) until the Germans agreed to sell the pharmacy to him in instalments. He still had not repaid this loan when the Warsaw Uprising broke out in the summer of 1944. Bielańska Street was burnt to the ground. Józef C. found a job working in a warehouse that supplied uniforms to the insurgents. He survived. Like thousands of others, he was expelled from the city after the defeat of the Uprising. He spent time in a transit camp and then lodged with a peasant near the city of Cracow. The war ended, and Józef C. returned to Leszno, which had once again become part of Poland. He found his business in good condition (it included a bookshelf left behind by the former German occupant) and resumed his pre-war life. Two years later, however, the communist authorities launched the 'battle over trade'. The rising tax burden made it impossible for Józef C. to run his business, so he decided to surrender it to the state. He tried to earn a living from a photography workshop that he set up in his home. Yet the problems continued: he became the victim of denunciations by a person who was interested in acquiring his apartment. Despite the surrender of his business, the tax authorities imposed a ruinous tax upon Józef C., and in the autumn of 1950, he was arrested by the political police. His apartment was opened to the public as the premises of a 'profiteer', and its furnishings were seized to make good the unpaid tax. Stocks of food, matches and soap discovered in the apartment were used as evidence of profiteering. The books left behind by the German administrator of the pharmacy, and Józef's acquisition of a Jewish business in occupied Warsaw, served to substantiate the charge of collaboration. In February 1951, Józef C. was sentenced to two years in a labour camp. His barrister made a plea for leniency, in which he wrote of his client:

> For quite some time, as a result of ... personal experiences, especially during the occupation, he has suffered very serious heart problems (angina pectoris), which have in turn given rise to a mental condition known as manic disorder. He has lived in seclusion and has shunned contact with other people.

The plea was rejected. The subsequent fate of Józef C. is not known.[102]

There are countless stories similar to the one cited above. In them we see individuals torn from their worlds; trying to go on as best they can; entangled in cooperation with changing regimes; and held to account for that cooperation by subsequent regimes. Józef C. tried to preserve his identity: he was a pharmacist and a Pole, although his knowledge of German helped him during the occupation. Thousands of people were drawn into even more complex games. Between 1938 and 1948, they metamorphosed from Czechs to Poles, Poles to Germans, Germans to Poles, Slovaks to Hungarians, Hungarians to Slovaks, Poles to Highlanders, Jews to Catholics, Catholics to atheists, merchants to proletarians, nationalists to socialists and socialists to communists. The stakes varied: saving one's life; saving one's work and property;

---

[102] The story of Józef C. is found in the records of the Special Commission for Combating Economic Abuses and Fraud, an institution set up by the post-war regime. These are now kept in the Central Archives of Modern Records (AAN) in Warsaw, catalogue no. 328.

acquiring work and property; avoiding deportation; being able to remain in a city; being able to migrate to a city. Official languages and place names continually changed. Capitals vanished (Vienna, Prague, Warsaw, Belgrade) and capitals of the 'national revolution' appeared (Bratislava, Zagreb). Carpathian Ruthenia, which after the First World War became a province of Czechoslovakia, briefly declared independence as Carpatho-Ukraine in 1939, only to return to Hungarian control; it subsequently became part of the USSR and its inhabitants suffered mass deportations. The constantly changing political geography altered the social geography, giving rise to revenge and ethnic cleansing in the later Yugoslavia and in Volhynia. These were the 'bloodlands', to borrow Timothy Snyder's phrase.[103] The quest for ethnic and religious homogeneity did not cease after the war; it took the form of mass expulsions, repatriation and the exchange of populations between countries.

Nothing would be as it was before: although towns could re-emerge and new communities flourish, the Jewish population, annihilated in the Holocaust, would never return. And with it disappeared the world of the *shtetl* and the Jewish districts of larger cities, which had, to a large extent, defined the Central and East European space. The void created by the Holocaust proved to be – also due to the practices of the post-war authorities – a moral void, in which the abandonment of memory about the Jewish population was symptomatic of a more general erosion of social ties within the towns and cities. It should be emphasized that Jewish towns, with their distinctive culture and economy, disappeared from territories under Soviet control as well, because of policies that were detrimental to their existence.[104] Occupiers, and later 'liberators', manipulated grievances and took advantage of long-standing economic and ethnic tensions. There were changes in ownership, often executed through the chaotic looting or seizure of abandoned property. After the war, this led to a syndrome of harbouring property of uncertain ownership (which included waiting in trepidation for former owners to return). The beneficiaries were significant in number. For decades, they remained silent about what they had done during the war – and what they had done was shrouded by the propaganda of national solidarity.

Between 1938 and 1948, revolutionary changes occurred in urban–rural relations. One must, of course, be wary of easy generalizations: the fate of each region was different. Such generalizations include portraying the experience of rural areas as traumatic and heroic. The image of the countryside as a victim of the invaders' ruthlessness, starving and burning, supporting the patriotic partisans, is as true as it is one-sided. It is an image that resonates with an earlier idealized vision of the peasantry as a bastion of national values. More recent historiography challenges this vision, especially when it tackles subjects such as the persecution of Jews by peasants during the Nazi occupation. Yet an image of the countryside created on that basis – peasants taking advantage of the hunger in the cities, plundering the property of displaced persons, hunting down Jews – would be similarly one-sided. What remains is a general assessment: the countryside was subjected to radical changes imposed from the outside, to which it tried to adjust; it suffered drastic shortages (remembered as 'eating potato peel') and often bloody pacification. Peasants were incorporated into the war economy and were expected to supply the required quotas of food. In the Protectorate of Bohemia and Moravia, strict control of agricultural production was introduced, and it was thus very hard to withhold supplies. Elsewhere – in Serbia, in parts of Yugoslavia under the Italian and Hungarian occupations, in the former Czechoslovakia and in the *Generalgouvernement* – the new authorities faced hostility

---

103 Timothy Snyder, *Bloodlands: Europe Between Hitler and Stalin* (New York: Basic Books, 2010).
104 Cf. A.S. Zamoysky, *Transformatsiia mestechek*.

Urban and rural development

from farmers and resorted to requisitioning.[105] Rural areas closed in on themselves and opted for self-sufficiency: they developed flax and fruit cultivation, weaving and leatherworking. On the other hand, farmers who lived close to large towns and cities were able to create trading networks. They supplied the starving urban population and managed to survive for several years in a situation of high risk but also of unprecedented income. The experience of rural artisans was similar. In Zebrzydowice (a large village in southern Poland), a network of shoemaker's workshops had developed in the interwar years that was barely able to withstand the competition from factory production. The Nazi occupation caused the market to collapse, but this was soon followed by prosperity: the factory production of footwear was incorporated into the war economy, and now artisans had a market to which they could sell their products. They grew rich, especially in 1943–1944.[106] The impact of even the most brutal occupation was not unequivocal and often ran contrary to collective memory. However, the enormity of the human and material losses necessarily took primacy.

It was assumed that in Yugoslavia and Poland the material losses amounted to one half of national wealth; in Hungary, slightly less (though Budapest suffered greatly); in Czechoslovakia, 25 per cent (especially in eastern Slovakia); and much less in Bulgaria and Romania, although in Romania the war was followed by famine. The devastation was caused not only by the hostilities, but also by planned exploitation, such as the export of machinery and equipment from the occupied territories (to Nazi Germany, and later to the Soviet Union), the planned destruction of cultural heritage (historic monuments), retaliatory burning and destruction, and finally spontaneous looting. There were many actors in these events, although national historiographies have focused on the losses caused by the enemy. Even deeper wounds were made to the collective psyche. These were associated with experiences on the front and in the camps, with rape, orphanhood and ill treatment.

Entire places disappeared from the face of the earth. The signs of physical damage done to the cities would remain for decades. Warsaw lost 70 per cent of its material infrastructure, and the few inhabitants who survived the winter of 1944–45 in the ruins, earned the epithet of 'Robinsons'. A similar fate befell the German cities of Breslau (now Wrocław) and Stettin (Szczecin), which found themselves part of Poland after the war. Among the ruins of Pest, people traded 'thread, candles, sausage, lard, and pogacha'.[107] The situation in Belgrade was equally dire. Niš, Leskovac, Kraljevo and Zadar all suffered huge losses. But there were also towns and regions that, in comparison, practically flourished. In the Karkonosze Mountains, which became part of Poland, one encountered well-appointed homes, offices and guest houses. Holidays in the Karkonosze provided some respite for people from devastated areas of the country. Although Cracow seemed like a vestige of old Europe to a party of Czechs who visited the city in 1947, further north they saw charred ruins, and Warsaw was a place they could not even describe.[108] Life in their own country seemed remarkably 'normal' compared to Poland or Romanian Moldavia where there was a famine and people made grits from acorns. 'The shop windows of Prague impart an impression of happiness and luxury', and in the stores one finds

---

105 E.A. Radice, 'Agriculture and Food', in *The Economic History of Eastern Europe 1919–1975*, vol. 2, eds M.C. Kaser and E.A. Radice (Oxford: Clarendon Press, 1986), 366–71, 392.
106 Adam Sarapata, *Studia nad uwarstwieniem i ruchliwością społeczną w Polsce* [Studies on stratification and social mobility in Poland] (Warsaw: Książka i Wiedza, 1965), 88–92.
107 Sándor Márai, *Dziennik 1943–1948* [Diary 1943–1948], transl. Teresa Worowska, (Warsaw: Czytelnik, 2016), 198.
108 A.C. Nor [Josef Kaván], *Cesta do Polska* [A journey to Poland] (Prague: Hynek, 1947), 93–9.

'coffee, tea, chocolate, powdered eggs, American canned food, and of course the famous Pilsen beer', reported a Bucharest daily.[109] Most goods were rationed, however, and the Polish poet Jerzy Zagórski noted that even in Czechoslovakia, 'such primitive things as salt, petrol, and cigarettes' were missing, a fact which 'seven years ago would have offended every European'.[110]

Nevertheless, despite the degradation, an atmosphere of pioneering cooperation took hold. The particular social energy of those years resulted from the very experience of war. As Elena Zubkova writes: 'The emotional temper of the war years was in many respects unique, not only by virtue of its extreme stress but above all because it required a reordering of previous priorities both in political and in human relations.'[111] Although Zubkova is referring to Stalinist totalitarianism, within which people experienced a special kind of freedom during the war years, her observation is also relevant to the region discussed here. Having shattered the past, the war enforced a reorientation of social attitudes and introduced the possibility of collective action, including mass migration. In Czechoslovakia, Poland, Hungary and Yugoslavia, the expulsion of Germans created a colonizing impulse: homes and farms were seized under the banner of moral righteousness. This logic of settling scores was used to legitimize power. The land reforms and nationalizations carried out from 1944 onwards encompassed not just the property of Germans and 'collaborators', but also that of native 'propertied classes' with whom scores had to be settled.

There were two competing needs: to resume life as it was before, and to break with the past. Both were subject to political machinations. The Polish regime supported the restoration of historic monuments, as this bolstered its legitimacy, but at the same time it announced a radical programme of redevelopment. In less destroyed countries, it was precisely this programme that came to the fore. The authorities promised to create 'new towns' and 'a new countryside' by destroying traditional economic ties and property relations. In regions beset by profound inequalities, the programme appealed to long-standing animosities between town and country. 'In times past, town-dwellers were suspect and to be avoided. They were the enemies of the people. Indeed, all that the peasantry got from the boyars and merchants was oppression and exploitation,' claimed the Romanian writer Mihail Sadoveanu.[112] Yet now the needs of those groups were to be met through a revolution led by the political elites. There was room for grassroots action too, however: the case of József C. is one such example.

From the end of the 1940s, the existing engines of growth were halted in countries that had come under Soviet control: private enterprise was crushed, and the flow of capital blocked. The state control of material resources was key to the implementation of large-scale investments. The new industrial centres absorbed labour, mainly from the countryside. More workers were needed for political reasons, but there was also a desire to accelerate urbanization and eradicate rural poverty, aims which won the support of wider society. However, investment in heavy industry took precedence over the development of public infrastructure and services – the gap between promises and reality continued to widen. In this investment effort, the greatest burden was shouldered by the rural population, which was forced to supply goods in a manner that often resembled the requisitioning of the war years. In return for this bounty, the authorities

---

109 A. Vogel, 'Praga 1947' [Prague 1947], *Jurnalul de Dimineaţa* (Bucharest, 17 March 1947): 1.
110 Jerzy Zagórski, *Indie w środku Europy* [India in Central Europe] (Warsaw: Książka, 1947), 7–8.
111 Elena Zubkova, *Russia After the War: Hopes, Illusions, and Disappointments, 1945–1957* (Armonk, NY: M.E. Sharpe, 1998), 15.
112 Mihail Sadoveanu, 'Însemnări pe marginea Articolului 80' [Notes in the margins of Article 80], in *Opere*, vol. 20: *Publicistica 1936–1955* (Bucharest: Editura de Stat pentru Literatură şi Artă, 1967), 590, 573–96.

promised electrification and a campaign against illiteracy, but these proclamations were generally made for propagandist reasons and did not engender substantial change – for that, people had to wait until the 1960s. But there were major problems associated with the very nature of the economy, which János Kornai termed 'the shortage economy'. In the initial phase, the shortages could be seen as a side effect of the great investment effort that was set to change the character of the region. Yet the adoption of this policy was not tantamount to a simple imitation of the Soviet model. As the Polish émigré journalist Jerzy Stempowski – hardly a communist sympathizer – commented in 1954:

> The government of [Bolesław] Beirut is currently implementing economic policies that were mooted during the period of independence [1918–1939]. It was not possible to implement them so long as Poland remained economically tied to Western Europe. The latter treated Poland as a kind of colony whose purpose was to supply agricultural products on the cheap. … Today, Poland has broken free of those chains. Admittedly, it is now carrying new chains, but it has embarked on a different path which must seem more promising to many, even if its consequences are less clear.[113]

This was not an isolated view, although the weight of those 'new chains' could undermine the whole argument.

Towards 'rural urbanization'

Until 1948–1949, the 'people's democracies' embraced a vision of agriculture that contained a strong element of private ownership. This vision was additionally bolstered by the post-war land reforms, which changed the socio-economic landscape, particularly in Poland (where the reform affected 50 per cent of all farmland), in Czechoslovakia and Hungary (40 per cent) and to a lesser extent in the Balkans (under 10 per cent). With the introduction of these reforms, the number of landless peasants decreased and almost all estates larger than 50 hectares were dissolved. While the reforms encouraged people to stay in rural areas and strengthened existing property owners, the newly created farms were hardly viable. On average, new holdings were two to three hectares in size.[114]

Although in Yugoslavia and Bulgaria the first cooperatives were set up almost immediately after the war, the transition from individual to collectivized ownership was not an openly declared goal. In a speech delivered just after the coup of 1948, Klement Gottwald stated: 'If somebody comes to your village and says that there will be kolkhozes in Czechoslovakia, be aware that he is an agent provocateur of the forces of reaction … There will be no collectivization in Czechoslovakia. We shall go our own way.'[115] Similar declarations were made by the leaders of neighbouring countries. Just a few months later, the first wave of collectivization

---

113 Jerzy Giedroyc and Jerzy Stempowski, *Listy 1946–1969* [Letters 1946–1969], part 1, ed. Andrzej Stanisław Kowalczyk (Warsaw: Czytelnik, 1998), 224–5.
114 Jozo Tomasevich, 'Agriculture in Eastern Europe', *The Annals of the American Academy of Political and Social Science* 317 (1958): 44–52, here 46, www.jstor.org/stable/1031076; W. Brus, 'Postwar Reconstruction and Socio-economic Transformation', in Kaser and Radice, *The Economic History of Eastern Europe 1919–1975*, vol. 2, 595.
115 Jan Rychlik, 'Collectivization in Czechoslovakia in Comparative Perspective', in *The Collectivization of Agriculture in Communist Eastern Europe: Comparison and Entanglements*, eds Arnd Bauerkämper and Constantin Iordachi (Budapest: CEU, 2014), 185–6.

began all over the region. In a brutal drive, the communist regimes competed with each other for the prize of being the first to achieve their goal. Only those peasants with the smallest plots of land were eager to join cooperatives. Others, closely tied to their property, could not easily be persuaded to become agricultural workers. In Yugoslavia, many claimed that they would gladly join if only their fathers (who owned the properties) would let them. Resistance was both economic and cultural. Fear of violating existing norms led to rumours that the family was to be abolished and replaced by a 'community of wives'. Cooperatives were so detested that even local party officials were reluctant to join. Fear of collectivization led to a decline in agricultural production and stagnation in land sales. Traditional fear of the city, regarded as the epicentre of repression, also intensified. Reactions to emissaries from the city (civil servants, officials and students bussed in to 'agitate' amongst the rural population) were sometimes violent. There would appear groups of peasants armed with pitchforks and rifles, or groups of peasant women, with whom the officials and militia were unable to cope. Repression ensued. When the historian Dariusz Jarosz writes that the 'beatings and insults hurled at peasants' in Poland were 'particularly brutal',[116] this does not do justice to the grim experience of collectivization in Romania and Bulgaria. On the other hand, those who joined cooperatives were rewarded with lower taxes and delivery quotas, and received generous supplies of seed, fertilizer and machinery, which were scarce at the time. Because of all the pressures, the campaign progressed at a slow pace. Collectivized peasants displayed an unwillingness to work. The productivity of cooperatives was low and the economic losses serious. The disorganization of agriculture had a detrimental effect on all aspects of life, especially the distribution of food to the towns and cities.

Despite the proclaimed 'worker-peasant alliance' and the 'campaign to link the city with the countryside' (help with harvests, excursions to the cities), the difficulties of urban life provoked anti-peasant feeling. Farmers were accused of hiding food, while migrants from the countryside were accused of selfishly combining income from industrial work with income from their own farms. The authorities took advantage of such sentiments to increase the pressure for collectivization. On the other hand, the real campaign to link the city with the countryside consisted of the black-market trade in food. The various forms of food rationing in the cities also recalled the war years.

For political and economic reasons, the collectivization drive had to be paused. In Yugoslavia (1953) and Poland (1956), most cooperatives were disbanded for good. In other countries, collectivization resumed in the late 1950s, after the turmoil in Hungary had subsided. This second wave was less repressive. To sweeten the pill, officials offered many social benefits (pensions, health insurance) to members of collective farms. At the beginning of the 1960s, the campaign was proclaimed a success: in Bulgaria, the share of individual holdings in total agricultural land had fallen to 1 per cent; in Romania to 9 per cent (individual holdings mainly survived in mountain areas); in Hungary to 6 per cent (mainly in the *puszta*); and in East Germany and Czechoslovakia to 6–7 per cent. Among Comecon countries, the proportions were reversed only in Poland. There, production cooperatives accounted for 1.5 per cent of agricultural land, state farms for roughly 15 per cent (mainly in the former German lands), and private farms for over 80 per cent.[117] But in Poland, too, profound changes occurred in relations between the cities and the countryside.

---

116 Dariusz Jarosz, *Polityka władz komunistycznych w Polsce w latach 1948–1956 a chłopi* [The politics of communist rule in Poland 1948–1956 and the peasants] (Warsaw: Neriton, 1998), 85.
117 *Kraje RWPG 1960–1975* [The Comecon countries 1960–1975] (Warsaw: GUS, 1976), 83.

Urban and rural development

One of the early promises of the 'people's democracy' was to eliminate the network of commercial agents, who were allegedly responsible for poverty in the countryside and high prices in the cities. In many regions, this network had been destroyed by the war and the Holocaust, but it was soon revived. However, the state took over the entire wholesale sector, before it broke up small trade and then created a purchasing system that was intended to provide farmers with stable sales and the cities with controlled prices. Peasants saw this purchasing system as part of the apparatus of repression, since deliveries were compulsory and the imposed prices very low. Depending on the size of the farm, households were divided into several categories. While delivery quotas for the lower categories remained relatively modest, quotas for medium or large holdings were set high, usually surpassing the economic potential of the household. When assessing yields, local officials often manipulated the data. This meant that well-off farmers were sometimes asked to deliver more crops than they had produced. As a result of various abuses, peasants were often left with seeds for the next harvest but no food. Because it was not possible to speak about the considerable economic power of farmers who owned more than 10–20 hectares of land, the term *kulak* was used to describe every 'enemy of socialism' in the countryside. The 'Great Leap Forward-style industrialization policy', which sought to take all grain surpluses from the peasants, crippled agricultural production; for this reason, the compulsory deliveries had to be gradually abolished (in Yugoslavia in 1951–52; in other countries, after 1953). However, the acquisition of large quantities of agricultural products enabled the communist authorities to supply the growing urban population with cheap food and thus keep wages low.[118]

Farmers (and cooperatives) retained (with some caveats) the ability to sell excess production in town markets. There were open-air markets that sold food and fairs that sold craft products. The local market was not, however, as important as it used to be. This was partly because the state supported factory production and made life difficult for rural craftsmanship. In Zebrzydowice, mentioned earlier, shoemakers thrived until 1948 and their prosperity was reflected in their Sunday appearance: suede shoes, silk shirts, hats and fur-lined coats. Marriage to a shoemaker was an attractive prospect for a country girl, who would thereby acquire the status of a 'lady'. Yet their businesses were destroyed by the communist 'battle over trade'. When shoemakers began to be forced to join cooperatives, many abandoned their workshops and moved into agriculture. Apprentice shoemakers, however, appreciated their change of fate. Once in a cooperative they were free of control by the owner and no longer had to provide informal services to him. They entered a regulated system of work and received vocational education.[119]

The growing urban-industrial sector absorbed labour and altered relations within rural communities. Consider, for instance, the village of Żmiąca in southern Poland, studied at the beginning of the twentieth century by the economist Franciszek Bujak, and after the Second World War, by the sociologist Zbigniew T. Wierzbicki. The village suffered heavily during the occupation, having been subject to requisitioning. Then there was the dramatic post-war period, when the area was engulfed in fighting between anti-communist partisans and the forces of the regime. Żmiąca escaped collectivization, however, and in the 1950s the structure

---

118 Nigel Swain, 'East European Campaigns Compared', in Bauerkämper and Iordachi, *Collectivization of Agriculture*, 518; Dobrivojević, *Selo i grad*, 299; Mark Pittaway, *Eastern Europe 1939–2000* (London: Hodder Arnold, 2004), 55; Felix Wemheuer, 'Collectivization and Famine', in *The Oxford Handbook of the History of Communism*, ed. Stephen A. Smith (Oxford: Oxford University Press, 2014), 409.
119 Sarapata, *Studia nad uwarstwieniem*, 93–8.

of its agricultural land and population (around 800 people) was similar to the way Bujak had described it. Yet now there were abandoned farms due to migration – something which had not occurred since the eighteenth century. In addition, the taxation policy of the regime led to the impoverishment of wealthier households and inhibited investment. At a time when young people were freeing themselves from parental control, possession of land was no longer the principal determinant of social position and marital choice. The workforce was also changing: the village was populated by an increasing number of the elderly and children. The old migration pathways – to Canada, Argentina, France and Latvia – were replaced by temporary employment on construction sites in the public and private sectors. Such work was so prevalent among men that it strengthened the position of women, who remained on the farms. At the end of the 1950s, Wierzbicki noted a previously unknown trend: parents attempting to prevent their children from leaving home.[120]

Retaining offspring on the land was not easy. Across the region, urban life acted as a magnet for young people from the countryside. In interviews conducted by the American anthropologist Andrei Simić, peasant migrants who came to Belgrade associated village life with unhappiness, boredom, hopelessness and frustration. One of the interviewees simply stated: 'That life kills a man.'[121] The desire to abandon rural life was pronounced among the young. In 1962, pupils in village elementary schools in Serbia were asked to write an essay about their career plans. Although they expressed positive views about their home villages, no one wanted to remain in the countryside or to pursue a career in agriculture. A boy from a remote mountain hamlet wrote: 'I do not want to become a peasant or agricultural worker. I want to be somebody. This can only be done by going to the city. Those who remain in the village have a difficult life, with much hard work.' Another noted: 'My desire to continue my studies becomes greater when I see how hard workers have to toil with their pick-axes. If I graduate from a university, I will become a gentleman. This is my greatest wish.' Others simply aspired to a better standard of living. A boy in southern Serbia expressed the wish 'to become an engineer, have a comfortable apartment, buy a television set, go to the movies, get a motorbike, travel to cities throughout Yugoslavia, and learn foreign languages.' Another commented: 'I would like to dress nicely in city clothes and be able to eat my fill.'[122]

Studies conducted in Poland in 1970 produced similar findings. One quarter of the villagers expressed their dissatisfaction with rural life, which was greatest amongst the young and more common amongst women than men. This suggested a need for emancipation. The respondents emphasized the unattractiveness of farming, the lack of services and entertainment and the poor public transport. Half of the respondents thought about emigrating to the city, and three quarters wanted their children to be free of manual labour. This was dictated by an aversion towards their own communities: one quarter of the villagers described rural life as dominated by vengeful, envious and – last but not least – ugly individuals. The positive self-stereotype of rural people included such elements as honesty and kindness, yet for the most part they saw themselves as overworked. The 'easier' life of the city was meant to liberate them from all this and allow them to rub shoulders with 'cultured' people. On the other hand, only a tiny minority (4.3 per cent) of rural respondents felt that urban dwellers represented high moral standards.

---

120 Zbigniew T. Wierzbicki, *Żmiąca w pół wieku później* [Żmiąca half a century later] (Wrocław: Ossolineum, 1963), 93, 285–6.
121 Andrei Simić, 'The Best of Two Worlds: Serbian Peasants in the Cities', in *Anthropologists in Cities*, eds George M. Foster and Robert V. Kemper (Boston, MA: Little, Brown, 1974), 192.
122 Joel Halpern, 'Farming as a Way of Life: Yugoslav Peasant Attitudes', in *Soviet and East European Agriculture*, ed. Jerry F. Karcz (Berkeley, CA: University of California Press, 1967), 371–2.

The elderly, in particular, considered them to be arrogant, greedy and lazy, while the city itself was seen as too crowded, expensive and offering unpleasant, mechanized work. It is telling that migrants from the countryside who settled permanently in the cities did not usually confirm this vision. Indeed, they came across as the most satisfied group.[123]

Characteristic of the societal changes taking place in the Eastern bloc at that time was the increase in rural inhabitants employed in the urban economy. Daily commuting became widespread. Peasant-workers combined urban and rural work. Well aware of their advantageous economic position, an especially high number of peasant-workers were willing to exist in this kind of transitional state throughout their life. In some countries, there was eventually a greater proportion of industrial workers in the rural population than in the urban population. In Yugoslavia in 1960, of a total of 2.9 million employees, 1.3 million were peasant-workers who commuted to their jobs.[124] This was an important phenomenon that accelerated rural urbanization. Permanent migration, however, was of fundamental importance. In the 1950–1970 period, the percentage of people employed in agriculture declined in every country of the Eastern bloc, most spectacularly in Bulgaria (from 80 to 32 per cent of total employment) and less dramatically in countries that abandoned collectivization (in Poland from 57 to 38 per cent, and in Yugoslavia from 70 to 57 per cent). Czechoslovakia, which already had a relatively low (40 per cent) share of people employed in agriculture, reduced it by half.[125] In most countries, migration caused an initially desirable and later problematic reduction in the rural workforce. Agricultural economies generally had low levels of mechanization and the loss of labour put economic plans at risk. These problems were less severe in Czechoslovakia, which gave generous subsidies to agriculture and pursued mechanization, and in Poland and Yugoslavia, where agriculture essentially remained in private hands (with the associated problem of land fragmentation), but very pronounced in Bulgaria, which was additionally oriented towards agricultural production within the so-called international division of labour in the Eastern bloc. To counter these difficulties, the authorities increased investment in rural infrastructure in the 1960s and 1970s and turned a blind eye to the cultivation of crops on plots next to peasant farms. Mechanization, irrigation and melioration led to higher productivity and higher incomes for members of cooperatives. The cultivation of industrial crops – flax, hemp, sunflower and sugar beet – became widespread. More attention was paid to the cultivation of orchards, vegetable gardens and vineyards. Animal stock, especially pigs and poultry, began to increase significantly. Pest control was intensified, and fertilizer production rose. According to the United Nations Food and Agriculture Organization, agricultural production in post-war Yugoslavia, Poland and Bulgaria increased by 50–60 per cent and more than doubled in Romania, Hungary and Czechoslovakia.[126] In spite of the tremendous advances in modernization, however, the structure of agricultural production remained traditional due to the prevalence of extensive grain cultivation. At the same time, daily bus services enabled frequent contact with nearby towns and cities. Health care became more accessible as hospitals and pharmacies were established close to rural areas. Residential housing also developed. Attempts were made to create conditions that would encourage young and resourceful people, in particular, to stay in the countryside. In Poland, support was given in the 1970s to private farms that focused on mechanized

---

123 Halina Szostkiewicz, *Wieś i miasto w opinii społecznej: Sprawozdanie z badań* [The village and the city in public opinion: a research report] (Warsaw: OBOP, 1974).
124 Halpern, 'Farming as a Way of Life', 362–4.
125 Ivan T. Berend, *Central and Eastern Europe, 1944–1993: Detour from the Periphery to the Periphery* (New York: Cambridge University Press, 1996), 185.
126 Ibid., 195.

animal production. Twenty years earlier, farmers with similar aspirations had been condemned as kulaks. The Bulgarian authorities applied a different model to control their collectivized agricultural economy. They tried to build new villages with a spatial arrangement and infrastructure that resembled a town. In Romania, in keeping with the radicalism of the regime, efforts were made to construct 'agro-towns'. The idea of such settlements, which were meant to eradicate the differences between town and country, had been circulating in the imagination of Soviet and Eastern bloc politicians, but only in the 1980s in Romania was it put into practice – with disastrous consequences.

In the imagination of the political elite, and probably in the collective imagination too, a vision dominated of 'rural urbanization', that is – according to a Polish study of 1975 – of 'progress' defined as: (1) a spontaneous process of overcoming 'socio-economic and cultural backwardness', leading to (2) a transformation of the occupational structure and work, (3) changes in the structure of the economy towards the 'rational use of labour in rural areas', and (4) changes in the landscape.[127] These processes were driven from above through the creation of press distribution networks and cultural centres, as well as rural cinemas, cafés and libraries. The aim of eliminating rural backwardness, in turn, was linked to a programme of secularization and homogenization (which in some regions was directed against national and religious minorities). Within this raft of ideas was the image of the cultured individual who took advantage of the facilities offered by modern civilization and who was influenced by the press, books, theatres, museums and other public institutions. Such facilities were concentrated in city centres, especially in capital cities, and this 'central' model was to spread to the suburbs and countryside in a planned fashion. Operating in parallel to this was a spontaneous process by which rural culture was urbanized through the diffusion of models. This was accelerated by migration and dual employment and, from the 1960s, by television. Young people were spontaneously drawn towards the urban lifestyle, symbolized in the 1950s by factory-made clothes and 20 years later by jeans; it signified the possibility to organize one's leisure time and the weakening of family control.

Relations between town and country also had another dimension. A great many people who settled in the cities, and were the first generation to be educated there, maintained ties with their families in the countryside (this was especially true in the less urbanized countries). It was common to send children on holiday to their grandparents and other relatives in rural areas, which led to some interesting cultural interactions. Grandmothers were also brought into the cities to look after children, and this forged links with traditional culture and religion.

Spontaneous economic relations developed in and around large towns and cities. Under the conditions of the shortage economy, the supply of food by individuals in the countryside played a special role. In countries where significant private ownership of agricultural land persisted, farms developed that were geared towards servicing the urban market: in Poland, a new group known as *badylarze* (owners of flower farms and greenhouses) emerged, and in many regions, especially in mountain and coastal areas, villages became focused on tourism. In the 1980s, almost every home in the Polish fishing village of Chałupy provided accommodation to holidaymakers, while in the village of Kuźnica, only 10 per cent of the homes which rented out accommodation had been doing so since the interwar period.[128] In highly urbanized

---

127 Witold Rakowski, *Procesy urbanizacji wsi na przykładzie woj. warszawskiego* [Village urbanization processes: the example of Warsaw voivodeship] (Warsaw: PWN, 1975), 25–6.
128 Elżbieta Dziegieć, 'Przemiany wsi rybackich pod wpływem rozwoju turystyki. Przykład Mierzei Wiślanej i Helskiej' [The transformation of fishing villages under the influence of tourism development: the example of the Vistula Spit and Hel Peninsula], in *Przemiany przestrzeni wiejskiej w Polsce i we Francji pod wpływem urbanizacji i turystyki* (Lodz: Uniwersytet Łódzki, 1991), 107–20, here 111.

Czechoslovakia, the vogue was to colonize the countryside as a space for recreation, which took the form of city-dwellers building summer cabins (*chaty*) and adapting peasant cottages (*chalupy*). The furnishings, gardens and lawns testified to a need for middle-class stability but also reflected the escapism of the politically despondent period of 'normalization' after 1970.

Ruralization and the big city

The big city was at the centre of the socio-cultural project imposed on the region after the Second World War. 'Imposed' does not mean that it was devoid of local support, but rather that it was created from the top down, essentially as a ready-made project, having grown out of the experiences of the USSR. Prior to 1956, the project treated the city as a productive and administrative cluster within which the 'New Man' would evolve. Capital cities were the focal point. From Sofia to East Berlin, capitals were subsumed in monumental propaganda, which combined a powerful media message with public spectacles and the aesthetics of Socialist Realism. All of this was inspired by Stalinist Moscow, which had been under construction for two decades, although the grandiose buildings that went up in Berlin, Bucharest, Tirana and Warsaw also betrayed attempts at a national style.[129] Moreover, this was part of the struggle against cosmopolitanism, which – in the context of forging closer ties within the anti-Western camp – included symbolic changes to the way in which the past and present were interpreted. Foreign capital and Western symbolism were eliminated. By the end of the 1940s, the old signs had disappeared from above the newly nationalized shops and cinemas. Budapest lost its Royal, City, Lloyd and Scala cinemas, gaining new ones instead: the Red Star, Worker, Brigade and Torch.[130] The cultural missions of the United States, Great Britain and France were closed down and their former frequenters persecuted. Propaganda campaigns were launched to combat the contamination of youth by 'American lifestyles'. These resembled the campaigns carried out several years earlier by the occupiers or by regimes allied with the Nazis. In Prague, the *Potápka*, and their female version, the *Bedla* – youth subcultures devoted to swing music – became the object of hateful propaganda as in the days of the Protectorate. Their *Malagambist* counterparts in Bucharest were treated in much the same way. Sergiu Malagamba himself, the leader of Romania's most famous jazz orchestra, spent the Stalinist years in prison, a fate he had already suffered under Ion Antonescu. In Poland, the communist press described the *Bażanty* and *Bikiniarze* subcultures of Cracow and Warsaw in a tone similar to that adopted by *Nowy Kurier Warszawski*, a propaganda organ of the *Generalgouvernement*. Such continuity was not conscious but rather stemmed from the structure of the system. Consciously, everything that could be considered as 'fascist' was rejected, and the meaning of this term was extended to include some of the interwar elites in their own countries. The bourgeois elites, if they had not become impoverished by war, were a target for repression from around 1948 onwards. The symbolism of the public space with which they were associated had to be erased, and the culture of their everyday life had to be transformed.

The 'bourgeois city' was seen as ugly (an assessment in keeping with the general view of Eclecticism and Art Nouveau in Europe at that time), but above all it was seen as hostile to the values of the 'people', whose task it now was to develop cities anew. There was a fundamental difference, therefore, between cities that had suffered major damage during the war,

---

129 Cf. Anders Åman, *Architecture and Ideology in Eastern Europe during the Stalin Era* (New York: Architectural History Foundation, 1987).
130 'Budapest Cinema Names: "Western Influence" Eliminated', *The Times* (London, 3 January 1950): 3.

which seemed the obvious sites upon which to build the new reality, and those cities that had survived – together with their elites, economic infrastructure and property. The consequences of this could be paradoxical. The huge reconstruction programme in Warsaw largely united the old and new elites, thus weakening the system's destructive impulses but at the same time legitimizing the regime. Bucharest, on the other hand, which had survived the ravages of war, became the target of a destructive campaign aimed at everything that was 'old'. Whereas Warsaw witnessed the reconstruction of monuments destroyed by the Nazis – Copernicus, Prince Poniatowski, Adam Mickiewicz – in Bucharest, the monuments to King Carol I and to the liberal Prime Minister Ion Brătianu, sculpted by Ivan Meštrović, were removed from their plinths. Nevertheless, in the early 1950s, the grand visions for the new city centres of these two capitals were similar: a Moscow-inspired narrative was combined with a quest for the 'ideal city' based on classical models, with allusions to modernism being smuggled in by architects educated before the war. The political elites demanded triumphal avenues and monumental frontage. An exception was Yugoslavia, whose exit from the group of countries subordinate to Stalin also implied a rejection of the dictates of the Stalinist aesthetic. Due to changed political circumstances, New Belgrade, whose construction began in 1948 as a symbol of progress, grew into one of the finest examples of modernism.[131] There was no monument to the Soviet leader in the Yugoslav capital, whereas in Bucharest, a figure of Stalin overlooked Stalin Park from Stalin Square. In Warsaw, the tallest skyscraper and the biggest square in the 'people's democracies' were named after him. The most imposing monument to Stalin (16 metres high and surrounded by a figural group) was put up in the centre of Prague. The one in the centre of Budapest, which was half as tall, did not survive the Hungarian Revolution in 1956; it was during this period that Stalinist names were removed from Warsaw. In other capitals, the symbolism did not change until 1961 and was pre-empted by changes to architectural designs. Socialist Realism, which attached importance to decoration and precious materials, was very expensive and thus readily abandoned. In around 1960, from Warsaw to Tirana (where monuments to Stalin would persist for another 30 years), architects began to design in a modernist spirit, with a focus on large-scale residential housing. This was a mostly belated reaction to the massive influx of people to the major cities of the region.

During the 1950s and 1960s, nearly half of the active workforce in the region abandoned agriculture. This was a manifestation of the escape from collectivization, but it had also been a long-time aspiration of rural youth. The main attraction was the change in the way that people settled in cities. Previously, the process had often been painful, marked by periods of undernourishment, casual work and vagrancy. The experiences of a young man from the countryside in interwar Budapest were described by László Németh in his novel, *Sin* (*Bűn*, Budapest 1936). At that time, the city absorbed such men as Lajos Kovács, the hero of the novel, through thousands of different avenues. They entered the city through servants' quarters and construction sites, and their fate depended on 'the owner' or 'the meister' or 'Mr and Mrs such and such'. These relationships were sometimes ruthless, but they also created a network of authorities and stabilized the urban culture, which was confronted with an influx of newcomers. In any case, the latter also joined trade unions and radical political parties, which formed a structure that destabilized the existing order. Families and rural communities, in turn, were a stabilizing force.

---

131 Ana Kladnik, 'Happy Living in a New Socialist Town: The Constitution, Distribution, Management and Inhabitation of Apartments in Post-War Yugoslavia and Czechoslovakia', in *Urban Planning and the Pursuit of Happiness: European Variations on a Universal Theme (18th–21st Centuries)*, eds Arnold Bartetzky and Marc Schalenberg (Berlin: Jovis Verlag, 2009), 116–27, here 119.

Their members who settled in the city created new pathways that facilitated the migration of friends and relatives.

The regimes of the 'people's democracies' brought about fundamental change. Large-scale industrialization required easy access for migrants to the centres of industry. The existing absorptive fabric of the cities, composed mainly of private entrepreneurs, was destroyed. In its place a system of planned employment was created, which absorbed migrants into the national economy, accommodated them and provided them with canteen food and other forms of assistance. This was a constant theme of the propaganda, although migrants were frustrated by the gap between the sugar-coated image and the reality. Nevertheless, they entered the cities more confidently than ever before, finding protection under the umbrella of public institutions and learning how to take advantage of the assistance on offer. This meant that workers usually conformed very rapidly, especially as most were afraid of getting on the wrong side of works councils and party organizations. At the same time, older authorities such as the *meister* (that 'god' of workers) lost their significance. Fear of dismissal was no longer so acute; workers themselves often abandoned jobs in order to find better ones. This turnover of staff – a problem that constantly threatened the achievement of targets – was a kind of arena of freedom for workers. Since the assistance provided did not include respect for workers' rights – the so-called trade unions represented the interests of the employer – abandoning work was a way of 'voting with one's feet' and of signalling dissatisfaction. Workers were generally confident of finding another job. The ranks of 'itinerants' – people who moved between building sites, cities and regions – swelled.

A typical place where young migrants would be socialized was in workers' hotels, especially those located in cities undergoing reconstruction or development. In Warsaw in 1951, there were around 130 such hotels, which gave shelter to 10,000 people. The majority of these hotels were very basic (two thirds had no sewage system), but this was hardly ever a deal breaker for the guests. The mere fact of being in the city opened up extraordinary opportunities. And, in any case, for many guests, being in a workers' hotel meant the freedom to drink and play cards rather than to attend talks in the common room. Indeed, in 1952, the head of Warsaw's communist party organization, Władysław Wicha, claimed that the hotels were a 'hide-out for yobs, who often engage in debauchery and hooliganism'.[132] This was hardly a sound basis for the creation of the 'New Man', all the more so in towns where the system of assistance was less developed. In Belgrade, as mayor Branko Pešić noted, migrants were forced to

> seek accommodation anywhere. Some manage to find an apartment, but they are the smallest percentage. A great many are forced to seek accommodation in cellars, in unhygienic apartments, or in barracks. Those who haven't seen it should see how it works … This no longer exists even in Africa.[133]

For newcomers, these 'African' conditions were a stage on their journey to a dream future, which meant gaining a foothold in the city and pursuing educational and professional advancement.

---

132 Marek S. Szczepański, *'Miasto socjalistyczne' i świat społeczny jego mieszkańców* ['The socialist city' and the social world of its inhabitants] (Warsaw: Uniwersytet Warszawski, 1991), 56; Błażej Brzostek, *Robotnicy Warszawy: Konflikty codzienne (1950–1954)* [Warsaw workers: everyday conflicts (1950–1954)] (Warsaw: TRIO, 2002), 164.
133 Mari-Janine Calic, *Istorija Jugoslavije u 20. veku* [The history of Yugoslavia in the 20th century], trans. from German by Ranka Gasic and Vladimir Babic (Belgrade: Clio, 2013), 260.

The policy of the 'people's democracies' responded to a deep-seated desire among rural inhabitants to obtain a higher education. This did not just mean earning a teaching qualification, with all the prestige that it traditionally conferred, but also gaining technical or even engineering qualifications, which were previously out of reach for rural youth. People could now forget about the various shortcuts into the city and instead take advantage of the broad pathways to advancement created by the machinery of the state. One consequence of this was the rise of a phenomenon known from the Moscow of the 1930s: the peasant metropolis.[134] The massive influx of people into the big cities damaged urban culture, which had already been weakened by the deliberate destruction of its economic and symbolic fabric. Some likened the influx of migrants to a destructive 'invasion', which in the minds of existing inhabitants was equated with political oppression. While all this was going on, owners had their stores, pharmacies, bars and craft shops – institutions rooted in local tradition – taken away from them. Models of success in both life and business were destroyed. The migrants, in turn, during the first phase of the changes, i.e. the 1950s, pinned their hopes on rapid advancement. In the second phase, however, having achieved stability, they began to adopt the anti-rural prejudices that had long been part of urban culture. The stigmatization of new arrivals was characteristic of the 1960s and 1970s. Entrenched communities perceived them as intruders who reduced the pool of available apartments and university places and who benefited from the support of their rural hinterland (especially supplies of food). Certain types of behaviour were also attributed to migrants from the countryside. These included poor hygiene (coal in the bathtub, pigeons on the balcony) and uncouth manners (jostling with their elbows, spitting on the pavement).[135] Very similar prejudices developed in the cities of the West, but mostly in regard to immigrants from Africa and Asia. In the region described here (except in Yugoslavia), these stereotypes mainly concerned the native community, within which the urban–rural divide was the key distinction. This was to some extent a repetition of processes that parts of the West had experienced in the nineteenth century.

According to György Enyedi, socialist urbanization in East-Central European countries 'was not a new model of modern urbanization'. Although countries in the region replicated stages of the global process of urban development, each stage of urbanization was marked by special characteristics. As in Western Europe, post-war industrialization led to the 'urban concentration of population, the spatial separation of home and workplace, the development of functional zones within cities, suburbanization, etc.' On the other hand, 'state socialism changed the content and functioning of urban society. Instead of middle-class development, proletarianization became widespread. Instead of autonomous, individual decisions made by citizens, centrally designated and strictly controlled rules dominated urban life, including leisure, culture, and political activity'.[136]

These changes differed, of course, depending on the country. Historically, the most urbanized was the German Democratic Republic, which had an old settlement network and, particularly in Saxony, a uniform network of small towns and several large industrial clusters. It also inherited a legacy of wartime destruction, the overcoming of which became part of the

---

134 Cf. David L. Hoffmann, *Peasant Metropolis: Social Identities in Moscow, 1929–1941* (Ithaca, NY: Cornell University Press, 1994).
135 Cf. Błażej Brzostek, 'The Ruralization of Bucharest and Warsaw in the First Post-War Decade', in Borodziej, Holubec and von Puttkamer, *Mastery and Lost Illusions*, 99–119.
136 György Enyedi, 'Urbanization under Socialism', in *Cities after Socialism: Urban and Regional Change and Conflict in Post-Socialist Societies*, eds Gregory Andrusz, Michael Harlo and Ivan Szelenyi (London: Blackwell, 1996), 102; György Enyedi, 'Urbanization in East Central Europe: Social Processes and Societal Responses in the State Socialist Systems', *Urban Studies* 29, no. 6 (1992): 869–80, here 876–7.

GDR's mission and which allowed the cityscapes of East Berlin, Leipzig and Dresden to be redesigned. A settlement structure similar to that of the GDR could be found in the Czech part of Czechoslovakia, which contrasted with the Slovak part and with Poland and Hungary in terms of its uniform development. Despite the pressure to expand heavy industry, it was mainly the medium-sized cities that evolved, and Prague basically retained its pre-war size. This was in part due to administrative obstacles, but also to the fact that investment was directed more towards Slovakia. Bratislava, which in 1939 had fewer than 140,000 inhabitants, by the early 1970s had in excess of 300,000. Around its small historic centre new housing estates sprang up: the largest in the 1960s was Ružinov, and in the following decade the huge Petržalka appeared. In Hungary, investment was focused on Budapest and the Northern Highlands. Several new industrial cities were built, including the flagship Sztálinváros (renamed Dunaújváros in 1961), but the settlement system was stable compared to Romania and Bulgaria, not least because Hungary's birth rate was lower than in those two countries. Despite the development of medium-sized cities, Budapest maintained its position: at the beginning of the 1970s, it approached two million inhabitants, while the second largest city, Miskolc, had only 200,000. Among the 'fraternal states', neighbouring Romania had the highest concentration of population in large cities: 13 of them had 100,000 inhabitants. This was the effect of ruthless industrialization, which did not slacken after 1956 but merely had a lower social cost. The consequences of the policy pursued earlier under the iron leadership of Gheorghe Gheorghiu-Dej recalled the Five-Year Plans in the Soviet Union. The pressure of collectivization pushed the rural population into the cities. Repression decreased in the 1960s, but the logic of development remained unchanged. The investment effort meant that in statistical terms Romania developed as rapidly as Japan. Between 1948 and 1969, the increase in the urban population fully accounted for the country's overall population growth, while the share of the rural population declined from 75 per cent to less than 60 per cent. Bucharest and the 12 largest cities accounted for 58.5 per cent of Romania's urban growth. Most large cities were remodelled, and vistas of huge housing estates were at the forefront of the propaganda message. This development took place largely at the expense of rural areas, whose poverty was masked by references to tradition and folklore. Bulgaria experienced even faster urbanization: between 1950 and 1970, not only did cities fully account for the country's overall population growth but the number of urban residents also increased by 0.8 million. At the beginning of the 1950s, only two cities had more than 100,000 inhabitants, with the number rising to six 20 years later. This was accompanied by rural depopulation that in some regions was drastic. In Poland and Yugoslavia, despite mass migration, such radical changes did not occur. Yugoslavia was marked by its decentralized management system, in which there was no general concept of human settlement development.[137]

However, the Yugoslav model, which gave cities and regions considerable autonomy, was the exception rather than the rule. Urbanization was closely tied to the allocation of funds, which was determined in centralized economic plans devised by planning institutions. Thus, in the 1950s, urbanization followed from industrialization. The development of heavy industry created a constant demand for labour. This allowed unemployment to be eliminated, at least amongst men. Full employment became a factor in the legitimization of power. On the other hand, the strong demand for labour in heavy industry and construction, which constantly

---

137 Jiří Musil, *Urbanizacja w krajach socjalistycznych* [Urbanization in socialist countries], trans. Květa Król (Warsaw: Książka i Wiedza, 1984), 335–70; F.E. Ian Hamilton, 'Urbanization in Socialist Eastern Europe: The Macro-Environment of Internal City Structure', in *The Socialist City: Spatial Structure and Urban Policy*, eds R.A. French and F.E. Ian Hamilton (Chichester: John Wiley, 1979), 177.

needed new workers, led to poor organization of the production process, an unskilled workforce and low productivity. Attempts were made to resolve these problems within the framework of the planning system – through training, recruitment and the relocation of personnel. This required hierarchical subordination and basically eliminated local government. Until the end of the 1940s, local authorities were at least able to manage their own revenues from taxes, loans and subsidies. The activity of associations and foundations was also tolerated. Later, all these forms of activity were suppressed, and local governments were transformed into 'popular councils', whose legal and financial tools allowed them to do little more than implement central government directives. In this situation, 'community action' – in other words, the mobilization of residents to build pavements and plant trees – became a surrogate for local investment and acquired a degree of notoriety. Similar actions were taken up by bodies established to replace local residents' associations. Usually called 'block committees', the purpose of these bodies was essentially to organize a system of supervision and mobilize people to participate in elections. At the same time, tenants had little influence over the administration of housing, which, in a situation of shortages, led to the deterioration of buildings and thus to the perceived 'greyness' of cities. Tenants responded by concentrating on their internal living space: polished parquet floors contrasted with unkempt exterior staircases. The authorities responded by periodically painting the facades on main streets, which only accentuated the contrast between the fronts of buildings and their backyards, and between presentable city districts and the outskirts. In any case, this was contrary to the aims of socialist town planning, whose purpose – in the words of one theorist – was to eradicate 'the eternal opposition between the centre and the periphery'.[138]

The aim was 'to introduce the people into the city centre'. In Warsaw, where this slogan was announced by 1950, such an introduction was to result from reconstruction and redevelopment. In the cities that had escaped war damage, this meant repurposing old houses. The authorities established administrative methods to accommodate people in private apartments, which might have seemed justified in cities ravaged by war (with the vague hope that the policy would only be temporary), but which was primarily associated with the struggle for the new face of the city. In Romania, members of the old elites (if they avoided arrest) were shunted out to the suburbs, their place taken by worker families, but the better buildings were taken over by the state apparatus. In Bucharest, the political elites colonized an elegant villa district in the north of the city previously inhabited by the old plutocracy. This was accompanied by the acquisition of movable property, a process that sometimes had a semblance of legality and other times did not. From 1950, the acquisition of property in Romania was based on a decree that mimicked 'revolutionary' Soviet legislation: buildings belonging – according to the deliberately vague criteria – to 'elements of the greater bourgeoisie' (and their families), and buildings which had been constructed 'for the purposes of exploitation' passed into state ownership without compensation. Those who attempted to obstruct the process risked ten years' hard labour and the confiscation of all their assets. The intensive colonization of old houses made it possible to save on investment. In Bucharest, whose population rose between 1948 and 1956 by around 200,000 inhabitants, only a few hundred apartments were built each year (and in 1951 – only 40, including 23 studio apartments).[139] Under such conditions, one feature of the system for allocating apartments – common to all countries of the region – was particularly striking: the

---

138 Edmund Goldzamt, *Architektura zespołów śródmiejskich i problemy dziedzictwa* [The architecture of the city centre complexes and problems of heritage] (Warsaw: PWN, 1956), 18.
139 *Viața Capitalei* [The life of the capital] (Bucharest, 20 April 1950), 1; *Anuarul statistic al orașului București 1960* [Statistical yearbook of the city of Bucharest 1960], 37.

most desirable housing stock was distributed among the political elite, managers, engineers and expert technicians.[140] Research conducted in Yugoslavia showed that 'the better the quality of a new housing complex or residential building, the more fully equipped and better located it was, the more likely that its tenants would be powerful people with a high social status'.[141] And it was the big administrative and industrial centres that offered their elites the best conditions.

These new spatial divisions, related to the status of selected political and professional groups, obliterated the old divisions, which were usually far more complex. Of huge importance here was the bureaucratic management of housing stock, but also economic policy (which severed the roots of local manufacturing) and more or less forced migration. The distinctiveness of neighbourhoods faded – there were no longer 'better' or 'worse' streets and houses. In mid-1950s Bucharest, which was home to 44,000 Jews, the south-eastern district was still colloquially referred to as the *cartierul evreiesc* (Hebrew neighbourhood). It is telling, however, that in subsequent decades, government policy would cause a tenfold decrease in that community and the disappearance of the neighbourhood. Similar homogenization could be observed in most major cities of the region. The determinants of social position likewise became blurred. Whereas a fairly narrow group of government employees was instantly recognizable – symbolized in the 1950s by the staff limousine – for many other people it was difficult to maintain distinctions, whether due to poverty or fear. Wartime pauperization had led to changes in habits. It was now acceptable, for instance, for middle-class women to walk down the street without stockings (or in trousers) and for their male counterparts not to wear a hat. From the late 1940s, uniformity was also encouraged by government policy. Signs of prosperity and success were camouflaged. It became common to leave private cars and shops in a deliberately shabby state so as not to attract the attention of the tax authorities. Everyday life in the cities underwent profound change as a result of chronic shortages, which also created a continuity with the war years. There were permanent queues outside shops, although their length varied from Prague to Bucharest. As in Moscow, attempts were made to conceal the shortages: shop windows on the main streets were laid out with wooden imitations of cured meats and citrus fruits. There emerged a wide variety of grassroots strategies to acquire goods and exchange information about them. Goods were often bought up when rumours spread about the outbreak of war or the introduction of new currency (the draining effects of this were experienced by all the societies of the region, in some cases several times). The extreme pragmatism of everyday clothing was dictated by the crowded conditions in trams, trolleybuses and shops. Throngs of commuters at peak hours strained public transport to breaking point. Private transport went into decline. Contrary to global trends, between 1950 and 1955 the number of passenger cars in Warsaw fell from 9,300 to 8,300; in that same period, the number of horse-drawn carts increased by one quarter.[142] Big cities swelled in the afternoon, with crowds swarming around shops, and then emptied in the early evening. This was connected with the rhythm of work as defined by the strict principles of socialist discipline, which caused widespread fatigue but also deprived people of their evening leisure time by forcing them to attend training courses and meetings. The desolation of cities was also caused by the disappearance of affluent consumers and the closure

---

140 John Sillince, 'Housing Policies in Eastern Europe and the Soviet Union', in *Housing Policies in Eastern Europe and the Soviet Union*, ed. John A.A. Sillince (London: Routledge, 1990), 13–14, 38; Ivana Dobrivojević, 'Urbanization in Socialism: Everyday Life in Yugoslav Towns, 1945 to 1955', in *Cityscapes in History: Creating the Urban Experience*, eds Katrina Gulliver and Helena Toth (Burlington, VT: Ashgate, 2014), 88.
141 Sreten Vujović, *Ljudi i Gradovi* [People and cities] (Budva: Mediteran, 1990), 83.
142 *Stolica* [The capital] (Warsaw, 2 September 1956): 5.

of entertainment venues. The strict energy policy, which meant that streets and shop-window displays were not properly lit, also made itself felt. All this created a new frame of experience that was difficult for the existing population, and especially its elites, to accept. When, in the autumn of 1955, the art history professor Karol Estreicher got his first opportunity in years to travel from Cracow to the West, his family and friends asked for the following items: a nylon blouse, thread, a pair of prescription glasses, a copy of *Life* magazine, a powder-case, a radio, rum, underwear, shoes and a pencil. In Belgium, he noted: 'I feel awkward because my clothes are so terribly unfashionable.'[143] Shortages had radically disrupted his habits. Yet people like Estreicher could, thanks to domestic helpers and institutional supply networks, avoid the common frustrations of the era, such as waiting for long hours in queues. That was the fate of the 'working population', and it contributed to the burgeoning of all sorts of rumours to explain the shortages, such as the export of food to the USSR or its hoarding due to an impending war.

Despite all the upheavals, in many large cities elements of the old culture of everyday life survived. In Prague, cheap popular pubs, *vyčepy piva*, remained a cultural institution. In Budapest, the elegant *Gerbeaud* café tried to maintain its reputation, albeit under the name *Vörösmarty*. On Warsaw's central street, the private *Blikle* patisserie, boasting a hundred-year-long tradition, prospered. In the surrounding area, dozens of private shops and craft workshops continued to ply their trade, yet they were now enveloped in an aura of shady business – their customers' incomes were deemed suspect and they ran the risk of repressive tax inspections. This kind of atmosphere was common in big cities, where a lot of trading was done in the grey economy and where corruption thrived, aided by the administrative and police apparatus. Writer Mircea H. Simionescu described the Bucharest of 1963 in his personal diary as a 'mass of questionable relationships and shady-goings-on, where danger is ever-present'.[144] Only clever citizens were able to fish in this murky water, and in this respect the large cities were very different to the provinces. This also flew in the face of propagandist assurances about equality of opportunity.

Aware of the growing urban problems, governments tried to curtail migration to capitals and other large cities. The issue of migration, which had begun soon after the war, was initially thought to be a temporary phenomenon, yet proved to be tenacious. During the late 1940s, Yugoslav communists tried to limit population growth in the capital in various ways, such as by expelling 'unproductive citizens' and by issuing special residence permits.[145] The governments of other Eastern European countries tried to control migration through administrative measures. City councils and central agencies had the authority to grant or refuse permission for non-residents to live and work within the boundaries of certain cities. In reaching their decisions, officials usually considered whether a given job was important for the national economy and whether the potential migrant was suitably qualified. However, the decisive factor was the availability of housing.[146] 'Do any countries in the world have such prohibited areas? – unless we're talking about military zones or imperialists in the colonies dividing up cities between whites and blacks', protested the author of a letter to Polish Radio in the summer of 1956.[147]

---

143 Karol Estreicher (jr), vol. 2 of *Dziennik wypadków* [A diary of events] (Cracow: Pałac Sztuki Towarzystwa Przyjaciół Sztuk Pięknych, 2002), 416–17.
144 Mircea H. Simionescu, *Febra: File de jurnal, 1963–1971* [The fever: leaves from a diary, 1963–1971] (Bucharest: EdituraVitruviu, 1998), 54.
145 Dobrivojević, 'Urbanization in Socialism'.
146 F.E. Ian Hamilton, 'Urbanization in Socialist Eastern Europe', 187–8; Daniela Koleva, 'Rural–Urban Migration in the Normal Biography', *Ethnologia Balkanica* 9 (2005): 120–21.
147 Polish Radio and Television Archive, Warsaw, catalogue no. 1050/17, *Biuletyn Listów* 52, no. 5 (August 1956): 6.

Strategies to bypass residency restrictions were so typical of the times that they became the topic of comedy films such as *No More Divorces* (*Rozwodów nie będzie*, directed by Jerzy S. Stawiński, Poland 1963) and *Bucharest Identity Card* (*Buletin de București*, directed by Virgil Calotescu, Romania 1982). People got into cities by marrying, by gaining specific qualifications or by paying bribes. Con artists sought out naïve migrants to exploit. One such charlatan, who was arrested in Romania in 1968, had 'promised to arrange permanent registration in Bucharest for several people from the provinces, taking from each the sum of 2,000 lei'.[148]

The 'deglomeration' strategies adopted by the Polish and Hungarian governments in the 1960s, which involved relocating certain factories, were also designed to limit the growth of large cities. The aim was to reduce pollution (which may be interpreted as the beginnings of an environmental strategy), lessen the strain on public transport and energize smaller towns. Planners also wanted to concentrate the precision engineering and electronics industries, which required higher qualifications, in the capital cities. This was a response to global technological (and export) challenges, but it was also linked to social change: the influence of relatively well-to-do engineers and managers, educated after the war, who were interested in the expansion of industry and in cooperation with developed economies. Such people formed the power base of regimes oriented towards increasing investment and seeking new forms of political legitimization. The latter could be based on pragmatism (technocracy), meaning the abandonment of many ideological taboos, but also on nationalism, which could complement existing Marxist dogma. Both these trends were accompanied by a change in the way propaganda portrayed the individual. Gone was the 'New Man' existing in the timeless harmony of the totalitarian imagination, and in came the 'Compatriot', who lived in the here and now, and whose particular interests gained recognition as they were deemed to be in tune with the common interest.

Between the old and the new

What would Teofil Kurczak have said about Wyszków in the 1950s? The town lost half of its population as a result of the war and the Holocaust and had been a scene of mass executions. After the war, the 'battle over trade' dealt the finishing blow to its craft industry. The more enterprising inhabitants either migrated to Warsaw or found jobs there, even if this meant commuting three hours one way: at the end of the 1950s, 2,500 inhabitants undertook this journey every day.[149] Wyszków shared the fate of towns that had lost their development potential and become 'dormitory towns', where workers returned only to sleep. Meanwhile, Moravian Vyškov, located in a country spared from war and more economically stable, retained its pre-war material infrastructure (around 2,500 homes) and population (13,000 people). All of its several dozen Jewish inhabitants had perished. Despite the severity of the occupation and the post-war regime, the cultural change experienced by Vyškov was not comparable to that of Wyszków. Yet there were towns where life was immeasurably different, even when compared to Wyszków. Consider Rügenwalde, which found itself in Poland after the war and was renamed Darłowo. Its population was almost entirely replaced, though its material infrastructure remained intact, or at least it did for a while: in 1950 there were 1,800 houses, yet 7 years later there were only 1,100! Local residents had dismantled not just the empty houses but also

---

148 Consiliul Naţional pentru Studierea Arhivelor Securităţii (CNSAS), Bucharest, catalogue no. D 012555, vol. 2, 56: *Buletin Informativ MAI* 53 (16 April 1968).
149 Janusz Szczepański, *Dzieje Wyszkowa i okolic* [The history of Wyszkowo and its surrounding area] (Warsaw: Mazowieckie Towarzystwo Kultury, 1998), 319.

the medieval ramparts because they needed the bricks: such was the price of instability, compounded by the inhabitants' lack of emotional connection with their place of residence.[150] Local development was also hindered by the economic practices of the regime. The Polish town of Stolp, which became Słupsk, rapidly lost its vitality: in January 1948, it was home to 655 private enterprises; a year later, there were only 163. The surviving firms struggled with the punitive tax policy and with the lack of apprentices and aspirants.[151]

Small towns and regions whose roots were severed by the centralized economic regime were divested of their workforce, which was symptomatic of Soviet-style economies.[152] In this situation, development depended on investment in industry, which local party authorities and administrations tried to secure. For Wyszków, an opportunity came in the form of a huge furniture factory, set up in the early 1960s. Projects of this kind were usually accompanied by investment in residential housing and services. New communities soon developed, sometimes marked by a high degree of structural imbalance, such as large groups of female workers in small towns. This phenomenon was portrayed in Miloš Forman's famous film, 'The Loves of a Blonde' (*Lásky jedné plavovlásky*, 1965), in which the female staff of a shoe factory attempt to 'hook up' with a troop of soldiers specially brought in for that purpose. Both the men and the women, the former residing in barracks, the latter in a dormitory, are depicted as transient communities shaped by orders from elsewhere.

Sometimes a decision by the central authorities would 'befall' a town, turning its life upside down. This is what happened to Slatina in Romania. Historically, the town had been associated with its market and craft workshops. After 1948, the latter were merged into cooperatives with revolutionary names, but this did not lead to development or to population growth: in 1956, the town had a population of less than 14,000, the same as before the war. At that time, however, a decision was taken in Bucharest to build an aluminium plant in Slatina. The work, begun in 1963, led to a spectacular influx of construction workers, some of whom were reclassified as factory workers. In 1969, the town had 24,000 inhabitants and was growing. The impact of the plant affected the nearby collective farms, whose poorly paid workers sought employment on the construction site as guards and later as production staff. Soon the collective farms began to suffer labour shortages; the women remained in the countryside.[153] This caused tensions between sectors within the planned economy, which was theoretically meant to eliminate the opposition between town and country.

The 'new city', erected in opposition to the 'old city', sometimes on its ruins or in a poorly urbanized region in order to display clear evidence of progress, represented the quintessence of propagandist ideas in the 'people's democracies'. As Katherine Lebow writes, in the 1950s such cities were to be 'glimpses of tomorrow's reality'.[154] No doubt they also raised the hopes of societies in the region, attracting considerable migration, especially from the countryside. All countries in the region built new cities, usually around industrial plants or mines: Sztálinváros in

---

150 *Gazeta Handlowa* (Warsaw, 26 July 1957): 4.
151 Józef Lindmajer et al., *Dzieje Słupska* [The history of Słupsk] (Słupsk: Polskie Towarzystwo Historyczne, 1986), 332.
152 A.S. Seniavskiĭ, *Rossiĭskiĭ gorod v 1960-e–1980-e gody* [The Russian city from the 1960s to the 1980s] (Moscow: Institut rossiĭskoĭ istorii RAN, 1995), 60, 67–8.
153 Miron Constantinescu and H.H. Stahl, eds, *Procesul de urbanizare în R. S. România. Zona Slatina-Olt* [Urbanization in the Socialist Republic of Romania: the Slatina-Olt region] (Bucharest: Academia de Ştiinţe Sociale şi Politice, 1970).
154 Katherine Lebow, *Unfinished Utopia: Nowa Huta, Stalinism and Polish Society 1949–1956* (Ithaca, NY: Cornell University Press, 2013), 7.

Hungary, Stalinstadt in the German Democratic Republic, Victoria in Romania, Dimitrovgrad in Bulgaria, Havířov and Poruba in Czechoslovakia, and Nowa Huta and Nowe Tychy in Poland. The motivations of migrants to these cities remained fairly traditional: a longing for higher earnings and better clothes, for example, attracted workers to Nowa Huta, the metallurgical plant that arose on the outskirts of Cracow.[155]

The case of Nowa Huta is telling. The city (later to become a district of Cracow) was a symbol of social disorganization and crime during the 'thaw' of the mid-1950s. In the following decade it became famous on account of the 'battle for the cross', an acrimonious conflict between the authorities and the local population, who demanded the construction of a church. At the same time, of all Cracow's districts, it was Nowa Huta that experienced the fastest growth in the number of television sets.[156] The stabilization of the Nowa Huta community was manifested in those two ways. People focused on doing up their apartments and stayed at home more frequently in the evenings to watch television, but they also reconstructed traditional family models characterized by religious rituals. This implied a failure of social engineering, which had assumed that the mass of migrants, plucked from their rural existence, could be moulded into a modern, secular community that embraced the ethos of the 'people's republic'. In the end, the authorities agreed to the construction of the church, which opened in 1977 and boasted a strikingly modernist architecture.

It was not so much the 'New Man' as petit-bourgeois tendencies that could be observed in the new cities. This typified, it would seem, the social atmosphere of the 1960s. In his novel, *The City in the Evening Light* (*Város, esti fényben*, Budapest 1968), Tamás Bárány portrays the imaginary Hungarian industrial city of Fűzfőpatona, a 'socialist city par excellence' that has been built from scratch. In the evenings, the footsteps of passers-by resound with 'the ghastly echo of an empty street', while the presence of the inhabitants is implied by parked cars and lights in the windows of tower blocks. Buying furniture and motorbikes is the inhabitants' prime concern. They have migrated to the city from different regions, often in the hope of quickly being allocated an apartment. The elite are the engineers, who are most adept at making money, and who present a model of success. Bárány suggests that this success is largely down to informal arrangements.

What was significant in Bárány's novel was the motif of trying to find an apartment, which determined migration decisions, one's choice of job and strategies in the workplace. From the mid-1950s, regimes sought to alleviate the housing shortage and used mass construction to legitimize their power. In the second half of the 1960s, the Romanian regime announced that more than two million people, a tenth of the country's population, had moved into new apartments.[157] These newfound hopes for housing, however, were accompanied by growing collective frustration over the way it was allocated and by the unmet needs of citizens. The new landscape, filled with prefabricated, late-Modernist housing estates, also aroused mixed feelings. This type of housing was essentially developed within the state sector (which included factory accommodation) and within the quasi-cooperative sector. The latter gave residents more independence and was also less of a burden on the state. Applicants would make a 'contribution', usually one third of the price of the apartment, which implied acknowledgement by the authorities that citizens could and did enrich themselves. The apartments became their personal prop-

---

155 Wierzbicki, *Żmiąca*, 93.
156 Tomasz Goban-Klas, *Młodzi robotnicy Nowej Huty jako odbiorcy i współtwórcy kultury* [The young workers of Nowa Huta as consumers and co-producers of culture] (Wrocław: Ossolineum, 1971), 117.
157 *Scânteia* (Bucharest, 5 March 1971): 1.

erty, which they did not have to share with others and could pass on to their children. Rigid standards were in force in both the state and cooperative sectors. Newly constructed apartments were uniform, each person was entitled to the same amount of space, and the residents of new estates belonged to different social strata. However, although officials tried to follow egalitarian principles, both in the older parts of towns and in new socialist estates, social segregation, especially in the realm of housing, never ceased. Aware of the existence of hidden rules for the allocation of apartments, citizens devised complicated strategies to circumvent them. These ranged from bribery, which allowed applicants to jump the queue, to the enlargement of living space through the illegal construction of loggias (aided, in 1960s Romania, by 'block committees', which were in theory supposed to prevent such practices).[158]

The informal sphere was even more important in the case of private construction. The practice of family house-building had a long tradition in the region, and it included many jerry-built structures, which began appearing in the nineteenth century, especially around large cities. The regimes of the 'people's democracies' did nothing to curtail this phenomenon, which was widespread in Bulgaria and Poland. Besides, without an extensive black-market supply of materials, even legal private construction would not have managed to survive. In the 1970s, one of the symbols of prosperity was the 'villa' – a metropolitan-style brick house that was coveted by rural and urban inhabitants alike. The growing appetite for education went hand in hand with a desire for family stability and a rejection of the nomadic lifestyle that had characterized the social changes of the 1950s. This was aided by both the economic climate (rising expenditure on welfare and on the production of consumer goods) and the political climate: a lessening of the fear that undermined social ties. In everyday life this signified the return to bourgeois aspirations and the paradigm of the 'cultured individual', which took shape in the nineteenth century and was fundamental to processes of mass social advancement.[159]

Advancement came at a price, however, for it intensified relative deprivation. Take, for instance, the young engineer Kamil Coufal, the hero of Jiří Švejda's novel *The Disaster* (*Havárie*, Prague 1975), who lives in a town of 30,000 inhabitants enveloped in the smoke of a vast chemical plant. Coufal works in the plant as a manager and is a victim of consumption neurosis. He considers his social advancement to be proceeding too slowly and is frustrated by the successes of others. An architect friend, who is not even 30, already has 'a car, a villa, and social status'. This prompts Coufal to look for ways to get ahead by illicit means (he installs a water supply in the villa of a local crook) and this causes him to neglect both his professional and familial duties, which leads to disaster. Although Švejda's novel contained a fair amount of social criticism, it was not 'dangerous' from the point of view of official doctrine: Coufal fell victim to his intoxication with the 'Western lifestyle'. The positive character in the novel is Coufal's father, who belongs to the generation that built the foundations of the system in the 1950s and which craves neither villas nor Ford cars. In the urbanizing societies of the 'people's democracies', changes did occur that were disturbing from the point of view of the system's ideology, but they were largely supported by the evolution of governance and the relative opening up of the regimes to the world.

The potential for change was linked to foreign travel, which in the 1960s became available to the better off. Against a backdrop of ever-expanding technological capabilities (including fashionable ideas about colonizing the cosmos) and the global tourist boom, the possibility of foreign travel

---

158 *Informația Bucureștiului* (Bucharest, 19 July 1968): 1.
159 Cf. Jonas Frykman and Orvar Löfgren, *Culture Builders: A Historical Anthropology of Middle-Class Life* (New Brunswick, NJ: Rutgers University Press, 1987).

was a minor development, but after the experiences of Stalinism it seemed astonishing; it was also more widespread than before the war, becoming a new possibility for the masses. In 1955, fewer than 200 foreign tourists visited Romania and only 172 Romanian tourists travelled abroad from a country of several million, but 5 years later the figures were 70,000 and 14,000 respectively.[160] Passport policy remained strict, however, and the tourist infrastructure was rudimentary, oriented primarily towards workers' holidays (which became increasingly important). In the mid-1960s, there were around 370,000 hotel beds in the European socialist countries, fewer than in Austria.[161] During this period, the Romanian and Bulgarian regimes took some remarkable decisions. The income from tourism prompted them to abandon dogma. Health spas for Western tourists were built on the Black Sea, attracting many visitors, although the Italian design of Bulgaria's Golden Sands was not able to mask the poor service, while the elegance of Romania's Mamaia was at odds with the atmosphere of police intrusion. The resorts were built in the vicinity of collective-farm villages, creating an almost 'colonial' contrast. As one Western visitor wrote in 1962:

> On Saturday afternoons, a different type of guest appears on the beaches of the Golden Sands. These are the workers and peasants who, together with their families, are brought in by lorry from the nearby factories and collective farms. They seem surprised to encounter thousands of bronzed tourists ... They camp in groups and view the strange scenes from a distance. They dare not bathe, since swimming costumes seem to be completely unknown to Bulgarian peasants and to workers who have recently migrated from the countryside. But once a bottle of homemade plum brandy has been passed around, the women summon up the courage to enter the water by lifting up their ankle-length skirts.[162]

Tourist enclaves became a powerful magnet for urban youth. On the Black Sea coast, they could at least observe the newcomers from the West, if not enter into commercial or sexual relationships with them. This was one element of the broader changes that were engulfing the young (especially urban) generation in the countries of the Eastern bloc. Highly symptomatic in this regard was the emotional fervour (and even street disturbances) that accompanied the concerts of the Rolling Stones in Warsaw (1967) and of Blood, Sweat and Tears in Bucharest (1970). The reaction of the authorities was to launch media campaigns against the 'parasites' or (in Romania) to seek out and arrest people with long hair or beards.[163] Only the Albanian regime was able to maintain a consistent policy of isolation.

The disintegration of doctrinal restrictions was also affected by a certain decomposition of the communist bloc in which new points of reference appeared alongside the 'Yugoslav model'. The latter had an enduring significance as a counterweight to the centralized Soviet model and seemed to create a better framework for prosperity. The American economist John Kenneth Galbraith wrote in 1958 that 'arriving in Belgrade from Warsaw makes a striking impression:

---

160 Em. Valeriu, 'Turism, recreație, cunoaștere, prietenie' [Tourism, recreation, acquaintances, friends], in *Almanah Turistic 1961* (Bucharest: ONT).
161 *Przegląd Gastronomiczny* [Gastronomic review] (Warsaw), no. 7 (1968): 21.
162 Franciszka Toruńczyk, 'Na czerwonej Rivierze' [On the red riviera], *Kultura* (Paris), no. 11 (1962): 91.
163 Bogdan Barbu, *Vin americanii! Prezența simbolică a Statelor Unite în România Războiului Rece* [The Americans are coming! the symbolic presence of the United States in Cold War Romania] (Bucharest: Humanitas, 2006), 310; see Kamil Sipowicz, *Hipisi w PRL-u* [Hippies in the Polish People's Republic] (Warsaw: Cyklady, 2008).

the well-stocked shops and the revival of the Yugoslav capital seem to belong to a different world'. A similar tone was adopted in reportage from Yugoslavia in the Polish press, but for political reasons the model could not be imitated. At the beginning of the 1960s, the 'Chinese alternative' emerged. This also sent tremors through the Eastern European regimes, though it largely failed to inspire their increasingly technocratic and consumption-obsessed elites. The latter were more enamoured with the 'Hungarian model', introduced by the Kádár regime in 1968, which permitted quasi-competitiveness in the economy. Its results impressed visitors arriving from other countries in the bloc. 'Paprikash with bread rolls – where on earth does a second-rate eatery find fresh bread rolls on a Sunday evening (not defrosted, mind you, but fresh)?' – wondered a visitor from East Germany in Budapest in the early 1970s.[164] Although the Hungarian model foundered politically and did not dismantle the rules that governed the poorly performing economy, it delayed the symptoms of its crisis by several years at least.

These symptoms, bearable in Czechoslovakia and Bulgaria, were very pronounced in Romania and Poland in the 1980s. They signified extreme shortages of consumer goods and housing, the breakdown of infrastructure, and declining productivity and autarkic tendencies in rural areas. At the same time, the countryside became an informal source of food supply for the cities on a scale unknown since the 1950s. This was especially significant in Romania, where the authorities imposed a drastic regime of frugality. The dictatorship's 'revolutionary' end in December 1989 revealed Romanian cities as an arena of street battles, the likes of which had not been seen in Europe for decades. The end of the 'Yugoslav model', which had long aroused so much jealousy, would be much more dramatic, however.

The realities of the 'transformation'

The year 1989 marked the beginning of the era of 'systemic transformation'. This was accompanied, from 1991 onwards, by the disintegration of multinational states – the Soviet Union, Yugoslavia and Czechoslovakia – creating a new regional landscape. The number of capital cities doubled, and the network of borders became more complicated than before the Second World War. In the south of the region, war returned, reviving the image of the 'Balkan powder keg', which had lain dormant for decades. Nothing could compare with the drama that was to unfold in Bosnia and Herzegovina, but the peaceful societies of Bulgaria, Slovakia and Poland experienced a deep depression as a result of the economic and cultural changes. The states of their economies were different at the outset, and this largely determined the character of the transformation – whether it was more or less painful – as well as its impact on urban–rural relations.

The 'shock therapy' model adopted in Poland coincided with the trough of the country's economic depression. Countries that were healthier in 1989 – Czechoslovakia and Hungary – escaped these drastic social consequences. Romania had already suffered them in previous decades, so there was little appetite among its elites and masses for shock therapy. Consequently, the changes in Romania proceeded at a slower pace and the social costs were spread out over time (which does not mean that they were smaller). After half a century or more – two or three generations of socialization – the societies of the region became reacquainted with the parliamentary system, the free market, convertible currencies, high inflation and mass unemployment. Price deregulation (in Yugoslavia in the 1980s, in Poland in the summer of 1989 and in Czechoslovakia at the beginning of 1991) rapidly led to an equilibrium between supply and demand (also for the first time in half a century) but likewise created the impression that the cost

---

164 Franz Fühmann, *Zweiundzwanzig Tage oder Die Hälfte des Lebens* (Rostock: Hinstorff Verlag, 1973).

of living was suddenly very high. In Czechoslovakia, prices jumped in 1991 by 20–30 per cent and inflation stood at around 56 per cent, compared to 35 per cent in Hungary. Those were the highest inflation rates in Czechoslovakia and Hungary in the 1990s and bore little relation to the experiences of Poland (585 per cent in 1990) and Romania (256 per cent in 1993), not to mention the former Yugoslavia. Poland also experienced record unemployment – 20 per cent by the middle of the decade; in other countries, it hovered around 10 per cent, while in the Czech Republic it remained under 3 per cent. However, Poland was the first country in the region to come out of recession, which it did in 1992, and in the following years it achieved a growth rate of 7 per cent. By the end of the decade, the majority of the countries in the region were experiencing solid growth, yet the dynamism of their economies also exposed the disparity between 'winners' and 'losers'.

The societies of the region were dominated by urban inhabitants. Data from 1995 show that in all the countries, with the exception of Albania (37.3 per cent) and Bosnia-Herzegovina (49 per cent), the share of the urban population was above 50 per cent.[165] Most of that population had stabilized in the 1970s – thereafter, migration rates steadily declined across the region and the trend was to remain on one's own property in the countryside. The destabilization caused by the economic changes, especially unemployment, was all the more painful. The generation born circa 1945, which had matured amid post-war poverty and an oppressive political system, and which had achieved limited prosperity in the 1970s, faced another fundamental challenge in its middle age. The more or less familiar institutional, economic and symbolic landscape was changing.

Traces of the communist past were erased almost everywhere – street names were changed, monuments taken down, and some of the most famous socialist buildings acquired a new function. The Georgi Dimitrov Mausoleum in Sofia was demolished, though it was harder to do the same – despite the exhortations – to the colossal Palace of Culture in Warsaw or the House of the People in Bucharest. However, the headquarters of the Polish United Workers' Party became the Warsaw Stock Exchange, and the headquarters of the Yugoslav Communist Party in Belgrade was transformed into a business centre. This was very significant as regards the formation of a new social elite. Socialist economies shifted towards capitalism, and state ownership rapidly declined, affecting both commercial and private life. A real-estate market was established, direct state financing of housing construction was abandoned, former public housing stock was privatized, and much of the housing that had been nationalized during the communist period was restituted to its former owners.[166]

International corporations entered the markets of the East. Of particular import was the opening of the first McDonald's restaurants in the capitals of the region. Their establishment in Belgrade and Budapest in the spring of 1988 gave those cities a symbolic position as outposts of Western civilization. In other capitals, McDonald's outlets appeared a few years later but – significantly – not until after the one in Moscow had opened in early 1990. Prague got its first McDonald's in March 1992, Warsaw in June 1992, Ljubljana in December 1993, Riga and Sofia in 1994, and Tallinn and Bucharest in 1995. The next year, the corporation gained a foothold in Zagreb, Vilnius and Minsk, in Kiev in 1997, and in Chișinău in 1998. Only Tirana

---

165 David Turnock, *The East European Economy in Context: Communism and Transition* (London: Taylor & Francis, 1997), 108–10.
166 F.E. Ian Hamilton and Francis W. Carter, 'Foreign Direct Investment and City Restructuring', in *Transformation of Cities in Central and Eastern Europe: Towards Globalization*, eds F.E. Ian Hamilton, Kaliopa Dimitrovska Andrews and Nataša Pichler-Milanović (Tokyo: United Nations University Press, 2005), 165–7.

had to settle for a local imitation of McDonald's called Kolonat. In each case, the first restaurants were besieged by customers who wanted a taste of America. This marked a cultural change that was characterized by the dominance of Anglo-Saxon content and consumer products, including 'Western' electronic goods (even though these were mainly manufactured in Asia), which became accessible due to changes in exchange rates. This soon affected the way in which homes were furnished, despite the statistical drop in earnings. Western supermarket chains appeared in major cities in the first half of the 1990s, followed in the middle of the decade by office buildings and shopping centres. The names of the shopping centres in Bratislava – Avion Shopping Park, Eurovea Galleria, Polus City Centre and Shopping Palace – reflected the new zeitgeist.

Bratislava itself was a good example of a city that symbolized the transformation, particularly as it acquired a new status in 1993 as a national capital. It had to fight for recognition on the map of Europe and to overcome the legacy of a city that had industrialized during the socialist era and had hitherto existed in the shadow of Prague. That the first McDonald's in Slovakia opened in 1995 not in the capital but in the provincial town of Banská Bystrica was interpreted as an act of scepticism towards Bratislava on the part of the international business community.[167] However, the city's proximity to Vienna and good road links with the West boosted development, which was symbolized by the new Volkswagen factory and Slovnaft petrochemical plant. Despite its newfound importance, Bratislava did not change much demographically (442,000 inhabitants in 1991 versus 450,000 in 2012), although by 2006 employment in the service sector was almost twice as high as it had been 20 years earlier. The medieval city centre was gradually restored, acquiring numerous bars and restaurants. Bratislava had 605 eating establishments in 1989, and 20 years later it rose to 1,570. Pizzerias and Chinese restaurants, in particular, experienced rapid growth in the 1990s. They added a superficial heterogeneity to the city's homogeneous culture. At the beginning of the twenty-first century, over 90 per cent of the city's inhabitants were Slovaks, the largest minorities being Hungarians (less than 4 per cent) and Czechs (2 per cent). This revealed the almost complete eradication of the city's ethnic diversity (in the 1930s, Germans and Czechs had each accounted for approximately 25 per cent of the population), a fact also underlined by the monotony of the housing estates surrounding the old city centre, the majority of which had fallen into disrepair. In spite of this, other residential districts and apartment buildings, inhabited by a newly affluent class, sprang up in the 1990s and indeed encroached onto the city's hitherto-protected green belt, spreading up the slopes of the Carpathian foothills. Such phenomena seemed to confirm the public view that corruption and dishonesty were thriving in the new era – a view that was conducive to political populism. Yet manifestations of distrust in the changes contrasted with the promotion of Bratislava as an open city. Indeed, whereas in 1990 the city had 4,000 hotel rooms, 20 years later it could boast 14,000. A multilingual throng of tourists colonized the old city centre, while the aforementioned shopping centres and office buildings brought with them a spirit of international business.[168] Many, moreover, represented the typical 'parachute' architecture of the region: buildings designed by international firms and dropped into the city, paying little heed to the local context. Architecture of this kind appeared more frequently in cities that were spatially disorganized, such as Warsaw and Bucharest. Preserved historic cities, such as Prague and Budapest, were more able to resist it.

---

167 Rick Zednik, 'McDonald's Coming to Banska Bystrica', *The Slovak* (19 July–1 August 1995), www.mcspotlight.org/media/press/banska_bystrika.html (accessed May 2016).
168 Waldemar Cudny et al., eds, *Tourism and the Transformation of Large Cities in the Post-Communist Countries of Central and Eastern Europe* (Lodz: Wydawnictwo Uniwersytetu Łódzkiego, 2012), 78–98.

Before the big international players arrived, however, the cities were, at least until the mid-1990s, a venue for spontaneous activity by (very) small-scale businesses, which were also international in character. From 1990 onwards, Warsaw was flooded by waves of traders from the former Soviet Union and then Vietnam. Networks of Chinese traders operated in the Czech Republic, Hungary and Romania. Bazaars selling clothing and household goods proliferated, lending a new, busy aspect to everyday life. The influx of tourists to Prague and merchants to Bucharest was accompanied by the expansion of stalls, booths, micro-catering businesses, etc. Noise levels rose on account of the automotive boom, which was especially felt in countries that had previously been starved of cars. Most shocking was the transformation of Tirana, a bucolic city of pedestrians and cyclists that suddenly turned into a Mercedes-congested marketplace. In Bucharest, the number of private cars increased from 100,000 in 1989 to one million in 2005, without any improvement in infrastructure. The impression of everyday chaos exacerbated public anxiety about crime and fraud, leading to widespread nostalgia for the 'peaceful times' of socialism.[169]

This nostalgia was associated with the processes of social advancement and decline that shook the societies of the region. Describing these processes, observers began to use the term 'middle class', which was to be the foundation of the new socio-economic order. The concept had been imported from the Anglo-Saxon world but quickly gained currency. In Poland after 1989, writes Henryk Domański, half of all respondents suddenly began to identify themselves as middle-class. This was connected with the growing importance of meritocracy and the linking of education with income.[170] At the same time, people across the region displayed an unwillingness to fend for themselves and tended to blame others for their failures. Inherited mindsets did not favour the development of a middle class. Indeed, in Bulgaria of the 1990s, there was a widespread belief that no such class existed. There was, of course, the 'old' or 'socialist' middle class, which had evolved since the 1960s and was now being demoted. It was mainly composed of professional and administrative staff who had been associated with the expansion of the centrally planned economy. The aspirations of this group were consumption-oriented, but it differed from similar groups in the West because it had less professional autonomy and private freedom and was less affluent. When it suffered a profound loss of status in the 1990s, a new middle class arose. The latter, being rooted in the private sector, was closer to the definition of the term, but it was relatively small in number and tied to the informal sphere.[171]

It seemed that the new generation – the descendants of Józef C., our pharmacist from Leszno – would be the mainstay of a successful systemic transformation. Yet, that generation matured in an atmosphere of legal instability and insecure property rights and was subject to the opaque and often cut-throat rules of market competition. Reprivatization was seen as a legal means of recreating a propertied class and compensating the victims of expropriation in the 1940s. Legislation was passed to restitute property (as in Czechoslovakia) or to provide compensation in the form of securities (as in Hungary): after 1990, all the countries of the region introduced such reforms, which inevitably led to litigation and political wrangling. The only exception was Poland, where there was no systematic reprivatization and where the new middle class had to start from scratch; its consumption, as in the rest of the region, was funded through the widespread use of mortgages and loans, made possible in the twenty-first century by a stable economy.

---

169 Mirel Bran, *București, dezghețul* [Bucharest during the thaw] (Bucharest: Humanitas, 2007), 18–19.
170 Henryk Domański, *Polska klasa średnia* [The Polish middle class] (Wrocław: Wydawnictwa Uniwersytetu Wrocławskiego, 2002), 5–13.
171 N. Tilkidjiev, ed. *The Middle Class as a Precondition of a Sustainable Society: Papers from a Sociological Conference in Bulgaria* (Sofia: Association for Middle Class Development, 1998).

The transformation proved difficult for agriculture, and not only for the land which had been collectivized. While the Czech economy withstood reprivatization in the countryside (1992) with surprising ease, not least because the country's agriculture was in relatively good condition, the vast collective farms in Romania and Bulgaria presented a picture of total disarray. As state subsidies were substantially reduced, agricultural production declined across the region and the indebtedness of agriculture deepened. The effect of this was mass protests of farmers, which occurred almost every year after 1990. Poland witnessed the emergence of a populist political movement called *Samoobrona* (self-defence), which brought farmers together under an anti-elitist and anti-urban banner. From 1992, *Samoobrona* organized farmers from all over the country to march on Warsaw (known as 'star marches' since they began at five different points and converged on the capital), although these events were never as disruptive or chaotic as the analogous 'Mineriade' marches of the Romanian miners. Significantly, Romania was the only country where employment in agriculture and the share of agriculture in national income (21.6 per cent in 1995) rose in the 1990s. This attested to deep recession in the cities rather than to prosperity in the countryside. In other countries, the corresponding figure ranged from 3.1 per cent (Czech Republic) to 6.4 per cent (Hungary) and was less than half the proportion in 1989,[172] reflecting the symbolic decline of rural areas. The chronic shortages of previous decades were soon replaced by food surpluses, which were difficult to sell. During the protests, farmers would spill wagons of grain and piles of apples on the ground. Meanwhile, grocery stores were bursting with processed products imported from the West. In 1991, 62 per cent of Hungarian agricultural cooperatives reported losses. Collective farms tried to survive by developing business plans that envisaged slashing production costs and cutting employee social funds. Collective farm workers resisted these changes and also participated in the theft of property, a practice that abated as employment fell.

The number of people employed in Czech cooperatives dwindled by half between 1990 and 1993. Those made redundant began to work for themselves or found jobs in the growing private sector. In the words of one researcher, the emergence of this private sector bore the hallmarks of 'grey primitive accumulation'.[173] In other words, it involved a large amount of illegal activity. The general trend, however, was towards more or less controlled de-collectivization. In Romania, this was done under the banner of restoring the traditional peasant class, although the habits learned in collective farms and the inherited material culture presented a huge challenge for new owners. In Hungary, where agriculture was considered to be quite prosperous before 1989, efforts were made to save the more efficient state farms. In Poland, where there had been little collectivization, ownership issues were neglected, which caused problems in regions where there were state farms (PGR) or private farms taken over from Germans who had emigrated or been expelled.

Poland was indeed a special case. Its individual agriculture, which had survived along with its culture and respect for private property, was suddenly confronted with the realities of an open economy. The agricultural sector had preserved its fragmented structure and was enormous compared to other European countries: in 2006, rural inhabitants accounted for 37 per cent of the country's adult population, and those employed in agriculture, together with their families, accounted for 19 per cent of all adult Poles. This group experienced huge frustration in

---

172 Maria Halamska, *Dekolektywizacja rolnictwa w Europie Środkowej i jej społeczne konsekwencje* [The de-collectivization of the peasantry in Central Europe and its social consequences] (Warsaw: PAN, 1998), 37.
173 Ibid., 40.

the 1990s and suffered higher levels of deprivation than urban inhabitants, a fact confirmed by sociological studies. The rural population was slightly older, more male and less educated than its urban counterpart; it was also more religious, although in European terms the urban population was very religious too: 67 per cent of rural inhabitants and 51 per cent of urban inhabitants declared that they regularly attended Sunday Mass. The countryside considered itself to be poorer than the city but more stable. In particular, it did not fear unemployment to the same extent. Further changes occurred in the twenty-first century, especially after Poland joined the European Union in 2004. A study conducted two years later revealed a significant increase both in the attractiveness of the countryside as a place to live and in the well-being of its inhabitants. The overall picture, however, seemed similar to that of the 1960s: rural inhabitants saw migration to the cities as a means of improving their life opportunities. They saw themselves as the guardians of tradition and considered themselves to be self-sufficient and more resilient to crisis. At the same time – and this was a new feature – they felt better able to take advantage of external support, in other words, EU funds.

A snapshot of this situation at the local level is provided by the research of Michał Łuczewski, who returned a few years ago to the aforementioned village of Żmiąca in southern Poland. He finds the village stagnant: between the mid-nineteenth century and 2009, its population decreased by one hundred people (from 818 to 718). For the first time in history, however, men are in the majority, and a phenomenon of old bachelors has appeared. The birth rate is very low, casting doubt over the future of the local school. The village is aging, and the pension system is becoming increasingly important. Traditional customs, such as home get-togethers to play cards, or May religious services beside wayside shrines, are restricted to the older (and poorer) residents. The villagers appreciate the improvements made to the infrastructure after 1989 (a water main, gas supply, a new parish house) and especially the subsidies from the Special Accession Programme for Agriculture and Rural Development (SAPARD) introduced after 2004. The combining of work on the land with work in the city, so characteristic of the communist era, is also disappearing.[174]

Yet the countryside and the cities are probably closer to each other than ever before. The view that the cities have permanently lost their central role is perhaps exaggerated,[175] but it is beyond doubt that the digital era has largely achieved that which the old slogans proclaimed about eradicating the differences between town and country. It is not the construction of 'agro-towns' in an attempt to build a collective utopia, but rather the emergence of digital networks connecting individual users, that has become the modern incarnation of the 'campaign to link the city with the countryside'. And no one needs to be urged to participate. As Łuczewski writes of Żmiąca: 'In the evenings, most of the local primary and secondary school pupils, and the college students, go on to Gadu-Gadu instant messaging, Facebook, and YouTube'.[176]

Further reading

Aldcroft, Derek H. *Europe's Third World: The European Periphery in the Interwar Years* (Aldershot: Ashgate, 2006).

Åman, Anders. *Architecture and Ideology in Eastern Europe during the Stalin Era* (New York: Architectural History Foundation, 1987).

---

174 Michał Łuczewski, *Odwieczny naród. Polak i katolik w Żmiącej* [The perennial nation: a Pole and a Catholic in Żmiąca] (Toruń: Wydawnictwo UMK, 2012), 36–8.
175 Cf. Florian Rötzer, *Miejskość w epoce cyfrowej* [Urbanity in the digital age], trans. Andrzej Kopacki (Warsaw: Instytut Goethego, 1996), 1–17.
176 Łuczewski, *Odwieczny naród*, 42.

Andrusz, Gregory, Michael Harlo, and Ivan Szelenyi, eds. *Cities after Socialism: Urban and Regional Change and Conflict in Post-Socialist Societies* (London: Blackwell, 1996).
Bartetzky, Arnold, and Marc Schalenberg, eds. *Urban Planning and the Pursuit of Happiness: European Variations on a Universal Theme (18th–21st Centuries)* (Berlin: Jovis Verlag, 2009).
Bauerkämper, Arnd, and Constantin Iordachi, eds. *The Collectivization of Agriculture in Communist Eastern Europe: Comparison and Entanglements* (Budapest: CEU Press, 2014).
Behrends, Jan C., and Martin Kohlrausch, eds. *Races to Modernity: Metropolitan Aspirations in Eastern Europe, 1890–1940* (Budapest: CEU Press, 2014).
Berend, Ivan T. *Central and Eastern Europe, 1944–1993: Detour from the Periphery to the Periphery* (New York: Cambridge University Press, 1996).
Berend, Ivan T. *Decades of Crisis: Central and Eastern Europe Before World War II* (Berkeley, CA: University of California Press, 1998).
Blau, Eva. *Shaping the Great City: Modern Architecture in Central Europe 1890–1937* (London: Prestel, 2000).
Borodziej, Włodzimierz, Stanislav Holubec, and Joachim von Puttkamer, eds. *Mastery and Lost Illusions: Space and Time in the Modernization of Eastern and Central Europe* (München: Oldenbourg, 2014).
Brzostek, Błażej. *Robotnicy Warszawy: Konflikty codzienne (1950–1954) [Warsaw workers: everyday conflicts (1950–1954)]* (Warsaw: TRIO, 2002).
Brzostek, Błażej. *Paryże Innej Europy: Warszawa i Bukareszt, XIX i XX wiek [The other Europe's Paris: Warsaw and Bucharest in the 19th and 20th century]* (Warsaw: WAB, 2015).
Burchardt, Jeremy. *Paradise Lost: Rural Idyll and Social Change in England since 1800* (London: I.B. Tauris, 2002).
Calic, Mari-Janine. *Geschichte Jugoslawiens im 20. Jahrhundert* (München: C.H. Beck, 2010).
Chirot, Daniel, ed. *The Origins of Backwardness in Eastern Europe: Economics and Politics from the Middle Ages until the Early 20th Century* (Berkeley, CA: University of California Press, 1989).
Conley, Tanja Damjanović, and Emily Gunzburger Makaš, eds. *Capital Cities in the Aftermath of Empires: Planning in Central and Southeastern Europe* (London: Routledge, 2010).
Cudny, Waldemar, Tomasz Michalski, and Rafał Rouba, eds. *Tourism and the Transformation of Large Cities in the Post-Communist Countries of Central and Eastern Europe* (Lodz: Wydawnictwo Uniwersytetu Łódzkiego, 2012).
de Jarcy, Xavier. *Le Corbusier: Un fascisme français* (Paris: Albin Michel, 2015).
Dobrivojević, Ivana. *Drzavna represija u doba diktature kralja Aleksandra 1929–1935 [State repression during the dictatorship of King Aleksander 1929–1935]* (Belgrade: Institut za savremenu istoriju, 2006).
Dobrivojević, Ivana. *Selo i grad: Transformacija agrarnog društva Srbije 1945–1955 [The transformation of rural society in Serbia 1945–1955]* (Belgrade: Institut za savremenu istoriju, 2013).
Fel, Edit, and Tamas Hofer. *Proper Peasants: Traditional Life in a Hungarian Village* (New York: Viking Fund, 1969).
Foster, George M., and Robert V. Kemper, eds. *Anthropologists in Cities* (Boston, MA: Little, Brown, 1974).
French, R.A., and F.E. Ian Hamilton, eds. *The Socialist City: Spatial Structure and Urban Policy* (Chichester: John Wiley, 1979).
Frykman, Jonas, and Orvar Löfgren. *Culture Builders: A Historical Anthropology of Middle-Class Life* (New Brunswick, NJ: Rutgers University Press, 1987).
Gee, Malcom, Tim Kirk, and Jill Steward, eds. *Culture and Society from 1800 to the Present* (Aldershot: Ashgate, 2003).
Gulliver, Katrina, and Helena Toth, eds. *Cityscapes in History: Creating the Urban Experience* (Burlington: Ashgate, 2014).
Gutkind, E.A. *Urban Development in East Central Europe: Poland, Czechoslovakia and Hungary* (New York: The Free Press, 1972).
Gyáni, Gábor. *Parlour and Kitchen: Housing and Domestic Culture in Budapest 1870–1940* (Budapest: CEU Press, 2002).
Hamilton, F.E. Ian, Kaliopa Dimitrovska Andrews, and Nataša Pichler-Milanović, eds. *Transformation of Cities in Central and Eastern Europe: Towards Globalization* (Tokyo: United Nations University Press, 2005).
Handlin, Oscar, and John Burchard, eds. *The Historian and the City* (Cambridge, MA: Harvard University Press, 1963).
Hoffmann, David L. *Peasant Metropolis: Social Identities in Moscow, 1929–1941* (Ithaca, NY and London: Cornell University Press, 1994).
Jarosz, Dariusz. *Polityka władz komunistycznych w Polsce w latach 1948–1956 a chłopi [The politics of communist rule in Poland 1948–1956 and the peasants]* (Warsaw: Neriton, 1998).

Jedlicki, Jerzy. *A Degenerate World*, ed. Elena Rozbicka, trans. Tristan Korecki (Frankfurt a.M.: Peter Lang Verlag der Wissenschaften, 2016).
Jelavich, Barbara. *The History of the Balkans: Twentieth Century*, vol. 2 (Cambridge: Cambridge University Press, 1983).
Karcz, Jerry F., ed. *Soviet and East European Agriculture* (Berkeley, CA: University of California Press, 1967).
Kaser, M.C., and E.A. Radice, eds. *The Economic History of Eastern Europe 1919–1975*, vol. 1 (Oxford: Clarendon Press, 1985).
Kaser, M.C., and E.A. Radice, eds. *The Economic History of Eastern Europe 1919–1975*, vol. 2 (Oxford: Clarendon Press, 1986).
Kula, Marcin. *Wybór tradycji [Opting for tradition]* (Warsaw: DiG, 2003).
Lebow, Katherine, *Unfinished Utopia: Nowa Huta, Stalinism and Polish Society 1949–1956* (Ithaca, NY: Cornell University Press, 2013).
Leder, Andrzej. *Prześniona rewolucja. Ćwiczenie z logiki historycznej [A revolution overlooked: an exercise in the logic of history]* (Warsaw: Krytyka Polityczna, 2013).
Lees, Andrew, and Lynn Hollen Lees. *Cities and the Making of Modern Europe 1750–1914* (Cambridge, MA: Harvard University Press, 2007).
Lenger, Friedrich. *European Cities in the Modern Era, 1850–1914* (Leiden and Boston: Brill, 2012).
Leszczyński, Adam. *Skok w nowoczesność. Polityka wzrostu w krajach peryferyjnych 1943–1980 [Jumping into modernity: the politics of growth in the countries of the periphery 1943–1980]* (Warsaw: Krytyka Polityczna, 2013).
Lukacs, John. *Budapest 1900: A Historical Portrait of a City and Its Culture* (New York: Weidenfeld & Nicolson, 1988).
Márai, Sándor. *Bekenntnisse eines Bürgers: Erinnerungen* (München: Piper Verlag, 2009).
Mathias, Peter, and Sidney Pollard, eds. *The Cambridge Economic History of Europe*, vol. 8 (Cambridge: Cambridge University Press, 2008).
Mišković, Nataša. *Basare und Boulevards: Belgrad im 19. Jahrhundert* (Vienna, Cologne and Weimar: Böhlau, 2008).
Murgescu, Bogdan. *România și Europa: Acumularea decalajelor economice (1500–2010) [Romania and Europe: the accumulation of economic disparities (1500–2010)]* (Bucharest: Polirom, 2010).
Musset, Jean. *Les villes de la Russie Subcarpatique (1919–1938): L'effort tchécoslovaque* (Paris: Librairie Droz, 1938).
Olsen, Donald J., *The City as a Work of Art: London, Paris, Vienna* (New Haven, CT: Yale University Press, 1986).
Pittaway, Mark. *Eastern Europe 1939–2000* (London: Hodder Arnold, 2004).
Pollak, Michael. *Vienne 1900: Une identité blessée* (Paris: Gallimard, 1992).
Popescu, Carmen. *Le style national roumain: Construire une Nation à travers l'architecture* (Rennes: Presses Universitaires de Rennes, 2004).
Purchla, Jacek, ed. *The Historical Metropolis: A Hidden Potential, International Conference 26–29.5.1996* (Cracow: Narodowe Centrum Kultury, 1996).
Sillince, John A.A., ed. *Housing Policies in Eastern Europe and the Soviet Union* (London: Routledge, 1990).
Smith, Stephen A., ed. *The Oxford Handbook of the History of Communism* (Oxford: Oxford University Press, 2014).
Snyder, Timothy. *Bloodlands: Europe Between Hitler and Stalin* (New York: Basic Books, 2010).
Tilkidjiev, N., ed. *The Middle Class as a Precondition of a Sustainable Society: Papers from a Sociological Conference in Bulgaria* (Sofia: Association for Middle Class Development, 1998).
Todorova, Maria. *Imagining the Balkans* (New York and Oxford: Oxford University Press, 1997).
Tomasevich, Jozo. *Peasants, Politics, and Economic Change in Yugoslavia* (Stanford, CA: Stanford University Press, 1955).
Turnock, David. *The East European Economy in Context: Communism and Transition* (London: Taylor & Francis, 1997).
Turnock, David. *The Economy of East Central Europe 1815–1989: Stages of Transformation in a Peripheral Region* (London: Routledge, 2006).
Wood, Nathaniel D. *Becoming Metropolitan: Urban Selfhood and the Making of Modern Cracow* (DeKalb, IL: Northern Illinois University Press, 2010).
Zubkova, Elena. *Russia After the War: Hopes, Illusions, and Disappointments, 1945–1957* (Armonk, NY: M.E. Sharpe, 1998).

2

SOCIAL STRUCTURE, MOBILITY AND EDUCATION

Zsombor Bódy and Stanislav Holubec

Introduction

At the beginning of the twentieth century, there were often no clear boundaries between social strata and groups in Central and Eastern Europe. As is well known, there were often no state-drawn borders between ethnicities in the multi-ethnic empires. Various local identities and loyalties were widespread within the different strata, especially among peasants, but at times among the aristocracy as well: Lithuanian nobility, for example, could not always be distinguished from Polish aristocracy. 'The pressure for national allegiance, standardizing a national society, was established only gradually.'[1] What is more, cohesive forces that could have established a differentiated society from the population of a geographical area were often lacking. Modern societies arose primarily through mechanisms of the market economy (which assigned each individual a position as employer, self-employed or employee), through a relatively homogeneous educational system, through the bureaucratic organs of the state, and in part, through political participation in overarching socio-political structures; in most cases, those of the nation state. These factors were absent in Central and Eastern Europe at the turn of the century. The history of this region in the twentieth century can be understood as the gradual establishment of societies, shaped by nation states from the First World War onward.

Wherever social integration was implemented through the market, the decisive social forms were classes, understood as structures of property inequality, regulated by market relations, and bearing consequences for the realms of education and power. Although classes in this sense were not unknown in the region, they did not constitute a predominant type of social grouping. Around the year 1900, classes were found primarily in larger cities. While the rural population long remained outside the market-based process of class formation, it could nevertheless be identified as a social stratum through specific forms of life. The village, as a spatially

---

1 Kerstin S. Jobst, 'Nationalitäten, Geschlecht und geographischer Raum: Anmerkungen zu dem "Sonderfall" Osteuropa', in *Zwischen Kriegen: Nationen, Nationalismen und Geschlechterverhältnisse in Mittel- und Osteuropa 1918–1939*, eds Johanna Gehmacher, Elizabeth Harvey and Sophia Kemlein (Osnabrück: Fibre Verlag, 2004), 132. See also Ralph Schattkowsky and Michael G. Müller, eds, *Identitätenwandel und nationale Mobilisierung in Regionen ethnischer Diversität: Ein regionaler Vergleich zwischen Westpreußen und Galizien am Ende des 19. und Anfang des 20 Jahrhunderts* (Marburg: Herder, 2004).

contained group of people encompassing all residents within a small and relatively transparent space, remained a separate social form with tight social controls through the community and through the patriarchal family, as a unit of property, labour and consumption. There were, of course, enormous differences within the region. For example, on the one hand, peasantry in the Czech lands and in the regions of Hungary that had a developed transportation infrastructure were thus familiar with the logic of the market economy, while on the other hand, peasants in several Balkan territories still focused on merely covering their needs, living in a subsistence economy, and lacked market rationality and acquisitiveness – in other words, they could be characterized as having a pre-capitalist mentality.[2] The cities were like islands within the vast expanses where the peasantry lived. Illiteracy, which still existed in many places, was another impediment to the cultural homogenization of these societies. In addition, state bureaucracy around the turn of the century was unable to penetrate society as fundamentally as it could during the interwar period or in the socialist era. Thus, rather than a society of cohesive forces with more or less differentiated strata, different social worlds coexisted in the region, frequently with no more than superficial contact with one another. Drawing on ethnographic studies, Holm Sundhaussen characterized Southeastern European societies as segmented societies in which individuals were integrated only in small groups like villages or clans, and argued that the mechanisms that could have transformed individuals into members of larger units were absent.[3] Religion was the only force that functioned as an institutionalized means of cultural homogenization extending beyond these smaller units. There were, however, multiple religions in the region: for example, there were diverse forms of Judaism, Orthodox Christianity, Roman Catholicism and Greek Catholicism, Calvinism, Lutheranism and Islam. Nor did the ethnicities and religions constitute homogeneous entities in themselves. There was an enormous distance from the assimilated Jews of Budapest and other large cities to the Orthodox rural Jews. Even the Romany of the region did not constitute a homogeneous group, but had several subgroups, not all of which were excluded from the existing integration mechanisms of the rest of society (as is often assumed).

A process of displacement from predominantly familial, kinship and communal forms in favour of primarily market-economic related structures (later supplemented by social services from the state and other public institutions) can be observed throughout the region: ties of heritage, birth and kinship gradually lost significance, and individual achievement on the market, established as an increasingly independent system, became an ever more important factor. The First World War significantly accelerated the dissolution of established forms of social integration. On the one hand, the mobilization of societies was accompanied by an expansion of the state apparatus, which after the war was able to control society much more profoundly than before. On the other hand, the war called into question the legitimacy of the previous social order and the acquisition of elite positions through inheritance. During the interwar period, the economic integration of producers into larger entities advanced significantly in all countries of the region, which meant the gradual dissolution of peasant self-sufficiency. This development was weakest in Southeastern Europe, where the prerequisites for an agriculture adapted to the market economy, or even to the production of goods for non-familial purposes, were often still lacking in rural regions.

---

2 Holm Sundhaussen, 'Südosteuropäische Gesellschaft und Kultur vom Beginn des 19. bis zur Mitte des 20. Jahrhunderts', in *Geschichte Südosteuropas: vom frühen Mittelalter bis zur Gegenwart*, eds Konrad Clewing and Oliver Jens Schmitt (Regensburg: Verlag Friedrich Pustet, 2011), 345–425.

3 Ibid. On pre-modern segmentary societies, see Wolfgang Reinhard, *Lebensformen Europas: Eine historische Kulturanthropologie* (München: C.H. Beck, 2004), 266–67.

The new states of the region sought to further the social integration of their populations through bureaucratic means by promoting economic integration on the level of the nation state – often through autarkic efforts. At the same time, they also attempted to raise education levels and to combat illiteracy with varying degrees of success. The results of these efforts differed from country to country of course, but did bring about changes in these societies that continued to have effects even in the second half of the twentieth century, such as greater mobility and rural–urban migration. But beyond urbanization, the forms of sociation for the people who remained in the countryside also changed. The dissolution of previous forms of sociation meant the individualization of women and men (i.e. the removal of, or emancipation from narrow circles, be they villages, small-scale religious communities or densely interconnected circles of people with equal status), and at the same time, it meant the inclusion of new mechanisms such as the market and education, as well as the ties of state citizenship in general.

After the Second World War, a state-coordinated bureaucratic homogenization of society replaced the principle of the market economy in virtually all countries in the region (several incipient forms of which had existed since the First World War, and to an even greater degree, since the global economic crisis). Familial, kinship and village-communal forms of sociation, where these were still present (i.e. especially among the peasantry), were also greatly reduced. While neither the market economy nor familial forms of social organization disappeared completely, bureaucratic homogenization became decisive for the majority of these societies. During this period, a surge of cultural homogenization in the modern sense of the term occurred in the societies of the region, insofar as state socialism was able to implement a powerful restructuring and expansion of the education system, which was accompanied by a strong wave of secularization.

Following the collapse of state socialism, an unambiguous class society began to develop once again in the region, after 1989–1991; that is, after the failure of the bureaucratic integration of these societies, market-economic processes once again defined and segregated workers in various sectors, such that part of the population had very little opportunity to participate in the market economy. These individuals can be regarded as orphans of bureaucratic integration since they were only mechanically and formally integrated into the working world by the socialist systems that had, in many cases, forced them out of their previous ways of life. Yet the re-emergence of a class society does not mean that sociation – which places people in multiple social relationships – also occurred on the basis of class differences. A highly nuanced sociological examination of Southeastern European societies has shown that in neither the pre-socialist nor the post-socialist period did class formation assume any defining structural significance.[4]

This cursory overview of the mechanisms that influenced, modified, and reproduced the social structure of societies in Central and Eastern Europe in the twentieth century indicates that they did not remain unaltered during that time. The mechanisms that ensured cohesion among social groups played a decisive role in establishing the boundaries between them, and in determining the channels of social mobility, which changed repeatedly and fundamentally from the turn of the twentieth century to the beginning of the twenty-first century. Iván Szelényi described these changes in the following way: in the first half of the twentieth century, social stratification was determined ideal, typically through status position (in the Weberian sense, i.e. the prestige resulting from birth, education and lifestyle) and through the market (economic

---

4 Anton Sterbling, 'Die Grenzen klassentheoretischer Analysekategorien in der Strukturanalyse südosteuropäischer Gesellschaften', in *Kontinuität und Wandel in Rumänien und Südosteuropa: Historisch-soziologische Analysen*, ed. Anton Sterbling (München: Südostdeutsches Kulturwerk, 1997), 193–219.

classes in the Weberian sense), whereas the market disappeared as a determining factor during the decades of state socialism. Thus, state socialist societies were, from a sociological perspective, a variation of estate-based societies (*Ständegesellschaften*), since in a bureaucratically coordinated economy the position of individuals was determined by education, lifestyle and rank. Thus, Szelényi disagreed with the famous thesis (originally formulated by Milovan Djilas) about a new bureaucratic ruling class in socialism because, he insisted, we cannot speak of classes in socialism. For Szelényi these societies recalled feudal societies, since – in addition to the formative power of status mechanisms of sociation – patronage and chains of personal loyalty also played a significant role.[5] Other, more nuanced positions also hold the status principle to be characteristic of socialist societies, but emphasize that there were no clearly defined estates (*Stände*) in socialist countries.[6] The lack of classes as forms of sociation – for example, when class formation was made impossible through the prohibition of market regulations – was accompanied by sociation in the form of status stratification, and by other forms of political and socio-cultural closure, as several scholars using sociological concepts to analyze Southeastern European societies have argued.[7] Holm Sundhausen found that even during the interwar period, the role of bureaucracy in the centralization and redistribution of national income had reached such a level in Southeastern European countries that, independent of ideological signs, we can already identify several incipient forms of state socialist systems.[8] Andrew C. Janos identified the same phenomenon in Central and Eastern European states.[9] Under the conditions of weakly developed capitalism during the interwar period, classes played only a limited role in these countries.[10] There is also agreement among scholars that only after 1989 did a social order once again emerge (and increasingly clearly) in which stratification according to economic class played an important role, although one that was still weaker there than in Western European societies, as other forms of sociation not based on class relations continued to be determining factors.[11]

The following chapter deals with the social structure of Central and Eastern European societies. First, it discusses the factors that shaped the social structures in the region over time and characterizes the main tendencies of social development (urbanization, the rise of industry and then the service economy, changes in mobility). The chapter then narrates the story of the four most significant social groups in the twentieth century: mainly the relationship between the traditional peasantry and elites, and the new industrial proletariat and urban middle classes. The chapter ends by discussing the expansion of education, which is universally understood to be an important factor shaping the structure of society.

---

5 Gil Eyal, Iván Szelényi and Eleanor Townsley, *Making Capitalism without Capitalists: The New Ruling Elites in Eastern Europe* (New York: Verso, 1998), 17–45.
6 Wolfgang Teckenberg, 'Ständische Ordnung, "Neue" Intelligenzija oder Klassenstrukturierung im Postsozialismus? Was aus der Revolte des Umbruchs geworden ist', in *Soziale Konstellation und historische Perspektive: Festschrift für M. Rainer Lepsius*, eds Steffen Sigmund, Gert Albert, Agathe Bienfait and Mateusz Stachura (Wiesbaden: VS Verlag für Sozialwissenschaften, 2008), 253–83.
7 Sterbling, 'Grenzen klassentheoretischer Analysekategorien', 199.
8 On the expansion of state property in industry and trade, see Marie-Janine Calic, *Sozialgeschichte Serbiens 1815–1941: Der aufhaltsame Fortschritt während der Industrialisierung* (München: Oldenbourg, 1994), 410–15.
9 Andrew C. Janos, *East Central Europe in the Modern World: The Politics of the Borderland from Pre- to Postcommunism* (Stanford, CA: Stanford University Press, 2000).
10 Eyal, Szelenyi, and Townsley, *Making Capitalism without Capitalists*, 20–24.
11 Anton Sterbling, 'Zur Rolle des sozialen Kapitals in fortgeschrittenen Industriegesellschaften und zur sozialen Schließung in Südosteuropa', in Sterbling, *Kontinuität und Wandel in Rumänien und Südosteuropa*, 221–31.

The main features of social change: mobility, educational expansion, urbanization

Several basic changes are evident in the societies of the region during the twentieth century and have been described frequently. Before the First World War, the majority of the population lived in villages and worked in agriculture. As illustrated in Table 2.1, a shift in labour power between the major employment sectors was one of the most important changes in these societies over the course of the century. The periodization of this change is also well known. While industry grew slowly during the interwar period, the industrial workforce expanded rapidly after the Second World War. An expansion of the service sector followed, beginning around 1970. It is also clear that the processes of industrialization and later of tertiarization deviated from the development rhythms of Western European societies. If we take the turn into the twentieth century as our starting point, the percentage of industrial labourers was significantly higher in the West than in the Central and Eastern European societies. Tertiarization also began earlier in the western part of Europe and proceeded more rapidly than in state socialist societies.

Although these major structural changes are a basic trend of social development, they are not sufficient in themselves to capture the nature and significance of the historical transformations of the social structure. While standard information about the percentages of major employment sectors does reflect the structures of modern labour societies, it cannot tell us much about historical changes in the nature of labour relations. There is a qualitative dimension to the social changes of the twentieth century which is not expressed in the percentages employed in the major branches of the economy. In the societies of Central and Eastern Europe at the beginning of the twentieth century, many groups did not yet work under the legally codified market-economy conditions of modern labour relations. In statistics from Hungary in 1910, for example, more than two thirds of women were registered as 'not gainfully employed'. That was not because peasants' daughters and wives did not work hard – on the contrary. Their incorporation in village familial structures, however, made them invisible as workers to the statisticians. In many cases, the household and larger units established on the logic of households still constituted the framework for their labour. Working as a family member, a farmhand, a day

Table 2.1 Percentage distribution of the labour force according to economic sectors in Central, Eastern and Southeastern European countries in the twentieth century

	Agriculture and Forestry				Industry				Service Sector and Civil Service			
	1920	1950	1980	2006	1920	1950	1980	2006	1920	1950	1980	2006
Bulgaria	82.4	75.5	36.9	9.3	8.1	10.3	38.8	33.2	9.5	14.2	24.3	57.4
Yugoslavia	82.2	70.7	30.6		11.0	16.1	33.0		6.7	13.2	36.4	
Poland	76.6	57.2	30.6	17.4	9.4	23.0	39.3	28.4	14.0	19.9	30.1	54.2
Romania	77.2	69.5	29.4	31.9	8.9	16.7	35.5	29.4	13.8	13.8	35.1	38.7
Czecho-slovakia	40.3	37.7	13.1	~5	36.8	37.3	48.8	38.5	22.9	25.0	38.1	56.6
Hungary	58.2	52.9	18.5	5.2	19.7	23.2	43.3	31.9	22.1	23.9	37.8	62.9

Notes: Czechoslovakia 2006 is the arithmetic mean of the data (values) from the Czech Republic and Slovakia; Romania has a different year of 1930, and includes pensioners.

Sources: Wolfram Fischer et al., eds, *Handbuch der Europäischen Wirtschafts- und Sozialgeschichte*, vol. 6, *Europäische Wirtschafts- und Sozialgeschichte vom Ersten Weltkrieg bis zur Gegenwart* (Stuttgart: Klett-Cotta, 1987), 93; Steffen Mau and Roland Verwiebe, *Die Sozialstruktur Europas* (Bonn: Bundeszentrale für politische Bildung, 2009), 144.

labourer or a servant on a large estate, or on a *zadruga*[12] (a multiple-family household), entailed completely different life circumstances than working in an agricultural production cooperative, or, following the collapse of state socialism, working in an agricultural business under a market economy. The same holds for industry. On the basis of general sociological categories, artisan journeymen around the turn of the twentieth century, workers in large factories during the interwar period, and workers in socialist industry are all considered industrial labourers. Nevertheless, their lifeworlds differed significantly in qualitative terms. Beyond the qualitative distinctions of this development (which will be illuminated in the subsequent sections that examine individual groups) further essential characteristics of the social order are hidden by numbers depicting macro-structural changes. The magnitude of circular mobility is concealed behind the structural mobility resulting from a shift in economic activity from agriculture to industry and later to the service sector. In addition to structural mobility, the number and the percentage of people who move down to a lower stratum, or conversely, up to a higher stratum, are also characteristic for a society; in other words, the openness of the social order. These trends of circular mobility also changed during the twentieth century.

The high percentage of people working in agriculture – characteristic for virtually all of the countries in Central and Eastern Europe – is partly indicative of the region's relatively low level of industrialization. There was also rural overpopulation arising from demographic developments that were especially pronounced in Southeastern European societies. The low level of industrial development in most Central and Eastern European countries was not sufficient enough to absorb the rural population surplus.

The high percentage of the population employed in agriculture even up to the Second World War did not mean, however, that mobility was insignificant during the first half of the twentieth century. The industrialization and urbanization of Central and Eastern Europe also brought about a certain degree of mobility. At the same time, the expansion of the state apparatus – in many places even prior to the First World War, elsewhere only after the war, but then all the more rapidly – also created new positions and thus new strata as well. This was the case even in states in which a new or significantly enlarged administrative apparatus expanded after the First World War, such as in the Baltics, Poland and Czechoslovakia, but also in the kingdoms of Romania and Yugoslavia.[13] Somewhat more detailed data are available for Hungary, where a census in 1930 recorded the employment not only of respondents, but also of their fathers. While in this particular case we cannot speak of an expansion of the state apparatus after the First World War, on the basis of these data we can identify a significant level of mobility. Although absolute mobility had not reached the level necessary to alleviate village unemployment, mobility was nevertheless significant from the perspective of establishing higher strata. According to the calculations of Hungarian sociologist Rudolf Andorka, the proportion of people whose employment or social status had changed in comparison to their fathers was 37 per cent for men and 48 per cent for women. Andorka further differentiated these figures, calculating that 18 per cent of the men and 25 per cent of the women here should be regarded as structurally mobile, as their change in social status had resulted from the mere expansion of certain strata (primarily the expansion of educated groups and industrial workers). The remaining 19 per cent of men and 23 per cent of women were, in contrast, products of circular mobility,

---

12 For more a more detailed description of the zadruga system, see Chapter 5 of the current volume.
13 On the formation of elites in Estonia, see Krista Hinno, *Bildung und Sozialstruktur: Das Fallbeispiel Estland* (Marburg: Tectum Verlag, 2004). On the Balkans, see Wolfgang Höpken and Holm Sundhaussen, eds, *Eliten in Südosteuropa: Rolle, Kontinuitäten, Brüche in Geschichte und Gegenwart* (München: Südosteuropa-Gesellschaft, 1998).

meaning substitution upward and downward among the different social groups. While the majority of workers' and peasants' sons did remain in the vocational categories of their fathers, the proportion of social climbers was not insignificant among the educated – 14.2 per cent of gainfully employed educated people (i.e. people with at least a secondary-school leaving certificate) were sons of peasants, and 7.4 per cent were sons of workers. Overall, less than half of the educated people came from families in which the fathers had enjoyed a similar education, indicating a modest percentage of self-recruitment for these groups. In comparison to the rapid social restructuring after the Second World War, the societies of the interwar period seemed to lack mobility. Nevertheless, the middle classes and elite groups in virtually all Central and Eastern European countries had emerged through social processes that increased membership in these strata and were thus in large part new social forms.

The extensive industrialization that occurred in the region under state socialism after the Second World War appeared to resolve the most important structural problem of the region: rural overpopulation. This structural transformation was especially pronounced in Hungary and Slovakia, somewhat less so in the Czech lands, Romania, Yugoslavia, and Poland (the Czech lands had industrialized earlier than other countries of the region; in the other three countries, a relatively large agricultural workforce continued to exist even during the socialist period, concomitant with the process of industrialization). In Hungary in 1964, for example, 59 per cent of of all Hungarians surveyed in a sociological research project had a profession different from their fathers. Of these people, 34 per cent were mobile because of structural changes, while 25 per cent had experienced circular mobility.[14] Similar figures are found for Poles. Back in 1963, Stanisław Ossowski, now recognized as one of the classic scholars of modern mobility, documented the unprecedented expansion of mobility in Central and Eastern Europe. For Ossowski, one essential issue was to determine how much mobility was due to economic developments, and how much was related to policy.[15] An even more interesting question was what these mobility trends would look like after periods of extensive industrialization. This is an issue that subsequent scholars of mobility have examined repeatedly. On the basis of numerous comparative studies, most sociologists today agree that mobility decelerated as rapidly after the 1960s as it had accelerated earlier.[16] An analysis comparing the Czech lands, Slovakia, and Hungary came to the following results: in all four countries, the three decades after the Second World War were a period of massive structural shifts, particularly in comparison with previous decades. But according to Max Haller, Tamás Kolosi and Péter Róbert, the 'process of postwar industrialization in the East European countries was, compared with Western Europe, much more labor-intensive and less due to increases in productivity.'[17] In Austria the tertiary sector increased by far the most, while the proportion of people employed in industry showed a significant decline after 1960, in contrast to the socialist countries. The explanation is evident: the preferential development of basic industries and a relative neglect of consumer goods industries, trade and other services

---

14 Rudolf Andorka, 'Changes in Social Mobility in Hungary, 1930–1983', in *Class Structure in Europe: New Findings from East-West Comparisons of Social Structure and Mobility*, ed. Max Haller (New York: M.E. Sharpe, 1990), 198–232, here 198–99.

15 Stanislaw Ossowski, *Class Structure in the Social Consciousness*, trans. Sheila Patterson (New York: Free Press, 1963).

16 Albert Simkus, *Class Divisions in East-Central Europe: Studies of the Consequences of the Socialist 'Experiments' of 1949–1988* (Armonk, NY: M.E. Sharpe, 1997).

17 Max Haller, Tamás Kolosi and Péter Róbert, 'Social Mobility in Austria, Czechoslovakia, and Hungary: An Investigation of the Effects of Industrialization, Socialist Revolution, and National Uniqueness', in Haller, *Class Structure in Europe*, 153–97, here 166.

that led to the pattern of structural shifts observable in Czechoslovakia and Hungary. This pattern was probably typical for most other Eastern European socialist countries. In the summary, the authors claimed that beyond basic similarities, a significant 'system difference' exists between capitalist and socialist societies. The volume of mobility was higher in the two socialist countries than in Austria, as collectivization and socialist industrialization had significant effects on higher absolute mobility. But the rate of changes in the occupational structure later decreased, especially in Czechoslovakia, while the shifts from the secondary to the tertiary sector were still an important factor in the continuing process of upward mobility in Austria: the rise of sons of blue-collar workers to lower white-collar jobs was more common in Austria than in the socialist societies.[18]

Between 1945 and 1990, social mobility in Central and Eastern European countries was not greater than in Western Europe overall. The peculiar feature of developments in this region was its division into two distinctively different periods: the first twenty years with significant mobility, and the next twenty years with relatively low mobility. Mobility trends in the West, in contrast, were much more balanced. Responsible for this peculiar Central European development were politically based processes of social restructuring. In the first period of state socialist regimes, significant industrial investments and a change in elites contributed to an increase in the mobility rate. Later, the relatively slow tertiarization of socialist economies and the lack of expansion in post-secondary-school education – which had characterized Western societies in the 1960s and 70s – led to a significant decrease in the mobility rate in these societies. In Central and Eastern European countries in the late 1980s, just over 10 per cent of people in their twenties were college students, a figure nearly identical to that twenty years earlier.[19] Mobility trends in Central and Eastern European countries were different for men and women. Women had a relatively higher mobility rate, even after the 1970s (when the mobility rate of men had already begun to sink), due to their leaving the agricultural and industrial sectors for jobs that required relatively little education but were nevertheless non-industrial.[20]

As a result of these restructuring processes, Central and Eastern European societies had several features in common. Around 1960, state socialist societies were integrated primarily through bureaucratic mechanisms, as the last niches of private economic activity had been eliminated for small businesses and the collectivization of the economy was complete. This meant that market-related distinctions played hardly any role in the systemic inequalities of these societies. Social capital – that is, favourable professional positions in formal organizations (such as the communist party, businesses, and official associations) – played a significantly more important role in socio-structural differentiation than did economic capital. Social capital had a greater effect on the distribution of goods than money because there was no market economy and opportunities for private accumulation were limited.[21] Starting in the mid-1960s a second economy evolved in practically all of these countries. Poland's socialist society, for example, has been described as the result of the following developments:

> 'real socialism' bore six structural characteristics, differentiating this country from capitalist countries at a similar level of development. These are: (1) the nomenclature system, being the structural implementation of directive-distributive management at

---

18 Ibid., 153–97.
19 Szonja Szelenyi, *Equality by Design: The Grand Experiment in Destratification in Socialist Hungary* (Stanford, CA: Stanford University Press, 1998), 12–20.
20 Bogdan W. Mach, 'Intergenerational Mobility in Poland: 1972–88–94', in *Social Mobility in Europe*, ed. Richard Breen (Oxford: Oxford University Press, 2004), 269–86.
21 Hinno, *Bildung und Sozialstruktur*, 21.

both the national and regional levels; (2) the heavy-industry working class, initially being a political slogan but soon becoming a distinct segment of the population and an important political force in the communist state; (3) the peasantry, defined by their individual ownership of arable land, yet dependent on state controlled access to agricultural products; (4) employees in redundant bureaucratic positions, actually representing hidden unemployment; (5) active organizers of the informal economy; and (6) semi-institutionalized opposition ... [22]

Apart from the facts that 'semi-institutionalized opposition' did not exist in all countries of the region, and that there was no private agricultural property in Czechoslovakia, Hungary, Romania and Bulgaria, this description could also be applied to the other socialist states in Central and Eastern Europe. The scope of the informal or second economy varied from country to country. But even in Czechoslovakia, where the population followed official norms relatively closely, in the 1970s a shadow economy developed, which the regime tolerated in part since without it, the limitations of the planned economy made it impossible to meet the daily needs of the population. This included illegal revenue in the service sector, as well as bribes and payoffs in health care, education and administration.[23] The development of both the legal economy and the 'black' or second economy led everywhere to increased social differentiation, or to market-economy relations playing a role in the integration of societies (albeit one subordinate to bureaucratic relations), in which the structures of inequality, again, were no longer determined solely by the status factors of education and social capital, but by economic capital as well.[24]

As is well known, the industrialization based on heavy industry and organized as a planned economy was oriented on the model of earlier waves of industrialization, and did not create any industry capable of competition or development in the long run. Consequently, after the collapse of state socialism there was especially high unemployment in these societies and a rapid rise in early pensioners among people over fifty.[25] Most countries of the region had low employment rates and high unemployment (in international comparison, this persisted even until 2000). The decline in employment for men varied in the region, ranging between 5 per cent (the Czech lands) and 15 per cent (Bulgaria). The only exception was Slovenia, which experience a decline of around one per cent. In 1990, the employment rate for men was practically identical with the employment rate for men in the West; in 2006, it was more than seven per cent lower in Central and Eastern Europe than in the old countries of the European Union. The development of female employment is even more interesting. In 1990, Central and Eastern Europe had a considerably higher employment rate for women than Western Europe (64.5 per cent versus 56 per cent). This heritage of the socialist system soon disappeared through a rapid decline in female employment (to 60.5 per cent in 2006), whereas the

---

22 Kazimierz M. Slomczynski, 'Social Structure, Its Changes and Linkages', introduction to *Social Structure: Changes and Linkages: The Advanced Phase of the Post-Communist Transition in Poland*, ed. Kazimierz M. Slomczynsk (Warsaw: IFiS Publishers, 2002), 15.
23 Lenka Kalinova, 'Mythos und Realität des "Arbeiterstaates" in der Tschechoslowakei', in *Arbeiter im Staatssozialismus: Ideologischer Anspruch und soziale Wirklichkeit*, eds Peter Hübner, Christoph Klessmann and Klaus Tenfelde (Köln: Böhlau, 2005), 87–107.
24 Ibid.
25 Péter Róbert and Erzsébet Bukodi, 'Changes in Intergenerational Class Mobility in Hungary, 1973–2000', in Breen, *Social Mobility in Europe*, 287–314; Tamás Kolosi and Péter Róbert, 'Key Processes of Structural Transformation and Mobility in Hungarian Society since the Fall of Communism', in *Social Report 2004*, eds Tamás Kolosi, István György Tóth and György Vukovich (Budapest: Tárki, 2004), 47–71.

proportion of women in Western Europe who performed paid labour increased during this period (to 64.5 per cent in 2006).[26]

The process of urbanization in the region occurred parallel to the increase in mobility. At the beginning of the twentieth century, the percentage of the urban population throughout the entire region was far below the Western level. In Hungary, Poland and the Czech lands, 20 to 30 per cent of the population lived in cities; in the countries of Southeastern Europe, the figure was less than 20 per cent. While in several areas there were older cities whose history dated back to the Middle Ages, they were often rather small during this period. Prior to the First World War, the largest city in the entire region was Budapest which, including its suburbs, had more than one million residents, a population size produced by the developments of the nineteenth century. The Hungarian capital was followed by Warsaw, Prague, Lodz, and Bucharest, in that order, each with populations of less than one million. Several capital cities still had fewer than 100,000 inhabitants in 1910 (Sofia, Belgrade and Zagreb). Urban development was due in part to the expansion of capitalism; in several capital cities, however, it was also partially the result of government policies that sought to establish a magnificent centre for the nation state.

Urban population continued to increase during the interwar period due to migration to the cities. Growth in the capitals of Southeastern European countries was particularly rapid, for example, in Belgrade, Bucharest, and especially Sofia, which was by far the most important destination of Bulgarian rural flight, and which had also grown 'mechanically' through the enormous flood of refugees from territories lost at the end of the First World War.[27] In a subsequent period of rapid industrialization during the initial decades after the Second World War, Central and Eastern European cities continued to grow through the progressive development of existing cities, and at times also through the founding of new 'socialist' cities. The rapid expansion of the urban population, however, raises questions about the actual character of this development. A number of authors have spoken of 'rurbanization', a neologism intended to underscore the fact that groups arriving from the countryside 'ruralized' the cities to a certain extent, as the numerous urban newcomers were unable to appropriate urban ways of life and mentalities. They brought with them to the cities rural customs, piety and mentalities.[28] The other side of this development was the decline of villages, which lost the youngest and most creative segments of their populations to rural flight.[29] In Bulgaria, migration to the cities gave rise for some time to the peculiar form of 'urban-rural households', in which parts of a family lived in the city, and others in the countryside, but nevertheless constituted a single unit in many respects.[30]

The collapse of state socialism also significantly altered the conditions of urban development in the countries of the region. The decline in industrial employment, which was accom-

---

26 See Michael Gebel, 'Labour Markets in Central and Eastern Europe', in *Europe Enlarged: A Handbook of Education, Labour and Welfare Regimes in Central and Eastern Europe*, eds Irena Kogan, Michael Gebel and Clemens Noelke (Bristol: The Policy Press, 2008), 44.

27 Grigor Doytchinov, 'Städtebau in Bulgarien vom 19. bis zum 21. Jahrhundert', in *Urbanisierung und Stadtentwicklung in Südosteuropa vom 19. bis zum 21. Jahrhundert*, eds Thomas M. Bohn and Marie-Janine Calic (München: Verlag Otto Sagner, 2010), 190.

28 See Mirjana Prosic-Dvornic, 'The Rurbanisation of Belgrade after the Second World War', in *Die Volkskultur Südosteuropas in der Moderne*, ed. Klaus Roth (München: Südosteuropa-Gesellschaft, 1992).

29 Klaus Roth, 'Soziokultureller Wandel im südosteuropäischen Dorf nach dem zweiten Weltkrieg', in *Das Dorf in Südosteuropa zwischen Tradition und Umbruch*, eds Frank-Dieter Grimm and Klaus Roth (München: Südosteuropa-Gesellschaft, 1997), 64–75.

30 Ulf Brunnbauer, 'Gesellschaft und gesellschaftlicher Wandel in Südosteuropa nach 1945', in Clewing and Schmitt, *Geschichte Südosteuropas*, 651–702.

Table 2.2 Urban population in Central and Eastern Europe, 1920–2006 (in %)

	Percentage of the population living in cities with over 20,000 residents				Percentage of the population living in cities with over 100,000 residents			
	1920	1950	1980	2011	1920	1950	1980	2011
Hungary	31	34	49	48	15	20	29	29
Poland	18	26	45	47	9	16	28	28
Czechoslovakia	17	22	34	43/38	10	14	17	22/12
Romania	12	18	37	44	3	9	24	28
Bulgaria	9	19	41	56	4	10	24	34
Yugoslavia	7	13	26	38/25	2	6	13	23/12

Notes: Czechoslovakia 2011 is for Czech Republic/Slovakia; Yugoslavia 2011 is for Croatia/Slovenia.

Sources: Wolfram Fischer et al., eds, *Handbuch der Europäischen Wirtschafts- und Sozialgeschichte*, vol. 6., *Europäische Wirtschafts- und Sozialgeschichte vom Ersten Weltkrieg bis zur Gegenwart* (Stuttgart: Klett-Cotta, 1987), 54. For 2011, own calculations with data taken from Eurostat population census 2011 (accessed 25.01.2019): https://ec.europa.eu/CensusHub2/intermediate.do?&method=forwardResult.

panied in several countries by an increase in the agricultural population, would have reduced the urban population all on its own, yet other factors also played a role. In Poland, the urban population loss varied between 4 and 16 per cent (Katowice); in the Czech lands, it was about 7 or 8 per cent.[31] Budapest lost 15 per cent of its population due to the surplus mortality rate, migration and suburbanization. In addition to sinking population figures, Central and Eastern European cities also changed internally. Commercialization, an expansion of retail and office space and a decrease in residential housing could be observed in most city centres. Central and Eastern European cities typically consist of three different elements. First, the old building areas (i.e. those constructed prior to 1945) which were sometimes integrated into the expanding downtown area and in some cases, were rediscovered and gentrified (Kazimierz in Cracow and Vinohrady in Prague). Second, the fate of the socialist housing block districts differed massively: several were modernized, most of them stagnated and some even turned into slums (the Chánov housing estate in the city of Most in the Czech lands; the borough Luník in Kosice, Slovakia; Stolipinovo district in Plovdiv and Fakulteta in Sofia, Bulgaria; and the Havana district in Budapest). The durability of these buildings continues to pose an enormous problem, even where they have been renovated over the past two decades. The third element is the suburban environs, where the driving forces have been expansive retail trade and residential suburbanization. These phenomena often transformed the urban area of the former socialist countries in Central and Eastern Europe into a space of contradictions, or at least strong contrasts. Thus, the various social and political trends of the twentieth century were inscribed into the built environment.

Elites

According to several scholarly studies, the role and significance of elites are crucial for the political stability or instability of a country, as well as for its medium and long-term economic and social development, and are in fact more important than either constitutional order or the

---

31 Annett Steinführer and Annegret Haase, 'Demografischer Wandel und städtische Schrumpfung in Ostmitteleuropa nach 1989', in *Von der 'europäischen Stadt' zur 'sozialistischen Stadt' und zurück? Urbane Transformationen im östlichen Europa des 20. Jahrhunderts*, ed. Thomas M. Bohn (München: Oldenbourg, 2009), 397–417.

social structure of the lower classes.[32] The evolving capacities of functional elites within the separate subsystems of society – a basic feature of modernity – is one of the key factors that determines how a society is able to respond to new challenges, and how it can develop under modern conditions. The responsibilities of the political elite – or power elite – include distributing a country's resources, securing the necessary means for the various functional elites, and identifying social conflicts of interest and addressing them peacefully within a consensual political and social order. If political elites assign functional elites inappropriate objectives, or if they are not prepared to secure the means necessary to realize these objectives, the development of a country may deviate from the best course possible under the historical conditions, or development may be slow. This was the case in Serbia or Yugoslavia, according to Sundhaussen, as the political elite of the country did not make available the means necessary to combat illiteracy. As is well known, elementary education can contribute significantly to an increase in agricultural production, and the lack of development of the Serbian school system meant that agricultural development there stagnated.[33] Dysfunctions can also arise from the inability of the political elites to achieve consensus, of course, as well as from blatant and possibly acrimonious opposition among various elite groups. Finally, it is clear that a predominance of the political elite over the functional elite can impede the latter's capacities, since social subsystems operate efficiently only when functional elites have some degree of autonomy.[34]

The character and the achievements of elites in Central and Eastern Europe is a contested issue. The evolving practices of the functional elite and the structures and modes of action of the political elite should be understood as the results of historical processes. The basic features of the new political, economic, and social systems established in rapid succession in the eastern parts of Europe during the twentieth century did not emerge 'naturally' in a gradual historical development, but were more or less consciously constructed and introduced from above by elites.[35] For this reason, the composition and achievements of elites in these countries have always been and continue to be a political issue. Assessments of the competence of these elites are dependent on the political position of observers, who tend to reduce the issue of elite capacities to the composition of elite personnel. In this way, the issue of the continuity and discontinuity of elites becomes the central focus of public debates. From a historical or social-scientific perspective, however, social origins, religious and ethnic affiliations, institutions and levels of education, career paths and the internal power relations of elite groups are also interesting subjects.[36] Nor is the issue of continuity or discontinuity easy to evaluate in historical terms, as is often desired in public discourses. There is no scholarly consensus about what should be regarded as an inadequate, sufficient or excessive circulation of elites. While continuity can be evaluated positively as a guarantee of stability, too much continuity can also be seen as rigidity

---

32 John Higley and Jan Pakulski, 'Elite Theory versus Marxism: The Twentieth Century's Verdict', in *Elites after State Socialism: Theories and Analysis*, eds John Higley and György Lengyel (Lanham, MD: Rowman & Littlefield Publishers, Inc., 2000), 229–41.

33 Holm Sundhaussen, 'Alphabetisierung und Wirtschaftswachstum in den Balkanländern in historisch-komparativer Perspektive', in *Allgemeinbildung als Modernisierungsfaktor: Zur Geschichte der Elementarbildung in Südosteuropa von der Aufklärung bis zum Zweiten Weltkrieg*, eds Norbert Reiter and Holm Sundhaussen (Wiesbaden: Harrassowitz, 1994), 21–36.

34 Georg Lowell Field and John Higley, *Elitism* (London: Routledge, 1980), 95–116.

35 Magarditsch A. Hatschikjan, 'Zeitenwende und Elitenwandel in Osteuropa', in *Eliten im Wandel: Politische Führung, wirtschaftliche Macht und Meinungsbildung im neuen Osteuropa*, eds Magarditsch A. Hatschikjan and Franz-Lothar Altmann (Paderborn: Schöningh, 1998), 252.

36 Ibid.

and thus deemed negative. The evaluation of discontinuity is fluid as well, as it can be seen as useful flexibility, but also as the cause of a decline in expertise and experience. There is no established benchmark for how much continuity or discontinuity is excessive or insufficient.[37]

Over the course of the twentieth century, Central and Eastern European nations experienced three or four political ruptures, some of which also entailed a change of elites. Virtually all of these countries experienced political change in 1918–1919, 1944–1945 and following the collapse of state socialism; several of them also underwent political change between 1938 and 1941. During the Nazi dictatorship, a total break with or abrupt dissolution of previous elite groups was attempted, and communist parties sought just as radically to remove existing elites through the appointment of a political counter-elite and the creation of a new functional elite. Nationalism, however, also caused some profound breaks. This was the case after the First World War in many of the newly founded or re-founded nation states, where the assumption of power by a new national elite meant the removal of previously established groups. In contrast, in Hungary, Romania and Bulgaria the economic and social orders remained relatively unchanged, as 'old' elites were able to retain their positions of power. After the Second World War, the fissure was significantly more radical, if not as total as party ideology might lead one to believe.[38] The new communist political elite could not dispense entirely with the expertise of the previous functional elite. The question of elite continuity or discontinuity was raised frequently after 1990 as one of the central issues of the transformation processes of these societies, but this time was also an important focus of sociological research. Thus, in contrast with previous regime changes in the twentieth century, an extensive database was collected to evaluate the actual transformation processes among elites.

If we look somewhat more closely at individual periods of elite change, the question of the actual continuity of elites can also be examined in connection with elites prior to 1914. Whereas political elites often depicted themselves as heirs to a long national history, they in fact emerged as the result of the restructuring processes of the late nineteenth century.[39] This is all the more the case for the functional elite that arose during the new institutional expansion of the nation state and in the differentiation processes of modernity. In Hungary as well as in the Austrian and parts of the Russian territories of Poland, aristocrats who could claim a truly unbroken lineage as an elite group continued to possess influence and relatively direct access to elite political positions. For a Hungarian count with large landholdings prior to the First World War, entrance to the political elite – in practical terms, becoming a member of parliament – was merely a question of personal decision. In contrast, Czech aristocrats with large landholdings consciously retreated from politics after the introduction of universal suffrage in 1906, as they were compelled to recognize that aristocratic forms of politics were outdated in the face of ethnic conflicts and mass politics.[40] In the countries of Southeastern Europe, no aristocracy existed as the leading group of the old estate-based society. For this reason, new elite groups tied to the nation state there did not have to wrestle with the remains of aristocratic society after attaining independence. Only in Romania did the large landowning group of 'Boyars' play a

---

37 John Higley, Judith Kullberg and Jan Pakulski, 'The Persistence of Postcommunist Elites', *Journal of Democracy* 7, no. 2 (1996): 133–47.
38 Magarditsch, 'Zeitenwende und Elitenwandel', 251–269.
39 On the agrarian elite, see András Vári, *Herren und Landwirte: Ungarische Aristokraten und Agrarier auf dem Weg in die Moderne (1821–1910)* (Wiesbaden: Harrassowitz, 2008).
40 Sarka Lellkova, 'Der konservative Großgrundbesitz in Böhmen und die Reichsratswahlen von 1907: Vom kampflosen Rückzug der böhmischen Herren aus den Wahlen', in *Adel und Politik in der Habsburgermonarchie und den Nachbarländern zwischen Absolutismus und Demokratie*, eds Tatjana Tönsmeyer and Lubos Velek (München: Martin Meidenbauer, 2011), 319–26.

significant role. South of the Slava and the Danube, long-established village authorities constituted the opposition to the new political and functional elite. A multiplicity of new institutions of the nation state attempted to break up the segmentary structures of village communities and to enforce the institutionalized standardization of the modern state vis-à-vis the local 'elite' of village elders and clan leaders. From schools to taxation, from the application of national law to military administration, modern functional elites had to ensure the acceptance of new institutions by local structures unfamiliar with the formalization and legalization of social relations.[41]

One impediment to the establishment of modern, state-integrated functional elites almost everywhere in the region was the lack of appropriately educated personnel. In Southeastern Europe, high-ranking state bureaucrats often came from the diaspora – for example, Serbs from the Habsburg Empire in the early decades of Serbian independence – and in many countries groups that were not ethnically part of the 'titular nation' of the respective state also played a certain role. Such people were disproportionately represented, especially among highly educated freelance professionals like lawyers and among the technical intelligentsia. In some countries Jews assumed this role, especially in Hungary, but also in Polish territories and to a certain extent in Romania; elsewhere it was Germans, for example, in the Baltics. In Estonia, Baltic Germans comprised 3.5 per cent of the total population, but made up 47 per cent of jurists and 48 per cent of physicians – almost identical figures could be found in Hungary for Jews – and 83 per cent of people in commerce. The reason for this was that these groups were primarily urban residents and were better educated than the rest of society. At the beginning of the 1920s, approximately one third of the inhabitants of Riga were Baltic Germans; in 1935, the figure was 10 per cent, a decline due less to emigration than to the rapid increase in the city's overall population.[42] In Budapest, Jews comprised almost one quarter of the city's total population prior to the First World War, and Jewish residents still made up more than one fifth of the population during the interwar period. In the cities of eastern Poland or Bukovina, the percentage of the Jewish population was often even higher. City dwellers with above average education were, of course, better able to attain positions within the functional elite that presupposed an academic background. In Estonia, for example, 24 per cent of Germans had attended secondary school, in contrast to 1.7 per cent of the overall population.[43] The education level of Jews was also significantly higher than the societal average. Nevertheless, these groups had opportunities often limited only to the functional elite (which was responsible for social integration within the new nation states), as they were not considered part of the nation, or at least their national affiliation could be called into question.

In the period after the First World War, new political elite groups obtained leading positions in many countries following the collapse of the multi-ethnic empires in Central and Eastern Europe and sought to complete the consolidation of the nation states. This set in motion an expansion of national functional elites, which profoundly affected the positions of the 'old' elites. In simplified terms, we can say that aristocrats in the Baltics and in Czechoslovakia lost their privileged status, and to a large extent their estates as well, whereas in Poland and Hungary they were able to maintain their positions, while in Bulgaria and Yugoslavia an aristocracy had long been absent due to the Ottoman Empire. If we look more closely, however, it is evident that, even in countries with great apparent continuity, the composition of the political elite did not

---

41 Holm Sundhaussen, 'Eliten, Bürgertum, politische Klasse? Anmerkungen zu den Oberschichten in den Balkanländern des 19. und 20. Jahrhunderts', in Höpken and Sundhaussen, *Eliten in Südosteuropa*, 5–30.
42 See Gert von Pistohlkohrs, 'Estland, Lettland und Litauen 1920–1940', in *Handbuch der Europäischen Wirtschafts- und Sozialgeschichte*, vol. 6, *Europäische Wirtschafts- und Sozialgeschichte vom Ersten Weltkrieg bis zur Gegenwart*, eds Wolfram Fischer et al. (Stuttgart: Klett-Cotta, 1984), 729–68, here 738–42.
43 Hinno, *Bildung und Sozialstruktur*, 12.

remain unaltered. In Hungary, for example, hardly any large landowners could be found among politicians in the interwar period. Since the famous counts of Hungarian politics had not originally been large landowners, upon losing their estates they became professional politicians or even scholars. A professionalization of politics can be observed throughout Central and Eastern Europe during the interwar period. Whereas high-ranking members of the functional elite or people from the upper classes had been able to enter the political arena previously, and to a certain extent even into the 1920s, politics increasingly became a monopoly of party activists who had made their careers (up to leadership positions) exclusively within a political party or political movement. There was hardly any room left for people coming from other professions. This development can be seen, for example, in Hungary during the 1930s, and especially after 1935, in comparison with the 1920s. This also meant that an increasing number of men from the middle classes or the petty bourgeoisie could be found in the political elite. Research on the recruitment of elites in Hungary has shown that people from the lower middle classes often occupied leading positions in the church, the military, and the university (professors), as meritocratic advancement was possible in these institutions through education and achievement, in contrast to the much more closed domain of the economic elite, predominated by wealthy heirs.[44]

Although the aristocracy continued to be held in high esteem (due to tradition, wealth, and its exclusive lifestyle), this class enjoyed hardly any political influence. The only group still capable of competing with the new political elite was the economic elite of industry, commerce and finance. The transformation of individual Central and Eastern European states into dictatorships, and the expansion of state control over the economy – especially beginning with the global economic crisis – should be evaluated in part within this context. The political elite sought to centralize ever more contributions to national income in order to promote the expansion of the nation state and to combat deficient social integration. These tendencies can be observed in the Baltic nations, as well as in Poland during the Sanacja period and in Hungary during the second half of the 1930s.

Whereas in Hungary, and to a certain extent in Poland, the new groups – primarily from the middle classes – attempted to push out previous elite groups from the political elite and to gain control over the economic elite, political elites in Southeastern Europe operated without significant competition at the national level. The ruling classes comprising the political and functional elite lived quite removed from the peasants. Only gradually did they succeed in establishing themselves over local elites and in gaining acceptance for the power of the state apparatus. On the national level, however, there was no aristocracy or economic elite capable of acting independently.[45] One sociological study concluded that in Southeastern European societies, processes of budgeting during the interwar period not only led to the establishment of authoritarian or semi-authoritarian political regimes, but also had far-reaching consequences for

---

44 Kovács I. Gábor, 'A két világháború közötti egyetemi tanárok rekrutációja és a középrétegek hierarchiája a társadalmi rangcímrendszer szerint a dualizmuskori Magyarországon' [The recruitment of university professors in the interwar period and middle-class hierarchy according to the order of social ranks in dualist Hungary], in *Elitek és iskolák, felekezetek és etnikumok*, ed. Kovács I. Gábor (Budapest: L'Harmattan, 2011), 99–198; Szakály Sándor, *A magyar katonai felső vezetés, 1938–1945* [The Hungarian higher-military leadership 1938–1945] (Budapest: Ister, 2003); Lengyel György, *A multipozícionális gazdasági elit a két világháború között* [The multi-positional economic elites between the two World Wars] (Budapest: ELTE Szociológiai Intézet, 1993); Gergely Jenő, *A katolikus egyházi elit Magyarországon, 1919–1945* [The Catholic Church elite in Hungary, 1919–1945] (Budapest: ELTE Szociológiai Intézet, 1997).
45 Maria Georgieva, 'Unternehmer, Staat und Politik: Zur Rolle der Wirtschaftselite in Bulgarien 1878–1941', in Höpken and Sundhaussen, *Eliten in Südosteuropa*, 105–28.

many occupational groups, making them 'directly dependent on opportunities of state support. This increased the general trend for politically significant groups to gain direct state access to the entire economy …'[46] The functional elite were in principle supposed to operate according to foreign models, but were in fact steeped in hierarchical relationships and personal networks, while the general population did not understand the internal logic of state administrative institutions. Functioning at a lower capacity overall, the elite was able to expand its control over resources – which did enable it to gratify patronage networks, but failed to increase capacities for social performance and adaptation.[47] The result, according to Sundhaussen, was an early form of 'state capitalism' with expanded state ownership in the various economic branches, state monopolies and high taxation – which from today's perspective suggests a special structural continuity beyond the Second World War in these countries. Such monopolies were by no means exclusive to Southeastern European countries, however. From Hungary to Poland up to the Baltic nations, the influence of the state on the economy increased in various forms, including state ownership, monopolies and compulsory economic measures.[48]

As is well known, there was a comprehensive change of elites in all nations of Central and Eastern Europe after the Second World War. In the years following, elite change was also attempted among the ranks of the functional elite – something facilitated by the war, which had often scattered these elite groups, when it had not destroyed them. However, nowhere was the change of functional elites as complete as that of political elite groups. In many countries, old experts remained in their positions to some degree because they could not be replaced. The war had eliminated or significantly weakened other potential elite groups – not least in Central and Eastern European nations, because these had been largely composed of Jews, although Germans disappeared as well. As a result, the new political elite was able to expand its power to all realms of social life without significant impediments. From this structural perspective, the process of expanding political power – simultaneous to a complete change of political elites – appears to be a continuation of developments that began in the 1930s.

Even if there is no accepted benchmark to gauge elite change, it is clear that in this particular case, the change of elites in the functional apparatuses was also accompanied by a profound decline in competence and capacities. Educated and experienced members of diverse elite groups fled the region, had died in the war, or simply lost their professional and social standing. Despite these events, some people – now designated throughout the region as 'old experts' – were able to find positions in the new system, which could not do without their expertise. Even when someone became 'déclassé', it remained uncertain whether this social decline was irreversible. According to Rudolf Andorka, at times the cultural capital of previous ruling groups enabled the progeny of once privileged elite families to find their way back into the functional or cultural elite in the 1960s.[49] Andorka was an example of this: the son of a general in the

---

46 Anton Sterbling, 'Grenzen klassentheoretischer Analysekategorien', 207–8.
47 Sundhaussen, 'Eliten, Bürgertum, politische Klasse?', 5–30.
48 Ágnes Pogány, 'Economic Anti-Semitism in Hungary after Trianon', in *History and Culture of Economic Nationalism in East Central Europe*, eds Helga Schultz and Eduard Kubů (Berlin: Berliner Wissenschafts-Verlag, 2006), 219–230; Ágnes Pogány, Jan Kofman and Eduard Kubů, *Für eine nationale Wirtschaft: Ungarn, die Tschechoslowakei und Polen von Ausgang des 19. Jahrhunderts bis zum Zweiten Weltkrieg* (Berlin: Berliner-Wissenschafts-Verlag, 2006).
49 Rudolf Andorka, 'Regime Transitions in Hungary in the 20th Century: The Role of National Counter-Elites', in 'Regime Transitions, Elites, and Bureaucracies in Eastern Europe', eds Hans-Ulrich Derlien and George J. Szablowski, special issue, *Governance: An International Journal of Policy and Administration* 6, no. 3 (1993): 358–71.

interwar period, he was sentenced to forced labour in the mines in the early 1950s, but went on to become a well-known sociologist in Hungary in later decades. Similar developments can be observed in the Baltic nations where at the end of the 1960s, the sons and grandsons of university graduates predominated within the elite. Family background was also a factor here, despite the crass, even brutal change in elites that occurred after the Second World War.[50]

Beginning in the late 1940s, the new regimes throughout the region attempted to replace the 'old' functional elite, establishing for this purpose substitute secondary schools as well as peasant and proletariat universities. While these institutions did enable numerous sons of farmers and workers – as well as a few daughters – to achieve relative social advancement, they did not prove adequately efficient over the long term.[51] Beginning in the 1960s, the various specialized apparatuses expanded rapidly, leading to an increase in functional elite positions requiring educated candidates. Political loyalty alone was no longer sufficient for entrance into the elite; expertise was also expected. For this reason, throughout the region traditional university education once again became the locus for recruiting the functional elite. Those entering the political elite after 1960 thus generally had university degrees, although there were, of course, still many older political elites without any post-secondary education. In all countries of the greater region, conflicts frequently occurred between the functional elite and the political elite. For a long time, however, these did not lead to real political confrontation, but remained merely scattered, continuous tensions within the system. Functional elites often sought to act in the spirit of technocracy, presuming that economic and social problems could be resolved with non-political, technical-scientific rationality. They felt that the opportunities for developing their expertise had been severely restricted through the political limitations set on the differentiation of partial subsystems. Despite the conflicts between the functional elite and the power elite (which at times sought to impose its political perspective on the functional elite), the two groups were dependent on one another. A coalition of technical functional elites and party leadership was virtually imperative in order to carry out the social and economic transformations needed to implement production increases.[52] The periods of reform resulting from the cooperation between the two elite groups were followed by periods in which the primacy of politics in state socialism was reasserted, as the power elite feared that technocratic reforms could jeopardize its political objectives.[53] Only in the 1980s did the conflict between functional elites and political elites reach a point at which it threatened to destroy the system, at least in Hungary, where previous reforms had gone far enough to obstruct the economic and social functioning of the subsystems and could not be resolved within the socialist political order.

Renowned intellectuals constituted a special elite group during the socialist period, fulfilling a peculiar role in state socialism. In the absence of a wealthy propertied class, this narrow circle was the only element (besides the expert apparatuses subordinated to politics) able to act with relative autonomy. The socialist system also needed a cultural and scientific elite, and these people were, or potentially could be, active in public life as well. Thus, intellectuals received

---

50 Hinno, *Bildung und Sozialstruktur*.
51 Majtényi György, *A tudomány lajtorjája: 'Társadalmi mobilitás' és 'új értelmiség Magyarországon a második világháború után* [Science's ladder: 'social mobility' and 'new intelligentsia' in Hungary after the Second World War] (Budapest: Gondolat, 2005), 11–15.
52 Dirk van Laak, 'Technokratie im Europa des 20. Jahrhunderts – eine einflussreiche "Hintergrundideologie"', in *Theorien und Experimente der Moderne: Europas Gesellschaften im 20. Jahrhundert*, ed. Lutz Raphael (Köln: Böhlau, 2012), 101–28.
53 Christoph Boyer, Introduction, *Zur Physiognomie sozialistischer Wirtschaftsreformen: Die Sowjetunion, Polen, die Tschechoslowakei, Ungarn, die DDR und Jugoslawien im Vergleich* (Frankfurt a.M.: Vittorio Klostermann, 2007), IX–XLII.

special attention from those in power – as well as from the secret police – and this attention could assume the form of a materially privileged status and, for example, the possibility of travel, as well as the withdrawal of such privileges or even simply the loss of a job.

The transformation process after the end of state socialism is perhaps the historical episode most frequently analyzed from the perspective of elite change. The public political debates focused especially on the issue of continuity in elite personnel. However, it is also worthwhile to consider the differences between elite change and elite restructuring. We can speak of elite change when dealing with the replacement of persons and groups within existing institutions. Elite restructuring, in contrast, is a process in which new institutional orders and positions are established that alter elite configurations (the basic relations between various elite groups).[54] Elite restructuring as well as elite change occurred in this sense everywhere in the region – although Szelényi's claim that the beginning of the transformation process was by no means a zero hour applies to both.

The restructuring of elites that occurred during the general transformation was similar in all countries. Previous party leaders disappeared, new centres of political power emerged, and functional elites could regard themselves as liberated from the strict supervision of the political elite. The most significant of these emancipation processes from the political elite was an increase in autonomy for functional elites, who were now supposed to operate under the conditions of the new market economy. The social character of the new economic elite – including its composition in terms of personnel – and its relations to the political elite appear to have been decisive from the perspective of this completely new social order. It was frequently claimed that during the transformation of elite configurations the political elite became in many respects dependent on the economic elite, and that the power relations between the two elite groups under socialism had thus been reversed. On closer inspection, however, this assertion seems dubious. There are reports from several countries in Central and Eastern Europe indicating the dependence of economic elites on political elites. The new economic elites were established in a process driven by politics, and this birth defect had a long-term influence on the features of this group. To some extent, these traits of a 'political capitalism' are present everywhere in the region.[55] Generally speaking, we can say that the differentiation of specific institutional realms and of corresponding elite groups made only gradual progress in Southeastern Europe. The significance of the centre of power continued to predominate over functional differentiation. Political elite groups at the centre of power mobilized nationalist, ethnic and religious convictions, while elites with specific expertise and representatives of economic interests remained in the background.[56] In other countries of the region as well, it is extremely doubtful that the relationship between political and economic elites was quasi-reversed.[57] State privatization agencies – together with large commercial banks controlled by the state – created a new economic elite. This elite was made and did not simply emerge. An autonomous property-owning bourgeoisie independent of the state barely existed, as members of the petty bourgeoisie from the second

---

54 Anton Sterbling, 'Elitenwandel in Südosteuropa: Einige Bemerkungen aus elitentheoretischer Sicht', in Höpken and Sundhaussen, *Eliten in Südosteuropa*, 31–47.

55 Cătălin Augustin Stoica, '"Our Martyrs of 1989 Did Not Die for This!": Political Capitalism in Post-Communist Romania', in 'Political and Functional Elites in Post-Socialist Transformation: Central and East Europe since 1989/90', special issue, *Historical Social Research* 37, no. 2 (2012): 26–52.

56 Anton Sterbling, 'Soziale Anerkennungsbedürfnisse und Autoritätsbeziehungen: Eliten und Konfliktpotenziale in südosteuropäischen Gesellschaften', in Sterbling, *Kontinuität und Wandel in Rumänien und Südosteuropa*, 247–61.

57 György Lengyel, 'Hungarian Economic Policy Makers and Businessmen in the 1990s: Similarities and Differences', in *Restructuring of the Economic Elites after State Socialism*, eds David Lane, György Lengyel and Jochen Tholen (Stuttgart: Ibidem Verlag, 2007), 97–114.

economy were rarely able to expand into large-scale manufacturing, and only a few returning émigrés (in the Czech Republic, Estonia, Latvia) attained the level of wealthy bourgeoisie, primarily due to the restitution of valuable real estate. By far the most powerful group of economic elites was the new managers, but they often attained their positions through precisely this interplay between foreign capital and the state.[58]

The biggest losers of the transformation processes among elite groups were intellectuals. Although intellectuals did appear to become much more influential the moment state socialism collapsed, their liberation from the political supervision of higher authorities had the consequence of reducing their social standing in relation to other elite groups. The economic elite became much more powerful than the previous economic apparatchiks of the party state, and developed into a partner for the political elite much more important than intellectuals. In the face of a market economy, a functioning mass media and commercial cultural production, intellectuals lost their previous interpretive monopoly in the public sphere. High culture and its producers were expected to survive on the market in competition with diverse forms of mass culture – and with ever decreasing state funding.

As to the magnitude of elite changes – that is, the replacement of individuals in elite positions in Central and Eastern Europe – soon after 1989–1990 it became clear that while a large number of people had been forced out of their previous posts, many of them continued to work in elite positions of some kind. It quickly became apparent, however, that this relatively high level of elite reproduction did not impede the transformation process. The 'old elites' did not turn out to be opponents of the new changes. A few years after the first free elections, political polarization did emerge in terms of important issues of foreign policy (entrance into the EU and NATO) and economic policy (privatization, etc.), but not along a dividing line of 'old' and 'new' elites.[59] Nevertheless, differences on issues of symbolic significance were at times so great that they played an important role in mobilizing voters – and this resulted in the enormous public attention paid to the composition of elite personnel.

Elite change was significant within some elite sectors, but there was also a certain degree of continuity. The magnitude and specific features of elite replacement was dependent on the given elite configuration in the 1980s. Generally speaking, in countries with a high level of elite circulation during the late phases of state socialism, the 'old' elites proved to be rather flexible and were able to apply their expertise so useful in the new circumstances – sometimes even in the face of a counter-elite – because elite activity had already been professionalized. This was the case, for example, for certain established economic elites in Central and Eastern European countries who were able to apply their managerial skills successfully during and after privatization. The former political elite, in contrast, had more difficulty holding its own vis-à-vis the new groups.[60] Only in those countries where transformation occurred slowly through political negotiation, for example, in Poland and Hungary, did they have a chance of retaining their earlier positions even in part. When the system collapsed abruptly, as in Czechoslovakia, or in

---

58 Hatschikjan, 'Zeitenwende und Elitenwandel in Osteuropa'; Iván Szelényi, 'The New Grand Bourgeoisie under Post-Communism: Central Europe, Russia and China Compared' (working paper no. 2010/63, UNU-WIDER, 2010).

59 Jacek Wasilewski, 'Die ehemaligen kommunistischen Eliten im demokratischen Polen: Sind sie noch interessant?' in *Alte Eliten in jungen Demokratien? Wechsel, Wandel und Kontinuität in Mittel- und Osteuropa*, ed. Hans-Joachim Veen (Köln: Böhlau, 2004), 177–93.

60 Petr Matějů and Eric Hanley, 'Die Herausbildung ökonomischer und politischer Eliten in Ostmitteluropa', in Hatschikjan and Altmann, *Eliten im Wandel*, 145–71.

Table 2.3 Percentage of elites in Central and Eastern Europe, 1993

	Czech Republic		Hungary		Poland	
Economic elites:						
Women	5.7		7.4		9.2	
Former functionaries	10.1		16.4		18.3	
Political elites:	Civil service	Parliament	Civil service	Parliament	Civil service	Parliament
Women	13.5	11.7	12.5	10.1	15.2	6.9
No university degree	25	19.4	0	5.1	2.7	16.7
Former CP member	32.7	37.9	46.3	15.4	33.2	23.6
Former functionaries	0	7.8	17.5	9	8.7	12.5

Source: Petr Matějů and Eric Hanley, 'Die Herausbildung ökonomischer und politischer Eliten in Ostmitteleuropa', in *Eliten im Wandel: Politische Führung, wirtschaftliche Macht und Meinungsbildung im neuen Osteuropa*, eds Magarditsch A. Hatschikjan and Franz-Lothar Altmann (Paderborn: Schöningh, 1998), 160–65.

individual Baltic countries where the nationalist dimensions of the change impeded the continuation of previous political engagement, virtually all political elites lost their posts. An early break with Moscow did allow a few politicians to remain active.[61]

Previous membership in the communist party says little about people's convictions, as both dissidents and career-conscious experts were frequently party members during certain periods of their lives. For example, one third of Solidarność had previously belonged to the Polish United Workers' Party. However, there is no consensus among scholars about the figures cited above. Using a broader definition of elites, Szelényi calculates significantly higher percentages of former elites. According to Szelényi, 40 per cent of elites in Poland in 1993 had also held elite positions in 1988, and 33 per cent in Hungary. Furthermore, a significant portion of elites from 1993 who had not been members of the *nomenklatura* had nevertheless held a leading position of some kind in 1988. This seems to affirm the well-known saying that the collapse of state socialism was a revolution of the deputies. The transition to a market economy does not appear to have altered patterns of elite recruitment, but merely accelerated generational change. According to Szelényi, only 20 per cent of elites in Poland and 21 per cent in Hungary came from non-elite classes.[62] Elite groups became more homogeneous overall. In the years of the transformation – and often already in the 1980s – elites as a group rapidly became younger and simultaneously more similar. In Hungary, for example, nine tenths of elites had a post-secondary education. The majority came from families of elite members and professionals with university degrees. The percentage of those whose fathers had been workers (or farmers)

---

61 Anton Steen, 'Elite and Mass Confidence in New Democracies – Towards Congruence? The Baltic States 1992–2007', in 'Elite Foundations', special issue, *Historical Social Research* 37, no. 1 (2012): 127–47.
62 Iván Szelényi and Szonja Szelényi, 'Circulation or Reproduction of Elites during the Postcommunist Transformation of Eastern Europe', *Theory and Society* 24 (1995): 615–38; György Lengyel, 'Die Zirkulation der ungarischen Wirtschaftselite in den 1990er Jahren: Verlangsamung und Abschluss', in Veen, *Alte Eliten in jungen Demokratien*, 267–84; Pavel Machonin and Milan Tucek, 'Czech Republic: New Elites and Social Change', in Higley and Lengyel, *Elites after State Socialism*, 25–45.

was significantly lower than it had been among previous elites. The reason for this was that the composition of the elite in the 1980s was in part the result of an earlier wave of mobility, whereas during the years of transformation people with inherited cultural and social capital had more opportunities to obtain leadership positions.[63] More newcomers were able to enter the political elite than the economic elite, but even these people routinely came from educated social classes. Only in Poland was it possible – through Solidarność – for men from the lower middle or the working class to become part of the political elite.[64]

Despite all the trends toward continuity, the magnitude of elite reproduction in Poland, Hungary and Czechoslovakia was lower than in Southeastern Europe. In the latter region, no potential counter-elite existed that could have assumed elite positions upon regime change. In Romania, the political elite of state socialism had been organized according to kinship and patronage relations and was divided into clans. The transformation there meant removing the clan that had monopolized power and replacing it with other elite groups.[65] The elite of the new era, however, came almost exclusively from the former political and functional elite, as no other potential elite existed. The situation was similar in Bulgaria and Serbia. In Croatia, the composition of the new elite was somewhat more complicated. Political activists of the 'Croatian Spring', returning émigrés (former communists and anti-communists), those members of the old apparatus with expertise who were prepared to accept the new ideologies, technocrats at large enterprises and members of the intelligentsia who had previously been politically passive, all became part of the new elite.[66]

In summary, we can say that elite configuration in Central and Eastern Europe has been uneven. The political elite has often been fractured and unable to create sufficient consensus but at the same time has retained its preponderance of power vis-à-vis professional functional elites.[67] The latter were not always able to develop their specialized expertise in the face of this. Nor did an independent economic elite, capable of functioning as a counterweight to the political elite, emerge in the first two decades after the collapse of socialism.

The middle classes

There is hardly an intellectual task as difficult as defining the so-called middle classes in historical terms or even outlining their contours. Numerous designations have been used in the literature to describe the middle zone of societies, many of them with ideological connotations. The problems of analysis are exacerbated in our region, where one is accustomed to speak of the absence of the middle classes, or at least of their weakness and heterogeneity. Our task here is

---

63 Luca Kristóf, 'What Happened Afterwards? Change and Continuity in the Hungarian Elite between 1988 and 2009', in 'Political and Functional Elites in Post-Socialist Transformation: Central and East Europe since 1989/90', special issue, *Historical Social Research* 37, no. 2 (2012): 108–22.

64 John Higley and György Lengyel, 'Introduction: Elite Configurations after State Socialism', in Higley and Lengyel, *Elites after State Socialism*, 1–24; Ákos Róna-Tas and József Böröcz, 'Bulgaria, the Czech Republic, Hungary, and Poland: Presocialist and Socialist Legacies among Business Elites', in Higley and Lengyel, *Elites after State Socialism*, 209–27; Jacek Wasilewski, 'Die ehemaligen kommunistischen Eliten im demokratischen Polen: Sind sie noch interessant?' in Veen, *Alte Eliten in jungen Demokratien*, 177–94.

65 Anneli Ute Gabanyi, 'Die rumänischen Eliten in der Systemtransformation', in Veen, *Alte Eliten in jungen Demokratien*, 313–31; Wasilewski, *Die ehemaligen kommunistischen Eliten*, 177–93.

66 Nenad Zakosek, 'Elitenwandel in Kroatien 1989–1995', in Höpken and Sundhaussen, *Eliten in Südosteuropa*, 279–88; Rumen Dimitrov, 'Elitenlosigkeit und Postkommunismus: Fragmente zum kulturellen Hintergrund der Mafiabildung in Bulgarien', in Hatschikjan and Altmann, *Eliten im Wandel*, 103–42.

67 Higley and Lengyel, 'Introduction: Elite Configurations after State Socialism', 1–24.

not to resolve the theoretical problems of conceptually identifying the middle class/the middle classes/the propertied and educated bourgeoisie, etc.[68] It is sufficient to note here that the perspective describing the development of the Central and Eastern European middle classes 'as a special and deficient path'[69] – implicitly in comparison to Western Europe – has long been criticized as inadequate, because it fails to illuminate the peculiar developmental path of the middle classes in this region. A number of authors have sought an alternative to the discourse of deficiency by insisting, first of all, that 'functional equivalents' of the Western European bourgeoisie were also present in these societies[70] – without them having formed a bourgeoisie in the sense of a relatively homogeneous social milieu. Second, it has been demonstrated that a number of aspects of bourgeois life were also present in Central and Eastern Europe and even in Southeastern Europe: theatres, parks, bourgeois social life and coffee houses existed in cities of the region, for example, in Warsaw, Budapest and Riga. The establishment of urban, bourgeois middle classes in Central and Eastern Europe can thus be described less as a deficient development than as the process of a diverse amalgamation of different social milieus that was fraught with tension and highly differentiated regionally. The ethnic and religious fragmentation of the middle classes constitutes a 'deficient' case only when measured against the examples of the much more homogeneous Western nation states.[71] Third, it can be argued that a middle zone did exist within the structural inequalities of wealth, education and power in these countries, even if the forms there were different from those in Western Europe.[72] Moreover, apart from the ethnic and, to a large extent, religious homogeneity of the social middle in the West, significant differences among the various middle-class groups existed there as well. In both the West and the countries of this region, independent artisans, merchants, tenement-building owners, and innkeepers possessed private property as well as a certain degree of autonomy, and usually strove for social advancement. Strata like civil servants and employees with mid-level education or academic training, as well as freelance professionals, also belonged to the relatively new groupings of the social middle. The intelligentsia – characteristic mainly in Poland and in Russia – was also an emerging group, comprising of mostly highly educated people, with ambitions to shape the social order, who often sought to play a role in political movements. The 'old' petty bourgeoisie – artisans, tradesmen and small property owners – distinguished itself from all other groups but was internally heterogeneous and never established a consensus about its own socio-cultural identity. The so-called 'new' middle class – employees in various branches, the intelligentsia, small entrepreneurs of the new type – was characterized not only by demarcation from the 'old' middle class (as well as from workers, peasants and aristocrats, where these existed),

---

68 For an overview of the applicability of the term bourgeoisie (or *Bürgertum*) in certain countries of the region, see Oliver Kühschelm, 'Das Bürgertum in Cisleithanien', in *Die Habsburgermonarchie 1848–1918*, vol. 9, part 2, *Soziale Strukturen: Von der Stände- zur Klassengesellschaft*, eds Helmut Rumpler and Peter Urbanitsch (Vienna: Österreichische Akademie der Wissenschaften, 2010), 849–907, especially 850–4; For further literature, see Peter Lundgreen, 'Einführung', in *Sozial- und Kulturgeschichte des Bürgertums: Eine Bilanz des Bielefelder Sonderforschungsbereichs (1986–1997)*, ed. Peter Lundgreen (Göttingen: Vandenhoeck & Ruprecht, 2000), 13–39.

69 Wolfgang Höpken, 'Die "fehlende Klasse"? Bürgertum in Südosteuropa im 19. und 20. Jahrhundert', in *Transformationsprobleme Bulgariens im 19. und frühen 20. Jahrhundert: Historische und ethnologische Perspektiven*, eds Ulf Brunnbauer and Wolfgang Höpken (München: Verlag Otto Sagner, 2007), 37.

70 Michael G. Müller, 'Die Historisierung des bürgerlichen Projekts: Europa, Osteuropa und die Kategorie der Rückstaendigkeit', *Tel Aviver Jahrbuch für deutsche Geschichte* 29 (2000): 163–70.

71 Joachim von Puttkamer, *Ostmitteleuropa im 19. und 20. Jahrhundert* (München: Oldenbourg, 2010), 173–4.

72 Höpken, 'Die "fehlende Klasse"?' 33–68.

but also by an internal heterogeneity.[73] Therefore, with all of these groups – present in varying proportions in the societies of the countries examined here – internal cultural homogeneity or a commonality of political and social guiding principles should be expected even less here than among similar groups in the West. The development of the new middle classes and the transformation of the old middle classes occurred in this region at times parallel to a certain degree of industrialization, and elsewhere without the establishment of industrialization, for example, in Galicia and in Southeastern Europe.[74]

The numerical weight of different groupings, the norms and practices of middle-class life, and the evaluation and the prestige of various middle-class groups changed significantly during the first half of the twentieth century. The Hungarian census of 1930, which recorded the employment of respondents' fathers, indicates significant mobility. Approximately 50 per cent of the broad middle classes did not come from middle-class families.[75] Similar figures can presumably be extrapolated for other Central European countries.

However, the qualitative changes during the decades prior to the Second World War appear to have been even more important than the significant expansion of the middle classes. Prior to the First World War, for example, around 24 per cent of adult men in Hungary had voting rights, which were granted on the basis of a tax threshold. This group, which ranged from wealthy peasants and artisans up to high-level government officials, could be understood as middle class in a broad sense of the term. Using a narrower definition, one could also count among the Hungarian middle class – according to the general understanding – those people who had at least a secondary school education and/or one servant employed in their household. This narrow strata of the 'true' middle class was, of course, distinguished, on the one hand, from those families who had enough wealth or income to implement an upper-middle-class lifestyle (including cultivating the arts and having multiple servants, etc.) and, on the other hand, from the strata of people who read newspapers, possessed voting rights and wore bourgeois clothing, but were unable to establish a middle-class lifestyle and had not completed secondary school.[76] In the semantics of public appearance, bourgeois clothing communicated to others that its wearers did not perform manual labour. Such clothing was, of course, worn not only by this narrower circle of the middle class, but also by broader strata of residents in Eastern European cities (for example, private employees and shop assistants), as it enabled them to distinguish themselves from workers and peasants.[77]

The origins of the strata in Central and Eastern Europe that wore bourgeois clothing prior to the First World War were quite diverse. State officials were among the first groups to belong to the middle classes. In Southeastern European countries, state officials – together with military officers – constituted the core group of the middle classes, which was the first to adopt

---

73 Gunther Mai, *Europa 1918–1939: Mentalitäten, Lebensweisen, Politik zwischen den Weltkriegen* (Stuttgart: Kohlhammer, 2001), 30–45.

74 See Maciej Janowski, 'Galizien auf dem Weg zur Zivilgesellschaft', in *Die Habsburgermonarchie 1848–1918*, vol. 8, part 1, *Politische Öffentlichkeit und Zivilgesellschaft: Vereine, Parteien und Interessenverbände als Träger der politischen Partizipation*, eds Helmut Rumpler and Peter Urbanitsch (Vienna: Österreichische Akademie der Wissenschaften, 2006), 805–58.

75 Rudolf Andorka, 'Changes in Social Mobility', 198–9.

76 Károly Halmos, 'Das Besitz- und Bildungsbürgertum in Ungarn', in Rumpler and Urbanitsch, *Die Habsburgermonarchie 1848–1918*, vol. 9, part 2, 909–50; Bódy Zsombor, 'Polgárok és munkások 1929-ben: Adalékok a fogyasztás történetéhez' [Citizens and workers in 1929: contributions to the history of consumption], *Korall: Társadalomtörténeti Folyóirat* 10 (2002): 187–99.

77 Manfred Hettling, 'Bürgerliche Kultur – Bürgerlichkeit als kulturelles System', in Lundgreen, *Sozial- und Kulturgeschichte des Bürgertums*, 319–39.

bourgeois behavioural patterns and to communicate these, often along with nationalist ideals and goals, to further strata.[78] In Central and Eastern European countries, state officials did not for the most part constitute the core group of the middle classes. In Hungary and certainly also in Poland, groups with noble heritage appropriated the new bourgeois behavioural norms and conveyed them to broader social strata, again often alongside nationalist ideals. Here bourgeois culture – as a specific constellation of cultural values and behavioural norms – was able to deviate from the bourgeoisie as a concrete group defined in terms of employment structure.[79] In the Baltic nations, in the Czech lands and in Poland prior to the First World War, state officials could assume only an ambivalent position, as they were incorporated into a political order that was not viewed as 'national' and possibly also belonged to other ethnic groups; nevertheless, they adopted a middle-class lifestyle and also represented this tendency to other local groups. State officials in Hungary, according to general opinion, did belong to the middle class, but were not a central part of it because other groups were more powerful and could outcompete them – those with an aristocratic heritage and, somewhat later, the bourgeoisie from the industrial and commercial sectors of the economy. In contrast to the generally accepted view, the majority of state officials did not come from aristocratic families, just as the majority of the imperial and royal officer corps were not aristocratic.[80] In the Czech lands, the middle classes emerged from the strata of wealthy peasants, artisans and other petty-bourgeois groups.[81]

In every country of the region, freelance professionals clearly belonged to the middle classes. In general, lawyers, physicians, engineers and pharmacists had relatively close ties to the state, although lawyers in Central European countries had begun to organize themselves into bar associations in the nineteenth century. Physicians followed this trend somewhat later in the twentieth century. In Southeastern European countries, the principle of professional organization was not established prior to the First World War. Members of these professions were often state officials in practice.[82] In Central and Eastern Europe these professions were subject to relatively powerful state supervision; nevertheless, forms of self-organization did exist – and with this, the claim to supervise independently the practical norms of these professions.

One common trait of the Central and Eastern European middle classes around the First World War was that only men could be members of the middle classes – here there was no distinction to the West. Women belonged to the middle class only as daughters and wives. If we accept voting rights as a contemporary description of the middle classes – universal male suffrage was adopted in the region only in Cisleithania beginning in 1906 – and thus regard those with voting rights as members of the middle classes, we can say that the social type implicit in the laws granting suffrage was the independent man – generally the head of a family – who possessed some wealth, whereby the trait 'independent' could be substituted by a higher-level

---

78 Holm Sundhaussen, 'Eliten, Bürgertum, politische Klasse', 5–30.
79 For articles that treat bourgeois culture and the bourgeoisie separately, see Ulrike Döcker, 'Bürgerlichkeit und Kultur – Bürgerlichkeit als Kultur', in *Bürgertum in der Habsburgermonarchie*, eds Ernst Bruckmüller, Ulrike Döcker, Hannes Stekl and Peter Urbanitsch (Vienna: Böhlau, 1990), 1: 95–104; Károly Halmos, 'Besitz- und Bildungsbürgertum in Ungarn', 909–50; for Galicia, see Kühschelm, 'Bürgertum in Ciesleithanien'.
80 Gábor Benedek, 'Die Beamten in Ungarn', in Rumpler and Urbanitsch, *Die Habsburgermonarchie 1848–1918*, vol. 9, part 2, 1211–43; Tibor Hajdu, *Tisztikar és középosztály, 1850–1914* [Officers and the middle class, 1850–1914] (Budapest: Ferenc-József magyar tisztjei, 1999).
81 Kühschelm, 'Bürgertum in Ciesleithanien', 849–907.
82 Wolfgang Höpken, 'Zwischen Bürokratie und Bürgertum: "Bürgerliche Berufe" in Südosteuropa', in Höpken and Sundhaussen, *Eliten in Südosteuropa*, 69–104.

position in the civil service that required academic qualifications. Beyond all distinctions of wealth and education, such people could be regarded as members of the middle classes. Yet even less than their Western European counterparts did they constitute a status group (in the Weberian sense) or a social milieu integrated through culture, values and/or behavioural norms. Nevertheless, their social position above the lower classes and beneath aristocrats, the upper middle class, and leading state functionaries is indisputable.[83]

The composition and internal proportions of middle-class groups, as well as their everyday life practices, were significantly reconfigured during the interwar period. The bourgeois lifestyle – with salons, the cultivation of both the arts and nature (parks, gardens), and specific forms of leisure time (expensive balls, vernissages, dinners, soirées at the opera, to mention a few) – often became obsolete even among the upper classes. In Southeastern European countries, bourgeois culture was thus hardly able to exert any social influence, since prior to the First World War it affected only a narrow leading circle in these societies: families of politicians with foreign contacts, high-level bureaucrats who had studied abroad, and the wealthiest businessmen. Bourgeois culture as a coherent value system and widespread behavioural forms had more impact on the broader middle classes in Central and Eastern Europe. In these societies, however, the relative spread of bourgeois norms and forms meant that the contours of those groups that had previously cultivated bourgeois culture became even more fluid. In the new or newly founded states, the emergence of national civil servants as well as officers and non-commissioned officer corps marked the (now significantly expanded) boundaries of the middle classes.

One of the most important changes in comparison to the period prior to the First World War was that women were now permitted to establish a middle-class existence, at least in Central European capitals and metropolises. In contrast to the turn of the century, the central social type of the middle classes was no longer the independent man with assets; instead, diverse groups of employees and lower-level civil servants with various levels of education and training – including women working as teachers, and in several countries, as lawyers or other professions – could claim affiliation to the middle classes and obtain middle-class social status through certain forms of consumption. In the metropolises, social distinctions were constructed during the interwar period in part through consumption. Middle-class people could use clothing, domestic culture and forms and forums of social life to set themselves apart from workers and members of the urban lower classes, even when these groups had the same income level, as was the case, for example, for qualified skilled labourers and lower-level employees, and even educated people in precarious work situations.[84] Of course, only a small minority in these societies participated in the first spheres of consumer society, whereas other groups in the lowest classes of society struggled merely to survive – especially in the countryside, but also in the cities during the global economic crisis.

It is somewhat peculiar that, simultaneous to the propagation of elements of bourgeois norms and forms during the interwar period – gradually underway in Southeastern European countries as well – explicitly anti-bourgeois ideas of the Left and Right became increasingly popular. The authoritarian or dictatorial expansion of direct or indirect governmental control

---

[83] Gábor Gyáni, 'Housing Patterns of Bürgertum: A Budapest Case Study from the 1920s', in *Wohnen in der Großstadt 1900–1939: Wohnsituation und Modernisierung im europaischen Vergleich*, eds Alena Janatková and Hanna Kozinska-Witt (Stuttgart: Franz Steiner Verlag, 2006), 391–405.

[84] Gábor Gyáni, 'Department Stores and Middle-class Consumerism in Budapest, 1896–1939', in *Cathedrals of Consumption: The European Department Store, 1850–1939*, eds Geoffrey Crossick and Serge Jaumain (Aldershot: Ashgate, 1999), 208–24; Zsombor Bódy, 'Közelítések Budapest két világháború közötti társadalmához a fogyasztás történetén keresztül' [Analyzing the society of Budapest through the history of consumption], *Fons* XVII, no. 4 (2010): 411–60.

over domains of social and economic activity also limited the autonomy of middle-class groupings and institutions, a development that in several countries frequently went hand in hand with inter-ethnic or anti-Semitic conflicts within the middle class. The actual course of these processes varied greatly. In Hungary, for example, the bar association for lawyers opposed with remarkable tenacity a division based on religious affiliation, whereas bitter anti-Semitic conflicts predominated among physicians.[85]

The Second World War and its consequences altered the configuration of the middle zone of Central and Eastern European societies much more than any of the other social strata. Among the most important upheavals were the consequences of genocide and ethnic cleansing, whose victims – practically from the Baltics to Serbia – frequently belonged to different middle-class groups. To single out just one example, in Estonia, Latvia and Lithuania, the middle classes were decimated, almost annihilated by the Holocaust, the disappearance of Baltic Germans, and the deportations of members of the 'national' middle class by the Soviets. In 1948, only sporadic remains of the 'old' middle classes existed.[86]

The war thus brought about a restructuring of the middle classes, whereby the extermination or expulsion of a number of groups was accompanied by a diffuse upward trend among the lower classes of society. The positions that had been held by the victims of genocides and ethnic cleansings were gradually assumed by others. In addition, the war strengthened the middle classes in other ways. The war economy created numerous new staff positions in industry, as well as with the railway and various branches of state administration concerned with the supervision and mobilization of societies. While these were subordinate positions, they were nevertheless stable and superior to those of workers and peasants. These trends could be observed not only in Romania, Hungary and even in the Czech lands, but also in territories occupied by the Nazis, for example, in the Polish General Government, where under the peculiar circumstances of war many new commercial and small industrial businesses sprang up, and simultaneously millions of women commenced gainful employment.[87]

Following a brief transitional period after the war, the expansion of state power over the various zones and functional domains of society that accompanied the communist seizure of power almost completely eliminated the autonomy of middle-class professions and activities. Certain groups were stigmatized as the 'old middle class' and many people became 'déclassé'. There was also a significant decline in professional expertise through emigration.

State socialism attempted to create a new 'intelligentsia' – a social type borrowed from Russia, since entrepreneurs, civil servants, freelance professionals and employees, as well as artists and writers who were dependent on the market, had previously belonged to the middle classes in these societies; but the results of these efforts remained limited and ambivalent. The influx into middle-class life forms, which could already be observed before the war, continued through the possibilities opened up by the state. The results of the various new educational forms, however, were not only numerically insufficient, but often did not correspond to the expertise required.[88] In the 1960s an amalgamation of 'old' and 'new' middle-class groups could already be observed.

---

85 Mária M. Kovács, *Liberal Professions and Illiberal Politics: Hungary from the Habsburgs to the Holocaust* (Washington, DC: Woodrow Wilson Center Press and Oxford: Oxford University Press: 1994), 106–11, 116–21.
86 Seppo Myllyniemi, 'Die Umwandlung der sozialen Strukturen der baltischen Länder während und infolge der deutschen Besatzung', in *Zweiter Weltkrieg und sozialer Wandel*, ed. Waclaw Długoborski (Göttingen: Vandenhoeck & Ruprecht, 1981), 279–87.
87 Waclaw Długoborski, 'Die deutsche Besatzungspolitik und die Veränderungen der sozialen Struktur Polens 1939–1945', in Długoborski, *Zweiter Weltkrieg und sozialer Wandel*, 303–63.
88 Majtényi, *A tudomány lajtorjája*.

In most of the countries of the region at this time, the political disadvantages of old middle-class heritage were balanced out by the greater cultural capital that could be claimed in middle-class professions even during state socialism. Other forms of continuity with the interwar period can also be identified: a guidebook on domestic culture from 1960 was almost indistinguishable from a book published in 1930 for members of the middle class with limited family budgets. Socialism thus did not create any new lifestyles prior to the popularization of television and the automobile. In most Central European countries during the 1960s and 70s, certain middle-class groups with higher education occupied the most favourable social and material position, or at least were clearly in a more favourable situation than skilled labourers. Because they possessed greater social and cultural capital, they were also able to reap more advantages from the redistributive system of state socialism (from utilizing their employer's vacation homes, to enrolling their children in nursery school) than industrial workers, to say nothing of agricultural workers on collective farms.[89] They were usually the first people to purchase a television set in the early 1960s and then later an automobile. Several groups of the ever-expanding stratum of lower-level employees, skilled labourers – also the leading groups in charge of agricultural collectives, plus private agricultural producers in villages in some countries – followed highly educated middle-class groups at a certain distance along the path to socialist consumer society.[90]

The socialist middle classes were characterized by two particular features. Property played only a modest role in the internal divisions of these classes. In contrast to the period prior to the Second World War, and in contrast to the West, private assets were not a decisive factor for an individual's social status. Much more significant was the individual's relationship to state organizations and the position he or she assumed within them. Often wealth was not a determining factor, but rather the consequence of the position occupied. The second feature was the flat salary structure. Teachers and other employees often earned less than skilled labourers. Thus, while the latter were able to follow the ideals of – state socialist – consumer society, underpaid middle-class members had to struggle to imitate Western middle-class standards.

The economic collapse of socialism and the development of the market economy around 1990 radically altered the social character and the internal composition of the middle classes. Many positions within the various branches of state institutions that had previously provided a relatively high salary and access to further services were reduced to mid- or low-level positions in the new private businesses. Under market conditions, previous participation in the redistributive system of state socialism no longer ensured a middle-class position. The acquisition of new middle-class consumer goods required a relatively high market income.

In certain regions of Central and Eastern European countries, where previous heavy industry had collapsed abruptly and no new businesses emerged as employers, the state socialist middle classes virtually disappeared. The cultural infrastructure and the institutions that had made a middle-class lifestyle possible were dismantled and educated people moved away, leaving these regions not only without any entrepreneurial groups, but now also lacking any highly educated population. Due to an absence of the middle classes, these regions often had no way out of the cul-de-sac of state socialism, despite support from the EU (for example, Ózd and the surrounding areas, Salgótarján, Komló in Hungary, as well as certain areas in the Czech

---

89 Sándor Horváth, *Két emelet boldogság: Mindennapi szociálpolitika Budapesten a Kádár-korban* [Two floors of happiness: everyday social policy in Budapest during the Kádár era] (Budapest: Napvilág, 2012).

90 Tibor Valuch, 'A társadalmi rétegződés és a társadalomszerkezet változásainak néhány jellegzetessége a rendszerváltás Magyarországán' [Some characteristics in the changes of social stratification and social structure in regime-change Hungary], *Aetas* 28, no. 4 (2013): 101–19.

Republic, Slovakia and Poland).[91] In those regions where economic development and immigration reached the critical mass necessary to retain the middle classes, a potential for development can be observed. Some parts of the middle classes were able to improve their position, for example those working in banking and law, and young professionals working for the multinational corporations now opening branches in Eastern European capitals.

There is a diversity of middle-class groupings in all Central and Eastern European countries. Their striving for consumer goods is universal, although there can be no question of an even relatively homogeneous middle-class lifestyle. There are no guiding standards regarding forms of clothing, interaction, housing and family, or shared political values that could unite these groups. Several 'old' groups, whose expertise is no longer of use in the globalized economy, have slowly sunk downward, while other groups of the socialist middle classes have been able to assert themselves. In addition, following the collapse of state socialism, new classes embarked in the direction of middle-class ways of life. Attendance at post-secondary schools tripled on average in the 1990s in comparison to the low matriculation levels of the ossified post-secondary institutions of socialism. This opening up of post-secondary schools to broader groups made possible a new wave of people 'becoming middle class'. From these divergent trends, a zone of the middle strata of society has emerged, in which market-induced inequalities and lifestyle communities are thoroughly intertwined.

The middle classes in Central and Eastern Europe at the end of the twentieth century were distinguished from their Western counterparts in numerous regards. The former in comparison were narrower, had a lower income and rarely possessed inherited wealth. What they did share with the middle classes of other regions, however, was the fact that without higher education and expertise enabling flexible adaptation to rapidly changing challenges, it was impossible to earn the income required for a middle-class lifestyle.

Workers

Portraying the history of workers entails covering a broad range of topics. Generally, two types of studies exist: the first type analyzes workers as a social milieu, or looks at their families, everyday culture or housing; the second concentrates on factory life, and particularly on labour conflicts. The first type of study is more common in investigations of the period before 1945, when industrial workers presented a social group clearly demarcated from the rest of society, while the second predominates in histories of Stalinist industrialization. The cultural turn in research on workers paid more attention to issues like the changing perception of workers, and to identity questions. The gender approach emphasized feminity and masculinity in the workplace. As for most of the topics discussed in the volume, a regional narrative on this social group has yet to be developed, such that the topic is addressed only in particular studies, or at best, in national narratives. Workers were a popular topic in historiography during the 1970s and 1980s, particularly in West Germany and the UK, but afterwards they lost much of their appeal and were replaced by studies of the socially déclassé; even later, these studies of class were overshadowed by studies on gender or ethnicity. A certain renaissance in Central and Eastern Europe took place in the 2000s, manifested in Polish and Hungarian research on workers under Stalinism,

---

91 Nicole Hirschler and Vladimir J. Horak, 'Dorf – Industrielle Vorstadt – Sanierungsgebiet: Eine Mikrostudie zur Geschichte und Sozialstruktur der Gemeinde Hrušov bei Ostrava im 19. und 20. Jahrhundert', in Bohn, *Von der 'europäischen Stadt' zur 'sozialistischen Stadt'*, 115–27; Tibor Valuch, *A jelenkori Magyar társadalom* [Contemporary Hungarian society] (Budapest: Osiris, 2015), 245–60.

a topic which had been impossible to investigate before 1989. At the same time, the research on workers before 1945, so strongly favoured by state socialist regimes, was largely abandoned.

As is the case with the middle classes, there is no agreement in sociology on the actual size of the social group we call workers.[92] Before the 1950s, the boundaries between industrial workers, industrial peasant-workers and agricultural labourers, who are discussed under the peasantry in this volume, were sometimes unclear. The borders between the self-employed and workers were also distinct, as were those between day labourers and the underclasses. The class of workers is just as heterogeneous as every other main social group in the region. Aspects influencing these boundaries are the level of sophistication in the branch of industry (textiles would be an example of a less sophisticated sector, while the automobile industry represents one more highly sophisticated), the workers' skill level (generally distinguished as skilled, semi-skilled or unskilled), the size of the factory and, finally, the degree of workers' autonomy within the production process. Historiography generally distinguishes among three different groups of workers, based on income and prestige: the best-paid category of workers is called the 'labour aristocracy' (personified before 1945 by printers, during Stalinism by miners and steel workers), the second is the bulk of the working class, and the last is unqualified workers partaking in capitalism in the form of day labour.

In terms of the strength of the industrial working class from 1900 to 1945, the region can be divided into areas with a significant working class, areas with rudiments of a working class and areas with a tiny or almost non-existent working class. The only part of our region where workers made up a majority of the population at the turn of century were the Czech lands. In the Kingdom of Hungary and in Russian Poland, they were around one quarter of the population, in Galicia and Bukovina about one fifth, in Southeastern Europe less than one tenth. Romania seems to have been the most industrial among them, with 10 per cent of employees working in industrial forms of production in 1913.[93] In the case of Southeastern Europe, only around one per cent worked in facilities we would call factories today; the majority of industrial workers were employed as craftsmen in workshops.

During the First World War, many industries in the areas of military operations were destroyed, but the growth of military industries burgeoned in the hinterland. The biggest decline due to destruction occurred in former Russian Poland: the number of workers in industrial production dropped 85 per cent from 1914 to 1918. Hundreds of thousands of Polish workers were transferred to Germany for forced labour, and agricultural workers from Russian Poland working in Germany for the 1914 summer season were forced into labour for the duration.[94] Urban famine became part of workers' everyday life. Industrial production was run by the military: many women were recruited for factory work, and military discipline was introduced over factory labour, including corporal punishment and the death penalty.[95]

The interwar period experienced moderate growth in the working class throughout the region. This growth was stronger in Southeastern Europe, although it remained minimal: for

---

92 For example, according to the scheme developed by Golthrope there are 29% of workers in contemporary European societies; according to the scheme developed by Wright, there are 55%, see Peter Robert, 'Stratification and Social Mobility', in *Handbook of European Societies: Social Transformation in the 21st Century*, eds Stefan Immerfall and Göran Therborn (New York: Springer, 2010), 505–7.
93 Tibor Iván Berend, *History Derailed: Central and Eastern Europe in the Long Nineteenth Century* (Berkeley, CA: University of California Press, 2003), 213.
94 Janusz Żarnowski, *Polska 1918–1939: praca, technika, społeczeństwo* [Poland 1918–1939: work, technics, society] (Warsaw: Książka i Wiedza, 1999), 175.
95 Rudolf Kučera, *Rationed Life: Science, Everyday Life and Working-class Politics in the Bohemian Lands, 1914–1918* (New York: Berghahn Books, 2016), 69–75.

example, there were only six thousand industrial workers in Serbia in 1900, but this number had risen to 16,000 by 1910, and to 55,000 by 1938. This growth is less impressive if we take into consideration the country's population growth.[96] An increase in industrial labour was also experienced in Romania and in Poland. In the most developed part of the region, Czechoslovakia and Hungary, the number of workers stagnated during the period: the share of those working in the industrial labour force remained constant between 1910 and 1950. According to international statistics on the share of the industrial workforce, in 1930 Czechoslovakia had 42 per cent, while the percentage in Hungary was 23, in Poland 17, in Yugoslavia 11, in Bulgaria 8 and in Romania just 7 per cent.[97] There were also stark regional differences within the countries: only the Czech lands were almost fully industrialized, while the industrial regions were much smaller in the other countries. Poland, Silesia and the area around Lodz were industrial; in Hungary, only Budapest and the northwest of the country were industrial. Romania had several islands of industry like the Grivita railway repair yards in Bucharest, the Resita steel mills and the coal mines of the Jiu Valley. The working class in Yugoslavia was concentrated in Slovenian coal mines and steel mills, armaments plants in Sarajevo and Kragujevac and railway construction in Croatia.[98]

During the interwar years, industrialization took place mainly in the textile and other consumer industries, which attracted unskilled workers (among them many women) and contributed to the decline of what had traditionally been a highly organized workforce in the north of the region. In Hungary, for example, the proportion of unskilled or semi-skilled workers rose from one sixth to one quarter during the period. The new workers were primarily recruited from the poorest groups of peasants, although some urban craftsmen joined factories as well. Those who opted for factory work often kept their small land holdings, becoming peasant-workers. Their number among factory workers was particularly high in Southeastern Europe. In Yugoslavia, for example, it is estimated that almost two thirds of industrial workers in the 1930s belonged to this category.[99]

The less developed countries of Southeastern Europe, with their smaller working classes, also had a higher proportion of unskilled workers.[100] The numbers of factory workers remained tiny here: in Yugoslavia, factory workers were only four per cent, and in Bulgaria only two per cent of the labour force, which was almost exclusively male. The workers of the first generation were not able to develop any collective identity and thus shared 'the egoism of small groups', in the words of Dragoş Petrescu,[101] so that families and local networks remained much more important than their class.

From the peasant's perspective, becoming a worker was not regarded as climbing up the social ladder. A peasant who owned land and a house, who was his own lord and enjoyed a secure source of food, was not very impressed by the fact that workers were covered by welfare security (pensions, sick leave) or had more finances at their disposal. In the eyes of the peasants, workers were vulnerable to unemployment, which was experienced on a mass scale in the region, first after 1918, and then even more so during the Great Depression. On the other

---

96 Calic, *Sozialgeschichte Serbiens 1815–1941*, 253.
97 Tibor Iván Berend and György Ránki, *Economic Development in East-Central Europe in the 19th and 20th Centuries* (New York: Columbia University Press, 1974), 306.
98 Mark Pittaway, *Eastern Europe 1939–2000* (London: Bloomsbury Academic, 2010), 90.
99 Calic, *Sozialgeschichte Serbiens 1815–1941*, 251.
100 Tibor Iván Berend, *Decades of Crisis: Central and Eastern Europe before World War II* (Berkeley, CA: University of California Press, 2001), 298.
101 Dragoş Petrescu, 'Workers and Peasant-Workers in a Working Class "Paradise": Patterns of Working Class Protests in Communist Romania', in Hübner, Klessmann and Tenfelde, *Arbeiter im Staatssozialismus*, 131.

hand, those many peasants without any chance of making a living in the countryside due to overpopulation were more likely to consider becoming workers instead.

While the political power of workers was rather low, the exception seems to have been Czechoslovakia, which was ruled by a social democratic party for a substantial period and home to a strong labour union movement, and, in 1918, became the only country in the region to introduce Labour Day as an official holiday. Although the Czechoslovak working class was as large as the working classes in Western Europe, according to Heumos, the number of peasant-workers was higher here, production was dominated by smaller enterprises, and the workers were divided politically between different parties, most notably Czech and German social democrats and communists.[102] In Hungary, too, social democracy and unions enjoyed a degree of strength. In all the other countries, workers' organizations were either insignificant, prohibited or loyal to authoritarian regimes. In contrast to Nazi Germany, the interwar authoritarian governments of Central and Eastern Europe never made a cult of the labour hero.

During the interwar period, Central and Eastern European workers were by no means ethnically homogeneous, although somewhat more so than the middle and upper classes, which had high proportions of ethnic Germans and Jews. In the late nineteenth century, both qualified and unqualified workers migrated to the industrializing regions, leading to an increased ethnic heterogeneity of workers. For example, in 1910 the lower qualified positions in Hungarian industry were held by Slovaks or Romanians, while their foremen were Germans, Czechs and Jews.[103] In Czechoslovakia, the German minority was over-represented among workers as the German-speaking regions tended to be more industrialized. In Poland, many industrial workers were Jewish, a phenomenon absent in the other countries of the region. According to Antony Polonski, in Warsaw (the city with the largest Jewish population in Europe during the interwar period), Jews could not be characterized as solely middle or upper class: one in three was a blue-collar worker, while among the Christian population it was about one in two.[104] Polonski has shown that the situation was different in Lodz, where Jewish workers were often rejected by factory owners due to anti-Semitism and for fear that their strict religious habits would have an impact on their working hours. As a result, they were compelled to work as self-employed handloom weavers or finishers of clothing, jobs which meant working much longer hours in order to earn a comparable wage.

Migrating to the cities for work meant the chance to experience different lifestyles and values, contrasting with the only gradually changing life of peasants in the countryside. The new lifestyles were copied from middle-class families. It seems that new values and cultural patterns, particularly interior furnishings and eating habits (for example, wall mirrors, nightstands, using a knife and fork),[105] were transmitted by housemaids and by the media of popular culture (the press, cinema). The nationalist middle classes were also sometimes willing to socialize with workers from their own ethnic community. Integration with the middle classes on the basis of religion was also possible. However, a significant portion of the middle classes distrusted and harboured various prejudices against workers, which are particularly striking in contrast to their idealization of peasants.

Interwar industrial workers thus remained rather isolated from the rest of urban society. The level of upward social mobility from the working to the middle classes was low due to the high

---

102 Peter Heumos, 'Die Arbeiterschaft in der Ersten Tschechoslowakischen Republik', *Bohemia* 29, no. 1 (1988): 50–72.
103 Berend, *History Derailed*, 214.
104 Antony Polonski, *Jews in Poland and Russia: 1914–2008* (Oxford: Littman Library of Jewish Civilization, 2012), 104.
105 Gábor Gyáni, *Parlour and Kitchen: Housing and Domestic Culture in Budapest, 1870–1940* (Budapest: CEU Press, 2002), 216.

cost of education and because economic development proceeded without raising the demand for technical education, which was to become a common path for workers' social mobility in later eras. According to statistics, workers clearly differed from the middle classes in terms of food consumption (a lower proportion of meat and milk in their diet), health (higher levels of infant mortality, rickets, tuberculosis) and housing (smaller, often one-room apartments without bathrooms but with shared toilets[106]). They were different in terms of culture as well, both in dress (males wore a flat cap and women a scarf, in contrast to the hats of the bourgeoisie) and in leisure time (shorter or non-existent holidays). Statistics indicate that working-class districts were located in the outskirts of cities, in the proximity of factories. In certain industries (mining, heavy industry, textiles) so-called 'worker colonies' were set up.[107] There were also slums in the metropolises of the region, inhabited by the most indigent of the labourers.[108]

The Second World War brought not only the destruction of industry in the war zones, but also a degree of development in the industrial sector in those regions occupied by Nazi Germany or the Axis states, which profited in the first war years from economic integration with the Nazi Regime. Cohorts of young peasants became the industrial workers during this period, either as forced labour in Germany or as workers in the new factories erected in their home countries. The absence of the urban famine experienced in the First World War made workers' experiences less dire during this conflict. Nazi repressions against workers took place mainly in cases of sabotaged factory production, but it seems that repression against workers in the Nazi-occupied territories was no stronger than against other social groups.[109]

The installation of Stalinist regimes constitutes a crucial turning point in the history of Central and Eastern European workers. For Marxists, the workers were the most productive and progressive social group, therefore 'industrial labour was absolutely central to the creation of socialist society'.[110] Under socialism, a modernized working class was to enjoy a central role in industrial society.[111] Several crucial tendencies marked the developments for workers during these four decades.

First, a tremendous increase in the number of industrial workers took place: the extensive growth of industry began in the late 1940s and lasted until the 1960s. Its proportion remained high in the 1970s and 1980s as communist governments proved unable or reluctant to carry out post-industrial restructuring. The extensive growth of the first decades closed the gap between the share of industrial labour in Central and Eastern Europe versus Southeastern Europe.[112] While the differences in the strength of working classes around the region were enormous in 1945, around 1965 they had nearly equalized: workers made up 40 per cent of the population in Romania and 42 per cent in Bulgaria in that year, numbers similar to those in Poland and Hungary. In Bulgaria, the working class (agrarian and industrial workers) grew from 19 per cent in 1946 to 60 per cent in 1975, and those working in industry from 8 to 38 per cent.[113]

---

106 Ibid., 154–69.
107 Martin Jemelka, *Na kolonii: život v hornické kolonii dolu Šalomoun v Moravské Ostravě do začátku socialistické urbanizace* [At the colony: life in the miner's colony of the Šalomoun Mine in Moravian Ostrava at the start of socialist industrialization] (Ostrava:VŠB-TU Ostrava, 2007).
108 Stanislav Holubec, *Lidé periferie: sociální postavení a každodennost pražského dělnictva v meziválečné době* [People of the periphery: the social status and everyday life of Prague workers in the interwar era] (Plzeň: Filosofická fakulta Západočeské University, 2009).
109 Gerhard Schild, *Die Arbeiterschaft im 19. und 20. Jahrhundert* (München: Oldenbourg, 2010), 44.
110 Mark Pittaway, *Eastern Europe 1939–2000*, 88.
111 Ibid., 89.
112 Ibid., 95.
113 Ulf Brunnbauer, *'Die sozialistische Lebensweise': Ideologie, Gesellschaft, Familie und Politik in Bulgarien 1944–1989* (Vienna: Böhlau, 2007), 259–62.

In the 1970s and 1980s, the state socialist countries had the highest proportions of workers in the world. Although the official statistics, in order to meet ideological demands, sometimes included among workers certain social groups that are not considered to be part of the working class in the West (such as the military), industrial workers were more numerous than anywhere else. From the 1960s on they also outnumbered peasants, previously the largest social group in these countries. Sometimes there was even talk of 'over-industrialization'. Many new workers were recruited among women, who made up no more than one quarter of industrial labour at the beginning of the state socialist period (in Czechoslovakia), but grew to comprise over one third of the industrial labour force by the late 1980s.

Not only did the socialist working class grow in number, it was also restructured: while pre-socialist workers were employed mainly in light industry or in agriculture, socialist industrialization shifted them predominantly to industrial labour, with an emphasis on heavy industry. The once common class of peasant-workers nearly disappeared; only in Poland and Romania did they remain a substantial group until the 1970s.[114] In most cases, urban workers gardened or worked on their dachas only as a hobby, or to grow better quality fruit and vegetables, but no longer as a second source of income.

Another transformation was the professionalization of workers. According to Hungarian statistics, between 1949 and 1990 the ratio of skilled workers among employees rose from 11 to 25 per cent, and semi-skilled workers from 5 to 18 per cent, while the unskilled declined from 12 to 6 per cent.[115] During the 1950s, workers were often recruited to join factory management, or to become party or union functionaries. Many members of the new political elites were originally of working-class origins. According to Heumos, this upward mobility affected at least 200,000 workers in Czechoslovakia.[116] In Hungary the same number of workers, especially skilled ones, became white-collar employees in the 1950s, which meant that about one third of skilled workers left the working class during that decade.[117] On the other hand, many white-collar employees were temporarily relegated to worker positions – the best known example is the Czechoslovak '77,000 to the productive sphere' action in 1951.

But the quantitatively most important development was 'turning peasants into workers', the largest rural–urban migration in the region's history. The new workers were predominantly young people from the country whose fathers had been peasants. According to research conducted from 1967 to 1973, in most countries of the region the majority of workers had peasant fathers (in Romania 65 per cent, in Bulgaria 61 per cent, in Hungary 54 per cent, in Poland 43 per cent). Only in Czechoslovakia were there more workers whose fathers were also workers than those with peasant fathers.[118] Moving from the village to the city meant more than simply changing jobs. It amounted to a complete change of life, a quasi-emigration to another

---

114 Paul M. Johnson, 'Changing Social Structure and the Political Role of Manual Workers in Eastern Europe', in *Blue Collar Workers in Eastern Europe*, eds Jan F. Triska and Charles Gati (London: George Allen and Unwin, 1981), 33.
115 Tibor Valuch, 'Changes in the Structure and Lifestyle of the Hungarian Society in the Second Half of the XXth Century', in *Social History of Hungary from the Reform Era to the End of the Twentieth Century*, eds Gábor Gyáni, György Kövér and Tibor Valuch (Boulder, CO: Social Science Monographs, 2004), 442.
116 Peter Heumos, 'Aspekte des Sozialem Milieus der Industriearbeiterschaft in der Tschechoslowakei vom Ende des Zweiten Weltkrieges bis zur Reformbewegung der sechziger Jahre', *Bohemia* 42 (2001): 324.
117 Valuch, 'Changes in the Structure', 551.
118 Johnson, 'Changing Social Structure', 33.

country. The new worker had to internalize a new time rhythm: while a peasant's work was autonomous and differed during the periods of the year, the worker had to obey factory regulations, accept the foreman's authority, punch a time clock and become accustomed to routinized work on an assembly line.[119] The worker's family also had to function differently from a family of peasants. In the city, both partners had a paid job, there were fewer opportunities to rely on help from grandparents and other relatives, and it was necessary to leave child rearing largely to the hands of the state. Some of the former peasants reacted to this stress by turning to alcohol or crime; for most, it made conflicts within the family inevitable. According to Sándor Horváth, post-Stalinist authorities actively pursued the goal of making peasants into true workers and cultivating urban inhabitants, for example, by promoting various cultural activities and educating people about modern lifestyles (e.g. by censuring those who kept animals in their bathrooms).[120]

Another aspect particularly visible during Stalinism was the politicization of the workplace. Stalinist propaganda portrayed industrial production as a battlefield and laziness as sabotage, and developed various rituals to celebrate labour (welcoming ceremonies for new workers, oaths of allegiance). Stakhanovite movements became the symbol of the epoch, almost immediately provoking hostility from colleagues who correctly understood them as tools of the regime to pressure other workers into increasing their labour efforts.[121] The traditional working classes were also appalled by the promotion of young workers to leading positions, and of women in sectors formerly perceived to be the realm of men (ironworks, mining). As the bulk of traditional workers was further outraged by a decline in living standards in the early 1950s,[122] high demands on work discipline and the lack of consumer goods, and was suspicious of the official rhetoric of the 'worker's state', the protests across the region from 1953 to 1956 (Poznan, Pilsen, Berlin) came primarily from this milieu. As Padraic Kenney argues, workers' willingness to protest was also fostered by the fact that during Stalinism, they were less likely to be persecuted for expressing their opinion than the intelligentsia; besides, they had been officially encouraged to criticize deficiencies in their factories.[123]

Violent conflicts forced the regimes into attempts to find a compromise with workers from the first half of the 1950s, an era that historian Mark Pittaway has called 'fundamental to the consolidation of socialist regimes'.[124] The regimes lowered their expectations on productivity, reduced working hours and put more emphasis on raising living standards. Holidays at nationalized spas and mountain resorts were used to reward the most loyal and diligent workers. As a result, the number of strikes declined everywhere. This did not mean that dissatisfaction disappeared completely. Indeed, Mary Fulbrook speaks of a shift from a 'collective form of protest to the more individualistic' between the 1950s and 1960s.[125]

---

119 Ibid.
120 Sándor Horváth, 'Ruralization, Urban Villagers, and Perceptions of Migration in Hungary during "De-Stalinization" (Budapest, Sztálinváros)', in *Mastery and Lost Illusions: Space and Time in the Modernization of Eastern and Central Europe*, eds Włodzimierz Borodziej, Stanislav Holubec and Joachim von Puttkamer (München: Oldenbourg, 2014), 159–80.
121 Anne Applebaum, *Iron Curtain: The Crushing of Eastern Europe 1944–1956* (London: Allen Lane, 2012), 341.
122 Pittaway, *Eastern Europe 1939–2000*, 93.
123 Padraic Kenney, *Rebuilding Poland: Workers and Communists* (Ithaca, NY: Cornell Univ. Press, 2012), 340.
124 Pittaway, *Eastern Europe 1939–2000*, 94.
125 Mary Fulbrook, 'Arbeiter in sozialen und politischen Konfliktkonstellationen', in Hübner, Klessmann and Tenfelde, *Arbeiter im Staatssozialismus*, 335.

The living standards that the regimes offered the working classes were perceived as a radical improvement, particularly in contrast to the rural or pre-war urban conditions of nutrition and housing. While the kitchen had been the centre of family life in the old working-class apartments, the new socialist workers adopted the living room as the new core of the household, with the kitchen reserved just for cooking. Further, separate rooms for children and parents, plus bathrooms and toilets in each flat, became a standard in every new housing block. The television reduced contact with the neighbours, which had been so important before 1945. The living standard of workers was clearly converging with that of urban professionals. What remained specific to the workers was their cultural life, the chances of their children receiving a higher education was still limited and their work was physically demanding.

If we compare the situation of workers in the East and in the West from the 1970s on, it is obvious that the workers' milieu remained more intact in the socialist bloc than in capitalist countries. There was no deindustrialization in the state socialist countries, and only a marginal presence of foreign labourers in the East in contrast to the West.[126] Much of the social life of Eastern European workers was organized around the workplace (holidays, child care, canteens, housing construction). Children of workers in the West had better chances of attending universities than in the East, where universities were more exclusivist. The working hours and welfare benefits of workers in the East were roughly the same as in the West, but Eastern workers tended to enjoy a somewhat more relaxed work tempo and better job security. In contrast to the development in the West since the 1970s, no underclass – dependent on welfare benefits and resigned to stagnation – developed in the socialist countries.[127] Compared to the West, the differences between the salaries of workers and the intelligentsia were smaller in the East. The overall standard of living of socialist workers was lower than that of professionals, however, as the latter could rely on their higher social capital to bring them benefits in many aspects of life (housing distribution, health care). Workers had the advantage over intelligentsia that they were not forced into political activities and had no reason to fear for their jobs because of their political attitudes. Further, workers tended to be better suited for life in the economy of shortage than the intelligentsia (for example, they could build their own homes, ply their trades in the household, repair their own cars, etc.) and could easily run their own businesses in the underground economy.

Although the workers were considered to be 'the ruling class' according to state ideology, and the communist party only its 'vanguard', sociological research has shown that workers did not share this vision, seeing the real power in the country to lie with political elites and management. Neither has research found a high level of pride in being a worker, particularly from the 1960s on. Therefore, as in the West, we can speak of an erosion of the working-class identity in state socialism. The reasons seem to be the rise of consumerism, the spread of informal entrepreneurial economic activities among workers and also mistrust in official propaganda. Gerhard Schild speaks in this context of the expropriation of the language of unions and other representatives of the working class by the communist regimes.[128] The official usage of the word 'working class' made it unattractive for the workers themselves.[129] It was difficult to believe the assertion that 'worker is the most honourable job' when it was widely known that the regime punished its opponents by relegating them to workers' positions.

---

126 Hartmut Kaelble, *A Social History of Europe, 1945–2000: Recovery and Transformation after Two World Wars* (New York: Berghahn Books, 2013), 142.
127 Béla Tomka, *A Social History of Twentieth-Century Europe* (London: Routledge, 2013), 132.
128 Schild, *Die Arbeiterschaft im 19. und 20. Jahrhundert*, 111.
129 Pittaway, *Eastern Europe 1939–2000*, 184.

However, one cannot say that workers were more willing to protest against the regimes than other social groups in the 1970s and 1980s. In fact, Poland was the only country where protests against the regime formed around workers. Here it became clear that worker strikes could hit the regime harder than petitions signed by the intelligentsia. The explanation for why this did not happen everywhere else emphasizes that in other countries anti-communism and religion were less popular, economic and housing conditions for workers were better and the governments were quick to nip nascent protests in the bud, as was the case in Romania. An example of a country with politically passive workers was Czechoslovakia, where organized opposition emerged mainly from the persecuted intelligentsia and religiously active minorities. If one analyzes the social background of Charta 77 signatories, half were purged communists (most of them with higher education), while workers made up only a few per cent (if we exclude those who were relegated to worker positions after 1968). It is also difficult to determine whether young workers were less content than students. Various sources report that young workers were more involved in protest activities, but students' passivity might be explained by their fear of being expelled from school. If we compare the social actors of the years 1953–1957 with the revolutions of 1989, it is no wonder that Mary Fulbrook notes the 'curious absence of the working class from the revolutionary upheavals'[130] in the latter case. On the other hand, it is clear that the workers also did not oppose the revolutions, and that the regimes failed to rally their support. One notable case was the workers' booing of the Prague party council secretary in November 1989 during a speech at the capital's largest factory, when he vowed that 'fifteen-year-old kids shall not make decisions for the country'.

The post-socialist era has been marked by the fast decline of the industrial sector and the shrinking number of industrial workers, which decreased between one half and one third within a decade. In spite of this decline, the industrial workforce stabilized at 28–34 per cent of the labour force by 2010, above the EU average. The differences in the decline and in the overall size of industrial production among the countries are quite small. In 2008, the strongest industry existed in the Czech Republic (38 per cent of the labour force) and the weakest in Romania and Bulgaria (28 per cent).[131] If we calculate the absolute numbers, the decline is much stronger. In the Czech town of Hradec Kralove, where the author was born (population 100,000), the three largest enterprises in 1990 were two machine factories and the Petrof piano factory; in 2005, the three biggest enterprises were the hospital, the regional administration and the university. Unemployment and declining wages are the main difficulties of post-socialist workers. In the Czech Republic, a person with a university degree earned 40 per cent more than one with workers' training (apprenticeship) in 1988; in 1996, the graduate earned 90 per cent more.[132] However, there were exceptions to the rule: some workers were able to start their own businesses, while some were able to switch to those branches of industry that were not closed down or even began to prosper (e.g. automobile production taken over by foreign capital was one of the most prosperous sectors in post-socialist economies).

The author of the book *Workers after Workers' States* mentioned how surprised Western scholars were to find that workers remained remarkably quiet in the face of the difficulties

---

130 Fulbrook, 'Arbeiter in sozialen und politischen Konfliktkonstellationen', 347.
131 Europäische Kommission Statistisches Amt, *Eurostat pocketbooks: Labour market statistics* (Luxembourg: Publ. Off. of the Europ. Union, 2011), 32, http://epp.eurostat.ec.europa.eu/cache/ITY_OFFPUB/KS-32-11-798/EN/KS-32-11-798-EN.PDF (Accessed 1 January 2016).
132 Petr Matějů and Jiří Večerník, *Zpráva o vývoji české společnosti* [Report on the development of Czech society] (Prague: Academia, 1998), 118.

they experienced, despite predictions in the early 1990s that intense social conflicts could be expected.[133] The level of strikes in the region nowadays is much lower than in the rest of Europe. One explanation is that the politics of labour was discredited under state socialism, another is the difficult situation overall, which leaves little latitude for collective action. Several authors point out various degradations of workers in the public discourse. David Kideckel, in his field research on Romanian miners during the transformation, even reported curious reactions by educated people as he made them familiar with his subjects.[134] When post-socialist workers were mentioned in the media, which was rarely the case, they were presented as the group unjustly privileged before 1989, who did not understand the modern world and were primitive and authoritarian. Whenever labour unions clashed with governments or entrepreneurs, the media sided with the latter. Young people were encouraged to study business or law, while apprenticeship was seen as an unattractive option and received the lowest priority in state educational policy. The word 'worker' almost disappeared from academic and public discourse. The recent trend, however, shows a certain rehabilitation of qualified industrial work in the region, which might in the future again be perceived as a more secure option for young people than earning a degree in the humanities, only to become an unqualified labourer in the service sector.

Peasants

On the eve of the First World War, peasants made up the majority of all European societies. Long into the twentieth century, the structural problems of this stratum – mainly the consequences of rural overpopulation – remained a decisive factor for Central and Eastern European societies, and the peasantry itself remained the group that continuously supplied other social strata with new men and women, especially the urban workforce, through mass mobility. The high proportion and influential role of peasants in these societies are often regarded as a sign of backwardness, of non-modernity. While such an assessment may be justified on the basis of comparisons with Western European societies, it remains an insufficient characterization. As in the West, twentieth-century village communities in Central and Eastern Europe no longer constituted closed, pre-modern worlds of tradition. This has been described in ethnographic terms as follows: 'Only in the modern state have all citizens become direct subjects of the state, whereas previously they had remained rooted since time immemorial in their primary group, be it family, lineage, village or guild, or at most their city … '.[135] In Central and Eastern Europe at the beginning of the twentieth century, these primary forms of sociation were no longer so wholly decisive in peasant life. Even in Southeastern European countries, where such primary groups still played a significant role, they faced a hopeless battle with the bureaucracies of the new nation states, which gradually but inexorably assumed the responsibilities of regulating the lives of members of these groups.[136]

Modernity not only surrounded the peasant world from outside but was already permeating it in myriad ways. Rural societies and peasants themselves adapted to the new challenges

---

133 David Ost and Stephen Crowley, 'The Surprise of Labour Weakness in Postcommunist Society', in *Workers after Workers' States: Labour and Politics in Postcommunist Eastern Europe*, eds Stephen Crowley and David Ost (Lanham, MD: Rowman & Littlefield, 2001), 2.
134 David A. Kideckel, 'Die Auflösung der ost- und mitteleuropäischen Arbeiterklasse', in *Postsozialismus: Transformationsprozesse in Europa und Asien aus ethnologischer Perspektive*, ed. Christopher Hann (Frankfurt a.M.: Campus, 2002), 175.
135 Reinhard, *Lebensformen Europas*, 267.
136 On this, see the description in Sundhaussen, 'Südosteuropäische Gesellschaft und Kultur', 345–425.

– which were mediated, on the one hand, through the market and, on the other, through the state, schools and the legal system – and also participated actively in the emergence of a rural modernity.[137] This included learning market-economic modes of behaviour and establishing new organizations that promoted the autonomy of rural society under the conditions of developing modernity. Among the latter we find associations, political organizations and, above all, a network of cooperatives, the development of which had already begun prior to the First World War in all countries of the region. The credit cooperatives, milk cooperatives and other networks secured access for peasants to (sometimes distant) markets and generally facilitated their adaptation to capitalist conditions.[138] This function was fulfilled particularly effectively by cooperatives in the Czech lands and in the Baltic territories of Russia prior to the First World War, whereas in Southeastern Europe, cooperatives played only a limited role in the development of an agricultural market economy, although such networks existed there as well.[139] The prerequisites for the development of an agriculture producing for a capitalist market – for example, specialized knowledge (not least literacy), access to markets, mental attitudes about profit-seeking, rational economic management – often did not exist among the peasants of Bulgaria and Serbia. Neither was the ownership structure favourable for capitalist development, insofar as very small plots of land predominated – except in Romania – on which families were able to engage only in subsistence farming.[140] In contrast to Southeastern Europe, the cooperatives in Hungarian and Polish territories contributed significantly to the development of agriculture and the loosening of ties in village communities, but not to the same degree as in the Baltic and Czech lands, where the transformation to a market economy went furthest.

The restructuring and cultural transformation of village worlds continued along other paths as well. Through emigration and, in part, re-emigration, a number of Hungarian and Polish rural regions maintained steady contact with North America – something that also required the exchange of information – and thus peasants, too, participated in the first wave of globalization. By returning from America, or possibly only through the money they sent home, re-emigrants were able to initiate structural changes within a village community even prior to the First World War.[141] Thus, in most areas of the region, the transformation of peasant communities,

---

137 For an overview of research on the emergence of modernity in rural Central and Eastern Europe, see Uwe Müller et al., 'Agrarismus und Agrareliten im östlichen Mitteleuropa: Forschungsstand, Kontextualisierung, Thesen', in *Agrarismus und Agrareliten in Ostmitteleuropa*, ed. Eduard Kubů (Berlin: Berliner Wissenschaftsverlag, 2013), 15–116. For an overview of the sociologically inspired literature on peasants, see Leo Granberg, Imre Kovách and Hilary Tovey, 'Introduction', in *Europe's Green Ring*, eds Leo Granberg, Imre Kovách and Hilary Tovey (Aldershot: Ashgate, 2001), XIII–XXXVII.

138 On the function of cooperatives, see Torsten Lorenz, ed., *Cooperatives in Ethnic Conflicts: Eastern Europe in the 19th and early 20th Century* (Berlin: Berliner Wissenschaftsverlag, 2006), 9–44. On cooperatives in Southeastern Europe, see Sundhaussen, 'Südosteuropäische Gesellschaft und Kultur', 345–425.

139 Marie-Janine Calic, 'Zur Geschichte der Genossenschaften in den jugoslawischen Ländern: Von den Anfängen bis zum Zweiten Weltkrieg', in *Genossenschaften in Osteuropa: Alternative zur Planwirtschaft*, eds Erwin Oberländer, Hans Lemberg and Holm Sundhaussen (Wiesbaden: Deutscher Genossenschafts-Verlag, 1993), 63–78.

140 'Keines der Balkanländer hatte zu Beginn unseres Jahrhunderts jenen Alphabetisierungsgrad erreicht, der als notwendige Voraussetzung für ein anhaltendes Wirtschaftswachstum betrachtet wird.' [At the beginning of our century, none of the Balkan states had attained that literacy rate which is regarded as the necessary presupposition for lasting economic growth.] Holm Sundhaussen, 'Alphabetisierung und Wirtschaftswachstum in den Balkanländern in historisch-komparativer Perspektive', in Reiter and Sundhaussen, *Allgemeinbildung als Modernisierungsfaktor*, 21–36, here 29.

141 Edit Fél and Tamás Hofer, *Proper Peasants: Social Relations in a Hungarian Village* (New Brunswick, NJ: Aldine Transaction, 2008).

and the loosening of their strong local ties, had already been set in motion around the turn of the century. Railways and literacy played a crucial role in this development. The expansion of the modern state bureaucracy placed villages that had previously been remote under closer control by the centres of the state; at the same time, however, this expansion secured channels through which peasants could acquire new information and knowledge, and also provided opportunities for a limited number of village inhabitants to find posts on the lowest, local level of the state apparatus. The development of modern state administration pushed some of the previous local elites into the background and absorbed others. In Southeastern Europe especially, this development also caused conflicts that pitted village communities against the state.[142] While traditional peasant elites saw their status threatened by state bureaucracy, many peasant families saw their way of life undermined by the reduction in the size of plots of land and by the effects of the market economy. These tensions could at times lead to severe conflicts, for example, in the 'agrarian socialist' movements in Hungary or in the peasant uprising in Romania in 1907.[143] Despite the 'modern' terms employed here, these can be regarded as the final expression of pre-modern peasant behavioural and thought patterns – religious egalitarianism and loosely organized, spontaneous community violence – set in motion precisely in reaction to modernity.

The First World War significantly accelerated the processes of the transformation of the peasantry through several interventions in village life. In practice, state or military authorities introduced a levy system for foodstuffs in all areas of the region, and the bureaucratic monitoring of peasant life increased everywhere. This resulted in a decrease in the significance of previous forms of village sociation (kinship, parish). But rather than imposing a one-sided subordination of the peasants, in order to ensure food production, state authorities also had to meet the villagers' exigencies. What is more, the war altered gender roles, as women frequently had to assume the responsibilities of the men on the front – which, as ethnographic studies have demonstrated, continued to have repercussions in later years.[144] The land reforms after the war provided a new stimulus that continued to advance the social and political emancipation of peasants. Land reforms were most radical where large landowners were regarded as foreigners in the new nation states following the First World War – in the Baltic states, in Czechoslovakia and in parts of Romania. In other countries, land reform remained limited either because there were no large estates to divide (as in Bulgaria and most of Yugoslavia), or because the influence of the property-owning elite was able to prevent extensive land reform, as occurred in Hungary. In the 1920s, the political power enjoyed by peasants did increase – less so, of course, for those without land – for the simple reason that because rural society still constituted a large proportion of the population, they commanded attention as part of the electorate; moreover, having undergone a process of politicization, they discovered that they were able to act relatively independently of other political actors.[145] Thus rurally-based political parties became crucial forces in most countries, even in Czechoslovakia, the

---

142 'The state was not an institution that the peasantry, and that is to say the overwhelming portion of the people, considered their own, but it remained to them a foreign, fearful, and often hated organisation [...] there was little cause for the peasants to look at the newly emerging state ... either with confiance or benevolence.' Jozo Tomasevich, *Peasants, Politics, and Economic Change in Yugoslavia* (Stanford, CA: Stanford University Press 1955), 144.

143 Phillip G. Eidelberg, *The Great Rumanian Peasant Revolt of 1907: Origins of a Modern Jacquerie* (Leiden: Brill, 1974).

144 Marie-Janine Calic, *Geschichte Jugoslawiens im 20. Jahrhundert* (München: Beck, 2010), 99. Kata Jávor, 'A magyar paraszti erkölcs és magatartás' [Hungarian peasant customs and behaviour], in *Magyar Néprajz: VIII. Társadalom*, ed. Attila Paládi-Kovács (Budapest: Akadémiai, 2000), 601–692.

145 Tomasevich, *Peasants, Politics, and Economic Change*, 230–2.

most industrialized nation in the region. Hungary was an exception in this regard: there, political consolidation after the war was based on the dissolution of the independent Agrarian Party, and the majority of farmers supported the ruling party, comprising a conservative coalition of various elite, middle-class and rural groups.[146] In the 1930s, when most of the countries of the region were ruled by dictatorships, peasantry as an independent political player disappeared, of course, parallel to the expansion of state control, which had become much more omnipotent and effective in all countries during the global economic crisis. Monopoly-like purchasing agencies, which had often developed out of the practically nationalized cooperative networks, expanded.[147]

During the interwar period these developments slowly eroded the originally peasant character of the rural population: the unity of production and consumption within families oriented around self-sufficiency, accompanied by the specific everyday peasant culture. In ever more families, peasant traits gradually disappeared, as economic activity was performed increasingly outside the family and, for the most part, no longer for the purpose of self-sufficiency. In addition to the increasing specialization of production in order to maximize monetary income – which in some areas was stimulated by the market economy, in others by state purchasing agencies – further new elements of peasant life could be observed. Gainful employment of individual family members outside the family, aspirations for positions with fixed salaries (for example, with the railway) and attempts to secure a relatively high level of education for their children, as well as the increased purchase of industrial goods: these are all signs that peasants no longer oriented themselves toward inherited patterns of life, even if the actual changes in their circumstances were realized more gradually than their desires. Besides everyday contacts with the urban world, one important factor in this cultural transformation was the cinema. Even in medium-sized villages, films were shown on a regular basis in makeshift cinemas. Southeastern European countries were somewhat backward in this regard as well. In 1947, there were only 697 cinemas in Yugoslavia, far fewer than in Central European countries (for example in Czechoslovakia, a country with similar population, there were 2619 cinemas in 1948).[148]

However, the gradual internal transformations of the peasantry were not able to resolve the structural problems of the agrarian population in the region. Especially in Southeastern Europe, increases in productivity could not keep up with demographic developments.[149] In 1930, the agrarian population per square kilometre of arable land was 101 in Yugoslavia, 81 in Bulgaria, 80 in Romania and 63 in Hungary, but only 28 in France.[150]

According to estimates, 50 to 60 per cent of the rural population in the Balkan states (75 per cent in Albania) and 22 per cent of the rural population in Hungary were superfluous as agricultural labourers.[151] Neither industrial development nor a transformation of agriculture toward

---

146 Bódy Zsombor, 'Ungarn als Sonderfall des mitteleuropäischen Agrarismus in der Zwischenkriegszeit', in *Bauerngesellschaften auf dem Weg in die Moderne: Agrarismus in Ostmitteleuropa 1880 bis 1960*, eds Helga Schultz and Angela Harre (Wiesbaden: Harraschowitz, 2010), 105–19.
147 For examples from the Baltic, see Martins Bumanis, 'Die Genossenschaftsbewegung in Lettland', in Oberländer, Lemberg and Sundhaussen, *Genossenschaften in Osteuropa*, 41–8; Ágnes Pogány, 'Wirtschaftnationalismus in Ungarn im 19. und 20. Jahrhundert', in Pogány, Kofman and Kubů, *Für eine nationale Wirtschaft*, 52–72; and Jan Kofman, 'Die nationale Wirtschaftspolitik der Zweiten Republik Polen (1918 bis 1939)', ibid., 135–68.
148 Brunnbauer, 'Gesellschaft und gesellschaftlicher Wandel', 651–702.
149 Calic, *Geschichte Jugoslawiens im 20. Jahrhundert*, 103.
150 Christian Giordano and Dobrinka Kostova, 'Die Reprivatisierung ohne Bauern in der bulgarischen Landwirtschaft nach der "Wende": Zur Persistenz einer unheilvollen Tradition', in Grimm and Roth, *Das Dorf in Südosteuropa*, 49–63, here 54.
151 Sundhaussen, 'Südosteuropäische Gesellschaft und Kultur', 345–425, especially 381–4.

labour-intensive forms of production was able to absorb so much surplus labour. Numerous factors impeded an intensification of agricultural production, and these arose in various combinations in the different countries. Global economic conditions were unfavourable during the entire interwar period; in many areas of the region – especially in Southeastern Europe – the average farm was too small to be profitable, and where large-scale farms constituted the

Table 2.4 Distribution of the peasant agrarian population according to farm size in Hungary (including unpropertied groups) in 1935

Cadastral yokes	Percentage of owners and workers	Percentage of arable land
> 100 cadastral yokes (≜ > 57.0 ha)	0.6	48.0
50 – 100 cadastral yokes (≜ 28.5–75.0 ha)	1.0	6.4
20 – 50 cadastral yokes (≜ 11.4–28.5 ha)	4.5	13.6
10 – 20 cadastral yokes (≜ 5.7–11.4 ha)	8.7	12.6
5 – 10 cadastral yokes (≜ 2.85–5.7 ha)	12.5	9.2
0 – 5 cadastral yokes (≜ 0–2.85 ha)	72.7	10.2

Source: Nagy József, *Földbirtok-politika Magyarországon a két világháború között* [Land ownership policy in Hungary in the interwar period] (Eger: Eszterházy Károly Főiskola Líceum K., 2003), 204.

Table 2.5 Distribution of farms according to size in Romania in the late 1930s

	Percentage of farms	Percentage of arable land
over 500 hectares	0.1	17.1
100–500 hectares	0.3	10.6
50–100 hectares	0.4	4.5
5–50 hectares	24.2	39.8
2–5 hectares	22.9	15.2
0–2 hectares	52.1	12.8

Source: Wolfram Fischer et al., eds, *Handbuch der Europäischen Wirtschafts- und Sozialgeschichte*, vol. 6, *Europäische Wirtschafts- und Sozialgeschichte vom Ersten Weltkrieg bis zur Gegenwart* (Stuttgart: Klett-Cotta, 1987), 805.

Table 2.6 Distribution of land according to ownership categories in Poland in 1925/26

	Percentage of farms	Percentage of arable land
over 50 hectares	0.9	47.3
20–50 hectares	2.4	7.1
10–20 hectares	9.6	13.8
5–10 hectares	22.5	17
2–5 hectares	30.7	11.3
0–2 hectares	33.9	3.5

Source: Andrzej Ajnenkiel, *Od rządów ludowych do przewrotu majowego: Zarys dziejów politycznych Polski, 1918–1926* [From peoples' governments to the May coup d'état: outline of the political history of Poland 1918–1926] (Warsaw: Wiedza Powszechna, 1977), 207.

predominant element in the ownership structure, the supply of superfluous labourers freed farms from the urgent necessity of increasing productivity that investments would have compelled, as in Hungary or in large parts of Poland and Romania. On the latter territories, the stratification of peasants resembled a pyramid, with broad lower classes of 'dwarf peasants', thin layers of medium-large peasant farms and a tiny group of wealthy peasants at the top of the pyramid.

In contrast to this internal structure of the Hungarian peasantry (and in part, the Polish and Romanian peasantry), medium-sized peasant farms predominated in the Czech lands, Estonia and Latvia. In the latter two countries, only 18.5 per cent of those working in agriculture were wage labourers; the broad majority were self-employed farmers and their family members. In Lithuania, only 15.5 per cent were agricultural labourers.[152] In Yugoslavia, the percentage of unpropertied peasants among the agrarian population was even lower, as more than 90 per cent of the rural population owned land (in Bulgaria 97 per cent), although this should not be taken as a sign of affluence, but rather the opposite.

In contrast to the situation in the Baltic states, where the predominantly medium-sized farms had access to secure markets due to the sea, Southeastern European countries had the least success. There, peasant farms became so small through inheritance that during the interwar period the average farm size in Bulgaria was only 5 hectares, in Yugoslavia 5.36 hectares, while in Poland, 60 per cent of farms were smaller than 5 hectares.[153] This made it impossible for families to engage in market-oriented economic activities. In many places in Southeastern Europe, peasant families followed a strategy aimed not at adaptation to capitalist, market-economy conditions, but rather at family subsistence independent of the market. Through 'an anti-innovation familial structure influenced by a patriarchal house community' – combined with the institutionalization of private property and an inheritance law that divided land – land ownership disintegrated into unproductive fragmentation.[154] This led, of course, to a subsistence economy, which – given the continual reduction in plot size through inheritance – offered no opportunity to escape extreme poverty.

> The basic motivation in the economic activity of the overwhelming portion of Yugoslav farm households was to provide food and other necessities for the family … [the] overwhelming majority of … households were thus primarily subsistence units and not agricultural business enterprises.[155]

Table 2.7 Distribution of peasant family farms in Yugoslavia in 1931

	Percentage of farms	Percentage of arable land*
over 20 hectares	3	22.7
5–20 hectares	29	49.3
2–5 hectares	34	21.5
0–2 hectares	34	6.5

Sources: Marie-Janine Calic, *Geschichte Jugoslawiens im 20. Jahrhundert* (München: C.H. Beck, 2010), 103.
*Wolfram Fischer et al., eds, *Handbuch der Europäischen Wirtschafts- und Sozialgeschichte*, vol. 6, *Europäische Wirtschafts- und Sozialgeschichte vom Ersten Weltkrieg bis zur Gegenwart* (Stuttgart: Klett-Cotta, 1987), 886.

---

152 Pistohlkohrs, 'Estland, Lettland und Litauen', 746.
153 Ibid., 886.
154 Calic, *Sozialgeschichte Serbiens 1815–1941*, 441.
155 Tomasevich, *Peasants, Politics, and Economic Change*, 431.

To secure survival, peasant families diversified their work activities and relied on occasional labour or seasonal employment by individual family members in industry or in mining.[156] Contemporary ethnographers reported that 'since there was simply not enough to do on the fragmented plots, people worked little and slowly there, despite abject poverty.'[157] Thus, in spite of the spread of agricultural cooperatives, government organizations for agricultural credit and the increased marketing of agricultural products, 'the ownership of a farm, in the case of a majority of the peasant households proved incapable of solving the peasant's quest for a decent living or for economic security'.[158]

The situation of agricultural labourers was not much better in other countries of Central and Eastern Europe, as agricultural wages were low everywhere due to a slump in global food prices. Servants on large estates and other groups of agricultural labourers were often paid in kind. In Bulgaria, for example, 58 per cent of the total agricultural income was in kind. The lack of wages paid in money meant that agricultural labourers of the region were unable to enjoy labour law regulations similar to those of industrial workers, who were protected not only by labour laws, but also through social insurance.[159] Thus, in essential aspects, agricultural labourers in Central and Eastern European countries still lived and worked in conditions removed from the modern world. The underemployment of the rural labour force remained characteristic.

To a certain extent, the political elites of Southeastern European countries actively neglected the promotion of agricultural development insofar as they secured few resources for the expansion of elementary education.[160] Theorists of rural modernization emphasize the close connection between a first phase of increasing average agricultural earning power and literacy.[161] The military expenditures of the Yugoslav state, for example, far exceeded the budget of the education ministry, while in 1930, 45 per cent of people older than 10 were illiterate (in Bulgaria, 31 per cent), and the literacy rate was even lower among peasants than in society at large.[162] Similar situations can be observed in the other nations as well. In Poland, 44 per cent of state expenditures went to the military, and in Czechoslovakia the military share of the national budget increased from approximately 12 per cent in the 1920s to 37 per cent in the 1930s.[163] Legal restrictions on market forces and other measures caused the social reform decreed from above in Serbia to fail, in contrast to the Stolypin reforms in Russia or those instituted in Central European states.[164] Farmers in Czechoslovakia struggled not with the problems of breaking free

---

156 Calic, *Sozialgeschichte Serbiens 1815–1941*, 236–46.
157 Calic, *Geschichte Jugoslawiens im 20. Jahrhundert*, 104.
158 Tomasevich, *Peasants, Politics, and Economic Change*, 430.
159 Juliane Brandt, 'Wohlfahrtsstaatlichkeit in Ungarn. Europäische Vorbilder und ungarischer Entwicklungspfad', in *Vorbild Europa und die Modernisierung in Mittel- und Südosteuropa*, eds Flavius Solomon, Krista Zach and Juliane Brandt (Münster: LIT, 2009), 145–88.
160 More than a quarter of state expenditures served military goals. Marie-Janine Calic, 'Bildung als Entwicklungsproblem in Jugoslawien (1918–1941)', in Reiter and Sundhaussen, *Allgemeinbildung als Modernisierungsfaktor*, 103–26.
161 Sundhaussen, 'Südosteuropäische Gesellschaft und Kultur', 345–425.
162 Ibid.
163 Piotr Stawecki, 'Wojsko Drugiej Rzeczypospolitej' [Army of the second republic], in *Polska odrodzona 1918–1939*, ed. Jan Tomicki (Warsaw: Wiedza Powszechna, 1982), 200–43, here 239; Jan Pavel, *Velikost a struktura výdajů na národní obranu v Československu v letech 1918–1938* [The size and structure of expenditure on national defence in Czechoslovakia, 1918–1938] (Prague: Národohospodársky ústav Josefa Hlávky, 2004), 35.
164 Calic, *Sozialgeschichte Serbiens 1815–1941*, 442; Tomasevich, *Peasants, Politics, and Economic Change*, 411–30.

from a subsistence economy, but rather with finding markets for their products. Poland and Hungary – both characterized by a high percentage of large landowners – in contrast, were familiar with both issues, depending on the region.

After the Second World War, the 'people's democracies' embraced a vision of agriculture that contained a strong element of private ownership. This vision was further bolstered by the post-war land reforms, which changed the socio-economic landscape, particularly in Poland (where the reform affected 50 per cent of all farmland), in Czechoslovakia and Hungary (40 per cent) and to a lesser extent, in the Balkans (under 10 per cent). With the introduction of these reforms, the number of landless peasants decreased and almost all estates larger than 50 hectares were dissolved. While the reforms encouraged people to stay in rural areas and strengthened existing property owners, newly created farms were barely viable. On average, new holdings were two to three hectares in size.[165]

An abrupt turn in agricultural policy took place between 1948 and 1949. Before this shift, Klement Gottwald stated in 1948:

> If somebody comes to your village and says that there will be *kolkhozes* in Czechoslovakia, be aware that he is an agent provocateur of the forces of reaction … There will be no collectivization in Czechoslovakia. We shall go our own way.[166]

Similar declarations were made by the leaders of neighbouring countries. Just a few months later, the first wave of collectivization began all over the region. In a brutal campaign, the communist regimes competed for the prize of being the first to achieve their goal.[167] Economic development according to the Stalinist model demanded huge resources. The main principles of economic policy were thus focused on extracting surpluses from the countryside. Taxation policy, compulsory consignments and collectivization were used as powerful means of class warfare against well-to-do peasants. Moreover, such measures were meant to convince the peasantry that individual farms were unsustainable and thus pave the way for the expansion of collectivized agriculture.

Only those with the smallest plots of land were eager to join cooperatives. Others, closely tied to their properties, could not easily be persuaded to become agricultural workers. In Yugoslavia, many claimed that they would gladly join if only their fathers (who owned the properties) would let them. Resistance was both economic and cultural. Cooperatives were so detested that even local party officials were reluctant to join. Fear of collectivization led to a decline in agricultural production and stagnating land sales. Repression ensued. While the historian Dariusz Jarosz writes that the 'beatings and insults hurled at peasants' in Poland were 'particularly brutal',[168] this does not do justice to the grim experience of collectivization in Romania and Bulgaria. The

---

165 Jozo Tomasevich, 'Agriculture in Eastern Europe', *Annals of the American Academy of Political and Social Science* 317 (1958): 46; Włodzimierz Brus, 'Post-war Reconstruction and Socio-Economic Transformation', in *The Economic History of Eastern Europe 1919–1975*, vol. 2, eds M.C. Kaser and E.A. Radice (Oxford: Clarendon, 1986), 595.
166 Jan Rychlík, 'Collectivization in Czechoslovakia in Comparative Perspective', in *The Collectivization of Agriculture in Communist Eastern Europe: Comparison and Entanglements*, eds Arnd Baukamper and Constantin Iordachi (Budapest: Central European University Press, 2014), 185–86.
167 Karl Eugen Wädekin, *Agrarian Policies in Communist Europe: A Critical Introduction* (The Hague and London: Rowman & Littlefield, 1982), 35.
168 Dariusz Jarosz, *Polityka władz komunistycznych w Polsce w latach 1948–1956 a chłopi* [Policy of the communist authorities in Poland in the years 1948–1956 and the peasants] (Warsaw: Wydawn. DiG, 1998), 85.

productivity of cooperatives was low and their economic losses grave. The disorganization of agriculture had a detrimental effect on all aspects of life, especially on the distribution of food to the towns and cities. At the beginning of the 1960s, the collectivization campaign was proclaimed a success: in Bulgaria, the share of individual holdings in total agricultural land had fallen to 1 per cent; in Romania to 9 per cent (individual holdings survived mainly in mountain areas); in Hungary to 6 per cent; and in East Germany and Czechoslovakia to 6–7 per cent.

Collectivization brought about a fundamental rupture in the development of the peasantry in Central and Eastern European countries.[169] Although the state had exercised increasing control over agricultural production and rural communities prior to this – during and after the Second World War, the rationing of the food supply led to bureaucratic regulation of agrarian production – it had left untouched the private economic basis of agriculture as well as the function of the family in this sector. With collectivization, the peasant family lost its function as a productive unit; with the expansion of the dictatorial surveillance state, the role of communities as self-governing bodies, in which wealthy peasants set the tone, was lost. The historical development of the peasantry in Central and Eastern Europe thus came to an end, for thereafter we can no longer speak of peasants in the strict sense.[170] After the disappearance of the basis of the peasantry – the family farm and the peasant village – those who continued to work in agriculture despite the wave of industrialization became, in effect, paid wage labourers, whose actual position on the farm no longer depended on abilities that had been crucial from the perspective of their former way of life as peasants. Instead, their role was determined by how well they were able to adapt to the new political and bureaucratic rules of the game. This also implied a decrease in the significance of the family, which until then had been the fundamental social unit in the village.[171] Gail Kligman and Katherine Verdery write: '[V]illages ceased to be primarily sources of community and became segments of formal organizations that reached upward into higher administrative levels.'[172] They go on to say, 'village life becomes bureaucratized and politicized. Instead of communities electing their mayors we find organizations staffed by political appointees ... Villages and households no longer circumscribe the life plans of their members.'[173] The new bureaucratically coordinated institutions – state farms, collective farms and village administration – attempted to promote the modernization of agricultural production. These attempts, however, did not lead to as rapid an increase in production as occurred in capitalist agriculture during the same time period. The reasons for the failure of these modernization attempts lay not only in the inefficiency of bureaucratic economic management, but also in the passive resistance of the rural population.[174] In Bulgaria, for example, collectivization turned

---

169 For an overview, see Arnd Bauerkämper and Constantin Iordachi, 'The Collectivization of Agriculture in Eastern Europe: Entanglements and Transnational Comparisons', in Baukamper and Iordachi, *The Collectivization of Agriculture*, 3–46.

170 József Ö. Kovács, *A paraszti társadalom felszámolása a kommunista diktatúrában: A vidéki Magyarország politikai társadalomtörténete, 1945–1965* [The liquidation of peasant society under communist dictatorship: the socio-political history of rural Hungary, 1945–1965] (Budapest: Korall, 2012), 395–422; József Ö. Kovács, 'The Forced Collectivization of Agriculture in Hungary, 1948–1961', in Baukamper and Iordachi, *The Collectivization of Agriculture*, 211–47; Gail Kligman and Katherine Verdery, *Peasants under Siege: The Collectivization of Romanian Agriculture, 1949–1962* (Princeton, NJ: Princeton University Press, 2011), 88–148.

171 Brunnbauer, 'Gesellschaft und gesellschaftlicher Wandel', 651–702.

172 Kligman and Verdery, *Peasants under Siege*, 408.

173 Ibid., 409.

174 Ivo Georgiev, 'Die Arbeiter als Modernisierungsbremse im realsozialistischen Bulgarien?' in Hübner, Klessmann and Tenfelde, *Arbeiter im Staatssozialismus*, 109–18.

peasants into wage labourers, as in Romania, whereby peasant know-how was lost. Work ethos, responsibility and peasant rationality disappeared, and often what emerged in its place on farms was pseudo-activity for a pseudo-salary.[175] Laws and regulations were circumvented by local leadership as well as by individual members of collective farms. Counter-strategies for collectivization led to passivity and indifferent attitudes about the cooperative.[176] Throughout the entire region many former peasants were concerned solely with receiving good land from collective farms for their private households.

Due to these profound qualitative changes in the social order, we cannot simply equate those employed in agriculture after collectivization with peasants of earlier periods on the basis of mere sectorial affiliation. In Bulgaria, collectivization brought 88 per cent of Bulgarian agricultural land into collective and state farms, a radical break from the peasant past. Landlessness remained rare in Bulgaria, but the average size of personal plots was 0.3 hectares. 'As had been the case before 1946, private plots were used mainly to produce food for household consumption.'[177] Poland and Yugoslavia were exceptions here, insofar as collectivization succeeded in only a small part of both countries.[178] The process of collectivization was halted in Poland and Yugoslavia before completion because the Polish and Yugoslav party leadership were unwilling to pay the political as well as economical price of violence against the peasants.[179] 'The cooperatives in practice proved ... to have a negative effect ... the producers' loss of interest and degradation of production', formulated a Yugoslav politician.[180] In Poland production cooperatives accounted for 1.5 per cent of agricultural land, state farms for roughly 15 per cent (mainly in the former German lands), and private farms for over 80 per cent.[181] But in Poland, too, profound changes occurred in relations between the cities and the countryside. Peasant farms adapted themselves to the conditions of the planned economy, which led overall to a curious conservation of the peasantry. 'Polish peasant farms were not collectivised but their Western-type farmerisation was blocked.'[182] A kind of re-peasantization could be observed in Poland in terms of agrarian structure (an average plot of 5 to 6 hectares) and also in the understanding of farming and the strategies for survival. One might argue that the typical clientelist relation between peasant and landlord was preserved to some extent in the relation between peasant farmers and the local state bureaucracy. As a result of this re-peasantization, in 1996 only 40 per cent of farms sold any of their produce on the market.[183]

---

175 Giordano and Kostova, 'Die Reprivatisierung ohne Bauern in der bulgarischen Landwirtschaft', 49–63.
176 Doroteja Dobreva, 'Arbeiten im Kollektiv: Offizielle Normen und tatsächliches Verhalten in einem bulgarischen Gebirgsdorf in den 50er Jahren', in Grimm and Roth, *Das Dorf in Südosteuropa*, 196–223; Gregory R. Witkowski, 'Collectivization at the Grass Roots Level: State Planning and Popular Reactions in Bulgaria, Romania, Poland, and the GDR, 1948–1960', in Baukamper and Iordachi, *The Collectivization of Agriculture*, 467–96.
177 Mieke Meurs, 'Peasant Production and Agricultural Transformation in the 1990s: How Distinct Are the Hungarian and Bulgarian Cases?', in *Actors on the Changing European Countryside*, eds Leo Granberg and Imre Kovács (Budapest: Institute for Political Science of the Hungarian Academy of Sciences, 1998), 74–86, cited sentence 76.
178 Dariusz Jarosz, 'The Collectivization of Agriculture in Poland: Causes of Defeat', in Baukamper and Iordachi, *The Collectivization of Agriculture*, 113–46.
179 Melissa K. Bokovoy, 'Collectivization in Yugoslavia: Rethinking Regional and National Interests', in Baukamper and Iordachi, *The Collectivization of Agriculture*, 293–327.
180 Ibid., 318.
181 Eugenia Krzeczkowska, *Kraje RWPG 1960–1975* [Comecon countries 1960–1975] (Warsaw: Główny Urząd Statystyczny, 1976), 83.
182 Krzysztof Gorlach and Paweł Starosta, 'De-peasantisation or Repeasantisation? Changing Rural Social Structures in Poland after World War II', in Granberg, Kovách and Tovey, *Europe's Green Ring*, 41–65, here 43.
183 Gorlach and Starosta, 'De-Peasantisation or Repeasantisation'.

In the other countries of Central and Eastern Europe, a certain amount of freedom for private domestic production was indeed restored beginning in the 1960s (which contributed significantly to improvement in the food supply) but this led neither to the re-establishment of peasant modes of life, nor to the emergence of agricultural entrepreneurship. The latter emerged only in Hungary to a certain extent, in a development in which broad strata of the rural population pursued a double strategy, namely of families working not only in state economic organizations, but also engaging in economic activities on their own account. In Hungary, 80 per cent of agricultural land was in the socialized sector by the early 1960s. Using private plots for subsistence was permitted, albeit initially only 0.5 hectares. Later, the size of household plots was expanded, for example, through subcontracting on socialized land. For some items, one third of production was private, and half of the household income was earned from private economic activity.[184] In Hungary an estimated 60 per cent of private production was sold on the market in the 1980s. In Estonia and Latvia – which served to a certain extent as laboratories of reform for the Soviet Union – a similar development could be observed.

> [T]he relaxation of various restrictions turned some kolkhozes into genuine collective farms which at times became relatively wealthy. By 1972 collective farmers' average income (including income from private plots) had exceeded that of urban workers in Estonia and Latvia, and the traditional labour flow from the countryside to the cities started to be cancelled out by an opposite flow.[185]

This strategy, which combined large-scale, state-controlled operations with household economic activities, remained relatively successful in Hungary for a considerable period.[186] The use of modern agro-technologies on collective farms beginning in the late 1960s, and the interest of small producers in making a profit led to a significant increase in agricultural productivity.[187] By the 1980s, however, this model proved to be unviable. The visible wealth of many villages was due precisely to the prohibition of capital accumulation and the purchase of further land, so that the relatively high incomes were expressed in consumption. Thus, the 'mini-farms' could not continue to grow, and the large-scale agricultural operations also wrestled with problems. Given the food prices, which had been set low for political reasons, expensive agro-technological investments did not pay off, especially since collective farms were supposed to retain even those workers who were in fact superfluous.[188]

Overall, state socialism did succeed in implementing a degree of modernization of rural infrastructure and everyday material culture, especially where the base level was low – for

---

184 Iván Pető and Sándor Szakács, *A hazai gazdaság négy évtizedének története, 1945–1985* [Four Decades of the Hungarian Economy] (Budapest: Közgazdasági és jogi, 1985); Imre Kovách, 'De-Peasantisation of the Hungarian Rurality', in Granberg, Kovách and Tovey, *Europe's Green Ring*, 66–88.
185 Romuald J. Misiunas and Rein Taagepera, *The Baltic States: Years of Dependence, 1940–1990* (London: Hurst, 1993), 230.
186 Pál Juhász, *Agrárpiac, Kisüzem, Nagyüzem* [Agrarian market, small factory, large factory] (Budapest: Medvetánc, 1982).
187 Zsuzsanna Varga, 'Conflicts and Compromises between the Hungarian Socialist State and the Peasantry: Contextualising the "Hungarian Agricultural Miracle"', in *Integration through Subordination: The Politics of Agricultural Modernisation in Industrial Europe*, eds Peter Moser and Tony Varley (Turnhout: Brepols Publishers, 2013), 203–22.
188 István Harcsa, Imre Kovách and Iván Szelényi, 'The Hungarian Agricultural "Miracle" and the Limits of Socialist Reforms', in *Privatizing the Land: Rural Political Economy in Post-Communist Societies*, ed. Iván Szelényi (London: Routledge, 1998), 21–42.

instance, in Bulgaria, where in the interwar period much of the rural population still lived in a pre-modern material culture (beds, for example, were a rarity).[189] During the second half of the socialist period, villages did acquire electricity, better transportation links with cities and greater access to higher education than before.

Following the collapse of state socialism, the bureaucratic coordination of agricultural production that had predominated was no longer able to function – least of all competitively. It turned out that state socialism had created no efficient structures that could secure productive employment for the rural population without the protection of the state. The collective farms had relinquished their social responsibilities for the village population to the central state administration. In most rural areas, the population was supposed to decrease, and where this did not occur, the return of a peasant subsistence economy was observed. After 1989–1990, land became private property again in virtually all countries of the region, and plots frequently ended up in the hands of their previous owners or their heirs. In most countries, this occurred in the form of restitution to previous owners; in Hungary, however, the process took place through 'compensation vouchers' that could be used to purchase land, and which were issued to previous owners according to a degressive formula. The larger the former property had been, the lower the percentage for which the owner was compensated. However, most of the former peasants compensated in this way were unwilling and unable to run an independent farm and find a footing on the free market. This is still the case to a certain degree in the Baltic states, where in addition to farms that produce for foreign markets, there is also limited production by poor households.[190] According to several authors, the factors differentiating the social and economic well-being of farms are: available machinery, the presence of pensioner income, the level of drinking and the availability of labour by family members.[191] The majority of the previously flourishing Hungarian mini-farms were not in a position to expand their production, as they lacked the necessary capital.[192] In the Czech Republic and Slovakia, the majority of owners leased their land to larger operations, and only 5 to 15 per cent of the new owners started up independent family farms. In Romania, Bulgaria and Poland, in contrast, family farms became the predominant form of the agrarian economy. In these countries, we can speak of a certain re-agrarianization, as the percentage of people employed in agriculture increased in the 1990s.[193] In Southeastern European countries, however, cultivation of plots remained at most a weekend activity for many who were employed in other economic branches or were pensioners. In Bulgaria, for example, part-time agricultural labour by new owners served only to supply food for the family. The village population in the 1990s was too old and too uneducated for capitalist agriculture to function, not to mention lacking the required capital. In many areas of Southeastern Europe, subsistence economy regained a certain degree of significance, as families sought to cover their own needs and in so doing supported themselves with the age-old model

---

189 Milena Benovska-Sabkova, 'Socialism as Modernisation: Observations on Bulgaria', in *Arbeitswelt – Lebenswelt: Facetten einer spannungsreichen Beziehung im östlichen Europa*, ed. Klaus Roth (Berlin: LIT Verlag, 2006), 25–41.
190 Ilkka Alanen, 'Baltic Agriculture After the De-Collectivisation', in Granberg and Kovács, *Actors on the Changing European Countryside*, 144–67.
191 Talis Tisenkopfs, 'Post-Collectivist Farmers as Social, Economic and Political Group', in Granberg and Kovács, *Actors on the Changing European Countryside*, 131–43.
192 István Harcsa, Imre Kovách and Iván Szelényi, 'The Price of Privatisation: The Post-Communist Transformational Crisis of the Hungarian Agrarian System', in Szelényi, *Privatizing the Land*, 214–44.
193 Karl Bruckmeier and Marina Olegowna Koptina, 'Post-Traditional or Post-Modern Rurality?', in Granberg, Kovách and Tovey, *Europe's Green Ring*, 167–96.

of mutual assistance.[194] Many old-new owners simply leased or sold their plots, thus initiating the gradual emergence of a new agricultural entrepreneurship, which, however, had virtually nothing to do with historical peasantry.[195] The exponents of this practice often came from the leading cadre of the earlier large-scale farms as they were the ones who possessed the knowledge and market contacts, as well as the best machines from the former collective farms. These enterprises were supposed to establish themselves in international competition, of course, as food markets opened quickly after 1990. In fact, it was the abrupt emergence of international competition that made it impossible for small Hungarian producers to follow their previous market strategies. Due to the lack of capital, they were unable to compete on the global market.[196] Poland was the exception here to a certain extent, as collectivization was never carried out in most of the country, such that we can speak of a continuity of peasant farming there, and of a slow development in the direction of modern enterprise after 1990. The development was somewhat similar in Hungary, where in 2000, approximately half of the land was used by large-scale farms, and the other half by family farms, whereby the cultivation of the plots was frequently, although not exclusively, performed as part-time labour to supplement pensions or other employment income.

Education

The following part deals with one of the most important aspects of social mobility – education. Education is often interpreted as a channel of mobility and a central factor reproducing social structures between generations, particularly as it influences vertical and upward mobility. The focus will be on the aspects of education which are considered symbols of modernity, the expansion of higher, secondary and post-secondary education, and on the problem of eradicating illiteracy in the period before 1945.

The quantitative growth of a literate population and of graduates in secondary and tertiary education during the twentieth century is one of the most impressive transformations in the region's social history. In 1880, two thirds of the population of Central and Eastern Europe was illiterate; the only regions where more than half of the population was literate were the Czech lands, the Baltic countries, Slovenia and western parts of Hungary. By contrast, only about 10 per cent of the population in Southeastern Europe was literate. Throughout the region, the literacy of women was below average. Secondary education was accessible to no more than three per cent, and university education to well under one per cent. The population of university students in Central and Eastern Europe in 1880 can be estimated at 15,000 young men. The early twenty-first century offers a different picture: the population is widely literate, most people have a secondary education and about one tenth also have university degrees. The population of university students is more than four million among both sexes. The educational gap between the genders no longer exists. The gap between countries with regard to the quality of education (for example as measured by PISA studies) and the percentage of adults with university degrees is much lower than the gap in literacy was between Central and Southeastern Europe in 1880.

As social history has generally associated primary education with the spread of literacy, which is well recorded in statistics and substantially documented in historiography, we will

---

194 Dobreva, 'Arbeiten im Kollektiv', 196–223; Klaus Roth, 'Soziokultureller Wandel im südosteuropäischen Dorf nach dem Zweiten Weltkrieg', in Grimm and Roth, *Das Dorf in Südosteuropa*, 64–75.
195 Giordano and Kostova, 'Die Reprivatisierung ohne Bauern in der bulgarischen Landwirtschaft', 49–63.
196 Harcsa, Kovách and Szelényi, 'The Price of Privatisation', 214–44.

only briefly characterize its most important currents here. There are certain methodological problems that affect comparability, however. For example, in some cases literacy was calculated from the population older than seven years of age, in others, older than 15 years of age; in some cases, reading and writing were required, and in others, only reading. The process of spreading literacy began in the late eighteenth century in the Habsburg Monarchy, which was one of the first countries on the continent to introduce obligatory school attendance. In Hungary, it was introduced in 1868. The emerging states of the Balkans adopted obligatory school attendance: Romania in 1864, Bulgaria in 1878 and Serbia in 1882. A 50 per cent literacy rate was reached in the Czech lands and Baltic countries as early as 1850, in the territory of Hungary in the 1880s and in the territory of Poland at the turn of the century (see Table 2.8). This rate was achieved in Romania, Bulgaria and Yugoslavia in the 1920s and in Albania only in the 1950s. In Kosovo, half the population was illiterate even in the 1970s. There were important differences between the sexes, religious groups, urban and rural areas, and between different regions within countries – the best example of this no doubt being Yugoslavia, where in 1930, Slovenia could boast a 95 per cent literacy rate, while in Bosnia-Herzegovina literacy was at 30 per cent).[197] Regional differences within other new countries (Poland, Czechoslovakia, Romania) were also striking, but not as dramatic as in the Yugoslav example. Illiteracy was concentrated mainly among disadvantaged groups like Muslims in Yugoslavia and Bulgaria, and the Romany people throughout the region. In the parts of the region without a developed culture of reading and writing, particularly in Southeastern Europe, illiteracy persisted even after the introduction of compulsory school attendance, as people tended to forget these skills in adulthood. In predominantly agricultural countries, compulsory school attendance did not bring the expected results, as child labour was needed at home during the harvests. In response, the authorities made the school year shorter in rural areas. While in countries like Czechoslovakia and Hungary the authority of the school was already afforded high respect in the interwar years, in Yugoslavia, cases were reported in which parents claimed that their child had died in order to avoid compulsory school attendance.[198] It seems that the state apparatuses of Southeastern Europe were not motivated enough to invest in elementary schools, while the universities were supported much more generously.[199] In the case of Albanians in Kosovo, the school minister from Belgrade declared

Table 2.8 Estimated rates of literacy in Central and Eastern Europe, 1900 and 1930 (in %)

	1900	1930
Czech lands/Czechoslovakia	88.0	95.3
Hungary	68.7	90.4
Poland	61.4	90.4
Romania	22.0	57.0
Bulgaria	29.6	68.5
Serbia/Yugoslavia	40.3	55.0

Source: Andrew Janos, *East Central Europe in the Modern World: The Politics of the Borderlands from Pre- to Postcommunism* (Stanford, CA: Stanford Univ. Press, 2002), 140, 167.

197 M.C. Kaser and E.A. Radice, eds, *The Economic History of Eastern Europe, 1919–75*, vol. 1, *Economic Structure and Performance between the Two Wars* (Oxford: Clarendon Press, 1985 [2006]), 139.
198 Holm Sundhaussen, *Geschichte Serbiens: 19.–21. Jahrhundert* (Vienna: Böhlau, 2007), 280–81.
199 Marie-Janine Calic, 'Bildung als Entwicklungsproblem in Jugoslawien: 1918–1941', in Reiter and Sundhaussen, *Allgemeinbildung als Modernisierungsfaktor*, 103–26.

openly that it was in the state's interest to keep them culturally inferior, because it would make their future assimilation easier.[200]

The primary school systems were different around the region up to 1945, and they were only unified in the course of Sovietization. During the interwar years, eight years of school attendance were obligatory in Czechoslovakia, although not everybody made it to the eighth class, as the number of those who had to repeat the classes was high. Estonia and Poland each required seven; Hungary and Latvia six; and Lithuania and Yugoslavia, only four years.[201] In Yugoslavia it was discovered that only 50 per cent of children between the ages of 7 and 10 went to school.[202] In Albania, four years of compulsory school attendance were introduced only in 1946; it was raised to seven years in 1952 and eight in 1963.[203] The little attention paid to elementary schools was contrasted with the high prestige of the gymnasium system, which were the centres of culture and knowledge. In most of the region, vocational schools were not developed; this tradition existed mainly in strongly industrialized Czech lands and in Hungary. In contrast to the later socialist vocational education, apprenticeships were organized by the factory or workshop, and the few schools that did exist offered regular classes for only a few hours per week.

In the first half of the century, the highest level of education for the majority of the population in all countries of our region was elementary school, or at least several classes of it. Those with higher levels of education remained a minority. In Estonia, the most developed country in terms of education, 12.6 per cent of the population had a secondary education and 1.9 per cent had attended university in 1934.[204] In Hungary, among the population older than 7, in 1948 only 3.3 per cent graduated from secondary school, and only 1.2 per cent went on to a university education.[205] In the Czech lands, among the population older than 15, in the year 1950, 10 per cent had a vocational school education, 5 per cent had completed secondary school with a graduation exam, and only 0.9 per cent had a university education.[206] In Yugoslavia in 1953, 42 per cent had no schooling at all or had attended school for 1–3 years, 46 per cent had 4–7 years, only 4 per cent finished elementary school, 6.5 per cent had a secondary school education and 0.5 per cent a university degree.[207] It seems that matriculation in secondary schools and universities was much more similar across the region than the levels of elementary education.

The pursuit and prestige of a university education grew during the nineteenth century. Before that time the number of university graduates was very few, and the knowledge provided by the university was very different from the needs of the economy and the state. As higher education become more practically oriented (with the establishment of technical universities and commercial academies, and the adoption of more practical curricula at gymnasiums beginning in the second half of the nineteenth century), it came to be perceived as the most important path to mobility in

---

200 Sundhaussen, *Geschichte Serbiens*, 281.
201 Pistohlkors, 'Estland, Lettland und Litauen', 748.
202 Martin Mayer, *Elementarbildung in Jugoslawien (1918–1941): Ein Beitrag zur gesellschaftlichen Modernisierung?* (München: Oldenbourg, 1995), 176.
203 Gert Geissler, 'Unterweisung-Schulen-Schulsysteme: Zur Geschichte institutionalisierter Bildungsprozesse in Europa', in *Die Bildungssysteme Europas*, ed. Hans Döbert (Baltmannsweiler: Schneider-Verl. Hohengehren, 2010), 27.
204 Hinno, *Bildung und Sozialstruktur*, 20.
205 Ignác Romsics, *Hungary in the Twentieth Century* (Budapest: Corvina Books, 1999), 151.
206 Alena Křížková and Marta Vohlídalová, 'The Labour Market and Work-Life Balance in the Czech Republic in Historical Perspective', in *Women and Social Citizenship in Czech Society: Continuity and Change*, eds Hana Hašková and Zuzana Uhde (Prague: Sociologický ústav AV ČR, 2009), 41.
207 *Jugoslavia 1918–1988, Statistički Godišnjak* [Yugoslavia 1918–1988, statistical yearbook], Socialistička Federativna Republika Jugoslavija, Savezni Zavod za Statistiku, Beograd, Februar 1989, 50.

modern society. It was by no means a continuous process over the twentieth century, however. The value of higher education tended to decline during periods of upheaval, economic depressions, military conflicts and under Stalinism, when upward mobility declined or depended more strongly on other aspects (such as opportunism or political loyalty) and education sometimes became a stigma or a reason to be persecuted. The most notable example is the decimation of the ethnic Polish intelligentsia during Nazi occupation. During less turbulent periods, education regained its importance. It also lost some of its relative value in the early twenty-first century because it has almost become universal (with 50 per cent of young people graduating from university). It seems that it has lost its former function as a 'lift' in the social structure and is instead becoming a sort of safeguard against unemployment or unqualified jobs. It seems that only a few fields of tertiary education are still a secure channel of upward mobility (engineering, computer science, medicine).

As to the quantitative growth of university students within the region over the century (see Table 2.9), we can identify constant growth during the entire period, although it differed wildly during particular decades. A considerable increase in the student population can already be observed in the period prior to the First World War, when an estimated 15,000 students in 1890 grew to 50,000 by 1914. We can also identify rapid periods of growth after the world wars, and the stagnation of or decline in the student population during the wars and the Great Depression. The growth in the period from the 1890s until the late 1930s was also faster than in Western Europe. The huge gap between the respective proportions of university students in our region and Western Europe in the late nineteenth century had been closed by 1950, and most countries from the region, including Yugoslavia, Poland and Bulgaria, were above the Western European average at that time.[208] According to Janos, the higher education system in Central and Eastern Europe developed much faster during this time than the economy.[209] Its

Table 2.9 University students in Central and Eastern Europe, 1920–2013 (in thousands)

	1920	1950	1990	2013
Bulgaria	5.5	33	152	284
Czechoslovakia	28.2	38.9	154	427/210
Hungary	12.9	32.5	47.5	359
Poland	25.9	125	158	1903
Romania	13.6	53.0	193	618
Yugoslavia	10.6	59.8	327	165/239
Total	96.7	342.4	1031.5	4205

Notes: Czechoslovakia 2013 is for Czech Republic/Slovakia; Romania 1920 subsequently includes the University of Cluj; Yugoslavia 2013 is for Croatia/Serbia; there is a different year for Yugoslavia, 1922.

Sources: Brian R. Mitchell, *International Historical Statistics: Europe 1750–2000* (New York: Palgrave Macmillan, 2003), 897–99. Data for 2013 taken from Eurostat 'Students enrolled in tertiary education by education level, programme orientation, sex, type of institution and intensity of participation' http://appsso.eurostat.ec.europa.eu/nui/show.do?dataset=educ_uoe_enrt01&lang=en (accessed 03 April 2019).

208 Kaelble, *A Social History*, 296. Whereas the percentage of university students among the 20–24-year-old population had been between 1 and 2% in the early 1920s, it reached 4.1% in Yugoslavia and Hungary, 5% in Bulgaria and 5.9% in Poland in 1950. By comparison, in France, Italy, Finland and Sweden 4% of the 20–24-year-old population attended university in 1950. In the same year, the percentage for the United Kingdom and Norway corresponds to that of Romania, where 3% of this specific age group attended university.
209 Janos, *East Central Europe in the Modern World*, 168–9.

faster growth than in Western Europe can be explained as a result of both state modernization policy and people's willingness to pursue better lives in those countries where chances for a career in private business were limited. The institution of higher education was much easier to adopt than the institutions of modern capitalism.

Concerning the centres of university education, there is a major difference between Central Europe, which had a medieval tradition of universities, and Southeastern Europe, where the first universities were founded only in the late nineteenth century in conjunction with the nation state-building processes. In the early nineteenth century, there were five important universities in the region, in Prague, Cracow, Lemberg/Lviv, Pest and Warsaw; however, the last of these was closed for several decades after the Polish uprisings and later Russified. The only universities offering classes in Polish were in Cracow and Lviv; ethnic Poles also went to study at the German universities of Berlin and Breslau, or to the Russian universities of Kiev and St. Petersburg. In the last decades of the Habsburg Empire, several new universities were established on its territory, which contrasts with the underdevelopment and even suppression of the university system in the parts of the region belonging to tsarist Russia. At the new university in Czernowitz/Cernauti (1885), instruction was in German, and three universities offered courses in Hungarian: in Kolozsvár/Cluj-Napoca (1872), Pozsony/Bratislava (1912) and Debrecen (founded in 1914, but only opened in 1922). Two minor nations of the monarchy, the Czechs and the Croats, also founded universities: The University of Zagreb was established in 1874, and Prague University divided into Czech and German sections in 1882. The Slovene struggle for a university, which began in the 1890s, remained unsuccessful.

In Southeastern Europe, the founding of universities taking place in the new states proceeded quite differently: the more suitable conditions in Romania (earlier independence and higher state revenues) made it the first country in the area to establish a university (Iasi in 1860, Bucharest in 1869). The Bulgarian and Serbian universities came three decades later: The University of Sofia in 1904 (lyceum in 1888) and Belgrade University in 1905 (la grande école in 1863). These universities had hundreds rather than thousands of students during the first years of their existence, in contrast to the thousands studying at Central European universities at that time, and they were strongly inspired by the French model. The proportion of university students in Cisleithania in the late nineteenth century did not differ from that in Western European countries, representing around one per cent of the male population.[210]

The end of the First World War, the birth of new states and border changes meant important changes affecting the development of all levels of education. Young men who were previously unable to study due to mandatory military service flocked to the universities, accompanied by increasing numbers of young women. New universities were established, and several existing ones dismantled due to the changes in borders. The first step was the re-founding of the Polish University of Warsaw in 1915, which had been opened when the city was occupied by German troops and the existing Russian university was evacuated. Other Polish universities were established right after the war in Lublin, Vilnius and Poznan. The country had the largest system of tertiary education in the region at the time: 6 universities, 13 institutions of higher learning and 690 professors. In Czechoslovakia, universities were established in Brno and Bratislava, the first named for President Masaryk; the second, surprisingly, not for a Slovak hero, but for the Czech education theorist, Jan Amos Comenius. In Hungary, new universities opened in Pécs and Szeged in 1921, replacing the lost universities in Cluj and Bratislava. Romania's territorial expan-

---

210 Walter Rüegg, ed., *A History of the University in Europe*, vol. 3, *Universities in the Nineteenth and Early Twentieth Centuries: 1800–1945* (Cambridge: Cambridge University Press, 2004), 245.

sion gave it universities in Czernowitz/Cernauti and Koloszvar/Cluj, which were subsequently Romanianized; the Czechoslovak state, on the other hand, did not dare to take the same steps in the case of the German university in Prague. The ethnic Hungarians of Romania were therefore the biggest national minority in the region without their own university. New universities were established in Latvia (Riga 1919) and Lithuania (Kaunas 1922), and the University of Tartu was Estonianized in 1918.[211] The Kingdom of Serbs, Croats and Slovenes had three universities, those already existing in Zagreb and Belgrade plus a newly established one in Ljubljana (1919). Albania remained the only country in the region without a university until 1945. Particularly important was the founding of medical schools, which were seen as a precondition for the modern state to develop and maintain a healthy population. Before 1918, they did not exist on the territory of future Yugoslavia and Bulgaria, so that doctors had to be trained abroad; but after the war, they mushroomed quickly (Sofia 1917, Zagreb 1919 and Belgrade 1919).

As to the size of the student body in different states, university students were still an exclusive group accounting for no more than five per cent of the youth. The differences between the countries were significant. Estonia had one student per 280 citizens,[212] in Latvia, one per 329, there was one per 453 in Czechoslovakia, one per 499 in Romania, one per 648 in Poland, one per 687 in Hungary, one per 888 in Bulgaria and one per 1,068 in Yugoslavia.[213] As for the number of female students, one cannot say that they correlated entirely with the socio-economic development of the country; for example, Romania had a higher proportion of female students than Hungary in 1930, while the economically weaker Baltic countries had a higher ratio than Czechoslovakia.[214]

The interwar universities were widely criticized for supporting traditional curricula. Between one third (Czechoslovakia) and two thirds of students (Yugoslavia)[215] graduated in law and the humanities. Technical and agricultural education became a priority only after 1945. Although the first faculties of agriculture and veterinary medicine were opened back in the nineteenth century, they remained marginal in the interwar years. In Romania, a country where 77 per cent of the population worked in agriculture, only 2 per cent of students were enrolled in the faculty of agriculture and 1 per cent in veterinary medicine.[216] Although tuition fees were charged throughout the region, they were relatively moderate.

Secondary and tertiary education in the region before 1939 was marked by the high proportion of Jewish students, which was much higher than the percentage of Jews in the population. In Cisleithania, Jews comprised a stable 14 per cent of students between 1881 and 1910, although they made up only 4.6 per cent of the population.[217] In Poland, Jews made up one quarter of the student population in the early 1920s, while accounting for only one tenth of the overall population. The ratio was similar in Romania and Hungary.

Right-wing forces attempted to reduce the high ratio of Jewish students by introducing *numerus clausus*, which was enacted as a law in Hungary in 1920. In response to international criticism,

---

211 Ibid., 41–4.
212 Pistohlkohrs, 'Estland, Lettland und Litauen', 748.
213 Brian R. Mitchell, *International Historical Statistics: Europe, 1750–2000*, 5th ed. (Basingstoke: Palgrave Macmillan, 2003), 897–8; Franz Rothenbacher, *The Central and Eastern European Population since 1850* (Basingstoke: Palgrave Macmillan, 2012), 30.
214 Dudley Kirk, *Europe's Population in the Interwar Years* (New York: Gordon and Breach, 1967, 24).
215 Sundhaussen, *Geschichte Serbiens*, 278–9.
216 Jan Sadlak, 'The Use and Abuse of the University: Higher Education in Romania, 1860–1990', *Minerva* 29, no. 2 (1991): 199.
217 Garry Cohen, 'Education, Social Mobility, and the Austrian Jews 1860–1910', in *Bildungswesen und Sozialstruktur in Mitteleuropa im 19. und 20. Jahrhundert*, eds Victor Karady and Wolfgang Mitter (Köln: Böhlau, 1990), 158.

in 1928 a new law was enacted that based the quota on certain social groups – however, it was phrased to preserve the practice of discriminating against Jews. In Romania and Poland, such legislation was not approved, but Jewish students were excluded from decision-making processes at particular universities, or they simply did not enrol because they were afraid of right-wing students. The universities in Poland initially attempted to persuade the government to enforce *numerus clausus*. When they failed, they introduced (mainly in 1937–1939) the so-called 'ghetto benches', which led to various upheavals and temporary closures of faculties. In the case of Romania, anti-Semitic protests were even directed at Jewish students in medical faculties that dissected Christian cadavers.[218] After 1939, without exception, Jews were expelled from universities in all of the states that had joined the Axis. German minorities were also over-represented in tertiary education in the region. According to Krista Hinno, in Estonia, Germans comprised only 3.5 per cent of the population before the First World War, but accounted for half of all lawyers, physicians and scientists, and even 83 per cent of business people. Despite the abolition of their privileges after 1918, they still retained much of their cultural capital until their resettlement in 1939.[219] Another over-represented group at universities in the region were the Protestants in Slovakia.

In all countries of the region, the Great Depression either reduced the number of students or caused their numbers to stagnate. In Czechoslovakia, the number of students declined by 21 per cent between 1930 and 1937, which could be also explained by the smaller cohorts of those born during the First World War; in Latvia, the decline was 23 per cent for the same period; in Estonia the decline between 1936 and 1938 was 50 per cent.[220] In Lithuania and Estonia, the number of students was suppressed by right-wing regimes: they were afraid of producing too many academics during the Great Depression[221] as students had a tendency to become politically radicalized during their studies.[222]

In most of the territories of the region directly occupied by the Nazis, such as Poland, the Czech lands, Ukraine and Belarus, the universities were closed. An exception was the territory of former Yugoslavia, where the University of Belgrade was allowed to exist under German rule, as was the University of Ljubljana under Italian occupation. In the Protectorate of Bohemia and Moravia the universities were closed as a consequence of student demonstrations in October 1939; in Poland, they were closed immediately following Nazi occupation while the University of Poznan was Germanized. Under Soviet occupation in 1939, the University of Lviv was forced to change its name to Ivan Franko University and to adopt Soviet curricula. When the Nazis invaded in June 1941, they arrested most of the professors who had survived the Stalinist purges and then closed the university. Although the Nazis supported several professional schools for Ukrainians, they did not allow the existence of a Ukrainian university.[223] The University of Vilnius experienced even more turbulent changes: when the territory was given to Lithuania in 1939, it was merged with the University of Kaunas and was Lithuanized. When the country was annexed by the Soviet Union it was Stalinized; when it was occupied by Nazi Germany, it was allowed to exist further and was given to Lithuanian nationalists. The final round of Sovietization came in 1944. The university thus experienced four purges within five years. The Polish universities, in contrast to the universities in the Protectorate of Bohemia and Moravia,

---

218 Sadlak, 'The Use and Abuse of the University', 200.
219 Hinno, *Bildung und Sozialstruktur*, 12.
220 Pistohlkohrs, 'Estland, Lettland und Litauen', 748.
221 Clewing and Schmitt, *Geschichte Südosteuropas*, 413.
222 Janos, *East Central Europe in the Modern World*, 170.
223 Adam Redzik, *Polish Universities during the Second World War* www.gomezurdanez.com/polonia/adamredzikpolishuniversitas.pdf, 12 (Acessed 10 January 2015).

were able to maintain their existence in the underground with six thousand students, or about 13 per cent of the pre-war enrollment.[224] An important difference between the Protectorate versus the General Government and the territory of the Soviet Union occupied by the Wehrmacht was that secondary schools were allowed to stay open in the Protectorate, although the presence of German in the curricula was stressed, while only elementary schools remained open in occupied Poland and the Soviet Union. As a reaction, the Polish underground state also developed a network of illegal secondary schools. The states of the region allied with the Axis were able to keep their universities running, unless they were closed due to military operations (for example, the universities in Hungary in autumn 1944), but they generally tightened up study requirements, with the army conscripting those students who failed their exams.[225]

State Socialism

From the perspective of education development, the socialist period can be divided into three phases. The 1950s were marked by the fast expansion of tertiary, secondary technical and secondary vocational education, deep and often chaotic reforms, and in Southeastern Europe, also by campaigns against illiteracy. The second phase, in the 1960s and 1970s, is marked by the continuation of growth, but also by the stabilization of the new system and in several cases a return to pre-Stalinist models. The third phase, the 1980s, is marked by the stagnation and even decline of universities, which is particularly remarkable in contrast to their parallel development in the West, and by renewed attempts to reform primary and secondary education.

Immediately after 1945 the growth rate for tertiary education and for the opening of the new universities and faculties was similar to that after the First World War. New borders meant, again, the relocation of universities, for example, the University of Lviv was relocated to Wroclaw. The German universities in Prague and Wroclaw/Breslau were dismantled. At this time, Romanian authorities did not repeat the Romanianization of the University of Cluj, but two parallel universities, one Romanian and one Hungarian, were allowed to exist. In Yugoslavia, each of the federal republics got its own university. New faculties were established in fields that had not been considered appropriate for university education before the Second World War, such as elementary school teacher training and pharmacology. Secondary vocational technical education also experienced a sharp increase. The entire education system, including universities, was Sovietized, implementing Soviet organizational structures, curricula, textbooks and teaching methods. Sovietization was accompanied by centralization, such that universities lost much of their autonomy. Sovietization also meant the ideologization of teaching. The level of this varied, depending on the country and the period. Most notably, in most of the countries, religious education in elementary schools and different philosophical approaches at the universities were replaced by training in Marxism-Leninism.

Stalinist educational policy attempted to increase educational opportunities for people from the lower social classes, mainly workers and small peasants, and to provide those who did not study with vocational training and the entire population with comprehensive elementary education. Beginning in the 1950s, most socialist countries required eight years of elementary school; in Czechoslovakia, it was nine. In Yugoslavia, the possibility of introducing 11 years of compulsory schooling was discussed.[226] As a part of the fight against former social privileges,

---

224 Ibid., 19.
225 Sadlak, 'The Use and Abuse of the University', 203.
226 Geissler, 'Unterweisung-Schulen-Schulsysteme', 27.

the former elite secondary schools were abolished (in Czechoslovakia even the word 'gymnasium' was banned) and replaced by the Soviet system of eight-year comprehensive elementary schools for everyone, followed by either comprehensive or specialized secondary schools, both of which permitted entry to the university or vocational schools. Emphasis was put on the technical secondary schools while private schools were abolished altogether.

In order to provide university education to those younger and middle-aged adults who had been unable to finish secondary schooling in their teens, short equivalency courses that allowed their graduates to study at the university spread in the early 1950s. In Czechoslovakia, one-year boarding schools for adults, substituting for what used to be eight years of gymnasium, became popular. Later on, evening secondary-school classes and correspondence courses for university became even more popular, as they allowed adults to further their education while staying in their jobs. The number of distance-learners at universities increased steadily until the 1960s, when they made up one third of all students.[227] During the 1960s, as the mission to alleviate inherited inequalities became obsolete, and a certain scepticism about the quality of distance studies took root, the share of distance students began to stagnate or decline.

The ambition to increase the proportion of people with a working-class or peasant background in higher levels of education was accompanied by discrimination toward the offspring of families considered disloyal to the new political power, those coming from 'bourgeois' or 'kulak' backgrounds or against students involved in anti-communist activities. A strategy of improving one's 'cadre profile', which was a precondition for enrollment, was to be employed as a worker for one or two years and then to apply to university again, or perhaps for a less prestigious field of study (engineering, agriculture). Prohibitions against youth with 'improper social backgrounds' were mostly abolished during the Thaw, however. Their reintroduction in Czechoslovakia during normalization seems to have been an exception.

The socialist system also introduced a system of entry exams following the Soviet model which contrasted with the situation before 1945, when the exam upon graduating from secondary school and paid tuition fees were the only preconditions for matriculation. Tuition fees were abolished (with the exception of Romania where fees existed until 1960), and various forms of scholarships were introduced. The fight against 'eternal students' was initiated, and universities were purged of those who failed to fulfil their academic requirements. Then the obligation of graduates to accept a certain job and spend several years in it was introduced. However, this measure varied by country and the period, and starting in the 1960s, it was abolished in most countries.[228] Despite official propaganda claiming that university graduates had no difficulties finding jobs in socialism, it was not always easy to get a position corresponding to one's education, so that graduates often had to take jobs for which they were over-qualified.

Another feature of socialist secondary and tertiary education was its 'polytechnization'.[229] The socialist states attempted to make universities comply with the demands of the economy better than the period before 1945, in order to contribute to the development of a strong industrial base. This led to increasing ratios of students in the technical sciences. While the university students in these fields of study had accounted for less than one quarter of all students before the war, under socialism this proportion climbed to two thirds. Romania offers a textbook example: students of engineering and architecture comprised 30 per cent in 1960, but 64 per cent

---

227 Andrzej Jezierski, *Państwo*, vol. 1 of *Historia Polski w liczbach* [The state, vol. 1 of Polish history in numbers] (Warsaw: Zakład Wydawn. Statystycznych, 2003), 529.
228 Brunnbauer, *'Die sozialistische Lebensweise'*, 599.
229 Ibid., 271.

of students in 1987;[230] in Czechoslovakia, 23 per cent of students were in technical fields in 1948, but this had risen to 40 per cent by 1989.[231] In Bulgaria, students of technical universities comprised 23 per cent of all students in 1953, but by 1989, the ratio had increased to 36 per cent.[232] An exception was Poland, where the proportion of students at technical universities actually stagnated.[233]

The Cold War and Stalinism caused a decline in academic cooperation between Eastern and Western Europe, which was more damaging for the East; although the attempt to revive it was made during the Thaw, it was not able to recover fully. On the other hand, student and academic exchanges with the Soviet Union were strongly supported (an exception was Romania under Ceaușescu).[234] The intensity of student exchanges was, however, much weaker than the exchange between the region and Western Europe after 1989. Nothing comparable to the Erasmus programme developed within the Comecon. For example, in the Erasmus-Socrates programme after 2000, nine thousand students from Romania and seven thousand students from Poland studied abroad each year, most of them in Germany and France,[235] whereas under socialism, the number of students enrolled in programmes in the Soviet Union or other Soviet bloc countries was in the hundreds rather than the thousands. An important feature of the state socialist tertiary educational sector was an influx of students from developing countries, but they were not accompanied by reciprocal numbers of students from the socialist countries studying in the developing world. Particularly high were the numbers of foreign students in Romania, which aspired to an active, independent policy in the developing world. The number of foreigners here ranged between four and nine per cent of all students.[236] In Czechoslovakia, there was even a special University of the 17th of November, the only such entity outside of Lumumba University in Moscow, which opened in 1961, granting scholarships to students from developing countries for a programme of study in English and French. However, this university was closed in 1974, having become too expensive.

As to quantitative changes in tertiary education under socialism, for most of the period, the student body was growing – although there were several exceptions, such as the faculties of fine arts and theology. The fastest growth was experienced during the 1950s, when its rate was higher than in Western Europe. On the other hand, stagnation occurred during the 1980s. The quantitative growth of the Western European tertiary education sector was 850 per cent between 1950 and 1990, while the growth of the same in Central and Eastern Europe during that period was only 440 per cent.[237] Why was the divergence in the growth of tertiary education between East and West so much stronger than the divergence in their overall economic growth? The answer seems to be that in the socialist states, the growth of higher levels of edu-

---

230 Sadlak, 'The Use and Abuse of the University', 223.
231 Milan Otáhal, *Studenti a komunistická moc v českých zemích 1968–1989* [Students and communist power in the Czech lands 1968–1989] (Prague: Dokořán, 2003), 166.
232 Aleksandar Kostov, 'Die neue technische Intelligenz: Zur Ausbildung bulgarischer Ingenieure zwischen 1945 und 1989', in Brunnbauer and Höpken, *Transformationsprobleme Bulgariens*, 202.
233 Jezierski, *Państwo*, 529.
234 Guy Neave, 'Patterns', in *A History of the University in Europe*, vol. 3, *Universities in the Nineteenth and Early Twentieth Centuries (1800–1945)*, ed. Walter Rüegg (Cambridge: Cambridge Univ. Press, 2004), 40.
235 Immerfall and Therborn, *Handbook of European Societies*, 559.
236 Sadlak, 'The Use and Abuse of the University', 216.
237 Kaelble, *A Social History*, 296, for Western Europe. Data for CEE, calculation compiled from Mitchell, *International Historical Statistics*, 15 f, 25, 32, 34, 44, 897 ff. Central and Eastern Europe here include the following countries: Bulgaria, Czechoslovakia, Hungary, Poland, Romania and Yugoslavia.

cation was more strongly derived from the growth of the economy, and only partly in order to fulfil the demands of the population, while in the Western countries the demands of the population played a more important role. In Eastern Europe, on occasion it even became a matter of policy to keep student numbers low for ideological reasons, as students had become the core group in public protests. Further, there were no student purges at universities in Western Europe as there were in Czechoslovakia after 1948 and in Hungary after 1956.

Tertiary education had great prestige in state socialism, as one can see in the high numbers of rejected applicants to the universities. There were several reasons for this: professionals made more money than workers and had better chances to accumulate social capital. Intellectual work was more interesting and less physically demanding. All of this made a university education attractive. The relatively high prestige of education under socialism is also sometimes explained by the impossibility of accumulating economic capital during the period, which was substituted by the ambition to accumulate cultural capital. These attitudes were especially predominant among the socialist intelligentsia. It seems that, contrary to many expectations, in contrast to the period before 1945, the working-class youth who could now afford higher education often did not have such ambitions; and particularly as the regimes stabilized from the late 1950s on, not many people with a working-class background had access to higher education.

Researchers have shown that while access to a university education became more socially equitable during the 1950s, in the following decade the proportion of middle-class students began to grow again. The explanation is not only that discrimination against students from the former upper and middle classes weakened, but also that the ambitious members of the working and peasant classes had become educated during the 1950s, and thus comprised the middle class under socialism, while the remaining workers and peasants had rather lower ambitions regarding educational mobility. Working-class children in Czechoslovakia had better chances of enrolling at university in the 1960s than in the 1980s.[238] University students in late socialism were thus recruited primarily from the intelligentsia, be it the old pre-communist one, which was thus able to reproduce its cultural capital, or the new socialist intelligentsia.

An example of a mechanism for getting into a prestigious school, which tells a lot about how state socialist society functioned, is the subject of a recent study by the Faculty of Arts and Philosophy at the Charles University in Prague in the 1970s and 1980s, where only a fraction of the applicants were allowed to enrol. Chances for admission there were determined not only by applicants' academic qualities, but often by their political attitudes and those of their families, individual corruption and nepotism, and also the regional origin of applicants. Admission was a highly bureaucratic process: the application was submitted not to the university, but to the secondary school, where the director, the class teacher and a representative of the Union of Socialist Youth wrote a joint appraisal of the applicant. The secondary school could even decide to reject any application. In the case of future teachers, local authorities were also asked for their opinion of the applicant and his or her family. If the applicant was an employee, he or she applied through the employer. The exam consisted of a test and an interview by the faculty's examining commission, which then decided whether or not to recommend the applicant for acceptance. The final decision, however, lay with a central commission at the faculty, comprised of not only professors, but also representatives of state and party. The commission had no clear criteria for acceptance; the vague formulation spoke of 'the complex evaluation of the candidate' (not only his knowledge and intellect, but also his and his parents' political attitudes and activities). The commission could actually ignore the applicant's secondary-school evalua-

---

238 Matějů and Večerník, *Zpráva o vývoji české společnosti*, 64.

tion and the results of the admission exam. This opened a space for corruption; and it seems that those who were favoured were not the most talented or politically loyal applicants, but rather people who had friends or relatives on the commission (social capital). Finally, the minister of education had the exclusive right to accept any applicant refused by the faculty, and this right was exercised frequently. In some prestigious subjects (psychology), the admission of as many as half of the students was facilitated by the minister.[239]

After 1989

In post-socialism, the region experienced a new wave of growth in tertiary education. While there were 964,000 students in 1989, by 2010 it was more than four million. The student population began to grow in the latter half of the 1990s, while from 1989 to 1994 the number of students had stagnated or even declined. As in the period after 1945, new faculties and universities were established. The growth of universities was, again, much faster than the growth of the economy. It was motivated by the desire of the youth population to increase their chances of mobility, the ambition of governments to be internationally competitive and by encouragement from the European Union to increase the number of students. This growth happened primarily in 'cheap' subjects like social sciences, law, economics and management, however, while the increase in the number of graduates in medicine or engineering has been much slower. The increased number of university students has not been accompanied by corresponding growth in investment in tertiary education. The result is a decline in the quality of teaching and a decline in academic faculty members' income. Other factors in this increase include the exponential growth of private universities in the late 1990s and the introduction of shorter, practically oriented programmes and distant learning. The quantitative gap in the percentage of university students between the East and the West during late socialism came to an end around 2005. Poland, Slovenia and the Baltic countries even climbed above the EU average during this time.[240]

As technical education had priority under socialism, it become somewhat devalued after 1989 and often experienced a relative decline: in Romania, which is the most extreme case, the percentage of students at technical universities declined from 70 to 30 between 1990 and 1995. In 2004, students of the social sciences, business and law comprised a very high percentage in most of the countries, from 50 per cent (Latvia) to 30 per cent (the Czech Republic, Slovakia). This was criticized as reminiscent of the one-sidedness of socialist tertiary education in its heavy orientation toward technical subjects. Private universities and colleges developed at a different pace. In some countries, the majority of all students enrolled in private institutions (75 per cent in Slovenia, 80 per cent in Lithuania and Latvia), and in others only a minority did (8 per cent in Bulgaria, 7 per cent in Slovakia).[241] Despite repeated attempts to introduce tuition at public universities, they have largely remained free; however, the system of scholarships and other stipends is less generous than in Western Europe and has been cut considerably since 1989. In Hungary, for example, a system was introduced that required students with poor marks in their

---

239 Jakub Jareš, 'Studentem na FFUK v době normalizace' [Students at Charles University in the age of normalization], in *Náměstí kransoarmějců 2: Učitelé a studenti filosofické fakulty UK v období normalizace*, eds Jakub Jareš, Matěj Spurný and Katka Volná (Prague: Filosofická fakulta, Universita Karlovya v Praze, Toogga, 2012), 299–322.
240 Steffen Mau and Roland Verwiebe, *Die Sozialstruktur Europas* (Bonn: Bundeszentrale für politische Bildung, 2009), 169.
241 Irena Kogan, 'Education Systems of Central and Eastern European Countries', in Kogan, Gebel and Noelke, *Europe Enlarged*, 27.

secondary school graduation exams to pay for university. In the Czech Republic, in the late 1990s tuition was introduced for those who already graduated and wanted to study at another university, and for students whose studies took longer than six years.

With regard to secondary education, a tendency to support a comprehensive curriculum developed, in contrast to the socialist specialization. Vocational secondary education experienced a crisis as it could no longer cooperate with closed-down or privatized industries and thus faced the declining prestige of manual professions. Several countries, such as the Czech Republic, Hungary and Slovakia, attempted to return to the more competitive system of secondary schools (gymnasium) and to lower the age of enrollment from 15 to 10, as it had been before 1945. This was perceived as a return to the pre-communist elite secondary education. In other countries, however, the model of keeping pupils together in elementary school until age 14 or 15 persisted (Bulgaria, Estonia, Poland, Slovenia). The most striking examples of the expansion of comprehensive secondary education can be found in the Baltic countries, where the ratio of pupils at the general secondary schools was between 60 and 80 per cent in 2005. In most of the other countries, professional secondary schools remained more common than comprehensive secondary schools. An extreme case is the Czech Republic where comprehensive secondary schools account for only about 20 per cent of the total (although their numbers have expanded since 1989). Attempts to establish private elementary and secondary schools have occurred as well; but, as with private universities, they remain in the minority. In several countries, the church resumed its role as an educational institution at the primary and especially at the secondary level (gymnasium), and the quality of education it offers is considered comparable with public education.

Irena Kogan distinguishes between three groups of post-communist countries with regard to education policy. The first group includes the countries of Central Europe that inherited the tradition of the Austrian-German gymnasium. Here, the post-socialist transition was marked by the reintroduction of early selection at around 10 to 11 years of age, and the retention of the exclusivist character of universities and of comprehensive secondary schools. A second group is represented by the Baltic countries which were influenced by both Russian and German educational traditions, and by contact with Scandinavian school systems after 1989. This group is marked by the predominance of comprehensive secondary education and the robust expansion of both public and private universities. Poland seems to lie between the first and second groups. A third group, comprised of Romania and Bulgaria, is characterized by the strong Soviet influence in the past. This group seems to have reformed its educational system only slightly by the 2000s.[242] The available data from post-Yugoslav countries and Albania allow us to add them to this group as well, albeit with some reservation. Here, the number of students at the secondary and tertiary level stagnated or even declined in the 1990s, and rapid growth came about only after 2000.[243] The differential impact of post-socialist transformation, in combination with deep historical traditions, is strikingly visible in the results of international research on the educational aptitude of 15-year-old students (PISA Study). Central and Eastern Europe fares worse than East Asia or Western Europe, but better than the post-Soviet countries, the Middle East or Latin America. Since the first study was conducted, Estonia has been at the top, whereas the countries of Southeastern Europe had the lowest results in the region.[244]

---

242 Ibid, 30–31.
243 World Bank Group, *The Road to Stability and Prosperity in South Eastern Europe: A Regional Strategy Paper* (Washington, DC: World Bank, 2000), 89.
244 Organisation for Economic Co-operation and Development, ed., *Science Competencies for Tomorrow's World: Results from PISA 2006* (Paris: OECD, 2007).

Further Reading

Applebaum, Anne. *Iron Curtain: The Crushing of Eastern Europe 1944–1956* (London: Allen Lane, 2012).
Baukamper, Arnd, and Constantin Iordachi, eds. *The Collectivization of Agriculture in Communist Eastern Europe: Comparison and Entanglements* (Budapest: CEU Press, 2014).
Berend, Tibor Iván. *Decades of Crisis: Central and Eastern Europe before World War II* (Berkeley, CA: University of California Press, 2001).
Berend, Tibor Iván. *History Derailed: Central and Eastern Europe in the Long Nineteenth Century* (Berkeley, CA: University of California Press, 2003).
Berend, Tibor Iván, and György Ránki. *Economic Development in East-Central Europe in the 19th and 20th Centuries* (New York: Columbia University Press, 1974).
Bohn, Thomas M., ed. *Von der 'europäischen Stadt' zur 'sozialistischen Stadt' und zurück? Urbane Transformationen im östlichen Europa des 20. Jahrhunderts* (München: Oldenbourg, 2009).
Bohn, Thomas M., and Marie-Janine Calic, eds. *Urbanisierung und Stadtentwicklung in Südosteuropa vom 19. bis zum 21. Jahrhundert* (München: Verlag Otto Sagner, 2010).
Borodziej, Włodzimierz, Stanislav Holubec, and Joachim von Puttkamer, eds. *Mastery and Lost Illusions: Space and Time in the Modernization of Eastern and Central Europe* (München: Oldenbourg, 2014).
Boyer, Christoph. *Zur Physiognomie sozialistischer Wirtschaftsreformen: Die Sowjetunion, Polen, die Tschechoslowakei, Ungarn, die DDR und Jugoslawien im Vergleich* (Frankfurt a.M.: Vittorio Klostermann, 2007).
Breen, Richard, ed. *Social Mobility in Europe* (Oxford: Oxford University Press, 2004).
Bruckmüller, Ernst, et al., eds. *Bürgertum in der Habsburgermonarchie*, vol. 1 (Vienna: Böhlau, 1990).
Brunnbauer, Ulf. *'Die sozialistische Lebensweise': Ideologie, Gesellschaft, Familie und Politik in Bulgarien 1944–1989* (Vienna: Böhlau, 2007).
Brunnbauer, Ulf, and Wolfgang Höpken, eds. *Transformationsprobleme Bulgariens im 19. und frühen 20. Jahrhundert: Historische und ethnologische Perspektiven* (München: Verlag Otto Sagner, 2007).
Calic, Marie-Janine. *Sozialgeschichte Serbiens 1815–1941: Der aufhaltsame Fortschritt während der Industrialisierung* (München: Oldenbourg, 1994).
Calic, Marie-Janine. *Geschichte Jugoslawiens im 20. Jahrhundert* (München: C.H. Beck, 2010).
Clewing, Konrad, and Oliver Jens Schmitt, eds. *Geschichte Südosteuropas: Vom frühen Mittelalter bis zur Gegenwart* (Regensburg: Verlag Friedrich Pustet, 2011).
Crossick, Geoffrey, and Serge Jaumain, eds. *Cathedrals of Consumption: The European Department Store, 1850–1939* (Aldershot: Ashgate, 1999).
Crowley, Stephen, and David Ost, eds. *Workers after Workers' States: Labour and Politics in Postcommunist Eastern Europe* (Lanham, MD: Rowman & Littlefield, 2001).
Döbert, Hans, ed. *Die Bildungssysteme Europas* (Baltmannsweiler: Schneider-Verl. Hohengehren, 2010).
Eyal, Gil, Iván Szelényi, and Eleanor Townsley. *Making Capitalism without Capitalists: The New Ruling Elites in Eastern Europe* (New York: Verso, 1998).
Fél, Edit, and Tamás Hofer. *Proper Peasants: Social Relations in a Hungarian Village* (New Brunswick: Aldine Transaction, 2008).
Fischer, Wolfram, et al., eds. *Handbuch der Europäischen Wirtschafts- und Sozialgeschichte*, vol. 6, *Europäische Wirtschafts- und Sozialgeschichte vom Ersten Weltkrieg bis zur Gegenwart* (Stuttgart: Klett-Cotta, 1987).
Gehmacher, Johanna, Elizabeth Harvey, and Sophia Kemlein, eds. *Kemlein Zwischen Kriegen: Nationen, Nationalismen und Geschlechterverhältnisse in Mittel- und Osteuropa 1918–1939* (Osnabrück: Fibre Verlag, 2004).
Granberg, Leo, Imre Kovách, and Hilary Tovey. *Europe's Green Ring* (Aldershot: Ashgate, 2001).
Granberg, Leo, and Imre Kovács, eds. *Actors on the Changing European Countryside* (Budapest: Institute for Political Science of the Hungarian Academy of Sciences, 1998).
Grimm, Frank-Dieter, and Klaus Roth, eds. *Das Dorf in Südosteuropa zwischen Tradition und Umbruch* (München: Südosteuropa-Gesellschaft, 1997).
Gyáni, Gábor. *Parlour and Kitchen: Housing and Domestic Culture in Budapest, 1870–1940* (Budapest: CEU Press, 2002).
Gyáni, Gábor, György Kövér, and Tibor Valuch, eds. *Social History of Hungary from the Reform Era to the End of the Twentieth Century* (Boulder, CO: Social Science Monographs, 2004).
Haller, Max, ed. *Class Structure in Europe: New Findings from East-West Comparisons of Social Structure and Mobility* (New York: M.E. Sharpe, 1990).
Hann, Christopher, ed. *Postsozialismus: Transformationsprozesse in Europa und Asien aus ethnologischer Perspektive* (Frankfurt a.M.: Campus, 2002).

Hašková, Hana, and Zuzana Uhde, eds. *Women and Social Citizenship in Czech Society: Continuity and Change* (Prague: Sociologický ústav AV ČR, 2009).
Hatschikjan, Magarditsch A., and Franz-Lothar Altmann, eds. *Eliten im Wandel: Politische Führung, wirtschaftliche Macht und Meinungsbildung im neuen Osteuropa* (Paderborn: Schöningh, 1998).
Higley, John, and György Lengyel, eds. *Elites after State Socialism: Theories and Analysis* (Lanham, MD: Rowman & Littlefield Publishers, Inc., 2000).
Hinno, Krista. *Bildung und Sozialstruktur: Das Fallbeispiel Estland* (Marburg: Tectum Verlag, 2004).
Höpken, Wolfgang, and Holm Sundhaussen, eds. *Eliten in Südosteuropa: Rolle, Kontinuitäten, Brüche in Geschichte und Gegenwart* (München: Südosteuropa-Gesellschaft, 1998).
Hübner, Peter, Christoph Kleßmann, and Klaus Tenfelde, eds. *Arbeiter im Staatssozialismus: Ideologischer Anspruch und soziale Wirklichkeit* (Köln: Böhlau, 2005).
Immerfall, Stefan, and Göran Therborn, eds. *Handbook of European Societies: Social Transformation in the 21st Century* (New York: Springer, 2010).
Janatková, Alena, and Hanna Kozinska-Witt, eds. *Wohnen in der Großstadt 1900–1939: Wohnsituation und Modernisierung im europaischen Vergleich* (Stuttgart: Franz Steiner Verlag, 2006).
Janos, Andrew C. *East Central Europe in the Modern World: The Politics of the Borderland from Pre- to Postcommunism* (Stanford, CA: Stanford University Press, 2000).
Kaelble, Hartmut. *A Social History of Europe, 1945–2000: Recovery and Transformation after Two World Wars* (New York: Berghahn Books, 2013).
Karady, Victor, and Wolfgang Mitter, ed. *Bildungswesen und Sozialstruktur in Mitteleuropa im 19. und 20. Jahrhundert* (Köln: Böhlau, 1990).
Kaser, M.C., and E.A. Radice, eds. *The Economic History of Eastern Europe, 1919–1975* vol. 3 (Oxford: Clarendon Press, 1985, 1986 [2006]).
Kenney, Padraic. *Rebuilding Poland: Workers and Communists* (Ithaca, NY: Cornell Univ. Press, 2012).
Kligman, Gail, and Katherine Verdery. *Peasants under Siege: The Collectivization of Romanian Agriculture, 1949–1962* (Princeton, NJ: Princeton University Press, 2011).
Kogan, Irena, Michael Gebel, and Clemens Noelke, eds. *Europe Enlarged: A Handbook of Education, Labour and Welfare Regimes in Central and Eastern Europe* (Bristol: The Policy Press, 2008).
Kolosi, Tamás, István György Tóth, and György Vukovich, eds. *Social Report 2004* (Budapest: Tárki, 2004).
Kovács, Mária M. *Liberal Professions and Illiberal Politics: Hungary from the Habsburgs to the Holocaust* (Washington, DC: Woodrow Wilson Center Press and Oxford: Oxford University Press, 1994).
Kubů, Eduard, ed. *Agrarismus und Agrareliten in Ostmitteleuropa* (Berlin: Berliner Wissenschaftsverlag, 2013).
Kučera, Rudolf. *Rationed Life: Science, Everyday Life and Working-class Politics in the Bohemian Lands, 1914–1918* (New York: Berghahn Books, 2016).
Lane, David, György Lengyel, and Jochen Tholen, eds. *Restructuring of the Economic Elites after State Socialism* (Stuttgart: Ibidem Verlag, 2007).
Lorenz, Torsten, ed. *Cooperatives in Ethnic Conflicts: Eastern Europe in the 19th and Early 20th Century* (Berlin: Berliner Wissenschaftsverlag, 2006).
Lundgreen, Peter, ed. *Sozial- und Kulturgeschichte des Bürgertums: Eine Bilanz des Bielefelder Sonderforschungsbereichs (1986–1997)* (Göttingen: Vandenhoeck & Ruprecht, 2000).
Mai, Gunther. *Europa 1918–1939: Mentalitäten, Lebensweisen, Politik zwischen den Weltkriegen* (Stuttgart: Kohlhammer, 2001).
Mau, Steffen, and Roland Verwiebe. *Die Sozialstruktur Europas* (Bonn: Bundeszentrale für politische Bildung, 2009).
Mayer, Martin. *Elementarbildung in Jugoslawien (1918–1941): Ein Beitrag zur gesellschaftlichen Modernisierung?* (München: Oldenbourg, 1995).
Misiunas, Romuald J., and Rein Taagepera. *The Baltic States: Years of Dependence, 1940–1990* (London: Hurst, 1993).
Mitchell, Brian R. *International Historical Statistics: Europe, 1750–2000*, 5th ed. (Basingstoke: Palgrave Macmillan, 2003).
Moser, Peter, and Tony Varley, eds. *Integration through Subordination: The Politics of Agricultural Modernisation in Industrial Europe* (Turnhout: Brepols Publishers, 2013).
Oberländer, Erwin, Hans Lemberg, and Holm Sundhaussen, eds. *Genossenschaften in Osteuropa: Alternative zur Planwirtschaft* (Wiesbaden: Deutscher Genossenschafts-Verlag, 1993).
Organisation for Economic Co-operation and Development, ed. *Science Competencies for Tomorrow's World: Results from PISA 2006* (Paris: OECD, 2007).

Ossowski, Stanislaw. *Class Structure in the Social Consciousness*, trans. Sheila Patterson (New York: Free Press, 1963).
Pittaway, Mark. *Eastern Europe 1939–2000* (London: Bloomsbury Academic, 2010).
Pogány, Ágnes, Jan Kofman, and Kubů Eduard. *Für eine nationale Wirtschaft: Ungarn, die Tschechoslowakei und Polen von Ausgang des 19. Jahrhunderts bis zum Zweiten Weltkrieg* (Berlin: Berliner-Wissenschafts-Verlag, 2006).
Polonski, Antony. *Jews in Poland and Russia: 1914–2008* (Oxford: Littman Library of Jewish Civilization, 2012).
Puttkamer, Joachim von. *Ostmitteleuropa im 19. und 20. Jahrhundert* (München: Oldenbourg, 2010).
Reinhard, Wolfgang. *Lebensformen Europas: Eine historische Kulturanthropologie* (München: C.H. Beck, 2004).
Reiter, Norbert, and Holm Sundhaussen, eds. *Allgemeinbildung als Modernisierungsfaktor: Zur Geschichte der Elementarbildung in Südosteuropa von der Aufklärung bis zum Zweiten Weltkrieg* (Wiesbaden: Harrassowitz, 1994).
Romsics, Ignác. *Hungary in the Twentieth Century* (Budapest: Corvina Books, 1999).
Roth, Klaus, ed. *Die Volkskultur Südosteuropas in der Moderne* (München: Südosteuropa-Gesellschaft, 1992).
Roth, Klaus, ed. *Arbeitswelt – Lebenswelt: Facetten einer spannungsreichen Beziehung im östlichen Europa* (Berlin: LIT Verlag, 2006).
Rothenbacher, Franz. *The Central and Eastern European Population since 1850* (Basingstoke: Palgrave Macmillan, 2012).
Rüegg, Walter, ed. *A History of the University in Europe, vol. 3, Universities in the Nineteenth and Early Twentieth Centuries (1800–1945)* (Cambridge: Cambridge University Press, 2004).
Rumpler, Helmut, and Peter Urbanitsch, eds. *Die Habsburgermonarchie 1848–1918, vol. 8, part 1, Politische Öffentlichkeit und Zivilgesellschaft: Vereine, Parteien und Interessenverbände als Träger der politischen Partizipation* (Vienna: Österreichische Akademie der Wissenschaften, 2006).
Rumpler, Helmut, and Peter Urbanitsch, eds. *Die Habsburgermonarchie 1848–1918, vol. 9, part 2, Soziale Strukturen: Von der Stände- zur Klassengesellschaft* (Vienna: Österreichische Akademie der Wissenschaften, 2010).
Schattkowsky, Ralph, and Michael G. Müller, eds. *Identitätenwandel und nationale Mobilisierung in Regionen ethnischer Diversität: Ein regionaler Vergleich zwischen Westpreußen und Galizien am Ende des 19. und Anfang des 20 Jahrhunderts* (Marburg: Herder, 2004).
Schild, Gerhard. *Die Arbeiterschaft im 19. und 20. Jahrhundert* (München: Oldenbourg, 2010).
Schultz, Helga, and Angela Harre, eds. *Bauerngesellschaften auf dem Weg in die Moderne: Agrarismus in Ostmitteleuropa 1880 bis 1960* (Wiesbaden: Harraschowitz, 2010).
Schultz, Helga, and Eduard Kubů, eds. *History and Culture of Economic Nationalism in East Central Europe* (Berlin: Berliner Wissenschafts-Verlag, 2006).
Sigmund, Steffen, et al., eds. *Soziale Konstellation und historische Perspektive* (Wiesbaden: VS Verlag für Sozialwissenschaften, 2008).
Simkus, Albert. *Class Divisions in East-Central Europe: Studies of the Consequences of the Socialist 'Experiments' of 1949–1988* (Armonk, NY: M.E. Sharpe, 1997).
Slomczynsk, Kazimierz M., ed. *Social Structure: Changes and Linkages: The Advanced Phase of the Post-Communist Transition in Poland* (Warsaw: IFiS Publishers, 2002).
Solomon, Flavius, Krista Zach, and Juliane Brandt, eds. *Vorbild Europa und die Modernisierung in Mittel- und Südosteuropa* (Münster: LIT, 2009).
Sundhaussen, Holm. *Geschichte Serbiens: 19.–21. Jahrhundert* (Vienna: Böhlau, 2007).
Szelényi, Iván, ed. *Privatizing the Land: Rural Political Economy in Post-Communist Societies* (London: Routledge, 1998).
Szelenyi, Szonja. *Equality by Design: The Grand Experiment in Destratification in Socialist Hungary* (Stanford, CA: Stanford University Press, 1998).
Tomasevich, Jozo. *Peasants, Politics, and Economic Change in Yugoslavia* (Stanford, CA: Stanford University Press, 1955).
Tomka, Béla. *A Social History of Twentieth-century Europe* (London: Routledge, 2013).
Tönsmeyer, Tatjana, and Lubos Velek, eds. *Adel und Politik in der Habsburgermonarchie und den Nachbarländern zwischen Absolutismus und Demokratie* (München: Martin Meidenbauer, 2011).
Triska, Jan F., and Charles Gati, eds. *Blue Collar Workers in Eastern Europe* (London: George Allen and Unwin, 1981).

Vári, András. *Herren und Landwirte: Ungarische Aristokraten und Agrarier auf dem Weg in die Moderne (1821– 1910)* (Wiesbaden: Harrassowitz, 2008).
Veen, Hans-Joachim, ed. *Alte Eliten in jungen Demokratien? Wechsel, Wandel und Kontinuität in Mittel- und Osteuropa* (Köln: Böhlau, 2004).
World Bank Group. *The Road to Stability and Prosperity in South Eastern Europe: A Regional Strategy Paper* (Washington, DC: World Bank, 2000).

3

TRANSPORT, INFRASTRUCTURE AND COMMUNICATION

Luminiţa Gatejel and Jerzy Kochanowski

Introduction

In the twenty-first century, we take transportation infrastructure and communication networks for granted. Only when they temporarily cease to function during a blackout, disaster or cyber-attack are we reminded of the fact that our lives are held together by multi-layered webs of communication and transportation. However, even when the railways, roads, cables and waves that make up these networks were coming into being during the last century, they attracted widespread public attention only during planning and construction phases. After the projects were completed, they would be slowly forgotten and were integrated into the 'natural' environment. For this reason, communication and transportation infrastructure remains invisible most of the time.[1] However, over the past few decades, historians have uncovered the importance of this topic for understanding the political, social and cultural dynamics set in motion by large-scale infrastructure. Infrastructure networks were built for various reasons, such as to enable a faster flow of information, goods and people inside and between certain territories, to ensure spatial and social integration and to expand state authority. At the same time, the decision to construct a particular connection was always determined by specific political, economic and social factors. This chapter focuses on the complexities of communications and transportation.[2] On the one hand, we consider the ways in which technological improvement took place throughout the long twentieth century. We are interested in exploring when and why certain projects were approved, how they were financed, who the actors involved were, and what types of technology were used. On the other hand, we seek to analyze the effects these projects had on politics and society after they were completed. We deal with different aspects of the impact and use of communications and transportation. New infrastructure accelerated processes of urbanization, lifestyle changes and both social segregation and homogenization. Users' responses ranged from violent resistance to enthusiastic embrace, which in turn led to polyvalent uses. The chapter focuses on some of the most important innovations in transportation and communication of the

---

1 Dirk Van Laak, 'Infra-Strukturgeschichte', *Geschichte und Gesellschaft* 27 (2001): 367–93, here 367.
2 Thomas J. Misa, 'The Compelling Tangle of Modernity and Technology', in *Modernity and Technology*, eds Thomas J. Misa, Philip Brey and Andrew Feenberg (Cambridge, MA: MIT Press, 2003), 1–31.

twentieth century: railways, automobiles and air transportation in the field of transportation, and telegraphs, telephones, computers and the internet in the field of communications. Due to space limitations, we cannot treat several other important fields, such as public transportation (trams, buses, metro), which is briefly described in this volume's chapter on rural–urban issues, and water transportation (channels, ports, ships). We also omitted media such as press, radio and television. Nevertheless, television culture is analyzed in *The Intellectual Horizons* volume in this series.

This chapter focuses on the distinguishing features of the development of communications and transportation infrastructure in Central and Eastern Europe. While we do not argue that these regions are wholly different from other parts of the world, we nevertheless seek to analyze the specific characteristics that defined the speed and intensity of transformations, the various factors that brought about changes in communication and transportation, and the complex historical heritages that conditioned their construction, reception and use. We also acknowledge that we are bringing together distinct European regions with their own historical traditions. Still, the regions of Central and Eastern Europe underwent similar historical changes during 'the long twentieth century' that were marked by the same ruptures in 1918, 1945 and 1989. Thus, four different historical periods are relevant for this chapter: the late imperial age up to the First World War, the interwar period of national consolidation, the state-socialist era and the post-socialist transformation that was followed, in many cases, by admission to the European Union (or in some cases an Association Agreement signed with the EU). Each of the three turning points set major processes of infrastructural linking and de-linking into motion. Each era was defined by the ways nations were integrated into different networks and by the physical and mental re-orientations brought about by new national and international connections. Nevertheless, while we use the same historical framework as a starting point for our analysis, we take care to highlight the divergent ways communications were planned, developed and used in different nations. Thus, our analytical aim is twofold: on the one hand, we are looking for common trends across the entire region, and on the other hand, we seek to uncover local and regional differences.

The chapter spans the 'long twentieth century', which we divide into the so-called (high) modernity of the 1880s to the 1970s and the subsequent post-modernist or post-industrial period up through the beginning of the twenty-first century.[3] Modernity is considered to be a period of time-space compression, of rapid industrialization and urbanization, of confidence in progress and of large-scale, state-driven projects.[4] It was a period during which communication and transportation technologies developed with unprecedented speed. Railways, motorways, air traffic, phone lines, radio and computer networks spread (unequally) throughout Central and Eastern Europe. For the former Eastern bloc countries, post-industrialism began only after the fall of the Berlin Wall, when the move towards 'flexible' market economies started.[5] The

---

3 James C. Scott, *Seeing Like a State: How Certain Schemes to Improve the Human Condition Have Failed* (New Haven, CT:Yale University Press, 1998), 4; Ulrich Herbert, *Geschichte Deutschlands im 20. Jahrhundert* (München: C.H. Beck, 2014), 18–19; David Harvey, *The Condition of Postmodernity:An Enquiry into the Origins of Cultural Change* (Cambridge: Blackwell, 1992).

4 Scott, *Seeing Like a State*, 4–8; Ulrich Herbert, 'Europe in High Modernity: Reflections on a Theory of the 20th Century', *Journal of Modern European History* 5 (2007): 5–21; Dirk van Laak, *Weiße Elefanten: Anspruch und Scheitern technischer Großprojekte im 20. Jahrhundert* (Stuttgart: Deutsche Verlags-Anstalt, 1999), 7–12. On the specific conditions of modernity in Eastern and Central Europe see:Włodzimierz Borodziej, Stanislav Holubec, and Joachim von Puttkamer, eds, *Mastery and Lost Illusions: Space and Time in the Modernization of Eastern and Central Europe* (München: De Gruyter, 2014), 4–9.

5 Herbert, *Geschichte Deutschlands*, 18.

results of this transformation remain ambivalent: while the quantity and quality of communications improved on the whole, their spatial distribution led to a great disparity between few, mostly urban places closely connected to the global economy and the disconnected rest.[6]

One important factor that set various processes of modernization in motion was the perceived backwardness of a given region by the ruling elites. During late imperialism, several 'civilizing missions' brought peripheral regions' infrastructure into closer connection with the imperial cores. This process also began a major transfer of resources and technical knowledge from the imperial centres to the provinces. Nation states used backwardness as justification for speeding up technological progress and consolidating their rule over newly established national territories.[7] Importing technological know-how was seen as a way to cut short the time needed for research and development or even skip over whole stages of technological evolution. This practice was later also adopted by state-socialist regimes: under the motto 'to catch up and overtake the West', they purchased knowledge from capitalist countries with the aim of streamlining their technological progress and surpassing the capitalist states.[8] As a consequence, entire transportation and communication networks relied on foreign technology and expertise. In this context, we are particularly interested in how the agenda of fighting backwardness and the importation of technology over the span of several regime changes coalesced to shape a particular history of modernization in the region.

A second feature of modernization specific to Central and Eastern Europe was the strong role played by the state in planning and executing large infrastructural projects. Although state actors were important in most modernizing schemes, their involvement was pivotal here. It is well known that during state socialism, resource allocation for new communication technologies and the use of already existing technologies was heavily controlled.[9] But during the phase of national consolidation after the First World War as well, the region's political elites were painfully aware that without a functioning infrastructure, the new states could not survive. Their financial contribution to national communication networks was considerable, but it also stretched their budgets.[10] In the same vein, the PHARE-Program of the EU for states aspiring to EU-membership – and, even more, the funds that they received after becoming members – are further examples of large-scale public investment programmes that triggered communications development.[11]

Strong state intervention influenced both decisions in favour of developing certain types of technology and infrastructure and the way communications and transportation were to be used. One such decision concerned whether transportation should be individual or collective. In Central and Eastern Europe, the decision in favour of one of the options was highly ideological.

---

6 Karl Schlögel, 'Europa in Bewegung: Die Transformation Europas und die Transformation des europäischen Verkehrsraumes', in *Neue Wege in ein neues Europa: Geschichte und Verkehr im 20. Jahrhundert*, eds Ralf Roth and Karl Schlögel (Frankfurt a.M.: Campus, 2009), 29–48.
7 Ian D. Armour, *A History of Eastern Europe 1740–1918: Empires, Nations and Modernisation* (London: Bloomsbury Academic, 2012), 2–8; Andrew C. Janos, *East Central Europe in the Modern World: The Politics of the Borderlands from Pre- to Postcommunism* (Stanford, CA: Stanford University Press, 2000), 407–10.
8 Katalin Miklóssy and Melanie Ilič, 'Introduction: Competition in State Socialism', in *Competition in Socialist Society*, eds Katalin Miklóssy and Melanie Ilič (London: Routledge, 2014), 1–9.
9 Iván T. Berend, *Central and Eastern Europe, 1944–1993: Detour from the Periphery to the Periphery* (Cambridge: Cambridge University Press, 1996), 72–9.
10 Ralf Roth and Henry Jacolin, eds, *Eastern European Railways in Transition: Nineteenth to Twenty-First Centuries* (Farnham: Ashgate, 2013), 1–23.
11 European Commission, Political Documents Related to the Enlargement Process, http://ec.europa.eu/enlargement/archives/key_documents/reports_2000_en.htm (accessed 4 October 2015).

State-socialist governments even claimed they had established a collective mode of transport and communications that could serve as an alternative to the individual, car-based Western model. In practice, however, none of the regimes throughout the twentieth century were able to implement just one type of transportation or communication. Quite striking is the fact that during state socialism, private and individual car transport reached an unprecedented high. Thus, over the course of the twentieth century, the preference for one type of transportation changed several times, but it always led to a hybrid of collective and individual forms.

Closely intertwined were decisions in favour of a predominantly private or public transportation network. When the first rail networks crossed Eastern Europe, they were entirely funded by private capital, but when the costs grew out of proportion and their profitability sank, they were nationalized bit by bit. During the interwar period, governments sometimes made desperate attempts to attract foreign private investors, but when such attempts failed, they tried to fill the gaps with public investments. Even in the 1980s, after infrastructures had long been nationalized under state socialism, governments allowed the creation of international joint-ventures that attracted capital from Western companies.[12] This was just as well, as after 1989 private and public investments co-existed. While neoliberal economics dictated the privatization of several existing infrastructures (for instance telephone companies), an important bulk of investments in new transportation and communication networks came from state and EU resources.

One last common regional denominator was the process of infrastructural re-orientation after every major turning point. After the dissolution of empires, the governments in the new nation states were called upon to ensure functional communication networks throughout the new state's territory by linking provinces that formerly belonged to different empires.[13] In the same vein, the Cold War was accompanied by a massive de-linking of infrastructure and the establishment of closer connections with the Soviet Union.[14] After the collapse of the Eastern bloc, the prospect of EU-membership set off new endeavours to re-connect Eastern Europe with Western Europe. How these re-established connections will determine European mobility remains an open-ended process. While the East–West divide has ceased to exist in Europe, new divisions have taken its place in the former socialist bloc, such as that between those within the EU and those outside, between the affluent cities and the impoverished countryside, or between the concentration of infrastructure projects in a few big transport hubs and diminished investment in local transport.[15] This still open-ended process seems to be highly ambivalent, closing historical gaps while at the same time increasing disparities across Europe.

The specifics of transportation under state socialism

The period between the end of the Second World War and the collapse of the Eastern bloc in 1989 was characterized by swift social, technological and economic changes, particularly after the late 1950s. The (tele)communications and transportation revolution that took place then was comparable only to the deployment of steam engines in shipping and overland transport

---

12 Rolf Eschenbach, *Ost-West-Joint-Ventures auf dem Prüfstand* (Vienna: Manz, 1989).
13 Gyula Horváth, *Spaces and Places in Central and Eastern Europe: Historical Trends and Perspectives of Regional Development* (London: Routledge, 2015), 25–6.
14 Thomas J. Misa and Johan Schot, 'Inventing Europe: Technology and the Hidden Integration of Europe', *History and Technology* 21 (2005): 1–19, here 9.
15 Wolfgang Kaschuba, 'Europäischer Verkehrsraum nach 1989 – die Epoche der zweiten Globalisierung', in Roth and Schlögel, *Neue Wege in ein neues Europa*, 175–95.

during the first half of the previous century.[16] Motorization was already widespread and had reshaped not just the economy, but also the landscape and everyday life. Container transport revolutionized the entire logistics of production and shipping and reduced the significance of once traditional ports and port cities. Seaports were replaced by international air terminals for intercontinental passenger transport. 1958 was the last year in which more people sailed across the Atlantic than flew, and traditional transatlantic liners were almost phased out over the next two decades. Meanwhile, increased social mobility and the development of tourism and motorization led to ferries becoming more popular, particularly car-ferries (e.g. in the Baltic Sea). Radical changes took place not only in travel and transit, but also in freight and shipping, which had never before been so common and simple.[17]

However, it would be wrong to claim that the development of transportation and (tele)communications was the same throughout Europe. There was a clear division between countries in the East and those in the West. The lack of development of Central and Eastern Europe,[18] most of which was under Moscow's control, was also affected by historical circumstances: with the exception of Czechoslovakia, the infrastructure in these regions was historically less developed than in the West. Indeed, the region was affected by the war in multiple ways, from occupying forces commandeering the vehicles and infrastructure of national carriers, to (post-)wartime destruction, shifting borders and the dismantling of industry carried out by the USSR not only in Germany, but also in Poland, Czechoslovakia and Hungary. Since the wartime losses could be compensated for quite quickly (although more quantitatively than qualitatively), the USSR's more than four-decade-long dominance – with all the political, social and economic consequences that went along with it – had a crucial impact on the state of Eastern European transportation.

Almost from the outset, all transportation in the Eastern bloc was subordinated to the military, political and economic aims of the USSR, which, for all practical purposes, became both the brain and the backbone of the region. One bloc now contained countries that had formerly belonged to different transportation networks, that were poorly interconnected and had no experience of mutual trade (e.g. Poland and Bulgaria), and that had traditionally been in conflict with one another (e.g. Czechoslovakia and Hungary or Hungary and Romania). Apart from Poland and the former Baltic states (which reverted to their pre-1918 situation as far as transportation is concerned), the remaining countries in the region were not connected to the USSR by rail, which was the most important means of transportation throughout nearly the entire period

---

16 See Jahan Salehi and Richard W. Bulliet, 'Łączność i komunikacja społeczna' [Connectivity and communication], in *Historia XX wieku*, ed. Richard W. Bulliet (Warsaw: Bertelsmann, 2001), 377–98; John C. Spychalski, 'Transport', ibid., 399–432.

17 Marc Levinson, *The Box: How the Shipping Container Made the World Smaller and the World Economy Bigger* (Princeton, NJ: Princeton University Press, 2008); Edna Bonacich and Jake B. Wilson, *Getting the Goods: Ports, Labor, and the Logistics Revolution* (Ithaca, NY: Cornell University Press, 2008); Christian Schäfer, *Kreuzfahrten: Die touristische Eroberung der Welt* (Nuremberg: Wirtschafts- und Sozialgeographisches Institut, 1998), 65–6; Gerd Wolf, *Die Entwicklung des Weltluftverkehrs nach dem Zweiten Weltkrieg* (Tübingen: J.C.B. Mohr, 1967); Axel Schulz, *Verkehrsträger im Tourismus: Luftverkehr, Bahnverkehr, Strassenverkehr, Schiffsverkehr* (München: Oldenbourg, 2009).

18 For general information about transport in this region, see, Werner Gumpel, *Das Verkehrswesen Osteuropas: Entwicklung und Gestaltung im Comecon* (Köln: Verlag Wissenschaft und Politik, 1967); Bogdan Mieczkowski, ed., *East European Transport: Regions and Modes* (The Hague et al.: Martinus Nijhoff, 1980); Bogdan Mieczkowski, *Transportation in Eastern Europe: Empirical Findings* (Boulder, CO: East European Quarterly and Columbia University Press, 1978); John Ambler, Denis J.B. Shaw, and Leslie Symons, eds, *Soviet and East European Transport Problems* (London: Croom Helm, 1985); Derek R. Hall, ed., *Transport and Economic Development in the New Central and Eastern Europe* (London: John Wiley & Sons, 1993).

considered here. Because of the differences in rail gauges, it practically had to be built up from scratch. This was extremely important in the case of transit countries such as Czechoslovakia, Hungary and particularly Poland. Poland offered the shortest route to East Germany, which the Soviets saw as a political and economic priority. On the one hand, transportation became an essential instrument for making the socialist states politically and economically dependent on the USSR, while on the other, it served as a means of building a 'socialist society'.

The creation of the Comecon (CMEA) in 1949 did not have a long-lasting effect on Central and Eastern European transportation. The Warsaw-based Permanent Commission on Transport – established in 1958 as a reaction to the creation of the European Common Market – had a greater impact.[19] Its aims were to coordinate prestigious many-year plans; to organize, unite and standardize international freight and passenger transportation; to streamline investments; and to coordinate research and development. For the first twenty years, it was divided into five departments: planning and economics; railways; waterways and shipping; road transportation; and passenger air transportation. In the mid-1970s, in an attempt to adapt to global changes in transportation, a separate department was created to deal with a wide range of transport issues and bring member nations into conformity with general economic and technological changes. Specialized departments were to deal with railways, waterways, motorized transport and motorways, and container transport. The former 'aviation' department was transformed into the Permanent Civil Aviation Commission.[20]

Although its achievements were great in terms of standardization, common tariffs and relieving transportation congestion (particularly on the railways), the Permanent Commission on Transport was unable to build a truly integrated transportation system. Problems that were not fully resolved were the difference in rail gauges between the USSR and most socialist countries, varying degrees of electrification (by the late 1970s, 28.2 per cent of lines had been electrified in the USSR, but only 10.3 per cent in Romania) and the 'motorization' of transportation. Thus, by the time Comecon had ceased to exist, the most important transport projects – the Trans-European North-South Motorway (TEM) and the Trans-European North-South Railway – had yet to be implemented. Although Comecon was created in order to isolate its member countries from Western economies, complete autarky was impossible. Soon after 1948, Yugoslavia was the first to turn towards the West, which continued to be a priority for it even after relations with the USSR had improved. With the demise of Stalinism, the margin of freedom increased in other countries in the region, such as Poland, Romania and Hungary, which were trying out their own transportation policies that would allow them to go beyond the Comecon borders, particularly for aviation and shipping.

Theoretically, economic integration – including transportation – should have been simpler in socialist countries than market economies because the state was capable of directing capital and human resources to key areas. However, transport turned out to be affected by all the problems that plagued top-down planned economies: huge losses, lack of competition and

---

19 On Comecon transport policy, see: Ignacy Tarski, ed., *Poland–RWPG–Świat. Współpraca krajów RWPG w zakresie transportu* [Poland – CMEA – the world: the cooperation of CMEA countries in the field of transport] (Warsaw: Państwowe Wydawnictwo Ekonomiczne, 1970); Ignacy Tarski, *System transportowy RWPG* [CMEA's transport system] (Warsaw: Wydawnictwa Komunikacji i Łączności, 1981); Jozef M. van Brabant, *Economic Integration in Eastern Europe: A Handbook* (New York: Routledge, 1989); Ewa Rumińska, *The CMEA-Integration of Planned Economies* (Warsaw: Central School of Planning and Statistics, 1992).

20 Bogdan Mieczkowski, 'The Influence of Transportation on the Development of Eastern Europe', in idem, *East European Transport*, 4.

irrational decision-making. On the one hand, industrialization reduced inter-regional inequality and differences in income distribution. It also changed consumption patterns and increased the number of 'modern' jobs in the provinces. But at the same time, it radically increased the burden and demands on the transport system, particularly since a considerable number of new industrial centres had been built from scratch in regions with poorly developed infrastructure, which led to certain sections of rail being overused while others were underused. The number of people employed in industry and mining rose from 5.9 to 6.7 million, while in the new centres, such industrial workers were in excess of 6 million.[21]

Like other processes of modernization (increased consumption, greater mobility due to changes in how people spent their free time, etc.), the development of industry and changes in the structure of trade (which, unlike the interwar period, involved more processed goods) radically increased the demand for goods and passenger transport in Eastern and Southeastern Europe.[22] Additionally, although the authorities in each country were developing their own heavy industry and automotive industry – which often served as proof that they enjoyed a certain autonomy from Moscow – they were also increasingly dependent on raw materials from the USSR (e.g. iron ore, coal, natural gas or crude oil), which obviously needed to be transported over long distances. For example, in 1965, the average distance for transporting hard coal and coke was 681 kilometres, crude oil 1,262 kilometres, ferrous metals 1,115 kilometres and timber 1,616 kilometres. For export, these already great distances grew even larger.

Throughout the entire region, the concentration of industry in larger centres coupled with widespread housing problems led to the emergence of a sizeable new group of people who lived in the countryside but worked in the cities, commuting to work every day (often distances as large as 100 kilometres). At the same time, the countryside and 'rusticity' came to be viewed as inferior in contrast to the cities and 'urbanity'.[23] This demanded that transportation between the cities and surrounding areas be improved, and indeed, these connections began to be bolstered throughout Central and Eastern Europe in the late 1950s.

Thus, it is hardly surprising that the transportation and freight industries in Central and Eastern Europe – particularly in former agricultural powerhouses like Romania, Bulgaria, Yugoslavia and Poland – began to employ increasingly more people.[24] However, this growth primarily resulted from a huge demand and the fact that labour productivity and technological capacity were much lower than in the West. In contrast, in developed market economies the number of people employed in transportation and freight was characteristically in decline: e.g. from 1950–1964 it fell from 7.7 to 5.8 per cent in the USA, from 10.5 to 8.2 per cent in France and from 9.1 to 7.5 per cent in Great Britain.[25]

---

21 Mieczkowski, *Transportation in Eastern Europe*, 17–19; Gumpel, *Das Verkehrswesen Osteuropas*, 30.
22 Mieczkowski, *Transportation in Eastern Europe*, 32–3.
23 Leszek Rudnicki and Henryk Woźniczka, *Chłopi-robotnicy* [Peasant workers] (Katowice: Fundacja dla Śląskiego Instytutu Naukowego, 1989); Dariusz Jarosz, '"Chłopskość" jako element stygmatyzacji w przestrzeni miejskiej w Polsce po 1945 r.' ['Peasantness' as a stigmatizing element in the urban sphere in Poland after 1945], in *Dzieje partii stronnictw chłopskich w Europie*, vol. 2, *W podzielonej Europie*, ed. Józef Ryszard Szaflik (Pułtusk: Akademia Humanistyczna im. Aleksandra Gieysztora, 2007), 393–408; Mieczkowski, *Transportation in Eastern Europe*, 36.
24 Szymon Balbin, *Rozwój i struktura zatrudnienia w krajach RWPG w latach 1950–1990* [Development and employment structure in CMEA countries, 1950–1990] (Warsaw: Centrum Informacji Naukowej, Technicznej i Ekonomicznej. Ośrodek Informacji Centralnej, 1974).
25 Mieczkowski, *Transportation in Eastern Europe*, 93 and 95.

Table 3.1 Employment in transportation and freight in socialist countries, 1950–1972 (percentage of the total number of employees)

Country	1950	1960	1972
Poland	4.6	5.4	6.5
East Germany	7.0 (1952)	7.2	7.5
Czechoslovakia	4.9	5.8	6.7
Hungary	4.2	6.8	7.6
Romania	2.2	2.8	4.4
Bulgaria	1.5 (1948)	4.1	6.0
Yugoslavia	2.0 (1952)	2.6	6.9

Source: Bogdan Mieczkowski, *Transportation in Eastern Europe: Empirical Findings* (Boulder, CO: East European Quarterly and Columbia University Press, 1978), 94.

By the 1960s, the aforementioned changes in all the socialist countries had already resulted in a similar, quite paradoxical situation: whereas in Western Europe and the USA the capacity of all types of transport exceeded the supply of goods to be transported, the opposite was true here. In the early 1970s, almost all types of transport in Eastern Europe had exceeded their limits, which affected the implementation (or rather non-implementation) of economic plans. Demography and social change were an important dimension of these economic problems. On the one hand, the exhaustion of labour 'reserves' from the post-war demographic boom led to a more rational management of the workforce. This was just as well, as new social expectations emerged, and even countries that had been less developed in the 1950s and 1960s such as Yugoslavia, Romania or Bulgaria made great strides thanks to education, media and improved connections with foreign countries. As in the West, there was a trend towards increased individual travel, so speed of movement, safety and comfort became more important. Yet people began to seek more convenient alternatives to their own cars (e.g. fast trains or aeroplanes), particularly for long journeys of over 200 kilometres. Also significant was the rise of a new, more technocratically oriented generation of political and economic leaders who (in the 1960s, for instance) resembled Western managers and had more realistic views on issues such as profitability and competition.[26] In the late 1970s and early 1980s, the USSR also profited from global trade, as it planned to connect the Trans-Siberian Railway to worldwide networks by linking it to the West with train ferries (e.g. from Mukran to Klaipeda) so as to avoid transit via politically unstable Poland.

Both at home and in joint ventures as part of Comecon, this encouraged the modernization that was required in order to keep up with global change and prevent the increasing likelihood of exclusion from the world market, particularly in shipping and aviation. Organizational and technological failures did prove to be an obstacle, however, and could often only be overcome through cooperation with Western companies or by buying licences. In the 1970s and 1980s, such cooperation provided a vital injection of know-how into the socialist economies. Examples include the construction of ship engines in Poland under French licence; the manufacture of certain helicopters and aeroplanes in Poland under foreign licences; Fiat factories in Poland, Yugoslavia and Bulgaria; and the production of train-carriage brakes for the Swiss firm Oerlikon in Poland and Yugoslavia.[27] There is no doubt that this transfer of knowledge,

---

26 Mieczkowski, 'Technological Change in Transportation in Eastern Europe', in idem, *East European Transport*, 282–316, here 289–90.
27 Mieczkowski, conclusion, in idem, *East European Transport*, 317–24.

technology and efficiency had a stronger effect than ideology and that it, to a certain extent, contributed to the collapse of the system.[28] However, it was unable to contribute to genuine transport reforms in Eastern Europe. The effects can still be felt today, even a quarter of a century after regime-change, economic transition and the fact that most countries in the region joined the European Union between 2004 and 2007.[29]

Railways

Opening up new regions of the empires through rail

Beginning in the mid-nineteenth century, empires that had access to territories in Central and Eastern Europe started building extensive railway networks. The Austrian, Bohemian and Moravian crown lands of the Habsburg monarchy had the most developed network. The very first railway lines of the Austro-Hungarian Empire ran from Linz to Budweis (1836) and from Vienna to Brünn/Brno (1838).[30] Between the 1860s and the 1870s, railway construction enjoyed a boom, so that all provinces were served by the railway system.[31] By the third quarter of the nineteenth century, the Austro-Hungarian Empire was linked with all neighbouring countries. The trains in the south were connected with the Italian network in the 1850s; northeastern trains were connected with the Prussian network, when Danzig (today Gdańsk) was linked with Vienna in 1862; and rails in Bukovina and Transylvania were connected with the Romanian railway network in the late 1870s.[32]

Another railway power in East Central Europe was the Kingdom of Prussia. The Prussian railway companies were important not only because of their extensive railway network, which stretched from Westphalia to East Prussia, but also because Prussian entrepreneurs, such as the famous Bethel Henry Strousberg, invested in foreign railway construction, for instance, in the newly founded state of Romania (Moldovia and Wallachia) between 1869 and 1873.[33] Starting in 1843, the first rail connections east of Berlin were built to Posen (today Poznań), Breslau (today Wrocław) and Stettin (today Szczecin).[34] Other eastern Prussian territories were linked up by the *Ostbahn* (Eastern Railway) in 1857, when the connection between Berlin and

---

28 Mieczkowski, 'The Influence of Transportation', 8–9. See Andrzej Korbonski, *CMEA, Economic Integration and Perestroika, 1985–1990* (Washington, DC: National Council for Soviet and East European Research, 1990); Paweł Bożyk and Józef Misala, *Stosunki gospodarcze Wschód–Zachód. Formy i mechanizmy* [East–West economic relations: forms and mechanisms] (Warsaw: PWE, 1988).

29 In Eastern Europe, one dollar of national income required twice as much for transport expenses. See Louis S. Thompson, 'Railways in Eastern Europe', in *What Role for the Railways in Eastern Europe?*, Report of the Hundred and Twentieth Round Table on Transport Economics, held in Cambridge (United Kingdom) on 12–13 September, 2001 (Paris: OECD Publications Service, 2001), 27–58, here 33–34.

30 Karl Bachinger, 'Das Verkehrswesen', in *Die Habsburgermonarchie 1848–1918*, vol. 1, *Die wirtschaftliche Entwicklung*, eds Adam Wandruszka and Peter Urbanitsch (Vienna: Verlag der Österreichischen Akademie der Wissenschaften, 1973), 278–322.

31 Ibid., 291–5.

32 Mariana Hausleitner, *Die Rumänisierung der Bukowina: Die Durchsetzung des nationalstaatlichen Anspruchs Großrumäniens 1918–1944* (München: Oldenbourg, 2001), 44; Jan Musekamp, 'The Royal Prussian Eastern Railway (Ostbahn) and its Importance for East-West Transportation', in Roth and Jacolin, *Eastern European Railways*, 117–27, here 120.

33 Ralf Roth, 'Introduction: Eastern European Railways in Transition', in Roth and Jacolin, *Eastern European Railways*, 1–21, here 7.

34 Musekamp, 'The Royal Prussian Eastern Railway (Ostbahn)', 118.

Königsberg (today Kaliningrad) was established and further linked with the Russian rail network in 1861. All passengers had to change trains at the border due to the differing rail gauges.[35]

The Russian Empire came to the game rather late with the construction of the Trans-Siberian Railway. At first there was little progress in the European part of the empire. The project to create a rail line between Moscow and Sebastopol was not initiated until Russia's defeat in the Crimean War.[36] Thus, constructed in 1848, the first connection from Warsaw did not go to Moscow, but to Vienna. The Russian section of the line to Warsaw was largely state-financed, while the Austrian section received private funding. In 1862, the capital of the Kingdom of Poland was finally connected with St. Petersburg, the capital of the Russian Empire.[37]

Railway construction on the Balkan peninsula was distributed unequally. The first lines within the Ottoman Empire were built in the 1860s, which was relatively late, and connected the Danube with the Black Sea between Cernavodă and Constanța and between Ruse and Varna. In 1869, Baron Maurice de Hirsch received a concession from the Ottoman government for the Compagnie de Chemins de Fer Orientaux (Oriental Railway) – of which he was the principal shareholder – to build a rail connection between Constantinople and Vienna. This route later became known as the Orient Express. Before the link was completed, rail construction was affected by the geopolitical consequences of the 1878 Congress of Berlin. The Treaty of Berlin, the final act of the Congress, compelled not only the remainder of the Ottoman Empire (specifically Eastern Rumelia), but also the Kingdoms of Bulgaria and Serbia to complete construction of a rail line that ran through their territory, so that in 1888, the first train to travel between Vienna and Constantinople via Belgrade and Sofia completed its trip.[38]

The early history of rail in Central and Eastern Europe has features that were, on the one hand, particular to the region, while on the other, were part of general developments on the continent. Until the mid-nineteenth century, passenger transport, information exchange and the movement of goods were primarily conducted via water. It is not by chance that the historical literature refers to the 'canal age', a period in which canals were frenetically built in order to guarantee the smooth flow of traffic on rivers and seas.[39] In the eastern part of the continent, for example, the Danube became one of the most important transport routes after the advent of steam power. The first railway lines in the adjacent countries were themselves short connections between cities and the Danube, such as the previously mentioned Linz–Budweis, Varna–Ruse and Cernavodă–Constanța lines. Not until trains were able to connect a number of different provinces and be expanded into networks could they offer a real alternative to water traffic.

After the first pioneering projects, which were motivated by enthusiasm for technology and the promise of quick profits, governments often stepped in to provide systematic coordination of construction projects that had initially been private ventures.[40] Since most railway

---

35 Ibid., 120–22.
36 Roth, 'Introduction: Eastern European Railways', 3.
37 Marcin Przegiętka, '1918, 1945 and 1989: Three Turning Points in the History of Polish Railways in the Twentieth Century', in Roth and Jacolin, *Eastern European Railways*, 131–44, here 131–2.
38 Alexandre Kostov, 'Entre l'influence occidentale et les efforts nationaux : Le choix des systèmes et du financement des chemins de fer dans les Balkans', *Balkan Studies* (Etudes balkaniques) 23 (2001): 11–20, here 12–14.
39 Peter Maw, *Transport and the Industrial City: Manchester and the Canal Age, 1750–1850* (Manchester: Manchester University Press, 2013), 69–80.
40 Ivan Jakubec, 'Integration or Decentralization? The Construction of Waterways and Railways in Cisleithania', in Borodziej, Holubec and von Puttkamer, *Mastery and Lost Illusions*, 183–204, here 194–5.

tracks were built on behalf of an empire, they often connected the respective imperial capital with the individual provinces. These connections were thus used as a means of imperial expansion, fulfilling both strategic and economic ends. The railroad was intended to improve the mobility and supply of troops in times of war and to further economic exchange in times of peace, even if this meant simply transporting raw materials from the provinces. But trains also contributed to the expansion of tourism and were supposed to make the imperial centres accessible to all subjects.[41]

The expansion of imperial railway networks had considerable social consequences. Although imperial class society was mirrored in the railroad classes, the shared perception among all social strata that the same train transported everyone, whether rich or poor, was not insignificant.[42] In practice, however, travel conditions differed considerably between the separate luxury compartments of first class and the 'wooden carriages' of fourth class. Still, the social spaces of the different classes were not hermetically sealed off from one another, and at the rail stations in particular, there was increased contact. In the late nineteenth century, the railway offered lower social groups such as seasonal labourers and peasants their first opportunity to take part in the acceleration brought about by modernity. In the end, the railway journey not only stirred up social hierarchies, but also defined new gender-specific modes of behaviour.[43]

The fact that railway construction in Eastern Europe was strongly oriented toward imperial interests also had considerable consequences for the states that gradually broke away from the imperial structure. The construction of the long-distance connection between Vienna and Constantinople, which necessarily passed through Serbian territory, left Serbian authorities with no leeway to develop competing rail projects.[44] Conversely, Romania greatly benefited from the competition between Prussia and the Habsburg monarchy and was able to expand its rail network extensively around the new Bucharest traffic hub between 1869 and 1873, shortly after declaring independence. It was built by Prussian entrepreneurs with Bismarck's support, who had hopes of breaking through Austria's command of the trade route along the lower Danube.[45] Even after the Congress of Berlin in 1878, which strengthened the independence of the younger countries in the Balkans, determining the specifics of infrastructure development remained the prerogative of the large European powers.[46]

Before the turn of the century, there were already international railway policies dedicated to establishing connections beyond imperial borders. Within this context, the policies aimed to create good links between the capitals of the important European empires. Two of the most famous railway lines traversed the continent from Paris in the west to St. Petersburg in the east, and from Paris or Berlin via Vienna to Constantinople. The Northern (Nord) Express and

---

41 Frithjof Benjamin Schenk, 'Mastering Imperial Space? The Ambivalent Impact of Railway Building in Tsarist Russia', in *Comparing Empires: Encounters and Transfers in the Long Nineteenth Century*, eds Jörn Leonard and Ulrike von Hirschhausen (Göttingen: Vandenhoeck & Ruprecht, 2011), 60–77, here 62–3.
42 Wolfgang Schivelbusch, *The Railway Journey: The Industrialization of Time and Space in the Nineteenth Century*, trans. Anselm Hollo (Oakland, CA: University of California Press, 1986), 72–5.
43 Frithjof Benjamin Schenk, *Russlands Fahrt in die Moderne: Mobilität und sozialer Raum im Eisenbahnzeitalter* (Stuttgart: Franz Steiner Verlag, 2014), 196–200, 216.
44 Henry Jacolin, 'Serbia's Access to the Sea, 1830–2006', in Roth and Jacolin, *Eastern European Railways*, 69–86, here 69–71.
45 Roth, 'Introduction: Eastern European Railways', 7.
46 Kostov, 'Entre l'influence occidental', 14–15.

the Orient Express were very special trains, not only because they connected famous cities, but also because they contained sleeping cars, which increased travel comfort significantly.[47]

State interventions contributed substantially to the funding of railway construction. Only a few years after the first lines had been built on the continent, companies came to discover that most lines either did not generate any profit at all or only did so on short sections of track. The first serious plunge in railway share prices in the Austro-Hungarian Empire came in 1845, which led the government to buy up most of the shares with the help of its own credit institution. Up until the First World War, state loans and guarantees played an important role in rail construction, either by guaranteeing a certain rate of interest for investors or by nationalizing unprofitable sections of track.[48] The Prussian Eastern Railway (Ostbahn) to Königsberg also received the support of King Friedrich Wilhelm IV and, as a state-owned enterprise, was financed using public bonds.[49] The problem of financing and the degree of state involvement continued to concern railway planners in the interwar period. Private capital was always desired for such complex and costly endeavours, but it was not always guaranteed, especially if strategic interests that did not necessarily contribute to the railways' profitability were at play.[50] The new countries in Eastern Europe before and after the First World War were particularly dependent on foreign loans. Similar to the aforementioned Prussian capital investments in Romanian railways in the 1870s, it was French loans that made it possible for the Republic of Poland to expand its rail network in the 1920s.[51]

Before the start of the First World War, the three empires built up an extensive rail network in Central and Eastern Europe. The varied density of rail lines both between and within individual empires was significant. This becomes clear if one considers the example of the Second Polish Republic, where the ratio of the lengths of railways that had been part of the Russian Empire to those that had been part of the Habsburg monarchy and Prussia was 1:2:6.[52] Even within the Habsburg monarchy itself, the difference between the individual crown lands was considerable. The density of the rail network decreased as the distance to Vienna and Budapest increased; it was most sparse in the peripheral regions of Galicia, Dalmatia, Croatia and Bukovina.[53]

During the war, the rail lines in the western part of the Russian Empire suffered serious damage, especially because of the destruction of bridges at the Bug and Vistula Rivers. Nevertheless, the German and Austrian occupiers had already begun replacing the broad-gauge tracks in the western part of the Russian Empire with the standard gauge in order to improve supply lines. The newly founded countries of Poland, Lithuania and Latvia profited from this technical adaptation after the war.[54] All in all, the empires left the new nation states a mixed legacy.

---

47 Musekamp, 'The Royal Prussian Eastern Railway (Ostbahn)', 121; Irene Anastasiadou, *Constructing Iron Europe: Transnationalism and Railways in the Interbellum* (Amsterdam: Amsterdam University Press, 2011), 35–6.
48 Bachinger, 'Das Verkehrswesen', 282–95.
49 Musekamp, 'The Royal Prussian Eastern Railway (Ostbahn)', 119–20.
50 Martin Kvizda, 'Czech Military Railways: History and a Comparative Analysis of the Czech Railway Network's Efficiency', in Roth and Jacolin, *Eastern European Railways*, 99–116, here 102.
51 Roth, 'Introduction: Eastern European Railways', 7; Przegiętka, '1918, 1945 and 1989: Three Turning Points', 135.
52 Włodzimierz Borodziej, *Geschichte Polens im 20. Jahrhundert* (München: C.H. Beck, 2010), 21.
53 Bachinger, 'Das Verkehrswesen', 301–3.
54 Christoph Kopper, 'Der Erste Weltkrieg als Eisenbahnkrieg', in Roth and Schlögel, *Neue Wege in ein neues Europa*, 222–34, here 232.

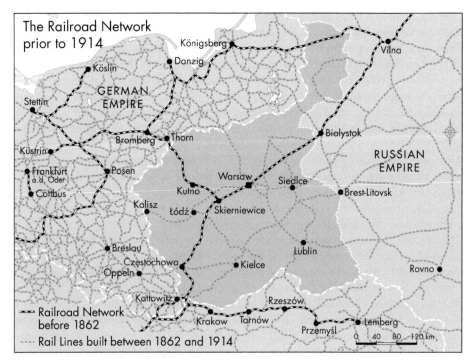

Map 3.1 The railway network before 1914
Source: Włodzimierz Borodziej, *Geschichte Polens im 20. Jahrhundert* (Munich: C.H. Beck, 2010), 483, copyright: Peter Palm, Berlin.

The railway in the service of the nation states

In many respects, the year 1918 only partly marked a turning point in railway history. Rails were no longer built by order of the imperial centre; instead, the newly emerged countries also wanted to prove themselves in this area. The objectives that were pursued, however, remained basically the same. In most of the newly established countries the most important urban centres were already linked to the train lines, while the regions that had belonged to different empires were poorly connected. For example, the former Austrian crown land of Galicia had eight connections to the other Habsburg territories and only two leading into the territory comprised by the former Russian Kingdom of Poland. In the end, it was the Polish government that had to take on the difficult task of creating a unified network, because parts of the new republic had previously belonged to three different empires. There were additional problems due to the vast damage caused by the First World War and the Polish–Soviet War. In the decades that followed, efforts concentrated on creating a functioning network with connections between the different railway sections inherited by the new nation. To take one example, economic and political concerns motivated the construction of a modern rail connection to the new Baltic Sea harbour at Gdynia, which was built to compete with the Free State of Danzig.[55]

---

55 Przegiętka, '1918, 1945 and 1989: Three Turning Points', 133–5.

The Kingdom of Serbs, Croats and Slovenes (SHS), which was founded in 1918, also had to merge existing lines and repair infrastructure damaged during the war, but things here took a different course than in Poland. As a consequence of the border drawn between the Kingdom of SHS (Yugoslavia) and Italy, the existing direct connections to Trieste and Fiume/Rijeka were now at the crossroads of a new political situation. Thus, one priority of the Yugoslav government was to build an alternative connection to the Adriatic Sea. Another consideration was to create a direct connection from Belgrade to the sea, as earlier plans had been blocked by the Habsburg monarchy. Most of these ideas never got beyond the planning stage until after 1945.[56]

Hungary was in many respects an exception. The Austria-Hungarian Compromise of 1867 gave the Hungarian government sovereignty in the area of infrastructure development. From this point on, railway construction was aligned with the interests of Budapest. Starting in the 1880s, 62 per cent of the largely unprofitable rail sections were nationalized and organized according to new principles. Returns were thus no longer the main criterion for the rail industry. Instead, the government pursued policies of social integration, which in turn also benefited the economy. Financed through taxes, a new system of tariffs with low prices was introduced, centred around Budapest. Passengers and freight that covered more than 400 kilometres paid the same price, no matter how far they travelled into Transleithania.[57] In contrast, lines going to Vienna were not subsidized and were thus disproportionately expensive. As a result, the subsidized lines were used to full capacity prior to the First World War.[58] After the war, Hungary lost about 60 per cent of its rail network due to the shifting of borders that followed out of the Treaty of Trianon. The history of Hungarian railways between the wars is thus one of disintegration or, at best, stagnation. Similar to many other countries in the region, lack of sufficient financial resources, which were further diminished during the world financial crisis, led to increasing neglect of the remaining train lines.[59] Not until 1939 did railway construction regain momentum. The expansion of the country's territory as a result of the First and Second Vienna Awards of 1938 and 1940[60] were also used as an opportunity to increase rail investment. Between 1938 and 1943, Hungarian authorities built and renovated more than the other countries in the region had in the preceding 20 years.[61] This short flourishing of the rail sector in Hungary demonstrates once again how imperial penetration and expansion of transportation went hand in hand.

Aside from these state-led projects that were motivated by either national, multinational or imperial interests, there were also international collaborations in the interwar period. In contrast to the age of empire, the new impulses of development in Central and Eastern Europe did not emanate from the German-speaking countries. After a fiasco with investments in Russia, France and French railway developers discovered East Central Europe for themselves and pursued

---

56 Jacolin, 'Serbia's Access to the Sea', 77–9.
57 These policies can be summarized by the term 'nationalizing empires'. See Jörn Leonhard, 'Multi-Ethnic Empires and Nation-Building: Comparative Perspectives on the Late Nineteenth Century and the First World War', in *Nationalizing Empires*, eds Stefan Berger and Alexei Miller (Budapest: Central European University Press, 2015), 629–46.
58 Imre Perger, 'The History of Railway Passenger Transportation in Hungary – From the Monarchy to the Twenty-First Century', in Roth and Jacolin, *Eastern European Railways*, 87–98, here 87–9.
59 Ibid., 90.
60 This territorial expansion included southern Slovakia, Carpathian Ruthenia (or less common: Transcarpathian Ukraine), northern Transylvania (formerly Romania) and the Bačka (formerly Yugoslavia).
61 Perger, 'The History of Railway Passenger Transportation', 92.

policies that deliberately excluded Germany and Austria. With an eye towards constructing international connections, the French wanted the countries of Central and Eastern Europe to serve as a *cordon sanitaire*, that is, as a buffer zone to contain Germany's feared expansionism. In concrete terms, this meant that the most important continental arterial routes were to circumvent German territory. Known as 'the line of the 45th parallel', the east–west axis was to be established farther south than the previous one, starting in the French port of Bordeaux and ending in Odessa via Lyon, Venice, Trieste, Zagreb, Belgrade and Bucharest. Of the more than 2,500 kilometres planned, only about 200 – at the Yugoslav–Romanian border – were ultimately ever built. Thus, one could hardly call it a new rail project; nevertheless, it signalled a new orientation of international economic cooperation and infrastructure links.[62] The line to Istanbul as well, the Orient Express, was relocated along the 45th parallel, running from Trieste through the Balkan States to Istanbul; today it is called the 'Venice Simplon-Orient-Express'.[63] In the wake of the world economic crisis, the International Labour Office of the League of Nations propagated a new form of internationalism. It proposed the massive expansion of international transportation networks as a way to exit the crisis and reduce unemployment. The project did not get beyond the conception phase, however, as it was overrun by the expansionist policies of Nazi Germany.[64] During the war itself, the German Reich Railway [*Deutsche Reichsbahn*] operated the rail network in the conquered territories in Eastern Europe. In 1942, this network achieved its greatest expansion, extending over 42,000 kilometres. The trains of the *Reichsbahn* facilitated the transport of troops as well as the 'resettlement' policies and deportations of Nazi Germany. National Socialist visions for the period after the war foresaw a new broad-gauge rail network that would integrate the conquered territories.[65]

In sum, it can be said that after the First World War fewer new railway lines were built than in the previous period. The focus of the new Eastern European countries was to use their railway policies to support the new political order. It was therefore either a matter of standardizing the nationalized traffic networks that had previously been part of several different empires or of creating new transportation hubs or connections. On the other hand, maintenance of the railway infrastructure overwhelmed most of the newly founded countries, which repeatedly had to rely on foreign loans until the world economic crisis finally dried up this source of capital too. This explains why electrification progressed only very slowly. It would remain a task for the post-war period.

State-socialist 'railway economics'

Throughout a large part of the post-war period, the railways remained the most important means of transportation in Central and Eastern Europe, both for freight and for passenger travel. This was in part due to the continental nature of the Comecon countries, their relative lack of development in terms of motorization and types of rail freight (which predominantly consisted of raw materials, often transported over great distances) as well as the weakness of ports and merchant fleets, particularly in the early years.

---

62 Anastasiadou, *Constructing Iron Europe*, 49.
63 Ibid., 69–70.
64 Ibid., 80–93.
65 Klaus Hildebrand, 'Die Deutsche Reichsbahn in der nationalsozialistischen Diktatur 1933–1945', in *Die Eisenbahn in Deutschland: Von den Anfängen bis zur Gegenwart*, ed. Lothar Gall (München: C.H. Beck, 1999), 220–43.

The railways were better able to cope with wartime damage.[66] It was also much easier to keep railways under strict control than road transport, for example. As already mentioned, the USSR's political, military and economic dominance played a significant role in this part of the continent. Until the mid-1950s, railways in Eastern European socialist countries (except Yugoslavia) were under the (in)formal supervision of the USSR: Soviet advisors worked in the ministries, while Soviet management models (central supervision of nationalization and organization of transportation[67]) and ideologization (together with labour productivity targets) were adopted. Productivity was often achieved by means of terror and fear.

During and directly after the war, the priorities of the Soviet authorities were to provide for their own departments and to take home wartime booty and the spoils of dismantled technology. Thus, as the frontline shifted, some railway lines in Poland, Czechoslovakia and Hungary were converted to broad gauge. With the help of often coerced labour from the local population, up to 25 kilometres of rails were widened every day! For example, over ten thousand people worked to widen the rails in Poland, mostly peasants using their own tools and horsepower. In 1945, half of all haulage (and approximately a quarter in 1946) in Hungary was done for the Soviet army – for free, of course.[68] Although Polish railways were officially under Soviet supervision only from November 1944 until July 1945, by the end of 1945 there were still 675 kilometres of broad-gauge (1520-mm) track, and by the end of 1946 there were 546 kilometres, and Soviet transports enjoyed a special, unmonitored status. The line from Katowice to Przemyśl, used to supply coal to the USSR, was converted to standard gauge in 1947.[69]

Several broad-gauge sections were not turned back to European standards. They were kept at major crossing points along the Polish–Soviet border, both for economic and military reasons.[70] One example was Line 217 in former East Prussia (the Elbing/Elbląg–Königsberg stretch of the Prussian Eastern Railway). Initially, it was used to appropriate booty and war reparations; then a military logistical centre was built nearby in the 1950s to duplicate the Soviet military base across the border in Mamonovo. The line was only ever used once for military purposes, namely during the deployment of troops into Czechoslovakia in 1968. During the 1970s and

---

66 For example, over half of Hungary's mainlines and a quarter of its branch lines, 85% of bridges and 28% of railway buildings were destroyed, while its rolling stock was either completely destroyed or commandeered. In Poland after the war, 38% of tracks had been destroyed, 46% of railway bridges and viaducts, 37% of railway buildings and 72% of rail traffic safety systems. The surviving rolling stock and infrastructure in East Germany, Poland, Czechoslovakia and Hungary was subject to dismantling by the Soviets. See Perger, 'The History of Railway Passenger Transportation', 92; Zbigniew Taylor, *Rozwój i regres sieci kolejowej w Polsce* [The development and regression of the railway network in Poland] (Warsaw: PAN IGiPZ, 2007), 58; Stanisława Zamkowska, *Odbudowa i funkcjonowanie kolei polskich 1944–1949* [The Reconstruction and the Functioning of Polish Railways 1944–1949] (Warsaw: Wydawnictwa Komunikacji i Łączności, 1984).

67 Until 1948–1949, for example, the Polish PKP owned a mainline for coal built during the interwar years that was formally the property of the French–Polish Rail Association, along with the standard-gauge, private Electric Commuter Railway built in 1927, as well as other private narrow-gauge railways designed for commuters, forestry (1,081 kilometres!) and sugar factories. Only industrial trains did not fall within the PKP's purview. See Taylor, *Rozwój i regres*, 61.

68 Zsuzsa Frisnyák, 'The Centrally Planned Economy and Railways in Hungary', in Roth and Jacolin, *Eastern European Railways*, 171–82, here 171; Mieczkowski, 'The Influence of Transportation', 2–3.

69 Taylor, *Rozwój i regres*, 58–60; Przegiętka, '1918, 1945 and 1989: Three Turning Points', 137–8; Gumpel, *Das Verkehrswesen Osteuropas*, 73.

70 Ogólnopolska Baza Kolejowa, 'Wykaz linii' [Railway timetables], www.bazakolejowa.pl//index.php?dzial=linie&sort=id&wask=0&norm=0&szer=1&przedzial=0 (accessed 8 August 2014).

1980s, it also played an important role as a transit route between East Germany and the USSR,[71] and it still exists to this day.

The situation was similar on other new borders of the USSR, where satellite states such as Romania, Czechoslovakia and Hungary would build or extend – often on their own initiative – routes that led to the border, allowing formerly insignificant stations to gain a new lease on life. This was the case with, for example, the Csap/Čop junction (which became Chop in Soviet Ukraine in 1946) in former Hungarian/Czechoslovak Subcarpathian Rus, where the railway lines from Lvov to Košice and Budapest forked. Both lines were strategically important for military and economic reasons and new border towns were even created near them. On the Slovak side, the railway town of Čierna nad Tisou was founded in 1946, with a huge railway junction that connected Czechoslovak tracks with newly laid broad-gauge tracks from Ukraine. The Hungarian border town of Záhony also grew more important, since a broad-gauge line ran from it to the industrial town of Kisvárda. In both cases, it turned out to be a long-term investment from which both towns still benefit today.

Improvements to heavy industry, particularly metallurgy, increased the demand for Soviet ore to such an extent that it became essential to build connections that guaranteed unimpeded transport from deposits in Krivoi Rog. The first plans for such a line were drawn up in the late 1950s, at the same time as the construction of a huge steelworks factory near Košice was being planned (construction was completed in 1965, and it is now U.S. Steel Košice). The idea of a route from Čierna nad Tisou was abandoned and a brand-new line from Uzhhorod was planned. The construction of this 88-kilometre stretch lasted from 1964 to 1966 and it was electrified in 1978.[72] The westernmost broad-gauge railway line was constructed under similar circumstances. Built between 1976 and 1979, the so-called Steelworks/Sulphur Line leading from the Soviet border in Hrubieszów to Sławków in Silesia (394.6 kilometres) was intended to supply ore to Poland's largest industrial investment of the 1970s – the Katowice Steelworks in Dąbrowa Górnicza. To prevent trains from being sent back empty, which was common when transporting raw materials, the same line was also used to send sulphur mined in Poland to the USSR.[73] Both lines became examples of Central and Eastern European railway investments from the period of 'real' socialism. Paradoxically, these projects continued to be viable after 1989: at the end of the first decade of the twenty-first century, they still compete for container cargo brought from the Far East on the Trans-Siberian Railway.

In the late 1950s, breaking away from the restrictive practice of imitating Soviet models had become possible, so that the autonomous development of transportation (including rail) considerably increased. The Warsaw-based Organization for Cooperation between Railways (OSJD) was set up in 1956, and, with the exception of the USSR, North Vietnam, Cuba and North Korea, all of its members were also members of the UIC (International Union of Railways), which had existed before the war. Technical and organizational contacts between the two organizations became especially crucial when the exchange of freight and passengers intensified

---

71 Wikipedia, 'Linia kolejowa nr 217' [Railway line no. 217], http://pl.wikipedia.org/wiki/Linia_kolejowa_nr_217 (accessed 8 August 2014); Zbigniew Tucholski, *Polskie Koleje Państwowe jako środek transportu wojsk Układu Warszawskiego* [Polish state railways as a means of transport for the Warsaw Pact troops] (Warsaw: Wydawnictwa Komunikacji i Łączności, 2009).

72 Petr Štefek, 'Słowacki LHS czyli Širokorozchodná trať (ŠRT)' [The Slovak LHS or broad-gauge track (ŠRT)], *Świat Kolei* 10 (2007): 16–17.

73 Tomasz Ciemnoczułowski, *Szerokim torem LHS* [Along the Sławków broad-gauge track] (Lodz: Dom Wydawniczy Księży Młyn, 2009).

between East and West after the end of Stalinism.[74] At the same time, the development of industry and motorization led to a heightened demand for raw materials (ore, coal, crude oil), which was sometimes imported from abroad, mostly from the USSR.

Lasting for almost a decade, post-war reconstruction mainly involved rebuilding old or destroyed infrastructure, sometimes in a temporary fashion. New investment was usually limited to the most essential tasks, which was an effect of the new political and economic realities, among them altered borders, Soviet domination, military issues and planned economies. These tasks included building railway lines from Czechoslovakia, Hungary and Romania to the Soviet border. In Poland, the 160-kilometre line from Skierniewice to Łuków was completed in 1954 to facilitate transit from the USSR to East Germany, avoiding the Warsaw junction. Another line leading to the hard coal mine in Turoszów opened in 1948.[75] In Romania, new lines were constructed to simplify coal transport from mines in the Jiu Valley.[76]

The situation was different in Yugoslavia. After 1948, it no longer had to deal with interference from the USSR, so it could build new lines according to the priorities of its individual republics (particularly Serbia's 'maritime' ambitions) and attempt to bring development standards in various parts of the federation up to par with one another. The most important investment was a line from Belgrade to the port of Bar in Montenegro, which would have radically shortened the journey from poorer regions (Southern Serbia, Kosovo, Sandžak and Montenegro) to the Adriatic Sea, thus making them more active and allowing them to exploit their natural mineral and timber resources. The distance from Belgrade to the port of Rijeka was 643 kilometres, while to Bar it was only 476 kilometres (from Niš, it was 865 and 560 kilometres respectively, and from Skopje 1,085 and 673 kilometres). Nevertheless,

> the Croats opposed the Adriatic Line in any form because its construction would have taken years. They put forward two other priorities: building a port near Rijeka on Yugoslavian territory close to the Zagreb–Rijeka railway line, and completing the line between Zagreb and the ports of Split and Šibenik, the extremities of which had already been built. ... For Croats, this project was as significant as the Adriatic Line was for the Serbs.[77]

Finally, in 1951, the Federal Economic Council of Yugoslavia decided to build a Belgrade–Bar line that was supposed to serve 49 per cent of the country's territory and ten million people. Construction began in 1952 and was completed in 1976, following enormous technical and financial complications. The line proved to be extremely vital after the breakup of Yugoslavia, when Bar became the main port of the post-1991 Yugoslavia.[78]

The four decades of 'real socialism', from the late 1950s until the system collapsed in 1989, was a calm, stable period for the railways only in appearance. In actual fact, they constantly faced new challenges, ranging from technological issues to rapidly growing numbers of passengers and their higher expectations. The two tables below provide an overview of Central and Southeastern European railways, as well as the starting point for an unavoidably superficial analysis.

---

74 Paul Véron, 'Railway Integration in Europe: UIC – A Key Player of East–West Railway Integration', in Roth and Jacolin, *Eastern European Railways*, 243–56, here 249.
75 Taylor, *Rozwój i regres*, 67.
76 Adelina Oana Ştefan, 'Passengers' Railway Identity in Socialist Romania during the 1950s and 1960s', in Roth and Jacolin, *Eastern European Railways*, 215–32, here 218–19.
77 Jacolin, 'Serbia's Access to the Sea', 78.
78 Ibid., 80–84.

Table 3.2 Length of railway lines in operation, 1950–2000

Country	Year	Total (thousand km)	Including electrified lines (thousand km)	Per 100 km^2 (km)	Per 10,000 inhabitants (km)
Bulgaria	1950	4	-	3.6	5.5
	1960	4.1	-	3.7	5.2
	1974	4.3	1.2	3.9	4.9
	1986	4.3	2.3	3.9	-
	1990	4.3	2.6	3.9	-
	2000	4.3	2.7	3.9	
Czechoslovakia	1950	13.1	0.1	10.3	10.6
	1960	13.1	0.8	10.3	9.6
	1974	13.2	2.7	10.4	9.0
	1986	13.1	3.5	10.3	-
	1990	13.1	3.9	10.3	-
Czech Republic	2000	9.4	2.8	12.1	
Slovakia	2000	3.7	1.5	7.5	
Yugoslavia	1950	11.6	0.1	4.5	7.1
	1960	11.9	0.2	4.6	6.4
	1974	10.3	2.5	4.0	4.9
	1986	9.2	3.5	3.6	-
	1990	9.5	3.7	3.7	-
Poland	1950	26.3	0.2	8.4	10.5
	1960	26.9	1	8.6	9.0
	1974	26.7	5.1	8.5	7.9
	1986	26.8	9.4	8.6	-
	1990	26.2	11.4	7.7	-
	2000	21.5	11.9	6.9	5.6
Romania	1950	10.9	0.06	4.6	6.7
	1960	11	0.06	4.6	6.0
	1974	11	1.1	4.7	5.3
	1986	11.3	3.4	4.7	-
	1990	11.3	3.7	4.8	-
	2000	11	3.9	4.6	-
Hungary	1950	9.9	0.4	10.7	10.6
	1960	10	0.5	10.8	9.7
	1974	8.6	1.2	9.3	8.2
	1986	7.9	2	8.5	-
	1990	7.8	2.3	8.4	-
	2000	7.7	2.7	8.2	

Sources: Rocznik Statystyczny [Statistical yearbook] (Warsaw: Central Statistical Office), 1969, 673; RS 1976, 603; RS 1988, 582; RS 1993, 574–5; Statistical Yearbook of the Republic of Poland 2004 (Warsaw: Central Statistical Office of Poland, 2004), 827; The World Bank, 'Rail lines (total route-km)', http://data.worldbank.org/indicator/IS.RRS.TOTL.KM. For Yugoslavia 1918–1988, 'Statistički Godišnjak, Socialistička Rederativna Republika Jugoslavija' [Statistical yearbook of the Socialist Federal Republic of Yugoslavia] (Belgrade: Federal Statistical Office, 1989), 282.

Table 3.3 Structure of loads per type of transport, 1955–2000

Country	Year	% of total loads transported (in tonnes) By rail	By road	% of total loads transported (in tonne-kilometres) By rail	By road	Loads transported by railway (billion t-km)	Passengers transported by railway (billion passenger-km)
Bulgaria	1955	37	60	80	14	4.1	2.8
	1970	35.2	62.9	72.8	17.6	13.9	7.3
	1980	19.2	78.8	56.8	32.4	17.7	7.1
	1990	6.9	91.3	42.0	51.2	8.7 (1991)	4.9 (1991)
	2000					Rail – 5.5 Road – 6.4	Rail – 3.5 Road – 14.7
Czechoslovakia	1955	38	61	90	8	28.2	20.9
	1970	24.7	73.4	77.3	12.8	55.9	18.9
	1980	18.4	79.7	67.8	19.9	72.6	18.0
	1989	18.1	80.0	65.7	21.8	72.0	19.6
Czech Republic	2000					Rail – 18.2 Road – 39.0	Rail – 7.3 Road – 16.5
Slovakia	2000					Rail – 11.2 Road – 21.4	Rail – 2.9 Road – 10.3
Yugoslavia	1960	38	56	74	11	13.9	10.3
	1970	6 (1974)	92 (1974)	32 (1974)	57 (1974)	23.1	10.4
	1978	8.6	87.3	33.0	54.3	25.0 (1980)	10.3 (1980)
	1989	17.1	74.9	35.6	47.6	25.8	11.7
Poland	1955	41	50	91	7	52.0	37.0
	1970	30.1	68.0	79.9	12.7	99.3	36.9
	1980	17.8	79.9	67.8	22.4	135	46.3
	1990	22.2	74.4	65.0	23.4	65.1 (1991)	40.1 (1991)
	2000					Rail – 54.4 Road – 72.8	Rail – 24.1 Road – 31.7
Romania	1955	84	11	91	2	14.14	12.5
	1960	55	40	88	4	18.8	10.7
	1970	39.9	55.9	-	-	43.7	17.8
	1980	36.1	59.3	77.1	13.9	65.0	23.2
	1985	41.4	52.8	83.0	7.7	64.3	31.1
	1991	-	-	-	-	37.8	25.4
	2000					Rail – 16.4 Road – 14.3	Rail – 11.6 Road – 8.7
Hungary	1955	-	-	-	-	8.8	10.3
	1960	57	42	87	6	13.3	14.3
	1970	21.8	76.5	71.0	20.9	19.8	16.3
	1980	17.6	79.8	64.4	25.0	24.4	14.7
	1989	17.1	79.6	51.1	34.6	19.4	9.6
	2000					Rail – 8.4 Road – 19.1	Rail – 9.7 Road – 18.7

Sources: Rocznik Statystyczny [Statistical yearbook]: 1969, 673–4; RS 1976, 603–4; RS 1983, 544; RS 1988, 581–2; RS 1991, 558–9; RS 1993, 574–5; Statistical Yearbook of the Republic of Poland 2004, 827–8.

Tables 3.2 and 3.3 both illustrate well how statistical data can sometimes be misleading. When one considers traditional criteria such as railway-line length per 100 square kilometres or 10,000 inhabitants, the region was still infrastructurally divided into the developed North (East Germany, Poland, Czechoslovakia and Hungary) and the undeveloped South (Romania, Bulgaria and Yugoslavia) right until the end of the 'short' twentieth century. When interpreting this data, however, one must also take into account a variety of factors and qualitative changes. This is vital, for example, when trying to understand the (apparently) surprising constancy or even reduced lengths of railway lines (except for the USSR). As mentioned above, most investments immediately after the war were designed to reconstruct ruined infrastructure, not to build new routes. Of course, new routes were built until the railways faced a crisis due to the transition, but they were either designed to develop transportation hubs (e.g. Prague and Česká Třebová in Czechoslovakia), to create lines that were mostly of economic importance and that aimed to improve services to former industrial and mining centres (Upper Silesia in Poland, or Ústí nad Labem, Most and Sokolov in Czechoslovakia), or to connect with new industrial centres (Polish examples included new brown coal mines in Bełchatów, the power station in Połaniec, and textile mills in Zambrów).[79]

However, these new investments were unable to balance the losses incurred due to economic transformation and modernization, particularly in the 1960s and 1970s. Railway use increased radically for both passengers and freight, and the demand could not be satisfied by old methods, which normally relied on increasing the workforce and using infrastructure to the extreme until it physically deteriorated. Attempts were made to resolve some problems through Comecon. Nevertheless, incompatible infrastructure and huge, empty transports became serious problems in moving freight between member countries. To a certain extent, the former issue was solved by modernizing lines (mostly by electrification) and standardization, and the latter by creating a joint pool of freight cars between Poland, Bulgaria, Hungary, East Germany, Romania, the USSR and Czechoslovakia. In the 1960s, this pool comprised approximately 100,000 wagons and succeeded in reducing (but not eliminating) empty transports. The Soviet border continued to be a bottleneck. The aforementioned broad-gauge sections had not resolved the problem in any systemic way, and still required arduous, protracted, labour-intensive and costly unloading and reloading, or the wheel bogies of the train carriages had to be changed.[80]

Only in the case of crude oil imported from the USSR was pipeline transport a solution that significantly reduced the burden on the railways. In 1960, 87.9 per cent of freight transport between the Comecon countries took place by train, whereas in 1965 it had fallen to 72.6 per cent. This difference was not due to road transport (which actually doubled, but only from 0.1 to 0.2 per cent) or shipping (from 7.5 to 10.5 per cent), but to pipelines (from zero to 12 per cent).[81] In 1958, the construction of the Friendship (Druzhba) oil pipeline was agreed upon, and the initial phase was completed in 1964. Two branches of the pipeline transporting crude oil from the USSR to Poland, East Germany, Czechoslovakia and Hungary were supplemented by auxiliary branches (e.g. the so-called Pomeranian Pipeline, completed in 1975, to transport crude oil from the Gdańsk seaport to the refinery in Płock; or the branch from Rostock to Schwedt). In turn, a network of internal pipelines were added to these auxiliary lines to

---

79 Z. Anthony Kruszewski, 'Transportation in Poland: Development, Problems and Policies', in Mieczkowski, *East European Transport*, 28; Karel J. Kansky, 'Regional Transport Development and Policies in Czechoslovakia since 1945', in Mieczkowski, *Eastern European Transport*, 147–64, here 148–52.
80 Gumpel, *Das Verkehrswesen Osteuropas*, 84; Mieczkowski, *Transportation in Eastern Europe*, 156–7.
81 Mieczkowski, *Transportation in Eastern Europe*, 154.

carry the end products from the refineries (Płock, Schwedt, Bratislava and Százhalombatta in Hungary). The pipeline made countries in the region dependent on oil supplies from the USSR. Unsurprisingly, this led to attempts at various forms of diversification, including the development of oil terminals in ports (Gdańsk and Rostock), not to mention Poland, Czechoslovakia and Hungary's planned joint Adria Pipeline. However, this investment, planned to start in 1964, was begun only in 1984 and completed in 1989, on the eve of an entirely new era.[82] A separate issue was gas pipelines, the most important being the 4,550-kilometre Orenburg gas pipeline built in 1975–1979, which carried gas to Poland, East Germany, Czechoslovakia, Hungary, Yugoslavia and Italy.

During the 1960s, oil became a strategic raw material for the satellite states thanks to the development of the chemical industry and, above all, motorization. Likewise, road transport began to compete with the railways in many parts of Central and Southeastern Europe, particularly for smaller cargo over shorter distances. By the end of the 1950s, more goods were delivered by road than by rail (see Table 3.2). Most journeys were short, e.g. bricks to building sites, bread to shops or specialized deliveries that needed a quick turnover. Passenger transport was a different matter altogether. In the motorized West, railways were mostly used for longer journeys by the mid-1960s, whereas in the East, they were still the main way for workers living in the suburbs to reach the cities. In 1965, the average railway journey length was 61.8 kilometres in France and 82.6 kilometres in Italy, but just 35.3 kilometres in Poland and 34.5 in Czechoslovakia. The average Pole made 30.8 journeys a year, Czechoslovak citizens almost 45, while the French made just 12.6 journeys, and Italians 6.2.[83] However, in the 1950s and 1960s, increasingly less profitable and less productive rail transport over shorter distances began to be superseded by more flexible road transport, an ultimately irreversible shift. This mostly concerned those sections of track that were the most technologically underdeveloped or ill-suited to modernization (suburban narrow-gauge, forestry and industrial railways), as well as sections of predominantly suburban, lesser-used (and therefore costly) standard-gauge routes. In Hungary, 1,888 kilometres of routes were closed down from 1959 to 1980 (712 narrow-gauge and 1,176 broad-gauge), and 60 per cent of narrow-gauge railways in Yugoslavia were closed between 1965 and 1974. In Poland, 1,230 kilometres had ceased to exist by 1978, and by 1990, over 1,700 kilometres of narrow-gauge lines had been put out of service (certain standard-gauge sections were also decommissioned).[84] The largest drop in rail passengers was recorded in Yugoslavia, where passenger-car transport grew by around 20 per cent per year between 1966 and 1970 and by almost 11 per cent per year between 1971 and 1974.[85] Yugoslavia was also the first country in the region where long-distance road haulage began to radically supersede rail freight.

The stabilization of the 1970s, subsequent drops in passenger numbers, and increased quantities of goods transported over the next decade were to a considerable extent caused by the authorities' focus on freight. As a result, passenger transport – although cheap in most countries

---

82 Werner Gumpel, 'Integration of the Comecon Transport System', in Mieczkowski, *East European Transport*, 212–18; David Pinder and Bridget Simmonds, 'Oil Transports: Pipelines, Ports and the New Political Climate', in Hall, *Transport and Economic Development*, 49–63; Wikipedia, 'Adria oil pipeline', http://en.wikipedia.org/wiki/Adria_oil_pipeline (accessed 30 August 2014).

83 Mieczkowski, *Transportation in Eastern Europe*, 38.

84 Frisnyák, 'Centrally Planned Economy', 178; Perger, 'The History of Railway Passenger Transportation', 93; Taylor, *Rozwój i regres*, 73; Oleg Zinam, 'Evaluation of Transport Capacity in Yugoslavia', in Mieczkowski, *East European Transport*, 165–92, here 171.

85 Zinam, 'Evaluation of Transport Capacity', 170–71.

of the region thanks to high state subsidies – was characterized by low service standards, unreliability, constant delays and low speeds in comparison to the West.[86] The situation was only improved partially by the gradual electrification of the railways, particularly in the 1960s and 1970s, which paved the way for larger, faster trains. The fastest growth of electrified lines was recorded in countries with undeveloped infrastructure (e.g. Bulgaria and Romania), while in absolute terms, most of them were constructed in Hungary (whose rate of electrification was equalled only by Finland in the 1960s), Czechoslovakia and Poland, where on average 200 kilometres of lines were electrified annually (and even more in the 1980s, due to liquid fuel shortages). However, even in the most developed countries of the region only one third of all lines had been electrified by 1989, much of which was for the busiest national and international trains (e.g. Lvov–Prague or Prague–Warsaw).[87] On all other routes, modernization entailed the introduction of expensive, inefficient diesel locomotives. The steam engine became rare in the 1980s, and the last regular passenger steam train in Poland (and also in Europe) ceased operation on 1 May 2014 on the line Wolsztyn–Leszno.[88]

Modernization, automation and computerization of the rest of the infrastructure were not always able to keep pace with electrification, a fact that inhibited higher speeds. In the Comecon countries, the only long section on which passenger trains could reach speeds exceeding 160 kilometres per hour was the so-called Central Rail Line, built from 1971–1977 between Upper Silesia and Warsaw. Plans to extend it to Gdańsk and Wrocław were shelved in the 1980s due to the crisis.[89]

In the late 1980s, Poland focused on electrifying lines leading to its eastern border. This was not a manifestation of servility, but a struggle over transit that had been going on for two decades. It was also a matter of money, which had not been a key factor in railway links between the socialist countries for many years. In 1951, a single tariff was introduced for Comecon members, which mostly suited the USSR's interests. However, when market conditions began to play a larger role in mutual relations in the 1950s and 1960s, certain countries raised their tariffs in 1964 – by 17.5 per cent in Bulgaria and Romania, and 35 per cent in Czechoslovakia, East Germany and Poland, amongst others. In 1976, Poland withdrew from all its tariff agreements dating from 1951. Czechoslovakia and Hungary followed suit in 1980 and, after 1981, Hungary began raising its tariffs annually (by as much as 92 per cent in 1981!). On the one hand, this competitive struggle between Comecon countries made the increasingly tangible economic crisis more acute, and on the other, it was clear that they needed to adapt to international transportation standards, and containerization in particular. Incidentally, attempts to create a common container network were made in 1971, when container trains would leave weekly from Děčín in Czechoslovakia bound for Berlin and then the port of Rostock. In 1973, regular container transport was initiated between Košice and the USSR as well as between Warsaw and Berlin, followed by preparations to open lines connecting Sofia with Bucharest, and Budapest, Bratislava, Prague and Berlin with Rostock.

---

86 Jakubec, 'Integration or Decentralization?', 153.
87 Gumpel, *Das Verkehrswesen Osteuropas*, 95–6; Frisnyák, 'Centrally Planned Economy', 178; Kansky, 'Regional Transport Development', 151–52.
88 TVN24, 'Ostatnia taka linia w Europie. Parowozy znikają z Wielkopolski' [The last such line in Europe: steam Engines disappear from Greater Poland], 20 March 2014, www.tvn24.pl/poznan,43/ostatnia-taka-linia-w-europie-parowozy-znikaja-z-wielkopolski,409607.html (accessed 25 July 2016).
89 Wikipedia, 'Linia kolejowa nr 4' [Railway line no. 4], http://pl.wikipedia.org/wiki/Linia_kolejowa_nr_4 (accessed 16 August 2013); Przegiętka, '1918, 1945 and 1989: Three Turning Points', 141. See also Taylor, *Rozwój i regres*, 91–8.

Cooperation soon turned into competition, e.g. Poland with East Germany, or Hungary with Yugoslavia and Czechoslovakia,[90] and the USSR became an increasingly important player in this game. While the shortest shipping route from Rotterdam to Japan (via the Suez Canal) was 20,000 kilometres, it was 14,000 kilometres via the Trans-Siberian Railway, which reduced the journey time from 28–30 to 20–25 days. The opening of the 4,300-kilometre Baikal–Amur Mainline in 1989 not only shortened the trip, but also radically improved the quality of the Trans-Siberian Container Service (TSCS). Unsurprisingly, Moscow strove to make access to its network the best possible. In the 1980s, two major transit countries – Poland to the west and Romania to the south – became politically and economically unpredictable. This motivated the USSR to revive an idea dating from the 1960s to develop train ferries in order to simplify transportation with Western Europe. The first such ferry was launched in 1986 between Mukran on Rügen Island in East Germany and Klaipeda.[91] However, bursts of modernization were still unable to conceal the fact that the whole region's rail infrastructure was outdated and far behind Western standards. The end of socialism soon exposed the sheer scale of this lack of development, as well as all the inherent challenges that it posed.

During the post-socialist period, the railways went from being one of the nineteenth century's most important symbols of modernity to the embodiment of decline, obsolescence and the past. Car transportation and highways began to be perceived as the symbol of 'catching up with the West'. Governments launched ambitious plans to develop highway systems according to Western European models. However, the Western European fast train systems were not viewed as something to be emulated. The lack of investment in railways led to the decline of both transported goods and passengers, declines in quality of service and the closure of less-travelled railway lines. For example, between 1989 and 2004, the number of passengers travelling on Polish railways sank from 951 million to 272 million.[92] Between 1990 to 2010, Poland closed one quarter of its railways and Hungary 17 per cent of its railways.[93] Other countries reduced their networks less drastically. After the breakup of the federations, the frequency of transportation between the individual republics decreased (particularly in the case of former Yugoslavia or Russia and the Baltic countries). There were, however, several positive trends: particularly after 2000, local railways, especially in tourist regions, began receiving greater support, and some were privatized or run by the local communes. Just as well, NGOs have become engaged in preserving the railways. In the Czech Republic, some railways were even renewed, for example those on the borders with Germany or Austria that were cut after 1945; nevertheless, out of 50 railway crossings operating between Czechoslovakia and Austria/Germany before 1938, only 20 continue to operate today. It seems that the railways in the region will take the German rather than the American or British path (in the USA and the UK, half of railways have been closed since the 1950s, while in continental Western Europe, the reduc-

---

90 Frisnyák, 'Centrally Planned Economy', 179; Mieczkowski, *Transportation in Eastern Europe*, 178–9.
91 Siegfried Köhler, *Die Fährverbindung Mukran–Klaipeda: Ein Sonderbauvorhaben im Griff der Staatsicherheit (1982 bis 1989)* (Schwerin: Landesbeauftragte f. Mecklenburg-Vorpommern für die Unterlagen des Staatssicherheitsdienstes der ehemaligen DDR, 2007); Gumpel, *Das Verkehrswesen Osteuropas*, 86; Igor M. Averin, 'Transocean and Transcontinental Bridges: Integral Parts of the Global Transport System', in *Ports as Nodal Points in a Global Transport System*, eds Antony J. Dolman and Jan van Ettinger (Oxford: Pergamon Press, 1992), 123–9, here 126. West Germany perceived the ferry as a threat to its own merchant fleet, so it is unsurprising that *Der Spiegel* (1 April 1985) described it as a 'Trojan ferry', see 'Trojanische Fähre', *Der Spiegel* 14 (1985): 29–30.
92 Przegiętka, '1918, 1945 and 1989: Three Turning Points', 95.
93 Perger, 'The History of Railway Passenger Transportation', 95. See World Bank, 'Rail Lines (total route-km)', http://data.worldbank.org/indicator/IS.RRS.TOTL.KM (accessed 26 October 2016).

tion was much smaller, for example about one quarter in Germany). Moreover, the European Union is supporting the modernization of railway transportation. For example, in Bulgaria, the contrast between highly modern local trains funded by the EU and the dilapidated countryside surprises every visitor. The plans to construct the Western European high-speed train networks will, however, most likely remain on paper for the next few decades.

Automobility

A reluctant start

Like no other consumer good, having one's own car symbolizes individuality and enables speed. In this respect, car ownership has dramatically changed our perceptions of property and of time and space. As the century of the automobile, the twentieth century coupled widespread social prosperity with the accelerated tempo of modernity. In contrast to the railway, the car's mobility is always accessible, independent of tracks and departure times. Over the last century, the automobile went from being technologically unreliable, reserved as a hobby for the wealthy, to being part of the everyday life of the industrial societies of East Central Europe.[94] Like in the West, having one's own car has come to be a matter of course, the dream of every adolescent. Road systems and other aspects of automobile infrastructure are part of our everyday world. The rise of the car was accompanied by massive political and social change.

The first motor cars resembled either coaches or bicycles. In the 1880s, Gottlieb Daimler and Carl Benz, independently of one another, combined existing technologies to construct the first automobiles.[95] The first companies that manufactured these new motorized vehicles had not yet become specialized in automobile construction. They were either former foundries or mechanical engineering companies that primarily produced metal products and manufactured, on the side, bicycles, motorcycles and, ultimately, automobiles.[96] Because of their relatively high degree of industrial development, it should come as no surprise that almost all factories that ultimately ended up producing cars in East Central Europe were initially located in Bohemia and Moravia. Important for the later mechanical engineering industry in Czechoslovakia were the Laurin & Klement company in Mladá Boleslav (Bohemia) and the Nesselsdorfer automobile company (Nesselsdorfer-Wagenbau-Fabrik) in Moravia. Both are considered pioneers of European passenger car manufacturing and, together with the Škoda and Tatra, would come to exert a great influence on the developing automobile society.[97]

It was not lucrative for European companies to exclusively manufacture cars during the interwar period because the costs associated with car ownership were still prohibitive for most people. Handcrafting cars was extremely expensive, and thus did not generate large yields for European producers in the 1920s.[98] Taxes on cars were high. And because early automotive technology was rather unreliable, maintenance costs were high too. In addition, most

---

94 Tim Dant and Peter Martin, 'By Car: Carrying Modern Society,' in *Ordinary Consumption*, eds Jukka Gronow and Alan Warde (London: Routledge, 2001), 143–58.
95 Kurt Möser, *Geschichte des Autos* (Frankfurt a.M.: Campus, 2002), 33.
96 Ibid., 35.
97 Valentina Fava, *The Socialist People's Car: Automobiles, Shortages and Consent in the Czechoslovak Road to Mass Production* (Amsterdam: Amsterdam University Press, 2013), 37.
98 Christoph Maria Merki, *Der holprige Siegeszug des Automobils 1895–1930: Zur Motorisierung des Strassenverkehrs in Frankreich, Deutschland und der Schweiz* (Vienna: Böhlau, 2002), 110–11; Möser, *Geschichte des Autos*, 48–9.

car owners also required a chauffeur, which increased the costs even further.[99] Among the first motorists were affluent members of the upper middle class, young aristocrats, artists and celebrities. These 'motorized dandies' were the only ones who could afford the new consumer good, and indeed, its features corresponded to their lifestyle.[100] Similar to the futuristic artist Filippo Tommaso Marinetti, they were fascinated by the intoxication of speed and the feeling of omnipotence that emanated from the new technology.[101] But it was not only celebrities who contributed to the popularity of the automobile, at least within the upper class. Members of royal and imperial families made the automobile socially acceptable as a symbol of status and progressive technology. The German emperor's brother-in-law, the Duke of Ratibor, was an avid motorist and president of the German Automobile Club, which was renamed the Imperial Automobile Club in 1905 by Emperor Wilhelm II.[102] Similarly, the automobile club in Romania was founded in 1904 by Prince George Valentin Bibescu.[103] Automobile clubs were also founded in the provinces that had not yet achieved independence prior to 1918, though not under the patronage of the monarchs. The Polish automobile club was founded in 1909 in Warsaw as *Towarzystwo Automobilistów Królestwa Polskiego* (The Motorists Society in the Kingdom of Poland). Its first president, Prince Władysław Drucki-Lubecki, was one of the most important large landowners and notables in Congress Poland.[104] These first motorized cars were used either for weekend outings or for car racing, which was becoming increasingly popular.[105] Patterned after the first Marseilles-Nice race and organized in 1897 by the Automobil Club de France, car racing quickly spread throughout the entire continent.[106] The first race in Eastern Europe was held in 1904 between Bucharest and the Danube port of Giurgiu over a distance of more than 120 kilometres, one of the first events organized by the newly founded Romanian automobile club.[107]

The First World War set off a new wave of motorization. At first, the automobile continued to gain prominence as a means for the aristocracy to present themselves to the masses. The assassination of Archduke Franz Ferdinand in his Gräf & Stift limousine in Sarajevo – the event that triggered the war – made it one of the most famous automobiles in history. The newspaper woodcut by Felix Schwormstädt immortalized the image of the motorized monarch facing his assassin, who ran up to him on foot.[108] Over the course of the war, the exclusivity of the automobile began to wane as many soldiers began having their first experiences with automobiles,

---

99 Merki, *Der holprige Siegeszug*, 46.
100 Möser, *Geschichte des Autos*, 79.
101 Thomas Kühne, 'Massenmotorisierung und Verkehrspolitik im 20. Jahrhundert: Technikgeschichte als politische Sozial- und Kulturgeschichte', *Neue Politische Literatur* 41 (1996): 196–229, here 203.
102 Möser, *Geschichte des Autos*, 81.
103 Chiriac Vasiliu, *Automobilul în România: Istorie și technica* [The automobile in Romania: history and technics] (Bucharest: Editura Flux, 1994), 39; Automobil Clubul Român, 'File de istorie 1904 – 2014', www.acr.ro/file-de-istorie-1904-2005.html (accessed 9 July 2014).
104 Borodziej, *Geschichte Polens*, 22. See also Automobilklub Polski, 'Historia: Początki: Towarzystwo Automobilistów Królestwa Polskiego (1909–1918)' [History – beginnings: the Automobilists' Society of the Kingdom of Poland (1909–1918)], www.automobilklubpolski.pl/historia/poczatki.html (accessed 20 July 2016).
105 Möser, *Geschichte des Autos*, 71–4; Merki, *Der holprige Siegeszug*, 62–3.
106 Merki, *Der holprige Siegeszug*, 53–7.
107 Automobil Clubul Român, 'File de istorie 1904 – 2014' [Pages from history 1904–2014].
108 The image can be viewed online at: www.imagno.at/webgate/preview.php?UURL=b725e89eaf225ce 30f058f3633542452&IMGID=00213549 (accessed 12 July 2014).

either as drivers or passengers of lorries and ambulances.[109] During the war the number of lorries and other utility vehicles grew, and after 1918 these vehicles continued to be used for civilian purposes, thus increasing their everyday presence.[110]

After the war ended, the passenger car continued to push on the motorization of Europe. This boom could not compete with the United States, however, especially not in the eastern part of the continent, where mass motorization had not yet begun.[111] The main difference between Europe and the United States lay not only in Europe's significantly lower degree of motorization, but also in the way the vehicles were manufactured. Despite fascination with the rationalization of Fordism and Taylorism, car production in Europe was largely carried out by hand until 1939. Czechoslovakia provides the best example of this difference. Škoda, which had previously been best known as an arms manufacturer, transferred its main office from Vienna to Prague after the end of the war; nevertheless, the company was not nationalized. In 1925 the Klement & Laurin company was bought up by Škoda, and Mladá Boleslav became one of Europe's most important production sites for automobiles.[112] After Škoda's new manager Václav Klement spent several months visiting American automotive plants, a new production site named 'America' was constructed in 1928. This new facility profited not only from American know-how, but also used machinery imported from overseas. However, despite the factory's name, its mode of production differed considerably from Ford's factories in the United States. In the name of rationalization and with the aim of increasing production, the product line was limited to three passenger vehicles and two lorry models. Production nevertheless remained low. Although Škoda used assembly-line technology, Czechoslovakia on the whole remained true to assembling cars by hand. Car manufacturing remained very scattered, with ten different locations and thirty different vehicle types, and the average annual output numbered less than 700 vehicles.[113] Until the mid-1930s, 90 per cent of automobile production in Czechoslovakia was concentrated in the hands of three main manufacturers: the Škoda Works, the Prague Automobile Factory (with the Praga brand for both passenger vehicles and lorries) and the Tatra brand's Ringhoffer factory in Kopřivnice.[114]

Although the production of and demand for passenger cars in Eastern Europe continued to lag behind that of Western Europe, the number of plants increased during the interwar period, which in turn boosted consumption. In many cases, these newly founded production sites were branch offices or franchises of already existing companies. In 1932, the Polish State Engineering Works (*Państwowe Zakłady Inżynierii*) signed a licensing contract with Fiat, producing the 508 and 518 models with a capacity of 3,000 automobiles per year. Starting in 1935, it also produced lorries under a contract with Fiat.[115] The Ford Romania factory was founded in 1935, and by 1938 American vehicles made up around 73 per cent of the total automobile stock in Romania.[116] In the 1930s Ford also produced both lorries and passenger vehicles in the new

---

109 Merki, *Der holprige Siegeszug*, 71–6.
110 Ibid., 87.
111 See David W. Jones, *Mass Motorization + Mass Transit: An American History and Policy Analysis* (Bloomington, IN: Indiana University Press, 2008), 3.
112 Fava, *The Socialist People's Car*, 36–7.
113 Ibid., 40–41.
114 Petr Pavlínek, *A Successful Transformation? Restructuring of the Czech Automobile Industry* (Heidelberg: Physica, 2008), 34.
115 Mariusz Jastrząb, 'Cars as Favors in People's Poland', in *The Socialist Car: Automobility in the Eastern Bloc*, ed. Lewis H. Siegelbaum (Ithaca, NY: Cornell University Press, 2011), 30–46, here 32.
116 Vasiliu, *Automobilul în România*, 62.

Gorkij factory in the Soviet Union.[117] Despite increasing production, the countries of Eastern Europe did not cross the threshold to mass motorization during the interwar period. Not only was the number of passenger automobiles still too low, but high taxes also curtailed consumption. Any upward trends were put to an end by the beginning of the Second World War, when most production facilities had to convert to war production.[118]

Mass motorization after 1945

The motorization of industrialized societies in the twentieth century depended on the mass production of reasonably priced passenger vehicles that were affordable for industrial labourers and low-level employees. The mother of all cars for the people was the Model T; Ford produced 15 million of them between 1908 and 1927. The price at the time, 370 US dollars – today almost 8,000 US dollars – made the Model T affordable for most people.[119] The *Volkswagen* – literally 'people's car' – was developed in Nazi Germany as a mass produced, reliable, economic automobile.[120] In the 1950s the compact VW, affectionately called the Beetle, contributed to the rapid rise of individual automobile use in West Germany.[121] In some other Western European countries as well, especially in the UK, France and Italy, there was a steep rise in ownership of passenger vehicles after the war, soon crossing the threshold to mass motorization, as in the United States.[122]

In Eastern Europe, state-socialist development policies initiated the transition to mass motorization after the end of the war. Even after the transition to Stalinism in most of Eastern Europe, Western influences on automobile production and consumption did not disappear entirely. On the contrary, the confrontation with the Western model of consumerism and the legacy of the capitalist past became a core aspect of automobility under state socialism. During the immediate post-war years, there were multiple competing notions of automobile consumption in the Eastern bloc. The Stalinist state allowed only the higher levels of the nomenklatura access to passenger vehicles (for official purposes); private cars and taxis remained rare commodities. With the transition from Stalinism to the different post-Stalinist forms of socialism came the fundamental question of whether automobiles should be primarily used for public transit or whether private ownership should be fostered.

Stalin's successor Nikita Khrushchev took this debate to a new level. The New Course and the Khrushchev Thaw aimed to improve living conditions, a shift in policy that was received very positively in Central and Eastern Europe. However, this 'new course' was adamantly opposed to

---

117 Lewis H. Siegelbaum, *Cars for Comrades: The Life of the Soviet Automobile* (Ithaca, NY: Cornell University Press, 2008), 40–43.

118 Jastrząb, 'Cars as Favors', 32; Marko Miljković, 'Western Technology in a Socialist Factory: The Formative Phase of Yugoslav Automobile Industry, 1955–1962' (Master's thesis, Central European University, Budapest, 2013), 45.

119 Robert Casey, *The Model T: A Centennial History* (Baltimore, MD: Johns Hopkins University Press, 2008).

120 Wolfgang König, *Volkswagen, Volksempfänger, Volksgemeinschaft: 'Volksprodukte' im Dritten Reich – Vom Scheitern einer nationalsozialistischen Konsumgesellschaft* (Paderborn: Schöningh, 2004), 151.

121 Erhard Schütz, 'Der Volkswagen', in *Deutsche Erinnerungsorte: Eine Auswahl*, eds Etienne François and Hagen Schulze (München: C.H. Beck, 2005), 351–68, here 354; Luminiţa Gatejel, 'Sozialistische Volkswagen: Trabant, Lada und Dacia im Kalten Krieg', *Osteuropa* 59 (2009): 167–83.

122 Manuel Schramm, 'Nationale Unterschiede im westeuropäischen Massenkonsum: Großbritannien, Frankreich, Deutschland und Italien 1950–1970', *Comparativ: Zeitschrift für Globalgeschichte und vergleichende Gesellschaftsforschung* 19, no. 6 (2009): 71–2.

private automobile ownership. Instead, Khrushchev endorsed a large-scale system of hired cars and the establishment of large car rental centres with moderate prices. The rental vehicle would have two advantages: it would make cars accessible to all citizens and its cars could be used more often than privately owned vehicles.[123] However, the promising idea of the rental centres was quickly eclipsed by the grey realities of state socialism. There were generally far too few rental centres with far too few cars, so that a passenger car had to be booked weeks in advance.[124]

Even prior to the failure of the rental system, East Germany was the first state-socialist country to focus on individual car use. The rise of the socialist 'people's car' began there in the late 1950s. The East German single-party state was at the frontlines of the Cold War, and the rivalry between the two German systems of government created pressure to advance mass motorization. East Germany clearly broke with Khrushchev's automobile policy with the production of the Trabant, and in doing so demonstrated that the developments in West Germany were more important for the decisions of the SED (Socialist Unity Party) leadership than prescriptions from Moscow. The conflict of the two systems of governance in the two Germanys ultimately served as the driving force for the need to develop a socialist counterpart to the West German VW Beetle.[125]

The development of the first Czechoslovak people's car, the Škoda 1.000 MB, was similar, though less dramatic, since there was no direct comparison with a counterpart in the West. Under the auspices of the 'new course', developing an affordable car that could be produced in large numbers became a high priority. Consequently, a new factory was built in Mladá Boleslav, where in 1964 the first Škoda 1.000 MBs began to be manufactured.[126] As early as 1962, Yugoslavia began producing its own people's car, the Zastava 750 which was a licensed version of the Italian Fiat 600. After the Tito-Stalin split in 1948, Yugoslav leaders turned to the West, which offered favourable loans and economic support. From the first contract with Fiat in 1943 until the collapse of Yugoslavia, all motor vehicles (cars and lorries) were manufactured in cooperation with the Italian manufacturer.[127]

In the 1960s, both Poland and the USSR also acquired licences from Fiat with the aim of increasing passenger vehicle production. Even though they were very expensive, the Polski Fiat (125) and the Soviet Lada became the most popular car brands in their countries, in part because they had virtual monopolies.[128] Poland first accomplished mass motorization with the compact Fiat 126p; between 1973 and 1990 more than three million were produced. Initially, its price was roughly twenty times the average monthly wage; that is, about one quarter of the price of the 'big' 125p. This made it affordable for a considerable segment of society, so that in the 1970s and 1980s a total of approximately 2.5 million Poles participated in the complicated instalment payment plan with special savings account passbooks. Waiting times for delivery of the 126p throughout the entire period were several years.[129]

Romanian economic planners were able to achieve substantial success by purchasing a Renault licence. It was the first time that a state-socialist country had managed to acquire a licence to produce a brand-new car model from a Western automobile manufacturer (as

---

123 Siegelbaum, *Cars for Comrades*, 84.
124 Ibid., 13.
125 Luminiţa Gatejel, *Warten, hoffen und endlich fahren: Auto und Sozialismus in der Sowjetunion, in Rumänien und der DDR (1956–1989/91)* (Frankfurt a.M.: Campus 2014), 38–43.
126 Fava, *The Socialist People's Car*, 49.
127 Miljković, 'Western Technology', 75–88.
128 Jastrząb, 'Cars as Favors', 35–7; Siegelbaum, *Cars for Comrades*, 99.
129 Marta Zaraska and Andrzej Krzysztof Wróblewski, 'Po Maluchu' [After little Fiat], *Polityka* 38 (2000): 3–9.

opposed to the Fiat licences mentioned above, which were for models that had been around for some time). The Renault 12 and the Romanian Dacia 1300 went into production simultaneously in 1970. But despite these favourable starting conditions, the motorization of Romania was plagued by the same problems as the other Eastern bloc countries. The first waiting lists formed in the mid-1970s, and waiting periods were still as high as ten years shortly before the fall of the Berlin Wall. The country also had a dearth of automotive repair shops, petrol stations and garages. In spite of the difficult production conditions, however, about two million vehicles were produced up through 1989. With a market share of more than 70 per cent, the Dacia gradually became the Romanian people's car.[130]

As the purchase of licences to manufacture cars clearly shows, the ideological distance to capitalism did not keep state-socialist leaders from drawing on the skills and know-how of capitalist countries. This divided stance towards the West was justified by claims that the importation of technology was solely for the purpose of building up socialism faster and more successfully. As soon as Western technology became part of the new socialist system, it was claimed, it would follow a very different economic logic and lose its capitalist qualities. The slogan of 'catch up and overtake' reflects well this intellectual balancing act that enabled the Eastern bloc countries to purchase Western licences to build a better society than the capitalist one.[131] Table 3.4 offers a survey of the quantitative development of car ownership in state socialism, contextualized with a comparison with the time before and after the system changes, with Germany as a point of reference.

Even though they were never able to truly satisfy demand, the countries of Central and Eastern Europe did manage to commoditize the automobile by 1989. In terms of quality, however, the development moved in the opposite direction: when they were first produced on a mass scale, the licensed products still appeared to symbolize the economic potential of socialist national economies; but in the 1980s, they became evidence of the weak innovation of state-socialist societies. Deficient resources and a viscous bureaucratic apparatus hindered all attempts to modernize car production from the 1970s on, and there was no longer any capital available

Table 3.4 Automobiles per 1,000 inhabitants, 1919–2012

Country	1919	1929	1939	1949	1959	1969	1979	1990	2000	2012
Germany (1949–1979: Federal Republic of Germany/German Democratic Republic)	1	7	20	7/4	69/8	207/54	369/151	390	532	530
Czechoslovakia (1990–2012: Czech Republic/Slovakia)	0.4	1	6	10	12	49	130	228/165	336/237	448/337
Hungary	0.1	1	2	1	2	19	87	185	232	301
Yugoslavia		1	1	0.4	2	28	102	135		
Poland	0.2	1	1	2	3	45	60	138	261	486
Romania						6.5	10.8	55	139	224

Source: Wolfram Fischer, 'Wirtschaft, Gesellschaft und Staat in Europa 1914–1980', in *Handbuch der europäischen Wirtschafts- und Sozialgeschichte*, vol. 6, *Europäische Wirtschafts- und Sozialgeschichte vom Ersten Weltkrieg bis zur Gegenwart*, ed. Wolfram Fischer (Stuttgart: Klett-Cotta, 1987), 143; Andrew C. Janos, *East Central Europe in the Modern World: The Politics of the Borderlands from Pre- to Postcommunism* (Stanford, CA: Stanford University Press, 2000), 415; Eurostat, 'Road traffic by type of vehicle until 2012', code: road_tf_veh_h (accessed 7 November 2016).

---

130 Gatejel, 'Sozialistische Volkswagen', 177–80.
131 Gatejel, *Warten, hoffen und endlich fahren*, 103–20.

for licences. All this was reflected in everyday motor vehicle use, leading to year-long waiting times for new vehicles, the poor quality of the cars actually delivered, a scarcity of replacement parts and a tenuous infrastructure with far too few petrol stations and repair workshops. Other effects were also the so-called 'long-term cars', which stayed with their owners for their entire life, as well as the semi-legal or illegal purchase of replacement parts or petrol, and countless hours that the owners invested in the care and maintenance of their vehicles.[132]

Transport infrastructure remained entirely underdeveloped, and road networks were unable to keep pace with the rate of motorization. There was no lack of concrete plans for the post-war period, which was supposed to meet the needs of the anticipated boom in transportation by car. Brigitte Le Normand's analysis of a 1950s master-plan for traffic in the city of Belgrade demonstrates that generous space was allocated for the modernization of the urban street grid. Due to insufficient resources and administrative conflicts over their distribution, however, the planned road network was only ever partially completed.[133]

Despite an overall lack of funds, roads were expanded extensively in Central and Eastern Europe after the Second World War. Between 1965 and 1988, the length of the road network increased by 24 per cent in Poland and by as much as 57 per cent in Yugoslavia.[134] The Prague–Bratislava motorway was a showcase project: at 317 kilometres in length, it was officially opened in late 1980.[135] In the end, however, Eastern European road networks remained far behind those in Western Europe. The socialist countries were never able to catch up with the nascent mass motorization of the late 1970s.[136]

Alongside domestic problems, road construction was also affected by international relations. In particular, Yugoslavia's exceptional position outside of the bloc allowed it to profit from the expansion of the international E-road network for Europe carried out by the United Nations Economic Commission for Europe (UNECE). One important European connection that resulted from the new geopolitical configuration of the Cold War linked Trieste with Istanbul, a route that largely ran through Yugoslav territory. The construction of this important route was made possible by loans from the World Bank. It had the positive side-effect of contributing to a dramatic improvement of Yugoslav roads: while in 1946 only 2 per cent had paved surfaces, in 1976 that number exceeded 40 per cent. Starting in the late 1960s, other countries of Central and Eastern Europe also participated in the European E-road network, though without the financial support of the World Bank.[137] This sort of international collaboration shows that the two blocs were by no means hermetically sealed off from one another; instead, there were at least some isolated examples of joint projects between the socialist and capitalist countries.

In Yugoslavia, the construction of an integrated system of roads began as early as 1948, when street planners used maps from the interwar period in order to connect the individual republics with a motorway officially called 'Brotherhood and Unity'. As the main artery of the Yugoslav traffic network with a total length of 1,182 kilometres, it was better known by the name

---

132 Lewis H. Siegelbaum, 'On the Side: Car Culture in the USSR, 1960s–1980s', *Technology and Culture* 50 (2009): 1–22.
133 Brigitte Le Normand, 'Automobility in Yugoslavia between Urban Planner, Market and Motorist: The Case of Belgrade, 1945–1972', in Siegelbaum, *The Socialist Car*, 92–105.
134 Berend, *Central and Eastern Europe*, 199.
135 Július Bartl, *Slovak History: Chronology & Lexicon* (Bratislava: Slovenské Pedagog. Nakl., 2002), 165.
136 European Commission, *EU Transport in Figures: Statistical Pocketbook 2012*, http://ec.europa.eu/transport/facts-fundings/statistics/doc/2012/pocketbook2012.pdf, 75 (accessed 25 September 2016).
137 Frank Schipper, *Driving Europe: Building Europe on Roads in the Twentieth Century* (Amsterdam: Aksant, 2008), 210–13.

Autoput.[138] As a showcase project in the midst of the post-war recession, supplies and labour were made readily available for the construction of the important section between Belgrade and Zagreb, thus allowing it to be completed in 1950.[139] The expansive 'Brotherhood and Unity' had still not been completed when Yugoslavia collapsed. Due to the growing volume of traffic it is among the most dangerous roads in Europe.

In the late 1960s the project was no longer viewed as a symbol of state cohesion, but as a sign of the rivalries between the different republics. Those responsible for distributing resources in the administrations of the individual republics pursued their own interests, which placed federal collaboration in jeopardy. For example, in 1969 Slovenia insisted that most of the World Bank funds be used for roads to Austria and not for roads within Yugoslavia.[140] Similar conflicts arose again and again. Nevertheless, in the two decades that followed, additional segments of the Autoput continued to be built, until they stretched clear across Yugoslavia, creating a connection to Austria in the north and to Greece in the south.[141]

In conclusion, we can safely say that the state-socialist countries did not develop an alternative to the mass motorization of the West. The only serious attempt was to establish rental cars as a standard, and this attempt failed miserably. Despite these shortcomings, however, it would be wrong to view the motorization of the Eastern bloc as a lesser imitation of Western models. The Western transfer of knowledge and technology did have a lasting effect on the Eastern bloc's breakthrough to mass motorization, but it also created many idiosyncrasies that had nothing at all to do with imitations of the West. These idiosyncrasies were a consequence of state-socialist politics and economics, and ultimately created a unique automobile culture. The elimination of the market, distribution quotas declared long in advance, and the centralized, top-down administration of the planned economies left deep traces on the automobile sector.

After 1989, car manufacturing underwent major changes, dividing the countries of Central and Eastern Europe into winners and losers. Surprisingly, the automobile tradition in state socialism only had a limited influence on further developments. The prime negative example is Poland, where no state-socialist car brand survived. The factories that had been successful up to 1989 were bankrupt by 1992. The state then gave these factories to Fiat, thus marking the beginning of a new chapter in the manufacturer's history in Poland. Even though only a few large companies moved their manufacturing plants to Poland,[142] it nevertheless became a major supplier for the automotive industry, making up 15 per cent of Polish exports in 2015. Further, Slovakia grew to become one of the most significant European automobile producers and suppliers, even though it had no prior experience to draw upon.[143] It was also common for Western companies to take over particular plants, such as Volkswagen taking over Škoda,

---

138 Sasa Vejzagic, 'The Importance of Youth Labour Actions in Socialist Yugoslavia, 1949–1950: A Case Study of The Motorway "Brotherhood-Unity"' (Master's thesis, Central European University, Budapest, 2013), 39–40, available online at: www.etd.ceu.hu/2013/vejzagic_sasa.pdf (accessed 6 November 2016); Miroslav Sić, 'Problematika razvoja autocesta u Hrvatskoj i Jugoslaviji na pragu 90. Godina' [Development of motorways in Croatia and Yugoslavia on the threshold of the nineties], *Geografski glasnik* 52 (1990): 13–28, here 23.
139 Vejzagic, 'Importance of Youth Labour Actions', 45.
140 Sabrina P. Ramet, *The Three Yugoslavias: State-Building and Legitimation, 1918–2005* (Bloomington, IN: Indiana University Press, 2006), 223–5.
141 Ibid., 281.
142 Gabriel Pankow, 'Doch kein JLR-Werk: So ärgern sich die Polen', *Automobil Produktion*, 12 August 2015, www.automobil-produktion.de/2015/08/doch-kein-jlr-werk-so-aergern-sich-die-polen/ (accessed 31 October 2016).
143 Christian von Hirschhausen and Jürgen Bitzer, eds, *The Globalization of Industry and Innovation in Eastern Europe: From Post-Socialist Restructuring to International Competitiveness* (Northampton, MA: Edward Elgar, 2000).

Fiat taking over Zastava, and Renault taking over Dacia. However, even such transfers did not always assure the survival of socialist company names, such as Zastava, whose factories now produce the Fiat 500L for the international market.[144] The take-overs also produced some success stories. After Škoda was bought up by Volkswagen in 1991, the firm advanced in the 2000s to become a European player.[145] The Dacia also experienced a serious crisis in 1989 but was given a new lease on life when Renault took over the run-down plant in 1999. Thanks to their low prices, the new, technically sound Dacia models are finding a growing number of buyers not only in Romania, but also on the international market.[146] In East Germany, there was also a different kind of 'survival' after the collapse of communism. Since production of the Trabant was discontinued in 1991 the car has achieved cult status, which is being maintained, among other things, by nostalgia for the East German car, as demonstrated by Trabi Safaris through the Berlin streets and annual meetings of Trabi enthusiasts.[147]

Air transport

According to a tourist guidebook for Warsaw published in 1938,[148] most people came to the Polish capital by car at the end of the interwar period, while air travel came in second place. Traditional rail transport came in third, and horse-drawn transport was not even mentioned. In truth, the guide is somewhat fantastic. Trains remained the most important means of transportation, and although one could fly to Warsaw's modern Okęcie Airport (opened in 1934) from Polish cities as well as from Berlin, Tallinn, Sofia and Athens, Polish civil aviation – as was the case all across the region – primarily served as an object of prestige and a symbol of modernity. It was more a testament of future possibilities than a real option for the present.

In a region dominated by nation states, increasing a state's presence on the international arena and proving its economic development and modernity were matters of importance. Despite its initially minor role in transportation and the economy, aviation fulfilled this function well. The first aviation companies in the region, which tended to be short-lived, concentrated on delivering mail and commodities, while passenger transport was seen as secondary. National post offices (e.g. in Poland, Romania and Bulgaria) issued commemorative postage stamps when these companies appeared. This was no accident, as these pioneering companies had received substantial state subsidies, despite being private initiatives largely funded by foreign investments (e.g. German capital in Poland and Hungary or French capital in Romania). For instance, founded in 1922, the Aeroexpress Rt. Airline received subsidies from the Hungarian government on the condition that it guarantee regular postal flights and keep passenger ticket prices at the same level as a first-class rail ticket for a similar journey. Established in the same year, the Polish airline Aerolloyd was also state-funded (in 1928, it operated five domestic routes and one foreign connection to Vienna).

---

144 Fiat Group, 'Fiat Group to Widen its Presence in Serbia', news release, www.fiatgroup.com/en-us/mediacentre/press/Documents/2008/Fiat_Group_estende_la_propria_presenza_in_Serbia_ing.pdf (accessed 13 September 2014).
145 Pavlínek, *A Successful Transformation*, 124–6.
146 Deutsch-Rumänische Industrie- und Handelskammer, *Rumänien Wirtschaftsnachrichten*, August 2013, http://rumaenien.ahk.de/fileadmin/ahk_rumaenien/Publicatii/DE/RW_August_01.pdf (accessed 31 October 2016).
147 Ina Merkel, 'Der Trabant', in *Erinnerungsorte der DDR*, ed. Martin Sabrow (München: C.H. Beck, 2009), 363–73.
148 Regina Zofia Danysz-Fleszarowa and Józef Kołodziejczyk, eds, *Warszawa: Przewodnik krajoznawczy* [Warsaw: a tourist guide] (Warsaw: Oddział Warszawski Polsk. Tow. Krajoznawczego, 1938).

Towards the end of the 1920s, civil aviation began to adapt the sort of modern equipment and infrastructure that was becoming a condition for survival on the market – especially during the crisis and when competing with much larger, stronger Western companies.[149] The only way to guarantee the viability of civilian carriers was more involvement from countries that were strongly interested in aviation for self-promotion and military reasons, or as a way to stimulate the most advanced sectors of the economy. During this period, civilian air traffic control was so simple that, at a conference to regulate aviation issues organized in Paris in 1919, each country was allowed to come up with its own regulations for its own airspace. A convention signed on 13 October 1919 also stipulated that every aircraft must belong to a specific country and be registered there.[150] The authorities could thus opt not to extend licences for aviation companies, a right they often put to use. As a result, state or joint state/private associations based on earlier companies were created. In the former Kingdom of Serbs, Croats and Slovenes, the first, short-lived airline was replaced by the Društvo za Vazdušni Saobraćaj Aeroput (Society for Air Traffic Aeroput) on 17 June 1927. In Romania, the CFRNA (Compagnie Franco–Roumaine de Navigation Aérienne) was established in April 1920, with major investment from France; in 1922, it began its first transcontinental flights from Bucharest to Paris. By the mid-1920s, it was competing with the Orient Express on the Bucharest–Belgrade line, and in 1928 was renamed SNNA (Serviciul Național de Navigație Aeriană). Due to the crisis, the state increased its share in the company, and in 1930 the state-run LARES (Liniile Aeriene Române Exploatate de Stat) was founded. Its abbreviation (but not its meaning) was retained in 1937 after it merged with the private airline SARTA (Societatea Anonimă Română de Transporturi Aeriene) to form Liniile Aeriene Române Exploatate cu Statul.[151] On 1 January 1929, the aforementioned Polish airline Aerolloyd was replaced by the state-run company LOT Polish Airlines.[152] Especially after

---

149 Airports were a particular problem: they were often makeshift airstrips on pastures (e.g. in Romania and Yugoslavia). In the early 1920s, the largest Yugoslav airport in the town of Jabuka near Pančevo was practically cut off from Belgrade since there was no bridge across the Danube, and the journey to the capital by boat sometimes lasted longer than the flight from Bucharest or Budapest. In Budapest, planes would take off from near Ferenc József Bridge over the Danube (now the Szabadság híd, or Liberty Bridge). Warsaw's airport was almost in the city centre, at Mokotów Field. In the 1920s, Chernovtsy's first airport was used so rarely that it normally served as grazing land that cows had to be chased off before planes came in to land. Ihor Zhaloba and Ihor Piddubnyj, 'Verkehrs- und Kommunikationsnetze in Czernowitz in der Zwischenkriegszeit (1918–1940)', in *Städte im europäischen Raum: Verkehr, Kommunikation und Urbanität im 19. und 20. Jahrhundert*, ed. Ralf Roth (Stuttgart: Franz Steiner Verlag, 2009), 63–86, here 72.
150 Małgorzata Polkowska, 'Perspektywy globalizacji komunikacji powietrznej' [Perspectives on the globalisation of aerial communication], *Ruch Prawniczy, Ekonomiczny i Socjologiczny* 68, no. 3 (2006): 117–36; International Civil Aviation Organization (ICAO), 'The Postal History of ICAO: The 1919 Paris Convention: The Starting Point for the Regulation of Air Navigation', https://applications.icao.int/postalhistory/ (accessed 20 January 2020). The next aviation conference held in Warsaw in 1929 was extremely important. On 12 October 1919 it hosted the signing of the 'Convention for the Unification of Certain Rules Relating to International Carriage by Air', also known as the Warsaw Convention (Dziennik Ustaw 1933 No. 8, par. 49), much of which still remains in force today.
151 Rob Mulder, 'Airline Companies in Rumania (1918–1945)', *European Airlines*, 17 June 2010, www.europeanairlines.no/airline-companies-in-rumania-1918-1945 (accessed 18 September 2014); Liviu Vălenaș, *Aviație și politică: o istorie comentată a aviației române: 100 de ani de la primul zbor mecanic din lume* [Aviation and politics: An annotated history of Romanian aviation; 100 years since the world's first mechanical flight] (Bucharest: Saeculum, 2007).
152 Andrzej Glass, *Polskie Linie Lotnicze LOT 1929–1989* [Polish Airlines LOT, 1929–1989] (Warsaw: Wydawnictwo Min. Obrony Narodowej, 1989).

the early 1930s, the Hungarian authorities highly subsidized the airline MALÉRT (Magyar Légiforgalmi Rt), which was all that had survived the collapse of Aeroexpress Rt. in 1925.[153]

These examples show the average state of Eastern European airlines between the wars (although the undisputed leader of this group was Polish LOT). However, there were worlds separating aviation in Bulgaria from aviation in Czechoslovakia. This points to the divergent levels of development and modernization in the region. To illustrate this more clearly, the private Bulgarian airline Bunavad, which was founded in 1927 and only offered domestic flights, did not survive the crisis and went bankrupt in 1930. Meanwhile, the first private Czechoslovak airlines, Ikarus and Falco, both founded in 1920, were merged into the Czech Joint-Stock Aviation Company in 1922, which soon collapsed and was replaced by the state-run ČSA (Czechoslovak State Airlines) in 1923. It was no accident that this occurred at the same time the Polish government had begun building its own seaport. In the early 1920s, Prague began to use a slogan the communists adopted after 1948: 'The air is our sea.'[154] Incidentally, Czechoslovakia was probably the only country in the region where private airlines were capable of competing effectively with state companies. Created in 1927 by the Škoda concern, the Czechoslovak airline ČLS began international flights from Prague to Vienna, Dresden and Berlin in 1928 (earlier than the state company). Just two years later, ČLS started flying to Zagreb, then to Bucharest in 1933, Moscow in 1936, and Paris, Rome, Budapest and Brussels in 1938.

The expansion of the Czech airlines was not unusual, since the late 1930s were a favourable period for all airlines, East Central and Eastern European airlines included. For example, the combined distance of Polish LOT flights was 6,285 km in 1938, and 10,207 km (of which 8,370 km were abroad) on the eve of the war. It operated regular flights between 7 Polish cities and 18 abroad (in 15 countries).[155] The crisis was a thing of the past, and state involvement allowed investment to surge forth. Modern airports that could handle international traffic were built in Belgrade (Dojno Polje, 1927; buildings, 1931), Warsaw (Okęcie, 1934) and Prague (Ruzyně, 1937). The existing fleet was upgraded to modern, metal aircraft, which were larger, safer and more comfortable. Models in use included the Dutch Fokker, the French Potez 56, German Junkers and the American Lockheed L-14 Super Electra and Douglas DC-2 and DC-3 aircraft. Poland, Czechoslovakia and Romania also began manufacturing their own planes. As a result, by the end of the 1930s, Eastern European airlines (particularly in Czechoslovakia and Poland) were as well equipped as certain large Western European companies.[156]

Cooperation between Western and Eastern European companies was close (sometimes running contrary to political alliances). Among other things, this was justified by changes in civil aviation's functions in the region: in the 1930s, there was a clear preference for international flights at the expense of domestic flights (which were mostly layovers). For example, in cooperation with Lufthansa, ČLS began flying to Munich, Leipzig, Zurich, Geneva and Marseille, and, thanks to French airlines, thus became a first leg on some passengers' trips to Africa. Flights operated in conjunction with Dutch KLM to Rotterdam and Amsterdam also allowed people

---

153 Paweł Bondary, 'Węgierskie linii lotnicze Malév' [Hungarian Airlines Malév], *Lotnictwo* 5 (2013): 62–9.
154 Stefan Albrecht, 'Luftverkehr als Zukunftsbranche in der Tschechoslowakischen Sozialistischen Republik', *Prager wirtschafts-und sozialhistorische Mitteilungen* 12 (2010): 15–29, here 16.
155 Janusz Żarnowski, *Polska 1918–1939: Praca-technika-społeczeństwo* [Poland 1918–1939: work-technology–society] (Warsaw: Książka i Wiedza, 1999), 203–4.
156 Adam Jońca, *Samoloty linii lotniczych 1931–1939* [The aeroplanes belonging to the airlines, 1931–1939] (Warsaw: Wydawnictwa Komunikacji i Łączności, 1985); Otto Poláček and Joachim Grenzdörfer, '60 Jahre tschechoslowakische Aerolinien ČSA', *Technisch-ökonomische Information der zivilen Luftfahrt* 20 (1984): 137–42.

to travel on to London. Together with Lufthansa and the Austrian ÖLAG, Hungarian airlines offered flights to Salzburg, Munich and Zurich and with British Imperial Airways to London; together with Romanian airlines to Bucharest, Prague and Berlin; and together with Yugoslav airlines to Belgrade and Athens. Hungarian, Polish and Italian airlines ensured connections from Gdynia to Venice and Rome via Gdańsk, Warsaw and Budapest.[157] Regular transatlantic flights (like those that Polish LOT planned to start in 1940) were also under serious consideration.

But the war put an end to all plans. The Czechoslovak airlines were the first to go under in Central and Eastern Europe. Prague initially attempted to merge ČLS and ČSA into ČMLS (Czecho–Moravian airlines), which would have offered flights to cities in Germany in cooperation with Lufthansa. These hopes turned out to be illusory, and both companies were banned in early August 1939 (although the administration of the non-state ČLS lasted right up until 1944). Polish LOT met its end on 1 September 1939, and Yugoslav airlines went under in April 1941. The airlines of the Axis powers were in a seemingly better position. They were officially neutral at first but became engaged in military action after 1941. Although Hungary failed in its attempts to establish flights to Paris, London and Moscow, MALÉRT still carried about 26,000 passengers in 1940. However, the airline's activity virtually ceased after mid-1941, and it was finished off by the German occupation in March 1944, when fighting destroyed its aircraft and airports. After the outbreak of the war, Romanian airlines acquired several dozen Polish civilian aircraft, including modern Douglas and Lockheed planes, which were later flown as part of the LARES fleet after the Polish authorities had evacuated numerous aircraft to safety in Romania.[158] The first year of the war was a period of prosperity for Romania's LARES airlines, but it was militarized in autumn 1940, and the war with the USSR radically restricted its capacities. By the end of 1944, Romanian airlines had also become a thing of the past.[159]

Being Axis members increased opportunities for Hungarian and Romanian aviation during the war. After the war, however, it complicated reconstruction and led to accelerated Stalinization. Paradoxically, the countries that had fought against Germany and whose airlines had ceased to exist in 1939–1941 were better able to rebuild their own civil aviation and maintain a semblance of autonomy after the war. At the same time, Romania, Hungary and Bulgaria did not so much (re)construct their national airlines but set up joint aviation companies with the USSR. As a result, LARES was replaced by TARS (Transporturi Aeriene Româno–Sovietice) in August 1945. The Hungarian Maszovlet (Hungarian–Soviet Joint-Stock Civil Aviation Company) was established in March 1946. Bulgaria even managed to set up a Directorate of Air Communications (DVS) in 1946, which then founded Bulgarian Air Lines a year later, even if it was national more in name than in substance. But in the same year, the authorities in Sofia were discouraged from having their own national airline, and the TABSO (the Bulgarian–Soviet Transport Aviation Corporation) was founded, an airline modelled on those of other countries in the region.

Viewed by the Soviets as a form of war reparations, these airlines usually took the form of joint-stock companies: half of the shares were held by the respective government and the other half by the USSR, which in turn guaranteed equipment, spare parts, staff training and, of course, strict supervision. While the majority of planes were Soviet, some airlines had Western

---

157 Rob Mulder, 'Društvo za Vazdušni Saobraćaj AD – Aeroput (1927–1948)' [Society for Air Traffic AD, Aeroput (1927–1948)], European Airlines, 17 June 2010, www.europeanairlines.no/drustvo-za-vazdusni-saobracaj-a-d-aeroput-1927-1948/(accessed 3 November 2016); Bondary, 'Węgierskie linii lotnicze Malév', 62–9.
158 For more detailed information, see Dan Antoniu, *Polskie konstrukcje lotnicze* [Polish aircraft structures], vol. 4, ch. 3: 'W Rumunii 1933–1946' (Sandomierz: Stratus, 2014).
159 Mulder, 'Airline Companies in Rumania'.

aircraft, such as the Hungarian fleet, which until 1961 used an American Douglas C-47 Skytrain that had been intercepted by Soviet fighters over the town of Pápa in 1951. Permission to operate flights abroad was rarely granted and was generally restricted to socialist countries. For example, the Hungarian Maszovlet began flying to Romania, Czechoslovakia, Bulgaria, Yugoslavia and Soviet-occupied Germany after 1947, and to Poland after 1950. At the end of 1954, the authorities in Budapest, Bucharest and Sofia bought out the USSR's shares, which ultimately enabled them to create their own national airlines. The Romanian and Hungarian airlines immediately changed their names to TAROM (Transporturile Aeriene Române) and MALÉV (Magyar Légiközlekedési Vállalat), while Bulgaria only did so on 1 January 1968, when Balkan Bulgarian Airlines was officially established. Since the Soviet-owned airlines had served as tools of exploitation and control, a fact particularly humiliating for countries with long histories of aviation like Romania and Hungary, the states' reacquisition of the national airlines served to further modernization and ushered in completely new standards of aviation.

Theoretically, the Allied countries (Poland, Czechoslovakia and Yugoslavia) could have reconstructed their aviation infrastructure on the basis of the pre-war companies. Poland and Czechoslovakia were both members of the International Civil Aviation Organization (ICAO), which was set up in December 1944 to supervise the drafting and implementation of international aviation regulations. Nevertheless, while LOT and ČSA retained their old names after 1945, parts of their fleets were made up of aircraft left behind after the Allied forces had demobilized, leaving them searching for new equipment. Thus, in the end, both countries were caught between the Scylla of striving for autonomy and the Charybdis of geopolitics and technological dependence on Moscow. Directly after the war, both countries tried to shape their own aviation policy: they joined international organizations (to which the USSR did not belong) and offered a relatively wide range of international flights (in 1946 ČSA flew to Zurich, Paris, Stockholm, London, Warsaw and Copenhagen, and LOT to Berlin, Paris, Stockholm and Prague). Due to feeble competition from Poland and none from Germany, Prague in particular, hoped to play a leading role in the region and become a central aviation hub between East and West.[160] However, it had to rein in its ambitions, at least for a while. In the 1940s and 1950s, the USSR required its satellite states to adopt Soviet aviation regulations and 'reconsider' their ICAO membership, which up until then had served as proof that Poland and Czechoslovakia were a part of Western 'aviation civilization'. Terminating ICAO membership was tantamount to accepting Soviet standards and regulations, which were often so far removed from international standards that the national carriers faced being banned from routes they had been flying since before the war. This was just as well, as Moscow soon forced its satellites to cancel most of their connections to Western Europe and the Middle East.[161]

In the mid-1950s, almost all of the airlines in the region seemed to have adopted Soviet standards and technology. One exception was JAT Jugoslovenski Aerotransport, which officially replaced Aeroput on 1 April 1947. Before it managed to establish itself, Yugoslavia was faced with a political crossroads. The resultant crisis (fuel shortages, plus the fact that it had become impossible to fly to socialist countries, let alone capitalist countries) was relatively short for JAT. In 1949, it began forging contacts with Western Europe, starting with Swissair. In 1954, the airline bought modern Convair aircraft, which allowed it to extend its international

---

160 Albrecht, 'Luftverkehr als Zukunftsbranche', 16.
161 Stefan Albrecht, 'Luftfahrt zwischen ICAO- und Sowjetstandards', in *Standardisierung und Integration europäischer Verkehrsinfrastruktur in historischer Perspektive*, eds Gerold Ambrosius et al. (Baden-Baden: Nomos, 2009), 183–96, here 183–7.

flights. Consequently, Yugoslavia, a country with no real aviation traditions, quickly became a model of modernization for other countries in the region.[162]

Additionally, the thaw of the mid-1950s could also be felt in civil aviation. Air France and SAS started flying to Moscow, and the airlines of the socialist countries began adhering to ICAO and IATA requirements more strictly, mostly at the insistence of Prague and Warsaw, which were increasingly interested in improving links with the West,[163] both for economic reasons and for prestige. Most airlines in the region were unprofitable, with domestic flights bringing the biggest losses, sometimes due to the relatively small size of the countries. In Poland (the largest socialist country in Europe after the USSR), for example, internal flights accounted for just 17.6 per cent of airline passengers in 1975.[164] Air transport was also a vital source of foreign currency – an eternal problem for the socialist countries. As far as matters of image are concerned, it is difficult to estimate or measure the role that airlines played in showcasing modernity, national sovereignty and their respective country's (limited) adherence to market principles.[165]

Likewise, although Comecon made it legally possible and economic factors seemed to support it, setting up joint airlines like SAS (Scandinavian Airlines) was out of the question in socialist Europe. The so-called Pool of Six (ČSA, LOT, the East German Interflug, TABSO/Balkan, TAROM and MALÉV) that had been set up in 1957 only cooperated on technical matters. The Comecon Permanent Commission on Civil Aviation was created in 1962 and three years later agreements dating from the 1950s were replaced by new ones (including with the USSR and Mongolia) intended to regulate cooperation, technical assistance, organizational matters, etc.[166]

Table 3.5 Central and Eastern European airlines: loads transported, 1937–2010 (million tonne-kilometres)

Country	1937	1950	1960	1970	1980	1990	2000	2010
Bulgaria	–	0.2	0.3	14.0	38.8	43.9 (1985)	No data	1.7
Czechoslovakia	0.23	2.7	13.8	34.4	42.4*	57.7	Cz. Rep. 38.7	Cz. Rep. 65.7
Yugoslavia	0.003	0.48	1.2	6.8	61.1	93.0 (1985)	–	–
Poland	1.1	0.6	1.8	10.5	30.1	57.9	87.5	114
Romania	–	1.16	2.0	3.5	7.5	9.7	11.8	4.0 (2009)
Hungary	–	0.23	1.5	10.5	9.2	8.4	No data	4.0 (2009)

Sources: Rocznik Statystyczny [Statistical yearbook]: RS 1959, 450; RS 1969, 676; RS 1976; 605; RS 1987, 603; RS 1988, 585; RS 1992, 549; RS 1993, 577; RS 2011, 861. *According to editions of Rocznik Statystyczny published after 1990, transport in 1980 totalled 14.6, and in 1985 21.2 million tonne-kilometres (RS 1992, 549; RS 1993, 577). Figures for 1970 seem equally problematic. See 'Statistická ročena české a slovenské federativní republiky' [Statistical yearbook of the Czech and Slovak Republic] (Prague: Federální statistický úřad, 1991), 425, www.czso.cz/csu/czso/nakladni_doprava_casove_rady.

---

162 Milutin Pršić, *The Story of Yugoslav Airlines: 40 Years of Yugoslav Airlines, 60 Years of Civil Aviation in Yugoslavia* (Belgrade, 1987).
163 Albrecht, 'Luftfahrt zwischen ICAO- und Sowjetstandards', 190.
164 Bogdan Mieczkowski, 'The Influence of Transportation', 5.
165 See Albrecht, 'Luftfahrt zwischen ICAO- und Sowjetstandards'; Vălenaş, *Aviaţie şi politică*; Robert Gruner, *Interflug und DDR-Aussenpolitik: Die Luftfahrt als diplomatisches Instrument* (Hamburg: Diplomica, 2009).
166 Mieczkowski, *Transportation in Eastern Europe*, 161; Gumpel, *Das Verkehrswesen Osteuropas*, 122–3.

Table 3.6 Central and Eastern European airlines: passenger transport, 1937–2010 (millions passenger-kilometres)

Country	1937	1950	1960	1970	1980	1990	2000	2010
Bulgaria	–	6.0	88.6	1201	2670	3231	3600	1248
Czechoslovakia (from 2000 on: Czech Republic)	9.2	46.1	390	1236	1539	2028	3972	6000
Yugoslavia	1.3	31.4	103	774	5091	6336	–	–
Poland	10.7	30.5	109	610	2714	4430	6034	8273
Romania	3.5	14.1	85.7	994	1112	1836	2508	4440
Hungary	–	10.5	75.2	424	102	1500	–	3852

Note: different years: Bulgaria 1985, 2009; Yugoslavia: 1985; Hungary: 2009.
Sources: *Rocznik Statystyczny* [Statistical yearbook]: *RS* 1959, 450, *RS* 1969, 676; *RS* 1976; 605; *RS* 1987, 603; *RS* 1988, 585; *RS* 1992, 549; *RS* 1993, 577; *RS* 2011, 861.

One might venture that the turn of the 1950s and 1960s signalled a new era in Eastern European air transportation, as illustrated in the table below:

Hard statistical data can tell us a lot, especially in the case of aviation, a mode of transport in which modern technology and adherence to international standards plays an incomparably more significant role than in railways or shipping. However, it does not reflect the complications of modernization or the political climate. Despite the amount of freight and passengers carried by the socialist airlines, none of them figured among the top airlines in the world, with the exception of Soviet Aeroflot, which accounted for 5.5 per cent of world traffic in 1951, 10.9 per cent in 1959 and 18 per cent in 1965. Even airlines from smaller countries like Belgium, Holland and Switzerland or those that had been less developed before the war, like Spain, transported much more than, say, LOT or ČSA.[167]

Unlike traditional means of transport (e.g. railways based on nineteenth-century infrastructure), aviation enabled unparalleled spurts of modernization, given the right domestic and international conditions. While Czechoslovak and Polish airlines continued to vie for first place in the region, companies in countries like Bulgaria and Yugoslavia – neither of which had any civil aviation from 1930 to 1946 – began to catch up, thus contradicting the previous division of Central and Eastern Europe into the modern northwest and backward southeast. The Western-oriented JAT Yugoslav Airlines continued the trend after their relations with socialist countries stabilized in the mid-1950s. They aimed to provide high-quality service, their own network of airports that adhered to European standards, better technical equipment, and modern aircraft with more carrying capacity. In the early 1960s, the JAT fleet was expanded to include French Sud Aviation Caravelle planes, in 1969, American McDonnell Douglas DC-9s and, in 1974, the first Boeing 727s in the region. As a result, and despite having had a worse start, Yugoslav airlines were able to overtake their Polish and Czechoslovak counterparts by a wide margin.[168]

A somewhat paradoxical combination of close cooperation with the USSR and the adaptation of some elements of market economies helped propel the development of Bulgarian airlines (see Table 3.1). One factor was the fact that the Bulgarian authorities opted to bolster the tourism industry, which had been the country's main source of foreign currency since the 1960s. The country's tourism bureau, Teksim, even set up its own charter airline, Bulair.

---

167 Gerd Wolf, *Die Entwicklung des Weltluftverkehrs nach dem Zweiten Weltkrieg* (Tübingen: J.C.B. Mohr, 1967), 12 and 46.
168 Oleg Zinam, 'Evaluation of Transport Capacity', 178; Pršić, *The Story of Yugoslav Airlines*.

Attempts to acquire French Caravelle planes came to nothing when the authorities pressured the firm into buying Soviet-made Ilyushins. In the end, when Teksim began to grow beyond the limits set by the state, its directors were arrested and accused of promoting capitalism, which led to the firm's bankruptcy in 1970. Still, thanks to effective policies from the central authorities, Bulgarian airlines had no problems buying the latest Soviet models (e.g. Tu-134As and Tu-154s). As a rule, they were also able to buy them earlier than airlines from other socialist countries. It was no accident that Andrey Tupolev was chairman of the Bulgarian–Soviet Society! As a result, by early 1970, this airline that had only been created after the war offered flights to 22 countries in Europe, Africa and Asia (not to mention nine internal routes), which was comparable with Polish and Czechoslovak airlines.[169]

The facade of cooperation between socialist countries concealed fierce rivalry over new, profitable routes around the region, as well as a race to modernize infrastructure and fleets in order to conform to international standards. This was inextricably linked to Moscow's dominance, since Moscow held sway over new routes and refused to allow other airlines to clash with Aeroflot's plans. Moscow also controlled options for purchasing new aircraft. This was particularly important for long-haul transcontinental/transoceanic flights, as the aircraft simply had to be up to international standards.[170] Socialist countries only manufactured smaller passenger and cargo planes, while all larger aircraft were available only through Moscow. It would only supply them infrequently, however, even to socialist countries, and would often sell second-hand planes or planes that could not be sold for foreign currency. Political views were also a deciding factor. From Moscow's standpoint, for example, Prague was better suited to be a transit hub from Western and Northern Europe and to/from socialist countries and the Middle and Far East than was unpredictable Warsaw. Unsurprisingly, Prague was given some state-of-the-art Tu-104 planes in 1957 (which made ČSA one of the first European airlines to have jets), as well as permission to begin flying to Cairo and to offer the first transoceanic flight in the region, a flight to Cuba in 1962 using Bristol Britannia aircraft that belonged to Cubana de Aviación.[171]

Soviet-made planes suffered from a number of problems. They had uncomfortable passenger cabins, high noise levels, bad fuel consumption – which became extremely important during the oil crises of 1973 and 1979 – and baggage compartments that were incompatible with IATA standard containers. Moreover, the Soviet manufacturers did not supply airworthiness certificates to confirm that the planes conformed to other countries' aviation regulations. It is thus no surprise that airlines in socialist countries also tried to buy aircraft from the West. We have already mentioned Yugoslavia, which had become autonomous. Poland bought three modern American Convair planes from Belgium in 1957. This stirred up jealousy among other airlines around the region, but it soon proved to be a troublesome purchase, requiring a huge amount of foreign currency. In the 1960s, ČSA's attempts to upgrade its fleet with Western

---

169 Wikipedia, 'Balkan Bulgarian Airlines', http://en.wikipedia.org/wiki/Balkan_Bulgarian_Airlines (accessed 24 September 2014); Todor Kambourov, *30 Years Balkan Bulgarian Airlines* (Sofia: Balkan Bulgarian Airlines, 1977); *35 godini Balkan Bălgarska Graždanska Aviatsiia* [35 years of Balkan Bulgarian Airlines] (Sofia: Balkan Bulgarian Airlines, 1982).

170 Internal flights were often made using old aircraft that were on the verge of obsolescence. An RFE report from April 1959 stated that 'LOT's internal flights [are] in short supply, mostly due to the terrible state of its ageing fleet, which is still usable thanks only to their genius mechanics', see 'Internal Difficulties of LOT Polish Airlines', Herder-Institut Marburg, Pressearchiv, 644. The situation was similar for other airlines. Unsurprisingly, most air disasters occurred on relatively short routes.

171 Stefan Albrecht, 'Die ČSA und ihre Expansion in die neuen unabhängigen Staaten Afrikas' (thanks to the author for making the paper available); idem, 'Luftverkehr als Zukunftsbranche', 17. LOT began its first flights outside Europe in 1963, to Cairo (and later to Baghdad, Beirut, Benghazi, Damascus and Tunis).

planes also failed due to political reservations, a lack of funds, and the embargo on supplying socialist countries with new technology. The only socialist country that managed to acquire a Western licence to manufacture (fairly small) Western planes was Romania, which began producing Britten-Norman Islander aircraft in 1969 and BAC One-Eleven planes in 1982 thanks to a contract with British Aerospace that had been signed in 1979.

This, however, only meant that *most* rather than all of TAROM's planes capable of making longer flights were Soviet-made. Yet despite their flaws, new Soviet models such as the Tu-134, Tu-144, Tu-154, Tu-154A and Il-62 allowed companies from socialist countries to expand into international travel, especially after the early 1970s. For example, LOT, which bought Il-62 aircraft in 1972, began regular flights to New York in 1973 and Bangkok (via Dubai and Mumbai) in 1976. LOT's passenger turnover (measured in so-called passenger-kilometres) rose more than fourfold between 1970 and 1980!

The growth and globalization of passenger transport in particular, soon demonstrated that the airports built or modernized during the early stages of the post-war boom, e.g. Budapest's Ferihegy (1960), Prague's Ruzyně (1960–1968), Bucharest's Otopeni (1965) and Warsaw's Okęcie (1969), were insufficient. In the 1970s, they were clearly lagging behind their Western European counterparts in terms of technology and services. During the 1980s, the gap between the modernity of airlines' fleets became ever greater. Polish LOT may have had the most painful experience: two of its Il-62s flying transatlantic routes crashed due to mechanical defects – one in 1980 (with 87 fatalities), the other in 1987 (with 183 fatalities). On the other hand, the mid-1980s also saw a return to the situation of the mid-1950s: the weakened USSR began allowing its satellite states more room for manoeuvre in aviation because the growing crisis in the whole bloc meant they were forced to think not only politically, but also economically.[172] For instance, Polish airlines decided to recall their most unreliable Il-18 and Tu-134 aircraft in 1986 and opted to buy American planes two years later, reasoning that it was the only way to ensure development and remain on the market. Two Boeing 767 aircrafts went into service in 1989 – the first in any Central and Eastern European fleet, which may be considered symbolic.

However, there is no doubt that, out of all forms of mass transportation, it was aviation that had long since crossed the Iron Curtain (not just in the geographical sense) and had potential for modernization throughout the entire region. During the transition period, this allowed it to outdistance rail transportation and shipping.

Table 3.7 Central and Eastern European airlines: number of planes, 1970–2000

Country	1970 Total	Jets	1975 Total	Jets	1985 Total	Jets	1990 Total	Jets	2000 Total	Jets
Czechoslovakia	73	9	73	26	48	40	32	32	66/18	28/10
Yugoslavia	38	17	46	36	62	48	55	47	–	–
Poland	36	5	39	14	39	14	41	30	35	22
Romania	–	–	–	–	–	–	89	38	53	26
Hungary	13	6	18	13	25	21	21	21	–	–

Notes: Czechoslovakia 2000 is for Czech Republic/Slovakia; no statistical data is available for Bulgaria.
Sources: RS 1973, 700; RS 1977, 509; RS 1988, 584; RS 1992, 549; RS 2002, 718.

---

172 Leslie Symons, 'Airlines in Transition to the Market Economy', in Hall, *Transport and Economic Development*, 67–81.

Telecommunications

Telegraph and telephone

The spread of the telegraph in Central and Eastern Europe is closely tied to the history of the railway. Not only did the establishment of the two infrastructure networks start at almost the same time in the mid-nineteenth century, but the first telegraph lines were also constructed along railway lines.[173] In the two German-speaking empires, Prussia and Austria-Hungary, first steps to establish a telegraph network were taken in the 1840s. In Prussia, the electric telegraph was introduced for the military in 1848, and only a year later it was made available for civilian use.[174] In Austria-Hungary, the state declared a monopoly on the telegraph in 1848 and rapidly expanded the network, so that by 1857 there were already 103 functioning stations.[175] In contrast to the first railway construction projects, which were carried out as private ventures, the telegraph continued to be state-run for decades due to its importance for transmitting news.[176] For areas near the Black Sea in particular, the start of the Crimean War was an important catalyst for the development of telegraphy. Bucharest was linked to the Austrian network, and from there a connection was built via Varna and the Black Sea to the French and British forces fighting in Crimea. On the other side, the German Siemens company built the main line in the Russian Empire: St. Petersburg–Moscow–Warsaw, with branches to Kiev, Odessa and Crimea.[177] This comprehensive network made it possible for the Crimean War to go down in history as the first media war.[178]

What came together quickly with foreign assistance in the Crimean War was continued in the following decades in the Ottoman and Russian Empires. The Tanzimat period of the Ottoman Empire and the era of Great Reform in Russia both placed an important focus on expanding telecommunications, which promised to facilitate improved administration and the modernization of the remote provinces.[179] East Central Europe was well-connected since it stood at the crossroads of important continental and intercontinental lines; for instance, the overland telegraph line between London and India crossed over this part of Europe.[180] The development of a worldwide network of telegraph lines between 1857 and 1865 not only promoted private and official correspondence, but also revolutionized the press and led to the founding of the first news agencies. Although fast communication allowed for improved management of state affairs, telegraphy was also available to other groups and individuals who pursued different goals than those that were officially desired, and this despite state control. They could use the new technology not only for private purposes, but also to gain political influence. Around the turn of the century, for example, organizers of strikes or revolts and members of

---

173 Marsha Siefert, '"Chingis Khan with the Telegraph": Communications in the Russian and Ottoman Empires', in Leonhard and von Hirschhausen, *Comparing Empires*, 83–6.
174 Werner Faulstrich, *Medienwandel im Industrie- und Massenzeitalter, 1830–1900* (Göttingen: Vandenhoeck & Ruprecht, 2004), 50–1.
175 Siefert, '"Chingis Khan"', 85.
176 Faulstrich, *Medienwandel im Industrie- und Massenzeitalter*, 50.
177 Siefert, '"Chingis Khan"', 90–1.
178 Winfried Baumgart, 'Der Krimkrieg 1853–1856: Ein historischer Überblick', in *Der Krimkrieg als erster europäischer Medienkrieg*, eds Georg Maag, Wolfram Pyta and Martin Windisch (Berlin: LitVerlag, 2010), 209–20.
179 Alfred J. Rieber, 'Interest-Group Politics in the Era of Great Reforms', in *Russia's Great Reforms, 1855–1881*, eds Ben Eklof, John Bushnell and Larissa Zakharova (Bloomington, IN: Indiana University Press, 1994), 58–83, here 61; Maurus Reinkowski, *Die Dinge der Ordnung: Eine vergleichende Untersuchung über die osmanische Reformpolitik im 19. Jahrhundert* (München: Oldenbourg, 2005), 45.
180 Siefert, '"Chingis Khan"', 96.

nationalist groups took advantage of this new capacity to rapidly disseminate information in order to better organize themselves and more effectively oppose their adversaries.[181]

On the other hand, state authorities had an interest in maintaining control of telegraph licences, and in most European countries, telegraphy remained a state monopoly until 1918. International contracts and exchange between state agencies were supposed to better protect this important technology. First, the two German-speaking empires joined forces in 1849 to form the German-Austrian Telegraph Union, which became the Western European Telegraph Union after Belgium and France joined during the Crimean War. Membership was denied to the British Empire because telegraphy there was controlled by private companies rather than by the government. Members agreed, for example, that only state telegrams should be allowed to be encoded. A series of international conferences aimed at standardizing and regulating the use of telegraphy took place in the years leading up to 1965, when the International Telegraph Union was ultimately established. It continues to exist today as the International Telecommunication Union (ITU), a specialized agency of the United Nations.[182]

During the July Crisis that led to the First World War, the connection between telegrams, accelerated communication and crisis escalation was particularly significant.[183] Exchanges between European chancelleries followed one another in rapid succession. Given the rapid flow of information, decision-makers everywhere believed that the situation could only be brought under control through similarly quick action. Instead of negotiating the crisis through the usual diplomatic channels, decisions were made rashly and, as was typical of the times, Austria-Hungary declared war on Serbia via telegram. This and subsequent telegrams triggered a series of interdependent, automatic responses as provided for in the agreements of the European alliances. Without the rapid means of communication and the resulting pressure on key state actors in July 1914, the crisis might have taken a different course with a different outcome.[184] Telegraphy did not bring any special advantage to either side during the war itself, since both sides had access to the same technology.

The beginnings of telephone use offer a clear contrast to telegraphy. Although the first telephone conversations in East Central Europe had taken place as early as the 1880s, it took some time before the new technology gained popularity.[185] Whereas telegraphy became a symbol of accelerated communication during the 1914 July Crisis, none of the chiefs of state involved reached for the telephone in order to communicate directly with the others. Thus, they avoided both the intimacy of real-time communication and the misunderstandings that can arise in direct dialogue.[186] During the war itself, the telephone contributed significantly to improved communication at the front. Field telephones were used on the Western Front for the first time in 1915, and by 1917, German troops had laid more than 216,000 miles of telephone cables on the Eastern Front.[187]

The construction of telephone cables to systematically connect the European continent only began after the war. In 1924 representatives of national postal and telegraph administrations

---

181 Ibid., 103–4.
182 Francis Lyall, *International Communications: The International Telecommunication Union and the Universal Postal Union* (Aldershot: Ashgate, 2011), 17–44.
183 Stephen Kern, *The Culture of Time and Space, 1880–1918* (Cambridge, MA: Harvard University Press, 2003), 259–86.
184 Siefert, "'Chingis Khan'", 104.
185 Eli Noam, *Telecommunications in Eastern Europe* (Oxford: Oxford University Press, 1992), 275–85.
186 Andreas Killen, 'Die Telefonzentrale', in *Orte der Moderne: Erfahrungswelten des 19. und 20. Jahrhunderts*, eds Alexa Geisthövel and Habbo Knoch (Frankfurt a.M.: Campus, 2005), 81–90, here 84.
187 Richard J. Schuster, 'Telephones', in *World War I Encyclopedia*, vol. 1, ed. Spencer Tucker (Santa Barbara, CA: ABC-Clio, 2005), 1160.

founded the Consultative Committee for International Telephony (CCIF), which was commissioned with coordinating the transnational expansion of cable telephony. The newly created international lines were used for both telephone conversations and radio transmissions.[188] The committee also contributed to the standardization of tariffs in the individual countries. The CCIF was able to convince all the countries to charge the same, fixed amount for the use of the network of any other country. One consequence of this development was that 'by the late 1930s, it was possible to make international phone calls throughout most of Europe. However, the cost was very high, especially in comparison with long-distance telephony in North America.'[189] Significant in this context is that the countries of East Central Europe played a considerable role in advancing the cabling of Europe. In 1927, representatives from Poland, Czechoslovakia, Germany and Austria met in Warsaw in order to push forward regional relay networks. In 1928, regular telephone calls were taking place between the four countries.[190]

The international expansion of the telephone network had critical repercussions on the nation states of Central and Eastern Europe. During the interwar period, private telephony became a part of urban life, even if the lines were generally overloaded and reception was poor. When contemporaries compared the telephone network of a country or a region with a nervous system, the national capitals represented the nerve centres.[191] Statistics on telephone use support this metaphor, as most people with telephone access lived in the capitals. For example, 60 per cent of all telephones in Hungary were in Budapest.[192] Warsaw was not only important as the site of the CCIF meeting; it was also the centre of Polish telephony. The number of telephones in the city grew rapidly, so that in 1934, there were already 95,500 numbers registered.[193] The Baltic states were also active members in the CCIF, which offered them the chance to quickly expand their telephone networks. In the late 1960s, two decades after the Soviets took power, they were among the Soviet republics with the highest number of telephones per capita. This ratio was 12 per cent in Latvia and 10 per cent in Estonia, which can be explained largely by the number of telephones that remained from the interwar period; it was not so much due to the infrastructure expansion of the Soviet state.[194]

This example demonstrates that after 1945, the governments of the countries of Central and Eastern Europe failed to transform the telephone into a medium of mass communication. On the one hand, communication at the highest state levels had been greatly improved through the introduction of direct international communication links. The best-known is without a doubt the so-called hotline between Moscow and Washington, DC, which was set up directly following the Cuban Missile Crisis and which would later outlive the Cold War.[195] Direct

---

188 Suzanne Lommers, *Europe – On Air: Interwar Projects for Radio Broadcasting* (Amsterdam: Amsterdam University Press, 2012), 98–104.
189 Per Högselius, Arne Kaijser, and Erik van der Vleuten, *Europe's Infrastructure Transition: Economy, War, Nature* (Basingstoke: Palgrave Macmillan, 2015), 45.
190 Lommers, *Europe – On Air*, 106–7.
191 Killen, 'Die Telefonzentrale', 85–7.
192 Zsusza L. Nagy, 'Transformation in the City Politics of Budapest, 1873–1941', in *Budapest and New York: Studies in Metropolitan Transformation, 1870–1930*, eds Thomas Bender and Carle E. Schorske (New York: Russell Sage Foundation, 1994), 50.
193 Edward D. Wynot, *Warsaw between the World Wars: Profile of the Capital City in a Developing Land, 1918–1939* (Boulder, CO: East European Monographs, 1983), 211.
194 Larissa Zakharova, 'Communication, Mobility and Control in the Soviet Union after World War II', in *Mobilities in Socialist and Post-Socialist States: Societies on the Move*, eds Kathy Burrell and Kathrin Hörschelmann (Basingstoke: Palgrave Macmillan, 2014), 23–44, here 30–31.
195 Christopher H. Sterling, *Military Communications: From Ancient Times to the Twenty-first Century* (Santa Barbara, CA: ABC-CLIO, 2008), 221–2.

telephone lines also existed between the individual power centres of the Eastern bloc countries and between them and Moscow. For communication within a particular country, there were the so-called government telephones: these phones had access to special lines, which were called *vertushka* in the Soviet Union and Bulgaria, named after the telephone dial. The picture of several telephones crowded on a desk was one of the most important symbols of the power of the heads of the nomenklatura.[196]

On the other hand, everyday personal use of the telephone network remained greatly restricted. Constructing telephone networks and connections proved to be the greatest challenge. The lack of investment in infrastructure hindered the expansion of the telephone network, which proceeded much more slowly than demand. As a result of this incongruence, people in Eastern bloc countries might have waited as long as 12 years for a telephone line, and the number of phones per capita remained far below that of Western Europe. Further, the distribution within the population itself remained very exclusive: members of the nomenklatura had priority and often had telephones both at their office and at home.[197] Up through the late 1980s, the distribution of telephones within the population remained extremely unequal, as was the case with all desired consumer goods. Unequal distribution between members of state and the rest of the population was not the only disparity. Urban dwellers were clearly at an advantage, and so were certain occupational groups, such as physicians.[198] Moreover, even if normal citizens did get a phone, there was still a hierarchy with respect to the kind of telephone line one received: in addition to the ordinary, private individual lines, there were also double or even four-way party lines that connected several telephones to a single line, such that only one subscriber could use the telephone at a time.[199] However, despite this unequal distribution, the telephone assumed a place in pop culture very early on, as demonstrated by the 1967 Romanian hit song by Margareta Pâslaru 'Cu cine vorbeai la telefon?' ('Who were you talking to on the phone?').[200]

Another factor that hindered communication within the population was the widespread wiretapping of private conversations by the secret police.[201] Even those lucky enough to have a telephone avoided using it for fear of surveillance, as illustrated in the following passage from György Dalos's novel *Der Versteckspieler* (The Hide and Seek Player):

> And now he had to tell Enikö that Tamás Cohen had disappeared. After all, it concerned her. He picked up the telephone receiver to call his wife. But after dialling the first three digits he hung up. Why should anyone who would be listening in on the conversation – uninvited but as a full-time job – even know that the escape of one of the assistants at the institute was so important to him?[202]

---

196 Michail S. Voslenskij, *Nomenklatura: Die herrschende Klasse der Sowjetunion* (Vienna: Molden, 1980), 354.
197 Noam, *Telecommunications in Eastern Europe*, 281.
198 Zoltán Pap, 'Das Telefon als Kennziffer der gesellschaftlichen Ungleichheit', in *Telefon und Gesellschaft: Beiträge zu einer Soziologie der Telefonkommunikation*, eds Ulrich Lange and Klaus Beck, vol. 2 (Berlin: Volker Spiess, 1990), 215–24; Ilko-Sascha Kowalczuk, 'Telefongeschichten', in *Fasse Dich kurz! Der grenzüberschreitende Telefonverkehr der Opposition in den 1980er Jahren und das Ministerium für Staatssicherheit*, eds Ilko-Sascha Kowalczuk and Arno Polzin (Göttingen: Vandenhoeck & Ruprecht, 2014), 24.
199 George Hari Popescu, 'Amintiri din comunism: Zeul Telefonul Fix' [Memories of communism: the telephone as god], www.cyberculture.ro/2014/04/30/comunism-telefoane (accessed 6 May 2016); Noam, *Telecommunications in Eastern Europe*, 281.
200 Margareta Pâslaru, 'Cu cine vorbeai la telefon?' [Who were you talking to on the phone?], 1967, www.youtube.com/watch?v=y1IlToERgl4 (accessed 6 May 2016).
201 Berend, *Central and Eastern Europe*, 248; Kowalczuk and Polzin, *Fasse Dich kurz!*
202 György Dalos, *Der Versteckspieler*, trans. György Dalos and Elsbeth Zylla (Frankfurt a.M.: Insel Verlag, 1994), 19.

It should be noted, however, that systematic wiretapping was impossible due to the low number of telephone lines. Aside from that, the technical equipment of the secret police was limited. For these reasons the state security forces services preferred to wiretap two groups: dissidents and people who had contact with foreigners. Focusing wiretapping on certain groups had the unintentional consequence that most other people could carry on their private conversations freely.[203] Despite this discrepancy, telephone surveillance robbed those affected of their private sphere. However, after the collapse of the Eastern bloc, recordings now serve as rich historical documents.[204] Not only do they offer information about the practices of the state security services; they also document how people radically changed their behaviour in order to reveal as little as possible. At the same time, however, this behaviour ultimately caused people to become alienated from themselves.[205] Besides, political leaders mistrusted the population in general. For instance, in the People's Republic of Poland the entire private telephone network was cut off during the first few weeks after martial law was declared in 1981. When it went back into operation, every conversation was accompanied by an automatic warning ('This conversation is being monitored'), which aimed to prevent users from exchanging unpopular information and opinions.

The development of telegraph and telephone lines over the course of the twentieth century offers more than just an index of the increasing speed and frequency of communication. It also demonstrates the desire for intimate and interactive exchange. However, in the beginning years of socialism in Europe, the telephone was slow to supplant telegraphs, a problem caused by both a lack of funding and the mistrust of political leaders toward their own populations. Not until the 1990s would mobile phone technology, which was far less expensive for the providers, solve the problem of mass telephone communication. This new technology spread simultaneously in the East and the West, making landlines on both sides of the Iron Curtain increasingly obsolete.

Table 3.8 Telephones per 1,000 inhabitants, 1920–1980

Country	1920	1929	1939	1949	1960	1970	1980
Germany	29	50	53	43/33	104/75	225/123	509/189
Czechoslovakia	6	10	15	31	-	138	206
Hungary	6	12	19	13	48	80	118
Bulgaria	2	3	5	8	26	56	141
Poland	2	6	8	9	30	57	95
Romania	2	3	5	-	12	32	-
Yugoslavia	1	3	4	7	13	36	95

Notes: Germany: from 1949 figures are for West Germany/GDR.
Source: Wolfram Fischer et al., *Handbuch der europäischen Wirtschafts- und Sozialgeschichte*, vol. 6, *Europäische Wirtschafts- und Sozialgeschichte vom Ersten Weltkrieg bis zur Gegenwart* (Stuttgart: Klett-Cotta, 1987), 150.

---

203 Zakharova, 'Communication, Mobility and Control', 41.
204 István Rév, *Retroactive Justice: Prehistory of Post-Communism* (Stanford, CA: Stanford University Press, 2005), 2.
205 Kowalczuk and Polzin, *Fasse Dich kurz!*; Dorin Tudoran, *Eu, fiul lor: Dosar de securitate* [I, their son: a security file] (Iași: Polirom, 2010).

Computer and information societies

Beginning in the 1970s, mass communication and multimedia capabilities were improved in both the Eastern bloc and in Yugoslavia. In light of this, one might ask if it is possible to speak of 'state-socialist information societies'. The term 'information society' has been used by social scientists since the 1970s to refer to a new phase of highly industrialized capitalist societies characterized by new, highly advanced forms of communication.[206] The use of computers and the rapid spread of new information technologies such as the internet spurred on this transition.[207] Behind the Iron Curtain, mass communication via radio and television underwent developments similar to those in the West, if with a small delay.[208] However, computer technologies were only comparable at the beginning. In the 1960s, parallel to the IBM models in the United States, Soviet companies developed their own computing machines, the most successful of which was the Minsk series.[209] In the late 1980s, the terms of the Comecon agreement made it possible for East Germany, Yugoslavia, Bulgaria and Romania to produce computers with the help of IBM technology.[210] However, numerous attempts to introduce the new computer technology in industry, research and state administration all failed due to problems typical of planned economies: a lack of coordination between authorities, insufficient financial support and, as a result, a lack of innovation.[211] For these reasons, one can say that the countries of East Central Europe did not become part of the information society until the 1990s.[212]

Nevertheless, beginning in the 1970s, the sort of creeping social change that was usually associated with capitalist societies with highly developed technology also began to take hold in the state-socialist societies. Increased consumer opportunities and access to various information media led to more sophisticated tastes and lifestyles.[213] Citizens of socialist countries could at least theoretically shape their own lifestyles, and the lives of many, mostly younger people no longer conformed with the ideals of the state and party elite.[214] For example, in 1980s Yugoslavia, a dynamic scene of hackers and hardware nerds developed at the margins of what

---

206 Christiane Reinecke, 'Wissensgesellschaft und Informationsgesellschaft', Version 1.0, in *Docupedia-Zeitgeschichte*, 11 February 2010, http://docupedia.de/zg/Wissensgesellschaft?oldid=106496 (accessed 28 April 2016), 1–2; Frank Webster, *Theories of the Information Society*, 4th ed. (London: Routledge, 2014), 263–73.
207 Jürgen Danyel, 'Zeitgeschichte der Informationsgesellschaft', *Zeithistorische Forschungen/Studies in Contemporary History* 9 no. 2 (2012): 186–211, here 186–8, www.zeithistorische-forschungen.de/2-2012/id=4441.
208 Sabina Mihelj, 'Television Entertainment in Socialist Eastern Europe: Between Cold War Politics and Global Developments', in *Popular Television in Eastern Europe During and Since Socialism*, eds Anikó Imre, Timothy Havens and Katalin Lustyik (New York: Routledge, 2013), 13–29; Dana Mustaţă, 'Television in the Age of (Post-) Communism', in Imre, Havens, and Lustyik, *Popular Television*, 47–64.
209 Felix Herrmann, 'Zwischen Planwirtschaft und IBM: Die sowjetische Computerindustrie im Kalten Krieg', *Zeithistorische Forschungen/Studies in Contemporary History* 9, no 2. (2012): 212–30, www.zeithistorische-forschungen.de/2-2012/id=3442.
210 R.J. Crampton, *Bulgaria* (Oxford: Oxford University Press, 2007), 373; Pál Germuska, *Unified Military Industries of the Soviet Bloc: Hungary and the Division of Labor in Military Production* (Lanham, MD: Lexington Books, 2015), 215–16.
211 Danyel, 'Zeitgeschichte der Informationsgesellschaft', 206.
212 Ibid., 207.
213 Paulina Bren and Mary Neuburger, 'Introduction', in *Communism Unwrapped: Consumption in Cold War Eastern Europe*, eds Paulina Bren and Mary Neuburger (Oxford: Oxford University Press, 2012), 3–19, here 10–14.
214 Caroline Fricke, 'Getting Off Track in East Germany: Adolescent Motorcycle Fans and Honecker's Consumer Socialism', in *Socialist Escapes: Breaking Away from Ideology and Everyday Routine in Eastern Europe, 1945–1989*, eds Cathleen M. Giustino, Catherine J. Plum and Alexander Vari (New York: Berghahn, 2013), 213–31.

was 'allowed'. This subculture of computer nerds was able to expand the most in Yugoslavia, where participants stood in close contact with the computer scene in the West, which in turn served as inspiration for them.[215] Aside from that, close economic cooperation between Yugoslavia and Western Europe greatly facilitated access to computer hardware and software. During the relative prosperity of the 1960s and early 1970s, a generation that wanted to lead a life based on the Western model was coming of age.[216] Although there was domestic production of a series of computers, the CER models (*Cifarski elektronski računar* – digital electronic computer), these young activists wanted Western-style home computers, whose programmes they could alter and further develop however they wanted. The first home computers entered the country from Trieste via the semi-legal smuggling trade, and it was common for friends and neighbours to share a computer because of prohibitive prices.[217]

This shared use of computers was also an initial step towards the development of an autonomous community of computer nerds and tinkerers who built their own devices. In 1984, the *Galaksiya* (Galaxies) magazine published diagrams and technical instructions explaining how to build a computer out of individual parts that could easily be purchased in a local electronics store. Consequently, individuals interested in computers put together about 8,000 such devices, which were of course independent of domestic production. These activists placed great value on having free access to hardware construction plans and software without restrictions due to copyright or state controls.[218] Similar do-it-yourself communities that familiarized young people with computers also formed around the same time in other state-socialist countries. These communities were characterized by informal economic practices, importing Western replacement parts via private means and using locally produced electronic parts intended for other purposes. The underground, decentralized nature of computer construction contributed to the fact that a small number of homemade computers found their way into private households.[219] Only in Yugoslavia did producers react positively to the construction plans and bring one of these computers into mass production.[220]

Despite this lively subculture, the former state-socialist countries did not close the technology gap with the capitalist countries until after the collapse of communism. Freedom of information and media diversity were among the most important wishes shared by a majority of the population in the former Eastern bloc.[221] This explains why so many were willing to invest

---

215 Bruno Jakić, 'Galaxy and the New Wave: Yugoslav Computer Culture in the 1980s', in *Hacking Europe: From Computer Cultures to Demoscenes*, eds Gerard Alberts and Ruth Oldenziel (London: Springer, 2014), 107–28.
216 Marie-Janine Calic, *Geschichte Jugoslawiens im 20. Jahrhundert* (München: C.H. Beck, 2010), 223–24; Predrag Marković, 'Where Have All the Flowers Gone? – Yugoslav Culture in the 1970s Between Liberalisation/Westernisation and Dogmatisation', in *The Crisis of Socialist Modernity: The Soviet Union and Yugoslavia in the 1970s*, eds Marie-Janine Calic, Dietmar Neutatz and Julia Obertreis (Göttingen: Vandenhoeck & Ruprecht, 2011), 120–21.
217 Jakić, 'Galaxy and the New Wave', 118. On the East-West smuggling trade via Trieste in general see Brenda Luthar, 'Remembering Socialism: On Desire, Consumption and Surveillance', *Journal of Consumer Culture* 6, no. 2 (July 2006): 229–59; Maja Mikula, 'Highways of Desire: Cross-Border Shopping in Former Yugoslavia, 1960s–1980s', in *Yugoslavia's Sunny Side: A History of Tourism in Socialism, 1950s–1980s*, eds Hannes Grandits and Karin Taylor (Budapest: Central University Press), 211–38.
218 Jakić, 'Galaxy and the New Wave', 120.
219 Patryk Wasiak, 'Playing and Copying: Social Practices of Home Computer Users in Poland during the 1980s', in Alberts and Oldenziel, *Hacking Europe*, 129–50.
220 Jakić, 'Galaxy and the New Wave', 124–5.
221 Katherine Verdery, 'The Start of a New Era? Romanians React to Ceaușescu's Fall', in *Post-Communist Romania at Twenty-Five: Linking Past, Present, and Future*, eds Lavinia Stan and Diane Vancea (Lanham, MD: Lexington Books, 2015), 3–22.

in personal communication early on, causing access to communication technology to grow exponentially over the past 25 years.[222] The former socialist countries constructed dynamic multimedia communication networks, which changed these societies considerably. One characteristic of these new information societies is the speed with which the digital technologies gained acceptance. Aside from this rapid acceptance, it is difficult to identify other specific features of Central and Eastern European information societies. Statistical surveys indicate growing disparities of use and accessibility of communication technologies among the former socialist countries.[223] The question as to how pioneers of computerization and media networking found their place in the new media landscapes is more significant. Recent studies have shown that by gaining new members, these groups have been able to create alternatives to mass media, which in some countries were still state-controlled in the 1990s. In Serbia during the Milošević era, it was the former computer enthusiasts of the 1980s who cunningly used the internet to break through the state monopoly on information and launch a resistance movement. The Otpor ('resistance') group that was founded in 1998 had a homepage before it even had a physical location. Its members used the internet extensively in order to avoid state intervention and organize protest actions. When the state-critical B92 radio station was banned, the group's computer experts managed to send the radio signal to Holland, where it was rebroadcast by the BBC via shortwave, making it possible to receive it in Serbia.[224] This is just one example of how the subcultures and informal economic practices of late socialism have continued to exert considerable influence on post-socialist mass communication. Just as the so-called cross-border shopping tourists were the first capitalists in Poland, it was the internet activists who forced the democratization of the media landscape in Serbia.[225]

Today, the internet and social media are regularly used to network like-minded Eastern Europeans and coordinate mass actions, as in the cases of the protest against pollution caused by the gold mining in the Roşia Montană in northern Romania and the wave of demonstrations in November 2015 against the Romanian government following a club fire in Bucharest.[226] A similar phenomenon occurred in Poland in 2012, when protests against the adoption of the ACTA (Anti-Counterfeiting Trade Agreement) was organized via social media. The protests ultimately moved the Polish government to reject the agreement.[227] These examples show not only that the countries of Central and Eastern Europe have become information societies, but also that their citizens know how to employ digital media for politically relevant objectives.

---

222 On statistical surveys see the conclusion of this article.
223 European Commission Directorate-General for Economic and Financial Affairs, 'Infrastructure in the EU: Developments and Impact on Growth', *Occasional Papers* 203 (December 2014), http://ec.europa.eu/economy_finance/publications/occasional_paper/2014/pdf/ocp203_en.pdf, 15–17 (accessed 3 May 2016).
224 Christopher R. Tunnard, 'From State-Controlled Media to the "Anarchy" of the Internet: The Changing Influence of Communications and Information in Serbia in the 1990s', *Southeast European and Black Sea Studies* 3, no. 2 (May 2003): 97–120.
225 Philipp Ther, *Europe since 1989: A History* (Princeton, NJ: Princeton University Press, 2016), 120–26.
226 Dan Mercea, 'Towards a Conceptualization of Casual Protest Participation: Parsing a Case from the Save Roşia Montană Campaign,' *East European Politics and Societies* 28, no. 2 (2014): 386–410; DIGI24, 'Fotogalerie: Revolta generaţiei Facebook' [Photo gallery: the revolt of the Facebook generation], www.digi24.ro/Stiri/Digi24/Actualitate/Stiri/FOTOGALERIE+Revolta+generatiei+Facebook (accessed 3 May 2016).
227 'Polen steigt aus Acta-Abkommen aus', *Die Zeit*, 4 February 2012, www.zeit.de/digital/2012-02/acta-polen-internet (accessed 2 June 2016).

Conclusion: post-socialism or the start of a new era?

In a volume that assessed Romania's post-socialist transition, the anthropologist Katherine Verdery decided to revisit the letters she received from her Romanian friends in the immediate aftermath of Ceaușescu's fall in December 1989. These letters expressed a boundless euphoria and the confidence that life could only improve after the gloomy 1980s.[228] These letters give us some idea of what personal expectations looked like at the beginning of the so-called 'transformation period'. 'What are my dreams? A small stereo system, a colour TV … a typewriter … various kitchen appliances …'[229] The letters' writers want more comfort, better access to information and more opportunities to express themselves. They also talk about the new freedom and the fears they have overcome: 'We are no longer afraid of the telephone.'[230] The bloodshed that accompanied Ceaușescu's removal from power set Romania apart from all the other socialist countries and their 'velvet revolutions'. However, many people in the former Eastern bloc shared the desire for freedom of information, freedom to travel and better access to consumer goods.

This helps explain why telecommunications have become one of the most dynamic economic sectors in these countries. Over the last 25 years, the access to communication technologies has grown exponentially. Radio and television ownership quickly increased, and the markets were nearly saturated.[231] Diverse television programmes and channels became available, and access to local, national and international broadcasts spread throughout the former Eastern bloc.[232] Furthermore, according to a survey commissioned by the European Union in 2012, the access to telephones increased dramatically, with at least 90 per cent of households having access either to a landline or a mobile phone.[233] The mobile phone network grew much faster than that of landlines: in Poland in 2012, 87 per cent of all households had a mobile phone compared to only 44 per cent with a landline; and in Romania, 82 per cent had a mobile phone compared to only 46 per cent with landlines.[234] The use of personal computers and the access to internet has been on the rise as well. In 2012, the number of households with a computer ranged from 46 per cent in Bulgaria to 64 per cent in Poland and 65 per cent in Latvia. With these numbers, all the new Central and Eastern European EU-member states (except Bulgaria) surpassed Greece, and Poland even surpassed Portugal, Italy and Austria.[235] Internet access has also expanded, ranging from 44 per cent of households in Bulgaria to 63 per cent in Latvia.[236] This spectacular distribution of communication technologies shows that at least those former socialist countries that joined the EU have managed to catch up with European standards.

---

228 Katherine Verdery, 'The Start of a New Era?'
229 Ibid., 14.
230 Ibid., 9.
231 UNESCO, 'The Media Landscape in 28 Countries: Results from a UIS Pilot Survey', 2012, www.uis.unesco.org/Communication/Documents/Media-statistics-pilot-survey-report.pdf, 14 (accessed 9 October 2015).
232 European Commission, 'Media Use in the European Union', *Standard Eurobarometer* 80, Autumn 2013, http://ec.europa.eu/public_opinion/archives/eb/eb80/eb80_media_en.pdf, 5–6 (accessed 9 October 2015).
233 European Commission, 'E–Communications Household Survey', *Special Eurobarometer* 381, http://ec.europa.eu/public_opinion/archives/ebs/ebs_381_en.pdf, 11 (accessed 9 October 2015).
234 Ibid., 17 and 22.
235 Ibid., 39.
236 Ibid., 41.

This evolution is all the more surprising if we consider that the Eastern bloc lacked a strong infrastructure that would have enabled the fast, reliable exchange of information. However, if we look at transportation instead of telecommunications, the results are less uniform. While passenger car ownership grew strongly, the road network improved only slowly.[237] Urban centres in particular are now overcrowded with cars.[238] Prestigious projects like the construction of highways have received high priority while regional road connections have been put off. Moreover, the discrepancy between the countries remains considerable: in 2012, Slovenia had 373 kilometres of motorways per million inhabitants, Croatia 292, Hungary 149, the Czech Republic 118, Bulgaria 82, Poland 78, Slovakia 77, Serbia 67 and Romania only 25. The gap with Western European countries persists. In terms of car ownership, most of the countries reached levels between 300 and 500 cars per thousand inhabitants, numbers comparable to the other EU-member states.[239]

With all this in mind, a preliminary conclusion might be that the various forms of communication and transportation infrastructure have developed unevenly over the past 25 years. While telecommunications have seen increased investment, the construction of new railways has largely been put on hold. These two forms of infrastructure are set apart by the type of investment they require. Communication technologies have spread throughout the region because they attract millions of individual users. The population of the former Eastern bloc found it worthwhile to invest heavily in communications after so many decades of being deprived. However, tolls and ticket prices could not make up for the billions needed to improve transport infrastructures. Allocations for transportation have largely depended on massive budgetary subventions. Generous sponsorship of road development by the EU helps explain why the construction of motorways has begun a rapid uptick. It is safe to assume that preference was given to international road transport because it better suits the needs of an economy heavily reliant on logistics and quick deliveries.[240] Only in recent years has rail transport attracted more interest, in part due to environmental concerns.[241] Thus, while many infrastructural problems have been solved since 1989, discrepancies between Eastern and Western Europe persist. Moreover, disparities remain between the countries of the former Eastern bloc themselves. For instance, there are considerable differences between the infrastructure of Romania (the least developed) and that of Slovenia or the Czech Republic. The disparities among the new EU-member states are more pronounced than the disparities between them and the Western member states.[242] In the future, it is possible that some of the countries will reach levels of development comparable to those of the older member states, while for the others the gap will be all the more pronounced.

---

237 European Commission, 'EU Transport in Figures', *Statistical Pocketbook* 2012, https://ec.europa.eu/transport/sites/transport/files/facts-fundings/statistics/doc/2012/pocketbook2012.pdf (accessed 9 October 2015).
238 Stefanie Peter, 'Mit dem Turbo in den Kapitalismus', *Frankfurter Allgemeine Zeitung*, 20 October 2008, www.faz.net/frankfurter-allgemeine-zeitung/feuilleton/mit-dem-turbo-in-den-kapitalismus-1711520.html (accessed 10 September 2014).
239 Romania is at the bottom with 202 per 1,000 inhabitants, followed by Hungary with 299. See European Commission, 'EU Transport in Figures.'
240 Richard Vahrenkamp, 'Die Logistische Revolution – Logistik und Güterverkehr in Europa 1950–2000, in Roth and Schlögel, *Neue Wege in ein neues Europa*, 452–75.
241 European Commission, 'Modern Rail Modern Europe: Towards an Integrated European Railway', 2008, http://ec.europa.eu/transport/media/publications/doc/modern_rail_en.pdf (accessed 20 October 2015), 5–7.
242 European Commission, 'European Economy: Infrastructure in the EU: Developments and Impact on Growth', *Occasional Papers* 203, December 2014, http://ec.europa.eu/economy_finance/publications/occasional_paper/2014/pdf/ocp203_en.pdf, 15–17 (accessed 21 October 2015).

In the end, a different type of segregation continues to organize space in Central and Eastern Europe, dividing it into metropolitan hubs and isolated provinces.[243] Cities have not been the only beneficiaries of investment into infrastructure. 'Corridors of globalization' around pipelines, motorways and airports that link the region to other parts of the world have also profited greatly.[244] For instance, new policies of deregulation have dramatically changed the nature of air transportation. The system of protected national companies was exchanged for a model open to competition. As a result, several low-budget air companies have changed the way people travel, as it has become easier to travel to European metropolises or desired tourist destinations by plane.[245] The same holds true for junctions along the newly built motorways.[246] However, surrounding provincial areas have hardly profited from this new boom. First, they were cut off in terms of roads and rails, and then in terms of wealth.[247] Such uneven development has only served to augment inequalities between those who profit from participating in the global economy and those who have been left out, as countries in Central, Eastern Europe have failed to redistribute new wealth to the provinces. It remains disputed whether few global hubs and corridors can sustain the economies of entire countries.

Further reading

Alberts, Gerard, and Ruth Oldenziel, eds. *Hacking Europe: From Computer Cultures to Demoscenes* (London: Springer, 2014).
Ambler, John, Denis J.B. Shaw, and Leslie Symons, eds. *Soviet and East European Transport Problems* (London: Croom Helm, 1985).
Ambrosius, Gerold, Henrich-Franke, C., and Neutsch, C., eds. *Standardisierung und Integration europäischer Verkehrsinfrastruktur in historischer Perspektive* (Baden-Baden: Nomos, 2009).
Anastasiadou, Irene. *Constructing Iron Europe: Transnationalism and Railways in the Interbellum* (Amsterdam: Amsterdam University Press, 2011).
Armour, Ian D. *A History of Eastern Europe 1740–1918: Empires, Nations and Modernisation* (London: Bloomsbury Academic, 2012).
Bender, Thomas, and Carle E. Schorske, eds. *Budapest and New York: Studies in Metropolitan Transformation, 1870–1930* (New York: Russell Sage Foundation, 1994).
Berend, Iván T. *Central and Eastern Europe, 1944–1993: Detour from the Periphery to the Periphery* (Cambridge: Cambridge University Press, 1996).
Berger, Stefan, and Alexei Miller, eds. *Nationalizing Empires* (Budapest: CEU Press, 2015).
Bonacich, Edna, and Jake B. Wilson. *Getting the Goods: Ports, Labor, and the Logistics Revolution* (Ithaca, NY: Cornell University Press, 2008).
Borodziej, Włodzimierz. *Geschichte Polens im 20. Jahrhundert* (München: C.H. Beck, 2010).
Borodziej, Włodzimierz, Stanislav Holubec, and Joachim von Puttkamer, eds. *Mastery and Lost Illusions: Space and Time in the Modernization of Eastern and Central Europe* (München: De Gruyter, 2014).
Bren, Paulina, and Mary Neuburger, eds. *Communism Unwrapped: Consumption in Cold War Eastern Europe* (Oxford: Oxford University Press, 2012).
Burrell, Kathy, and Kathrin Hörschelmann, eds. *Mobilities in Socialist and Post-Socialist States: Societies on the Move* (Basingstoke: Palgrave Macmillan, 2014).
Calic, Marie-Janine. *A History of Yugoslavia*, trans. Dona Geyer (West Lafayette, IN: Purdue University Press, 2019).
Calic, Marie-Janine, Dietmar Neutatz, and Julia Obertreis, eds. *The Crisis of Socialist Modernity: The Soviet Union and Yugoslavia in the 1970s* (Göttingen: Vandenhoeck & Ruprecht, 2011).
Casey, Robert. *The Model T: A Centennial History* (Baltimore, MD: Johns Hopkins University Press, 2008).

---

243 Ther, *Die neue Ordnung auf dem alten Kontinent*, 143–56; Borodziej, *Geschichte Polens*, 401–09.
244 Schlögel, 'Europa in Bewegung', 36–41.
245 Javier Vidal, 'Tourism and Transport in Europe, 1930–2000', in Roth and Schlögel, *Neue Wege in ein neues Europa*, 476–90, here 485–6.
246 Schlögel, 'Europa in Bewegung', 37.
247 Kaschuba, 'Europäischer Verkehrsraum', 193–4.

Crampton, R.J. *Bulgaria* (Oxford: Oxford University Press, 2007).
Dolman, Antony J., and Jan van Ettinger, eds. *Ports as Nodal Points in a Global Transport System* (Oxford: Pergamon Press, 1992).
Eklof, Ben, John Bushnell, and Larissa Zakharova, eds. *Russia's Great Reforms, 1855–1881* (Bloomington, IN: Indiana University Press, 1994).
Faulstrich, Werner. *Medienwandel im Industrie- und Massenzeitalter, 1830–1900* (Göttingen: Vandenhoeck & Ruprecht, 2004).
Fava, Valentina. *The Socialist People's Car: Automobiles, Shortages and Consent in the Czechoslovak Road to Mass Production* (Amsterdam: Amsterdam University Press, 2013).
François, Etienne, and Hagen Schulze, eds. *Deutsche Erinnerungsorte: Eine Auswahl* (München: C.H. Beck, 2005).
Gatejel, Luminița. *Warten, hoffen und endlich fahren: Auto und Sozialismus in der Sowjetunion, in Rumänien und der DDR (1956–1989/91)* (Frankfurt a.M.: Campus, 2014).
Geisthövel, Alexa, and Habbo Knoch, eds. *Orte der Moderne: Erfahrungswelten des 19. und 20. Jahrhunderts* (Frankfurt a.M.: Campus, 2005).
Germuska, Pál. *Unified Military Industries of the Soviet Bloc: Hungary and the Division of Labor in Military Production* (Lanham, MD: Lexington Books, 2015).
Giustino, Cathleen M., Catherine J. Plum, and Alexander Vari, eds. *Socialist Escapes: Breaking Away from Ideology and Everyday Routine in Eastern Europe, 1945–1989* (New York: Berghahn, 2013).
Grandits, Hannes, and Karin Taylor. *Yugoslavia's Sunny Side: A History of Tourism in Socialism, 1950s–1980s* (Budapest: CEU Press, 2010).
Gronow, Jukka, and Alan Warde, eds. *Ordinary Consumption* (London: Routledge, 2001).
Gruner, Robert. *Interflug und DDR-Aussenpolitik: Die Luftfahrt als diplomatisches Instrument* (Hamburg: Diplomica, 2009).
Hall, Derek R., ed. *Transport and Economic Development in the New Central and Eastern Europe* (London: John Wiley & Sons, 1993).
Harvey, David. *The Condition of Postmodernity: An Enquiry into the Origins of Cultural Change* (Cambridge: Blackwell, 1992).
Hausleitner, Mariana. *Die Rumänisierung der Bukowina: Die Durchsetzung des nationalstaatlichen Anspruchs Großrumäniens 1918–1944* (München: Oldenbourg, 2001).
Herbert, Ulrich. *Geschichte Deutschlands im 20. Jahrhundert* (München: C.H. Beck, 2014).
Hirschhausen, Christian von, and Jürgen Bitzer, eds. *The Globalization of Industry and Innovation in Eastern Europe: From Post-Socialist Restructuring to International Competitiveness* (Northampton, MA: Edward Elgar, 2000).
Högselius, Per, Arne Kaijser, and Erik van der Vleuten. *Europe's Infrastructure Transition: Economy, War, Nature* (Basingstoke: Palgrave Macmillan, 2015).
Horváth, Gyula. *Spaces and Places in Central and Eastern Europe: Historical Trends and Perspectives of Regional Development* (London: Routledge, 2015).
Imre, Anikó, Timothy Havens, and Katalin Lustyik, eds. *Popular Television in Eastern Europe During and Since Socialism* (New York: Routledge, 2013).
Janos, Andrew C. *East Central Europe in the Modern World: The Politics of the Borderlands from Pre- to Postcommunism* (Stanford, CA: Stanford University Press, 2000).
Jones, David W. *Mass Motorization + Mass Transit: An American History and Policy Analysis* (Bloomington, IN: Indiana University Press, 2008).
Kern, Stephen. *The Culture of Time and Space, 1880–1918* (Cambridge, MA: Harvard University Press, 2003).
König, Wolfgang. *Volkswagen, Volksempfänger, Volksgemeinschaft: 'Volksprodukte' im Dritten Reich – Vom Scheitern einer nationalsozialistischen Konsumgesellschaft* (Paderborn: Schöningh, 2004).
Korbonski, Andrzej. *CMEA, Economic Integration and Perestroika, 1985–1990* (Washington, DC: National Council for Soviet and East European Research, 1990).
Kowalczuk, Ilko-Sascha, and Arno Polzin, eds. *Fasse Dich kurz! Der grenzüberschreitende Telefonverkehr der Opposition in den 1980er Jahren und das Ministerium für Staatssicherheit* (Göttingen: Vandenhoeck & Ruprecht, 2014).
Laak, Dirk van. *Weiße Elefanten: Anspruch und Scheitern technischer Großprojekte im 20. Jahrhundert* (Stuttgart: Deutsche Verlags-Anstalt, 1999).
Lange, Ulrich, and Klaus Beck, eds. *Telefon und Gesellschaft: Beiträge zu einer Soziologie der Telefonkommunikation*, vol. 2 (Berlin: Volker Spiess, 1990).
Leonard, Jörn, and Ulrike von Hirschhausen, eds. *Comparing Empires: Encounters and Transfers in the Long Nineteenth Century* (Göttingen: Vandenhoeck & Ruprecht, 2011).

Levinson, Marc. *The Box: How the Shipping Container Made the World Smaller and the World Economy Bigger* (Princeton, NJ: Princeton University Press, 2008).
Lommers, Suzanne. *Europe – On Air: Interwar Projects for Radio Broadcasting* (Amsterdam: Amsterdam University Press, 2012).
Lyall, Francis. *International Communications: The International Telecommunication Union and the Universal Postal Union* (Aldershot: Ashgate, 2011).
Maag, Georg, Wolfram Pyta, and Martin Windisch, eds. *Der Krimkrieg als erster europäischer Medienkrieg* (Berlin: Lit Verlag, 2010).
Maw, Peter. *Transport and the Industrial City: Manchester and the Canal Age, 1750–1850* (Manchester: Manchester University Press, 2013).
Merki, Christoph Maria. *Der holprige Siegeszug des Automobils 1895–1930: Zur Motorisierung des Strassenverkehrs in Frankreich, Deutschland und der Schweiz* (Vienna: Böhlau, 2002).
Mieczkowski, Bogdan, ed. *East European Transport: Regions and Modes* (The Hague: Martinus Nijhoff, 1980).
Miklóssy, Katalin, and Melanie Ilič, eds. *Competition in Socialist Society* (London: Routledge, 2014).
Misa, Thomas J., Philip Brey, and Andrew Feenberg, eds. *Modernity and Technology* (Cambridge, MA: MIT Press, 2003).
Möser, Kurt. *Geschichte des Autos* (Frankfurt a.M.: Campus, 2002).
Noam, Eli. *Telecommunications in Eastern Europe* (Oxford: Oxford University Press, 1992).
Pavlínek, Petr. *A Successful Transformation? Restructuring of the Czech Automobile Industry* (Heidelberg: Physica, 2008).
Ramet, Sabrina P. *The Three Yugoslavias: State-Building and Legitimation, 1918–2005* (Bloomington, IN: Indiana University Press, 2006).
Rév, István. *Retroactive Justice: Prehistory of Post-Communism* (Stanford, CA: Stanford University Press, 2005).
Roth, Ralf, ed. *Städte im europäischen Raum: Verkehr, Komunikation und Urbanität im 19. und 20. Jahrhundert* (Stuttgart: Franz Steiner Verlag, 2009).
Roth, Ralf, and Henry Jacolin, eds. *Eastern European Railways in Transition: Nineteenth to Twenty-First Centuries* (Farnham: Ashgate, 2013).
Roth, Ralf, and Karl Schlögel, eds. *Neue Wege in ein neues Europa: Geschichte und Verkehr im 20. Jahrhundert* (Frankfurt a.M.: Campus, 2009).
Rumińska, Ewa. *The CMEA-Integration of Planned Economies* (Warsaw: Central School of Planning and Statistics, 1992).
Sabrow, Martin, ed. *Erinnerungsorte der DDR* (München: C.H. Beck, 2009).
Schäfer, Christian. *Kreuzfahrten: Die touristische Eroberung der Welt* (Nuremberg: Wirtschafts-und Sozialgeographisches Institut, 1998).
Schenk, Frithjof Benjamin. *Russlands Fahrt in die Moderne: Mobilität und sozialer Raum im Eisenbahnzeitalter* (Stuttgart: Franz Steiner Verlag, 2014).
Schipper, Frank. *Driving Europe: Building Europe on Roads in the Twentieth Century* (Amsterdam: Aksant, 2008).
Schulz, Axel. *Verkehrsträger im Tourismus: Luftverkehr, Bahnverkehr, Strassenverkehr, Schiffsverkehr* (München: Oldenbourg, 2009).
Scott, James C. *Seeing Like a State: How Certain Schemes to Improve the Human Condition Have Failed* (New Haven, CT: Yale University Press, 1998).
Siegelbaum, Lewis H. *Cars for Comrades: The Life of the Soviet Automobile* (Ithaca, NY: Cornell University Press, 2008).
Siegelbaum, Lewis H., ed. *The Socialist Car: Automobility in the Eastern Bloc* (Ithaca, NY: Cornell University Press, 2011).
Stan, Lavinia, and Diane Vancea, eds. *Post-Communist Romania at Twenty-Five: Linking Past, Present, and Future* (Lanham, MD: Lexington Books, 2015).
Sterling, Christopher H. *Military Communications: From Ancient Times to the 21st Century* (Santa Barbara, CA: ABC-CLIO, 2008).
Ther, Philipp. *Europe since 1989: A History* (Princeton, NJ: Princeton UP, 2016).
van Brabant, Jozef M. *Economic Integration in Eastern Europe: A Handbook* (New York: Routledge, 1989).
Wandruszka, Adam, and Peter Urbanitsch, eds. *Die Habsburgermonarchie 1848–1918, vol. 1, Die wirtschaftliche Entwicklung* (Vienna: Verlag der Österreichischen Akademie der Wissenschaften, 1973).
Webster, Frank. *Theories of the Information Society*, 4th ed. (London: Routledge, 2014).
Wynot, Edward D. *Warsaw between the World Wars: Profile of the Capital City in a Developing Land, 1918–1939* (Boulder, CO: East European Monographs, 1983).

4
WOMEN BETWEEN THE PUBLIC AND PRIVATE SPHERES

Kateřina Lišková and Stanislav Holubec

Introduction

The status of women changed dramatically over the course of the long twentieth century.[1] Women's social standing improved overall in the public and private spheres, although rather unevenly in the various segments of social life. The rise in women's access to education proved to be advantageous: from low literacy and negligible high school graduation rates at the turn of the century, to their outnumbering men in higher education today. Their involvement in paid work was rather low in the first half of the century but rapidly increased under state socialism; yet, it was followed by a decline during the post-socialist years, both in absolute numbers and compared to the West. With the exception of suffrage, the field of politics marks the smallest, most uneven gains for women, particularly in terms of elected office. In the private realm, women gradually gained more freedom with marriage equality in the mid-twentieth century and divorce became more readily accessible (which women in Central and Eastern Europe sought more often than men). Abortion became available to most women in our region by 1957, about a dozen years before this crucial reproductive right was legalized in the West (and with the infamous exception of Romania, it was never repealed in our region). The recognition of same-sex desire was by far the longest and most arduous of sexual liberation processes, which marked some early victories (i.e. with the decriminalization of homosexuality in Hungary and Czechoslovakia in 1961, also long before the West), yet which still has a long way to go (as not a single country in our region bestows equal rights on gays and lesbians in the realm of the family).

Education for girls at the elementary level became compulsory in the nineteenth century; during the later decades, high schools for girls were established and, although they were reluctant at first, universities eventually opened up to women. Surprisingly, admitting women into universities did not correspond to the country's level of urbanization and industrialization: while Romania in 1883 had already let women into their universities, it took the Czech university system more than a decade to follow suit. Moreover, these women graduates were met

---

[1] Parts of this chapter were previously published in Kateřina Lišková, *Sexual Liberation, Socialist Style: Communist Czechoslovakia and the Science of Desire, 1945–1989* (Cambridge: Cambridge University Press, 2018). They have been published with permission of the Licensor through PLS Clear.

with resistance. Indeed, the first women with medical degrees, which they could only obtain abroad, had to wait decades for their credentials to be acknowledged in their home countries. By the 1920s, virtually all fields of study in Central and Eastern Europe were accessible to women, which is precisely when the backlash hit: right-wing governments tried to limit women's education by explaining that women who were university graduates stood in the way of men and their careers. During state socialism, the number of female university students further rose, mainly in technical disciplines. Indeed, the ratio of male to female engineers in Bulgaria was nearly one to one. At the time of the collapse of communism, men and women were almost equally represented in tertiary education, with some differences based on persistent cultural patterns (men dominating in technical and natural sciences, women dominating in the humanities); the gender gap, however, remained strong among higher academic levels (PhDs, professorships).

With the rise of industrialization, women entered into paid employment positions in increasing numbers. Professional women had an especially difficult time with the pre-1945 laws explicitly discriminating against them. By law, women's salaries were lower than men's in the public sector: once a woman married, she had to abandon her job, otherwise she could be fired if a man demanded her position. The situation dramatically changed with state socialism when women legally became equal to men, and their participation in the labour force became strongly supported. While most Western women were stay-at-home mothers, most women in the East were full-time employees. By the 1980s, Southeastern Europe caught up with Central Europe in the ratio of employed women; women across our region comprised well over 40 per cent of the workforce. After the demise of state socialism, many countries in our region re-traditionalized, which meant, among other things, a certain decrease in the number of women in the labour market. With the turn of the millennium, fewer Eastern European women had paid jobs compared to their Western counterparts.

Prior to 1918, most of the countries had enacted laws that maintained men's superiority over women in political, social and economic rights. Hungary was an exception where adult women – not their fathers, not their husbands – had control over the family property. After the First World War, women gained the right to vote in most countries. For a long time, conservatives had denied suffrage to women – until they realized that women tended to vote in their favour, at which point conservatives switched to supporting the woman's right to vote. During state socialism, the number of women elected to parliament rose to one third; rarely though, did women reach the highest echelons of power. There were a few exceptions to this rule, however: in Bulgaria and Czechoslovakia, women had made it to the politburo; Romania had a female minister of foreign affairs in the late 1940s; and Yugoslavia had appointed female prime ministers for its various republics beginning in the 1960s. After socialism ended, women vacated their parliamentary seats, their representation thus dropping to single digit percentages. However, Poland and the Baltic countries saw their first ever female prime ministers and presidents take office.

The turn of the nineteenth/twentieth century witnessed a profound change in the perception of sexuality and gender, including shifting attitudes towards prostitution, increasing demand for fertility control and debates about marriage that in our region had a peculiarly nationalist flavour. Further, the prostitution debates featured a particularly ethno-religious aspect as Jews were often blamed for pimping out and profiting from such a trade. The spread of venereal diseases, often associated with prostitution, fuelled the eugenic efforts that defined the first half of the twentieth century. Only those who were fit were supposed to reproduce. Thus, contraception and abortion were legalized in the 1930s in Romania (and was attempted in several other countries), not as a liberatory tool for women, but as a way to rid society of 'degenerates'. Sterilization was then yet another means to achieve the eugenic end. In a similar vein, several countries attempted (but failed) to introduce obligatory premarital health examinations that would search for venereal disease and tuberculosis in both partners and, if found, prohibit them from marrying.

During the interwar period, the way marriage was perceived continued to change, if not legally (wives remained under the guardianship of their husbands, without legal property or rights over themselves and their children), then symbolically. Both world wars accelerated that change: with husbands and fathers on the front, women experienced the sovereignty of running their own families. Some women, like the Yugoslav female fighters (*partizankas*) during the Second World War, even fought side by side with the men. However, the wars also subjected women to sexual violence as many women were raped by enemy soldiers.

The socialist regimes that were established in the wake of the Second World War dramatically reformulated not only class, but also gender and sexual relations. Equality between men and women was legislated in marriage (and beyond), granting spouses the same rights and responsibilities over children and property. The communist government in Bulgaria had already introduced these changes in 1944, while other Central European countries followed suit in the early 1950s. Socialist marriage was to be a union based in love, and no other factors, such as financial constraints, were to interfere. Since matrimony was now strictly voluntary, it was only logical that divorce should be liberalized. Hungary introduced a no-fault divorce as early as 1952. On the other hand, Polish authorities looked down on marital dissolution and local divorce rates never resembled those of the rest of Central Europe. In any case, the importance placed on women's equality by the early socialist governments faded over time, and by the 1970s, countries returned to policies promoting motherhood and family. Curiously, the same late socialism that entrenched gender in traditional terms, openly discussed sexuality, with experts in Czechoslovakia and Poland advising women and men on how to lead sexually satisfying lives. While the early transition years in many countries witnessed a re-traditionalization in family life, the turn of the millennium brought non-traditional gender arrangements, such as career-oriented women and child-caring men, closer to the mainstream.

The crucial reproductive right to terminate a pregnancy was bestowed upon women (and taken away several times in various countries) throughout the twentieth century. The states tried to balance family stability with women's rights, negotiated national interests in population growth and women's health: from the early decriminalization of abortion in post-revolutionary Russia, through Stalin's retraction of that right, to the right-wing authoritarian regimes attempting to tighten control (the most extreme case was fascist Croatia introducing capital punishment for terminating pregnancy), to legalizing abortion in most of the Cold War East after Stalin's death. After legalization, socialist states in back-and-forth moves tightened and relaxed the access to abortion but never rescinded the law (with the extraordinary exception of Ceaușescu's Romania in 1966). In the early years of post-socialist 'transition', conservatives in several countries targeted these liberal legislations. They ultimately failed everywhere, with the exception of Poland, which legislated some of the harshest anti-abortion provisions in Europe in 1993.

However it is related to gender, homosexuality is part of this chapter on women mostly because of its relation to sexuality that we discuss here. National legal systems have approached the sexual 'other' in a very uneven way throughout history. One step forward might have often meant two steps back at some later point. Strikingly, the Ottoman penal code legalized same-sex intercourse in 1858, only six years after its Austrian counterpart criminalized 'perversion against nature'. Yet the liberal approach disappeared by the end of the century. Homosexuality was legalized for the first time in the twentieth century in post-revolutionary

Russia. Socialist states generally tended to ease their legal approaches to homosexuality, yet Bulgaria even criminalized women for same-sex activities in 1951, while Romania's approach kept getting harsher up until 1957. Decriminalization in two countries, Czechoslovakia and Hungary, in 1961 was inspired by Czechoslovak medical research conducted in the 1950s. While silence surrounded homosexuality most of the time and in most of the countries, some homosexual lives flourished outside of public scrutiny. In any case, there is no contemporary research suggesting any widespread persecution during state socialism. Immediately after 1989, many countries made the age of consent for homosexuals the same as the age of consent for heterosexual couples. The re-traditionalization of family values that followed the demise of socialism and continued in some countries well into the new millennium, legislated marriage as the union of a man and a woman, barring gays and lesbians from ever gaining equal rights in the family realm. However, registered same-sex partnership became available in most countries of the region.

Women and higher education

Concerning women in higher education, the period from the late nineteenth century until 1945 is marked by significant achievements, particularly with regard to a decline in illiteracy and an increase in higher education. In the late nineteenth century, while the need to fight illiteracy was not disputed, and nearly everywhere primary education became obligatory for girls,[2] equal access for women to secondary and post-secondary education was met with resistance. The universities finally opening their gates to female students has been celebrated by the feminist movement as a huge achievement and turning point. Although secondary and university education did not become a mass phenomenon until 1945 – with about five per cent of young people throughout the region enrolling in the former, and one per cent in the latter – the process of providing access to post-secondary education can be considered just as important in understanding the transformation of gender and is also deserving of a brief characterization.

In the late nineteenth century, in most European countries including Central and Eastern Europe, women were not allowed to study. In this regard, the UK and Switzerland were pioneers as they already had substantial numbers of female students enrolled in universities. Since the 1870s, the question of access to higher education for women had been a topic of public discussion, and dozens of women from the region attended university in those countries in Europe that permitted it, mainly in Switzerland. The most notable example is Polish student Stefania Wolicka who was the first European woman to receive a doctorate in Philosophy; she did this in 1875 at the University of Zurich, despite having been ordered (along with other Russian students) by tsarist authorities to leave her studies one year before graduation as they were suspicious of a liberal conspiracy. The first Hungarian woman physician Vilma Hugonnai graduated at the same university in 1879, followed by the first Czech woman physician Bohuslava Kecková one year later. Dr Hugonnai, however, had to wait two decades for her diploma to be recognized in her home country. Dr Kecková was somewhat more fortunate; although she could not get a position back at home, she was offered one in Bosnia, where the Austrian

---

2 The only exception was Albania where obligatory school attendance for girls was only introduced in 1936. In the countryside, obligatory school attendance started at 7 years, in the cities, at 4, as pre-school was obligatory. Zuzana Finger, 'Die Albanischen Elementarschulen in der Zogu Zeit', in *Allgemeinbildung als Modernisierungsfaktor: Zur Geschichte der Elementarbildung in Südosteuropa von der Aufklärung bis zum Zweiten Weltkrieg*, eds Norbert Reiter and Holm Sundhaussen (Wiesbaden: Harassowitz, 1994), 171.

authorities were surprisingly willing to engage women, as the local Muslim population were often reluctant to let male doctors examine female patients.[3]

In Europe, the first step towards getting women into higher education was to create institutions of secondary education that were exclusively for women, as this was much easier than trying to persuade existing gymnasiums (similar to the UK grammar school system) to open their doors to young women. Indeed, the number of such schools increased greatly from the 1860s to the 1900s. The first all-girl gymnasium in the region was opened in the Russian partition of Poland in the 1860s (Marie Skłodowska Curie was one of its graduates in 1883). The first Czech all-girl gymnasium opened in Prague in 1890. In Hungary, gymnasiums for girls were allowed in 1896; until then, girls could study only as private students at gymnasiums that were exclusively for boys.[4] The first Bulgarian all-girls gymnasium opened in 1897.[5] Co-education at the secondary level was generally approved of in the region after the First World War, but Hungary, which was the most reluctant in this respect, only approved co-education after the Second World War.

The first university departments opened their doors to women at the turn of the century. Here, the forerunner was Romania, which may have been inspired by France, with the University of Bucharest admitting female students in the 1880s.[6] Between 1901 and 1905, women made up seven per cent of all university students in Romania.[7] In Serbia, women were admitted to the *Grande école*, the highest educational facility in the country as early as the late 1880s, well before its transformation into a university in 1905. It seems that the lead taken by Southeastern Europe (over Central Europe) was influenced by the fact that, inasmuch as institutions of higher education were rather new in the region, they were more open to such reforms than Central European institutions. Also, the influence of relatively liberal France, which was stronger here than in Central Europe, may have played a role. In the Austrian monarchy, the opening wave started around 1895 and Bulgaria followed suit around 1900. In Russian Poland, women were not allowed to study at all until 1915, but they flocked to the Polish universities in Austrian Galicia.[8]

Women were not admitted into all divisions of a university at once but were first granted access to those considered more 'suitable' to them. In Romania, the faculty of philosophy opened its doors to women in 1883, the faculty of sciences in 1887 and the faculty of medicine in 1890. In the Czech case, philosophy opened its doors in 1895, medicine in 1896; women were only allowed to study law in 1918, and technical universities began admitting women in 1920. In 1930, according to the statistics of female professionals in Czechoslovakia, 600 women were doctors, 500 were gymnasium teachers, 200 were pharmacists, 160 were engineers and

---

3 Bulgaria copied this practice after 1918, sending the first woman graduate of the medical school to serve in Muslim districts. Krassimira Daskalova, 'Bulgarian Women's Movement', in *Women's Movements, Networks and Debates in Post-Communist Countries in the 19th and the 20th Centuries*, eds Edith Saurer, Margareth Lanzinger and Elisabeth Frysak (Köln: Böhlau, 2006), 413–38, here 426.
4 Claudia Papp, *Die Kraft der weiblichen Seele: Feminismus in Ungarn, 1918–1941* (Münster: LIT Verlag, 2002), 305.
5 Daskalova, 'Bulgarian Women's Movement', 417.
6 Ovidiu Bozgan and Bogdan Murgescu, eds, *Universitatea din București 1864–2014* [University of Bucharest 1864–2014] (București: Editura Universității din București, 2014), 99.
7 Theodora Eliza Văcărescu, Abstract 'Women's Education in Romania and the Provinces Inhabited by the Romanians, 1880–1930: A Case Study', www.cooperativag.ro/gustian-sociologists-interwar-university-abstract/ (accessed 1 September 2016); also in Romanian, published as a chapter in *Universitatea interbelica a sociologior gustieni*, ed. Zotán Rostás (Bucharest: Universității din București, 2014).
8 Katarzyna Sierakowska, 'From Partitions to an Independent State: The Feminist Movement in Poland in the First Half of the 20th Century', in Saurer, Lanzinger and Frysak, *Women's Movements, Networks and Debates*, 475–94, here 478–9.

90 were attorneys.[9] In 1895 in Hungary, women were admitted to the university in the faculties of pharmacy, medicine and the humanities; the faculties of law, engineering and agronomy remained closed to them until 1945. In the 1920s, the authoritarian decade after the defeat of the Hungarian revolution, the faculty of medicine at the University of Budapest banned all female students.[10] In Poland, women were allowed to study all disciplines after 1918 (however, at the University of Warsaw, women have been allowed to study all disciplines since 1915, during German occupation). Between 1936 and 1937, women made up the following percentages of university students: Hungary, 15 per cent; Czechoslovakia, 17 per cent; Bulgaria, 23 per cent; Yugoslavia, 23 per cent; Romania, 26 per cent; and Poland, 28 per cent.[11] One can see that this did not correlate with the overall economic development in these respective countries.

During the interwar years, when a right-wing regime came into power, it often attempted to restrict the number of female students allowed to enrol in university. These attempts, however, rarely came to fruition and instead remained on paper as the emancipation process was already in full swing. During the 1920s for example, the political right in Hungary unsuccessfully attempted to exclude women from universities altogether.[12] After Slovakia gained its independence in 1938, the government attempted to reduce the number of female students (who made up about one sixth of the university student population) by introducing *numerus clausus* in all universities and by excluding women entirely from the faculty of law. This was justified by the claim that these married women, whose education was subsidized by the government, posed a threat to the careers of young male university graduates, thus increasing social inequality. It was argued, in a society where the number of well-paid professional jobs is scarce, the rule should be one family, one job. The proposed governmental decree was not approved, however, and the number of women enrolled in universities further increased during the war as men were drafted into the army.[13]

Under socialism we can see an increase in the female student population from roughly one third in the beginning of the period to more than half by the end. That rate, however, is similar to the growth rates in the period from the late nineteenth century up until 1945. The rapid growth in the number of women among university students is noteworthy particularly with regard to technical education, which before 1945 was considered a male domain; and in several countries, technical universities were not open to women at all.[14] In this field, however,

---

9 S. Štrbáňová, 'The Institutional Position of Czech Women in Bohemia 1860–1938', in *Women Scholars and Institutions, Proceedings of the International Conference (Prague, June 8–11, 2003), Studies in the History of Sciences and Humanities*, eds S. Štrbáňová, I.H. Stamhuis and K. Mojsejová, vol. 13 A and 13 B (Prague: Research Centre for the History of Sciences and Humanities, 2004), 69–97.
10 Papp, *Die Kraft der weiblichen Seele*, 322.
11 Sharon L. Wolchik, 'The Precommunist Legacy, Economic Development: Social Transformation and Women's Roles in Eastern Europe', in *Women, State and Party in Eastern Europe*, eds Sharon L. Wolchik and Alfred G. Meyer (Durham, NC: Duke University Press, 1985), 31–46, here 33–4.
12 Maria M. Kovács, 'Hungarian Women Entering the Professions: Feminist Pressures from Left to Right', in *Bildungswesen und Sozialstruktur in Mitteleuropa im 19. und 20. Jahrhundert*, eds Victor Karady and Wolfgang Mitter (Köln: Böhlau, 1990), 247–57, here 254.
13 Matej Šemšej, 'Študentky počas prvej slovenskej republiky' [Female students at the time of the First Slovak Republic], in *Na ceste k modernej žene. Kapitoly z dejín rodových vzťahov na Slovensku*, ed. G. Dudeková et al. (Bratislava:Veda, 2011), 373.
14 Aleksandar Kostov, 'Die neue technische Intelligenz: Zur Ausbildung bulgarischer Ingenieure zwischen 1945 und 1989', in *Transformationsprobleme Bulgariens im 19. und 20. Jahrhundert: historische und ethnologische Perspektiven*, eds Ulf Brunnbauer and Wolfgang Höpken (München:Verlag Otto Sagner, 2007), 191–203, here 198.

the female population was growing faster than before 1945 and faster than in the West: for example, the percentage of female students in all universities increased during the decades of socialism in Bulgaria from 33 per cent to 51 per cent; but at the technical universities, their percentage increased from 8 per cent to 42 per cent! The higher academic ranks, however, remained largely male dominated. In many countries in the region, the first female professors were appointed after 1945, but even in late socialism, the ratio of female to male professors was no more than one to five, a statistic which remains unchanged to this day (see Table 4.1).

Women in the workforce

A steady entrance into the labour market and the legal discrimination of women

Entering into the labour market was a much more radical process for women than it was for men. In the 1850s, we can estimate that less than one tenth of the adult population in the region had paid work, only a very small fraction of them being women; by the 2000s, however, two thirds of the adult population were employed, with women making up more than 40 per cent.[15] Women's participation in the labour market particularly accelerated during the world wars and under state socialism, stagnated during the Great Depression and then declined in post-communism.

Women's participation in the paid labour market was initiated mainly due to the demands of the capitalist economy to engage a female labour force in certain sectors of industrial labour (notably, the textile industry) and services (sales, domestic service, etc.), corresponding with the traditional gendered discourse of the role of women. On the other hand, figures for women amongst qualified workers or workers in the heavy labour industry, like construction or mining, were negligible. Women were successful in their attempts to gain employment as professionals in social

Table 4.1 Proportion of female students at universities in Central and Eastern Europe, 1950–2010 (in %)

Country	1950	1960	1970	1980	1990	2010
Albania	33	18	33	50	52	56
Bulgaria	33		51	56	51	56
Yugoslavia	33	29	39	45	52	
Poland	36	41	47	56	56	59
Romania	33	33	43	43	47	56
Czechoslovakia	20	34	36	40	44	57/59
Hungary	24	33	43	50	50	57
Western Europe	22	29	34	41	49	55

Notes: Western Europe 2010 is the overall European average; there is a different year for Czechoslovakia of 1946, for 2010 Czech Republic/Slovakia.

Source: Hartmut Kaelble, *Sozialgeschichte Europas: 1945 bis zur Gegenwart* (München: C.H. Beck, 2007), 396. Sharon L. Wolchik, 'Ideology and Equality: The Status of Women in Eastern and Western Europe', *Comparative Political Studies* 13 (1981): 449. For 2010, United Nations, 'Statistical Yearbook 2013 Fifty-eighth Issue' (New York, 2016), 71–90.

---

15 Michael Gebel, 'Labour Markets in Central and Eastern Europe', in *Europe Enlarged: A Handbook of Education, Labour and Welfare Regimes in Central and Eastern Europe*, eds Irena Kogan, Michael Gebel and Clemens Noelke (Bristol: The Policy Press, 2008), 35–63, here 44.

services, education and medicine, for which higher education was a requirement. This met with resistance, however, as women were seen as a threat; and from the end of the nineteenth century on, conservative politicians made attempts to curtail the number of women working in public services using different measures (i.e. paying lower wages or firing them after they got married).

For example, while women were permitted to work as governmental employees in the last decades of the nineteenth century in the Austro-Hungarian Empire, they had to leave their position after their wedding day, with no severance pay and no pension. A good example of this is Bulgaria where around the turn of century, the government regulated the exclusion of (mainly middle class) women from public service. Between 1899 and 1905, every female teacher was fired after they got married with the justification that it was not fair for a family to have two salaries.[16] Following protests, however, the law was repealed. Another regulation stated that the number of women with teaching positions in a single district must not exceed that of men, and further, that her salary be capped at 10 per cent less than that of her male colleagues.[17] Another regulation which was approved after 1918 forced women teachers into retirement at age 40 or after 20 years of employment, whichever came first. In Czechoslovakia, there was an enforced celibacy law for female teachers which was legally abolished in 1919 – after which, they even instituted a short paid-maternity leave. However, this law focused on schoolteachers, while other female employees of the government remained outside of the purview of the law.

We only have the global data on women's paid labour from the late nineteenth century from the most developed part of the region – the western half of the Habsburg monarchy. This data shows a very low rate of employment for women: in 1880, about 60 per cent of adult women had no income of their own; 30 per cent of women were workers or servants; and about 10 per cent were property owners, widowed peasants, artisans, independent shop owners and clerks.[18] These statistics, however, do not cover women who helped their husbands in workshops, shops or on their farms. Before 1945, no country in the region had a paid female labour force of over 30 per cent. According to what little statistical data is available, in 1930 women made up 30 per cent of the paid labour force in Czechoslovakia[19] and 26 per cent in Hungary;[20] we can assume that in the less industrialized countries of Central Europe, this share did not exceed 20 per cent, and that in Southeastern Europe, women comprised no more than 10 per cent of the paid labour force. A more detailed picture of Czechoslovakia shows that in 1930, women counted for 26 per cent of all clerical workers (which included schoolteachers) and 33 per cent of industrial workers. They dominated, however, amongst domestic servants, comprising 99 per cent of this sector.[21]

---

16 Krassimira Daskalova, 'The Women's Movement in Bulgaria in a Life Story', *Women's History Review*, 1 (2004): 91–104, here 93.
17 Krassimira Daskalova, 'Women, Nationalism and Nation-State in Bulgaria, 1800–1940', in *Gender Relations in South Eastern Europe: Historical Perspectives on Womanhood and Manhood in 19th and 20th Century*, eds Miroslav Jovanovic and Slobodan Naumovic (Beograd: Udruženjezadušstevnuistoriju, 2001), 15–38, here 28.
18 P. Horská and L. Fialová, 'Česká žena očima statistiky posledních sto let' [Czech women seen from the perspective of statistics in the last one hundred years], in *Historické listy* 1 (1991): p. 15.
19 Václav Průcha, *Hospodářské a sociální dějiny Československa 1918–1992* [The economic and social history of Czechoslovakia] (Brno: Doplněk, 2004) 366.
20 Béla Tomka, *A Social History of Twentieth-Century Europe* (New York: Routledge, 2013), 67.
21 In more industrialized parts of the region, domestic services absorbed only a minority of the women workers. For example, in the Czech lands at the turn of the century, the domestic labour force accounted for no more than 6% of all paid jobs (and about 20% of paid female labour). No more than one tenth of young women between the ages of 18 and 25 were employed as housemaids. Ludmila Fialová, 'Domácí služebnictvo v českých zemích na přelomu 19. a 20. století ve světle statistik' [House servants in the Czech Lands at the turn of 19th and 20th century], *Historická demografie* 26 (2002): 154.

Until the Second World War, paid employment for married women was considered inappropriate in many middle-class families and in the families of qualified workers. Attitudes changed, however, with the younger generation of middle-class families, particularly as women increasingly had access to higher education, and due to their large-scale paid employment during the First World War. The number of female professionals increased particularly in the 1920s as more and more women graduated from universities. Clerical jobs were also becoming more feminized: in Poland, there were even female police officers and tram conductors at the time. In 1927 in Yugoslavia, the first female judges and lawyers were appointed. In Romania, women were permitted to serve as judges and attorneys in 1929, and in Czechoslovakia in 1930. Bulgaria, Albania and Hungary were the only countries that on the eve of the Second World War continued to prohibit this.[22] Women were increasingly teaching not only in elementary schools, but in gymnasiums as well, and in some countries even in universities.

The situation was significantly worsened by the Great Depression when unemployment skyrocketed and the married women who were gainfully employed were particularly scapegoated for taking valuable jobs away from men who were perceived as the rightful breadwinners.[23] The installation of right-wing authoritarian regimes, and later the Nazi occupation, sometimes entailed attempts to dismiss women from public positions. After the Munich Agreement in 1938, as Czech clerical workers were losing their jobs in the recently annexed territories, all female public service workers were dismissed by government decree in order to give their positions to their male counterparts.[24] Jewish families, furthermore, were forced to fire their housemaids. In order to avoid the threat of burgeoning unemployment for housemaids in Slovakia, the government even decreed in 1939 that it was the duty of every Christian family with a relatively high income to employ one or two servants. The middle class interpreted this measure as an unacceptable interference in their lives.[25]

During this period, it was not uncommon to find men from all social classes participating in housework. Also, modern technology had not yet significantly reduced the woman's workload in the household. Refrigerators and gas stoves found their way only to middle class families who could also afford domestic servants. The urban working-class woman only benefitted from the expansion of the water pipeline, along with electricity and the sewing machine. Laundry, cleaning and cooking remained highly time-consuming. Nevertheless, the distribution of some products on the market – bread or canned food, for example – did somewhat reduce the woman's workload. For women living in rural areas, life did not change much. Interestingly, in Yugoslavia, the state's modernization attempts involved abolishing the institution of *zadruga* (an extended family, or clan of families, living together with common property and jointly organized labour) in order to liberate the population from pre-modern institutions. The *zadruga*, however, has never been a prevailing family form and at that time, was already in decline. Indeed, many women complained about its abolition in the 1930s, when they argued that within the *zadruga*, they had less work because of the division of labour with other female members, whereas in the new system of nuclear families, they were burdened with more duties.[26]

---

22 Daskalova, 'Bulgarian Women's Movement', 420.
23 Melissa Feinberg, *Elusive Equality: Gender, Citizenship, and the Limits of Democracy in Czechoslovakia, 1918–1950* (Pittsburgh, PA: University of Pittsburgh Press, 2006), 99–128.
24 Květa Jechová, 'Cesta k emancipaci', [The way to emancipation] in *Pět studií k dějinám české společnosti po roce 1945*, eds Oldřich Tůma and Tomáš Vilímek (Prague: Ústav pro soudobé dějiny AV ČR,, 2008), 99.
25 Šemšej, 'Študentky počas prvej slovenskej republiky', 399.
26 Holm Sundhaussen, *Geschichte Serbiens, 19. – 21. Jahrhundert* (Wien: Böhlau, 2007), 274.

State socialism and the sharp rise in employment

The advent of state socialism brought about gender equality laws. This change was indeed radical for all the socialist countries, although there were major differences between the countries that adopted the equality laws after 1918 and those that did not. Women were also engaged throughout the region in the labour force, partly as a programme to create social equality, and partly as a solution to the lack of workers as in some countries the male population had been decimated during the war (e.g. Poland had the highest percentage of female workers in the region between 1945 and 1970). From a woman's perspective, taking a paid job was not necessarily connected to emancipation, but could simply mean a way out of poverty. Female employment rates grew faster in this region than in Western Europe, with the exception of Scandinavia. Further, the establishment of kindergartens and the promotion of women in higher education spread faster here during the 1950s than in Western countries. The difference between East and West in terms of female employment may have been even greater than it seems from the statistics, as many of the jobs for women in the West were part-time, while this option hardly existed in the East.[27] The gap in female employment rates between the East and the West began to close after the mid-1970s as the rate slowed in communist countries but continued to increase in Western Europe. In the 1950s, there was a strong difference between Southeastern Europe, where women constituted 24–27 per cent of the entire labour force, and Poland, Czechoslovakia, Hungary, where the proportion ranged from 29 to 44 per cent. In the 1980s, the difference was only 44–47 per cent throughout both regions; Yugoslavia was the only exception with 39 per cent. While the accomplishment of emancipation policies in communist countries was attested by the high rates of female employment and also by the high number of educated women, there were still considerable disparities between men and women in terms of career prospects and earnings. Such discrepancies ultimately point to the limits of the communist countries' emancipation strategies.

The first setbacks after Stalinism

During Stalinism, women's role in the labour force was prioritized over other aspects of gender equality such as the equal division of tasks in the household or in child care. In a range of professions typically associated with men, young women came to epitomize the epoch: as tractor drivers, tram conductors, foundry workers or lathe operators. Authors such as Katherine Verdery[28] or Gail Kligman[29] have argued that the Stalinist regimes attempted to erase the differences between genders as part of their goal to homogenize the population. According to Joanna Goven the policy of the Stalinist state had both gender-homogenizing and gender-differentiating effects.[30] As she has shown, Stalinist discourse did not question that child-rearing and housework were the main responsibilities of women, and that women could only be helped in this regard via institutional care, not by their male counterparts. However, such appeals were also rare in the West at that time.

---

27 Katja Boh, 'European Family Life Patterns – a Reappraisal', in *Changing Patterns of European Family Life: A Comparative Analysis of 14 European Countries*, eds Katja Boh et al. (London: Routledge, 1989), 265–96, here 269.
28 Katherine Verdery, 'From Parent-State to Family Patriarchs: Gender and Nation in Contemporary Eastern Europe', in *East European Politics and Societies* 8, no. 2 (1994): 225–55.
29 Gail Kligman, *The Politics of Duplicity: Controlling Reproduction in Ceausescu's Romania* (Los Angeles, CA: University of California Press, 1998).
30 Joanna Goven, 'Gender and Modernism in a Stalinist State', *Social Politics* 9, no. 1 (2002): 3–28, here 8.

Table 4.2 Female employment rates in Central and Eastern Europe, 1930–2010 (in %)

Country	1930	1940	1950	1960	1970	1980	1990	2000	2010
Estonia							48.4	48.7	50.3
Latvia							50.0	48.0	49.8
Lithuania							48.3	49.5	50.3
Poland			44.7	44.3	46.0	45.4	45.8	46.2	44.8
Czechoslovakia	30		38	42.4	45.5	45.4			
Czech lands			37	43.7	46.5	45.8	47.6	44.8	43.3
Slovakia			40.7	38.7	42.8	44.6	46.9	45.7	44.7
Hungary	26.1	27.3	29.2	35.5	41.1	43.4	44.5	44.7	46.3
Romania				27.1	30.1		46.1	46.0	44.3
Yugoslavia/Serbia			24.2	26.3	31.3	35.5	39.4	44.5	43.3
Bulgaria			27.4	33.5	41		47.0	46.5	46.9
Albania				25.1	38.7		45.8	41.2	43.5

Notes: the female labour force as a per cent of the total labour force or the economically active population (all recipients who are either employed or unemployed); Serbia: data from 2000 does not cover Kosovo and Metohija; there are different years for Latvia: 1989; Lithuania: 1989; Poland: 1978, 1992; Czech R.: 1991; Hungary: 1941, 1949; Bulgaria: 1951, 1993; Albania: 2009; Yugoslavia: 1953, 1988.

Sources: Time Series of Historical Statistics, 1867–1992, Budapest: KSH, 1993, 36–37 (Hungary 1900–1990); *UNECE Statistical Database*, https://w3.unece.org/PXWeb2015/pxweb/en/STAT/STAT__20-ME__3-MELF (accessed 20 January 2020) Estonia 1990–2010, Latvia 1989–2010, Lithuania 1989–2010, Poland 1992–2010, Czech R. 1991–2010, Slovakia 1990–2010, Hungary 2000–2010, Romania 1990–2010, Serbia 2000–2010, Bulgaria 1993–2010, Albania 1990–2009). Historická statistická ročenka ČSSR [Historical statistical yearbook ČSSR] (Prague: Federální Statistický Úřad, 1985), 149, 464, 664; Jugoslavija 1918–1988: Statistički Godišnjak, [Yugoslavia 1918–1988: statistical yearbook] (Beograd: Socijalistička Federativna Republika Jugoslavija Savezni Zavod za Statistiku, Februar 1989), 59–60; Historia Polski w Liczbach: *Państwo, społeczeństwo* [History of Poland in numbers: state, society] (Warsaw: Główny Urząd Statystyczny, 2003), 412; Václav Průcha et al., *Hospodářské a sociální dějiny Československa 1918–1992* [Economic and social history of Czechoslovakia] (Brno: Doplněk, 2004), 366; Sharon L. Wolchik, 'Ideology and Equality: The Status of Women in Eastern and Western Europe', *Comparative Political Studies* 13 (1981): 452.

Concerning the post-Stalinist period, historian Małgorzata Fidelis argues that the Khrushchev Thaw in Poland represented a departure from the Stalinist policy of employing women in heavy industry and mining, and even speaks of the 'strong anti-feminist characteristic' of the Thaw.[31] During this period, women were forced to leave their jobs in the heavy industry, which was perceived as being harmful to their 'reproductive biology'.[32] We cannot say if this is specifically Polish because the comparative research on these issues has not yet been conducted. The introduction of laws banning women from performing physical, heavy labour in the 1960s had a certain negative effect on women as it did in fact prevent them from having higher paid jobs.[33] Researchers have shown, however, that the performance of physically demanding work was not in fact a problem for women's health. Their health problems were instead caused by sleep deprivation resulting from the triple burden of their paid work, their household work and

---

31 Małgorzata Fidelis, *Women, Communism, and Industrialization in Postwar Poland* (New York: Cambridge University Press, 2010), 204.
32 Fidelis, *Women, Communism, and Industrialization*, 252.
33 Barbara Havelková, 'The Three Stages of Gender in Law', in *The Politics of Gender Culture under State Socialism: An Expropriated Voice*, eds Hana Havelková and Libora Oates-Indruchová (London: Routledge, 2014), 43.

from taking care of their children, not from working conditions at their place of employment. As historian Katherine Lebow summarizes, the post-Stalinist period 'was characterized by the abandonment of plans to reshape gender roles in the workplace, a renewed understanding of the social sphere as the appropriate realm of female activity, and a return to traditional family values.'[34] However, the presence of women in the paid workforce was not reduced. The necessity to retain and to further increase the female labour force was too strong, particularly because the state had invested in their training and education.[35]

According to Fidelis, 'in the 1960s and 1970s, the gender segregation of jobs became more pronounced' which meant fewer women working in industrial jobs where the majority of the male workers opposed the employment of married women.[36] Women in the 1970s were predominantly understood in the familial context: their role as mothers and homemakers came to the forefront; their paid work came to be seen as a subsidy to the family budget; 'the vocabulary focused on the "appreciation" of women's multiple roles and sacrifices that seemed to be inevitable.'[37] In 1968, the Polish state adopted a voluntary one-year unpaid leave for mothers of children under the age of four, and a three-month paid maternity leave was introduced. Four years later, the voluntary leave was extended to three years, and the paid maternity leave was prolonged to four months. In 1981, mothers going on family leave became eligible to receive up to 100 per cent of the minimum wage, and within a year, 'more than 90 per cent of qualified working mothers had left employment to take advantage of this policy.'[38]

An unequal burden at home during state socialism

For working women, it was difficult to maintain a balance between their paid work and their household work. In the 1960s, the gender gap in household chores existed both in the East and the West.[39] However, while sociologists have identified an increase in male participation in household chores in the West since the 1970s, such a shift does not appear to have occurred in the socialist countries. Housework was more time-consuming in the East as a substantial amount of time was spent searching for scarce goods, queuing in long lines, etc.[40] There are many country-wide studies that document the unequal division of housework. Data from Bulgaria and Yugoslavia show that a woman's total workload was between 60 and 70 hours per week, of which 20–30 were unpaid.[41] In 1967, Bulgarian men worked on average 2 hours and 38 minutes per day in the household, while women worked an average of 5 hours and 19 minutes.

---

34 Katherine Lebow, *Unfinished Utopia: Nowa Huta, Stalinism and Polish Society 1949–56* (Ithaca, NY: Cornell University Press, 2013), 123.
35 Jechová, 'Cesta k emancipaci', 124.
36 Fidelis, *Women, Communism, and Industrialization*, 242–3.
37 Ibid., 244.
38 Ibid., 245.
39 Liana C. Sayer, 'Trends in Housework', in *Dividing the Domestic: Men, Women and Household Work in Cross-National Perspective*, eds Judith Treas and Sonja Drobnič (Stanford, CA: Stanford University Press, 2010), 19–38, here 28.
40 The first attempt to compare people's daily routines between the East and the West was led by Hungarian sociologist Alexander Szalai and his team in the mid-1960s. This research did not bring satisfactory results, however, as some countries only sampled specific towns while others conducted country-wide surveys. Göran Therborn, *Die Gesellschaften Europas 1945–2000: Ein Soziologischer Vergleich*, (Frankfurt a.M.: Campus, 2000), 78.
41 Ulf Brunnbauer, 'From Equality without Democracy to Democracy without Equality? Women and Transition in Southeast Europe', *South-East Europe Review* 3 (2000): 151–68.

Men were more likely to be involved in household chores if the family had a garden or kept animals; cooking, laundry and caring for the children were perceived as the woman's tasks.[42] In 1977, only one per cent of Bulgarian men took part in such activities.[43] In the Czechoslovak case, women did four times the amount of housework than men. A Czechoslovak survey from the 1960s showed that the average daily schedule for a woman with two children consisted of 9 hours of paid work, 5.5 hours of shopping and taking care of the home, 1.5 hours of childcare, 6 hours of sleeping and only 1 hour and 40 minutes for herself (while the husband had 4 more hours of free time than his wife).[44] Between 1960 and 1980 there was an increase in leisure time for women, yet during the same period, men's contribution to the household stagnated. This increase in leisure time was due to the introduction of household technology (refrigerators, washing machines, etc.) and the expansion of child care institutions, not in fact by an increase in the amount of help they received from their male counterparts.

An increase in divorce rates and the subsequent expansion of single-parent families represented a new challenge for the mother's daily routine. Single-parent families existed in the period before 1945 as well, but this was rather due to the death of a parent than to divorce. The proportion of single-parent families decreased in the 1950s because of rising health standards and the insignificant divorce rates. However, this began to change in the 1960s. For example, in Czechoslovakia in 1961, single-parent families with dependent children made up only 4.7 per cent; by 1980, it was already up to 10 per cent.[45]

The decline and precariousness of the female labour market in post-socialism

The first years after the collapse of state socialism were rather bleak for women. The 1990s were marked by rising female unemployment rates and deteriorating incomes for those who managed to keep their jobs. Indeed, women continued to be invisible in the public sphere and there was a backlash against what some saw as the state socialist 'emancipation from above'.[46] There was also hostility towards feminism as it was criticized for being an import from the West.[47] Men emerged as the beneficiaries of the privatization of local economies while women crowded the lower echelons of the job market where the work was underpaid and precarious.[48] The shift towards a liberal free market triggered anxiety in the citizens and some men turned their anger towards women who were then pushed back in the home in an effort to 'return their femininity' to them and to 'remasculinize men'.[49]

---

42 Ulf Brunnbauer, *Sozialistische Lebensweise: Ideologie, Gesellschaft, Familie und Politik in Bulgarien (1944–1989)* (Wien: Böhlau, 2007), 550.
43 Juljana Konstantinov, 'Nahrung vom Dorf, Beziehungen durch die Stadt: Über den gegenwärtigen Charakter des bulgarischen Land-Stadt-Haushalts', in *Vom Nutzen der Verwandten: Soziale Netzwerke in Bulgarien*, eds Ulf Brunnbauer and Karl Kaser (Wien: Böhlau, 2001), 693.
44 Havelková, 'The Three Stages of Gender in Law', 40.
45 Radka Dudová, 'The Rise of Lone-Parent Families – Challenging the Norm', in *Women and Social Citizenship in Czech Society: Continuity and Change*, eds Hana Hašková and Zuzana Uhde (Prague: Institute of Sociology, Academy of Sciences of the Czech Republic, 2009), 135–70, here 137.
46 Marilyn Rueschemeyer and Sharon L. Wolchik, *Women in Power in Post-Communist Parliaments* (Bloomington, IN: Woodrow Wilson Center Press and Indiana University Press, 2009).
47 M. Molyneux, 'Gendered Transitions in Eastern Europe', *Feminist Studies* 21, no. 3 (1995): 637–46.
48 Susan Gal, 'Gender in the Post-Socialist Transition: The Abortion Debate in Hungary', *Eastern European Politics and Societies* 8, no. 2 (1994): 256–86.
49 Tatiana Klimenkova, 'What Does Our New Democracy Offer Society?', in *Women in Russia: A New Era in Russian Feminism*, ed. Anastasia Posadskaya, trans. Kate Clark (London: Verso, 1994).

One of the most important socio-economic trends in post-socialism was the decline in female employment rates that was mainly caused by economic depression. Anti-communist political discourse referred to the 'unnatural inclusion' of women in the workforce under socialism and argued for a substantial change. This change has been manifested by the decisions of several post-communist governments to close child day-care facilities and to extend maternity leave. Although in the first half of the 1990s the number of women in employment decreased faster than that of men,[50] when looking at the period between 1990 and 2006, we see the overall decline in employment was the same for both sexes (see Table 4.3). This is in contrast, however, with development in Western Europe, where women's participation in the labour force increased during the same period. While in the 1990s women in the region were more present in the labour market than women in Western Europe, by 2006 the situation had reversed, and a higher ratio of women in Western Europe were employed than in the post-socialist countries. Important exceptions are the Baltic countries, the Czech Republic and Slovenia, which along with the Scandinavian countries, still have the highest female employment rates in Europe (see Table 4.3).[51]

The perennial gender pay gap

Another indicator of inequality between the sexes is the gender pay gap. This also existed under socialism, but was less pronounced than in the West, as overall wage differences were lower. Not surprisingly, the gender pay gap has continued to exist since 1989 and in several cases has even increased slightly: in Slovenia from 13 per cent in 1987 to 15 per cent in 1996; in Bulgaria from 26 per cent in 1990 to 31 per cent in 1997.[52] Nowadays, however, it does not differ much from that of Western Europe, with the exception of Scandinavia where it is lower. It was primarily the differentiation of wages based on sector and qualification in post-socialism which led to the

Table 4.3 Labour force participation by gender in Central and Eastern Europe in 1990 and 2006 (in %)

	Male			Female		
	1990	2006	change	1990	2006	Change
Bulgaria	77.8	62.2	-15.6	72.2	51.6	-20.6
Latvia	83.6	72.0	-11.6	75.3	63.1	-12.2
Poland	79.2	68.2	-11.0	65.1	57.3	-7.8
Romania	77.2	66.9	-10.3	61.1	54.4	-6.7
Estonia	83.1	73.7	-9.4	76.2	64.6	-11.6
Lithuania	81.7	72.5	-9.2	70.4	66.4	-4
Hungary	74.4	66.6	-7.8	57.3	53.7	-3.6
Slovakia	82.5	76.3	-6.2	70.6	62.3	-8.3
Czech Republic	82.1	77.0	-5.1	74.0	64.4	-9.6
Slovenia	76.9	75.6	-1.3	63.3	67.0	3.7
CEE 10	**79.9**	**71.1**	**-8.8**	**68.6**	**60.5**	**-8.1**
EU 15	**80.0**	**78.3**	**-1.7**	**56.1**	**64.5**	**8.4**

Source: Michael Gebel, 'Labour Markets in Central and Eastern Europe', in *Europe Enlarged: A Handbook of Education, Labour and Welfare Regimes in Central and Eastern Europe*, eds Irena Kogan, Michael Gebel and Clemens Noelke (Bristol: The Policy Press, 2008), 44.

---

50 Therborn, *Die Gesellschaften Europas 1945–2000*, 78.
51 Female Labour Market Participation, 8, http://ec.europa.eu/europe2020/pdf/themes/31_labour_market_participation_of_women.pdf (accessed 5 May 2016).
52 Brunnbauer, 'From Equality without Democracy'.

increasing gender pay gap as many women were concentrated in lower positions. On the other hand, the gender pay gap has somewhat decreased by the fact that many women professionals have experienced a rise in income as a group, most notably in banking or law. As Fidelis argues: 'the cultural capital that some women were able to acquire under communism and then utilize in the post-communist professional world was to an extent a result of occupational segregation and the feminization of the service sector of the economy.'[53] As co-authors Mira Marody and Anna Giza-Poleszcuk claim, 'for the few women who are relatively young, have the requisite job skills, and are unburdened by children, the post-1989 transition has been filled with rewards and opportunities ... Nevertheless, this is a relatively small new elite.'[54] Gender inequalities seem to be less grave than the developing inequalities between social strata, rural and urban areas or generations. Reaching the same education levels as men during state socialism, women seem to be immunized to some extent against the growing inequalities in capitalism.

Like Western Europe, the region is still marked by an unequal division of labour in the home. According to a 1995 survey from the Czech Republic, it is estimated that women spent about 18–20 hours per week on housework, whereas men spent only about 6 hours.[55] An international comparison in which only Hungary was included from the region has shown, however, that the differences are not higher than in Western Europe (again, with the exception of Scandinavia).[56] In any case, the post-socialist abundance of goods and services, in contrast with the socialist 'shortage economy', has helped to ease the woman's daily workload that is required to maintain a family (microwaves, disposable nappies, big shopping centres). That is to say, women no longer have to go shopping every day, wait in queues and carry heavy bags.[57]

Women and political representation

The right to vote

Another important aspect of the emancipation of women was the gaining of equal rights before the law which included the right to vote. Indeed, women's suffrage was part of the platform of socialist and liberal movements, and although it originated in the West, it was soon received in the countries of the region (as can be seen by the quick translation of John Stuart Mill's *The Subjection of Women* into the many different languages of Central and Eastern Europe). Before 1918 in Central and Eastern Europe, women were by law unequal to men throughout the region, albeit there were differences between the countries. Under Hungarian law, for example, women were legally better off than those under Austrian law, where a woman was first subordinate to her father, then to her husband. In Hungary, women became fully independent after reaching the age of majority, or adulthood. In Cisleithania (the Austrian half of the monarchy), if a woman were to get divorced, she would lose all possessions that she either did not earn for herself, or initially bring with her into the marriage; however, under Hungarian law, a divorced woman had the

---

53 Fidelis, *Women, Communism, and Industrialization*, 252.
54 Mira Marody and Anna Giza-Poleszcuk, 'Changing Images of Identity in Poland: From the Self-Sacrificing to the Self-Investing Woman?', in *Reproducing Gender: Politics, Publics and Everyday Life after Socialism*, eds Susan Gal and Gail Kligman (Princeton, NJ: Princeton University Press, 2000), 151–75, here 174.
55 Alena Křížková and Marta Vohlídalová, 'The Labour Market and Work-life Balance in the Czech Republic in Historical Perspective', in Hašková and Uhde, *Women and Social Citizenship*, 35–76, here 65.
56 Shirley Dex, 'Can State Policies Produce Equality in Housework', in Treas and Drobnič, *Dividing the Domestic*, 79–104, here 86.
57 Marody and Giza-Poleszcuk, 'Changing Images of Identity in Poland', 165.

right to half of the property. Also under Hungarian law, a widow had the right to govern the property after the death of her husband; in Austrian law on the other hand, adult descendants had priority in the inheritance.[58] In Serbia and other countries with an Ottoman legacy, the civil code of 1848 considered women to be on the same level as children and thus did not grant them the right of autonomous decision-making.[59] This period before the First World War also saw the first attempts by women to run for political office, namely, a group of Czech activists. The law of Bohemia did not explicitly deny their passive electoral rights, as it simply did not occur to the lawmakers to do so. In 1908, three women ran for office in the Bohemian Diet for the first time, albeit unsuccessfully. And in 1912, the first Czech woman, a nationalist-feminist writer, was elected to office, but the governor of Bohemia refused to approve her mandate.[60]

After 1918, gender equality laws appeared in the constitutions of Poland, Czechoslovakia and the Baltic countries, and equal rights in politics, both passive (the right to run for office) and active (the right to vote), were granted to women.[61] However, in Hungary, and later in Bulgaria and Romania, women were only granted limited electoral rights. In Yugoslavia and Albania, there was no suffrage for women at all. In Hungary in 1920, the electoral right was given only to literate women, while this was not required of men. According to historian Maria Kovács, the law was approved not with the ambition to emancipate but, 'in order to please the victorious Entente and partly as an instrument of a conservative stabilization.'[62] The conservative forces in Hungary, however, campaigned against the exclusion of illiterate women, as there was a fear this would increase the influence of liberal and Jewish women. After 1922, this right was considerably curtailed: women retained their voting rights only if they were above the age of 30, had a university degree or were married with at least three children. This meant that the number of Hungarian women above the age of 24 who were previously allowed to vote, decreased by 40 per cent.[63] In Slovenia, all political parties requested the right to vote in 1918, but as the country seceded to the Kingdom of the Serbs, Croats and Slovenes, this was not implemented.[64] In Bulgaria, women's voting rights were limited: women were allowed to vote in communal elections for the first time in 1937, but only those who were married with children; and while voting was obligatory for men, it was optional for women. A few months following that decision, voting rights were extended to all women and they were allowed to vote in every election, but the passive right was still denied them.[65] Romanian women were enfranchised in 1938, but this was also restricted to certain categories, and the passive right was only granted in the case

---

58 Gabriela Dudeková and Tünde Lengyelová, 'Premeny právneho postavenia žien' [Changes in the legal status of women], in *Na ceste k modernej žene: kapitoly z dejín rodových vzťahov*, eds Gabriela Dudeková et al. (Bratislava:Veda, 2011), 312.
59 Sabrina Ramet,'In Tito's Time', in *Gender Politics in the Western Balkans:Women and Society in Yugoslavia and the Yugoslav Successor States*, ed. S.P. Ramet (University Park, PA: Penn State Press, 2010), 89–106, here 92.
60 D. Musilová, *Z ženského pohledu, Poslankyně a senátorky Národního shromáždění ČSR 1918–1939* [From the female point of view: female members of parliament and senators of national assembly of ČSR 1918–1938], (Univerzita Hradec Králové:Veduta, 2007), 30. For more information on the legal position of European women in comparative perspective, see the subchapter on partnership and patriarchy.
61 Anna Zarnovska, 'Women's Political Participation in Inter-War Poland: Opportunities and Limitations', *Women's History Review* 13, no. 1 (2004), 57–68, here 58.
62 Kovács,'Hungarian Women Entering the Professions', 250.
63 Papp, *Die Kraft der weiblichen Seele*, 235.
64 Milica Antić Gaber and Irena Selišnik, 'Slovene Women's Suffrage Movement in a Comparative Perspective', in *Suffrage, Gender and Citizenship: International Perspectives on Parliamentary Reforms*, eds Irma Sulkunen, Seija-Leena Nevala-Nurmi and Pirjo Markkola (Newcastle: Cambridge Scholar Publishing, 2009), 219–41, here 231.
65 Daskalova,'The Women's Movement in Bulgaria in a Life Story', 97.

of the Senate, not for the Chamber of Deputies.[66] The establishment of the royal dictatorship several months afterwards, however, prevented the law from coming into being.

Throughout the countries with women's suffrage, conservative forces (who originally opposed voting rights for women) quickly realized that women would rather vote conservative than liberal or left. In Hungary, granting women the right to vote helped the agrarian conservative Christian National Union Party in its electoral success in 1920.[67] In Slovakia, suffrage perhaps assured the victory of Andrej Hlinka's Slovak People's Party in 1920. As Ursula Bauman has written regarding the whole of interwar Europe, 'It is doubtless rather ironic that precisely those political forces which had most vehemently opposed women's political equality profited most from women's votes.'[68] It seems that in the countries where women had the right to vote, many would vote according to their husbands' wishes or according to the recommendation of their priest. With regard to Czechoslovakia, according to one popular joke in the more secular Czech part, women's suffrage meant two votes at the disposal of a married man; while in Slovakia, which was more religious, it meant 100 votes at the disposal of the priest.

The right to be elected

Passive enfranchisement soon brought the first female representatives to the parliaments, although the numbers remained in the single digits throughout the 1920s and 1930s. Poland's interwar parliament had female representatives as early as 1919; but they rarely made up more than two per cent of representatives in the Sejm and around four per cent in the Senate.[69] In Czechoslovakia, women made up four per cent of the parliament between 1925 and 1929, and only three per cent between 1929 and 1935. Lithuania had the highest percentage of women in parliament with seven per cent in 1920.[70] After Antanas Smetona established his authoritarian regime in 1926, women were pushed out of Lithuanian politics. Although women's suffrage was not abolished, an obstacle was created which granted passive electoral rights only to property owners, thus excluding some female candidates, since by law, family property belonged to the husband.[71] Estonia and Latvia also granted passive rights to women. In Hungary, there were only four women representatives in parliament during the interwar period. On the other hand, women were denied passive franchise in all of Southeastern Europe.[72] Concerning political affiliation, women were present across the political spectrum with the exception of the extreme right, which as Karen Offen has characterized as 'profoundly antifeminist'[73] (several fascist movements in the region did not even accept women as party members).

Before taking office, many suffragists had been involved in feminist movements or in public education and charity, and they remained faithful to these affiliations in their parliamentary work

---

66 Roxana Cheschebec, 'Toward a Romanian Women's Movement, An Organizational History, (1880s–1940)', in Saurer, Lanzinger and Frysak, *Women's Movements, Networks and Debates*, 439–56, here 454.
67 Kovács, 'Hungarian Women Entering the Professions', 250.
68 Ursula Baumann, 'Religion, Emancipation, and Politics in the Confessional Women's Movement in Germany, 1900–1933', in *Borderlines: Gender and Identities in War and Peace 1870–1930*, ed. Billie Melman (London: Routledge, 1998), 285–306, here 295.
69 Zarnowska, 'Women's Political Participation', 58.
70 Virginija Jurénienė, 'The Lithuanian Women's Movement at the Beginning of the 20th Century', in Saurer, Lanzinger and Frysak, *Women's Movements, Networks and Debates*, 457–74, here 470–73.
71 Jurénienė, 'The Lithuanian Women's Movement', 473.
72 Musilová, *Z ženského pohledu*, 57.
73 Karen Offen, *European Feminisms, 1700–1950: A Political History* (Stanford, CA: Stanford University Press, 2000), p. 279.

as well. 'Hard' politics (diplomacy, economy, military) remained the realm of men. This was similar to the position of women in Western Europe: in none of these countries did women attain a cabinet position in the government or any other position where they might chair a body of men. Quite often, the gender equality that was promised in the constitutions was not realized in everyday life since the civil codes contained several provisions that did not correspond to actual gender equality. For instance, the definition of a husband was that he was the head of the household and was thus the one who could decide if his wife were allowed to work outside the home.[74]

Although gender equality was one of the demands of the social democratic and communist movements from the beginning, this failed to become a reality after these movements came to power. Shortly after 1945, the role of women in communist governments and apparatuses in the region seems to have become more important. During this time, the first women ministers were named almost exclusively for health or social policy. Yet, one woman made it to the highest ranks of the Romanian regime: Ana Pauker became the minister of foreign affairs (1947–1952), whom *Time* magazine called 'the most powerful woman alive'. In Czechoslovakia and Bulgaria, women were present in the highest ranks of party leadership (politburo). However, the number of women in the highest ranks started to decline in the early 1950s, and important female-politicians were purged in Czechoslovakia, Bulgaria and Romania. For the rest of their existence, the communist regimes remained male dominated and this became increasingly obvious from the 1970s onwards as Western Europe took the lead in engaging women in politics.

Although there was a rising proportion of women with communist party membership during the socialist period (for example, in Yugoslavia women made up 19 per cent of the party in 1948, 23 per cent in 1977 and 31 per cent in 1986),[75] their attainment of higher positions tended either to stagnate or to decline. This discrepancy was the case all over the region. Again, in Yugoslavia, women counted for 19 per cent of the Communist Party's membership in 1948, but only 9 per cent of delegates to congress, 5 per cent of the central committee members and 4 per cent of MPs were women. Even Tito addressed this problem as an important issue,[76] possibly as a part of his attempt to represent a democratic alternative to the Soviet model. As a result, several quotas were introduced, and Yugoslavia went on to be the first of the socialist countries to have women become the heads of government and of regional parties (Savka Dabčević-Kučar, Prime Minister of Croatia 1967–1969, Head of the League of Communists of Croatia 1969–1971, Latinka Perović, Secretary of the Central Committee of the League of Communists of Serbia 1968–1972, and Milka Planinc, Head of the League of Communists of Croatia 1971–1982, and then Prime Minister of Yugoslavia 1982–1986).

Although the introduction of different quotas began in the 1970s, it did not really improve the position of women throughout the Soviet bloc – while their presence increased (mainly in political bodies), they still lacked any real power (e.g. in parliament). Their position in governments, central committees and politburos remained much weaker. For example, there was not a single woman amongst the 12 members of the politburo of the communist party in Czechoslovakia in the 1970s and 1980s, nor amongst the two dozen members of government; while in the central committee women made up 10 per cent, in parliament, the figure was between 25 per cent and 30 per cent.[77] It seems that women came closest to the highest

---

74 Feinberg, *Elusive Equality*, 51
75 Ramet, 'In Tito's Time', 99, 102.
76 Ibid., 99.
77 Složení vedoucích orgánů KSČ [Composition of the leading organs of the Communist Party of Czechoslovakia], www.ustrcr.cz/data/pdf/projekty/funkcionari-ksc/nejvyssi-organy.pdf (accessed 8 September 2016).

ranks of power in those countries of Southeastern Europe where the regimes took on dynastic features. In Bulgaria, for example, Ludmila Živkovova was considered a successor to her father until her premature death in 1981. Romania was the only case amongst the socialist countries where the general secretary's wife, Elena Ceaușescu, became the second most important person in the country – second only to her husband. Margot Honecker (of the GDR) was the only other wife of a general secretary who made it to the higher ranks; however, her power and influence were much more limited. By the time her husband became the head of the state, she had already held office as the Minister of People's Education, but in contrast to the Romanian situation, no powerful ruling couple was created in the GDR.

Women as political opponents

Women were often engaged as oppositional activists either directly (as activists, spokespersons, writers) or indirectly (as wives and mothers). As direct activists, their roles were rather minor. For example, from the first signatories of Charter 77, only 14 per cent were women, none of whom became important representatives of the oppositional movement;[78] yet, the Charter was the first to introduce the rule that one of the three speakers must be a woman. Among Solidarity leadership, women were even less present: although women made up half of its members and one of its first leaders was a woman (a crane operator and dissident activist named Anna Walentynowicz, whose dismissal from her position sparked the movement), at Solidarity's first national congress held in 1981, women made up only 7.8 per cent of the delegates, and only one woman was elected to its national executive membership council.[79] Women, however, played an important role in the everyday activities of the oppositional movement and they were often secondary victims of political repression during the arrests of their husbands. As historian Shana Penn showed, Polish activists were involved in highly political activities, most notably, the publication of the samizdat *Mazowsze Weekly* (*Tygodnik Mazowsze*),

Table 4.4 Political positions held by women in Central and Eastern Europe, 1972–1975

Country	Party members 1972 in %	Parliament 1975 in %	Central Committee 1975 in %
Albania	24	26	
Bulgaria	26	18	17
Czechoslovakia	27	26	11
Hungary	25	23	8
Poland	23	15	4
Romania	25	14	5
Yugoslavia	16	13	8

Note: There are different years for Czechoslovakia: 1966; Romania: 1974; Yugoslavia: 1964.

Sources: Barbara Wolfe Jancar, *Women under Communism* (Baltimore, MD: Johns Hopkins University Press, 1978), 92–93. Mary Ellen Fischer, 'Women in Romanian Politics: Elena Ceaușescu, Pronatalism and the Promotion of Women', in *Women, State and Party in Eastern Europe*, eds Sharon L. Wolchik and Alfred G. Meyer (Durham, NC: Duke University Press, 1985), 128, 132; Sabrina Ramet, 'In Tito's Time', in *Gender Politics in the Western Balkans: Women and Society in Yugoslavia and the Yugoslav Successor States*, ed. Sabrina Ramet (University Park, PA: Pennsylvania State University Press, 1999), 100.

---

78 Květa Jechová, *Lidé Charty 77: Zpráva o biografickém výzkumu* [The people of Charter 77: a report on the biographical research] (Prague: ÚSD AV ČR, 2003), 69.
79 Barbara Jancar, 'Women in the Opposition in Poland and Czechoslovakia in the 1970s', in Wolchik and Meyer, *Women, State and Party*, 168–85, here 169–70.

an important discussion platform which appeared after Solidarity had been chased underground. This group of women, who called themselves *Damska Grupa Operacyjna* (Ladies' Operation Unit), was not discovered by the secret police as it kept the identities of its authors and editors hidden, and it did not occur to the officers that women could even be behind such a publication. In keeping their identities secret, they were trying to avoid police interrogation and prison which was regarded as more difficult for women to withstand. Penn mentions cases in which women served as speech writers for the Solidarity leaders, or even gave interviews that were published in the Western press under the names of male leaders. Keeping the identity of these authors secret is the reason why the Solidarity movement is strictly perceived as a male affair and why the founding mothers of the Polish opposition remain unknown.[80] In the cases in which their husbands were arrested, they established circles of mutual aid; or, if one of their husbands lost his job, the roles in the household were reversed, he would take care of their children and his wife would get a paid job.[81] According to Petra Schindler-Wisten, state repression rather increased the cohesion of the family, as divorce among dissenters was fairly rare.[82] However, if we take into consideration the number of illegitimate children which were born amongst these groups of dissenters, we can perhaps speak about group rather than family cohesion.

The attempts of Western feminist activists to spread their ideas among the anti-communist opposition were unsuccessful. There were almost no feminist oppositional organizations with the exception of the GDR's *Frauen für Frieden*, or Women for Peace. Indeed, feminism was never a matter of discussion in oppositional circles. In Eastern Europe, feminist topics were seen as irrelevant in comparison with the question of universal human rights. In 1985, Václav Havel commented on the difficulties of finding a common language between Western feminists and Eastern dissidents:

> I do not wish to ridicule feminism; I know little about it and am prepared to believe that it is far from being the invention of a few hysterical women, bored housewives, or cast-off mistresses. Still, I have to note that in our country, even though the position of women is incomparably worse than in the West, feminism seems simply 'dada'.[83]

With the world 'dada', Havel meant that feminist issues were irrelevant or even crazy-sounding within the context of state socialism, where he believed both sexes were facing the repression of the regime. The idea that dissent is also unequal in terms of gender was difficult for him to understand.

Women in politics after socialism

Concerning women in politics, it is difficult to speak of either an improvement or a decline after 1989. The first post-socialist election saw a decline throughout the region in the number of women in elected bodies. For example, in Croatia, only four per cent of the delegates in the first post-communist assembly were women; in Romania, only three per cent, and in 1998 in

---

80 Shana Penn, *Solidarity's Secret: The Women Who Defeated Communism in Poland* (Ann Arbor, MI: University of Michigan Press, 2005), 10–12.
81 Petra Schindler-Wisten, 'Der Einfluss auf die Tätigkeit im Dissens auf das Familienleben in der Zeit der so genannten Normalisierung', in *Geschlechterbeziehungen in Ostmitteleuropa nach dem Zweiten Weltkrieg: Soziale Praxis und Konstruktion von Geschlechterbildern – Vorträge der Tagung des Collegium Carolinum in Bad Wiessee vom 17. bis 20. November 2005*, ed. Claudia Kraft (München: Oldenbourg, 2008), 231–50, here 244.
82 Schindler-Wisten, 'Einfluss auf die Tätigkeit im Dissens auf das Familienleben', 249.
83 Václav Havel, 'Anatomie jedné zdrženlivosti' [The anatomy of restraint], in *Do různých stran: Eseje a články z let 1983–1989* (Scheinfeld: ČSDS, 1989), 70–71.

Macedonia, also only three per cent.[84] In Central Europe, the situation was only slightly better: 19 per cent of the first democratic parliament in Czechoslovakia were women, while Poland had 13 per cent, and Hungary had 7 per cent.[85] This has aroused the concern of feminists but it does not necessarily indicate a real decline in the influence of women in politics as the socialist parliaments were not the real centres of power as they were in the post-socialist parliaments.[86] Gender quotas have gone rather unused in the region as they are associated with the previous regimes. In post-socialist countries, the word feminism continues to be pejorative, and at times, even 'women's emancipation' is called into question as a legacy of socialism. An infamous example is that of Romania, where for a long time, Elena Ceaușescu discredited feminist issues. On the other hand, the 1990s saw the first women prime ministers and presidents of the countries in the north of region: Kazimira Prunskienė (Prime Minister of Lithuania 1990–91), Hanna Suchocka (Prime Minister of Poland 1992–93) and Vaira Vīķe-Freiberga (President of Latvia 1999–2007). The development of civil society and the founding of various NGOs (against domestic violence, labour discrimination, etc.) also represent an important improvement for the feminist movement. As we can see from Table 4.5, the position of women in politics in Slovenia and the Baltic countries is quite strong, while Romania, Bulgaria and most of the Post-Yugoslav countries are on the other end of continuum.

Women and (hetero)sexuality

The nationalization of desire

National accents resonated in the politics of love and marriage in the nineteenth century. At that time, Central and Southeastern Europe was a mix of cultures, languages and ethnicities

Table 4.5 Women in politics in Central and Eastern Europe in 2009 (in %)

	Women senior ministers in national government	*Women members of single/lower house of parliament*	*Country had a female prime minister or president between 1989 and 2009*
Romania	0	10	
Hungary	13	11	
Slovakia	6	13	
Slovenia	17	13	
Czech Rep.	11	16	
Poland	25	20	Hanna Suchocka (1992–93)
Estonia	21	21	
Bulgaria	26	22	
Lithuania	13	23	Kazimira Prunskienė (1990–91) Dalia Grybauskaitė (2009–19)
Latvia	21	21	Vaira Vīķe-Freiberga (1999–2007)
EU 27	26	23	

Source: Gillian Pascall, Anna Kwak, 'Gender Regimes in Transition: Gender Equality in CEE Countries?' in *Welfare States and Gender in Central and Eastern Europe: Continuity and Post-Socialist Transformation in the EU Member States*, eds Christina Klenner and Simone Leiber (Brussels: European Trade Union Institute, 2010), 140.

---

84 Brunnbauer, 'From Equality without Democracy'.
85 Ann Taylor Allen, *Women in Twentieth-Century Europe* (Houndmills: Palgrave Macmillan, 2008), 135.
86 Peggy Watson, 'The Rise of Masculinism in Eastern Europe', *New Left Review* 198 (1993): 71–82, here 73.

where people who claimed shared ethno-national roots often lived separated by state borders, while their neighbours claimed allegiance to different ethno-national communities. As the century progressed and national movements gained traction, a special emphasis was placed on national endogamy. Women were to marry men from their own ethnic community (for men the dictum applied in a limited capacity, as we will show). Many a national song extolled the virtues of a people's 'own' men and women falling in love while warning against foreigners, mostly the ones who were physically the closest. Thus, Slovak women were warned against Hungarian and German men; Hungarian maidens were to lock their doors against Slovak men; Slavic girls in the Balkans were threatened by 'a fate worse than death' had they married a Turk; and Polish brides would rather die than marry a German.[87] Patriotic poets disparaged the sexuality of the ethnic 'others' that allegedly caused adultery and social disintegration in the imperial centres of Vienna and Berlin. By the end of the century, patriots 'saw exogamy as national degeneration, while their predecessors had described it as merely undesirable.'[88] Erotic love was portrayed as 'sweet' for a compatriot couple, and women were encouraged to enjoy it as long as they did not fall for a foreigner; that is, female sexual desire was celebrated if the woman desired a man of her own nationality. While female chastity, so often present in nineteenth-century literature, was 'conspicuous by its absence,'[89] another double standard applied to women. As Alexander Maxwell argues, 'exogamous marriage denationalized women, but men could swell the nation's ranks by converting foreign brides.'[90] He presents examples of several prominent figures of national movements (all men) who in their writing urged endogamy, while in their own lives married a foreign woman without it damaging their credentials. The nation was thus 'a brotherhood of men' in which the weight of biological reproduction was carried by women who, however, could lose their national status by making the 'wrong' sexual choices.

Women and their perceived attractiveness in the eyes of men delineated national boundaries. Men from within, and outside of, the Habsburg Empire sang praises of female beauty. Thus, pan-Slavists praised the looks of Czech women over the physical attributes of their Germanic counterparts, and while they did not contest the claims of beauty in Hungarian women, they eagerly sought those with 'Slavic' features. The purity of women's beauty was conflated with national purity as patriots claimed the 'purer' beauty was found in the countryside because it was unspoiled by 'blood mixing'.[91] While national women were portrayed as alluring (yet chaste) future wives, men were represented as heroic brethren of considerable sexual prowess. Interestingly, even across national allegiances, men kept masculine loyalties over the ethno-national ones and refrained from attacking men of 'other' nations on account of their sexuality. As Maxwell argues, this 'conspiracy of politeness' served the purpose of avoiding conflicts and tension.[92] Nationalized fantasies of desire were projected on women with an understanding nod shared among men.

Women's status fundamentally depended on men. Even after the constitutions of newly created nation states refused to recognize the privileges of sex, and after voting rights were bestowed upon women in the wake of the First World War, women's position within marriage and in the eyes of the public remained unequal. Women not only lacked rights over themselves and

---

87 Alexander Maxwell, 'National Endogamy and Double Standards: Sexuality and Nationalism in East-Central Europe during the 19th Century', *Journal of Social History* 41, no. 2 (2008): 413–33, here 416–23.
88 Ibid., 416.
89 Ibid., 425.
90 Ibid., 425.
91 Alexander Maxwell, 'Nationalizing Sexuality: Sexual Stereotypes in the Habsburg Empire', *Journal of the History of Sexuality* 14 (2005): 266–90, here 274–6, doi:10.1353/sex.2006.0026.
92 Maxwell, 'Nationalizing Sexuality', 288.

their children, their claim to any rights at all – the rights guaranteed by the state – hinged upon the citizenship of their husbands. For example, in interwar Czechoslovakia, a married woman automatically received the citizenship of her husband and if he chose to emigrate or was stateless, she lost her citizenship.[93] The state thus ensured a kind of national purity of marriage and the family, insofar as it was possible in the ethnically mixed interwar societies. The woman's role was to bear children, and any equality women aspired to, needed to bow first to this tradition.

Prostitution and marriage: between venereal disease and eugenics

Prostitution had long demarcated the line between respectable and fallen women, yet during the nineteenth century, it became publicly identified as an institution parallel to that of marriage: middle class men sustained their marriages thanks to periodic ventures into the red-light districts. Activists who called for a prostitution ban subsequently invoked miserable working conditions for the women involved, as well as a sexual double standard that allowed men to be promiscuous while at the same time condemning women who transgressed the bounds of marital fidelity. Sexual standards played a crucial role in constructing citizens (and divides among them) during the late decades in the Habsburg, Ottoman and Romanov imperia. Regulation of sexual behaviour shifted from the church to the state as the civic codes began to encompass behaviours such as prostitution. The Habsburg Empire enacted a decree in 1854 that subjected prostitution to police control.[94] With people moving from the countryside to the cities, panic arose around sexual promiscuity. Women who had recently left their peasant communities in partitioned Poland in order to work in factories in places like Lwów, were suspected of spreading venereal disease. New regulations, adopted at the turn of the century, gave doctors the authority to examine all working women for venereal disease, in effect treating them like prostitutes. Historian Keely Stauter-Halsted argues that moral panic surrounding prostitution was triggered by broader anxieties about social status in a rapidly changing Polish-speaking community in early twentieth-century Poland. Women from poor backgrounds fell prey to these growing social fears.[95] Real or imagined, women as sexualized objects centred in newspaper stories which greatly excited the increasingly literate readership of the urban centres. Stories of rape and murder titillated citizens in urbanizing Cracow.[96] The horrific 'white slave trade', in which innocent country girls were supposedly sold to brothels in exotic lands, roused the imagination of the people. Often, moral degeneration intertwined with ethno-religious differences as the perceived pimps were portrayed as Jews willing to sacrifice women in order to further their own economic prospects.[97] Women transgressing strict norms of home-bound wives and mothers risked accusations of immorality. Once they set foot into the public world, they might have been targeted as 'fallen women'. Without guardianship of their fathers or

---

93 Feinberg, *Elusive Equality*, 72–98.
94 Keely Stauter-Halsted and N. Wingfield, 'Introduction: The Construction of Sexual Deviance in Late Imperial Eastern Europe', *Journal of the History of Sexuality* 20, no. 2 (2011): 215–24, here 219.
95 Keely Stauter-Halsted, 'The Physician and the Fallen Woman: Medicalizing Prostitution in the Polish Lands', *Journal of the History of Sexuality* 20, no. 2 (May 2011): 270–90, doi:10.5555/jhs.2011.20.2.270.
96 Nathaniel Wood, 'Sex Scandals, Sexual Violence, and the Word on the Street: The Kolasówna Lustmord in Cracow's Popular Press, 1905–1906', *Journal of the History of Sexuality* 20, no. 2 (May 2011): 243–69, doi:10.5555/jhs.2011.20.2.243.
97 Nancy M. Wingfield, 'Destination: Alexandria, Buenos Aires, Constantinople; "White Slavers" in Late Imperial Austria', *Journal of the History of Sexuality* 20, no. 2 (2011): 291–311, doi:10.1353/sex.2011.0024.

husbands, women in increasing numbers made their own choices about who to spend time with. Yet, their community scrutinized their preferences. In occupied Belgrade during the First World War, a special 'native police' was set up to control the behaviour of Serbs and the extent to which they fraternized with the occupiers. Women seen as too close to foreign soldiers were castigated as prostitutes, irrespective of the nature of the relationship in question (whether they engaged in sexual behaviour, if money changed hands, or not).[98] Indeed, women ran the risk of being labelled as prostitutes; this risk was even more pronounced during times of rapid social change (such as urbanization) or acute conflict (such as war).

While most who spoke publicly loathed prostitution, there were outliers who celebrated it for preserving the chastity of women. As an Austro-Hungarian author wrote in the first decade of the twentieth century, in garrison towns with dozens of soldiers, respectable wives and daughters were safer if brothels were nearby where these young men could release their sexual tensions.[99]

Unlike prostitutes, married women stood on the other end of the indecency–respectability spectrum. Yet even wives, historically perceived as chaste and fundamentally uninterested in sex, began to expect sexual fulfilment in marriage. In 1926, a Dutch gynaecologist Theodoor van de Velde published a book called *Ideal Marriage: Its Physiology and Technique*, which would come to be described as the best-selling sex manual of all time. In the book, van de Velde posited sexual pleasure for both husband and wife at the crux of marriage and went on to claim that 'happiness within marriage depended on sex being fulfilling for both partners.'[100] Translation into Eastern European languages followed closely behind the original publication date: in 1928, the book appeared in Hungarian; two years later, in Czech (with subsequent interwar editions in 1933 and 1936); and in Polish in 1935 (with a sixth Polish edition in 1939). Conjugal sex advice became an instant hit in the countries of Central Europe. Sexual enjoyment in marriage was such a foreign idea to traditional mores that the Catholic Church put van de Velde's text on its index of prohibited books.[101]

The international sexual reform movement which was striving for women's equality, divorce rights and safe birth control, spilled over from Western Europe into the East. The World League for Sexual Reform's last congress took place in 1932 in the Czechoslovak city of Brno (it was moved there from Moscow after having been banned by Stalin).[102] In May of the following year, the Nazis destroyed the *Institut für Sexualwissenschaft* in Berlin, whose founder, Magnus Hirschfeld, was also a founder of the World League for Sexual Reform. The Nazis burned books on sexuality that were gathered by the Institute, giving a loud and clear signal that the Nazi regime would not tolerate any perversities and novel sexual mores.

During the 1920s and 1930s, progressive policies of sex reform became intertwined with eugenics, which contained its infamous racial component. Both movements shared beliefs in reason and social engineering, which they viewed as essential in the march of progress. Thus, in

---

98 Jovana Knežević, 'Prostitutes as a Threat to National Honor in Habsburg-Occupied Serbia during the Great War', *Journal of the History of Sexuality* 20, no. 2 (1 May 2011): 312–35, doi:10.5555/jhs.2011.20.2.312.
99 Dagmar Herzog, *Sexuality in Europe: A Twentieth-Century History* (Cambridge: Cambridge University Press, 2011), 14.
101 Ibid., 50.
100 Ibid., 50.
102 Dan Healey, *Homosexual Desire in Revolutionary Russia: The Regulation of Sexual and Gender Dissent* (Chicago, IL: University of Chicago Press, 2001); Ralf Dose and Pamela Eve Selwyn, 'The World League for Sexual Reform: Some Possible Approaches', *Journal of the History of Sexuality* 12, no. 1 (2003): 1–15, doi:10.1353/sex.2003.0057.

interwar Poland, eugenicists 'propagated social hygiene, combatted prostitution and supported women's emancipation and all the progressive social movements'[103] while calling for sterilization of criminals and the mentally ill. Further, eugenicists and sex reformers shared the idea of sexual education for the young; while the former saw in it a means to tackle venereal disease, the latter perceived sex education as a necessary step on the path of self-determination. Both movements favoured secular marriage, free from the oversight of the church. Eugenicists' calls for limiting procreation were seconded by sex reformers. In 1929, a Polish eugenicist claimed that, 'in very many instances, conception should have never taken place'; he went on to say that, '[a]ll forms of mental suffering, moral and mental degeneration, alcoholism, epilepsy, severe conditions of hysteria are passed on through offspring and those burdened with these conditions should not reproduce'; these sentiments were echoed by Polish sex reformers who stated in the resolution from their first congress in 1934 that 'accidental selection should be replaced by conscious selection based on eugenic guidelines.'[104] Deciding whether or not to have children was not to be an individual decision, but a matter of state importance to which governmental authorities would intervene. Yet, eugenic dreams 'in interwar Poland suffered a total defeat.'[105]

Hungary experienced a similar interweaving of reformist and eugenic drives. In 1919, a right-wing regime displaced a communist venture and birth control was propagated by eugenicists: only those viewed as 'hereditarily ill or mentally deficient [were prevented] from propagating, and [the authorities] had absolutely no interest in contraception as a means toward female self-determination.'[106] States tried to replenish their citizenry which was decimated by the Great War, but not just anyone was free to reproduce. Public health officials across Eastern Europe worried about the quality of the population that would be coming out of diseased bodies; only healthy people should be allowed to marry and beget offspring. Thus, a new measure was conceived: premarital eugenic counselling. In 1920s Hungary, it was being debated specifically with the purpose of combatting venereal disease. Serious efforts to make marital counselling obligatory were conducted during the 1930s and 1940s when those 'seen as a threat to the body of the nation' were to be banned from reproducing.[107] However, obligatory premarital health exams introduced in 1941 failed: young people remained uninterested in consulting experts about whom to marry and rates of venereal disease remained the same until antibiotics were introduced in the mid-1940s. Similarly, in Romania in 1940, obligatory premarital health exams were introduced for soldiers and were later to become a required procedure for everyone wanting to enter a marriage.[108]

While universal health checks in Romania never materialized, one group became particularly targeted by eugenicists: women. Defined and celebrated as procreators, interwar Romanian

---

103 Magdalena Gawin, 'The Sex Reform Movement and Eugenics in Interwar Poland', *Studies in History and Philosophy of Science Part C: Studies in History and Philosophy of Biological and Biomedical Sciences, Eugenics, Sex and the State* 39, no. 2 (June 2008): 181–86, here 181, doi:10.1016/j.shpsc.2008.03.001.
104 Eugenicists and sex reformers quoted respectively, Gawin, 'The Sex Reform Movement', 184.
105 Ibid., 185.
106 Herzog, *Sexuality in Europe*, 55.
107 Gábor Szegedi, 'Veszélyes kapcsolatok – Házassági tanácsadás a biopolitika korai diskurzusa és gyakorlata Magyarországon' [Dangerous liaisons – marriage counselling as an early discourse and practice of biopolitics in Hungary], *Művelődés-, Tudomány- és Orvostörténeti Folyóirat/Journal of History of Culture, Science and Medicine* 3, vol. 5 (2012): 286–306, here 304, www.kaleidoscopehistory.hu/download.php?cikkid=118 (accessed 8 September 2016).
108 Marius Turda, 'The Nation as Object: Race, Blood, and Biopolitics in Interwar Romania', *Slavic Review* 66, no. 3 (2007): 413–41, here 439, doi:10.2307/20060295.

women were to see the quintessence of their political subjectivity in their reproductive capacities: they were building the new nation by the physical activity of childbearing. In the 1930s, eugenicists successfully pushed for abortion to become legal in cases 'of those considered mentally and socially degenerate.'[109] Both penal codes of 1930 and 1936 contained provisions for such an abortion 'where the life of the mother was in danger and when it was carried out to prevent the transmission of mental hereditary disorders.'[110] By the 1940s, the role of women shrank to motherhood without fanfare. 'They had to give birth if they wanted to maintain their health and identity.'[111] Women became suspected of weakening the strength of the nation by being allowed to bear defective babies. Men, as long as they were ethnically Romanian, were not perceived as similarly dysgenic. Thus, gender trumped any other feature of a woman's identity in a way that did not apply to men.[112]

Eugenics was a common answer to many ailments in the first half of the twentieth century.[113] Coming from both the left and the right, eugenicists hailed the proposed measures as progressive and medically apt while propagating national values. However, with the notable exception of abortion in Romania, the eugenic proposals did not become a reality.

The interwar period witnessed a major shift in gender and sexuality. In Russia, unprecedented (and for a long time unparalleled) laws came into effect. In 1920, abortion was legalized and in 1922, homosexuality was decriminalized. While abortion was made available mostly to offset the economic hardships women faced (and abortion was predicted to be abandoned after communism arrived), a strong current of liberatory thought existed in early communism. Alexandra Kollontai, probably the best-known Bolshevik spokesperson for sexual change, promoted a radical view of sexuality unconstrained by class and gender inequalities or hypocritical morality.[114] On the other hand, Lenin never fully subscribed to the ideal of sexual liberation. According to him, self-discipline was paramount, sex was to be enjoyed only in moderation and traditional marital and family bonds never to be dissolved. The course definitely changed under Stalin when 'an era of sexual Thermidor set in.'[115] Abortion was recriminalized in 1936 (and so was homosexuality) with the official explanation that 'industrialization had done away with the social conditions making abortion necessary.'[116] It would take two decades for socialist countries to reinstitute a woman's right to terminate her pregnancy. The Soviet Union legalized abortion again in 1955 and most of its comrade countries followed suit (with two notable exceptions: Romania under Ceaușescu harshly recriminalized abortion in 1966 and East German women were only granted the right to abort in 1972 [more in the subchapter on abortion]).

---

109 Marius Turda, 'To End the Degeneration of a Nation: Debates on Eugenic Sterilization in Inter-War Romania', *Medical History* 53 (2009): 77–104, here 84.
110 Marius Turda, 'Romania', in *The History of East-Central European Eugenics, 1900–1945: Sources and Commentaries*, ed. Marius Turda (London: Bloomsbury Publishing Plc, 2015), 271–362, here 284.
111 Maria Bucur, 'In Praise of Wellborn Mothers: On the Development of Eugenicist Gender Roles in Interwar Romania', *East European Politics & Societies* 9, no. 1 (1 December 1994): 123–42, here 141, doi:10.1177/0888325495009001007.
112 Maria Bucur, *Eugenics and Modernization in Interwar Romania* (Pittsburgh, PA: University of Pittsburgh Press, 2010).
113 Christine Leuenberger, 'Cultures of Categories: Psychological Diagnoses as Institutional and Political Projects before and after the Transition from State Socialism in 1989 in East Germany', *Osiris* 22 (2007): 180–204.
114 Healey, *Homosexual Desire in Revolutionary Russia*, 111.
115 Jelena Batinić, *Women and Yugoslav Partisans: A History of World War II Resistance* (New York: Cambridge University Press, 2015), 175.
116 Frances Lee Bernstein, *The Dictatorship of Sex: Lifestyle Advice for the Soviet Masses* (DeKalb, IL: Northern Illinois University Press, 2007), 171.

Women and sexuality during the world wars

Female civilians often fell prey to sexualized violence. After the Soviet annexation of eastern Poland in 1939, many people were forcibly resettled into the Soviet hinterland. Many of these exiled women were raped repeatedly by the Soviets as the violence continued to escalate. Women felt sullied, and eventually lost the ability to speak about these crimes as crimes committed by the enemy. Indeed, their experiences silenced them.[117] As if the horror of mass rape were not enough, women were subjected to the ire of their families and their communities who deemed them traitors who have dishonoured their kin and the nation. Interestingly, the same treatment befell them had they 'fraternized' with the enemy.[118] When sex was involved, be it forced or voluntary, women were seen as damaged goods and were at fault. In the Protectorate of Bohemia and Moravia, locals saw Czech women who 'fraternized' with the occupiers as participating in the Germanization of the Czech nation. After the war ended, the fraternizing women were brutally attacked and even those who had lawfully married a German man faced discrimination and often violence. However, local men who married German women were treated differently, and their wives came under the auspices of the citizenship decree.[119]

Women joined the fight and battled alongside men in both world wars. Many decided to leave the home front and bypass the usual positions of nurses and administrators providing support to male soldiers. Upending gender stereotypes proved difficult particularly for all survivors after the war was over. Women who never left home became self-reliant, managing entire households in a way unforeseen before the war. Reuniting with their veteran husbands was often 'fraught with tension, because family relations had been realigned during the war.'[120] Women returning from the battlefield faced traditional gender norms, which rendered their wartime lives unintelligible. People 'at home could only make sense of their heroic actions as manly (read: unfeminine) and out of the ordinary (read: abnormal).'[121] In rare cases where women were celebrated as war heroes, popular mythology desexualized them. A Romanian volunteer named Ecaterina Teodoroiu fought in the Great War, was twice wounded and died. Although she was in her twenties and engaged to be married, she was immortalized as a young girl and a virgin; it took stripping her of her womanly attributes for her to be glorified as a fighter.[122]

While female fighters did not become the norm, there existed at least one notable exception during the Second World War: the *partizankas* who were involved en masse in the Yugoslav liberation movement. Popular images of *partizankas* presented fearless warrior women side by side with men. Fascist propaganda portrayed these women as sexually debauched in order to weaken the anti-fascist struggle. In reaction, the Yugoslav Partisans mounted claims and regulations of sexual asceticism describing the relations between women and men in the battlefield

---

117 Katherine R. Jolluck, 'The Nation's Pain and Women's Shame: Polish Women and Wartime Violence', in *Gender and War in Twentieth-Century Eastern Europe*, eds Nancy Meriwether Wingfield and Maria Bucur (Bloomington, IN: Indiana University Press, 2006), 193–219, http://public.eblib.com/choice/publicfullrecord.aspx?p=282521.
118 Nancy Meriwether Wingfield and Maria Bucur, eds, *Gender and War in Twentieth-Century Europe* (Bloomington, IN: Indiana University Press, 2006), 7, 9.
119 Benjamin Frommer, 'Denouncers and Fraternizers: Gender, Collaboration, and Retribution in Bohemia and Moravia during World War II and after', in Wingfield and Bucur, *Gender and War*, 111–32, http://public.eblib.com/choice/publicfullrecord.aspx?p=282521.
120 Frommer, 'Denouncers and Fraternizers', 6.
121 Ibid., 7.
122 Ibid., 7.

as characterized by 'respect, honesty, and camaraderie.'[123] Yet, the Partisans were torn when it came to sex. As part of the communist party, they did not aim to defeat only fascism but bourgeois order as well, the order that subjugated women. Communists embraced the ideology of women's equality, yet in the reality of peasant society, traditional attitudes towards the roles of men and women survived. The chasm was further exacerbated by the ambivalent Soviet approach to sexuality: by the time the Partisans were fighting, Stalin's repressive attitudes towards sex had fully taken hold. So, as Jelena Batinić argues, a double standard was set that punished women for sexual 'transgressions' more than men: it was the woman who was transferred to another unit in case an intimate relationship was discovered, and in case a woman got pregnant, access to abortion was decided by her commander. Generally, women were 'identified as culprits in incidents of sexual nature, and even blamed for thwarting men's commitment to combat.'[124] The gender equality with which women could fight alongside men was not matched by equal treatment in sexual matters.

The centrality of sexuality to the socialist project

The socialist regimes that sprouted in the region after the Second World War introduced gender equality, a topic which many of these countries had debated, but never implemented. Communist legal codes adopted between the mid-1940s and early 1950s ruled equality within marriage so that wives no longer needed their husband's approval to study, work or live outside the home; paternal power over children was abolished, and property came to be shared equally by both spouses. In many countries, divorce was liberalized at the same time: the previous lengthy two-step process that involved several years' separation and the agreement of the other spouse before the marriage could be legally dissolved was abandoned. Sexuality for socialist states was far from an insignificant private matter. As historian Dagmar Herzog points out, 'discussion of sex constantly circled around hopes for the future ... sex became a crucial focus for the regime in its efforts to encourage citizens to endorse more fully the socialist project.'[125] Gender and sexual relations were reformulated simultaneously with class.

While there was no unified 'socialist' path for gender emancipation and sexual liberation, there were striking similarities in the timing of emancipatory versus traditionalizing measures in various countries: the gender and/or sexual progressiveness of the first decade or so was offset by a return to traditional family policies during the 1960s which was cemented by the 1970s and continued to define the regimes until their demise in 1989. Gender regimes were then mapped onto sexuality as it was being discussed by experts and talked about in the media. Also, shared demographic patterns existed that distinguished the socialist camp from the West. First and foremost, marriage and divorce rates were higher in Eastern Europe. Marriage was universal (and often repeated as divorcees entered new matrimonies) across the region; indeed, less than 10 per cent of women aged 50 were never married.[126] As divorce laws became more and more relaxed over the years (the courts stopped attributing blame for the breakdown of the marriage), the frequency of marriage dissolution increased: during the last two decades of state socialism, divorce rates doubled in all countries except for Albania, Romania and Yugoslavia. Yet, there were divorce champions

---

123 Batinić, *Women and Yugoslav Partisans*, 177.
124 Ibid., 212.
125 Dagmar Herzog, *Sex after Fascism: Memory and Morality in Twentieth-Century Germany* (Princeton, NJ: Princeton University Press, 2005), 7.
126 Jean-Paul Sardon, 'Mariage et divorce en Europe de l'Est', *Population* 46, no. 3 (1991): 547–97, www.persee.fr/web/revues/home/prescript/article/pop_0032-4663_1991_num_46_3_3695.

that by far exceeded the region's averages. In Czechoslovakia, Hungary and East Germany, the proportion of divorces reached 30 per cent, compared with only 20 per cent in most of the other countries.[127] Also, it was more often women who sought divorce than men.[128]

From the onset, socialist states guaranteed women equal rights within marriage. The communist-led Bulgarian government decreed equal rights for men and women in 1944. The 'Decree on Marriage' issued the following year stripped the church of the right to confer marriage, it gave both spouses the right to choose their profession and the obligation to contribute to the family budget.[129] In Czechoslovakia, equal rights for men and women were professed by the 1948 constitution and translated into the Act on Family Law which was adopted the following year. Both spouses received equal standing in marriage obliterating the husband's 'head of the household' status. Women and men were equally entitled to the property acquired during marriage. Fathers lost their paternal power and both parents enjoyed the same rights and responsibilities over their children. Also, the distinction between marital and out-of-wedlock children disappeared from the law. Supporting one's children became a legal obligation and the employer could dock the wages of a parent who was not 'fulfilling his duty towards the society.'[130] The 1949 Hungarian constitution declared equality between the sexes and the 1952 Family Law specified what it would mean for the family. Women were guaranteed joint ownership rights which meant that a woman had the right to reside in a family flat that belonged to her husband even after their divorce and until the state assigned her new housing. This policy protected women and children in cases of family dissolution. The law also required that a child had two recognized parents and if a mother was unwed, the welfare agency actively sought the father, encouraged him to marry the mother of his child and if he refused, they docked 20 per cent of his wages for child support.[131] Poland also adopted a new Family Code in 1950 that granted men and women equal rights in marriage and over their children.[132]

The early socialist authorities believed that with the advent of socialism, the times were gone when women married for money due to a lack of choice. Socialist marriages were to be based on love and companionship, not on economic necessity. Thus, virtually all the family legislations that were newly adopted around 1950 liberalized divorce. The 1949 Czechoslovak Act on Family Law made divorce an option even when both spouses did not agree (as had been the case during the interwar period when both spouses had to agree to the divorce before they could get it). Yet in cases where one spouse apparently caused the breakdown, the divorce could not be granted against the will of the other spouse. This 'proof of fault' was alleviated in 1955 and abolished in 1963.[133] The Hungarian 1952 Family Law 'introduced a version of no-fault divorce, which allowed either partner to initiate divorce proceedings' only having to 'demonstrate that their marriage had decayed.'[134] Apart from the East Germans who divorced in record numbers early on, the Hungarian divorce rate had already spiked in 1959 at levels

---

127 Sardon, 'Mariage et divorce en Europe de l'Est', 573.
128 Ulf Brunnbauer, '"The Most Natural Function of Women": Ambiguous Party Policies and Female Experiences in Socialist Bulgaria', in *Gender Politics and Everyday Life in State Socialist Eastern and Central Europe*, eds Shana Penn and Jill Massino (New York: Palgrave Macmillan, 2009), 77–96, here 87.
129 Brunnbauer, 'The Most Natural Function of Women', 80.
130 Havelková, 'Three Stages of Gender in Law', 31–56.
131 Lynne Haney, *Inventing the Needy: Gender and the Politics of Welfare in Hungary* (Berkeley, CA: University of California Press, 2002), 28–30.
132 Winiarz 1954 quoted in Fidelis, *Women, Communism, and Industrialization*, 177.
133 Havelková, 'Three Stages of Gender in Law', 33–34.
134 Haney, *Inventing the Needy*, 29.

that would only be approximated by other Central Europeans in the 1970s.[135] In Poland, where the role of the Catholic Church was strong, divorce was a rare occurrence that could only be granted when 'socialist morality cannot create normal conditions for cohabitation and the upbringing of children.'[136] As a result, Polish divorce rates remained by far the lowest in comparison with its Central European neighbours.

The socialist states' retreat from women's equality

The unequivocal accent on women's emancipation did not last too long. Some argue that emancipatory rhetoric and policies were abandoned as early as de-Stalinization. Other scholars identify various points throughout the 1960s – but surely by 1968 – as the time when most socialist countries switched from emancipatory discourses and policies to maternal and familial measures. The last two decades of state socialism were marked by an ambiguous mix of rising levels of female employment with only perfunctory repetitions of the importance of women's equality, while traditional approaches of framing women as child-bearers came to the fore.

As early as the mid-1950s in Poland, according to Małgorzata Fidelis, de-Stalinization met with nationalist tendencies that identified the 'forced' emancipation of women, and particularly their entry into masculine jobs, as a distinctly Soviet phenomenon. As a result of the efforts to cleanse the nation of 'imposed' Soviet practices, women were forced to leave their 'masculine' jobs such as underground coalminers, and the party-state began to insist on either placing them in feminine jobs such as in textiles or dairy production, or that they go back to their homes and only work part-time.[137] The motivation for removing women from underground work was explained by their reproductive health: horrific cases of dying newborns were presented during the ministerial debates about the necessity of change in employment policies in 1954. Indeed, motherhood became more valuable to the state than women as producers and wage earners. These changes were, to an extent, fuelled by circulating images of debauched young women working in factories in industrialized regions such as Silesia. Young women working in places like Nowa Huta were allegedly so promiscuous that they would go to parties, get drunk and have sex, sometimes getting pregnant as a result. A contemporaneous journalist lamented such morals:

> I did not hear from any of these young mothers of the so-called out-of-wedlock children ... a confession that seems natural: 'I fell in love, the boy deceived me, he promised marriage.' Instead of this, they said tersely: 'I was at a party.'[138]

This 'degeneracy of private life' was linked to the work environment where the sexes intermingled, which was blamed on the Stalinist system. In the mid-1950s, 'the upsurge of powerful journalistic accounts regarding morality, gender roles, and domesticity indicated a powerful reclaiming of pre-communist notions of private life by large segments of Polish society.'[139] Indeed, Polish society reversed its course and gender began to re-traditionalize.

---

135 The Hungarian divorce rate in 1959 was 24.2 divorces per 100 marriages, virtually similar to the East German rate which they had reached by 1950: 23.2 divorces per 100 marriages. In Czechoslovakia, the rates only exceeded 20 in 1970, and then rose steadily. Poland never reached a 20 per cent divorce rate; its highest was 19.6 in the mid-1980s. Source: *Statistical Office of the United Nations, 1949–1991: Demographic Yearbook, issues 1948–1990* (New York: United Nations).
136 Winiarz 1954 quoted in Fidelis, *Women, Communism, and Industrialization*, 177.
137 Fidelis, *Women, Communism, and Industrialization*, 203–37.
138 Wigura 1955 quoted in Fidelis, *Women, Communism, and Industrialization*, 181.
139 Fidelis, *Women, Communism, and Industrialization*, 175.

According to Hana Havelková, the backlash against the policies of emancipation in Czechoslovakia began in the late 1960s with the period of 'normalization' that followed the failed Prague Spring, and which lasted until 1989; this backlash was characterized by the return to a conservative understanding of gender relations.[140] Lynne Haney shows how welfare regimes changed in Hungary and with them the understanding of the role of women. Between 1948 and 1968, welfare policies focused on 'centralized wage structure, employment guarantees, and price subsidies.'[141] In other words, men and women were above all seen as workers. In 1968, the state redeployed to focus on 'women's needs as mothers [that] were separated from those of other social groups.'[142] Broad social institutions that had been marshalled to support people in their everyday lives shrank in order to focus on families and the role of women within them. A new cadre of family experts emerged in newly established child guidance centres that were to assist if children experienced educational or behavioural problems. Mothers were targeted as both the source of and the solution to these problems. Women in 1968 received new childcare grants and other financial incentives, and with them came the close scrutiny of their mothering abilities, namely, domesticity tests and psychological exams. Among other things, a mother's sex life could come under the experts' purview. 'Mothers could not win: counsellors blamed both asexual and highly sexual mothers for transmitting pathologies' to their children.[143] If girls acted out sexually, their mothers were reproached for either being celibate (which compelled their daughters to seek the missing sexuality for themselves) or for being promiscuous (which presented their daughters with the wrong model). If boys were not seeking the company of girls, mothers were faulted for smothering them with maternal love which made their sons unable to view women sexually.

Similarly in Bulgaria, '[b]eginning in the mid-1960s, the initially revolutionary vector of state gender policy, which aimed at establishing equality between the sexes, gave way to an emphasis on women's reproductive role as the state began to intensively pursue pro-natalist policies.'[144] In 1968, the Bulgarian government adopted pro-population measures: they significantly increased child benefits up to the third child (so as not to encourage ethnic minorities in having more babies), paid maternity and child care leave were extended 'from 120 days leave prior to 1968 for any child, to 150 days for the second child and 180 days for the third'.[145] Unmarried people and childless couples had to pay up to 10 per cent more in tax. 'In 1973, the child care leave was extended by an additional six to eight months during which women received the minimum wage.'[146] Also, mothers could take an extra unpaid leave for up to three years in order to take care of the child.

Some authors explain these various gender regimes as a result of pragmatic governing: the early communist state needed labour and thus forced women into employment, embellishing its move by talk about equality; in the later stages, the state needed more children and thus pushed women into motherhood, praising this as the 'natural' role of women.[147] Communist rulers were supposedly motivated by 'social engineering'.[148] The pragmatic explanation does

---

140 Havelková and Oates-Indruchová, *The Politics of Gender Culture under State Socialism*, 7 and 14.
141 Haney, *Inventing the Needy*, 9.
142 Ibid., 11.
143 Haney, *Inventing the Needy*, 122.
144 Brunnbauer, 'The Most Natural Function of Women', 78.
145 Ibid., 88.
146 Ibid., 89.
147 Ibid., 79.
148 Fidelis, *Women, Communism, and Industrialization*, 252.

not give any credit to the ideational background of state socialism. Yet, the socialist project pivots around equality: of workers as well as women. The emancipation of women has been high on the agenda since the birth of socialism, and the laws and policies implemented immediately after communist takeovers attest to its importance. Moreover, the pragmatic explanation of the turn towards 'women as mothers first and foremost' disregards the fact that birth-rates had been steadily and unmistakably falling since the early 1950s – since 1949 in Romania, 1950 in Yugoslavia, 1951 in Poland, 1952 in Czechoslovakia and Bulgaria, 1954 in Hungary[149] – and the fact was hardly lost on local governments. Yet, the game-changing shifts in state policies on women and the family did not materialize until 1968. Furthermore, if the preoccupation with fertility rates were the utmost concern, socialist governments would likely not have legalized abortion, as most of them did in 1956 and 1957. With the exception of Romania in 1966, legal abortion was not withdrawn in any socialist country despite their pro-natalist turn. What this suggests is that the state's deliberations are more complex than simple 'emancipation vs. pro-natalism' and that state policies reflect more than just pragmatic imperatives.

While pragmatic concerns about population size linked to economic productivity or ethno-national importance are surely consequential, symbolic concerns about the 'normal' and 'proper' way of life are at play with undiminished significance. States wedded their populace to the (changing) project of socialism through (changing) discourses on desirable forms of intimate life. Marriage and (hetero)sexuality underwent shifts from the celebration of equality and mutuality in love, to a gender hierarchy that was pictured as essential for satisfying conjugal life. Expert pronouncements played a crucial role in cultivating socialist subjects' views on sex and love. Sexology proved a particularly potent expertise which informed people about sexual physiology, intercourse, contraception and happiness in intimate life.

Two distinct approaches to sexuality and gender existed in communist Czechoslovakia. The first one wanted sex to be between men and women who were to be equal and free of the bourgeois shackles of property. Before entering marriage, a couple should take the time to get to know each other, either in the workplace or at collective volunteer work units. The other approach stipulated that men and women were different and marriage could only work if husbands were superior to their wives. If gender arrangements differed from this, women would suffer a pain similar to that of sexual dissatisfaction. Only the nuclear family and one's spouse were perceived as safe social bonds. The first approach was typical of a period shortly after the communists took power in 1948 and throughout the 1950s. The other depiction sums up the attitudes of the late stages, the period called 'normalization', after the failed attempts of the Prague Spring of 1968. At the inception of communism, love, sex and family were understood in close connection to the public world of work. Intimacy in the 1950s was closely connected to the broader society and its political economy. Socialist subjects were constructed as authentic in the public realm of work and equal to one another, including gender equality. When normalization arrived in the 1970s, intimacy was severely privatized. Close ties were to be enjoyed only in the safety of a family circle detached from the workplace. The authentic self was to be cultivated within domestic confines. While women's equality enjoyed its discursive heyday in the 1950s, the 1970s returned to a traditional parlance connecting women with housework and child-rearing.[150]

---

149 The highs reached in these respective years were: 31 births per 1,000 inhabitants in Poland, 30.2 in Yugoslavia, 27.6 in Romania, 23.0 in Hungary, 22.8 in Czechoslovakia and 21.1 in Bulgaria. Source: *Statistical Office of the United Nations, 1949–1991: Demographic Yearbook, issues 1948–1990* (New York: United Nations).

150 Kateřina Lišková, 'Sex under Socialism: From Emancipation of Women to Normalized Families in Czechoslovakia', *Sexualities* 19, no. 1–2 (February 2016): 211–35, doi:10.1177/1363460715614246.

Sexual pleasure was presented as an important part of marriage on the pages of women's magazines such as *Zhenata dnes* in Bulgaria which discussed issues like 'sexology, premarital sex and single motherhood',[151] or in the manuals authored by sexologists in 1950s Czechoslovakia which stressed the importance of a satisfactory sex life for marriage, accentuated female pleasure and advised on contraception. By the 1970s, sexuality became even more openly discussed, sometimes with instructive depictions of sexual positions and detailed advice on how to counter 'sexual dysfunctions' such as premature ejaculation or the lack of female orgasm. Yet, the late socialist discussion of sexuality sometimes became entrenched in rather conservative notions of gender. In Poland, sexological books ran large print runs which reflected the hunger of readers for sexual advice. Sexologists firmly held that only proper gender positions – with feminine women and masculine men – could bring about sexual pleasure. The 1978 *Sztuka kochania* (The art of love), the first post-war book on sex in Poland (and written by a female sexologist), presented 'the woman's proper gender behaviour as the route to satisfactory sex.'[152] Another title, published five years later, described successful (and sexually satisfied) marriages as those where 'strong male and female qualities give a feeling of complementary but distinct psychological worlds.'[153] The emancipation of women was time and again blamed for women's lack of desire and for men's feelings of inferiority.

> One can educate herself, have an academic or other career, be an activist, but at home and when it comes to love, a woman has to be a woman, and a man has to be a man, if they want to live the full life and avoid disappointments and complexes.[154]

Similarly, Czechoslovak sexologists in the bestselling book *Mladé manželství* (Young marriage) first published in 1970, warned against gender role reversal. The authors presupposed inequality and differences between potential partners and strove to provide advice on how to choose a partner so that the inequalities balanced themselves out. According to sexologists, some characteristics could not be put in harmony: 'The situation is easier for couples where the man has a higher intellect than the woman. These settings complement the patriarchal family system. It is truly a stumbling block if the situation is reversed.' Such situations could, sexologists warned, lead to neurosis and inferiority complexes in men and permanent dissatisfaction in women; a dissatisfaction similar to sexual dissatisfaction, yet more unbearable and painful.[155]

Shifting gender and sexual patterns during post-socialism

As Janet Elise Johnson and Jean C. Robinson sum up in their book *Living Gender after Communism*, the problems of the early post-socialist years

> range from women being unemployed because they are seen as mothers to being employed as sex workers because they are seen as whores; being glorified as the symbol of the nation to experiencing rape in ethnic conflicts because they are symbolic

---

151 Kristen Ghodsee, 'Pressuring the Politburo: The Committee of the Bulgarian Women's Movement and State Socialist Feminism', *Slavic Review* 73, no. 3 (2014): 538–62, here 549.
152 Agnieszka Kościańska, 'Sex on Equal Terms? Polish Sexology on Women's Emancipation and "good Sex" from the 1970s to the Present', *Sexualities* 19, no. 1–2 (February 2016): 236–56, here 244, doi:10.1177/1363460714557662.
153 Lew-Starowicz 1983, quoted in Kościańska, 'Sex on Equal Terms?', 245.
154 Wislocka 1978, quoted in Kościańska, 'Sex on Equal Terms?', 246.
155 Mellan and Šípová, 1970, quoted in Lišková, 'Sex under Socialism', 222.

of the nation ... needing state social services because they are entrusted with the responsibility to raise children while wanting secure and loving families but facing unrecognized violence in those families.[156]

Marriage and the family became even more fragile during the first years of 'transition' than they had been during the last decades of communism. The marital dissolution had already become rampant in some countries (Hungary, Czechoslovakia, the GDR), yet the divorce rates increased further in the 1990s while the likelihood of marriage dropped. Alarmed by these developments, the conservative and religious parts of society clamoured for a return to the 'good old values'. However much traction conservatives gained, they ultimately failed, as '[a]lternative forms of committed intimacy, with their non-traditional sexual rules, continued to gain popularity among the new generations in "the East."'[157]

Throughout the 1990s, Eastern European countries exhibited diverging attitudes towards sexuality compared to Western Europe: fewer 'Eastern' women used contraception (albeit rates varied across countries with 92 per cent of married Slovenian women using some form of contraception compared to only 35 per cent in Estonia); systematic school-based sex education was missing; and tolerance towards homosexuality was lower (again, attitudes varied from widespread acceptance in the Czech Republic to extreme homophobia in Albania).[158] In some countries, young people lacked reliable information about sexuality and reproduction. In a 1993 Romanian reproductive health survey, one third of respondents aged 16 to 25 had no idea that a woman can get pregnant from her first sexual intercourse. Also, Romanian youths held sexually restrictive beliefs with 63 per cent of women in their late teens believing that a woman must be a virgin until she marries, and 84 per cent of youngsters of both genders claimed never to have had sexual intercourse.[159] In Bulgaria, a more conscious approach to sexuality emerged compared to both its neighbour and to the socialist period. The use of modern contraceptives rose between 1995 and 2000, especially among women younger than 25 who had entered their reproductive years at the end of state socialism.[160]

The new millennium brought non-traditional arrangements to the fore. Women with successful careers and men changing nappies ceased to be such a rare sight. These arrangements brought what some Polish sexologists perceived as new sexual dysfunctions such as 'premature female orgasm' and 'erectile dysfunctions related to male involvement in childcare.' The former problem afflicted the career-oriented women who

> have an orgasm very quickly and behave 'abnormally' after having sex: they are able to return to work right away, for instance, 'they take their laptops and start to work in bed'; they are not interested in 'holding their partners for hours, as normal women do.'[161]

---

156 Janet Elise Johnson and Jean C. Robinson, *Living Gender after Communism* (Bloomington, IN: Indiana University Press, 2006), 5.
157 Aleksandar Štulhofer and Theo Sandfort, *Sexuality and Gender in Postcommunist Eastern Europe and Russia* (New York: Haworth Press, 2005), 7.
158 Štulhofer and Sandfort, *Sexuality and Gender*, 10–15.
159 Adriana Baban, 'Women's Sexuality and Reproductive Behavior in Post-Ceausescu Romania: A Psychological Approach', in Gal and Kligman, *Reproducing Gender*, 240–41.
160 Elwood Carlson and Vicki Lamb, 'Changes in Contraceptive Use in Bulgaria, 1995–2000', *Studies in Family Planning* 32, no. 4 (December 2001): 329–38, doi:10.1111/j.1728–4465.2001.00329.x.
161 Kościańska, 'Sex on Equal Terms?', 237.

The latter dysfunction befell 'men who stay at home to take care of children while their wives or female partners go back to work after childbirth [and such men] may experience erectile dysfunction.'[162] Yet again, shifting gender patterns triggered sexual rearrangements.

Abortion

Under the Habsburg reign, the Criminal Code of 1852 criminalized any attempt at terminating a pregnancy. Women were punished with six months to one year in jail even if they failed to abort. If they achieved the desired abortion, they were sentenced from one to five years of hardened jail time. An abortionist faced up to five years of hardened jail time or up to ten years if the pregnant woman's health was threatened or if she died. These laws stayed on the books in successor states until the mid-twentieth century when they were replaced by communist codes that allowed abortion if there were valid medical reasons. Abortion, that is the termination of a pregnancy upon the woman's request due to 'social reasons', was legalized in most countries of our region in the mid-1950s.

In a historically unprecedented move, abortion was first legalized in revolutionary Russia in 1920, yet the right was taken away from women in 1936 as part of Stalin's repressive measures. Legalizing abortion meant that women could request the procedure on social grounds (the detailed measures varied slightly across time and geographical location); prior to full legalization, grounds for abortion were usually based on the health of both the mother and the foetus, and sometimes paired with criminal conception (i.e. rape, incest). While abortion was illegal in many countries, the state was often lax about enforcing this law, and many people performed abortions – from the backstreet abortionists whose amateur interventions sometimes led to serious health problems, to luxurious private clinics that provided abortion for the upper classes, as in 1930s Prague.[163] It is possible that the number of births was equivalent to the number of abortions, as was thought to be the case in interwar Germany.[164] Even the relatively efficient Czechoslovak state apparatus was able to discover and punish just about one out of every thousand cases of abortion in the 1920s,[165] usually only when there were some complications and the woman had to seek professional medical assistance, and only then if the doctor fulfilled his obligation to report it to the police.

The demand for legal abortion has existed since the nineteenth century in liberal and socialist circles. As early as 1918, the conservatives in Czechoslovakia expressed concern that the progressive forces would not be satisfied with only female suffrage, that they wanted to legalize abortion as well.[166] In 1920 and 1930, one leftist (woman) MP indeed proposed such a legislative initiative, but the public reaction was generally negative, and the proposal did not make it through the legislative committee to the parliament. The later initiative nevertheless found the sympathies of the social democratic and communist press. The overall discourse focused on social justice and

---

162 Ibid.
163 Stanislav Holubec, *Lidé Periferie: Sociální postavení a každodennost pražského dělnictva v meziválečné době* [People on the periphery: the social status and everyday life of Prague workers in the interwar period] (Plzeň: Západočeská Univerzita v Plzni, 2009), 87–9.
164 Andreas Gestrich, *Geschichte der Familie im 19. und 20. Jahrhundert* (München: Oldenbourg, 2010).
165 Ludmila Fialová, 'Domácí služebnictvo v českých zemích na přelomu 19. a 20. století ve světle historických statistik' [House servants in the Czech Lands at the turn of 19th and 20th century], in *Historická demografie* 26 (2002): 165.
166 Feinberg, *Elusive Equality*, 129.

social responsibility,[167] since it was mostly working-class women whose health was at risk, for they could not afford the procedure provided by doctors and had to resort to back alley abortions.

Fascist regimes implemented eugenic laws that supported the reproduction of some while suppressing the propagation of the others. In Germany, 'unworthy lives' were to be nipped in the bud: since 1935, 'eugenic justification' for terminating a pregnancy was on the books. Yet the 'vitality of German people' was protected by the implementation of the death penalty for abortion in 1943.[168] The Ustashe (*Ustaša*) in Croatia went to extremes in the fight against illegal abortions, and in 1941, declared that abortionists would be sentenced to death. Any woman who tried and failed to rid herself of an unwanted foetus would go to prison for five to ten years, and women who were successful in their attempt would be sentenced to life imprisonment.[169] Nevertheless, even in this case it seems that the act was not enforced in practice. Such policies didn't apply in Nazi-occupied territories, where occupation authorities tolerated abortion because it would decrease the birth rate of the racially inferior population. Polish and Russian female forced labourers were even driven to undergo abortions against their will.

Access to abortion was liberalized in most socialist countries in the mid-1950s as a reaction to its decriminalization in the Soviet Union in 1955. The new legislations instituted social and economic hardship as a reason to demand the procedure. In some countries, abortion commissions existed whose task it was to approve a woman's claim in each individual case. By 1968, most countries embarked upon pro-natalist policies marked by increased incentives to give birth and raise children (higher childcare bonuses, significantly longer maternity leave), which in some countries was accompanied by restricted access to abortion. Yet, the procedure remained available to women for the duration of state socialism.

Romania, in stark contrast to other state socialist countries, decided to ban abortion completely in 1966. This ban was perhaps a reaction to the fact that the country had the highest abortion rate in the region in the mid-1960s.[170] The regime's nationalist ideology and its understanding of ethnicity as a natural category were probably factors along with a strong tradition of Romanian eugenics. In her seminal study, *The Politics of Duplicity*, Gail Kligman painted a shocking picture of the 'politicization of demography': traumatized women whose health was ravaged as a result of illegal abortions in the 1970s and 1980s, with high penalties for performing illegal abortions and terrifying conditions in homes for unwanted and abandoned children.[171]

In the 1970s and 1980s, Central and Eastern Europe had one of the highest abortion rates in the world, surpassed only by the Soviet Union. There were, however, significant differences from country to country. In the Baltic countries, the abortion rate was as high as it was in the Soviet Union; high levels were recorded particularly among the large Russian population there. Although abortion was banned in Romania, there was a high miscarriage rate. Above-average values were also recorded in Bulgaria and Yugoslavia, but it was significantly lower in the Catholic and Muslim parts of those countries. In Hungary, where until 1973 abortions exceeded births by about one third, the citizens took an unprecedented action to prevent the

---

167 Ibid., 130.
168 Myra Marx Ferree, *Shaping Abortion Discourse: Democracy and the Public Sphere in Germany and the United States* (Cambridge: Cambridge University Press, 2002), 27.
169 Rory Yeomans, 'Fighting the White Plague: Demography and Abortion in the Independent State of Croatia, 1941–1945', in *Health, Hygiene and Eugenics in Southeastern Europe until 1945*, eds Sevasti Trubeta, Christian Promitzer and Marius Turda (Budapest: Central European University Press, 2011), 385–426, here 402.
170 Henry Philip David, ed., *From Abortion to Contraception: A Resource to Public Policies and Reproductive Behavior in Central and Eastern Europe from 1917 to the Present* (Westport, CT: Greenwood Press, 1999), 11.
171 Kligman, *The Politics of Duplicity*.

recriminalization of abortion: a public collection of signatures to protect 'a woman's right to self-determination'.[172] The lowest abortion rate – one fifth of the rate in the Baltics – was recorded in Poland. According to demographer Libor Stloukal, the great willingness to undergo the procedure can be attributed to liberal legislation, the lack of contraception and a lack of sex education in schools.[173] While in the West, the mass availability of contraception preceded the legalization of abortion, in the Eastern bloc the opposite was true. A high rate of abortions led to attempts to introduce and promote contraception or more gentle methods of abortion (such as vacuum aspiration) beginning in the late 1970s.

The number of abortions has declined rapidly in all post-communist countries. In 1989, the Czech Republic recorded its all-time high: 49.3 per cent of all pregnancies ended in either miscarriage or abortion. By 1996, that figure had dropped to 20.6 per cent, and in 2010, it fell to 15 per cent. The abortion rate is, however, still higher than in most Western European countries. The same tendency can be seen in all countries of our region. Declining abortion rates can be attributed mainly to cheap and easily available contraception.

The issues of reproduction were among the first taken up by post-1989 governments.[174] In a typical scenario, the liberal abortion laws inherited from socialism were targeted by conservative forces and church authorities. Romania, with its living memory of Ceaușescu's terrifying policy, was the only exception and repealed all laws limiting access to abortion. Conservative initiatives in the rest of our region, however, brought about change only in the existing law in Poland in 1993 and, temporarily, in Hungary, where 'the wording of the new law was more restrictive than its implementation.'[175] The well-documented, unsuccessful attempt to take such a measure in Catholic Croatia at the peak of the right-wing conservative Croatian Democratic Union's (HDZ) power shows how difficult it is to take this step in the context of European liberal democracies.[176] In Poland, the prohibition of abortion, approved in 1993, was certainly helped by strong public opposition to abortion during the socialist period which culminated in the 1980s, and by the strengthening of the Polish Catholic Church. The anti-abortionists used religious arguments while also warning of a looming demographic crisis. In any case, with its radical anti-abortion legislation, post-communist Poland remains an exception within the region.

Abortion between criminalization and legalization

Albania: Abortion was criminalized until 1991 apart from cases in which there was a serious danger to the woman's health and life. The Criminal Code of 1977 'punished repeat offenders or those performing an abortion that resulted in the woman's death or serious disruption of her health with eight years in prison. Otherwise, the punishment

---

172 Judit Takács, 'Disciplining Gender and (Homo)Sexuality in State-Socialist Hungary in the 1970s', *European Review of History: Revue Européenne d'Histoire* 22, no. 1 (January 2015): 161–75, here 164, doi:10.1080/13507486.2014.983426.

173 Libor Stloukal, 'Understanding the "Abortion Culture" in Central and Eastern Europe', in David, *From Abortion to Contraception*, 23–37.

174 Susan Gal, *The Politics of Gender after Socialism: A Comparative-Historical Essay* (Princeton, NJ: Princeton University Press, 2000), 15; Gal and Kligman, *Reproducing Gender*, 3.

175 David, *From Abortion to Contraception*, 36.

176 Hannes Grandits, 'Kinship and the welfare state in Croatia's twentieth century transition', in *Family, Kinship and State in Contemporary Europe*, vol. 1, ed. Hannes Grandits (Chicago, IL: University of Chicago Press, 2010), 466.

was re-education through work or detention for up to two years. A woman performing an abortion on herself without help was punished by a social reprimand or by re-education through work.'[177] This policy resulted in the second highest infant mortality ratio in Europe (after Romania). Abortion was legalized in steps between 1991 and 1995. Currently, it is available upon the woman's request. She has to state psychological or social problems and undergo compulsory counselling a week prior to the procedure.

Baltic countries: As part of the USSR, all three countries were under the Soviet law until 1991. The Soviet law had prohibited abortion since 1936 (after having it made legally accessible for the first time in the world in 1920 in the Russian Soviet Republic; the law applied across the USSR after 1921), except for cases in which the woman's life was in severe danger or the foetus ran the risk of heritable disease. Abortionists were punishable by a three-year sentence, and a woman who repeated the offence was to pay a fine.[178] The Decree of 1955 repealed the ban and made abortion accessible up to the 12th week of pregnancy, if performed in a hospital by a medical doctor. This legislation inspired a swift change across the region. Yet, the problem with illegal abortions in the USSR did not disappear. As a result of revived pro-natalism, oral contraceptives became 'effectively banned' in 1974.[179] Abortion became the primary method of family planning. The Soviet government doubled down, and in 1982, allowed for abortions for health reasons up to the 28th week.[180] In 1987, this decree was extended to cover a vast array of social circumstances (such as the death of the husband or divorce during pregnancy), and allowed any social reason to be weighed by a commission. In 1933, **Latvia** made abortion punishment-free for the woman in cases where 'the birth of a baby will financially ruin the expectant mother or her family,' penalties for providers, however, remained. Yet, this legislation was repealed two years later.[181] Nowadays, abortion is available on request up to the 12th week of pregnancy and up to the 20th week in the case of rape.[182] In **Lithuania**, the decree of 1935 made abortion accessible upon medical indication; that is, the decision was up to the doctors.[183] The Soviet abortion law was replaced

---

177 United Nations, Abortion Policy: Albania – The Population Policy Data Bank maintained by the Population Division of the Department of Economic and Social Affairs of the United Nations Secretariat, www.un.org/esa/population/publications/abortion/profiles.
178 *Decree on the Prohibition of Abortions. 27 June 1936*, www.revolutionarydemocracy.org/archive/abort.htm (accessed 15 July 2016).
179 United Nations. Dept. of Economic and Social Affairs. Population Division, *Abortion Policies: A Global Review. Volume I: Afghanistan to France* (New York: United Nations, 2001), 111, www.un.org/esa/population/publications/abortion/.../lithuania.doc (accessed 15 July 2016).
180 Ibid., 98.
181 Ineta Lipša, 'Over-Latvianization in Heaven' – Attitudes towards Contraception and Abortion in Latvia 1918–1940', in *Baltic Eugenics: Bio-politics, Race and Nation in Interwar Estonia, Latvia and Lithuania 1918–1940*, eds Björn M. Felder and Paul J. Weindling, vol. 35. (Amsterdam: Rodopi, 2013), 169–201, here 185.
182 IPPF European Network, *Abortion: Legislation in Europe* (Brussels: IPPF European Network, 2012), 48–49, http://humanistfederation.eu/ckfinder/userfiles/files/our-work/SRHR/Abortion%20Legislation%20in%20Europe_September2012.pdf (accessed 15 July 2016).
183 Björn M. Felder and Arūnas Germanivičius, 'Eugenics against State and Church: Juozas Blažys (1890–1939), Eugenics, Abortion and Psychiatry in Interwar Lithuania 1918', in Felder and Weindling, *Baltic Eugenics*, 203–32, here 218.19.

in 1994 and limited to the 12th week.[184] Nowadays, consultation prior to abortion is mandatory and parental consent for women under the age of 18 years is requested, and while not mandated by law, a waiting period of 10 to 12 days is frequent. However, the relatively high cost of 250 LTL (equivalent to $456 USD) in public clinics (and more in private establishments) together with limited access in rural areas is driving abortion rates down.[185] **Estonia** has kept abortion accessible up to the 12th week for any woman, and up to the 22nd week in the case of a girl under the age of 15.[186]

Bulgaria: In 1936, abortion was permitted as long as there were sound medical reasons. After the Second World War, an amendment was passed that abolished the punishment of providers and women who underwent the procedure in medical establishments. In 1956, abortion upon request was legalized (up to the 16th week of pregnancy and up to the 24th in medically indicated cases). Medical staff was to dissuade the woman from having the procedure, yet if she insisted, the abortion was performed. The procedure was free of charge until 1960, then a small fee was paid. Vacuum aspiration became available in 1963. In 1967, regulations tightened making abortion available only up until the 12th week and only to mothers of three or more children; other women had to apply at a special commission. A further restriction was implemented in 1973 when abortion became prohibited for women who were unmarried, childless or mothers of only one child. In 1990, first-trimester abortion became available to all women.[187]

Czechoslovakia: In 1920, medical reasons were (narrowly) defined which allowed for abortion. A 1936 legal interpretation restricted abortion to situations when the woman's life was in danger. The 1950 criminal code pronounced abortion a criminal offence (up to one year of imprisonment for a woman, up to 10 years for an abortionist). Medical grounds for the procedure applied and were gradually widened. Terminating a pregnancy for 'reasons worthy of special consideration', aka upon a woman's request, during the first trimester (upon commission's approval) was legalized in 1957. The access was restricted in 1962, relaxed in 1966 and restricted again in 1973. While the recommendations listed women over the age of 40 and having at least three living children, the list always included vague formulations such as 'special difficulties of the unmarried woman' or 'disturbed family life'[188] which allowed for abortion to be granted. Commissions were abolished in 1987 and abortion up to the twelfth week became freely available to all women.[189] Both successor states kept the legislation. In **Slovakia**, however, conscientious objection on the part of physicians makes it difficult for women to find an abortion provider.

---

184 IPPF European Network, *Abortion: Legislation in Europe* (Brussels: IPPF European Network, 2012), 50, http://humanistfederation.eu/ckfinder/userfiles/files/our-work/SRHR/Abortion%20Legislation%20in%20Europe_September2012.pdf (accessed 15 July 2016).

185 Ibid., 50–51.

186 Peter Roudik, 'Estonia: Access to Abortions Simplified for Minors', in *Global Legal Monitors*, from Library of Congress, 28 July 2015, www.loc.gov/law/foreign-news/article/estonia-access-to-abortions-simplified-for-minors/ (accessed 15 July 2016).

187 Vassilev in David, *From Abortion to Contraception*, 75–8.

188 Wynnyczuk and Uzel in David, *From Abortion to Contraception*, 108–10.

189 Radka Dudová, *Interrupce v České republice: Zápas o ženská těla* [Interruption in the Czech Republic: the struggle for women's bodies] (Sociologický ústav AV ČR, 2012); Radka Dudová, 'Regulation of Abortion as State-Socialist Governmentality: The Case of Czechoslovakia', *Politics and Gender* 8, no. 1 (2012): 123–44.

Hungary: In 1933, the high court decided that abortion should be legal for medical reasons. In 1945, rape became a legal reason for terminating pregnancy, free of charge, upon a commission's approval.[190] Abortion for social reasons was legalized as early as 1953; commissions remained in place. Three years later, the access was further liberalized when committees that were set up to sanction women's requests were tasked to say yes to every demand within the first trimester. In 1973, the law turned more restrictive enumerating the acceptable grounds for abortion. In 1988, the committees' power was weakened and only a medical specialist could assist in the woman's decision-making. In 1992, the law mandated a 'situation of crisis' for abortion to be performed; this vague formulation was specified in 2000 as causing 'bodily or mental impairment, or a socially intolerable situation.'[191] The 2011 Constitution declared life as sacred upon conception, which has opened the door for further restrictions (so far, not yet acted upon).

Poland: Abortion was made accessible in Poland in 1932 in the instance that there were sound medical reasons, and in cases of incest or rape. Although the draft had included a clause allowing 'the difficult economic situation of a woman' as legitimate grounds for abortion, the final law did not make it possible.[192] The situation did not change in the aftermath of the Second World War. Abortion was legalized in 1956 including the 'woman's difficult living conditions' as a valid reason. Self-induced abortions and women seeking illicit abortions were also decriminalized.[193] The law remained in place throughout the socialist period (the only modification being the ministerial instruction of 1981 which demanded that abortion providers give contraceptive counselling as well). In 1993, a new law banned abortion in all cases except for pregnancies resulting from rape or incest, pregnancies that posed a health risk to the mother, or cases in which the foetus was severely deformed. This law, already among the strictest in Europe, has been repeatedly attacked from the right with conservative groups demanding the access be limited only to cases where the woman's life is in danger.

Romania: In the 1930s, abortion (like sterilization) was possible solely on eugenic grounds and only upon scientific approval.[194] Inspired by Stalin's ban on abortion, the communist government recriminalized abortion in 1948. It was then legalized in 1957 which made the Romanian law the most liberal in Europe. For the next decade, abortion was readily available at low cost, 'quickly acquir[ing] social legitimacy.' Abortion then became the primary method of birth control which, by 1965, resulted in the highest rate reported by any country at that time: for every child born there were four abortions. An abortion ban was then put in place in 1966: only women above the age of 45 and women who gave birth and cared for four or more children could get the procedure approved. Women who had an illicit procedure, and the abortionists who performed them, were punishable, and the state went after both vigorously. Ceaușescu held that 'the foetus is the

---

190 Andrea Peto, 'Women's Rights in Stalinist Hungary: The Abortion Trials of 1952–53', trans. by Eva Kossuth, *Hungarian Studies Review* 29, no. 1–2 (2002): 49–76, here 51.
191 United Nations, Abortion Policy: Hungary – The Population Policy Data Bank maintained by the Population Division of the Department of Economic and Social Affairs of the United Nations Secretariat, www.un.org/esa/population/publications/abortion/profiles.htm.
192 Zielinska in Gal and Kligman, *Reproducing Gender*, 25, n5.
193 Ibid., 25.
194 Turda, 'To End the Degeneration of a Nation'.

socialist property of the whole society.' Contraception was exceedingly limited, available only on the black market at extremely high prices. By 1980, the measure had become even stricter: now women had to have at least five children under the age of 18 in order to qualify for abortion. Compulsory gynaecological check-ups were held annually at enterprises. The policy led to the deterioration of life for women and children and to the highest recorded infant and maternal mortality rates in Europe. The government that replaced Ceaușescu repealed every and all limits on abortion and contraception on its very first day in office.[195] Legal abortion became, yet again, the preferred method of controlling fertility.

Yugoslavia: Abortion was legalized in 1952 for medical, eugenic and legal reasons; in 1960, the social indication was added. The law was further liberalized in 1969 when the previously required approval of a medical commission prior to the 10th week of pregnancy, was removed.[196] In 1977 (Slovenia, **Bosnia and Herzegovina**) and 1978 (Croatia), laws were passed guaranteeing 'the right to freely decide on the birth of children.'[197] In practice, it means free access to abortion up until the 10th week of pregnancy after which point, a special commission decides. This law is still in effect in all the successor states. In **Croatia**, this law still remains despite the 1990s debates about restricting access to abortion. To the contrary, in 2014, the Croatian government declared that all public hospitals need to provide access to abortion, despite any possible conscientious objections on the part of the doctors. In **Slovenia**, the human rights clause was modified by the 1991 Constitution to include that 'the decision to bear one's own children is free.' However, the 10-week threshold for free access to abortion was preserved.[198]

Homosexuality

From legality to criminalization in the nineteenth century

While the penal codes of the first two thirds of the nineteenth century typically did not punish same-sex acts, by the end of the century homosexuality was listed in most criminal books. The Romanian Penal Code of 1864, inspired by French legislation that did not interfere with private matters, did not mention same-sex acts.[199] The Ottoman Empire legalized same-sex intercourse in 1858 during the period of legal reforms.[200] The law was reversed in the Principality

---

195 Baban, 'Women's Sexuality and Reproductive Behavior', 225–8.
196 Mirjana Rašević, 'Yugoslavia: Abortion as a Preferred Method of Birth Control', *Reproductive Health Matters* 2, no. 3 (1994): 68–74, doi:10.1016/0968-8080(94)900833.
197 See 'Law No. 1252–1987 of 21 April 1978, Act concerning the medical measures for materialization of the right to freely decide on the birth of children', www.hsph.harvard.edu/population/abortion/CROATIA.abo.htm (accessed 10 September 2016). Similarly, in other socialist republics, see UN, Abortion Policy.
198 United Nations, Abortion Policy: Slovenia – The Population Policy Data Bank maintained by the Population Division of the Department of Economic and Social Affairs of the United Nations Secretariat, www.un.org/esa/population/publications/abortion/profiles.htm.
199 Viviana Andreescu, 'From Legal Tolerance to Social Acceptance: Predictors of Heterosexism in Romania', *Revista Română de Sociologie* 22, no. 3 (2011): 209–31, here 214.
200 Ishtiaq Hussain, *The Tanzimat: Secular Reforms in the Ottoman Empire; A Brief Look at the Adoption of Secular Laws in the Ottoman Empire with a Particular Focus on the Tanzimat Reforms (1839–1876)* (Faith Matters, 2001), 10, http://faith-matters.org/images/stories/fm-publications/the-tanzimat-final-web.pdf (accessed 9 May 2016).

of Serbia in 1860 when sexual intercourse 'against the order of nature' between males became punishable by a minimum of six months up to four years imprisonment.[201] Further, the liberal Ottoman approach disappeared in the principality of Bulgaria in 1896 when the penalty for same-sex acts between men was that of confinement to a dark cell for a period of six months.[202] The sodomy laws of Russia, Prussia and Austria were applied on the Polish territory until it gained independence after the First World War.[203] The Austrian Penal Code of 1852 contained a clause punishing 'perversion against nature', defined as acts with animals or between two people of the same sex. The punishment was set at one to five years of hardened jail and in special cases, up to ten years.[204] In nineteenth-century Hungary, homosexuality was not on the books which, as a contemporaneous source explained, was because 'the Hungarian people have attained virtue and chastity to such a degree that there was no need for a special law like this'; the punishment for acts of sodomy depended on the wisdom of the judge.[205] In 1878, the law changed and defined 'perversion against nature' as sexual acts between men or with animals, and the punishment was up to one year in the least severe prison.[206]

Same-sex activities flourished in cities that provided anonymity and with it a relative lack of public scrutiny. Budapest in the nineteenth century 'embraced the public sex culture', and buying and selling anything from titillating photographs to sex earned it the title, 'Sinful City.'[207] Same-sex desire, however small in numbers, figured in the life of the city. With its bathhouses and metropolitan life, Budapest became an ideal Eastern European spot for men who desired other men. Here, in the Rudas spa, a resident writer Károly Kerbeny coined the terms 'heterosexual' and 'homosexual' in the late nineteenth century. In the interwar period, journalists and the police estimated the homosexual population at five to ten thousand people, less than one per cent of the city inhabitants. The police attempted to surveil the places where men gathered, yet detection proved rather difficult.[208]

Politicians running for office ran the risk of being criminalized for their alleged homosexuality. For example, the mayor of Ljubljana, who was elected in 1921, was refused ministerial approval and subsequently lost his court battle, thus resulting in the overturning of the election results.[209] However, Yugoslavia did not seem to prosecute its homosexuals either before or after the Second World War despite the anti-homosexual articles that were on the books.

---

201 Kriminalni (Kaznitelni) zakonik za Kraljevinu Srbiju [Criminal Code of the Principality of Serbia], www.smrtnakazna.rs/Portals/0/SrbijaPropisi/Kaznitelni%20zakonik%201860.pdf. (accessed 18 May 2016).
202 Sasha Roseneil and Mariya Stoilova, 'Heteronormativity, Intimate Citizenship and the Regulation of Same-Sex Sexualities in Bulgaria', in *De-Centring Western Sexualities: Central and Eastern European Perspectives*, eds R. Kulpa and J. Mizielińska (Farnham, UK: Ashgate, 2011), 167–90, here 170.
203 Łukasz Szulc, 'Queer in Poland: Under Construction', in *Queer in Europe: Contemporary Case Studies*, eds Robert Gillett and Lisa Downing (Farnham: Ashgate, 2012), 159–72, here 160.
204 Jan Seidl, *Od žaláře k oltáři: emancipace homosexuality v českých zemích od roku 1867 do současnosti* [From jail to the altar: the emancipation of homosexuality in the Czech lands from 1867 to the present] (Brno: Host, 2012), 22–23.
205 Judit Takács, 'Hungary', in *The Greenwood Encyclopedia of LGBT Issues Worldwide*, ed. Chuck Stewart (Santa Barbara, CA: Greenwood Press, 2010), 219–33, here 226.
206 Anita A. Kurimay, *Sex in the 'Pearl of the Danube': The History of Queer Life, Love, and its Regulation in Budapest, 1873–1941* (PhD diss., Rutgers University-Graduate School-New Brunswick, 2012), 235.
207 Description of Kurimay in *Sex in the 'Pearl of the Danube'*, Rutgers University Community Repository, http://hdl.rutgers.edu/1782.1/rucore10001600001.ETD.000066850 (accessed 10 September 2016).
208 Takács, 'Queering Budapest', in Cook and Evans, *Queer Cities, Queer Cultures*, 191–210, here 192–4.
209 Roman Kuhar, 'Ljubljana: The Tales from the Queer Margins of the City', in *Queer Cities, Queer Cultures: Europe since 1945*, eds Matt Cook and Jennifer M. Evans (London: Bloomsbury, 2014), 135–50, here 136–7.

Homosexuality has been historically cast in nationalist struggles. 'Our' side usually depicted 'them' as weak-minded debauched homosexuals, and homosexuality as entirely 'their' vice. Similarly, the 'homosexual affairs' of the 1930s and 1940s created a space for nationalist identifications. The most notorious, according to Mark Cornwall, was the case of Heinz Rutha (1897–1937), a Sudeten German political leader and the main advisor of its pro-Nazi Leader Konrad Henlein for youth education. Rutha blazed a trail of versatile education for young men which focused on friendship and love of the nation, and was inspired by the German idea of *Männerbund*, an elite 'at the heart of the state.'[210] The homosocial environments he kept creating around himself were stimulating in more than one sense, yet were a thorn in the side of the Czechs – when presented with an opportunity in 1937, Czech police did not hesitate to prosecute Rutha, who subsequently committed suicide. During the Second World War, communist radio alluded to the case as 'a stinky swamp' where 'abnormal men ruin our boys'; after the liberation, a Czech author labelled the case 'a typical German depravity.'[211] National self-awareness was at stake and Rutha, the 'other', hated by Nazis, was denigrated as a sexual outcast.

It is well known that homosexuals were prosecuted in Nazi Germany. The Reich's punishment was severe, counting the sentence in cumulative fashion and not allowing for probation. The Protectorate of Bohemia and Moravia with its own laws was, surprisingly, a relatively safe haven for men who preferred to have sex with other men (except for the cases in which a German citizen was involved, since Germans were under the jurisdiction of the Reich). Police did not seek homosexuals in any organized way, nor were the punishments particularly harsh when homosexual men happened to be found. The Protectorate law, again unlike its German counterpart, did not even penalize homosexual prostitution any more harshly than the instances of (homosexual) sex where money did not change hands. Moreover, interwar forensic practice had cultivated a method of medically determining whether the 'homosexuality' of the accused was congenital (vs. acquired), and if so, the courts were more lenient. The expert culture, both legal and medical, contributed to the fact that 'the situation of ethnically Czech homosexuals worsened relatively little during the occupation.'[212]

State socialist silence and the gradual acceptance of homosexuality

While a rather taboo subject, homosexuality was slowly finding its way into the public consciousness. Most countries eased their approach to the sexual 'other' over time. Southeastern European countries such as Romania and Albania, however, offer a strikingly different image to the gradual relaxation of attitudes towards homosexuality that were well under way in Central Europe. In Romania, the law became exceedingly worse with its peak in 1957 when consenting adults who performed homosexual acts could be sent to prison for up to 10 years.[213] In 1977, Albania recriminalized homosexuality (which had been legal since the Ottoman reforms in the mid-nineteenth century) with a sentence of up to 10 years. Some argue that 'oppressing and suppressing homosexuals was one of the very issues where the regime and society silently agreed.'[214]

---

210 Cornwall in Pavel Himl, Jan Seidl and Franz Schindler, '*Miluji tvory svého pohlaví*': homosexualita v dějinách a společnosti českých zemí [I love the creatures of my own sex: homosexuality in the history and society of the Czech lands] (Prague: Argo, 2013), 187.
211 Cornwall in Himl, Seidl and Schindler, '*Miluji tvory svého pohlaví*', 176.
212 Seidl in Himl, Seidl and Schindler, '*Miluji tvory svého pohlaví*', 251.
213 Andreescu, 'From Legal Tolerance to Social Acceptance', 214.
214 Henry F. Carey, *European Institutions, Democratization, and Human Rights Protection in the European Periphery* (Lanham, MD: Lexington Books, 2014), 349.

In most other countries, at the beginning of state socialism, homosexuality was listed in the criminal codes, yet penalties were much less severe than in Romania (Poland is an exception here because homosexuality was never criminalized.) In Bulgaria in 1951, homosexuality became punishable with a three-year prison sentence. Not only penetration, but any act of sexual satisfaction constituted an offence; and for the first time, the definition included women. A state campaign targeted 'intellectual homosexuals', sending them to labour camps for correction, although no women seemed to have been sentenced.[215] In 1964, an exemplary trial against 26 men from all walks of life was held on the charges of 'practising homosexualism' and endangering socialist morality. Some were convicted for up to six years. In this trial, homosexuality was understood as a chosen behaviour that 'could be eradicated by corrective labour or another form of legal punishment.'[216]

The entire socialist era did not approach homosexuality in the same manner. Anna Borgos classifies the first two decades of states socialism as a 'complete closet' for Hungarian homosexuals, while the last two decades are marked by 'informal communities' formed in the capital.[217] Hungary and Czechoslovakia decriminalized homosexuality in 1961, first among the socialist states and preceding Western countries by several years (in comparison, England and Wales legalized homosexuality in 1967, West Germany softened its criminal articles in 1969, and in the United States, sodomy laws were finally repealed by the Supreme Court's decision in 2003). In our region, abolishing the penalties for consensual sex between two adult men was inspired by Kurt Freund's (1914–1996) medical research conducted in 1950s Czechoslovakia. Freund attempted a behaviourist reconditioning of self-identified homosexuals by administering emetic drugs while subjects watched images of desirable men; following this treatment, subjects were injected with male sex hormones while they watched provocative images of women. In order to increase scientific objectivity, Freund invented a device that measured a 'true' desire in his subjects: a phalloplethysmograph. This apparatus attached to the penis and followed the changes in blood flow – if the man was getting aroused by the projected images, the device would note it. The combination of his research techniques persuaded Freund that homosexuality was incurable. This realization led him to actively lobby for decriminalization.[218] In effect, the official explanation of the need to decriminalize homosexuality included expert reasoning: 'According to medical findings, these perpetrators are sexually deviant and at the current stage of medical science, cannot be cured.'[219] Similarly in Hungary, homosexuality was decriminalized based on medical arguments that 'the most sound therapy could hardly ever lead to the desired result. Homosexuality is a biological phenomenon and can therefore not be handled legally as a crime.'[220] Also in Yugoslavia, a legal expert initiated the process of decriminalization with proposals 'based on scientific research.'[221]

While homosexuality remained stigmatized, people sought same-sex experiences in places such as bathhouses and public toilets.[222] Oral histories of gay men who lived during state

---

215 Roseneil and Stoilova, 'Heteronormativity, Intimate Citizenship', 170, 173.
216 Monika Pisankaneva, 'The Forbidden Fruit: Sexuality in Communist Bulgaria' (University of Amsterdam, 2003 online) (accessed 19 May 2016), www.iisg.nl/womhist/pisankaneva.doc, 11–12.
217 Anna Borgos, 'Secret Years: Hungarian Lesbian Herstory, 1950s–2000s', *Aspasia* 9, no. 1 (March 2015): 87–112, here 105, doi:10.3167/asp.2015.090106.
218 Seidl, *Od žaláře k oltáři*, 286–95.
219 From a report of the Minister of Justice addressed to the Secretary of the Communist party. Quoted in Seidl, *Od žaláře k oltáři*, 282.
220 Quoted in Takács, 'Disciplining Gender', 169.
221 Kuhar, 'Ljubljana: The Tales from the Queer Margins of the City', 138.
222 Takács, 'Disciplining Gender', 170.

socialism recount gay life ('veselej život'; in Czech 'veselý' means 'cheerful' yet might translate as 'gay') despite heteronormative pressures. Men talked about the places where they could meet other men interested in sex: they voluntarily participated in Kurt Freund's experimental treatment of homosexuality in the 1950s, placed classifieds in magazines and made use of the somewhat open borders in the 1960s. The building of the subway in 1970s Prague brought about a change in the topography of public restrooms, and with it, a limited number of meeting places. The year 1983 marked the HIV pandemic and the breaking of the expert's public silence in Czechoslovakia. The mid-1980s also saw the publishing of the first openly gay story and the founding of the Socio-therapeutic club which paved the way for post-1989 gay civic activities.[223]

Female narrators also recount the ease with which they could meet partners in Czechoslovakia and abroad and the fullness and meaningfulness of their sexual experiences. In a country with high divorce rates, some were able to create non-heterosexual families with children from previous marriages. As one such woman recalls: 'It was unimaginable [during state socialism] that anyone would ask directly if we were lesbians. Impossible! I was not afraid of this question a single bit. Who would dare to ask? And in what words?'[224] Similarly in Hungary, lesbians recalled how divorce sheltered their non-normative desires: 'It was terrible, people used to keep asking "How come you aren't married yet?" By then being a divorced woman was much better; that provided a completely different social status. And afterwards I was glad that things had turned out the way they had because I could always say I had been married once. Of course, I didn't mention that it lasted only half a year.'[225] The lack of public language for homosexuality, unexpectedly, made the situation easier for women who loved other women.

The same lack of language that liberated the lives of some proved to be isolating for others. Some older Hungarian lesbians remember the state socialist period as 'a hopeless desert' since it was miserable trying to find a partner. Yet others were inventing new ways. When placing ads in magazines, for example, some referenced a 1982 movie called 'Another Way' (*Egymásranézve*), the first mainstream motion picture to portray a lesbian relationship in the region. The novel, which the movie was based upon, disappeared from the bookstores within weeks. The movie won a FIPRESCI award in Cannes and sparked a vivid discussion among film critics about portraying a 'passion that can defy social conventions.'[226]

The fact that homosexuals were somewhat invisible in the public eye meant that they could live their lives relatively free of scrutiny. There is no evidence (so far) of any widespread prosecution of homosexuality during state socialism. The exception seems to be the aforementioned 1964 trial in Bulgaria and the 1950s trial in Budapest (but not elsewhere in Hungary) where police compiled '"homosexual inventories" providing potential blackmail victims to be coerced into becoming police informers.'[227] The extent to which the police actually used the inventories remains unknown. In Yugoslavia, oral histories of the lives of gay men bring about a picture of hassle-free lives: 'I didn't like the previous political system [communism], but it was quite open in this regard. It is true they have punished the political dissidents, but they did allow

---

223 Schindler in Himl, Seidl and Schindler, '*Miluji tvory svého pohlaví*'.
224 Věra Sokolová, 'State Approaches to Homosexuality and Non-Heterosexual Lives in Czechoslovakia during State Socialism', in Havelková and Oates-Indruchová, *The Politics of Gender Culture under State Socialism*, 82–109, here 101.
225 Borgos, 'Secret Years', 102.
226 Takács, 'Queering Budapest', 196–7.
227 Ibid., 194.

people to live as they wish and to love whom they wanted. They didn't interfere with one's private life.'[228] Metropolises continued to provide anonymity that sheltered the sexual 'other'. Ljubljana printed its first gay guide in 1970, and by the 1980s, became a Yugoslav gay hotspot with several permanent queer spaces.[229] Budapest continued its pre-war bathhouse tradition and offered some cafes, which were known as meeting spots.[230]

The slow equalization in family status during post-socialism

Equalizing the status of gays and lesbians with the rest of the citizenry is still an unfinished project. However, many important improvements in the status of homosexuals have occurred, mostly in family law. The Hungarian Constitutional Court ordered to put gay and lesbian partnerships on a par with heterosexual partnerships in 1995. The Hungarian Civil Code thus recognizes any couple, of whatever sex, that live together permanently in a state of 'financial and emotional communion'. Such a relationship does not require any official registration which might, however, bring about the problem of proof.[231]

Important steps towards equality have often coincided with an aspiring accession into the European Union. In Bulgaria, for example, various discriminatory paragraphs needed to be revoked in order to harmonize the legislation with the European standards of non-discrimination.[232] While there is recognition of same-sex relationships in the form of 'registered partnerships' in many countries across the region, nowhere is marriage accessible to same-sex couples and neither are there many marriage-like rights surrounding childcare (i.e. access to reproductive assistance, adoption or custody rights in case of one partner's death), material benefits (i.e. inheritance and tax relief, right to pension) and other forms of special consideration (i.e. receiving information about the health of one's partner). For example, in Croatia, only 2 out of 27 rights bestowed upon legally married spouses are available to homosexuals (the right to inherit half of the joint assets accrued by the couple, and the duty of care for the partner).[233] Indeed, states are holding onto traditional ideas of marriage as a union between a man and a woman, and some even introduced such wording to their laws for the first time in history (such as Bulgaria in 1991,[234] Croatia in 2003[235] or Romania in 2008[236]).

Despite these pitfalls, LGBT lives are gaining more and more recognition. Same-sex desire is visible on the streets of many capitals, manifest during the pride marches that began in the late 1990s (e.g. in Budapest in 1997) and which, during the first dozen or so years, did not spark

---

228 A Slovenian film director quoted in Kuhar, 'Ljubljana: The Tales from the Queer Margins of the City', 138.
229 Kuhar, 'Ljubljana: The Tales from the Queer Margins of the City'.
230 Takács, 'Queering Budapest'; Borgos, 'Secret Years'.
231 Craig Kaczorowski, GBLTQ archive (Budapest, 2015), www.glbtqarchive.com/ssh/budapest_S.pdf (accessed 19 May 2016); Legislation Online, 2016, *Crimal codes: Hungary*, 2016, www.legislationline.org/documents/section/criminal-codes (accessed 19 May 2016).
232 Roseneil and Stoilova, 'Heteronormativity, Intimate Citizenship', 175.
233 Ivana Jugović, Aleksandra Pikić, and Nataša Bokan, 'Lesbians, Gays and Bisexuals in Croatia: How the Stigma Shapes Lives', in *Beyond the Pink Curtain: Everyday Life of LGBT People in Eastern Europe*, eds Roman Kuhar and Judit Takács (Ljubljana: Mirovni Inšt., 2007), 345–62, here 346.
234 Roseneil and Stoilova, 'Heteronormativity, Intimate Citizenship', 179.
235 Croatia: Constitutional Amendment Banning Gay Marriage Passed by Referendum, www.loc.gov/law/foreign-news/article/croatia-constitutional-amendment-banning-gay-marriage-passed-by-referendum/ (accessed 22 May 2016).
236 Andreescu, 'From Legal Tolerance to Social Acceptance', 215.

much controversy.[237] The countries that had been 'beyond the pink curtain'[238] are now flashing more colours of the rainbow.

Decriminalization of homosexuality and legalization of same-sex partnership

Albania: In 1858, the Ottoman Empire legalized same-sex intercourse;[239] in 1977, severe punishment for same-sex intercourse – up to 10 years in prison (the same as paedophilia); in 1994, the prison sentence was reduced to 3 years; same-sex intercourse was decriminalized in 1995;[240] in 2001, the age of consent was established at 14 years of age.[241]

Baltic countries: The Russian legislation of 1832 and subsequent laws penalizing *muzhelozstvo* (sex between men) was applicable, yet was not strictly enforced;[242] after independence was gained in 1918, these laws were repealed;[243] after Soviet occupation in 1940, anti-sodomy laws were reintroduced.[244] **Estonia** decriminalized homosexuality in 1992,[245] equalized the age of consent at 14 years in 2002[246] and introduced registered partnership in 2014 (which entered into effect in 2016), including the ability to adopt the partner's biological child,[247] yet legally still prohibiting marriage. **Latvia** prohibited marriage for same-sex couples in 1991;[248] the legal age of consent for homosexuals remained unclear until 2006 when it was set at 16;[249] in 2006, marriage was constitutionally

---

237 Unfortunately, that changed around the year 2008 when pride marches in Serbia, Poland, Romania, Croatia, Latvia and Russia have faced violent right-wing attacks. Hadley Z. Renkin, 'Homophobia and Queer Belonging in Hungary', *Focaal* 2009, no. 53 (March 2009): 20–37, doi:10.3167/fcl.2009.530102.
238 Kuhar and Takács, *Beyond the Pink Curtain*.
239 Hussain, *The Tanzimat*, 10.
240 Carey, *European Institutions, Democratization, and Human Rights*, 349.
241 *Age of Consent in Albania*, AgeOfConsent.net. 2016, www.ageofconsent.net/world/albania (accessed 19 May 2016).
242 Siegfried Tornow, 'Homosexuality and Politics in Soviet Russia', in *Sexual Minorities and Society: The Changing Attitudes toward Homosexuality in the 20th Century Europe; Facts about Homosexuality in Soviet Russia and Current Estonia*, eds Udo Parikas and Teet Veispak (Tallinn: Institute of History, 1991), 78–93, here 82.
243 Teet Veispak, 'Homosexuality in Estonia in the 20th Century: Ideological and Juridical Aspects', in Parikas and Veispak, *Sexual Minorities and Society*, 105–114, here 108.
244 Lilian Kotter, *Estonia, IGLHRC Book Estonia*, 2003 (accessed 13 July 2016), www.outrightinternational.org/sites/default/files/42-1.pdf, p. 53.
245 David A. Gerstner, ed., *Routledge International Encyclopedia of Queer Culture* (London: Routledge, 2012), 655.
246 Estonian Human Rights Centre, Global Rights, ILGA Europe, SeksuaalvähemusteKaitseÜhing, *The Status of Lesbian, Gay, Bisexual and Transgender Rights in Estonia: A Shadow Report*, 2010 (online) (accessed 13 July 2016), www2.ohchr.org/english/bodies/hrc/docs/ngo/EstoniaShadowReportLGBT.pdf, 2; Criminal Code of the Republic of Estonia (2001, amended 2013) (English version online) (accessed 13 July 2016) www.legislationline.org/documents/section/criminal-codes.
247 Peter Roudik, 'Estonia: Legalization of Civil Partnerships', Global Legal Monitor, 14 January 2016, www.loc.gov/law/foreign-news/article/estonia-legalization-of-civil-partnerships/.
248 ILGA, *Equality for Lesbians and Gay Men: A Relevant Issue in the EU Accession Process* (Brussels: ILGA, 2001), 36, www.ilga-europe.org/sites/default/files/Attachments/2001_equality_in_accession_process.pdf (accessed 13 July 2016).
249 *What is the Latvia Age of Consent?* www.ageofconsent.net/world/latvia (accessed 13 July 2016).

defined as a union between a man and a woman;[250] cohabitation remains unrecognized by Latvian law.[251] In **Lithuania**, consensual gay sex between men remained criminalized until 1993;[252] the age of consent was equalized at 16 in 2002;[253] same-sex marriage was constitutionally prevented in 2006.[254]

Bulgaria: in 1896, the sentence for homosexual acts was set at confinement to a dark cell for six months;[255] between 1944 and 1951 the sentence was increased to five years imprisonment for sex between men;[256] in 1951, the law punished up to three years for 'sexual acts or sexual gratification between people of the same sex' which included women,[257] unlike elsewhere in our region; in 1968 Bulgaria decriminalized homosexual acts, yet until 1986, the age of consent was set at 18 (as opposed to 14 years of age for heterosexual intercourse); in 2002, a paragraph was removed that sanctioned any expression of homosexuality in public.[258]

Czechoslovakia: the 1852 Penal Code punishes 'lewdness against nature' with animals and between men;[259] the law (amended in 1873) became part of the criminal code of the Czechoslovak republic in 1918;[260] a new criminal code emerged in 1950, yet homosexuality was still punishable by up to one year, or up to five years for prostitution or intercourse with minors;[261] decriminalization in 1961 for consenting adults (the age of consent set at 18 for homosexuals, 15 for heterosexuals), excluding prostitution and public nuisance; the age of consent was equalized to 15 in 1990; registered partnership was adopted in the **Czech Republic**[262] in 2006 (but not in **Slovakia**, and still to this day).

Hungary: in the nineteenth century, there was no law criminalizing homosexuality; in 1878, a light punishment was introduced; in 1961, it was decriminalized for consenting adults, yet women could now also be prosecuted (age of consent was 14 for heterosexuals, 20 for homosexuals, then decreased to 18 in 1978, and equalized to 14 in 2002);[263] in 1995, the Constitutional Court opened up cohabitation (a factual, legal relationship) to same-sex couples; in 2007, the Parliament adopted registered partnership, which has been in effect since 1 July 2009.[264]

Poland: same-sex sexual activity was always legal which was confirmed in 1932 when the age of consent was uniformly set at 15;[265] in 1969, homosexual prostitution

---

250 *The Constitution of the Republic of Latvia*, http://saeima.lv/en/legislation/constitution/ (accessed 13 July 2016).
251 ILGA, *Equality for Lesbians and Gay Men*, 36.
252 Ibid., 44.
253 Gerstner, *Routledge International Encyclopedia of Queer Culture*, 660.
254 Constitueproject.org, *Lithuania's Constitution of 1992 with Amendments through 2006*, www.constituteproject.org/constitution/Lithuania_2006.pdf (accessed 13 July 2016).
255 Kulpa and Mizielińska, *De-centring Western Sexualities*, 170.
256 Pisankaneva, 'The Forbidden Fruit', 11.
257 Ibid., 11.
258 Ibid., 12.
259 Seidl, *Od žaláře k oltáři*, 22.
260 Ibid., 28.
261 Ibid., 258–59.
262 *Předpis č. 115/2006 Sb. Zákon o registrovaném partnerství a o změně některých souvisejících zákonů*, [The act on registered partnership] www.zakonyprolidi.cz/cs/2006-115 (accessed 29 May 2016).
263 Takács, 'Disciplining Gender'.
264 Takács, 'Queering Budapest', 201.
265 Wayne R. Dynes, ed., *Encyclopedia of Homosexuality*, vol. 2 (New York: Routledge, 1990), 1013.

disappeared from the criminal code;[266] same-sex marriage was constitutionally prevented in 1997.[267]

Romania: the Penal Code of 1864 did not include punishments for same-sex acts; since 1878, only violent same-sex acts such as rape were punishable; in 1937, the law criminalized homosexuality for the first time (if the acts in question produced a 'public scandal', the penalty was between six months and two years' imprisonment); in 1948, punishment was increased, up to five years; a 1957 law hardened again and any homosexual act could be punished with incarceration from three to ten years; in 1968, prison time was set at one to five years; in 1996, only public or scandalous homosexual acts became punishable (one to five years' imprisonment);[268] in 2002, the age of consent was equalized at 15;[269] in 2008, the senate changed the legal definition of marriage (which as of 1953 had been 'a union between spouses') to a 'union between a man and a woman';[270] to date, there is no form of registered partnership for same-sex couples.

Yugoslavia: the 1929 Criminal Code banned anal intercourse as 'lewdness against nature' and the 1959 law limited the definition to acts between men only with punishment of up to one-year imprisonment.[271] Same-sex sexual activity has been legal since 1977 in Slovenia, Croatia and Montenegro (also in the province of Vojvodina yet has remained illegal in the rest of Serbia;[272] interestingly, Vojvodina recriminalized same-sex activity in 1990[273]). Same-sex sexual activity has been legal since 1994 in Serbia, 1996 in Macedonia, and 1998 in Bosnia and Herzegovina.[274] In 1977 in Slovenia and Croatia[275] the age of consent was equalized at 14 years of age (it was increased to 15 for everyone in 2003[276]). The age of consent was equalized at 14 in Bosnia and Herzegovina in 1998[277] and 2006 in Serbia.[278] Registered partnerships have been legal in Croatia since 2003[279] and since 2005 in Slovenia.[280] Same-sex marriage has been constitutionally banned in

---

266 Dynes, *Encyclopedia of Homosexuality*, 1013.
267 *The Constitution of the Republic of Poland of 2nd April 1997*, www.sejm.gov.pl/prawo/konst/angielski/kon1.htm (accessed 22 May 2016).
268 Andreescu, 'From Legal Tolerance to Social Acceptance', 214.
269 *Age of Consent: Romania*, www.ageofconsent.net/world/romania (accessed 23 May 2016).
270 Andreescu, 'From Legal Tolerance to Social Acceptance', 209–31.
271 Katja Kahlina, 'Contested Terrain of Sexual Citizenship: EU Accession and the Changing Position of Sexual Minorities in the Post-Yugoslav Context', *The Europeanization of Citizenship in the Successor States of the Former Yugoslavia (CITSEE), CITSEE Working Paper Series* 33 (2013): 1–30.
272 Francis Tapon, *The Hidden Europe: What Eastern Europeans Can Teach Us* (Library of Congress: Sonic-Trek, Inc., 2011), 339.
273 America Pink, *LGBT rights in Serbia, LGBT rights in Serbia: Issues*, http://america.pink/lgbt-rights-serbia_2508111.html (accessed 17 May 2016).
274 Kuhar, 'Ljubljana: The Tales from the Queer Margins of the City'.
275 Gerstner, *Routledge International Encyclopedia of Queer Culture*, 653.
276 *Kazneni zakon* [Criminal Code], www.zakon.hr/z/98/Kazneni-zakon (accessed 23 May 2016).
277 Svetlana Durkovic, *Study on Homophobia, Transphobia and Discrimination on Grounds of Sexual Orientation and Gender Identity – Legal Report: Bosnia and Herzegovina*, 3–4, www.coe.int/t/Commissioner/Source/LGBT/BosniaHerzegovinaLegal_E.pdf (accessed 22 May 2016).
278 Tapon, *The Hidden Europe*, 339.
279 ODLUKU O PROGLAŠENJU ZAKONA O ISTOSPOLNIM ZAJEDNICAMA [Proclamation of Partnership Act], http://narodne-novine.nn.hr/clanci/sluzbeni/306172.html (accessed 23 May 2016).
280 Uradni List, 2005, *UKAZ o razglasitvi Zakona o registraciji istospolne partnerske skupnosti (ZRIPS)* [Law on Registration of Same-Sex Partnership Community (ZRIPS)], www.uradni-list.si/1/content?id=56999 (accessed 17 May 2016).

Croatia since 2003,[281] in Serbia since 2006 and in Macedonia since 2015;[282] the Slovenian Parliament approved a bill in 2015 legalizing same-sex marriage, yet citizens rejected it in a referendum later that year.[283] The ability to adopt one's step-child has been legal in Slovenia since 2011 and in Croatia since 2014.[284]

Further Reading

Allen, Ann Taylor. *Women in Twentieth-Century Europe* (Houndmills: Palgrave Macmillan, 2008).
Batinić, Jelena. *Women and Yugoslav Partisans: A History of World War II Resistance* (New York: Cambridge University Press, 2015).
Bernstein, Frances Lee. *The Dictatorship of Sex: Lifestyle Advice for the Soviet Masses* (DeKalb, IL: Northern Illinois University Press, 2007).
Boh, Katja, et al., eds. *Changing Patterns of European Family Life: A Comparative Analysis of 14 European Countries* (London, New York: Routledge, 1989).
Brunnbauer, Ulf. *'Die sozialistische Lebensweise': Ideologie, Gesellschaft, Familie und Politik in Bulgarien (1944–1989)* (Wien: Böhlau, 2007).
Brunnbauer, Ulf, and Wolfgang Höpken, eds. *Transformationsprobleme Bulgariens im 19. und 20. Jahrhundert: historische und ethnologische Perspektiven* (München: Verlag Otto Sagner, 2007).
Brunnbauer, Ulf, and Karl Kaser, eds. *Vom Nutzen der Verwandten: Soziale Netzwerke in Bulgarien* (Wien: Böhlau, 2001).
Bucur, Maria. *Eugenics and Modernization in Interwar Romania* (Pittsburgh, PA: University of Pittsburgh Press, 2010).
Carey, Henry F. *European Institutions, Democratization, and Human Rights Protection in the European Periphery* (Lanham, MD: Lexington Books, 2014).
David, Henry Philip, ed. *From Abortion to Contraception: A Resource to Public Policies and Reproductive Behavior in Central and Eastern Europe from 1917 to the Present* (Westport, CT: Greenwood Press, 1999).
Dynes, Wayne R., ed. *Encyclopedia of Homosexuality* vol. 2 (New York: Routledge, 1990).
Feinberg, Melissa. *Elusive Equality: Gender, Citizenship, and the Limits of Democracy in Czechoslovakia, 1918–1950* (Pittsburgh, PA: University of Pittsburgh Press, 2006).
Felder, Björn M., and Paul J. Weindling, eds. *Baltic Eugenics: Bio-politics, Race and Nation in Interwar Estonia, Latvia and Lithuania 1918–1940*, vol. 35 (Amsterdam: Rodopi, 2013).
Ferree, Myra Marx. *Shaping Abortion Discourse: Democracy and the Public Sphere in Germany and the United States* (Cambridge: Cambridge University Press: 2002).
Fidelis, Małgorzata. *Women, Communism, and Industrialization in Postwar Poland* (New York: Cambridge University Press, 2010).
Gal, Susan. *The Politics of Gender after Socialism: A Comparative-Historical Essay* (Princeton, NJ: Princeton University Press, 2000).

---

281 Peter Roudik, 'Croatia: Constitutional Amendment Banning Gay Marriage Passed by Referendum' (13 January 2014), www.loc.gov/law/foreign-news/article/croatia-constitutional-amendment-banning-gay-marriage-passed-by-referendum/ (accessed 22 May 2016).
282 Michael K. Lavers, 'Macedonian Lawmakers Approve Same-Sex Marriage Ban', *Washington Blade* (21 January 2015), www.washingtonblade.com/2015/01/21/macedonian-lawmakers-approve-sex-marriage-ban/ (accessed 18 May 2016).
283 STA, 'Constitutional Court Allows Gay Marriage Referendum', *The Slovenia Times* (22 October 2015), www.sloveniatimes.com/constitutional-court-allows-gay-marriage-referendum (accessed 17 May 2016).
284 Sexual Orientation and Gender Identity Working Group, *Croatia Country report for use in Canadian refugee claims based on persecution on the basis of sexual orientation or gender identity* (January 2015), 12, https://ihrp.law.utoronto.ca/utfl_file/count/documents/WorkingGroup_Clinic/IHRP%20SOGI%20Croatia%20Report%20FINAL%202015.pdf (accessed 23 May 2016).

Gal, Susan, and Gail Kligman, eds. *Reproducing Gender: Politics, Publics and Everyday Life after Socialism* (Princeton, NJ: Princeton University Press, 2000).
Gerstner, David A., ed. *Routledge International Encyclopedia of Queer Culture* (London: Routledge, 2012).
Gillett, Robert, and Lisa Downing, eds. *Queer in Europe: Contemporary Case Studies* (Farnham: Ashgate, 2012).
Grandits, Hannes, ed. *Family, Kinship and State in Contemporary Europe*, vol. 1 (Chicago, IL: University of Chicago Press, 2010).
Haney, Lynne. *Inventing the Needy: Gender and the Politics of Welfare in Hungary* (Berkeley, CA: University of California Press, 2002).
Hašková, Hana, and Zuzana Uhde, eds. *Women and Social Citizenship in Czech Society: Continuity and Change* (Prague: Institute of Sociology, Academy of Sciences of the Czech Republic, 2009).
Havelková, Hana, and Libora Oates-Indruchová, eds. *The Politics of Gender Culture under State Socialism: An Expropriated Voice* (London: Routledge, 2014).
Healey, Dan. *Homosexual Desire in Revolutionary Russia: The Regulation of Sexual and Gender Dissent* (Chicago, IL: University of Chicago Press, 2001).
Herzog, Dagmar. *Sex after Fascism: Memory and Morality in Twentieth-Century Germany* (Princeton, NJ: Princeton University Press, 2005).
Herzog, Dagmar. *Sexuality in Europe: A Twentieth-Century History* (Cambridge: Cambridge University Press, 2011).
Johnson, Janet Elise, and Jean C. Robinson. *Living Gender after Communism* (Bloomington, IL: Indiana University Press, 2006).
Jovanovic, Miroslav, and Slobodan Naumovic, eds. *Gender Relations in South Eastern Europe: Historical Perspectives on Womanhood and Manhood in 19th and 20th Century* (Beograd: Udruženjezadušstevnuistoriju, 2001).
Karady, Victor, and Wolfgang Mitter, eds. *Bildungswesen und Sozialstruktur in Mitteleuropa im 19. und 20. Jahrhundert* (Köln: Böhlau, 1990).
Kligman, Gail. *The Politics of Duplicity: Controlling Reproduction in Ceausescu's Romania* (Los Angeles, CA: University of California Press, 1998).
Kogan, Irena, Michael Gebel, and Clemens Noelke, eds. *Europe Enlarged: A Handbook of Education, Labour and Welfare Regimes in Central and Eastern Europe* (Bristol: The Policy Press, 2008).
Kraft, Claudia, ed. *Geschlechtberbeziehungen in Ostmitteleuropa nach dem Zweiten Weltkrieg: Soziale Praxis und Konstruktion von Geschlechterbildern – Vorträge der Tagung des Collegium Carolinum in Bad Wiessee vom 17. bis 20. November 2005* (München: Oldenbourg, 2008).
Kuhar, Roman, and Judit Takács, eds. *Beyond the Pink Curtain: Everyday Life of LGBT People in Eastern Europe* (Ljubljana: Mirovni Inšt., 2007).
Kulpa, Robert, and Joanna Mizielińska, eds. *De-Centring Western Sexualities: Central and Eastern European Perspectives* (Farnham, UK: Ashgate, 2011).
Lebow, Katherine. *Unfinished Utopia: Nowa Huta, Stalinism and Polish Society 1949–56* (Ithaca, NY: Cornell University Press, 2013).
Lišková, Kateřina. *Sexual Liberation, Socialist Style: Communist Czechoslovakia and the Science of Desire, 1945–1989* (Cambridge: Cambridge University Press 2018).
Melman, Billie, ed. *Borderlines: Gender and Identities in War and Peace 1870–1930* (London: Routledge, 1998).
Offen, Karen. *European Feminisms, 1700–1950: A Political History* (Stanford, CA: Stanford University Press, 2000).
Papp, Claudia. *Die Kraft der weiblichen Seele: Feminismus in Ungarn, 1918–1941* (Münster: LIT Verlag, 2002).
Parikas, Udo, and Teet Veispak, eds. *Sexual Minorities and Society: The Changing Attitudes toward Homosexuality in the 20th Century Europe; Facts about Homosexuality in Soviet Russia and Current Estonia* (Tallinn: Institute of History, 1991).
Penn, Shana. *Solidarity's Secret: The Women Who Defeated Communism in Poland* (Ann Arbor, MI: University of Michigan Press, 2005).
Penn, Shana, and Jill Massino, eds. *Gender Politics and Everyday Life in State Socialist Eastern and Central Europe* (New York: Palgrave Macmillan, 2009).
Posadskaya, Anastasia, ed. *Women in Russia: A New Era in Russian Feminism*, trans. Kate Clark (London: Verso, 1994).

Ramet, Sabrina P., ed. *Gender Politics in the Western Balkans: Women and Society in Yugoslavia and the Yugoslav Successor States* (University Park, PA: Penn State Press, 2010).

Reiter, Norbert, and Holm Sundhaussen, eds. *Allgemeinbildung als Modernisierungsfaktor: Zur Geschichte der Elementarbildung in Südosteuropa von der Aufklärung bis zum Zweiten Weltkrieg* (Wiesbaden: Harassowitz, 1994).

Rueschemeyer, Marilyn, and Sharon L. Wolchik. *Women in Power in Post-Communist Parliaments* (Bloomington, IL: Woodrow Wilson Center Press and Indiana University Press, 2009).

Saurer, Edith, Margareth Lanzinger, and Elisabeth Frysak, eds. *Women's Movements, Networks and Debates in Post-Communist Countries in the 19th and the 20th Centuries* (Köln: Böhlau, 2006).

Stewart, Chuck, ed. *The Greenwood Encyclopedia of LGBT Issues Worldwide* (Santa Barbara, CA: Greenwood Press, 2010).

Štrbáňová, Sona, Ida H. Stamhuis, and Kateřina Mojsejová, eds. *Women Scholars and Institutions, Proceedings of the International Conference (Prague, June 8–11, 2003), Studies in the History of Sciences and Humanities*, vol. 13 A and 13 B (Prague: Research Centre for the History of Sciences and Humanities, 2004).

Štulhofer, Aleksandar, and Theo Sandfort. *Sexuality and Gender in Postcommunist Eastern Europe and Russia* (New York: Haworth Press, 2005).

Sulkunen, Irma, Seija-Leena Nevala-Nurmi, and Pirjo Markkola, eds. *Suffrage, Gender and Citizenship: International Perspectives on Parliamentary Reforms* (Newcastle: Cambridge Scholar Publishing, 2009).

Sundhaussen, Holm. *Geschichte Serbiens, 19. – 21. Jahrhundert* (Wien: Böhlau, 2007).

Tapon, Francis. *The Hidden Europe: What Eastern Europeans Can Teach Us* (Library of Congress: SonicTrek, Inc.: 2011).

Therborn, Göran. *Die Gesellschaften Europas 1945–2000: Ein Soziologischer Vergleich* (Frankfurt a.M.: Campus, 2000).

Tomka, Béla. *A Social History of Twentieth-Century Europe* (New York: Routledge, 2013).

Treas, Judith, and Sonja Drobnič, eds. *Dividing the Domestic: Men, Women and Household Work in Cross-National Perspective* (Stanford, CA: Stanford University Press, 2010).

Trubeta, Sevasti, Christian Promitzer, and Marius Turda, eds. *Health, Hygiene and Eugenics in Southeastern Europe until 1945* (Budapest: Central European University Press, 2011).

Turda, Marius, ed. *The History of East-Central European Eugenics, 1900–1945: Sources and Commentaries* (London: Bloomsbury Publishing Plc, 2015).

Wingfield, Nancy Meriwether, and Maria Bucur, eds. *Gender and War in Twentieth-Century Eastern Europe* (Bloomington, IN: Indiana University Press, 2006).

Wolchik, Sharon L., and Alfred G. Meyer, eds. *Women, State and Party in Eastern Europe* (Durham, NC: Duke University Press, 1985).

5
POPULATION AND FAMILY

Stanislav Holubec and Béla Tomka

Introduction

The twentieth-century history of population and family in Central and Eastern Europe has claimed scholarly attention from multiple perspectives. Population changes have a significant impact on modernity, which, in contrast to premodern times, can be characterized as a period of swift demographic transformations. Demographic behaviour influences several important aspects of social life. It shapes gender roles, particularly by decreasing the number of children and postponing the age of birth. It also affects social stratification, as different social classes have historically exhibited different birth rates. By influencing the structure and size of the labour force it exerts a major impact on the economy, for example by creating agrarian overpopulation or what is called the demographic 'window of opportunity', a period of time when the population of adults starts to prevail over the population of children, and the population of the elderly has not expanded yet, thus presenting a chance for economic breakthrough. Population change also shapes consumption patterns in various ways, for example declining birth rates result in a drop in the share of income spent on basic necessities. Demography has a major impact on the development of education, as changes in birth rates create pressure to adjust the size and structures of education systems. The history of migration is closely intertwined with the history of transportation, and out-migration from the countryside is one of the most important factors in the development of urban–rural relations. Demographic transformation is among the most significant factors shaping modern social life.

As to the family, Central and Eastern Europe, like other regions, witnessed not only the transformation of the family in the twentieth century as a consequence of wider social changes, but an evolution of family structures that also had an impact on a number of major social processes and institutions, including the development of fertility, the welfare state and the labour market. Moreover, family became a focal point of interest of various political systems throughout the twentieth century, as regimes attempted to advance their political agenda by controlling family behaviour as well. Finally, a more general analytical interest may also lead to the study of Central and Eastern European family history. In recent decades, many historians and social theorists have claimed that the divergences in historical family patterns in Europe are significant manifestations, or indeed, sources of regional differences. Therefore, variations in family development have often played an important role in attempts to designate political-cultural boundaries within Europe. It was even proposed that there was a straightforward connection between the nuclear family and the evolution of political democracy, while societies with multiple household systems occasionally produced authoritarian rule and communist dictatorship.[1]

Although the scholarly focus on twentieth-century Central and Eastern European population and family history is substantiated in several respects, the study of these fields poses particular challenges. Historical research on Central and Eastern European population and family has to cope with specific difficulties. The first of these is more general and related to the very nature of the discipline of these fields. Population history and family history have become well-established fields within social history in the last couple of decades. They are often regarded as closely related (sub)disciplines with similar methodology. This practice originates from the period of the institutionalization of family history – the late 1950s and the 1960s – when the 'demographic approach' clearly dominated the field. Since then, however, family history has become much more diversified, employing such approaches as the 'sentiment' or cultural approach, and the 'household economy approach' which deals primarily with the transformation of the functions of the family.[2] The divergence of these two areas of scholarship poses a considerable difficulty for any common treatment of the two themes.

Another major problem we have to face is the asymmetries of research on twentieth-century Central and Eastern Europe. The demographic research carried out was of high academic quality throughout the century in several countries of the region, and many plausible analyses have been offered to explain and interpret demographic processes that were related to family development. However, partly because of the characteristics of the discipline, demographers were able to study only certain aspects of family development. What is more, in demographic research dealing with family, the historical perspective usually remained secondary. While demographic studies are available in abundance for the twentieth century, European family history has clearly focused on the period from the seventeenth to the nineteenth century and has neglected the last century. In contrast, family sociology has produced tangible results. From the 1960s, family sociology produced numerous high-quality studies on the region, but these works, obviously, examined only the last few decades of the century; consequently, earlier decades remain largely unexplored in international scholarship.

It is also a case in point here that the diversity of the Central and Eastern European region alone calls for a comparative perspective. However, one can hardly name any comparative research on twentieth-century Central and Eastern European family history. Not only are there no overall studies covering the whole region, or larger parts of it, but even comparative research is quite sporadic and tends to concern only specific aspects of family development. Most of the more extensive demographic comparisons have investigated changes in fertility and mortality over the last couple of decades.[3] The scope of comparative sociological research on the family

---

1 E. Todd, *The Explanation of Ideology: Family Structures and Social Systems* (Oxford: Blackwell, 1985).
2 Michael Anderson, *Approaches to the History of the Western Family, 1500–1914* (London: Macmillan, 1980); Michael Mitterauer, *Historisch-Antropologische Familienforschung: Fragestellungen und Zugangsweisen* (Vienna: Böhlau, 1990), 87–90.
3 For these demographical comparisons, see for example: Alain Monnier and Jitka Rychtarikova, 'The Division of Europe into East and West', *Population: An English Selection* 4 (1992): 129–60; David Coleman, 'European Demographic Systems of the Future: Convergence or Diversity?' in *Human Resources in Europe at the Dawn of the 21st Century*, ed. Eurostat (Luxembourg: Office for Official Publications of the European Communities, 1992), 141–80; András Klinger, 'Magyarország demográfiai helyzete Európában' [The demographic situation of Hungary in a European context], *Demográfia* 34 (1991): 1, 19–60; László Hablicsek deals with an earlier period in his study, *Az első és második demográfiai átmenet Magyarországon és Közép-Kelet-Európában* [The first and second demographic transition in Hungary and in Central and Eastern Europe] (Budapest: KSH, 1995).

in Central and Eastern Europe has been restricted to relatively narrow aspects and a limited number of countries.

The perspectives and themes addressed in this chapter are determined largely by the fact that most of the twentieth-century trends in population and family development in the region conform to larger trends that also apply to Western Europe and the industrial world. These convergent tendencies include the fall in fertility and mortality, which in the first half of the century can be conceptualized as part of the demographic transition, and as important manifestations of the second demographic transition in the last decades of the century; the nuclearization of family households; the decline in the average size of the households; the fall of patriarchy and growing symmetry between family members; and the growing activity of governments in matters of population and family – all of which will be addressed in this chapter.

However, the population and family development in the region also showed a number of distinct characteristics in twentieth-century Central and Eastern Europe. To address these peculiarities, it might be productive to emphasize two phenomena that had a profound and specific impact on Central and Eastern Europe: military conflicts, and communism or state socialism.

The impact of military conflicts and genocides on population change does appear in standard demographic accounts. However, demographers prefer presenting major trends and continuous processes to investigating the ruptures caused by political violence or other political developments. The occasional lack of wartime data encourages such approaches. This rather implicit treatment of the demographic effects of wars seems unsatisfactory in a region so strongly affected by political turbulence and military destruction during the century that several influential historical accounts of the twentieth-century history of Central and Eastern Europe take these events as their focus.[4] The Second World War hit the region particularly hard – Poland lost 18–20 per cent of its pre-war population, Hungary and Yugoslavia about 10 per cent – which moves this period to the foreground as an important research subject of population history. Thus, the chapter sets out to develop this theme, while also examining the erosion of human capital and other social consequences. At the same time, it also intends to connect with the volume on *Violence*. Forced migration, a much more researched topic, is a further concern of the chapter. The hundreds of thousands of refugees or forced migrants during the First World War were only the prelude to the Second World War, which resulted in 12 million Germans expelled, and 3 million Poles deported from the lost Polish territories in the East. A total of 2.3 million refugees are estimated to have fled during the Yugoslav Wars. In addition, these events generated population imbalances, distorting the age structure and gender ratios.

As for state socialism and its effects on population and family, several trends conformed to those surfacing in industrial societies, and can even be interpreted as improvements to quality of life and progress for social emancipation. Health care advanced considerably, manifested in the substantial decline in infant mortality and rising life expectancy in the 1950s. Corporal punishment of children in schools was abolished, and the full legal equality of women was declared in every respect. In some cases, the spread of female employment was accompanied by strong pronatalist and maternalist welfare policies (Czechoslovakia and Hungary from the late 1960s), which were welcomed by many observers as a new synthesis of strategies for the emancipation of women.

Other developments, however, can be interpreted as peculiar and sometimes even conflicting with preceding trends. The life expectancy for men began to stagnate and even to fall from the mid-1960s in most parts of the region, which can be considered unique in the peacetime population history of the industrialized world. A total ban on induced abortion was imple-

---

4 Mark Mazower, *Dark Continent: Europe's Twentieth Century* (London: Penguin, 1998); Timothy Snyder, *Bloodlands: Europe between Hitler and Stalin* (New York: Basic Books, 2010).

mented in several countries (in the early 1950s in Hungary, in the late 1960s in Romania), in some cases followed by wholesale liberalization, resulting in an extremely high number of abortions. Forced sterilization of Romany women occurred in Czechoslovakia in the 1970s. Suicide rates rose to new highs (Hungary had the highest suicide rates in the world in the early 1960s).

The strict control of migration – in fact, travel – to the Western world belonged to the repressive measures of the socialist state. Specific phenomena related to migration included forced, or, quasi-forced, migration within countries; illegal migration to the West; the almost total lack of immigration in the post-war era; and such corrupt polices as the 'sale' of German-speaking citizens to West Germany by the Romanian government in exchange for hard currency in the late 1970s and the 1980s. The reproductive and familial behaviour of the Central and Eastern European population also showed distinct features in the last decades of communist rule. Marriage rates were extremely high even in the 1970s; at the same time, excessive divorce rates emerged throughout the region, most notably in the Baltic states. The young age of mothers at the birth of their first child and the relatively low rate of extramarital births also contributed to the emergence of family patterns that were distinct in a European context.

It seems that not only the Central and Eastern European state-socialist demographic regimes showed remarkable features, but also their post-socialist successors. Especially important are the birth rates, which dropped to among the lowest levels in the world; massive economic immigration to Western Europe; and the resulting decline in population – the most extreme case being Latvia, which lost 22 per cent of its population between 1990 and 2012. However, in most respects, the region seems to have followed Western European trends in this era, including, among others, a decline in marriage rates, the acceptance of unions between homosexuals, and the postponement of the birth of a first child.

The considerations referred to so far, and the research literature, which has been barely touched upon here, all designate the major themes investigated in this chapter, structured as follows: first, the concept of demographic transition will be introduced, allowing us to cover the most important changes in fertility and mortality; second, several types of migration will be addressed. The next subchapter addresses the historical patterns of family formation and changes in Central and Eastern European family and household structures; this is followed by a section examining historical changes in the interpersonal relationships between family members and the attitudes towards children; then, population and family policies are discussed; the final part of the chapter suggests some particular characteristics of twentieth-century Central and Eastern European population and family history.

In covering these themes, the chapter also applies a number of specific analytical perspectives. First of all, the following questions are raised:

- Which fields of population and family history transformed most quickly, and which aspects of this transformation were more sluggish? What were the dynamics of change?
- What factors underlying these changes could be identified? Which of these were distinctly characteristic of the region or some parts of it?
- How far did the Central and Eastern European region differ from other parts of Europe and to what extent was this region internally uniform?

It also seems necessary to make a couple of remarks about the methods of the investigation and the limits of the research.[5] As for methods, the historical processes of Central and Eastern

---

5 For the methodology of comparisons in general, see Larry J. Griffin, 'Comparative-historical Analysis', in *Encyclopedia of Sociology*, vol. 1, eds Edgar F. Borgetta and Marie L. Borgetta (New York: Macmillan,

Europe have also been examined by statistical tools, although the comparability of available data frequently presents obvious difficulties, and the formal and measurable similarities/differences can often be misleading with regard to functionality.

The outlined study of the Central and Eastern European region poses a difficult task for the researcher from multiple perspectives. The examined period is quite long, a whole century, and the number of countries involved in the analysis is also high. These circumstances themselves necessitate certain simplifications regarding the scope of analysis. Although the investigation aims at comparisons, it cannot be a systematic endeavour for the reasons listed above. However, these difficulties must not prevent us from applying comparisons as an important tool of history writing, which might offer new perspectives on Central and Eastern European social history.

Therefore, we hardly need to emphasize that our investigation has limitations, some of which are drawn consciously, and others which remain unintentional. The former are indicated clearly by the fields and questions elaborated above. Constraints emerging from the unintentional, practical difficulties are not only due to the authors' limited scope of knowledge. During the research, we were not able to compensate fully for the deficiencies of the available research literature discussed above, the imbalances of which are thus reflected in our work as well. The most obvious of these disproportions is a chronological one: because of the lack of sources and relevant research, we had less opportunity to discuss the processes in play during the period before the Second World War. What is more, the study undoubtedly suffers from thematic inequalities as well: for example, the cultural characteristics of the family (norms, values, rituals), despite all of our efforts to include them, were pushed to the background for the same reasons.

Population growth, fertility and mortality

To discuss the issues of population growth, fertility and mortality, it is plausible to begin the chapter by briefly outlining the concept of demographic transition, which although not new, still offers us a means of explaining population development in the nineteenth and twentieth centuries. Demographic transition had a profound effect on the social history of Europe, being one of the main factors of nineteenth- and early twentieth-century overseas migration, and along with industrialization, a crucial factor in urbanization. The first foundations of the concept were laid by the American demographer Warren Thomson in the late 1920s;[6] it was further elaborated a decade later by the French demographer Adolph Landry, who used the term '*la révolution démographique*', with the term 'demographic transition' appearing shortly after 1945.[7] According to this model, premodern society is characterized by high rates of mortality and fertility, resulting in very slow population growth. With the advent of modern society, a steady decline in mortality occurred, first due to improved nutrition, later to advances in public health and sanitation. However, fertility still continued to be high, leading to rapid population growth. After a certain period (sometimes years, sometimes decades), fertility also began to fall significantly, leading to a deceleration in population growth. The main reasons were contraception, abortions and later marriage. Increasing migration, too, is considered to be a factor leading

---

1992), 263–71; Else Oyen, ed., *Comparative Methodology* (London: Sage, 1990); for comparative studies in the sociology of family and social history, see Gary R. Lee and Linda Haas, 'Comparative Methods in Family Research', in *Sourcebook of Family Theories and Methods: A Contextual Approach*, eds Pauline G. Boss et al. (New York: Springer, 1993), 117–31.

6 Warren S. Thompson, 'Population', *American Journal of Sociology* 34, no. 6 (1929): 959–75.

7 Frank W. Notestein et al., *The Future Population of Europe and the Soviet Union: Population Projections, 1940–1970* (Geneva: League of Nations, 1944).

to declining birth rates. Cultural transformations were also of importance, mainly in the sphere of women's education and emancipation. As a result of these factors, the rate of population growth started to slow down. The new, 'modern' demographic regime is characterized by low mortality and low fertility and very slow population growth.

The geographic spread of the transition is also noteworthy. The process started in the early nineteenth century in Western Europe, before gradually spreading to Central Europe and later to Southern and Eastern Europe. Time differences in the progression of demographic transition from country to country can be explained with reference to the economic development within a given country, opportunities for education, and the emancipation of women, as well as specific cultural and religious values.

Several critiques of the concept were formulated: First, contrary to the model, the pre-modern population regime was not stationary, but showed important fluctuations. Second, the global applicability of the model has been questioned. It is not certain that so-called 'Third World' countries will ever reach this last phase of growth. Third, the decline in fertility often does not correlate with urbanization or industrialization as the model assumes. Fourth, the model fails to explain some phenomena such as the Western baby boom after 1945, and the deteriorating mortality rates in the Soviet bloc since the 1960s. Fifth, in many cases the difference between declining mortality and fertility was very short, and therefore had little influence on overall population growth. In spite of these shortcomings, the concept is still widely used, as it reveals important historical processes and offers a heuristic framework for discussion.

It has been argued that, although the modern demographic regime is characterized by a stable population, steadily falling fertility rates will eventually result in population decline and a greater proportion of elderly people in developed countries. So far, however, the massive population decline of the Western countries has not occurred because most of the countries where it was expected to occur have also experienced significant in-migration by adults of productive age. Population decline in many countries in the region can best be explained by out-migration and declining birth rates in the context of the post-socialist socio-economic crisis.

At the beginning of the period covered by our volume, 1890, the region (including today's countries of former Yugoslavia, Bulgaria, Romania, Poland, Hungary, Czech Republic, Slovakia and the Baltic states) had a total population of around 70 million, which had risen to about 125 million by 2010. If we look at the evolution of the region's population, it becomes clear that it is broadly similar to demographic developments in twentieth-century Western and Southern Europe. The region was somewhat outpaced by the population growth of its eastern neighbour – Russia – whose population (within the borders of the former Soviet Union) was twice as large in 1890 and 2.3 times greater in 2000. It could not keep up with the population dynamics of its neighbour to the southeast, Turkey, which was demographically similar to other Near East countries.

From the available data it is clear that the First World War had generally disastrous effects on the population of the region. The greatest population losses were experienced by countries and regions at the centre of war operations – Serbia, Lithuania and Latvia lost more than a quarter of their respective populations. The territory of the future Latvia lost perhaps the greatest proportion of its population: in 1914 it had 2.5 million inhabitants, but by 1920 that figure had dwindled to 1.5 million, mainly as a result of emigration.[8] In terms of military casualties, however, Serbia suffered the most. The country mobilized almost its entire population of men

---

8 Derek H. Aldcroft, *Europe's Third World: The European Periphery in the Interwar Years* (Farnham: Ashgate, 2006), 98.

aged between 18 and 55, about half of which were killed. Around one quarter of the pre-war population was lost as a result of war casualties, famine and epidemics (e.g. a Balkan typhoid fever epidemic that lasted from late 1914 to mid-1915,[9] and the Spanish flu epidemic from the end of 1917). If one adds to that figure the estimated number of children not born due to the war, the result is a loss of about a third of the population. Above-average population losses were also recorded in Romania and Poland, where military operations continued until 1921 and the eastern regions were hit particularly hard. While population losses in the former Austria-Hungary and Bulgaria were lower, they surpassed the losses in Western European countries.[10] Yet some countries recorded a marginal increase in population growth between 1914 and 1919, for example Bulgaria, Hungary and the Czech lands. This can be explained by the fact that Bulgaria and Hungary were forced to give up territories after the defeat and experienced an influx of people from the ceded areas. Population growth in the Czech lands at the time was due to the fact that its territory was far away from the front lines, unlike most other parts of the region.

During the interwar period, the population of the region increased from 86 to 102 million, which signalled a slowdown in growth compared to the pre-war decades. Population growth was still uneven across the region. As in the late nineteenth century, Southeastern Europe still found itself in the midst of demographic transition and its population continued to grow rapidly. For example, the population of Albania increased by 32 per cent in just two decades, while population growth in Bulgaria and Yugoslavia in the same period was 30 per cent and 31 per cent respectively. Poland also experienced high growth (30 per cent), which was evenly distributed across the country. The lowest growth was experienced by the most advanced countries in the region – Czechoslovakia, Hungary and the Baltic countries. In comparison with Western Europe, the population of the region continued to grow rapidly, mirroring the population growth of its eastern and south-eastern neighbours – the Soviet Union and Turkey. This growth, however, was still stronger in rural areas. Only two cities in the region – Budapest and Warsaw – had over one million residents in the interwar period (the population of Bucharest passed the one-million mark in the early 1940s).[11]

The region suffered devastating population losses during the Second World War. If we compare the total number of inhabitants of the Central and Eastern European countries between 1938 and 1946 including the Baltics, we see the population decline by 10 per cent in the period from 1938 to 1946, from 102 to 90 million. Yet the number of casualties was even higher: nine million military personnel were killed and the number of civilian victims of the war was in excess of seven million (however, another four million people were born during the war). Jews, Belarusians, Poles, Ukrainians and Serbs were the main victims of war; 90 per cent of the first group were killed. By 1945 the territory of the Baltic states and Poland (in particular, parts of Western Ukraine and Belarus) had lost more than a quarter of their pre-war populations. The decline in the region's population was also due to the flight and expulsion of Germans, and to Central and Eastern Europeans going into exile or being deported from their countries to the east by Soviet authorities, particularly Poles and natives of the Baltic states.

---

9 Christian Promitzer, 'Typhus, Turks, and Roma: Hygiene and Ethnic Difference in Bulgaria, 1912–1944', in *Health, Hygiene and Eugenics in Southeastern Europe*, eds Christian Promitzer, Sevasti Trubeta, and Marius Turda (Budapest: Central European University Press, 2010), 87–126, here 93.
10 Notestein et al., *The Future Population of Europe*, 78.
11 Dudley Kirk, *Europe's Population in the Interwar Years* (Geneva: League of Nations, 1946), 24, 34.

The region experienced relatively rapid population growth during the socialist period, albeit incomparable with the growth seen in the late nineteenth century. The population grew from 93 million in 1950 to 128 million in 1990. Population increases in the countries examined ranged from 11 per cent to 53 per cent in the period from 1950 to 1990. Albania was an exception: Its population grew by a phenomenal 168 per cent. Poland had the fastest growth in the region after Albania and other Southeastern European regions with mainly Muslim populations. The lowest growth rate was experienced in Hungary, whose population actually began to decline from the early 1980s due to very low birth rates. During this period, the rate of population growth in the region was lower than that of its eastern and south-eastern neighbours (37 per cent as opposed to 60 per cent in the Soviet Union and 167 per cent in Turkey), yet it was still higher than in Western Europe (24 per cent).

In the post-communist period (between 1990 and 2005), the region experienced a slight decline in its population from 130 to 125 million. The main reasons for this were a sharp drop in the birth rate, combined with emigration to Western Europe, especially after 2004. The real decline is even larger than the statistics show, because many emigrants living in Western Europe maintain residency in their native countries. The greatest population loss was experienced by Latvia, which witnessed a drop from a population of 2.7 million to 2.2 million. Many ethnic Latvians left for better jobs in the West, and many members of the Russian minority there decided to return to their homeland. Bosnia represents another extreme case. In the context of the Yugoslav Wars, its population fell from 4.3 to 2.3 million in the period from 1993 to 1995,[12] but partially recovered to 3.7 million by 2000. Significant population losses were also observed in other parts of Southeastern Europe that were severely hit by the economic crisis of the 1990s but did not experience war or mass flight and expulsions. Other

Table 5.1 Population growth in Central and Eastern Europe, 1920–2009 (in %)

Country	1920–1950	1950–1980	1990–2009
Albania	32	118	12
Bulgaria	43	22	-19
Czechoslovakia	-5	23	-1/3
Hungary	18	15	-4
Poland	4	43	1
Romania	32	36	-3
Yugoslavia	31	33	
Slovenia (data from 1991 on)			0.4
Croatia (data from 1995 on)			-0.2
Serbia (data from 1995–2006)			-4
Estonia	7	22	-17
Latvia	9	19	-16
Lithuania	33	24	-4

Notes: For 1990–2009, Czechoslovakia is Czech Republic/Slovakia, Serbia includes Montenegro and Kosovo; different years are as follows: Estonia, Latvia & Lithuania data from 1930–1960, 1960–1980. Own calculations based on figures from Angus Maddison, *Statistics on World Population, GDP and Per Capita GDP, 1–2008 AD*, www.ggdc.net/maddison/oriindex.htm (accessed 1 January 2014) and Franz Rothenbacher, *The Central and East European Population since 1850* (London: Palgrave 2012), 29.

---

12 Károly Kocsis, ed., *South Eastern Europe in Maps* (Budapest: Geographical Research Institute of the Hungarian Academy of Sciences, 2007), 62.

countries experienced population stagnation or even slight population growth. This group includes countries in Central Europe that were not as severely affected by economic difficulties and mass emigration. Indeed, these countries have sometimes been the destination of migrants from the east and south. Macedonia and Kosovo, countries with large Albanian populations marked by high birth rates, also belong in this group, in contrast to Albania, which was hit severely by out-migration, mainly to Italy.

However, the population decline of Central and Eastern Europe is unprecedented: 11 of the 15 countries with the highest population losses in the world in the last two decades are post-communist states (the remaining four are small islands in the Pacific). It is therefore no wonder that some demographers are predicting that the region will lose one tenth to one fifth of its population in the period from 2010 to 2050, not only because it has one of the lowest fertility rates in the world, but also because it is not attractive enough for immigrants from less developed countries.[13] Looking at the countryside in Southeastern Europe, there is a distinct possibility that some parts of the region will one day be as sparsely populated as they were in the early modern period.

There are two population groups that made up a significant share of the population and showed peculiar features as far as their demographic characteristics are concerned, but which are often neglected in most accounts of the region's population history, mainly because they remained a minority everywhere: Jews and Romany. The population of Jews migrating to the religiously tolerant Polish-Lithuanian commonwealth from the increasingly intolerant west of Europe grew from the sixteenth century on. At the beginning of the period examined, more than half of the world's Jews lived in the Central and East European region, primarily in western parts of the Russian empire, including the former Kingdom of Poland, Austria-Hungary and Romania (a total of approximately 5.6 million in 1900).[14] Today, there are fewer than 80 thousand. These Jewish populations were quite heterogeneous. In most of the territories, Jews with Germanic roots (Ashkenazi) prevailed, only south of the Sarajevo-Belgrade-Bucharest line did Sephardic Jews dominate, having settled there at the time of Ottoman expansion. Jews in the western part of the region, in Hungary and the Czech lands, had the sociocultural characteristics of Western European Jewry (urban, educated, relatively well-off), while those living in the rest of the countries in the east of the region are referred to in the literature as 'Eastern European Jews'.

As a result of the fact that the decline in mortality took place earlier for the Jewish population than for other ethnic groups, the proportion of Jews in the population increased in the late nineteenth century (a statistic which was exploited in anti-Semitic campaigns); yet this growth slowed before the First World War, as other ethnic groups began to grow faster. Both the Holocaust (described briefly in demographic terms in the subchapter on migration) and migration to Israel after 1945, put an end to Jews as a significant minority in the region. Hungary was the only country in Central and Eastern Europe where a notable Jewish minority still remained. The second significant Jewish population in the post-war era existed in Romania, but as the population was getting older or emigrating, their numbers were rapidly declining. Today, each country of the region (including Poland) has a Jewish population of less than 10 thousand. The population of Hungarian Jews, in contrast to Soviet Jews, did not experience a new wave of

---

13 Eurostat, 'Bevölkerungsprognosen', http://epp.eurostat.ec.europa.eu/tgm/table.do?tab=table&init=1 &language=de&pcode=tps00002&plugin=1 (accessed 1 January 2014).
14 Calculated on data by Victor Karady, *The Jews of Europe in the Modern Era: A Socio-Historical Outline* (Budapest: Central European University Press, 2004), 44–5.

emigration after 1989 and amounts to about 50 thousand persons today. The reliability of these estimates is limited, however. If Jews are defined as people practising the Jewish religion, the number is much smaller; if one counts by ethnic identity, the number would also be low; yet, if they are defined as people with Jewish ancestors, the numbers are much higher.

The Romany population, a significant minority in the countries of Southeastern Europe, presents a different case. At the beginning of the twentieth century, the Romany represented a small ethnic minority in the region (accounting for just two per cent of the population in Bulgaria, Romania and Hungary). Their population in the late 1930s was estimated at 650 thousand, about 0.5 per cent of the region's inhabitants. Although it is commonly believed today that they lead a nomadic life, statistical evidence shows that most of them were already sedentary in the late nineteenth century (in Hungary in 1893, 88 per cent were characterized as sedentary), albeit often living separately from the societies of the countries' given majorities.[15] The Romany were persecuted and murdered during the Holocaust in areas occupied by the Nazis or by Romanian and Croatian fascists (the number of Romany victims is estimated between 10 and 30 per cent of the pre-war population; almost the entire Romany population was killed in Croatia, Estonia and Lithuania).[16] In contrast to Jews, they rarely emigrated from the region afterward. The Romany genocide and the role played in it by locals were long neglected and have only recently become a topic of public discussion (for example, people are now discussing the Romany concentration camp, Lety, in South Bohemia, which was run by the Czech police from 1940 to 1943).

The post-1945 years saw fast demographic growth of the Romany. Based on some estimates, although disputed, they currently represent over eight per cent of the populations of Romania, Bulgaria and Macedonia, four to eight per cent of the populations of Slovakia and Hungary, and two to four per cent of the populations of the Czech Republic and Serbia.[17] Zoltan Barany estimated their number in the 1990s at about 4.1 million, making up about 3 per cent of the region's population.[18] There are no accurate statistics, however, since most Romany are reluctant to declare their ethnicity for fear of racist discrimination, or because they identify more strongly with a subgroup of Romany, or even with the majority populations. The 'Romany question' is perceived from Prague to Sofia as one of the region's most serious social problems, even though it designates widely diverging issues for specific segments of local societies: from the social exclusion and deprivation of the Romany, to increasing shares of those belonging to this group in the general population.

Fertility

The total fertility rate in Central and Eastern Europe in the nineteenth century was similar to that in previous centuries, with the average woman giving birth to four or five children. If she married at the age of twenty and lived until her fiftieth birthday, a woman usually gave birth to between six and nine children. However, a certain proportion of women remained childless, died young, or lost their fertility before the end of their reproductive cycle. The first

---

15 Viorel Achim, *The Roma in Romanian History* (Budapest: Central European University Press, 2004), 135.
16 Donald L. Niewyk, *The Columbia Guide to the Holocaust* (New York: Columbia University Press, 2000), 422.
17 Kocsis, *South Eastern Europe in Maps*, 57.
18 Zoltan Barany, *The East European Gypsies: Regime Change, Marginality and Ethnopolitics* (New York: Cambridge University Press, 2002), 123–4, 160.

documented signs of declining fertility in the region were seen in the Czech lands and Hungary in the 1890s. Before the First World War, the total fertility rate in the Baltic states had fallen to 2.5 children per woman – sometimes considered the endpoint of demographic transition. The Czechoslovak Republic and Slovenia declined to this level in the 1920s, Hungary and Bulgaria by the 1930s, and Romania followed in the 1940s. In most other parts of the region the process was completed in the 1950s (Slovakia, Poland, Serbia, and Croatia) and the 1970s (Macedonia, Montenegro and Bosnia-Herzegovina). However, in Albania and Kosovo, the end of demographic transition was only reached in the new millennium.

When the communist regimes were established, families with an average of two to three children prevailed in the region, with the exception of countries that had large Muslim and Albanian populations (in the extreme case of Albania in 1950, there were seven children per woman!). Differences in birth rates became a topic of political disputes, as in Yugoslavia, where the birth rate in Kosovo was more than twice the Yugoslav average and was a matter of concern for the Serbs.[19] Serbs and Croats living in Bosnia and Herzegovina were also alarmed by the high birth rates among local Muslims.[20] In Latvia and Estonia, the locals were similarly afraid of Russian immigrants' fertility, which was twice as high as their own.

The post-communist period was characterized by a strong decline in birth rates throughout the region. During the collapse of communism, it had a slightly higher birth rate than Western Europe. In 1990, the total fertility rate in the region was typically between 1.8 and 2.0. Special cases could be found only in Southeastern Europe, where Albania and Kosovo bucked the trend with 3.3 and 3.7 children per woman, respectively.[21] In 2000, none of the countries in the region had a total fertility rate higher than 1.4 children per woman, again, with the exception of Albania and Kosovo. Currently the birth rates in Central and Eastern Europe are among the lowest in the world. According to World Bank data from the year 2000, of the twenty countries in the world with the lowest birth rates, twelve were in this region and three were in the former Soviet Union.[22] After 2000, birth rates recovered somewhat in many parts of the region. It is not clear, however, whether this recovery is permanent, and it is by no means a return to the high birth rates before the fall of communism. Fertility levels are still below the Western European average and below the replacement level.

The social sciences have attempted to explain post-socialist fertility patterns. Some observers have stressed economic hardship as a factor, while others pointed to new opportunities that are more attractive than having children, which supposedly had been one of the few paths to self-realization for young people before 1989.[23] The arguments in favour of state support for families were countered by neo-liberal arguments about individual responsibility. In the early 1990s there was speculation that the decline in the birth rate meant not a renunciation of parenthood, but rather its postponement until a more appropriate time. Sociological studies indicated that

---

19 Fred Singleton and Bernard Carter, *The Economy of Yugoslavia* (London: Croom Helm, 1982), 229.
20 Ibid., 229.
21 European Commission, Eurostat, 'Total fertility rate, 1960–2011 (live births per woman)', http://epp.eurostat.ec.europa.eu/statistics_explained/index.php?title=File:Total_fertility_rate,_1960-2011_(live_births_per_woman).png&filetimestamp=20130129121040 (accessed 1 January 2014). GaëlDupont, Pension Reforms in acceding countries, Revue de l'OFCE, 5/2004, 61 (accessed 1 June 2014)
22 The World Bank, 'Birth rate crude (per 1000 people)', http://data.worldbank.org/indicator/SP.DYN.CBRT.IN?order=wbapi_data_value_2000+wbapi_data_value&sort=asc&page=2 (accessed 1 January 2014).
23 Ladislav Rabušic, *Kde ty všechny děti jsou? Porodnost v sociologické perspektivě* [Where have all the kids gone? Natality in sociological perspective] (Prague: Sociologické nakladatelství, 2001), 214–15.

a very low birth rate coexisted with the desire of most women to have children sometime in the future. (For example, only one per cent of Croatian women expressed a reluctance to have children, while 77 per cent wanted to have two or more children). The extremely low Croatian birth rate, however, reveals a huge gap between aspirations and their realization.[24]

Data from the first decade of the new century have to some extent supported the thesis of postponed births: birth rates increased slightly after 2000, although they remained below the levels of the 1980s; but it also seems that a greater number of women will remain childless in comparison to late socialism. For example, according to some estimates, about one fifth of Polish women born around the year 1970 will remain childless.[25] The data on childlessness in the twentieth century suggest that this proportion of permanently childless women is not unusual if we compare it with times before 1950. However, the reasons for childlessness are different: before 1950, it was often due to illness-related infertility, a lack of opportunities to marry, and the exercise of certain professions that made motherhood impossible. Particularly, the cohort of women born around the year 1900, who had fewer opportunities to marry due to the absence of potential partners during the war and the high number of male casualties of war, was marked by significant lifelong childlessness.[26]

Furthermore, the pattern of women in the East giving birth at an earlier age than women in the West no longer applied in the post-socialist period. In the two decades after 1990, the gap in age at first delivery between our region and the West narrowed from five to two years. The average age of a woman in Central and Eastern Europe at the birth of her first child was between 24 and 28 in 2009, compared to 22 in 1990.[27]

Age at first childbirth is also connected to age at first marriage, although this correlation is now weaker than it was in the early twentieth century, as more individuals have children out of wedlock, while others marry but postpone parenthood. There are, however, striking differences between the different countries in the region in terms of the development of marriage age. In the Muslim or Albanian-dominated parts and in the former Soviet Union, the pattern of early marriage (at around 23 years of age for women) persists. In Central Europe, the marriage age has climbed upwards with the age of first childbirth, and both indicators now range from 25 to 29 years for women.[28]

As a consequence of both the decreasing birth rate and higher life expectancy, there was a steady decrease in the proportion of children and young people in the population during the twentieth century. Table 5.2 illustrates major differences in the proportions of persons aged 0–14 in the populations of countries in the region. Not only was the level of economic development of significance in the 1920s, but also cultural-religious traditions: Bosnia, with

---

24 Hannes Grandits, 'Kinship and the Welfare State in Croatia's Twentieth Century Transition', in *Household and Family in the Balkans: Two Decades of Historical Family Research at University of Graz*, ed. Karl Kaser (Vienna: LitVerlag, 2012), 453–78, here 468.

25 Maria Letizia Tanturri et al., 'State of the Art Report: Childlessness in Europe', in *Families and Societies: Working Paper Series* 32 (2015): 1–53, here 11, www.familiesandsocieties.eu/wp…/WP32Tanturri-EtAl2015.pdf (accessed 1 January 2016).

26 Lenka Juříčková, 'ANALÝZA: Bezdětnost v České republice' [Childlessness in the Czech Republic], www.demografie.info/?cz_detail_clanku&artclID=118 (accessed 1 January 2014).

27 'Age of mothers at childbirth and age-specific fertility' (2012), www.oecd.org/els/…/SF_2_3_Age_mothers_childbirth.pdf (accessed 1 November 2016), 2.

28 Franz Rothenbacher, *The Central and East European Population since 1850* (Houndmills: Palgrave Macmillan, 2012), 1000; Jean-Paul Sardon, 'Women's First Marriage Rates in Europe: Elements for a Typology', *Population: An English Selection* 5 (1993): 119–52, here 150–52.

Table 5.2 Persons aged 0–14 in the population of Central and Eastern Europe, 1920–2000 (in %)

Country	1920	1960	2000
Albania		40.2	30.3
Kosovo	43.7	41.2	33
Bosnia and Herzegovina	59.6	38.6	20.7
Bulgaria	36.2	32.3	15.7
Romania	40.1	27.5	18.5
Serbia	34.2	29.6	20.5
Poland	33.4	33.8	19.6
Slovakia	32.7	31.5	19.7
Croatia	32.5	27.2	17.3
Slovenia	31.3	27.3	15.8
Lithuania	30.8	35.6	20.0
Hungary	30.5	25.4	16.8
Latvia	28.0	29.9	17.9
Czech lands	27.8	25.4	16.4
Estonia	25.5	22.7	17.6

Notes: 1920, 1960 are for Kosovo with Metohija; Serbia with Central Serbia, Kosovo and Vojvodina; Bulgaria 1960 is 0–19 yrs; there are different years as follows: Kosovo: 1921; Bosnia and Herzegovina: 1921, 1961; Bulgaria: 1966; Romania: 1900, 1956; Serbia: 1921; Poland: 1921; Slovakia: 1961; Croatia: 1921, 1961; Slovenia: 1921, 1961; Lithuania: 1923, 1959; Latvia: 1959; Czech Lands: 1961; Estonia: 1922, 1959.

Sources: Based on figures in: Franz Rothenbacher, *The Central and East European Population since 1850* (London: Palgrave, 2012), 75–76; Franz Rothenbacher, *The European Population since 1945* (London: Palgrave, 2004), 160, 161, 429, 665; Vladimír Srb, *Tisíc let obyvatelstva českých zemí*, [A thousand years of Czech Lands' population] (Prague: Karolinum, 2004), 101; Brian R. Mitchell, *International Historical Statistics: Europe 1750–1993* (Basingstoke: Palgrave, 1998), 25, 32, 34; Branislav Šprocha and Pavol Tišliar, *Demografický obraz Slovenska v sčítaniach ľudu 1919–1940* [Demographic picture of Slovakia in Censuses 1919–1940] (Brno: Tribun EU, 2012), 63; The World Bank, 'Population ages 0–14', http://data.worldbank.org/indicator/SP.POP.0014.TO.ZS?page=2 (accessed 1 July 2016); Statistical Office of Kosovo, 'Demographic, Social and Reproductive Health Survey in Kosovo', November 2009, 11, www.unfpakos.org/wp-content/uploads/2012/05/DHSreportEng-pdf.pdf, (accessed 1 July 2016)

its significant Muslim population, was on one end of the continuum, while the countries with Protestant traditions were on the other. As we can see, strong convergence took place during the century and the only countries with a high proportion of children remaining are Albania and Kosovo.

Mortality

One of the fundamental demographic shifts in the region in the twentieth century is the rapid decline in mortality. The most used indicator is the crude death rate, which is measured as the number of deaths per 1,000 people per year. We can best review this process using age-specific indicators such as infant mortality and life expectancy.

Statistical data on infant mortality, understood to be a major indicator of social development, have been available for the Czech lands since the early nineteenth century, and from the rest of the Habsburg Empire since the second half of the nineteenth century. In Southeastern Europe, the data were first recorded in Bulgaria; from Romania and Yugoslavia, we have them only after 1920. Infant mortality statistics in the nineteenth century show large fluctuations associated with good or bad harvests and mass infections. In most countries, the rate started to decrease in the early twentieth century and continued to decline rapidly until the 1960s.

An examination of infant mortality across the region before 1950 suggests that we must be cautious with the quality of data. For example, Czechoslovakia and Hungary had similar infant mortality to Bulgaria and Yugoslavia in the 1920s and 1930s.[29] In of all these countries about 15 per cent of children died before completing the first year of life. The situation was better in the Baltic countries, which had an infant mortality of around 10 per cent.[30] It seems that in some countries not all cases of infant mortality were recorded. Another possible explanation could be that the quality of the health-care system or the economic development of a given country was not able to affect the rate of infant mortality significantly until roughly the mid-twentieth century. Urbanization sometimes even led to an increase in infant mortality. All in all, even though the data might be dubious, it makes clear that the region clearly lagged behind Western Europe with respect to this indicator.

Concerning the impact of the world wars on infant mortality, we have rather divergent or even contradictory data, and they are often lacking, particularly for countries that were subjected to military devastation. In Hungary, there was a surprising decline in infant mortality in the early years of the First World War. The mortality rate here declined from 199 per thousand in 1914 to 107 per thousand in 1915, but later began rising again. The initial fall can be explained by the fact that the number of births declined unevenly in specific social groups. The largest fall was recorded in the lower classes, because most of the men who were drafted came from the lower classes, and they generally had a higher rate of infant mortality than the upper classes. Concerning the Second World War, we also find the pattern of an increase in mortality in the later years of military conflict. Bulgaria saw an increase in infant mortality from 124 to 144 deaths per thousand infants between 1941 and 1945; Hungary experienced an increase from 115 to 169; and the rate in Romania rose from 166 to 187.[31]

The data on infant mortality since the early 1950s shows a great breakthrough everywhere in the region. It decreased rapidly during the 1950s and 1960s, significantly converging to the level of Western European countries. This was mainly due to the advent of antibiotics, better vaccination and the expansion of maternity clinics across the region. A somewhat higher infant mortality rate remained in the regions of Southeastern Europe that had large Muslim and Albanian populations. By contrast, the rate was very low in Czechoslovakia, where effective measures were taken soon after the war. The country had one of the lowest rates in the world at this time. The Baltics also had a low mortality rate inherited from the pre-war decades. From the 1960s on, the decline in infant mortality slowed, and the region clearly lagged behind Western Europe when communism collapsed. In the 1980s, a small part of the region resembled the most developed Western countries, with an infant mortality rate of less than one per cent (the Czech lands, Slovenia). Yet infant mortality was higher in the south (between 2.5 per cent and 5 per cent), mainly in poorer parts of Yugoslavia (Kosovo, Macedonia) and in Romania. While a less authoritarian birth culture developed in the West from the 1970s on, changes in

---

29 A good example of the development of the health-care system is the establishment of medical faculties. While the medical faculties in Poland, the Czech lands and Hungary had medieval traditions, the first medical faculty in Southeastern Europe was founded in Bucharest in 1857, the second in Sofia in 1918, the third in the Kingdom of Yugoslavia in 1920 and the fourth in Albania in 1952; see Brigitte Fuchs, 'Orientalizing Disease: Austro-Hungarian Policies of Race, Gender, and Hygiene in Bosnia and Herzegovina, 1874–1914', in Promitzer, Trubeta and Turda, *Health, Hygiene and Eugenics*, 57–86.
30 *Annuaire statistique de la Societé des Nations 1938/40* (Geneva: League of Nations, 1940), 40.
31 *Demographic Yearbook 1948* (New York: United Nations, 1949), 406.

the socialist countries were slow in this respect (no home births permitted, no father present at the birth, isolation of the mother from the child after delivery, etc.). Progressive approaches to birth came to the region only in the post-socialist era.

After 1989, infant mortality continued to decline (thanks to imports of Western medicine), but the pace of this decline was slower in countries that experienced serious economic difficulties during the transition. Nowadays, the Czech Republic and Slovenia are among the top 20 in the world, while Romania and Albania are the countries with the highest infant mortality rates in Europe. According to experts, the extraordinarily good position of the Czech Republic is due not only to the quality of prenatal and postnatal care, but also to the fact that women are advised to have an abortion in case of even the slightest risk of foetal defect, which is, in fact, a legacy of socialist health care.[32]

Unlike the crude death rate, data on life expectancy are more difficult to obtain. The existing data for the years before 1950 are often unreliable. Prior to 1900, registrars often had to estimate the age of deceased persons where the population was illiterate. The available data for the early twentieth century suggest that the Baltic countries and the Czech lands had a higher life expectancy at birth (in 1900 in Lithuania, 41.7 years and the Czech lands 40.2 years; Latvia, 44.9 years in 1896) than other parts of the region. The countries of Southeastern Europe lay at the bottom of the pile. However, comparisons are sometimes difficult to make. For example, in the case of Albania we have just one value for the first half of the century: 35.4 years in 1929, which is similar to the life expectancy in the Czech lands in 1890. While public health-care was somewhat successful in combating infant mortality and tuberculosis in the interwar period, it was not able to cope with other diseases, and sometimes measures supposedly implemented to improve the health of the population in fact served to marginalize ethnic minorities who were accused of spreading epidemics (e.g. the Romany and Pomaks in Bulgaria).[33]

The well-documented development of life expectancy under state socialism can be divided into two phases: in the 1950s there was a rapid increase in life expectancy, which even surpassed the growth rate in the Western countries. An example is the Czech lands, which experienced a rapid increase in life expectancy in the 1950s over previous decades. While the average life expectancy grew by about two years per decade in the last decades of the nineteenth century, and by four years per decade in the early twentieth century, the rate of increase peaked at about six years during the 1950s. Life expectancy converged both within the states and within the regions of the states. For example, in Slovenia in 1952, the life expectancy for men was 63 years compared to 48.6 years in Kosovo. Over the next 20 years, the gap between the two countries was largely closed.[34] Slovakia also caught up with the Czech lands in terms of life expectancy over the same period.

From the mid-1960s onwards, however, there was very slow growth, or even stagnation and decline. The stagnation of and decline in life expectancy was first recorded in the Soviet Union, including the Baltic republics in the mid-1960s. In Czechoslovakia, there was a slight decline in life expectancy in the 1960s and very slow growth of less than one year per decade in the 1970s and 1980s. Romania experienced a decline in life expectancy during the economically

---

32 Jaroslava Hasmanová Marhánková, 'Konstrukce normality, rizika a vědění o těle v těhotenství: Příklad prenatálních screeningů' [The construction of normality, risks and body-knowledge during pregnancy: an example of prenatal screenings], *Biograf* 47 (2008): 56, www.biograf.org/clanky/clanek.php?clanek=v4702 (accessed 1 January 2014).
33 Promitzer, 'Typhus, Turks, and Roma', 112.
34 Fred Singleton and Bernard Carter, *The Economy of Yugoslavia* (London: Croom Helm, 1982), 216.

miserable 1980s. Stagnation was also recorded in Poland and Hungary. The stagnation of or decline in life expectancy from the 1960s on can be attributed mainly to lifestyle (alcoholism, smoking, unhealthy diet), everyday stress, bad working conditions and environmental problems. The decline in life expectancy was particularly strong for men.

This stagnation in life expectancy continued until the mid-1990s, and in some countries, this measure even deepened after 1990 (in the Baltics, Bulgaria, Albania, Hungary).[35] Poverty, unemployment and the erosion of health services, as well as psychological factors (uncertainty, stress) contributed to this phenomenon.[36] The important exceptions included Poland, Czechoslovakia and most of the former Yugoslavia, which did not experience such a decline.

The most extreme case is Latvia, where life expectancy fell by more than two years during post-socialism and the process lasted for more than 15 years. In this respect, the country resembles Russia, where the post-socialist decline in life expectancy has also been very strong. The Latvian case can be explained in part by the presence of a large Russian minority. Comparing native Latvians to ethnic Russians, the evidence suggests that the two groups differed significantly after 1991, not only in their lifestyles, but also in their psychological well-being, with Russians losing their former sense of superiority. According to research conducted by Juris Krumins and Uldis Usackis, the declining life expectancy in Latvia in the period from 1989 to 1994 affected both ethnic groups but was more pronounced among ethnic Russians.[37]

The post-socialist decline in life expectancy did not affect both sexes and all social groups equally. Women lived longer than men everywhere in the twentieth century, but the gender gap in life expectancy in post-socialist countries has been deepest in international comparisons, representing the continuation of the trends from the previous decades. Other studies have also shown a correlation between education and life expectancy,[38] with college graduates living an average of five years longer than people who complete only elementary school. A study of mortality in Latvia revealed that while mortality was higher in rural areas before 1989 due to the lack of doctors and other medical services, in the years of transition the situation was reversed, such that the inhabitants of rural areas started to live longer than the town people in Latvia. The authors of the study explain that this was a result of the better food supply in the countryside.[39]

In most countries of the region, the trend reversed in the second half of the 1990s, and life expectancy began rising again. With an average life expectancy of between 74 and 80 years in the year 2015, the region is currently on a par with Latin America and China; it lags behind Western Europe (79–83) but surpasses Russia (69) and other post-Soviet countries. The Baltic states have the lowest life expectancy in the region, arguably a legacy of Soviet times. In Slovenia and the Czech Republic, life expectancy is approaching that of Western Europe. According to current statistics, a surprisingly long life-expectancy is found in the countries of Southeastern Europe, even in those affected by war and deep social crisis. Bosnia and Herzegovina, Serbia

---

35 D. Stuckler, L. King and M. McKee, 'Mass Privatization and the Post-communist Mortality Crisis: A Cross-National Analysis', *The Lancet*, 373/9661 (2009): 399–407.
36 Giovanni Andrea Cornia and Renato Paniccia, 'The Transition and Mortality Crisis: Evidence, Interpretation and Policy Responses', in *The Mortality Crisis in Transitional Economics*, eds Giovanni Andrea Cornia and Renato Paniccia (Oxford: Oxford University Press, 2000), 3–37, here 31.
37 Juris Krumins and Uldis Usackis, 'Mortality Consequences of the Transition to Market Economy in Latvia, 1991–1995', in Cornia and Paniccia, *The Mortality Crisis in Transitional Economics*, 280–302, here 289.
38 Vladimir M. Shkolnikov and Giovanni Andrea Cornia, 'Population Crisis and Rising Mortality in Transitional Russia', in Cornia and Paniccia, *The Mortality Crisis in Transitional Economies*, 253–78, here 267.
39 Krumins and Usackis, 'Mortality Consequences of the Transition to Market Economy', 302.

and Albania, for example, have a higher life expectancy than the Baltic states, and the disparity between the life expectancy of men and women is lower there. The explanation seems to be the lower incidence of alcoholism and a healthier diet.

There are two modern causes of death which appeared during state-socialist times and continue to exist today: an unhealthy lifestyle (diet, smoking, lack of physical activity) and car accidents. The unhealthy lifestyle began to be perceived as a serious problem back in the 1970s. The danger of obesity was addressed for the first time on TV and in other media.[40] It seems that the problem of obesity even worsened after 1989, particularly among youths. World Health Organization (WHO) data suggest that the region has an obesity problem similar to that in Western Europe.[41] According to available statistics the consumption of tobacco also increased in the region after 1989 contrary to its decline in the West of Europe. The Balkans and the Baltic countries top the European rankings for smoking. People in these countries smoke, on average, twice as much as in Scandinavia.[42]

Traffic accidents and related deaths are another negative aspect of late modernity. Not surprisingly, they increased with rising levels of motorization in the second half of the twentieth century and became the most frequent cause of death among certain age groups (children, young adults). In the West, accidents began to decline with the introduction of safety measures in the 1960s. In the 1970s the only decline in the number of road accidents was recorded in Czechoslovakia and Hungary. In other parts of the region, including Poland, the death rate on the roads grew right up to the new millennium, as motorization increased while road infrastructure remained in poor condition. It is only in recent years that even the less developed parts of the region have experienced a decrease in road fatalities. The region still records higher numbers of road deaths than Western Europe. In 2010, for example, 6.5 per hundred thousand deaths in the European Union were the result of car accidents; in some parts of the region the rate was twice as high. Romania is the most dangerous country in the EU for motorists due to the poor condition of both roads and vehicles, the driving behaviour of the motorists and alcoholism.[43] Albania, Bosnia and Herzegovina, and the Baltics are also some of the most dangerous parts of Europe in this respect.

Modernity also witnessed major changes in the culture of dying. In the late twentieth century, people not only died later than they did one hundred years before, they also died under different conditions. There has been a shift from dying at one's home to dying in the hospital. As a reaction to the often-inhuman conditions in socialist hospitals in the 1990s, the hospice movement gained strength in several countries of the region. Another remarkable feature of modernity is the transformation of burial rituals, which was manifested in the shift to secular funerals and cremation. The twentieth century brought more changes in burial rituals than the previous millennium. At the beginning of the period, burials had an exclusively religious

---

40 Martin Franc, 'Socialism and the Overweight Nation: Questions of Ideology, Science and Obesity in Czechoslovakia, 1950–1970', in *The Rise of Obesity in Europe: A Twentieth Century Food History*, eds Derek J. Oddy, Peter J. Atkins and Virginie Amilien (Farnham: Ashgate, 2009), 193–205.

41 World Health Organization, 'Overweight and Obesity', www.who.int/gho/ncd/risk_factors/overweight/en/index.html (accessed 1 January 2014).

42 Steffen Mau and Roland Verwiebe, *Die Sozialstruktur Europas* (Bonn: Bundeszentrale für politische Bildung, 2009), 220, 222–23.

43 European Commission Eurostat, 'Causes of Death – Standardised Death Rate, 2010', http://epp.eurostat.ec.europa.eu/statistics_explained/index.php?title=File:Causes_of_death_-_standardised_death_rate,_2010_(1)_(per_100_000_inhabitants).png&filetimestamp=20121022145128 (accessed 1 January 2014).

character. Rural funerals were still accompanied by a number of folk traditions and superstitions, and the corpse was handled not by trained professionals but by family members. Even in the relatively modernized Czech countryside, at the beginning of the twentieth century old rituals persisted, such as getting the oldest member of the family to close the corpse's eyes, opening the windows to allow the soul to go to heaven, and burying the corpse in a shroud or one's best clothes.[44] There was a move away from church burials after communist regimes came to power, but it proceeded differently across the region. While the socialist state usually managed to convince its citizens of the futility of church weddings (state weddings were often mandatory), it was less successful in its attempt to end church burials. It seems that funerals were more resistant to secularization than other rites of passage. For example, in highly secular Bulgaria in 1965, only 36 per cent of weddings were held in churches, while 52 per cent of children were baptized, and 71 per cent of funerals had a religious character.[45] Only in the Czech lands – the most atheist part of the region – did the number of religious burials decline significantly during state socialism (from 1955 to 1987, from 75 to 39 per cent).

Cremation as a Modern Practice

Modernity brought changes in funeral rituals, particularly the idea of cremation, which came to Central and Eastern Europe from Germany in the late nineteenth century. At that time, the first pro-cremation clubs were founded in the Habsburg Monarchy by anticlerical activists, but the authorities did not permit this type of funeral. Those who wanted to be cremated had to be transported after their death to Germany, where cremation was allowed (the first crematorium in Germany was opened in Gotha in 1878). Similar clubs were founded in Serbia or Romania around the turn of the century. Although the first Czech crematorium was built in Liberec before the First World War, it could only be used after 1918 when the new republic legalized cremation. In interwar Czechoslovakia, 13 crematories (symptomatically called 'temples of progress') were constructed, some of which were architecturally impressive. Atheists and members of Protestant churches predominated among the cremated, while the Catholic Church forbade its members to choose this option.[46] The idea of cremation was closely associated with the socialist movement. Socialist parties and associations encouraged its members to be cremated after death. Growth in the number of cremations was slow, however. In 1940, only six per cent of corpses were cremated, although in Prague the ratio was much higher at one fifth.

Apart from Czechoslovakia, Romania was the only country in Central and Eastern Europe where cremation was already legalized in the interwar period. The first crematorium was opened there in 1928 at a time when the efforts of cremationist associations in

---

44 Olga Nešporová, 'Století proměn v pohřbívání: od církevního uložení do země ke zpopelnění bez obřadu' [A century of changes in burials: from church funerals to cremation without ceremonies], *Český lid. Etnologickýčasopis* 2 (2013): 187.
45 Ulf Brunnbauer, *Sozialistische Lebensweise: Ideologie, Gesellschaft, Familie und Politik in Bulgarien (1944–1989)* (Vienna: Böhlau, 2007), 556.
46 Nešporová,'Století proměn v pohřbívání', 190.

neighbouring countries remained unsuccessful. Cremation did not become very popular here, however, and even stagnated in the socialist era, while it experienced rapid growth in Yugoslavia and Hungary. Although the first crematorium in Hungary was built in Protestant Debrecen in 1930, the authorities did not allow it to begin operations until 1951. In Yugoslavia, there were several initiatives, but only the foundations of the crematorium in Belgrade had been laid by the end of the 1930s. The Second World War suspended the project so that the city did not open its first crematorium until 1964. In interwar Poland, cremation was illegal and was permitted only after 1945 when the country gained several crematories on the territory acquired from Germany. It is possible that the image of cremation in Poland was tainted by its misuse by the Nazis. In some countries, cremation is still illegal (Albania), and in others it has been introduced only very recently (Bulgaria in 2001). According to statistics, the Czech Republic has the highest level of cremation in Europe (76 per cent of corpses are cremated). Even the corpses of Polish and Slovak citizens are incinerated in the Czech Republic today due to better geographical proximity of Czech crematoria and lower prices. In 2001, other countries in the region came behind the Czech Republic in the following order: Slovenia (42 per cent), Hungary (33 per cent), Slovakia (13 per cent), Latvia (12 per cent), Romania (12 per cent in 1999), Poland (6 per cent in 2007), and Bulgaria (4 per cent).[47]

Jews and Romany, the two minority groups we selected for deeper analysis, showed specific patterns of fertility and mortality. The available demographic data on Jews at the end of the nineteenth century show them as a demographically more modern group than the majority populations. Although mortality declined in the whole region, Jews fared better than other populations. In the case of Jews in Hungary, their mortality was lower than that of ethnic Hungarians in the late nineteenth century. The same pattern can be found in Galicia and Romania.[48] According to data from the interwar period, Jews had about one half to one third of the rate of infant mortality experienced by the majority populations.[49] The decline in Jewish fertility proceeded even faster than the decline in mortality. Less than 20 births per thousand annually, which is considered to be a boundary between populations of high and low fertility, were reached three or four decades earlier than by the majority population. During the interwar period, the Jewish birth rate was half that of the majority populations; and as they were getting older, in certain cases their numbers even declined, for example in Hungary or in the Czech lands where their mortality rates were higher than their fertility rates.[50] The different demographic behaviour can be explained both by their cultural traditions and by their actual social status. The Jewish population might not be so different if it were compared with the part of majority population exhibiting the same socio-economic characteristics as Jews. For example, better mortality numbers are explained by the higher

---

47 Douglas J. Davies and Lewis H. Mates, eds, *Encyclopedia of Cremation* (Aldershot: Ashgate, 2005), 87, 252–3, 364, 419.
48 Evyatar Friesel, *Atlas of Modern Jewish History* (Jerusalem: Carta, 1990), 21.
49 Victor Karady, *Gewalterfahrung und Utopie, Juden in der europäischen Moderne* (Frankfurt a.M.: Fischer Taschenbuch, 1999), 44.
50 Jana Vobecká, *Demographic Avant-Garde: Jews in Bohemia between the Enlightenment and the Shoah* (Budapest: Central European University Press, 2013), 77–111; Karady, *The Jews of Europe*, 46.

educational level of the Jewish minority and by very low illegitimacy, as illegitimate children have higher mortality rates. Also, certain religious rules might be important factors (i.e. ritual hygiene, no alcohol).[51]

The Romany presented a radically different picture in terms of fertility and mortality before 1945, having high birth rates but also higher mortality than local majority populations, although the evidence is sparse. The demographic situation of the Romany improved significantly during the socialist era as a result of various social and health programmes adopted by the states. The declining mortality rates, in combination with high birth rates, led to a significant increase of the Romany population in the region. Their birth rate reached 30 per thousand annually, and the population doubled every 20 to 30 years (in Hungary, for example, the total fertility rate of Romany women was twice as high as for ethnic Hungarians).[52] As Romany reproductive practices were, however, perceived by the socialist regimes as incompatible with modern life, they were often labelled as a 'socially degraded stratum' or by similar terms, whose population growth should not be supported or even prevented. In Czechoslovakia, according to Radka Dudová, the attempts by the state to 'influence the quality of the population by implementing a reproduction policy can only be classified as eugenics.'[53] In the 1960s, the press began publishing articles on the 'degree of defectiveness of Gypsy children,' calling for a 'socialist solution ... respecting the current knowledge of genetics, biology and social sciences and supporting ... the birth of physically and mentally healthy individuals.'[54] State measures soon followed: from the 1970s, all applications for abortions by Romany women had to be accepted according to the directive of the Ministry of Health; the procedure was free of charge for them and had to be performed immediately. Doctors were also instructed to recommend abortion to Romany women even when only minor signs of foetal damage were detected. A more radical measure was the sterilization of Romany women. Those allegedly 'socially needy' women who decided to undergo this procedure were paid two thousand crowns by the state, which was equivalent to more than a woman's average monthly wage. In 1988, this payment was increased to ten thousand, or five monthly salaries. In some cases, patients were not sufficiently informed, or sterilization was performed without their consent. The law stipulated that women could be sterilized only if they were over 35 or already had more than four children, but these conditions were not fulfilled in at least one third of all sterilizations of Romany women. There were also proposals to reduce the high birth rate among the Romany population by reducing child allowance payments to the first three children and ending them with the fifth child.

The post-socialist Romany population and its demographic behaviour is heavily influenced by their disadvantaged economic conditions and social exclusion. It is still characterized by a higher birth rate than the majority populations, although a significant decline has been recorded here as well. As far as life expectancy is concerned, the Romany fare the worst in every society in the region. According to qualified estimates their life expectancy was an average of 10 years shorter than that of the general population around 1990.[55]

---

51 Karady, *Gewalterfahrung und Utopie*, 47.
52 Barany, *The East European Gypsies*, 128.
53 Dudová Radka, *Interrupce v České Republice: zápas o ženská těla* [Abortion in the Czech Republic: a struggle over women's bodies] (Prague: Sociologický ústav AV ČR, 2012), 117.
54 Ibid., 117.
55 M. Braham, *The Untouchables: A Survey of the Roma People in Central and Eastern Europe* (Geneva: UNHCR, 1993), 42.

People on the move: voluntary and forced migrations

Mass migration is a key feature of modern society. Premodern society is usually characterized as stationary, with a very low (but not negligible) level of migration. The two processes of establishing modernity, industrialization and urbanization, are often accompanied by migration from the countryside to the city, from poor to rich areas, and between sparsely and densely populated regions. The period examined here was called by Stephen Castles and Mark Miller 'the age of migration'.[56] At no other time in the region's history was there so much movement of populations. In historical demography, the issue of migration has long received less attention than birth, death and marriage rates. While data on birth, marriage and death rates for the whole region are available for the last 150 years, data on migration are far less common. With the emergence of theories of globalization in recent decades, the topic of migration has increasingly become a focus of research in social history and historical demography. Recent studies have particularly explored gender and migration, and cultural aspects of migration.

In describing the migration history of the region, it makes sense to distinguish between forced and voluntary migration, the latter of which might be also called politically and economically motivated migration, as these two types dominated the region during the period examined. However, these are only two extremes at either end of a continuum. For example, the term 'forced migration' may be used to describe a situation in which someone chooses to leave their country because state authorities prohibit them from working in their profession. It is difficult to speak about voluntary migration if an individual's only choice is between going abroad or living in abject poverty at home. Therefore, forced and voluntary migration are closely related to politically and economically motivated migration. While political migration is always forced, economic migration is based either on push factors (bad conditions at home) or pull factors (better conditions abroad) or a combination of both. Demographers also distinguish between internal (intra-national) and external (international) migration, and categorize it by its duration, whether it is conceived as permanent or temporary, and whether whole groups migrate or merely individuals (collective and individual migration). The fate of migrants in this new country is also important, i.e. whether they remain isolated (as many illegal immigrants do) or whether they integrate or even assimilate. Integration entails taking on certain cultural aspects of the host society such that the immigrant is not immediately recognized as an outsider, while keeping certain aspects of his or her former identity (ethnic identity, language, religion, internal habits in family life). Assimilation means relinquishing one's former identity and habits and accepting the complete identity of the host society. In this chapter, we intentionally set aside urban–rural migration, as it is discussed in the chapter on rural–urban issues. Also, since forced migrations appear in the volume on violence, we describe it here rather briefly.

There are a variety of approaches explaining why people migrate. Neoclassical economics stress that individuals seek to maximize profits. As there are different wages and different levels of unemployment in different countries caused by differences in the supply and demand for labour, an individual's decision whether or not to migrate also takes migration costs into account. Premodern migration is interpreted here as the flow of people from countries with a lack of land to the countries with available land, and modern migration as a flow of workers from labour-scarce to labour-abundant countries. The 'new economics of migration' argues that the process concerns not only the labour market or land availability, but the importance of

---

56 Stephen Castles and Mark J. Miller, *The Age of Migration: International Population Movements in the Modern World* (New York: The Guilford Press, 1993).

the family as a unit; the family then migrates seeking better education for their children, a better social system or improved housing conditions. It also assumes that decisions are not made by individuals, but rather within households. The dual market theory stresses the demand explicitly for immigrant labour in developed countries. In this perspective, migrants are needed because they are willing to work for less money and less likely to ally with domestic workers in fighting to improve labour conditions. For migrants, it is acceptable to take a low status job, as they do not care much about their prestige in the host country. The high status that migration might earn them in their home country is sufficient. The world-systems theory stresses the transfer of capitalist relations from the core to peripheral countries, yet migration from the peripheries to the core is an issue more complex than mere differences in labour markets. It also depends on the ideological attractiveness of the core, colonial relations, and the destruction of peripheral economies through the penetration of capitalist mechanisms. This perspective also points to the migration of experts and managers from the core to the peripheries. Network theory stresses the role of diasporas in reducing the costs and risks of migration (as through offering help to find work and housing, and with learning the language). The culture of migration approach stresses that if someone has migrated once, he or she is more likely to migrate again. This implies that migration has become acceptable behaviour in modern societies.[57]

The issue of forced migration (sometimes also called deracination or forced displacement) lacks such a sophisticated theoretical framework, as its motivations are quite visible. Studies generally differentiate between the different causes of forced migration: war and civil war, human trafficking, slavery, flight from political repression or natural catastrophes, or displacement due to construction projects (e.g. hydroelectric dams). Holm Sundhaussen develops his typology on the different levels of violence forcing people to leave by distinguishing between command (force), violence, threats of violence and fear of violence. He lists four reasons why the twentieth century in Central and Eastern Europe can be called the age of forced migration: the growth of nationalism, the crisis of the great multi-ethnic empires, the mass destructive character of wars and the existence of great dictatorships – Nazism and Stalinism. He also points to another important trend in the international perception of forced migration: the paradigm shift from the acceptance of forced population transfers to refusal, resulting from the mass inhumanity associated with the forced migrations during the century. He calls this shift from 'Lausanne to Dayton', the places where the two most important conferences on forced migration in Europe were held, the first in 1922, legalizing the population exchanges interpreted as the humane way of avoiding interethnic conflicts; the second in 1995, which instead rejected this principle and demanded the return of all displaced persons.[58]

If we try to periodize the waves of migration in the twentieth century, there were two main waves of voluntary (economically motivated) migrations and four waves of expulsions or forced migrations: the first wave of voluntary migration took place between the 1890s and 1914, and the second after 1989. Both started rather equally around the region and went westward: in the first case to Western Europe and America, in the second, mainly to Western Europe. The omnipresent pattern of involuntary migrations was of national minorities being expelled by state authorities, particularly after lost wars to the countries considered to be the minorities' homelands, or of people fleeing before military operations during the wars. The first wave of

---

57 Douglas S. Massey et al., 'Theories of International Migration: A Review and Appraisal', *Population and Development Review* 19 (1993): 431–66.
58 Holm Sundhaussen, 'Forced Ethnic Migration, 2010', http://ieg-ego.eu/en/threads/europe-on-the-road/forced-ethnic-migration/holm-sundhaussen-forced-ethnic-migration (accessed 1 June 2016)

forced migration was confined to Southeastern Europe in the context of the disintegration of the Ottoman Empire. The second wave involved the whole region during and after the First World War. The third wave occurred during and immediately after the Second World War, and its impact was particularly strong in Central Europe. The fourth wave was prompted by the Yugoslav Wars of the 1990s. These four waves changed the ethnic structure of the region, particularly in the north. The forced (politically motivated) migrations during socialism were also significant following political upheaval in various countries (Hungary in 1956, Czechoslovakia in 1948 and 1968, and Poland in 1981).

As Table 5.3 shows, forced and voluntary migrations and ethnic cleansing in the twentieth century resulted in the ethnic homogenization of most of Central and Eastern Europe. Before 1945, the states of the region were characterized by ethnic heterogeneity, which was the case both for the empires before 1918 and the new states that emerged from them. For example, in 1910 Germans and Hungarians accounted for a mere 44 per cent of the population in Austria-Hungary, and in 1930 Serbs made up only 44 per cent of the population in Yugoslavia; the Czechs represented only 51 per cent of the population of Czechoslovakia, and Poles made up 69 per cent of Poland's population.[59] The ethnic heterogeneity of the region was particularly a result of the presence of two ethnic minorities: Germans and Jews. Before 1939, the German minority comprised 22 per cent of the population of Czechoslovakia, 6.9 per cent in Hungary, 4 per cent in Romania and Yugoslavia and 2.3 per cent in Poland. At the same time, Jews represented 8.6 per cent of the population in Poland, 7.6 per cent in Lithuania, 6 per cent in Hungary, 4 per cent in Romania, 1.3 per cent in Czechoslovakia and 0.6 per cent in Yugoslavia. The period between 1939 and 1949 meant the destruction of this ethnic heterogeneity.

Based on these data, we can distinguish three different groups of countries. The first – those that became very homogeneous in character – would include Poland, the Czech lands and

Table 5.3 Proportions of the ethnic majority of populations in selected Central and Eastern European countries in 1930 and 2001 (as a percentage of the whole population)

Country	1930	2001
Poland	69	97
Czech Republic	68	95
Slovakia	68	86
Romania	72	89
Albania	92	99
Hungary	92	97
Bulgaria	87	84

Note: There are different years as follows: for Poland, 1931; Romania, 2002; Bulgaria, 1934.

Sources: Michael Charles Kaser, ed., *The Economic History of Eastern Europe 1919–1975*, vol. 1 (Oxford: Clarendon Press, 1986), 25. Data on Bulgaria: R.J. Crampton, *Bulgaria* (Oxford: Oxford University Press, 2007), 424. Data on Poland: Andrzej Jezierski, *Historia Polski w liczbach* [History of Poland in numbers], (Warsaw: Główny Urząd Statystyczny, 2003), 383. Data on Slovakia: Branislav Šprocha and Pavol Tišliar, 'Demografický obraz Slovenska v sčítániach ľudu 1919–1940' [Demographic picture of Slovakia in censuses 1919–1940] (Brno: Tribun EU, 2012), 155.

---

59 Michael Charles Kaser, ed., *The Economic History of Eastern Europe 1919–1975*, vol. 1 (Oxford: Clarendon Press, 1986), 25.

Kosovo. While in the Czech case homogenization can be attributed to the expulsion of three million Germans after 1945, in Poland this was a more complex set of events: changes in borders, the murder of the Jewish population, the flight and expulsion of the Germans and the so-called 'population exchange' between Poland and the USSR. The homogenization of Kosovo's population was facilitated by the fast demographic growth of the Albanian majority and the expulsion of the Serbian minority towards the end of the twentieth century.

The second group includes those countries that underwent moderate ethnic homogenization. Slovakia represents a borderline case. It witnessed a substantial fall in its Hungarian and Rusyn/Ukrainian minorities, while the German and Jewish populations almost disappeared. Romania lost most of its Jewish and German minorities, yet it continues to have a strong Hungarian minority. Hungary and Albania also experienced limited ethnic homogenization. The ethnic makeup of Bulgaria remained unchanged, but it should be stated that, contrary to the rest of the region, the ethnic homogenization of that country had already taken place between 1880 and 1920, the era of flight and expulsions of the Turks, when the proportion of Bulgarians rose from 67 per cent to 83 per cent. Despite bloody wars in Bosnia, there was no substantial change in the proportions of any of the three ethnic groups there. In this case, we may speak of the homogenization of individual parts of the country in the 1990s, when the previously multi-faceted fabric of the country was divided into three rather separate parts. In several countries of this group, including Hungary and Bulgaria, it is likely that no ethnic homogenization took place at all, due to the growing Romany minority (which does not appear in the statistics); for the same reason, the ethnic homogenization of Romania and Slovakia may be slower than the data suggest.

The third group includes those countries whose ethnic diversity actually increased during the period under review: the Baltic states and the republics of former Yugoslavia, with the exception of Kosovo. Lithuania gained a Polish minority in 1939 as a result of the annexation of Vilnius, a city with a Polish population of 60 per cent and a Jewish population of more than 30 per cent, but only a very small percentage of Lithuanians prior to 1939. Vilnius lost its German and Jewish minorities during the Second World War and experienced the migration of various ethnic groups from the Soviet Union beginning in 1950. The story was similar in Estonia and Latvia where the influx of Russians was even higher, as a programme of strong industrialization was launched in these strategically situated republics in the 1950s and standards of living were correspondingly higher. Slovenia, too, the most successful part of Yugoslavia, attracted migrants from other parts of the federation; and Macedonia, like Kosovo, experienced rapid growth of its Albanian minority.

Migration before 1939

As mentioned above, migration in the nineteenth century was motivated mainly by poverty and overpopulation, which prevented a large part of the population from earning their living in agriculture. While there had been substantial migration to the region in previous centuries (e.g. German colonization, Jewish migration), the nineteenth century saw a prevailing out-migration, chiefly to the USA, in line with the overall trend in Europe.

Although throughout the nineteenth century there was substantial migration to Germany, France and other Western European countries, the mass migration overseas became the most remembered feature of the period. According to statistics, the first migrants to the US from the region came from the most developed parts of the Habsburg Empire, parts of the former Polish Kingdom under German rule and the Baltics. People from Central and Eastern Europe, together with Italians after the 1880s, became the strongest group of migrants to the US, outpacing the Western Europeans. The emigration of Poles from Germany peaked in the 1880s, and Polish migrants from the Habsburg Monarchy and Russia followed later.[60] In 1907, there were 1.7 million Polish native speakers in the USA, making them the most numerous ethnic group from Central and Eastern Europe.[61] Jews, Ukrainians, Slovaks and Hungarians began to leave the region in great numbers at the beginning of the century.[62] Of the 1.7 million Jews emigrating from Europe to the USA in the years 1899 to 1924, 1.2 million were from the Russian empire, 260,000 came from Austria-Hungary and 103,000 from Romania, which had the highest Jewish emigration per capita.[63] Emigration to the US meant the departure of about one fifth of the Jews living in the region. The volume of migrants from the Balkan states was much smaller before 1900. In the 1880s, the annual number of migrants leaving the Balkans was merely in the hundreds, and even by the late 1890s, only about four thousand were emigrating each year, while the Habsburg Monarchy lost between thirty and seventy thousand people per year to migration. This changed in the new century, as migration rates from Bulgaria, Serbia and Romania rose to equal that of the Habsburg Monarchy.[64]

The intensity of migration was influenced by several factors: relatively low living standards in the region, increasing cultural and educational standards that supported people's attempts to improve their social position, a degree of accumulated wealth that could cover the cost of travel, and the presence of a diaspora in the target country. Railways and better ships provided an important transport infrastructure. While the northern half of the region had been connected to Western European ports via railways as early as the 1860s and 1870s, the south followed in the 1880s and 1890s. The usual route to the USA from the Habsburg Empire and Southeastern Europe was via Bremen or Hamburg. As a result of better shipbuilding technology, travel times and costs were gradually reduced. While crossing the Atlantic took 44 days in 1850, the same journey took just 10 days in 1875 and 4.5 days in 1914.[65] The governments either tried to stop emigration, fearing the loss of labourers (in the case of Serbia, by raising the cost of a passport),[66] or supported it, as it promised to reduce the number of minorities perceived as hostile (in the case of Hungary).

Although migration to other countries in Europe is less prominent in historical memory than migration overseas, there were several strong currents. Czech and Galician workers travelled to work in Saxony or Prussia. In response, Germany introduced a restrictive system of work permits and began to organize foreign workers in an almost military fashion to prevent their integration and ensure that their employment remained seasonal.[67] There were also several ethnographically characteristic travelling workers in the region, for example, Ursari peddlers from Bosnia, Slovak tinkers and Romany craftsmen. Migration within Europe was very easy

---

60 Dorota Praszałowicz, 'Polen', in *Enzyklopädie Migration in Europa: Vom 17. Jahrhundert bis zur Gegenwart*, eds Klaus J. Bade et al. (Paderborn: Schöningh, 2007), 258–72, here 261.

61 Ibid., 262.

62 Hermann Zeitloher, 'Tschechien und Slowakei', in Bade et al., *Enzyklopädie Migration in Europa*, 279.

63 Friesel, *Atlas of Modern Jewish History*, 132.

64 Marvin R. Jackson, 'Comparing the Balkan Demographic Experience 1860 to 1970', *Journal of European Economic History* 14, no. 2 (1985): 223–72, here 235.

65 Paul Robert Magocsi, *Historical Atlas of East Central Europe* (Seattle, WA: University of Washington Press, 1995), 93.

66 Aleksandar Miletćić, *Journey under Surveillance: The Overseas Emigration Policy of the Kingdom of Serbs, Croats and Slovenes in Global Context, 1918–1928* (Vienna: LitVerlag, 2012), 69–70.

67 Klaus J. Bade and Jochen Oltmer, 'Polnische Arbeitskräfte in Preussen–Deutschland vom späten 19. Jahrhundert bis zum Zweiten Weltkrieg', in Bade et al., *Enzyklopädie Migration in Europa*, 881.

at that time due to the almost total absence of passports and border controls. The latter were found only in Austria-Hungary along the border with Russia, and, for a time, with Serbia and Romania. There were no patrols on Austria's borders with Germany and Italy. Passports were only introduced on a massive scale with the outbreak of the First World War, but this measure was thought to be only temporary at the time.

During this period, the first wave of forced (politically motivated) migration from the south also got under way. The countries that had gained independence from the Ottoman Empire refused to grant citizenship and other rights to certain ethnic minorities, even though some of them had been present for generations. Some one million Jews fled racial persecution in the Russian parts of former Poland-Lithuania and migrated to the USA or Palestine; however, it seems that the more important motivation was economic. Romanian Jews left for the USA because of religious persecution at home.[68] The Turks were also targets of persecution. One and a half million Turks are thought to have fled the Balkans after 1876, mainly from Bulgaria. Michael Schwartz even speaks of a 'national liberation through expulsion'.[69] In the context of the Balkan Wars, an agreement on the exchange of citizens was reached between Bulgaria and Turkey in 1913. While that agreement was based on voluntary migration, in a later agreement reached in Lausanne in 1923 the exchange of citizens between Greece and Turkey was already obligatory.[70]

After 1918, the creation of new states and changes in borders caused a strong wave of migration. Several diasporas decided to return to newly created nation states (Poland, Czechoslovakia), or were forced to leave territories lost to their nations (Hungary, Turkey, Germany). Drawing up new borders and establishing systems of strict control were not always welcomed by the rural population, which was accustomed to seasonal migration. For a short period of time, the region also became a target of migration from a Russia ravaged by civil war, mainly in the direction of Serbia, Bulgaria and Czechoslovakia. Shortly after the end of the war, overseas migration resumed. Yet this migration did not reach its pre-war levels, as the USA enacted strict regulation in 1924, which set up quotas stipulating how many members of each nationality should be allowed in. Migration from Central and Eastern Europe thus shifted to Latin America, and by the end of the 1920s, migration to Western Europe overtook migration overseas. Polish emigration to France comprised the strongest stream in the region.[71] Czechoslovakia, the only country in the region which maintained a liberal democracy during the 1930s, became the target for emigration of those politically persecuted by authoritarian or fascist regimes. Polish students of Jewish origin, for example, facing discrimination at their home universities, opted to study in Czechoslovakia, as did refugees from Nazism, the most well-known example being Thomas Mann, who received Czechoslovak citizenship in 1936.

Migration between 1939 and 1989

With the expansion of Nazi Germany, the largest wave of forced migrations and expulsions in the history of the region began, lasting until 1947/1948. It started with the flight of Czechs, Jews and German antifascists after the annexation of Sudetenland in September

---

68 Holm Sundhaussen, 'Südosteuropa', in Bade et al., *Enzyklopädie Migration in Europa*, 301.
69 Michael Schwartz, *Ethnische 'Säuberungen' in der Moderne: globale Wechselwirkungen nationalistischer und rassistischer Gewaltpolitik im 19. und 20. Jahrhundert* (München: Oldenbourg, 2013), 238.
70 Sundhaussen, 'Südosteuropa', 96–106.
71 Kirk, *Europe's Population in the Interwar Years*, 99.

1938. The Czechs were subsequently forced to leave Slovakia and Subcarpathian Rus.[72] The Nazi invasion of Poland and Yugoslavia prompted the flight of the local population, especially political elites. Even after the end of military operations in Poland, the Nazi occupation administration continued to expel Poles from the part of Poland annexed by Germany into the General Government. Slovenians and Croats were expelled from Nazi-occupied parts of Yugoslavia in 1941. Populations were forced to migrate out of the territories occupied by the Soviet Union. After it occupied Eastern Poland in 1939, part of the population fled and more than 300,000 were deported, mainly to Siberia and Kazakhstan. Similar deportations followed after the Soviet occupation of the Baltic states and Bessarabia in 1940. The last one – in all the annexed territories – took place immediately before the German attack in June 1941.

At the beginning of the war the Nazi occupation administration also attempted to move people of German origin who lived in Eastern Europe to occupied territories.[73] The Germans from the territories occupied by the Soviet Union in 1939 and 1940 were relocated mostly to the parts of Poland that were annexed by Germany. Other Germans were resettled from Ukraine to the annexed part of Poland after the attack on the Soviet Union and during the German retreat in 1943. Partial population transfers also took place between the allies of the Axis powers. A population exchange was organized between Romania and Bulgaria after the handover of Southern Dobruja to Bulgaria in 1940. After Bulgaria occupied Macedonia in the same year, many Bulgarians settled there.[74] Jews were driven out of their homes and into the ghettos in the months after the Nazis invaded Poland (the biggest ghettos were in Warsaw and Lodz), and their systematic transfer to extermination camps started in the summer of 1942. Other allies of Nazi Germany took part in the extermination organized by the Nazis. Yet Romania and Bulgaria adopted a different policy. The former did not hand over its Jews to the Nazis, but placed them in Romanian concentration camps, where their chances of survival were somewhat better. Jews living in Soviet Bessarabia were saved by fleeing to the Soviet Union after it was attacked by the Nazi coalition.[75] Bulgaria's small Jewish minority was not affected at all. Millions of young people from the region, mainly from the Soviet Union and Poland, were brought to Germany to work as forced labourers from 1942 on. By August 1944, 2.7 million Soviet citizens, 1.7 million Poles, 280,000 Czechs and about 160,000 people from Southeastern Europe were working in Germany. The region's population, mainly Germans, Baltic peoples, or Nazi collaborators from various ethnic groups, fled again as the Soviet army approached westward in great numbers in 1944.[76] The biggest retreat took place when over seven million Germans fled from the Red Army (in the case of the Germans from Vojvodina and Banat, they

---

72 Miloš Havelka, 'Tschechische Republik – Migrationen, Vertreibungen, Interventionen', in *Migrationsprozesse: Probleme von Abwanderungsregionen, Identitätsfragen*, ed. Anton Sterbling (Hamburg: Krämer, 2006), 143–9, here 144.
73 Bundeszentrale für Politische Bildung, *Zwangsumsiedlung, Flucht und Vertreibung 1939–1959: Atlas zur Geschichte Ostmitteleuropas* (Warsaw: Demart, 2009), 162. For the German perspective on expulsion, see Detlef Brandes, ed., *Lexikon der Vetreibungen: Deportation, Zwangsaussiedlung und ethnische Säuberung im Europa des 20. Jahrhunderts* (Vienna: Böhlau, 2010); also, Eva Hahn and Hans Henning Hahn, *Die Vertreibung im deutschen Erinnern: Legenden, Mythos, Geschichte* (Paderborn: Schöningh, 2010).
74 Kocsis, *South Eastern Europe in Maps*, 50.
75 Rainer Ohliger, 'Vom Vielvölkerstaat zum Nationalstaat – Migration aus und nach Rumänien im 20. Jahrhundert', in *Migration in Europa: historische Entwicklung, aktuelle Trends und politische Reaktionen*, eds Heinz Fassmann and Rainer Münz (Frankfurt a.M.: Campus Verlag, 1996), 285–302, here 291.
76 Matthew Kott and Harald Runblom, 'Estnische und lettische Flüchtlinge in Schweden seit dem Zweiten Weltkrieg', in Bade et al., *Enzyklopädie Migration in Europa*, 553.

fled from the Yugoslav partisan army).[77] Hungarians fled the territories annexed in the period from 1938 to 1941 in anticipation of repressions by Soviet, Romanian and Yugoslav troops, and many of those who remained were deported to the gulags.[78]

After the Second World War there was a general continuation of ethnic homogenization in countries across the region, taking more radical forms in the countries occupied by Nazi Germany. While Poland, the Czech lands and Ukraine were almost completely cleansed of their national minorities, the south witnessed a comparatively smaller wave of expulsions and forced migrations. The largest population transfers were organized in Poland. Poles and Jews from the territories occupied by the Soviet Union were transferred westward. They came together with the Poles from the centre of the country to the newly acquired western territories, which gained 2.9 million new inhabitants in this way. Many Jewish Holocaust survivors left for Palestine. Some 5 million Germans had fled before the end of the war; 3.5 million remained and were expelled afterwards.[79] There was also an exchange of populations between Soviet Lithuania and Poland, but most Lithuanian Poles were allowed to stay.[80] Many anti-communist Poles, Balts and Yugoslavs in the West decided not to return. At the end of 1946, there were still 700,000 people from Central and Eastern Europe in the American and British occupied zones in Germany who refused to return to their homeland.[81] After numerous protests, the Western powers decided not to transfer back any inhabitants of territories occupied by the Soviets after 1 September 1939. Only those who lived in the Soviet Union before that time were transferred back.

Another organized transfer took place in the Czech lands, mainly in former Sudetenland, from where nearly three million ethnic Germans were expelled and replaced by two million Czechs from the inland regions. Approximately one third of the Germans living on Czechoslovak territory in May 1945 were expelled during the 'wild' expulsions between May and the autumn of 1945, while the rest were transferred in an organized manner. Tens of thousands of people lost their lives during the expulsions. Unlike in Poland, where about a million former citizens of the Reich were declared Polish and allowed to stay in their homes, only a few Germans remained in the Czech lands, mainly those who were indispensable to Czech industry. The Czechoslovak government also planned to expel the Hungarian minority, but this plan was not accepted by the Allied powers. Some Hungarians were expelled from Slovakia, however, right at the end of war. As the Allies did not want to tolerate another expulsion on a massive scale, some were exchanged for Hungarian Slovaks, and some were deported to the Czech lands to work in agriculture for a certain period of time. Organized expulsions also took place in the southern part of the region, albeit on a far smaller scale. About half of the 500,000 Hungarian Germans were expelled. Italians were transferred from Istria, which was annexed by Yugoslavia after 1945. Turks were also expelled again from Bulgaria.

During state socialism, certain patterns of migration from the previous period continued and several new patterns emerged. Several remaining national minorities that had not been expelled during/after the world wars continued to emigrate: Jews, Germans, Turks and Hungarians. The

---

77 Zoltán Dövényi, 'Zeitliche und räumliche Aspekte der Migrationswellen in Ungarn 1918–1995', in *Migrationen und ihre Auswirkungen. Das Beispiel Ungarn 1918–1995*, ed. Gerhard Seewann (München: Oldenbourg, 1997), 7–33, here 18.
78 Ibid., 18.
79 Bundeszentrale für Politische Bildung *Zwangsumsiedlung, Flucht und Vertreibung*, 185.
80 Michael Garleff, 'Ostmitteleuropa: Baltikum–Estland, Lettland und Litauen', in Bade et al., *Enzyklopädie Migration in Europa*, 253; Praszałowicz, 'Polen'.
81 Frank Caestecker, 'Displaced Persons (DPs)', in Bade et al., *Enzyklopädie Migration in Europa*, 530.

most notable cases were the Germans sold to West Germany by the Ceauşescu regime during the 1980s, and the emigration of Bulgarian Turks after a virulent xenophobic campaign by the Zhivkov regime during the same period. Another case was the emigration of forty thousand Hungarians from Romania to Hungary in the 1980s, to escape both national oppression and a miserable economy.

State socialism is often seen as a period of political emigration, but this was only one aspect of emigration during this period, as there were other kinds which have often been ignored. Political emigration took place on various scales in individual countries and during different periods. It is difficult to estimate how many people left Central and Eastern Europe for political reasons at the time, because these were often intertwined with economic motives and/ or national discrimination. It may be estimated that around three million people emigrated between 1945 and 1989, the majority of them young and well qualified. The migration was not unidirectional, however, as a certain number also returned home. There were also possibilities to travel westward legally, but they varied from country to country and during different periods. Travel to the West was made difficult, and in some periods, we can even speak of an almost complete ban in several countries. The early 1950s were obviously the most restrictive; later the situation grew more relaxed, with only temporary retreats to restriction. Yugoslavia was the country with probably the most relaxed travel policy. Yet even here, oppositional activities by Yugoslavs living abroad could lead to their visas being cancelled by the Yugoslav administration. Poland and Hungary also had rather liberal travel policies. On the other hand, travelling to the West was very difficult for the citizens of the Soviet Union, including the Baltic republics, and for Romanians. Albania, with its policy of voluntary self-isolation, represents the most extreme case.

There were also the political refugees who came to Central and Eastern Europe from elsewhere, most notably the eighty thousand or so Greeks emigrating after the civil war in the late 1940s.[82] Less known episodes include the migration of several thousands of Italian communists to the region in the 1950s, the decision of foreign students from Yugoslavia to stay in the Soviet bloc after it broke with Tito, and emigration by Chileans in 1973, most of whom found asylum in East Germany. The number of Greek refugees who found asylum in Yugoslavia and other Eastern bloc countries is estimated at about a hundred thousand; the other cases mentioned above amounted to no more than several thousand.

Another aspect is legal labour migration, most notably from Yugoslavia to Western Europe from the 1960s on, which is estimated at around 800,000 during the 1970s,[83] and the much smaller labour migration among socialist countries and from the Third World (Vietnam, Cuba, Nicaragua) to socialist countries. This immigration never exceeded more than dozens of thousands, however, and was strongly controlled from above. There was also strong labour migration between the republics in federations, often leading to ethnic tensions, most notably the work migration to the Baltic region from the rest of the Soviet Union, which, combined with the higher birth rates of the newcomers,[84] created a population of more than two million Russians, Ukrainians and Belarusians in the region by the late 1980s, threatening to outnumber the ethnic majority of Latvians and Estonians in their home countries.

---

82 Theodoros Lagaris, 'Griechische Flüchtlinge seit dem Bürgerkrieg 1946–1949', in Bade et al., *Enzyklopädie Migration in Europa*, 609.
83 Jackson, *Comparing the Balkan Demographic Experience*, 267.
84 Romuald Misiunas and Rein Taagepera, *The Baltic States, Years of Dependence, 1940–1990* (Berkeley, CA: University of California Press, 1993), 215.

Migration after 1989

The post-communist period, especially the 1990s, saw the largest wave of migration in the region since the Second World War. Although the Western fear of a new age of migration was surely too pessimistic, the Yugoslav Wars brought hundreds of thousands of refugees to Western countries, and in several cases the citizens of former Yugoslavia became the largest foreign population in their host countries (Austria, Sweden). In other countries of the region, labour migration predominated. In this respect, the post-communist period began to resemble the period before 1914.

The first major wave in the early 1990s was the departure of many foreign workers and students from developing countries, and the withdrawal of Soviet troops stationed in East Germany (GDR), Hungary, Poland and Czechoslovakia (Soviet troops had already left Romania and Bulgaria at the end of the 1950s).[85] If we account for their family members, we can estimate that about half a million Soviet citizens had to leave the region, and another half a million the former GDR. About 150,000 had to leave the Baltic states, and most of them did so between 1992 and 1994, although the last Russian soldiers did not leave Latvia until 1999. At the beginning of the 1990s, some political emigrants returned from the West. Most of them did not gain as much influence on politics and the economy as they had expected, and many were frustrated with the existing conditions. Thanks to its large and well-organized Western diaspora, the Baltics were an exception. Here returnees become the presidents of all three countries in the period from 1998 to 2006. In other countries, the émigrés successful in politics included the former Bulgarian Tsar Simeon, who became prime minister of the country in 2001. Several other exile returnees, mainly of royal origin, were warmly received, for example, the former Romanian King Michael I, who became the most respected public person in the country; the son of the King of Albania, Leka, who enjoyed short popularity in the country until the crisis in 1997, and Karel Schwarzenberg, who became the Czech minister of foreign affairs in 2007.

Also, historical ethnic minorities continued to return to their former homelands. About 190,000 Hungarians left Romania for economically more successful Hungary. Yet, due to the proximity of both countries, their return was not always permanent. Of the Turks who left Bulgaria in masses during 1989 due to national and religious discrimination, only some returned after the collapse of the communist regime; many soon migrated back to Turkey, now mainly for economic reasons. A last substantial part of the German minority in Romania also left for home in the early 1990s. This migration overshadowed even the number of people in the German minority infamously sold to West Germany in the 1970s and 1980s.[86] Small historical minorities of Czechs and Romanians also returned from the former Soviet Union to their respective homelands. Also, some Poles who were transferred to the Soviet Union under Stalin returned only after 1990.

The Romany played a significant role in post-socialist emigration. In the early 1990s they left Romania and Bulgaria in large numbers for Western Europe; it is estimated that more than

---

85 The largest contingent of troops was in the GDR (363,000), followed by Czechoslovakia (73,000), Poland (58,000) and Hungary (49,000). Numbers from Elaine M. Holoboff, 'National Security in the Baltic States: Rolling back the Bridgehead', in *The International Politics of Eurasia*, vol. 5, *State Building and Military Power in Russia and the New States of Eurasia*, eds S. Frederick Starr and Karen Dawisha (Armonk, NY: Bruce Parrott, Sharpe, 1995), 112.

86 Hans Heinrich Rieser, 'Abwanderung der Deutschen aus dem Banat', in Sterbling, *Migrationsprozesse: Probleme von Abwanderungsregionen*, 131–41, here 135.

250,000 Romany came to Germany between 1990 and 1993.[87] Their migration was prompted by the rapid deterioration of their economic situation and an increase in racist attacks. Most Romany asylum seekers were sent back home, however, so their migration had no impact on the rapidly growing Romany population in the region. The post-Yugoslav Wars also had an impact on the Romany. Thousands of them fled from war-torn Bosnia to the West. Those living in Kosovo also became a target of violence from the Serbian army in 1999, and later from Albanian nationalists accusing them of collaboration with the Serbs. About 30,000 Kosovo Romany fled or were expelled to Serbia and Montenegro.[88] Some Western European countries even introduced visa requirements for Central European countries because of the influx of Romany.

The breakup of multinational federations raised the question of granting citizenship to those who became new national minorities (for example, Slovaks in the Czech lands). This process was fairly smooth in former Czechoslovakia and Yugoslavia, but rather different in the case of the large Russian minorities in Latvia and Estonia, which were refused automatic citizenship after the republics declared independence. Citizenship was granted only to those who had been citizens in 1940 and their descendants. Those who settled during Soviet rule had to pass a language exam in order to get citizenship, which was difficult for many. As a result, many set out to emigrate once more, not only to Russia, but after the EU accession, to Western Europe as well. For example, in Estonia the Russian minority decreased from 35 to 25 per cent of the population between 1991 and 2005, and half of the Russians remaining still lack citizenship.[89] The thesis of the region's ethnic homogenization therefore is also valid for Baltic countries over the last 20 years, with the perspective of this trend continuing in the near future.

Quantitatively, the most significant trend was the out-migration motivated by economic reasons experienced in most of the countries during the two decades after 1989. It was particularly strong in countries suffering from acute economic crises – Romania, Bulgaria, post-war Yugoslavia and Moldova.[90] Moldova has become the country with the highest out-migration in Europe. Different ethnic groups tended to migrate in different directions: ethnic Moldavians went westward, Moldavian Ukrainians and Russians migrated eastward, and members of the Gagauz community headed to Turkey as well. In 2012, about 45 per cent of migrants from Moldova lived in Russia and 45 per cent in the EU countries, mostly in Italy.[91] It is estimated that about half the total population of Moldova is currently working abroad.[92] A high

---

87 Klaus J. Bade, *Europa in Bewegung: Migration vom späten 18. Jahrhundert bis zur Gegenwart* (München: C.H. Beck, 2000), 402.
88 Donald Kenrick, 'Former Yugoslavia: A Patchwork of Destinies', in *Between Past and Future: The Roma of Central and Eastern Europe*, ed. Will Guy (Hertfordshire: University of Hertfordshire Press, 2001), 405–25, here 415.
89 Marek Okólski, 'Migration Patterns in Central and Eastern Europe on the Eve of the European Union Enlargement', in *Migration in the New Europe: East-West Revisited*, eds Agata Górny and Paolo Ruspini (Houndmills: Palgrave Macmillan, 2004), 23–48, here 28.
90 Calculations of net migration defined as the number of migrants per thousand inhabitants, yielding the following numbers for the period between 2004 and 2008: Croatia 1.51, Hungary 1.37, the Czech lands 0.97, Slovenia 0.39, Slovakia 0.29, Bosnia and Herzegovina 0, Serbia 0, Romania -0.26, Poland -0.47, Macedonia -0.48, Lithuania -0.73, Latvia -2.34, Bulgaria -2.84, Estonia -3.33, Albania -3.33, Moldova -10.02. 'Net migration rate – Europe', www.cia.gov/library/publications/the-world-factbook/rankorder/2112rank.html (accessed 1 January 2014).
91 MPC-Migration Profile, Moldova, www.migrationpolicycentre.eu/docs/migration_profiles/Moldova.pdf (accessed 10 September 2016).
92 Milan Cuc, Erik Lundbäck, and Edgardo Ruggiero, *Migration and Remittances in Moldova* (Washington DC: International Monetary Fund, 2005), 13–19.

emigration rate is also to be found in Albania. The fact that two thirds of all Albanian migrants were men even caused a crisis on the Albanian marriage market.[93]

Only a handful of countries experienced higher in-migration than out-migration. This was the case for Hungary and Croatia, both of which had large minorities in countries hit by economic and political crisis. The same was true of economically quite successful countries such as Slovenia and the Czech Republic. Labour migrants to these countries have usually been young, predominantly male, and have tended to concentrate in metropolitan areas. There were only 30,000 foreigners living in the Czech Republic in 1989, but this number had increased to 424,000 by 2010, mainly due to immigration from Slovakia, the former Soviet Union and Vietnam, while expats from Western Europe and North America made up only about 10 per cent in 2010.[94] In Prague, residents of foreign nationalities already accounted for one tenth of the population in 2007.[95] However, in terms of incoming migrants, the Czech Republic and Slovenia are still below the level of most Western European countries.[96] A similar migration flow to better-situated countries of Central and Eastern Europe can be observed among students: young Slovaks went to study in the Czech Republic, ethnic Hungarians from Romania went to Hungary, and students from the former Yugoslavia went to Slovenia.

The main factors behind migration from Eastern and Central Europe were a sharp reduction in real wages at the beginning of the 1990s and a rise in unemployment, combined with the relaxation of travel policy and agreements between governments, which permitted certain forms of labour (temporary, supplementary). Many labour migrants worked illegally, however. It was only after the countries of the region joined the European Union that the labour market gradually opened up to them and those Central and Eastern Europeans working in the West were able to do so legally. Most migrants from Central and Eastern Europe preferred to work in Germany and Austria as salaries were up to ten times higher than in their own countries and they were in geographic proximity. Almost two thirds of all migrant workers from Central and Eastern European countries settled in Germany in the 1990s. Only Albanians tended to settle in great numbers in Greece and Italy.[97] In the second half of the 1990s, the flow of migration from Southeastern Europe began heading toward the south of Europe (Romanians to Italy and Spain, Bulgarians mainly to Greece and Spain).

The wage gap in the 1990s meant that even highly qualified people from the region could earn more money doing menial jobs in the West. In the new millennium, the West's lead on the wage front has narrowed somewhat. For example, in 2010, German salaries were only three to six times higher, but this was still enough to make the West attractive for migrants. By that time, the demand for experts from the region – particularly people in technical professions, medicine and sciences – had risen in the West. Remittances from professionals who migrate to the West are, however, a welcome source of income for those remaining at home and may contribute to the development of their countries upon their return.[98]

---

93 Karl Kaser, 'The History of the Family in Albania in the 20th Century: A First Profile', in Kaser, *Household and Family in the Balkans*, 441–52, here 449.
94 R04 Cizinci v ČR podle státního občanství 1994–2015 [R04 foreigners in the Czech Republic by citizenship 1994–2015], www.czso.cz/csu/cizinci/4-ciz_pocet_cizincu (accessed 31 December 2015).
95 Dušan Drbohlav et al., *Migrace a (i)migranti v Česku: kdo jsme, odkud přicházíme, kam jdeme?* [Migration and (i)mmigrants in the Czech Republic: who we are, where we come from, where are we going?] (Prague: Slon, 2010), 54.
96 Havelka, 'Tschechische Republik – Migrationen, Vertreibungen, Interventionen', 148.
97 Marek Okólski, 'Migration Patterns in Central and Eastern Europe', 38.
98 Andrei Roth, 'Abwanderung aus Rumänien', in Sterbling, *Migrationsprozesse: Probleme von Abwanderungsregionen*, 61–73, here 71.

Marriage migration – in most cases the departure of women from the region to marry in the West – is a notable post-socialist phenomenon. The number of men from the region who marry women from the West was – and still is – much lower.[99] For every marriage of a Czech man to a French woman, there are 35 marriages of French men to Czech women.[100] Usually, the couple settles in the husband's country and the wife internalizes her husband's culture, language and sometimes even his ethnic identity. Moreover, the mass migration of students became remarkable when the Central and Eastern European countries joined the Erasmus programme in 1998, with Romania and Bulgaria also enrolling somewhat later. The interest of students from the region in studying in the West grew fast; however, applications from the West to study in the region were less frequent. In 2004, 224,000 students from the region studied in Western Europe and North America, while at the same time only 14,000 students from Western Europe studied in Central and Eastern Europe.[101]

An important change was the relaxation of travel policy of former socialist countries to the West. Back in the 1980s, Hungarian citizens already enjoyed an almost automatic right to one tourist visit in the West per year, and Poland was also rather liberal in this respect; in Czechoslovakia and the GDR, it was fully liberalized during the Revolutions of 1989. The Federal Republic of Germany introducing the visa for Polish citizens in early 1980s abolished this in 1991. This contrasts with the visa requirements introduced by Western countries for visitors from the Soviet Union and the Balkans in the early 1990s. The requirement was abolished for the Baltic countries only in 1999, for Bulgaria in 2001 and for Romania in 2002. For citizens of Yugoslavia, used to unrestricted travel, the introduction of visa requirements by the EU countries after the collapse of the federation came as an unpleasant surprise. Only Slovenia and Croatia were granted visa-free regimes for travel to Western European countries from the beginning of their existence; Serbia and Macedonia had to wait until 2009 and Albania and Bosnia until 2010. Citizens of Kosovo needed a visa to enter Western Europe until 2019. After 1989, the Central and Eastern European countries also decided to introduce visa requirements for the former Soviet Union. This was requested by the EU, which was concerned that Central and Eastern Europe could become a transit zone for immigrants from developing countries. As early as 1991, the Baltic states introduced visa requirements for Russian citizens; other countries followed around 2000 (the Czech Republic in 2000, Poland in 2003).

Forced migrations after 1989 were confined to the republics of the former Yugoslavia. An estimated four million people (one fifth of the pre-1991 Yugoslav population) were forced to leave their homes during the Yugoslav Wars in the 1990s. For example, the population of Bosnia declined from 4 million to 2.3 million in the period from 1991 to 1995, although most of the refugees later returned. In 1996 the country already had a population of 3.6 million, and since 2004 it has stagnated like the other countries of the region due to out-migration and a low birth rate. Those who did return to Bosnia frequently settled in new, ethnically homogeneous enclaves rather than in their original homes. About 350,000 Serbs fled Croatia, and only 100,000 had returned by 2003.[102] Given that most of those who came back were elderly, it is

---

99 Krystyna Iglicka, 'The Revival of Ethnic Consciousness: A Case of Poland', in Górny and Ruspini, *Migration in the New Europe*, 141.
100 Stanislav Holubec, *Sociologie světových systémů: Hegemonie, centra, periferie* [The sociology of world-systems: hegemonies, cores, peripheries] (Prague: Slon, 2010), 131.
101 Stefan Immerfall and Göran Therborn, *Handbook of European Societies: Social Transformations in the 21st Century* (New York: Springer, 2010), 557.
102 Pascal Goeke, 'Flüchtlinge aus dem ehemaligen Jugoslawien in Europa seit 1991', in Bade et al., *Enzyklopädie Migration in Europa*, 580.

likely that the Serbian minority in the country will decrease further. The conflict in Kosovo led to the flight of about 700,000 Albanians (half of the Albanian population of Kosovo) to Albania and Macedonia, but most of them returned after the conflict. The departure of Serbian military forces resulted in the flight and expulsion of about 200,000 Serbs, Montenegrins and Romany from Kosovo, most of whom never returned. The arrival of Albanian refugees from Kosovo to Macedonia in 1999 led to a short-term increase in the Albanian minority there and heightened ethnic tensions in the country, but Macedonia remained the only multi-ethnic republic of the former Yugoslavia that was not hit by civil war.

Many refugees from the former Yugoslavia settled abroad permanently. Germany became the main country of asylum for Yugoslav migrants and has accepted more refugees than the rest of the EU combined.[103] However most of them had to leave after several years, while those who were granted asylum in other countries were able to stay. Austria and Sweden also opened their doors to large numbers of refugees.[104] The Bosniaks represented the largest group of refugees. Unlike Croats, Serbs or Albanians, they had no 'mother republic' that would accept them. In contrast to the previous pattern of Muslim migration from the Balkans in the twentieth century, this time the Bosniaks went to Western Europe rather than Turkey. The direction of Bosniak emigration not only confirms the appeal of the West, but also the strong connection Yugoslavs established with West Germany back in socialist times. Although the status of expelled Serbs and Croats who left Bosnia for their 'mother republics' was more favourable than that of the Bosniaks, they were not always welcomed and have often been perceived by their compatriots as less cultured (Bosnian Croats) or conceited (Bosnian Serbs).[105]

It seems that in the 1990s Central and Eastern Europe returned to its state in the decades before 1918 to some extent, with relatively high rates of labour migration and more open borders. The 'century of ethnic cleansings' appears to be a closed chapter. This is due not only to today's international rejection of 'ethnic cleansing' (known as the 'Dayton paradigm') and the ethnic 'purification of the region' over the century, but also to the declining ethnic hatred among the European nations.

Family formation and family structure: marriages and households

Traditional approaches to family history often rely on demographic variables to record the most important transformations of the family. Although this type of analysis cannot provide a full understanding of how family arrangements evolve, it does offer many analytical advantages. It enables us to measure the dynamics of developments, and thus to discern the fields most affected by change. Eventually, the understanding of these processes might help assess how other factors – such as cultural and political – had an impact on the lives of families.

Thus, this subchapter discusses the region's most important demographic aspects of twentieth-century family development. First, the historical patterns of family formation are outlined; then the process of the pluralization of family forms is addressed; third, the changes in Central and Eastern European family and household structures are dealt with.[106]

---

103 Bade, *Europa in Bewegung*, 367.
104 Holm Sundhaussen, 'Südosteuropa', 303–4.
105 Carolin Leutloff, 'Im Niemandsland: Kollektive Identitäten von Krajina-Serben in der Emigration in der BR Jugoslawien', in *Umstrittene Identitäten: Ethnizität und Nationalität in Südosteuropa*, ed. Ulf Brunnbauer (Frankfurt a.M.: Lang, 2002), 149–72, here 161–2.
106 On family history in Europe, see Anderson, *Approaches to the History of the Western Family*; Michael Mitterauer and Reinhard Sieder, *The European Family: Patriarchy to Partnership from the Middle Ages to the Present* (Chicago, IL: University of Chicago Press, 1982); for methodology and the larger context,

Marriage patterns

The marriage system greatly affects the structure of the family and the household and thereby reproduction, so scholars studying European family history have paid special attention to the changes in these patterns. Nevertheless, only a few works on the history of European family formation do not start with John Hajnal's famous thesis on European marriage patterns; similarly, there are only a few studies that do not conclude with a revision of the validity of Hajnal's proposition. We, too, regard Hajnal's findings as an important point of departure, because they shed light on the distinctiveness of the region within Europe from the perspective of family history, and on the internal uniformity of the region.[107]

John Hajnal identified two fundamental marriage patterns in historic Europe, emerging in the late Middle Ages. The dividing line between the two patterns ran approximately from St. Petersburg to Trieste. The so-called 'European marriage pattern' prevailed west of the line, while east of it, a diverging type of family formation persisted, basically conforming to nuptiality found in other regions of the world, and which was therefore considered by Hajnal the 'non-European marriage pattern'. In a European context, it is also often called the 'Eastern European marriage pattern'. The first arrangement was typified by a relatively late age at first marriage and a high ratio of lifelong celibacy, that is, of those never marrying. In north-western European societies, the customary mean ages of marriage in early modern rural areas were 27–28 for men and 25–26 for women, with no signs of any significant change between the seventeenth and mid-nineteenth centuries. Following the mid-nineteenth century a further increase in the average age of marriage is visible in many parts of Western Europe. As to lifelong celibacy, before 1800 the share of the population that never married was around 10 per cent, but in some regions, this share increased to 20 per cent or even higher later in the nineteenth century. In contrast to this pattern, in much of East Central Europe and Southeastern Europe, couples married at a relatively young age, and only a very small share of the population remained unmarried.[108]

Hajnal's thesis was published in 1965. At that time, the idea that north-western Europe had been demographically unique since the early modern era was not unknown. However, Hajnal systematically analyzed and statistically documented the thesis on distinct marriage patterns, and thus nurtured theorization and informed discussion. The model was fiercely debated, both regarding its geographical divides and the explanations behind the patterns. Jean-Louis Flandrin introduced a north–south line that cut France into two parts, while Peter Laslett delineated a fourth region embracing Central Europe. Both modifications refined the original formulation of marriage systems.[109] Hajnal's proposition, however, was challenged most as it pertained to Western and Southern Europe, and to a much lesser extent regarding Eastern Europe. As Hajnal's data ran roughly up to the end of the

---

see Tamara K. Hareven, 'Historical Analysis of the Family', in *Handbook of Marriage and the Family*, eds Marvin B. Sussmann and Suzanne K. Steinmetz (New York: Plenum Press, 1987), 37–57; Göran Therborn, *Between Sex and Power: Family in the World, 1900–2000* (London: Routledge, 2004).

107 On family history in the Central and Eastern European region in comparison, see Alain Monnier and Jitka Rychtarikova, 'The Division of Europe into East and West', in *Population: An English Selection* 4 (1992): 129–59; Michael Mitterauer, 'Family Contexts: The Balkans in European Comparison', *The History of the Family* 1, no. 4 (1996): 387–406; David Coleman, 'European Demographic Systems of the Future', 141–80.

108 John Hajnal, 'European Marriage Patterns in Perspective', in *Population in History*, eds D.V. Glass and D.E.C. Eversley (London: Edward Arnold, 1965), 101–43.

109 Jean-Louis Flandrin, *Families in Former Times: Kinship, Household, and Sexuality* (Cambridge: Cambridge University Press, 1979); Peter Laslett, 'Family and Household as Work Group and Kin Group: Areas of Traditional Europe Compared', in *Family Forms in Historic Europe*, ed. Richard Wall (Cambridge: Cambridge University Press, 1983), 513–63.

nineteenth century, the question also arose as to whether the model could be applied to the twentieth century. In the following, we will argue that while it remained valid in Central and Eastern Europe in the first decades of the twentieth century as well, profound changes took place in the marriage patterns of European societies later, which also extended to Central and Eastern Europe.[110]

Although marriage systems were not separated exactly by the St. Petersburg–Trieste line in Europe, marriage patterns at the turn of the twentieth century complied with Hajnal's 'non-European' type in much of Central and Eastern Europe. The most notable exception was the Baltic region, which already adhered to the Western European marriage pattern in Hajnal's original model. What is more, in the early twentieth century Central and Eastern Europe represented only a somewhat restricted version, while in the second half of the century, as will be demonstrated below, it became a fully fledged manifestation of this pattern.[111] With these qualifications, marriage was characteristically undertaken at a considerably younger age in the late nineteenth and early twentieth centuries in Central and Eastern Europe than in north-western Europe, and it was almost universal. In 1900, the average marriage age for women was 20.1 years in Serbia, 20.8 years in Bulgaria, and 23.6 years in Poland, while for men it was 23.0, 24.2 and 26.6 years, respectively. In Southeastern Europe, merely one to three per cent of women and three to five per cent of men never married in their lifetime. The celibacy rate in Poland, the Czech lands and Hungary exceeded these levels somewhat (Tables 5.4 and 5.5). All in all, the region as a whole was separated from Western Europe, but it was also one of the fields of family life where the north–south divide was most visible.

Table 5.4 Mean age of women at first marriage in Central and Eastern European countries, 1900–2010 (year)

Country	1900	1930	1950	1980	2010
Estonia				22.6	27.9
Latvia				22.8	27.4
Lithuania				23.0	26.4
Poland	23.6	24.9		22.8	25.6
Czech R.	25.4	24.7	24.7	21.4	29.4
Slovakia		22.6	22.2	22.3	26.9
Hungary	22.5	23.8	22.8	21.3	28.7
Romania	20.3			22.0	26.0
Serbia/Yugoslavia	20.1	21.7	22.3	22.2	27.1
Bulgaria	20.8	21.6	20.9	21.7	26.9
Albania				22.2	23.4

Notes: Poland in 1900: figure includes German, Russian and Austrian territories later becoming parts of Poland; Czech R. in 1900: figure includes Bohemia, Moravia and Silesia; Hungary is the present territory; there are different years as follows for Poland: 1931, 1978, 1984; Hungary: 1948; Romania: 1899, 1977; Yugoslavia: 1931; Bulgaria: 1926, 1956, 1975; Albania: 2008.

---

110 John Hajnal and others in his wake defined the ratio of lifelong celibacy based on those people in the cohort of 45–49-year-olds who never married (Hajnal, 'European Marriage Patterns in Perspective', 101–4). In the following discussion, because of a greater availability of data, the ratio is usually based on the cohort of 45–54-year-olds. This difference, however, does not alter the results significantly.

111 Hajnal, 'European Marriage Patterns in Perspective', 103; Paul Demeny, 'Early Fertility Decline in Austria-Hungary: A Lesson in Demographic Transition', in *Population and Social Change*, eds David V. Glass and Roger Revelle (London: Arnold, 1972), 164–8; Máire Ni Bhrolchain, 'East–West Marriage Contrasts, Old and New', in *European Population*, vol. 2, *Demographic Dynamics*, eds Alain Blum and Jean-Louis Rallu (Montrouge: John Libbey Eurotext, 1993), 461–79.

Sources: Patterns of First Marriage: Timing and Prevalence (New York: United Nations, 1990), 9 (Czech Lands 1900, Bulgaria 1900–1934); 10 (Poland 1900, 1931; Romania 1899; Serbia 1900, Yugoslavia 1931–1948); 224 (Poland 1960–1984; Romania 1977; Yugoslavia 1950–1980; Bulgaria 1956–1975); Ludmila Fialová, 'Changes in Nuptiality in Czech Lands and Slovakia, 1918–1988', *Journal of Family History* 19, no. 2 (1994): 108 (Czech Republic 1920–1980, Slovakia 1920–1980); Józsefné Csernák, 'Házasság és válás Magyarországon' [Marriage and divorce in Hungary], in *Magyarország történeti demográfiája (896–1995)*, ed. József Kovacsics (Budapest: KSH, 1997): 352 (Hungary 1900–1930); *Time Series of Historical Statistics, 1867–1992* (Budapest: KSH, 1993), 130 (Hungary 1948–1990); Franz Rothenbacher, *The Central and Eastern European Population since 1850* (Houndmills: Palgrave Macmillan, 2012), 100 (Estonia 1980–2000, Latvia 1980–2000, Lithuania 1980–2000, Bulgaria 1970); UNECE Statistical Database, http://w3.unece.org/pxweb/DATABASE/Stat/30-GE/02-Families_households/?lang=1 (Estonia 2010, Latvia 2010, Lithuania 2010, Poland 2010, Czech R. 2010, Slovakia 2010, Hungary 2010, Romania 2010, Serbia 2010, Bulgaria 2010, Albania 2008) (accessed 20 October 2013).

Table 5.5 Female celibacy in Central and Eastern European countries, 1900–2000 (percentage of women never married in the 45–54 age group)

Country	1900	1920	1930	1950	1960	1980	1990	2000
Estonia		15.8	17.3				6.5	7.6
Latvia		12.3	14.1				5.2	8.8
Lithuania			11.3				5.3	5.8
Poland	7.8	8.2	7.1		9.1	5.9	4.8	6.0
Czechoslovakia		8.9	6.0	9.2	6.5	3.7	3.5	3.3/6.7
Hungary	4.8	5.5	6.1	8.2	7.3	3.8	3.8	4.4
Romania	3.0					3.6	3.2	5.4
Serbia/Yugoslavia	1.0		4.7	5.8	6.1	5.0	3.9	
Bulgaria	1.0	1.0	1.4		2.1	2.1	2.9	3.9
Albania							1.4	2.6

Notes: Czechoslovakia 1921: figure includes Bohemia, Moravia and Silesia, and 40–49-year-old cohort; Czechoslovakia, Poland 1900–1931: figures are for 45–49-year-old cohort unless otherwise indicated; Poland 1900: figure includes German, Russian and Austrian territories later becoming parts of Poland, and 40–49-year-old cohort; Bulgaria, Yugoslavia, Romania, Spain: figures are for 45–49-year-old cohort unless otherwise indicated; Czechoslovakia 1947–1980, Poland 1960–1980, Romania 1977, Bulgaria 1956–1975, Yugoslavia 1960–1980: figures are the ratio of those married by the age of 50; Czechoslovakia 2000: figure is for Czech Republic/Slovakia; Hungary 1920, 1980–1990: figures are for 45–49-year-old cohort, 1900, 1930–1960: figures are for 45–54-year-old cohort; Yugoslavia 1931–1948: figures are for 50–54-year-old cohort; there are different years as follows for Estonia: 1922, 1934, 1989; Latvia: 1989; Lithuania: 1923, 1989, 2001; Romania: 1992, 2002; Yugoslavia: 1991; Czechoslovakia: 1921; Poland: 1921, 1931; Hungary: 1949; Romania: 1899, 1977; Yugoslavia: 1931, 1948; Bulgaria: 1934, 1956, 1975, 1992, 2001; Albania: 1989, 2001.

Sources: Franz Rothenbacher, *The European Population since 1945* (Houndmills: Palgrave, 2005), 33 (Czechoslovakia 1950–1990, Poland 1960–2000; the whole of Europe 2000); *Patterns of First Marriage: Timing and Prevalence* (New York: United Nations, 1990), 9 (Czechoslovakia 1920–1930; Bulgaria 1900, 1934), 10 (Poland 1900–1931, Romania 1899, Serbia 1900, Yugoslavia 1931–1948), 235 (Czechoslovakia 1947–1980, Poland 1960–1980, Bulgaria 1956–1975, Romania 1977, Yugoslavia 1960–1980); Eurostat, *European Social Statistics: Demography* (Luxembourg: Eurostat, 2000), Table F11 (Czech Republic/Slovakia 2000); *Time Series of Historical Statistics, 1867–1992* (Budapest: KSH, 1993), 8–9, 12, 14 (Hungary 1900–1990, author's calculations); Franz Rothenbacher, *The Central and Eastern European Population since 1850* (Houndmills: Palgrave Macmillan, 2012), 94–95 (Estonia 1922–1934, 1989–2000, Latvia 1920–1930, 1989–2000, Lithuania 1923, 1989–2001, Romania 1992–2002, Bulgaria 1910–1920, 1992–2001, Yugoslavia 1991, Albania 1989–2001).

The Eastern European marriage pattern faded somewhat in the region in the first decades of the twentieth century, but changes remained moderate.[112] After the Second World War, the willingness to join in matrimony rose again in Central and Eastern Europe, conforming to Western European and North American trends in the first two post-war decades. The propensity to marry increased, particularly among those widowed or divorced, and the average age of those entering their first marriage declined. Moreover, whereas in Western Europe nuptiality declined from the late 1960s, in Central and Eastern Europe there was only a moderate change in the appeal of marriage. In fact, in several societies the lowest levels ever were found in the average ages at first marriage in the 1970s: for instance, in 1975 in Bulgaria brides were 20.8, and in Romania 21.1 years old on average. In parallel, the age gap between marriage partners widened.[113]

From the mid-1970s the inclination to marry began to diminish somewhat in Central and Eastern Europe as well. The average age at marriage gradually began to rise, while a more rapid change was seen in the marriage rate, which was revealed more clearly by annual marriage ratios than by the celibacy ratio, which is less sensitive to short-term changes. For example, in Hungary, had the age-specific nuptiality rates observed in 1987/1988 persisted in the long run, 82 per cent of men and 92 per cent of women born in the second half of the 1960s would have been married by the time they were 50, which was a considerable drop compared to earlier times.[114] Parallel changes were identified in the Balkan countries as well. Notwithstanding the developments in the 1980s, the relatively high ratio of married people and the young age at marriage clearly demonstrate the exclusiveness of marriage in partnerships in most parts of Central and Eastern Europe and the Balkans until the 1990s. This feature of the Central and Eastern European marriage system is especially striking, if one considers that in the meantime the decline in the popularity of marriage had advanced much further in Western European societies. Thus, in this respect the two regions diverged until the last decade of the century.[115]

Approaching the new millennium, a major trend in union formation was the decline in nuptiality throughout Europe.[116] The last decade of the twentieth century saw significant, sometimes even dramatic changes in the marriage patterns of Central and Eastern European societies as well. It was part of a broader process: the fall of communism accelerated population and family changes in the region so much that in these societies the post-1990 era can be plausibly conceptualized as a new period of population and family development. The decline in the ratio of those entering marriage first appeared in the early 1990s; however, those who still did marry did so at a relatively young age. By the new millennium, the mean age of brides and bridegrooms also started to increase considerably in the Central and Eastern European and Balkan countries – except Albania. Hungary and the Czech Republic especially had approximated the Western European patterns by 2010 (Table 5.4).[117]

---

112 UN, *Patterns of First Marriage: Timing and Prevalence* (New York: United Nations, 1990), 9–10.
113 Ibid., 224.
114 Józsefné Csernák, 'Házasodási szokások Finnországban és Magyarországon' [Marriage patterns in Finland and Hungary], *Statisztikai Szemle* 71, no. 10 (1993): 801.
115 Kathleen E. Kiernan, 'Partnership Behaviour in Europe: Recent Trends and Issues', in *Europe's Population in the 1990s*, ed. David Coleman (Oxford: Oxford University Press, 1996), 62–91, here 62–4.
116 Elina Haavio-Mannila and Anna Rotkirch, 'Sexuality and Family Formation', in Immerfall and Therborn, *Handbook of European Societies*, 465–97.
117 Hana Maříková, 'The Czech Family at Present and in the Past', in *Families in Eastern Europe*, ed. Mihaela Robila (Amsterdam: Elsevier, 2004), 31–49, here 33.

Three of the phenomena investigated thus far demand explanation most: first, the differences between marriage patterns in the West and the East, which had already existed at the beginning of the century; second, the considerably high level and even intensification of the willingness to marry that persisted until the end of the communist era in Central and Eastern Europe; and third, the decrease in the willingness to marry after the system change.

1. In the scholarly literature, the most influential interpretations link historical changes and variations in nuptiality to Christian religious doctrines and their influences, or to a lack thereof; to the scarcity of resources, particularly of land, in traditional rural economies; and, finally, to inheritance practices.[118] These scholarly explanations for the emergence of European marriage patterns were only partly in accordance with the historical realities of Central and Eastern Europe. Even if one accepts these arguments with regard to marriage patterns in the early twentieth century, the factors mentioned above still have a limited and, even more importantly, fading validity when explaining differences in the rest of the twentieth century. The significance of Christian religious doctrines in determining the everyday life of people was declining. Since famine no longer posed a threat and land had ceased to be the most essential resource for life in this century, the scarcity of land could no longer have influenced family behaviour decisively. The same applies to inheritance practices in societies where industrial labour increasingly pushed rural classes into the background. It can be argued that marriage-related social norms, which had been institutionalized earlier, continued to exist in the twentieth century. However, the inertia of norms can offer only a partial explanation, particularly since the dynamics of marriage changes often contradicted the dynamics of how traditional social norms evolved. For this reason, other factors have to be taken into consideration as well. Several of these underlying factors will be addressed later, including value changes (secularization and individualization), and alterations in economic and employment structures (the considerable growth of female employment, urbanization, and industrialization) in the section examining the emerging diversity of family forms in the twentieth century.

2. As to the second major set of developments yet to be explained, the changes promoting marriage as a universal phenomenon in Central and Eastern Europe in the post-war decades were the outcome of a number of factors. It is evident that the transformation of marriage as the almost exclusive type of partnership arrangement in the region was largely impeded by the isolation of communist regimes from the rest of the world. This also arrested economic and social diffusion processes, including the spread of alternative family forms from Western societies, where many of these became common from the late 1950s. Moreover, the preservation of the Eastern European marriage pattern was strongly facilitated by the social and cultural uniformity prevailing in the communist regimes, which permitted little diversity in individual life courses. Furthermore, the relatively high degree of social security based on full employment enabled individuals to plan important life events such as marriage. In other words, those willing to marry generally did not have

---

118 Michael Mitterauer, 'A "European Family" in the Nineteenth and Twentieth Centuries?', in *The European Way: European Societies during the Nineteenth and Twentieth Centuries*, ed. Hartmut Kaelble (New York: Berghahn, 2004), 146–7; Michael Mitterauer, 'Europäische Familienformen im interkulturellen Vergleich', in *Historisch-anthropologische Familienforschung: Fragestellung und Zugangsweisen* (Köln: Böhlau, 1990), 38; UN, *Patterns of First Marriage*, 41; John Hajnal, 'Two Kinds of Preindustrial Household Formation System', *Population and Development Review* 8 (1982): 449–94.

to worry about their future economic situation. An even more compelling explanation is that in communist countries social policy prioritized married couples in the allocation of several goods and services, most importantly housing, which was a major incentive to marry under the circumstances of the shortage economy. Finally, the very nature of dictatorial regimes was also instrumental in producing higher marriage rates. Here, the public sphere was dominated by indoctrination and hypocrisy, which made civic activities unappealing and led to citizens seeking refuge in privacy, particularly in the sanctuary of family.

3. Finally, the decrease in nuptiality in Central and Eastern Europe at the end of the twentieth century is equally underlain by numerous, neatly interrelated factors. Most of all, after the regime change, the factors incentivizing marriage, a characteristic feature of communist family policy and the socio-economic system in general, disappeared. The transformation crises created massive unemployment for a considerable time, and later the labour market proved to prefer a young, unmarried and childless labour force, especially in the case of women. Prominent among the causes one can identify foreign cultural influences that found a highly recipient region with a longing for Western lifestyles, which at the same time raised the standard of living aspired to by the population. The postponement of marriage and childbirth was also reinforced by the expansion of educational opportunities, especially affecting university students, whose numbers increased almost everywhere in the region in the 1990s. Moreover, educated people, even after finishing college, are more prone to delay matrimony than the less educated segments of society.[119]

The moderation of nuptiality levels in the late twentieth century went in tandem with the increasing popularity of cohabitation without marriage. Not only was lower fertility achieved by modern methods of birth control (intrauterine devices and the contraceptive pill), but they also facilitated 'nubile cohabitation' and influenced the timing of marriages. The modern birth control methods, which arrived in the region relatively late, made it easier to lengthen the time people could spend in premarital partnerships, as fewer marriages were sought primarily because of pregnancy. Also, as it will be pointed out, since pregnancies and births outside marriages grew to be more tolerated by society, they did not lead to marriages as often as before.

Divorce and the pluralization of family forms

Towards the end of the century, the change in marriage rates became less relevant to describe partnerships, and the explanatory power of marriage rates began fading in European societies, because partnership forms underwent profound transformations, albeit with different dynamics in various countries of the continent. Some elements of these changes, often referred to as the pluralization of marriage and family forms, arrived relatively early in Central and Eastern Europe, while others took root much later, only towards the new millennium. The intricate process of transforming attitudes to marriage and family, and the limits to this process, are manifested in the diffusion of divorce as well as cohabitation and extramarital births. Thus, we first examine these developments in detail, moving on in the next subchapter to examine other relevant attitudinal aspects of family change.

---

119 Tomáš Sobotka et al., 'Demographic Shifts in the Czech Republic after 1989: A Second Demographic Transition View', *European Journal of Population* 19, no. 3 (2003): 249–77.

The *union dissolution* rates of the Czech lands and, especially, Hungary were already among the highest in Europe in the early twentieth century and remained so in the interwar period.[120] The fragmented information we have suggests a similarly high frequency of divorce in the Baltic countries, while divorce rates were much lower in the Balkans. After the Second World War, the stability of marriages further eroded in the region, where divorce laws were liberalized earlier than in most Western European countries. Although the rapid increase in the frequency of divorces was a general tendency in the first decades of the communist regimes, in this respect one can differentiate among three major areas within the region: the Baltic states belonging to the Soviet Union, where by far the most divorces were registered; Czechoslovakia and Hungary, which occupied an intermediate position in the region, but still ranked rather high among European countries; and finally, the Balkan countries, where divorce was far more infrequent. Poland was also nearer the latter model; nonetheless, notably more marriages were disrupted here in the post-war decades than in other Catholic European countries.

The significant increase in divorce frequency during communism is shown quite straightforwardly by the number of divorces per 10,000 married persons (Table 5.6). However, this indicator is sensitive to the dynamics of family formation and life expectancy. Other indices that are not so widely available, such as the total divorce rate, which control for the variation in the number of marriages, signalled a more moderate increase in the 1970s and a slight decline in the second half of the 1980s in several East Central European and Baltic countries. In the post-war decades, the social composition of divorcees also changed significantly in the region, because they became younger – as did those getting married – and spouses with children also increasingly filed for divorce.[121]

The rising marital disruption figures in the second half of the twentieth century thus point to a fairly distinct and arguably even inconsistent attitude towards marriage in several Central and Eastern European societies. While traditional marriage patterns basically persisted in the region to the 1990s, divorce rates greatly increased throughout the century and were above those of most Western European societies.

The quality of partnerships had undoubtedly become a major concern in life by the late twentieth century in Europe. Somewhat paradoxically, the growing importance of an agreeable relationship further increased the vulnerability of unions, as reflected in the divorce rates. The rise in divorce rates typically slowed down or declined to some extent at the end of the twentieth century but did not return to mid-century levels. High frequencies of divorce were observed in the Baltic states and in East Central Europe (the Czech Republic and Hungary), where the total divorce rate – expressing the rate of marriages that would end in dissolution if the divorce intensity were constant – exceeded 40 per cent. In those countries which had high divorce ratios, marriages were disrupted even sooner, and union breakups were increasingly common in the case of couples with young children. This change also influenced the structure of families: more parents qualified as single, children and fathers were more often geographically separated and an increasing number of children lived in 'patchwork' families, that is, with step-parents and step-siblings.

---

[120] For family dissolutions in different Western European countries, see Robert Chester, ed., *Divorce in Europe* (Leiden: Netherlands Interuniversity Demographic Institute, 1977); Francis G. Castles and Michael Flood, 'Why Divorce Rates Differ: Law, Religious Belief and Modernity', in *Families of Nations: Patterns of Public Policy in Western Democracies*, ed. Francis Castles (Aldershot: Dartmouth, 1993), 293–326, here 300–01.

[121] Józsefné Csernák, 'Házasság és válás Magyarországon' [Marriage and divorce in Hungary], in *Magyarország történeti demográfiája (896–1995)*, ed. József Kovacsics (Budapest: KSH, 1997), 350, 362.

Table 5.6 Number of divorces per 10,000 married persons in Central and Eastern European countries, 1930–2000

Country	1930	1950	1960	1980	1990	2000
Estonia	27	28	99	178	165	189
Latvia	40		109	205	173	116
Lithuania			41	133	144	137
Poland		21.3	22.7	45.9	45.8	
Czechoslovakia	19.3	44.2	46.1	89.1	107	
Hungary	29.5	52.9	66.9	98.6	97.6	
Romania			88	62	60	53
Yugoslavia		53	54	41		
Bulgaria	11	51	32	52	48	52

Note: The Estonian data for 1930 is from 1928.

Sources: Franz Rothenbacher, *The European Population, 1850–1945* (Houndmills: Palgrave, 2002), 161 (Czechoslovakia 1930), 357–9 (Hungary 1930); Franz Rothenbacher, *The European Population since 1945* (Houndmills: Palgrave, 2005), 165 (Czechoslovakia 1950–1990), 433 (Hungary 1950–1990), 671 (Poland 1950–1990); Franz Rothenbacher, *The Central and East European Population since 1850* (Houndmills: Palgrave Macmillan, 2012), 108–9 (Estonia 1950–2000, Latvia 1930–2000, Lithuania 1960–2000, Romania 1960–2000, Bulgaria 1930–2000, Yugoslavia 1950–1980, Albania 1990–2000), 519 (Estonia 1928).

Not only did divorces soar in Europe after the Second World War, but other major changes in family life occurred, including the rapid diffusion of cohabitations and extramarital births.[122] Couples living together without joining in matrimony had been a well-known family arrangement long before the twentieth century, particularly in specific underprivileged groups of the population. The frequency of marriages decreased in most Western European countries from the 1960s on, and in parallel to this, cohabitation diffused rapidly.[123] In contrast, by the 1980s cohabitation was not increasing in Central and Eastern Europe, once again with the exception of part of the Baltic region, namely in the case of Estonia. The moderate decrease in nuptiality that can be identified in the 1980s only lengthened premarital relationships in most societies of the region rather than inducing more cohabitation. What is more, the region also presented distinct cohabitation features. The trial marriage type of cohabitation characteristically prevailed in the younger generation from the 1960s on in Western Europe, which had no direct connection with social disadvantages.[124] In contrast, in Central and Eastern European societies, women who cohabited frequently had poor education, were divorcees with children, or

---

122 On major trends of family formation, see Therborn, *Between Sex and Power*, 192–225.
123 On this issue, see also Sybille Meyer and Eva Schulze, 'Nichteheliche Lebensgemeinschaften – Alternativen zur Ehe?' *Kölner Zeitschrift für Soziologie und Sozialpsychologie* 35 (1983): 735–54; Kathleen Kiernan, 'Leaving Home: Living Arrangements of Young People in Six West-European Countries', *European Journal of Population* 2, no. 2 (1986): 177–84, here 182; Nico Keilman, 'Recent Trends in Family and Household Composition in Europe', *European Journal of Population* 3, no. 3/4 (1987): 297–325, here 309–12.
124 François Höpflinger, 'Haushalts- und Familienstrukturen im intereuropäischen Vergleich', in *Die Westeuropäischen Gesellschaften im Vergleich*, eds Stefan Hradil and Stefan Immerfall (Opladen: Laske + Budrich, 1997), 97–138, here 109.

widows.[125] In fact, in the 1970s a couple of Central and Eastern European countries showed the lowest ratio of cohabitation in the cohorts of 20–24 and 25–29-year-olds – the very same cohorts for which the ratio of cohabitation was highest in Western Europe. With regard to the over-30 cohorts, cohabitations increasingly prevailed and peaked among those over 60. In the oldest age groups, most cohabiting partners had been widowed. The fact that younger generations were underrepresented was due primarily to the housing shortage in Central and Eastern European societies, as teenagers and young adults in their twenties were hardly ever able to own or rent their own flat.

In the European societies of the new millennium, cohabitation increasingly developed into an alternative to marriage.[126] Although the main thrust of transformation has been the same in the continent, significant divergences prevailed between countries regarding both the acceptance and prevalence of cohabitation, and the dynamics of changes. The divergence among the former communist countries was also significant concerning the levels of cohabitation and public acceptance of this living arrangement. In much of the Balkans nubile cohabitation had barely taken root by 2000, but Slovakia and Poland, too, were considered by some demographers as 'immune' to cohabitation.[127] In contrast, it is clear that in Romania and in the Czech Republic more couples preferred this arrangement, while in Hungary and Slovenia the figures fell to the mid-range of European national averages (Table 5.7).[128]

Table 5.7 Ratio of married and unmarried persons among women aged 25–34 in Central and Eastern European countries, 2000–2002

Country	Married (%)	Cohabiting without marriage (%)	Non-married cohabitation as % of all couples
Slovakia	60.3	2	3.2
Poland	60.2	2.1	3.4
Czech Republic	57.7	4.5	7.2
Lithuania	61	5.7	8.6
Romania	68.6	7.1	9.4
Latvia	40.6	4.3	9.6
Hungary	56.9	11.5	16.8
Slovenia	45.2	12.1	21.1
Estonia	40.4	21.2	34.4

Source: Zsolt Spéder, 'Változások az ezredfordulón' [Changes at the turn of the millennium], in Rudolf Andorka, Bevezetés a szociológiába (Budapest: Osiris, 2006), 417.

---

125 Elwood Carlson and András Klinger, 'Partners in Life: Unmarried Couples in Hungary', European Journal of Population 3, no. 1 (1987): 85–99; Zoltán Szűcs, Az élettársi kapcsolatban élő családok társadalmi-demográfiai jellemzői [Demographic characteristics of cohabiting unions] (Budapest: KSH, 1996), 7.

126 Kiernan, 'Partnership Behaviour in Europe', 67–8; Zsolt Spéder, 'Változások az ezredfordulón' [Changes around the turn of the century], in Bevezetés a szociológiába, Rudolf Andorka et al. (Budapest: Osiris, 2006) 416.

127 Tomáš Sobotka and Laurent Toulemon, 'Changing Family and Partnership Behaviour: Common Trends and Persistent Diversity across Europe', Demographic Research 19, no. 6 (2008): 85–138.

128 In Poland 21.4 per cent of young adults assessed the increasing number of people cohabiting positively, while 37.5 per cent of their Czech counterparts expressed approval. Zsolt Spéder, 'Childbearing Behaviour in the New EU Member States: Basic Trends and Selected Attitudes', in The New Generations of Europeans, eds Wolfgang Lutz et al. (London: Earthscan, 2006), 59–82, here 66–7 and 72–3.

Table 5.8 Extramarital births as a percentage of all births in Central and Eastern European countries, 1930–2010

Country	1930	1960	1980	1990	2010
Estonia	8.2	13.8	18.3	27.2	59.1
Latvia	8.2	11.9	12.5	16.7	44.1
Lithuania	6.7	3.7	6.3	7.0	28.7
Poland	5.8	5.7	4.8	5.8	20.6
Czechoslovakia	11.3	4.9	5.7	7.7	40.3/33.0
Hungary	8.9	5.7	6.6	13.1	40.8
Romania				16.9	27.7
Serbia		10.8		19.0	23.9
Bulgaria	1.8	7.1	10.9	12.4	54.1
Albania					0.5

Notes: Czechoslovakia 2010: figure is for Czech Republic and Slovakia. There are different years as follows for Poland 1927; Estonia 1928; Serbia 1961, 1995; Lithuania 1970; Romania 1993, 2001; Bulgaria 1946–1950 (average), 1962; Albania 2003.

Sources: Franz Rothenbacher, *The European Population, 1850–1945* (Houndmills: Palgrave, 2002), 160 (Czechoslovakia 1930, own computation), 566 (Poland 1927, own computation); Franz Rothenbacher, *The European Population since 1945* (Houndmills: Palgrave, 2005), 164 (Czechoslovakia 1950–1990, own computation), 670 (Poland 1955–1990, own computation); Franz Rothenbacher, *The Central and East European Population since 1850*, (Houndmills: Palgrave Macmillan, 2012), 344–6 (Bulgaria 1930–1990), 518–28 (Estonia 1928–1990), 562–4 (Latvia 1930–1990), 602–4 (Lithuania 1930–1990), 981–3 (Serbia 1961–1995); *Time Series of Historical Statistics, 1867–1992* (Budapest: KSH, 1993), 148 (Hungary 1930–1990); Data for 2010 and for Latvia 1960, Lithuania 1970 and Romania 1993 were calculated from Eurostat datasets: see Population and Migration Statistics, 'Live births by mother's age and legal marital status', Code:demo_fagec: http://epp.eurostat.ec.europa.eu (accessed 10 January 2019); UN World Fertility Report 2003, www.un.org/esa/population/publications/worldfertility/World_Fertility_Report.htm (Albania 2003) (accessed 25 October 2013).

Despite all of these developments, alternative forms of partnerships have not replaced marriage. The survival of traditional marriage norms has been significant: around the turn of the millennium the huge majority of the population (75–90 per cent of women in the 20–34 age group) in all of Europe, and not only in Central and Eastern Europe, still considered marriage as the most desirable form of partnership. Moreover, in Central and Eastern Europe the ratio of married couples considerably surpassed that of unmarried couples, even in the 25–34-year-old female cohort, in which non-married cohabitation was most frequent (Table 5.7).[129]

Like cohabitation, 'extramarital' births had become relatively common before the twentieth century in certain social groups of Europe. Research differentiates between specific periods in the history of illegitimacy: a phase of increase started in the mid-eighteenth century in most European societies, while a second phase of decline began around 1880. As a result of this process, apart from Austria and Sweden, all Western European societies subsequently showed extramarital births with rates below 10 per cent in the early twentieth century. Significant change in this respect occurred again in the 1960s, with the Nordic countries playing a pioneering role (Table 5.8).[130]

---

[129] Zsolt Spéder, 'Az európai családformák változatossága: Párkapcsolatok, szülői és gyermeki szerepek az európai országokban az ezredfordulón' [Varieties of European family forms: couples, parenting and the role of children in European countries at the turn of the century], *Századvég* 22, no. 3 (2005): 3–48.

[130] Ron Lesthaeghe and Guy Moors, 'Living Arrangements, Socio-economic Position, and Values Among Young Adults: A Pattern Description for France, West-Germany, Belgium, and the Netherlands, 1990', in Coleman, *Europe's Population in the 1990s*, 211–12; Höpflinger, 'Haushalts- und Familienstrukturen', 110.

In a European context, the Central and Eastern European levels of extramarital births can be regarded as low (Bulgaria), medium (Poland), medium to high (Czechoslovakia, Hungary) or high (Latvia, Estonia) in the first two thirds of the century.[131] From the 1960s, however, considerably more extramarital births were observed in most Western European societies than in East Central Europe and the Balkans, and by 1990 the gap had opened wide. In Central and Eastern Europe, the Baltic region and particularly Estonia, constituted an exception, with high numbers of children born outside marriage. A further disparity between European regions was that births outside marriage were much more prevalent among underprivileged women in Central and Eastern European societies than in Western Europe throughout the twentieth century, especially from the 1960s on, when in the latter region well-educated social groups were increasingly represented, resembling what we found in the case of cohabitation. However, dramatic changes occurred in extramarital births after the collapse of the communist systems: in two decades, the number of births outside marriage multiplied in the region. As an example, the Bulgarian level has already approached the Estonian level in 2010, which can be considered high even in a Western European context (Table 5.8).[132]

The pluralization of family forms is a complex process originating in factors that are often interwoven and appear in most industrialized countries. The most important of these include changes in employment structure, urbanization, the expansion of female employment, value changes and the welfare activity of the state.

Among economic changes, families were greatly influenced by alteration in the structure of employment, which was especially stormy in the 1950s and 1960s in Central and Eastern Europe. The decline of agricultural labourers' share in the overall employment and the growth of the industrial and service sectors also advanced urbanization as well as the expansion of female employment, which, in turn, are major factors in the decline of traditional family forms. Among the numerous causal mechanisms, it is worth highlighting that the number of divorces and extramarital cohabitations, as well as the number of births outside marriage, are all traditionally higher in urban populations. This is related to the lower level of social control in cities, which results in less successful enforcement of traditional family norms. A further factor is the changing status of women within the family, which was above all a consequence of female employment. Earning an independent income enabled women to redefine their position in the family and to strive for a more equal distribution of burdens and recognition. This process itself increased the possibility of conflict, as women were less willing to tolerate their disadvantages than before. The development of female employment was also enhanced by the rapid growth of women's educational levels in the twentieth century, and this process also inspired women to pursue their own career objectives.

A newer but no less significant challenge to traditional family forms was the value change palpable in European societies after the Second World War, which can be best described by the concepts of individualization and secularization and was interwoven with the changes discussed above. Individualization, that is, the increasing emphasis on the rights and autonomy of the individual in relation to other entities such as the family, resulted in individuals becoming less willing to accept the obligations associated with marriage and family. Secularization prevailed

---

131 Ferenc Ájus and István Henye, 'Illegitimacy in Hungary, 1880–1910', *Journal of Family History* 19, no. 4 (1994): 369–88.
132 Tomáš Sobotka, 'The Diverse Faces of the Second Demographic Transition in Europe', *Demographic Research* 19, no. 8 (2008): 171–224, here 188–93.

especially in Bulgaria, the Baltics, Hungary and the Czech lands, and weakened the prevalence of the church's doctrines towards family.[133]

The expansion of the states' social commitments also affected the family because welfare states took over much of the family's responsibilities in caring for the children and the elderly, that is, the states guaranteed social security. Welfare benefits paid to singles and single parents with child(ren) enabled many to pursue and realize their individual aims as opposed to the traditional patterns of family life.[134]

Changes in family law acted as a catalyst in many fields: after the communist takeover, the procedure for divorce was simplified according to the Soviet model in the entire region, thus playing a prominent role in the increase of the divorce rate. The only exception was Romania, where the acceptable reasons for divorce were restricted in 1966, thus decreasing the number of those filing for divorce. However, the regulation also proved to be temporary, as restrictions were eased again in 1974.[135] In addition, the constraints put on private property after the Second World War, which were also characteristic for this region, similarly facilitated divorces, because considerations about keeping property played hardly any role in deciding whether or not to begin divorce proceedings. The combined effect of these factors largely explains the extent to which the traditional system of family gave way to alternative forms of family in the last decades of the twentieth century in Central and Eastern European societies.

Changes in family and household structure

The decline in fertility, shifts in marriage patterns and several other social changes in the twentieth century examined thus far had a significant impact on the structure of families and households. This transformation deserves attention, as the composition of family households arguably affects interpersonal relations within the family as well as children's socialization, and thereby the quality of family life.

Both family research and popular tradition have long assumed that in pre-industrial Europe, large families and households predominated. These families and households emerged as a result of the high number of children and because several generations lived together, along with extra kin. Households reached high complexity, since various relatives were living together with the family core, including cousins, nieces and nephews, uncles and aunts, thus creating heterogeneous household forms.[136] From the mid-1960s, however, Peter Laslett and his colleagues began

---

133 Sabrina P. Ramet, *Social Currents in Eastern Europe: The Sources and Consequences of the Great Transformation* (Durham, NC: Duke University Press, 1995), 156–9.
134 Franz Rothenbacher, 'Social Change in Europe and its Impact on Family Structures', in *The Changing Family: Family Forms and Family Law*, eds John Eekelaar and Thandabantu Nhlapo (Oxford: Hart Publishing, 1998), 3–31, here 5–10.
135 Rothenbacher, *The Central and Eastern European Population*, 92.
136 Peter Laslett distinguished the following types of households in his well-known typology based on the composition of the household: 1. solitaries: widows or widowers; single people; 2. no family households: households in which none of the members belong to the same family; 3. simple family households: nuclear family households, with only the couple and their dependent children and no other type of relative or non-relative present; 4. extended family households: nuclear families plus one or more relatives, such as a parent, a sibling or siblings, who do not form other couples; 5. multiple family households: households comprised of more than one couple, who are closely related in some way, such as nuclear families living together; most often parents and their married child with his/her spouse (*stem family*); parents with more married children and their spouses (*joint family*); or married siblings with their spouses. Peter Laslett, 'Introduction: The History of the Family', in *Household and Family in Past Time*, eds Peter Laslett and Richard Wall (Cambridge: Cambridge University Press, 1972), 1–89.

to accumulate new evidence challenging the view that large and complex households had been prevalent since the early modern period, at least regarding north-western Europe. Relying on empirical evidence gleaned from a wide application of what is called the 'family reconstitution method', they claimed that between the late sixteenth and the late nineteenth centuries, the mean household size was both relatively stable and moderate, including, for instance, about 4.75 members in England. They also suggested that the nuclear family form was the major type in the Western family system.[137] Demographic constraints particularly rendered the formation of large and complex family households more difficult: high infant and child mortality as well as the prevalence of premature deaths in later stages of life hampered the emergence of large households. The relatively low average household size also suggests that a high number of kin and servants, boarders and lodgers normally could not have lived together with the core family in a single household.

Thus, it seems plausible that changes in both the size and the structure of families and households were moderate in Europe from the early modern period until the end of the nineteenth century. However, scholarship has yet to reach a full consensus on this, and the Balkans are one of the candidates that underwent significant family changes in the eighteenth and nineteenth centuries. However, the shifts that took place in the twentieth century were undoubtedly significant all over Europe, with regard to both the contraction of families and households, and the simplification of family and household structures. These tendencies prevailed in Central and Eastern Europe as well, but family systems in the early twentieth century and the dynamics of the following changes diverged widely within the region.

In the first decades of the twentieth century, the *mean household size* in several countries of East Central Europe did not differ significantly from that observed in Western Europe. In 1930 a typical household comprised 3.8, 3.9 and 4.4 members in Czechoslovakia, Hungary and Poland, respectively, declining further by the mid-century, to 3.3 in Czechoslovakia and 3.6 in Hungary. The decline has been uninterrupted since 1950; thus, from the 1960s on, households in East Central Europe resembled their Western European counterparts in this regard, with the three Baltic countries coming close. The process of contraction was less remarkable in Poland, where the average household size remained considerably higher throughout the second half of the twentieth century (Table 5.9).[138]

The Balkan region undoubtedly had larger households in the early twentieth century. However, except for Yugoslavia and Albania, this gap had been almost entirely closed by the end of the century. Although Yugoslavia showed considerable internal disparities regarding household patterns, as in other fields of social and economic development, these differences were not as extensive in terms of household size at the beginning of the century: Slovenia lagged only slightly behind the Yugoslav average even in 1930. Internal disparities built up by the 1980s, while at the turn of the millennium, after the dissolution of the country, different household sizes of the region's societies converged. In the Balkans, Albania represented a special case, with its average household size towering far above the European average even at the turn of the millennium.

---

137 Peter Laslett, 'Mean Household Size in England since the Sixteenth Century', in Laslett and Wall, *Household and Family in Past Time*, 125–58.
138 Franz Rothenbacher, *The European Population, 1850–1945* (Houndmills: Palgrave, 2002), 51; Idem, *The European Population since 1945* (Houndmills: Palgrave, 2005), 43; Lajos Thirring, 'Magyarország népessége 1869–1949 között' [The population of Hungary between 1869 and 1949], in Kovacsics, *Magyarország történeti demográfiája*, 295.

Table 5.9 Mean household size in Central and Eastern European countries, 1900–2010 (persons)

Country	1900	1920	1930	1950	1960	1980	1990	2010
Estonia		2.9	3.2		2.6	2.6	2.6	2.3
Latvia								2.5
Lithuania								2.4
Poland		4.8	4.4		3.5	3.1	3.1	2.8
Czechoslovakia			3.8	3.3	3.1	2.8	2.6	2.5/2.8
Hungary		4.3	3.9	3.6	3.1	2.8	2.6	2.6
Romania							3.1	2.7
Yugoslavia		5.1	5.1	4.3	4.0	3.6	3.6	
Bulgaria	5.6	5.3	4.7	3.4		3.1	2.8	2.9
Albania			5.6		5.5	5.8	4.7	

Notes: Unless indicated otherwise, data are for private households; Estonia 1922 is for total household members; Czechoslovakia 2010 is for Czech R./Slovakia; there are different data for Hungary, i.e. 1920 & 1930 are for average habitants per dwelling; there are different years as follows for Estonia: 1922, 1934, 1959, 1979, 1989; Poland: 1921, 1931, 1978, 1988; Czechoslovakia: 1961, 1991; Hungary: 1949; Romania: 1992; Yugoslavia: 1921, 1931, 1953, 1961, 1981, 1991; Bulgaria: 1934, 1975, 1992; Albania: 1923, 1989.

Sources: Franz Rothenbacher, *The European Population since 1945* (Houndmills: Palgrave, 2005), 43 (Poland 1960–1988; Czechoslovakia 1950–1991); Franz Rothenbacher, *The European Population 1850–1945* (Houndmills: Palgrave, 2002), 51 (Poland 1921–1931; Czechoslovakia 1930); Tamás Faragó, *Nemek, nemzedékek, családok és rokonok a XVIII–XX. században* [Sexes, cohorts, families and relatives in the XVIII–XXth Centuries] (Doctoral dissertation) (Budapest: MTA Kézirattár, 1994), appendix 59 (Hungary 1910); József Kovacsics, ed., *Magyarország történeti demográfiája* [Historical demographics of Hungary] (Budapest: KSH, 1963), 295 (Hungary 1930, 1949); *Time Series of Historical Statistics, 1867–1992* (Budapest: KSH, 1993), 82 (Hungary 1920, 1941, 1960–1990); Franz Rothenbacher, *The Central and East European Population since 1850*, (Houndmills: Palgrave Macmillan, 2012), 94–5 (Estonia 1922–1990, Romania 1992, Bulgaria 1900–1990, Yugoslavia 1921–1991, Albania 1923–1990); Eurostat: http://appsso.eurostat.ec.europa.eu/nui/show.do?dataset=ilc_lvph01&lang=en (Estonia, Latvia, Lithuania, Poland, Czech R., Slovakia, Hungary, Romania, Bulgaria 2010) (accessed 25 October 2013).

The transformation of household size was related to the retreat of larger households on the one hand, and the increase in the share of solitary households on the other. The decline in the share of larger households with five or more members followed a developmental path similar to that of the average household size in Central and Eastern Europe. Around 1930, the share of large households was the lowest in Estonia (where comparability of the data is fairly limited, however), in Czechoslovakia (31.3 per cent) and in Hungary (33 per cent).[139] Large households were much more common in Poland, and even more so in the Balkans, especially in Albania and Yugoslavia, but also in Romania and Bulgaria. However, fertility, that is, the number of children per family, also diminished rapidly over the next decades in most regions of Central and Eastern Europe, fundamentally influencing the size of households. Yet, this process did not proceed in a uniform manner. In Czechoslovakia, the share of large households was 16.7 per cent in 1961 and 8.4 per cent in 1991, barely different from the Western European pattern. Hungary followed a similar path, but large households survived to a much greater extent in Poland, Romania, Yugoslavia and Albania – mostly reflecting differences in fertility levels.

---

139 Rothenbacher, *The European Population since 1945*, 45. The distribution of dwellings in Hungary in 1930 over the number of habitants in settlements with more than 10,000 inhabitants is from Faragó Tamás, *Nemek, nemzedékek, családok és rokonok a XVIII–XX. században* [Gender, nations, families and relatives from the 18th to the 20th centuries] (PhD Diss., Budapest: MTA Kézirattár, 1994), Appendix 49.

Solitary households amounted to less than 10 per cent of all households in almost all Western European societies before the First World War. The spread of this type was quite moderate in the following decades, but diffusion accelerated in the post-war era. A similar development can be observed in Central and Eastern Europe, where the share of single-person households also grew rapidly. Nevertheless, it departed from rather low initial levels, with 7.3 per cent in Czechoslovakia, 9 per cent in Poland and 6 per cent in Hungary in 1930, and remained lower than the Western European mean in the following decades. In 1990, the share of solitary households in both Czechoslovakia and Hungary reached almost one fourth, and in Poland one fifth, of all households. Estonia stood out with its unusually high ratio of single-person households throughout the century. Quite remarkably, in several Balkan societies the number of solitary households was as high as in eastern Central Europe, but in the post-war decades this living arrangement spread only moderately (Yugoslavia, Romania), or was increasingly pushed into the background (Albania). Thus, in this regard, the gap between the societies of Central and Eastern Europe and Western Europe continued to be more significant than has been found for both the mean household size and the proportion of large households (Table 5.10).

Table 5.10 Percentage of solitary households among all households in Central and Eastern European countries, 1920–2010

Country	1920	1930	1950	1960	1980	1990	2010
Estonia	(37.8)	22.3		33.2	31.2	28.7	34.5
Latvia							27.9
Lithuania							34.7
Poland	6.1	9.0		16.4	17.4	18.3	20.7
Czechoslovakia		7.3	10.8	14.2	22.9	25.3	27.2/20.8
Hungary		6.0	10.0	14.5	19.6	24.3	23.6
Romania					13.9	17.1	20.9
Yugoslavia/ Serbia			12.2	13.6	13.1/13.2	13.9/17.4	
Bulgaria	5.3	7.4		17.7	16.8	19.7	30.8
Albania			8.9	6.1		4.2	6.3

Notes: Unless indicated otherwise, data are for private households; Serbia: data do not cover Kosovo and Metohija; Czechoslovakia 2008: data are for Czech R./Slovakia; there are different data for Estonia 1922, and they include persons living in institutions and dormitories; Hungary 1949 is an estimate; there are different years as follows for Estonia: 1922, 1934, 1959, 1979, 1989; Latvia: 2011; Lithuania: 2011; Poland: 1921, 1931, 1988, 2011; Czechoslovakia: 1961, 1991; Czech R.: 2008; Slovakia 2011; Hungary: 2011; Romania: 1977, 1992, 2011; Yugoslavia: 1953, 1961, 1981, 1991; Serbia: 1981, 1991; Bulgaria: 1934, 1956, 1975, 1992, 2011; Albania: 1989, 2008.

Sources: Franz Rothenbacher, *The European Population, 1850–1945* (Houndmills: Palgrave, 2002), 53 (Poland 1921–1931; Czechoslovakia 1930); Franz Rothenbacher, *The European Population since 1945* (Houndmills: Palgrave, 2005), 46 (Czechoslovakia 1950–1991, Poland 1960–1988); Tamás Faragó, *Nemek, nemzedékek, családok és rokonok a XVIII–XX. században* [Genders, generations, families and relatives in the 18th–20th century] (PhD diss., Budapest: MTA Kézirattár, 1994), appendix 38 (Hungary 1949); *Time Series of Historical Statistics, 1867–1992* (Budapest: KSH, 1993), 76 (Hungary 1960–1990); Franz Rothenbacher, *The Central and Eastern European Population since 1850* (Houndmills: Palgrave Macmillan, 2012), 135–136 (Estonia 1922–1989, Romania 1966–1992, Bulgaria 1900–1992, Yugoslavia 1953–1991, Albania 1950–1989); UNECE Statistical Database,http://w3.unece.org/pxweb/DATABASE/Stat/30-GE/02-Families_households/?lang=1 (Estonia 2010, Czech R. 2008, Serbia 1981–1991, Bulgaria 2011); Eurostat, (accessed October 20, 2013)http://epp.eurostat.ec.europa.eu/statistics_explained/index.php/File:Private_households_by_household_composition,_2011.png (Latvia 2011, Lithuania 2011, Poland 2011, Slovakia 2011, Hungary 2011, Romania 2011) (accessed 25 October 2013).

However, the transformation of households in the twentieth century was much more complex than a simple decline in the size of households: the structure of households also underwent significant changes. The nuclear family, often referred to as the 'conjugal family', consisting of spouses and their dependent children, became the dominant type – a development enhanced by the withdrawal of non-family members from the household, the decline of the extended family and the growing popularity of marriage in the two post-war decades.[140]

Even though a remarkable stability of marriage patterns in Central and Eastern Europe could be observed until the last decade of the twentieth century, the character of family life changed considerably throughout the region. The complexity of Central and Eastern European family structures further decreased throughout the century. Relatives other than members of the core family gradually retreated from the household, and less complex family households were established, for instance, by kin in the ascending line living together.

This change in family structure materialized more slowly in Central and Eastern Europe than in Western European societies. In 1949, an estimated 22–24 per cent of all households in Hungary still included more than one core family or accommodated kin besides the nuclear family.[141] The persistence of the relatively high level of household complexity in Hungary is demonstrated by the fact that in 1990, 11.8 per cent of all households still belonged to this category, such that 19.1 per cent of the total population resided in such households. These ratios are substantially higher than those prevailing in Western Europe. The most characteristic situation was of parents and married child(ren) or a widowed parent and the child's family forming one household.[142]

As far as the complexity of family households is concerned, the case of the Balkans has attracted great attention in social and historical research.[143] In this region, complex household structures constituted a long-standing tradition prior to the twentieth century.[144] Although if scant statistical information is available on Southeastern European family structures in the nineteenth and early twentieth centuries, a vast body of ethnographical and anthropological evidence suggests the existence of large and highly complex multiple family households called *zadruga* in nineteenth-century rural communities of the Balkans. The zadruga was a household and kinship organization, with a membership varying between 20 and occasionally even 90. It consisted of two or more nuclear families related by blood or adoption. They jointly owned the means of livelihood – the land, the livestock and the tools – and regulated the use of property and labour as well as consumption communally.[145] Major decisions in the zadruga were made by the married males, and by the head (*starshina*) in particular, who was designated by seniority,

---

140 K. Schwarz, 'Household Trends in Europe after World War II', in *Modelling Household Formation and Dissolution*, eds Nico Keilman, Anton Kuijsten and Ad Vossen (Oxford: Clarendon Press, 1988), 74.
141 Faragó, *Nemek, nemzedékek, családok és rokonok*, Appendix, 38.
142 Béla Tomka, *Családfejlődés a 20. századi Magyarországon és Nyugat-Európában* [Families in 20th century Hungary and Europe] (Budapest: Osiris, 2000), 46–62.
143 Maria N. Todorova, *Balkan Family Structure and the European Pattern: Demographic Developments in Ottoman Bulgaria* (Budapest: CEU Press, 2006); Ulf Brunnbauer, *Gebirgsgesellschaften auf dem Balkan: Wirtschaft und Familienstrukturen im Rhodopengebirge – 19./20. Jahrhundert* (Vienna: Böhlau, 2004), 309–440; Karl Kaser, 'The Balkan Joint Family: Redefining a Problem', *Social Science History* 18, no. 2 (1994): 243–69.
144 For this issue in a Balkan context, see Michael Mitterauer, 'Family Contexts: The Balkan in European Comparison', *History of the Family* 1, no. 4 (1996): 387–407.
145 Maria Todorova, *Myth-Making in European Family History: The Zadruga Revisited* (Washington, DC: Wilson Center, 1989), 20.

descent or election. Residence was patrilocal – the bride moved to her husband's place – and inheritance was patrilineal.[146]

However, the existence of the zadruga does not imply that this family type dominated in the Balkans in the eighteenth or nineteenth century, let alone in the early twentieth century. The Balkan societies showed great diversity of family patterns. The zadruga was confined to certain regions and even there it was not the exclusive organizational principle of households. It prevailed mostly in the remote mountainous regions of the western Balkans, and even there, it could be divided into at least three types.[147] Moreover, E. Hammel argued that the zadruga – just like other types of the extended and multiple families in the region – should be considered 'as a process'.[148] Where parents lived to see their children marry and start a family, they often formed a joint household with the families of their children. Consequently, complex households such as the zadruga may have been common indeed at a particular stage of the family cycle, even if their share within the whole population was observed to have been moderate. Hammel's approach helps reconcile different scholarly perspectives to a great extent and also facilitates interpretation of the often-intricate paths of family development in the Balkans. In spite of the fact that the fully fledged form of the joint family had almost completely disintegrated by the interwar period, its traces could still be observed in certain distant rural communities in the mid-century.[149]

Complex households were common not only in the Balkans, but also elsewhere in Europe, including East Central Europe, for instance in southern Estonia and in some parts of Hungary in pre-industrial times.[150] On the basis of this consideration, several scholars claimed that the study of zadruga is simply 'myth-making', part of 'Balkanism', so that the use of the notion of the zadruga should be entirely abandoned.[151] However, what makes zadruga still unique and thereby important for family history, despite its above-mentioned limitations, is that it was not simply an extensive and complex family household – the relations between the members were also peculiar in a European context. They showed very strong features of patriarchalism and occasionally even practised ancestor worship and swore blood vengeance.[152]

Having said this, we cannot establish a direct link between the nineteenth-century peasant joint family and most of the prevailing forms of extended or multiple family households in the twentieth-century Balkans and Central and Eastern Europe, since the functions of such living arrangements had changed entirely. The urban population was highly represented in complex households in the decades after the Second World War, which indicated that it was not, or not mainly, production processes that facilitated their formation, since households hardly

---

146 Philip E. Mosely, 'Adaptation for Survival: The *Varžić* Zadruga', in *Communal Families in the Balkans: The Zadruga*, ed. Robert F. Byrnes (Notre Dame: University of Notre Dame Press, 1976), 31.
147 Mitterauer, 'Family Contexts', 403.
148 Eugene Hammel, 'The Zadruga as Process', in Laslett and Wall, *Household and Family in Past Time*, 370; for similar findings, see Andrejs Plakans, 'Interaction between the Household and the Kin Group in the Eastern European Past: Posing the Problem', *Journal of Family History* 12 (1987): 163–75.
149 The same even holds for some regions of Central and Eastern Europe. See Judit Morvay, 'The Joint Family in Hungary', in *Europa et Hungaria: Congressus Ethnographicus in Hungaria*, eds G.Y. Ortutay and T. Bodrogi (Budapest: Akadémiai Kiadó, 1965), 231–42, here 231 and 239; Edit Fél and Tamás Hofer, *Proper Peasants* (Chicago, IL: Aldine Publishing, 1969), 103.
150 Heldur Palli, 'Estonian Households in the Seventeenth and Eighteenth Centuries', in Wall, *Family Forms in Historic Europe*, 207–16; Rudolf Andorka and Tamás Faragó, 'Pre-Industrial Household Structure in Hungary', in Wall, *Family Forms in Historic Europe*, 281–308.
151 Todorova, *Myth-Making in European Family History*, 20.
152 Mitterauer, 'Family Contexts', 387–406.

functioned as institutions of labour organization in the urban environment.[153] The same holds for rural areas where, mostly as a result of collectivization and industrialization, the functions of the family also underwent a major change in the twentieth century: family households lost many of their tasks in running agricultural production. The still relatively high share of extended and multiple family households signalled a housing shortage, the survival of norms promoting them, and only to a lesser extent the persistence of economic functions in both the urban and rural environments.[154] In those countries where collectivization was not fully realized – Poland and Yugoslavia – villages bore the traces of family labour to a greater extent. However, it only postponed the transformation process in these areas.

Moreover, not only did the structure of households become less complex all over Europe in the twentieth century, but, as a major thrust of transformation, their separation from each other also advanced. In the late nineteenth century, formally individual households were often intertwined, a case in point being a tenant employed by his landlord in a shop or a workshop, and often also paying for his housing with labour. In Budapest, as late as 1910, only 42.6 per cent of all households occupied a dwelling alone, the remaining were often one-person households of lessors, lodgers, night lodgers or persons actually renting a part of the residence. By 1930, the share of the separate households increased to 60.8 per cent of all households.[155] Therefore, what we can observe is not simply a crystallization of nuclear family households, but also a growing spatial separation of nuclear families from kin and others, in parallel with the emergence of the spatial preconditions for intimacy in the dwelling. This process further progressed in the second half of the century, with a decline in the number of non-kin household members, who eventually disappeared almost entirely from most Central and Eastern European societies by the end of the twentieth century.

The most significant factor causing the sharp decrease in the size of households in twentieth-century Europe was a great reduction of the number of children in families, resulting from diminishing fertility, which was examined in one of the preceding sub-chapters. The drop in the number of fourth and further births had already begun in the first half of the century in Western Europe. After the Second World War, even though fertility boomed temporarily, this development sped up and embraced third births as well. In the first decades of the century, similar patterns emerged in Southern Europe, then in Central and Eastern Europe and in the Balkans. While third births amounted to 15 per cent of all births in Hungary in 1935, after a practically permanent downturn they represented only 9–10 per cent in the 1970s, and it was only in the second half of the 1980s that this share rose moderately. Of all births, an even stronger decline occurred in the percentage of fourth and further births.[156] In parallel with the fall in the number of families with three and more children, the share of childless families did not increase in the region; rather, it diminished between the first decades of the century and the 1980s. As suggested earlier, this development originated primarily in the decline of infertility,

---

153 In Hungary in 1970, the ratio of households with relatives in the ascending line was 6.4 per cent in villages, 3.6 per cent in the capital, Budapest, and 3.8 per cent in the towns of the country. László Cseh-Szombathy, 'A mai magyar család legfőbb jellegzetességei' [Major characteristics of contemporary Hungarian families], in *A változó család*, ed. László Cseh-Szombathy (Budapest: Kossuth, 1978), 46.
154 Statistical distortion may also have increased the percentage of complex family households. Because of the special system of allocating council apartments, in larger towns relatives would often register as living together (e.g. grandchildren with grandparents) as a measure to keep or gain the right to rent.
155 Tamás Faragó, 'Housing and Households in Budapest, 1850–1944', *History and Society in Central Europe* 1, no. 1 (1991): 29–63.
156 *Time Series of Historical Statistics, 1867–1992*; vol. 1 (Budapest: KSH, 1993), 163.

mostly due to the containment of venereal diseases, and to medical progress in treating infertility resulting from other causes such as inflammations. As an outcome of these processes, particularly in the two or three post-war decades, there was a concerted spread of the two-child family, in addition to the fall in average family size.[157]

A further element that reduced the average household size and simplified household structure throughout Europe was the diminishing number of household members who were not actually related to the family, including servants, maids and other employees in farms and small shops or workshops. In most regions of Central and Eastern Europe, there were no strong traditions for employing non-relatives on family farms who would also join the household, as observed in many parts of north-western Europe. After the communist takeover, the employment of such workers was explicitly prohibited, as a result of which even the few existing workers disappeared. This policy also led to the disappearance of domestic servants, who formerly lived in more affluent households and thus increased the average size of households, and whose number was considerable even in the interwar period, especially in larger Central and Eastern European cities.

Finally, the diffusion of single-person households contributed significantly to the decline in average household size. The increase in the share of single-person households in Central and Eastern Europe resulted mostly from the growth in the number of elderly people living alone and was partly a result of the advance in life expectancy, but also of the increasing separation of families. The growing number of divorces, too, produced more solitary households. Up to the end of the century, changing youth lifestyles contributed to this process much less than in Western Europe, since the pattern of early marriage survived and thus the incidence of independent premarital households was low in Central and Eastern Europe, even in the last three decades of the century. Significant change in this respect occurred only after the transformation of the political system, when, to mention a few relatively well-known factors, the lifestyle of young people started to alter more rapidly than before, higher education went through a phase of strong expansion and Western consumption patterns increasingly permeated these societies.

Patriarchy and partnership in the twentieth century

Besides transformations of the demographic characteristics of families – and partly as a result of them – the quality of family life and the personal relations in families in particular underwent considerable changes in twentieth-century Europe. It was part of a long-term development dating back to the early modern period or even earlier. During this process, the emotional ties between spouses gained greater importance in family formation, and child rearing became the centre of family life, which is sometimes called the emergence of the privatized family, or the romantic revolution in family life. Arguably, the middle classes were the first to go through this, and later the new attitudes and preferences spread from the middle classes to the upper and lower classes.[158] While these processes had advanced considerably in earlier periods, the retreat of patriarchy and the breakup of the rigid hierarchies in family structure took place mostly in the twentieth century and were among the most significant consequences of modernity in

---

157 Rudolf Andorka, *Determinants of Fertility in Advanced Societies* (London: Methuen, 1978).
158 On these changes, see Martine Segalen, *Historical Anthropology of the Family* (Cambridge: Cambridge University Press, 1996), 201–56; Lawrence Stone, *The Family, Sex, and Marriage in England, 1500–1800* (New York: Harper and Row, 1979); Edward Shorter, *The Making of the Modern Family* (New York: Basic Books, 1976).

family history in Europe. In the following, these aspects of family change will be examined, as they concern Central and Eastern Europe.

Interpersonal relationships in the family are very difficult to grasp systematically, especially from a historical and comparative perspective. The concept of patriarchy can be used as an expedient analytical tool for this purpose. In scholarly discourse, patriarchy often refers to a system of gender relations in which male members of a society predominate in positions of authority.[159] However, the notion will be used below in a narrower sense, as follows: patriarchy will be interpreted as the presence of an institutionalized power asymmetry in the family. It has two aspects: the first is what the word literally means, 'the rule of the father', that is, paternal power over children; the second is the power of husbands over spouses, which historically cannot be separated from the previous element, and arguably determines it, such that it seems plausible to study this dimension of patriarchy in depth. Yet it also seems obvious that, while the concept of patriarchy may direct our attention to power asymmetries within the family, it cannot grasp other important aspects of the transformation of family life, especially the changes concerning the intimacy of family life.

At the beginning of the twentieth century, the power of the father and the husband was extensive everywhere in the continent and legally well-entrenched as well. Married women traditionally lived under their husband's authority with regard to employment, disposal of property and several other aspects. Irrespective of their ages, unmarried women were subject to their father's authority. Both boys and girls needed their father's consent in order to be able to marry. Women were not admitted to the franchise anywhere in Europe in 1900, and if they were permitted to attend an institution of higher education, they needed a special warrant. There were some countries where women gradually gained rights that provided economic autonomy and legal maturity from the 1850s, above all Norway, Sweden, Denmark and England. However, in many other European countries – particularly in Latin countries which were strongly influenced by the Napoleonic Code, and in Eastern Europe – this improvement of women's legal position was not realized until the turn of the century, and even in the following decades it was only allowed under various restrictions. Thus, patriarchy varied in specific societies in the early twentieth century, and it was already being challenged, as reflected in the feminist movement unfolding at the time.

Central and Eastern Europe did not show uniformity in this respect, either. The existence and functioning of patriarchy are documented best in the case of the Balkans. In several parts of this region, but by no means everywhere, the co-residential patterns within households and the specific family ideology reproduced patriarchal structures, but the intact survival of these arrangements was constrained by economic conditions nonetheless.[160] The internal diversity of the Central and Eastern European region is well reflected by Göran Therborn's typology, which reconstructs early twentieth-century types of legal patriarchy. He distinguishes between two traditional and two modern conceptions of patriarchy based on the legal stipulations for husband–wife relations. The societies of the region were represented in three out of four types. One form of the traditional legal patriarchy originated directly in canon law, which was highly

---

[159] For the historical aspects of patriarchy, see Gerda Lerner, *The Creation of Patriarchy*, vol. 1 (Oxford: Oxford University Press, 1986). Recent research has also suggested that upper classes and artists were the avant-garde of romantic love. Sharon Marcus, *Between Women: Friendship, Desire, and Marriage in Victorian England* (Princeton, NJ: Princeton University Press, 2009).

[160] Joel M. Halpern, Karl Kaser and Richard A. Wagner, 'Patriarchy in the Balkans: Temporal and Cross-Cultural Approaches', *The History of the Family* 1, no. 4 (1996): 425–42.

conservative with regard to gender relations. Serbia, Bulgaria and Albania stood for this type. In the latter country, for Muslims, who constituted the majority of the population, family relations were regulated by the Hanafite school, that is, the law of the Ottoman Empire. Local customary law also played a great role in Albania, and in other parts of the Balkans as well. A further traditional notion of patriarchy was manifested in and buttressed by secular law and arose primarily from the established role of males as caretakers. The modern forms of patriarchy were closely connected to the traditions of the Enlightenment and regulated family relations via the means of modern law. One major type relied on explicit legal formulations to guarantee paternal authority in the family. Family arrangements were regulated in this way in Romania. The other arrangement was more moderate, since it required cooperation and favoured companionship in family relations, including both husband–wife and father–children ties, but assigned the final legal authority to the father and the husband. Of the countries of Central and Eastern Europe, Hungary belonged to this category (Table 5.11).[161]

Changes concerning patriarchy in the first decades of the twentieth century can be regarded as gradual in Central and Eastern Europe. Although the Bolshevik revolution brought about full legal equality between men and women within the family in the eastern part of Europe, radical changes in this respect did not unfold in the Nordic countries until after the First World War. In Central and Eastern Europe, the new Baltic states were mostly occupied with replacing their former religious regulation with state regulation. This policy emphasized partnership within the family in Estonia and Latvia, but eventually also assigned the rights of decision to the husband and the father in cases of major differences of opinion. Lithuania held on to the former Russian canon law of marriage in general, and to German law in the Memel territory. As a result of its earlier division, Poland witnessed the survival of multiple family law traditions in its different regions. The legal setting was similarly mosaic-like in Serbia/Yugoslavia and in Romania, but legal patriarchy prevailed on the whole. The alteration of family law in Czechoslovakia was primarily intended to offer the possibility of a choice between secular and church marriage. This opportunity strengthened the influence of the church in Slovakia as compared to under earlier Hungarian regulations, while it weakened the sway of the church in the Czech lands as opposed to previous Austrian legislation.[162]

Table 5.11 Forms of legal patriarchy in Europe in the early twentieth century

Traditional patriarchy based on church law	Traditional patriarchy based on secular law	Modern legal guarantee of moderate patriarchy	Modern legal guarantee of extreme patriarchy
Albania	Great Britain	Germany	Austria
Bulgaria	Denmark	Hungary	Belgium
Greece	Finland	Netherlands	France
Russia	Norway	Switzerland	Italy
Serbia	Sweden		Portugal
			Romania
			Spain

Source: Göran Therborn, *European Modernity and Beyond* (London: Sage, 1995), 105.

---

161 Göran Therborn, *European Modernity and Beyond: The Trajectory of European Societies, 1945–2000* (London: Sage, 1995), 104–6.
162 Therborn, *Modernity and Beyond*, 106–7.

Legal patriarchy has often been consolidated by prevailing employment regimes. Female employment rates in Central and Eastern Europe was close to the Western European average between 1900 and 1945 and could be considered relatively low in Southeastern Europe.[163] What is more, the level of women's education was also far behind that of men's in the first half of the century in Central and Eastern Europe. It practically compelled women to enter into jobs with lower qualifications. However, the period witnessed a successive fading away of differences in education according to gender, as is shown by the increasing ratio of female students at universities: the most striking figure is from Poland in 1930, which reached 34 per cent, while the same figures are 19 per cent for Czechoslovakia, 16 per cent for Hungary, 21 per cent for Yugoslavia and 22 per cent for Bulgaria.[164]

While one can identify gradual transformations of patriarchal relations in the first decades of the century, these changes accelerated after the Second World War. The shifts in husband–wife relationships surfaced on many dimensions, including new legal regulations, the change of women's position in education and the labour market, a new division of labour within the family, and finally, the diffusion of novel normative conceptions about the relationship between husband and wife and their tasks within the family.

Family law became a terrain of radical changes in Central and Eastern Europe after the Second World War. The advancement of gender equality and the secularization of marriage were parts of the political agenda of the communist parties seizing power. Gender equality in the family and in society was incorporated into the new post-war constitutions in Central and Eastern Europe. Egalitarian and anti-patriarchal family legislation, for example emphasizing free marriage choice and women's right to work outside the household, was enacted quickly. New family laws were also passed in the early post-war years (in Bulgaria in 1945, Albania in 1948, Czechoslovakia and Poland in 1950, Hungary in 1953, Romania in 1954). These new laws abolished the legal foundations of patriarchy in the region. Secularization and gender equality were legally secured in the Baltic region after Soviet occupation, even though a few regressive steps were introduced in this respect in 1944, for example, making extramarital paternity suits and divorces more difficult.[165]

Female employment increased greatly after the Second World War in Central and Eastern Europe. On the one hand, the growth in female employment demonstrated the change in women's social positions; on the other, a number of sociologists and historians argue that the work of women outside the household can be considered the most significant single factor that transformed family relationships. In this regard, it is worth considering not only the increase of the rate of female employment, but also what kind of work women were engaged in and how women's relative wages changed – in comparison to those of men.[166] When seen in an international context female employment increased rapidly in the 1950s and 1960s. The communist

---

163 For female employment rates in different countries up to the mid-twentieth century, see E. Boserup, ed., *Female Labour before, during and after the Industrial Revolution* (8th International Economic History Congress) (Budapest: Akadémiai Kiadó, 1982); for later periods, see Katja Boh, 'European Family Life Patterns – A Reappraisal', in *Changing Patterns of European Family Life: A Comparative Analysis of 14 European Countries*, eds Katja Boh et al. (London: Routledge, 1989), 265–96, here 271–2; Riitta Jallinoja, 'Women between Family and Employment', in *Changing Patterns of European Family Life*, 118; Manfred G. Schmidt, 'Gendered Labour Force Participation', in Castles, *Families of Nations*, 182.
164 Wolfram Fischer, 'Wirtschaft, Gesellschaft und Staat in Europa, 1914–1980', in *Handbuch der europäischen Wirtschafts- und Sozialgeschichte*, vol. 6, eds Wolfram Fischer et al. (Stuttgart: Klett-Cotta, 1987), 82.
165 Therborn, *Between Sex and Power*, 98.
166 John Ermisch, 'The Economic Environment for Family Formation', in Coleman, *Europe's Population in the 1990s*, 144–62.

countries, led by Poland and East Germany, were at the forefront in Europe in the 1960s. Only Finland was able to match their levels of female employment, with some other Scandinavian countries approaching them. Employment rates do not even properly reflect the real disparities, as part-time jobs had hardly existed in communist countries, while this type of working schedule was common in Western Europe.[167] The gap in female employment between the countries of East Central and Western Europe began to decrease after the mid-1970s, because in the communist countries levels had peaked by then, while a rising tendency continued in Western European societies. In parallel, the remaining gaps in female employment patterns had been significantly reduced in the Central and Eastern European region by the 1980s. The differences between societies with the highest and lowest female employment rates amounted to only a few percentage points in 1990.

As suggested earlier, the diffusion of female employment already attested to the fact that women's aims and aspirations, and public attitudes with regard to their social position, changed considerably in post-war Europe. A couple of surveys revealed that the majority of the population in most of the Western European countries in the 1960s believed that women should seek gainful employment, and that partners should share household tasks equally.[168] Though the actual practice of the division of labour in the family reflects expressed preferences to a lesser extent, there has been a balancing process between men and women which began in the 1960s.[169] Central and Eastern Europe witnessed a more tempered transformation concerning the actual equality of women in the family, and even less than what could have been anticipated, considering the stormy socio-economic transformations after the Second World War. The change in normative relations, popular views on women's roles, and the sharing of household tasks from the 1960s was not as rapid in Central and Eastern Europe as in Western Europe.

The expectations concerning marriage in post-war Central and Eastern Europe have changed in a similar direction to that in Western Europe, even if they also reflected some contradictions of family development. In all social groups, personal choice and romantic love had largely replaced instrumental criteria and parental influence when selecting a spouse by around the 1960s. Companionship and mutual support became the ideal of couples forming unions, or, to use Lawrence Stone's expression, the sentimentalization of family life prevailed.[170] The survival of some traditional elements of spouse selection could still be identified. A number of value surveys with a scope of international comparisons show that considerably more people in this region regarded the availability of material goods, such as good housing conditions, to be essential for a happy marriage in the early 1990s than in Western Europe. What is more, they considered mutual understanding and tolerance to be less important.[171]

After the system change, several observers claimed that a kind of patriarchal backlash took place in the Eastern societies of the continent. These arguments were based on changes in family law, as divorce and abortion were made more difficult in some countries (e.g. Poland).

---

167 Boh, 'European Family Life Patterns', 269.
168 Hartmut Kaelble, *A Social History of Western Europe, 1880–1980* (Dublin: Gill and Macmillan, 1990), 129; S. Harding, D. Philips and M. Fogarty, *Contrasting Values in Western Europe: Unity, Diversity and Change* (London: Macmillan, 1986), 120–29; Ronald Inglehart, Miguel Basanez and Alejandro Moreno, eds, *Human Values and Beliefs: A Cross-Cultural Sourcebook* (Ann Arbor, MI: University of Michigan Press, 1998), Tables V 198–V 210, V 223.
169 Alexander Szalai, ed., *The Use of Time: Daily Activities of Urban and Suburban Populations in Twelve Countries* (The Hague: Mouton, 1972), 643, 662.
170 Stone, *The Family, Sex, and Marriage*, 221–69.
171 Inglehart, Basanez and Moreno, *Human Values and Beliefs*, Tables V 198–V 210.

Irrespective of whether divorce and abortion regulations are a major indication of patriarchy, the legal changes pointing to the revival of patriarchy can be regarded as quite marginal. That is why G. Therborn, already referred to above, calls the period after the turn of the millennium the 'era of post-patriarchy', not only in Western Europe but in Central and Eastern Europe as well. Therborn's claim is substantiated by the fact that the legal autonomy of adult children from their parents, and that equal rights for men and women in the family have been realized. Yet, as has been pointed out above, this was not a truly novel development in Central and Eastern Europe, since these rights had been enacted decades before.

There are other signs of the growing equality in families in post-communist Central and Eastern Europe: the difference between the leisure time of men and women also decreased somewhat. In 2006, the free time of 20–74-year-old women amounted to 85 per cent of that of men of the same age in Poland, and to 84 per cent in Estonia, Hungary and Slovenia.[172] However, what is a significantly new and adverse development in this respect in the region is that income inequalities increased considerably after the system change – especially in the early 1990s – which also influenced gender gaps. As a result, women were less able to realize their legally guaranteed opportunities. In 2000, the average level of earnings by women reached only 61 per cent of men's in Poland, and 58 per cent in the Czech Republic, Hungary and Romania. However, this sizeable gender gap was still smaller than in most Western European countries.[173] What is more, the participation of women in the higher echelons of education increased as well, reaching a very high level in many countries of the Central and Eastern European region. Women comprised more than two thirds of all students in higher education in Poland and Hungary after the turn of the millennium. Consequently, the qualification level of women in the younger generations began to exceed that of men in these societies.

Although research on the history of childhood contributed greatly to the formation of modern family history as a discipline from the 1960s, European research has focused mostly on what childhood meant and how the situation of children changed in the seventeenth and eighteenth centuries.[174] Much less scholarly attention has been devoted to, and even fewer comparative studies written, on the twentieth century. Central and Eastern Europe appears to be a particularly blank spot in this respect. Still, the secular trend of the increasing attention paid to the education and well-being of children prevailed without interruption throughout the century.[175] This process was manifested in the intensification of governmental programmes and public institutions established in order to care for children – a case in point that will be discussed in the next chapter of the study. Notwithstanding the latter development, the century has nonetheless also witnessed the transformation of values, norms and social conceptions related to children.

Considering the family and public attitudes towards children, there were fewer differences between Central and Eastern Europe and other European regions than in other aspects of family history. Notwithstanding the fact that only a limited amount of comparative data are available from Central and Eastern Europe from the early twentieth century regarding cultural values

---

172 Judit Takács, "'Ha mosogatógép nem lenne, már elváltunk volna ... ' " Férfiak és nők otthoni munkamegosztása európai összehasonlításban' ['If there were no dishwasher, we would have already divorced ... ' – the division of household chores in a European comparison], *Esély* 19, no. 6 (2008): 52.
173 Therborn, *Between Sex and Power*, 128.
174 In addition to the studies by Philippe Ariès, see: Lloyd DeMause, ed., *The History of Childhood* (New York: Psychohistory Press, 1974); Stone, *The Family, Sex, and Marriage*; Shorter, *The Making of the Modern Family*; for a more recent publication, see Joseph M. Hawes and N. Ray Hiner, eds, *Children in Historical and Comparative Perspective* (New York: Greenwood Press, 1991).
175 Stone, *The Family, Sex, and Marriage*, 423.

related to children, it can be claimed that the major thrust of development was the growing appreciation of children's personality and autonomy.[176] In addressing the regulations of the husband–wife relationship in an earlier part of this study, numerous legal aspects of this transformation were already examined. However, there were a couple of legal developments which directly affected the status of children in family and society.[177]

Although ideas about childhood have changed considerably since the early modern period, and laws were passed to protect children in the nineteenth century, these measures mostly addressed child labour rather than the status of children within families. Thus, at the beginning of the twentieth century, children's rights did not exist in the sense in which they are understood today in any European countries.[178] Men and women did not have equal rights with regard to their children. Children born from an extramarital relationship were discriminated against without exception: children born inside or outside marriage did not have equal rights with regard to inheritance or paternity.[179] The most obvious manifestation of child discrimination was the common use of adjectives, such as 'illegitimate' and 'illicit', and usually not because of some worn-out legal tradition, but on the basis of fairly recent legislation.[180] Other legal considerations were more important than the interests of the children; for example, custody decisions in divorce cases were often made according to the guilt or lack thereof of the parties involved, and not based on the children's best interest. Also, children's personal integrity was not guaranteed legally, that is, corporal punishment by parents and guardians was not prohibited by law.

One can see astonishing differences when examining the changes of family law in Europe. Some of the Nordic countries pioneered the introduction of legal equality between spouses and between children born in and out of wedlock during the First World War. Only Scotland and England were able to catch up with them to a certain extent, when these countries changed their family laws in the interwar period. However, other Western European countries reached this level of legal development only in the 1970s and 1980s. As has already been pointed out, family law in communist countries also went through a considerable transformation in the early post-war years. The initial steps were set out to secure the equality of women in the family. New laws also greatly emphasized the need to protect children; last but not least, children born outside marriage were supposed to enjoy the same rights as those who were born within marriage. However, the communist system failed to realize what is known as the 'third generation of children's rights', that is, the rights to personal autonomy and personal integrity primarily manifested in 'non-spanking laws'. What is more, they were hardly enforced in Central and Eastern Europe in the 1990s. Only Latvia and Croatia prohibited all corporal punishment of children, the former in 1998 and the latter in 1999.[181]

Obviously, one has to be very careful when interpreting legal developments, because laws may be implemented in a different way in different societies, and popular behaviour

---

176 Linda Clark, 'France', in Hawes and Hiner, *Children in Historical and Comparative Perspective*, 294.
177 Göran Therborn, 'The Politics of Childhood: The Rights of Children in Modern Times', in Castles, *Families of Nations*, 241–91.
178 Colin Heywood, *A History of Childhood: Children and Childhood in the West from Medieval to Modern Times* (Cambridge: Polity Press, 2006), 39.
179 The lack of right to paternity meant that the name of the father was not required to be disclosed if the father decided not to identify himself.
180 Therborn, 'The Politics of Childhood', 255.
181 Peter Newell, 'Global Progress towards Giving Up the Habit of Hitting Children', in *The New Handbook of Children's Rights*, ed. Bob Franklin (London: Routledge, 2002), 374–87, here 382.

may not necessarily comply with regulations. This is all the more the case since research has shown smaller differences in attitudes to children than could be seen in the case of family law. Notwithstanding the lack of long-term comparative value studies for this area, value surveys conducted at the end of the twentieth century revealed considerable similarities in expectations towards children in all of Europe.[182]

According to the World Values Survey of the early 1990s, after the Second World War no distinct pattern of parenting values developed in Central and Eastern Europe, or even in East Central Europe. Czechoslovak parents regarded the independence of children as less important than any other Europeans surveyed. In contrast, Hungarian parents considered their roles and tasks to be fairly in line with what was surveyed in most of the Western European countries, encouraging children's autonomy and independence.[183] Some characteristics prevailed all over Europe, but in other cases an East-West divide was palpable. One could regard the emphasis on good manners as a shared European trait, but hard work and thrift were stressed more in Central and Eastern European countries than in most Western European ones, where tolerance mattered less than in Western Europe.[184] However, all in all, the Central and Eastern European patterns of parental attitudes towards raising children fit much better with Western European patterns than most of the other aspects of interpersonal relations in the family.[185]

Among the developments examined so far, two phenomena require explanation: first, why the dissolution of patriarchy showed its distinct dynamics; second, why the sentimentalization of family relations and the change in attitudes to children in Central and Eastern Europe fit better with European trends than most of the other developments in family history.

As has been shown, patriarchy followed a peculiar dynamic in Central and Eastern Europe: in the first half of the century, slow changes unfolded and then gained momentum. A number of social and economic shifts that ensued in the second half of the nineteenth century and in the first decades of the twentieth century eroded patriarchy all over the continent. As a result of industrialization, the place of work separated from the household, thus undermining paternal power. Industrialization regularly brought about proletarianization, leading to the growth of non-propertied classes, and thus the transfer of family properties to the next generation lost much of its significance as a means of parental control. Urbanization also weakened patriarchal norms and several other kinds of traditional authority, since social control is more difficult to practise in an urban environment. As a matter of fact, industrialization and urbanization started to develop long before the twentieth century in the Central and Eastern European region as well, but accelerated noticeably in the twentieth century, and especially in the second half of the century. The expansion of the welfare functions of the state was a further factor. The introduction of compulsory schooling removed children from the parental household and from the rule of the father for a considerable time.[186] Normative and ideological challenges to patriarchy originated from diverse directions, only a few of which can be touched upon briefly here. In Central and Eastern Europe, the socialist labour movement played the most

---

182 Harding, Philips and Fogarty, *Contrasting Values in Western Europe*, 19–24; Inglehart, Basanez and Moreno, *Human Values and Beliefs*, Tables V 226–V 236.
183 Inglehart, Basanez and Moreno, *Human Values and Beliefs*, Table V 227.
184 Ibid., Tables V 224–V 236; for similar results of another, more limited survey, see Rossella Palompa and Hein Moors, 'Attitudes towards Marriage, Children, and Population Policies in Europe', in *Population, Family and Welfare: A Comparative Survey of European Attitudes*, vol. 1, eds Rossella Palompa and Hein Moors (Oxford: Clarendon Press, 1995), 245–53.
185 Takács, '"Ha mosogatógép nem lenne, már elváltunk volna ..."', 66–9.
186 Therborn, *Between Sex and Power*, 22–3.

significant role ideologically, and especially during the years of Stalinism, communist countries imported ideological blueprints and role models from the Soviet Union. The figure of Aleksandra Kollontay was presented in the official discourse as the archetype of the 'modern socialist woman' throughout the region.

However, in the first half of the century several social and economic processes supported the survival of patriarchy as well. These socio-economic developments originated in part from processes similar to those that led to the dissolution of patriarchy. Three of them will be highlighted here. On the one hand, the working class was increasingly recruited from men as a result of the relative decline of the textile industry towards the end of the nineteenth century. The expanding manufacturing industry required such devotion from the labour force – for example, regarding working schedules – that it was difficult for married women or women with children to comply. Moreover, while proletarianization was often accompanied by pauperization and the dissolution of families in the first phase of the industrial revolution, by the beginning of the twentieth century the majority of the working class had enough income to be able to imitate the middle-class family model in both Western Europe and the industrial centres of Central and Eastern Europe. The 'male breadwinner' model was increasingly a reality.[187] The earlier stages of industrial revolution witnessed working-class families adopting a strategy of aggregating the incomes of its members – husband, wife and children – but by the beginning of the twentieth century they tended to rely on the income of the husband/father. This was because incomes were generally increased and laws regarding child- and female-labour were regulated and restricted. Finally, the normative patterns of societies were also instrumental for the survival of patriarchy. It had such programmatic representations as the 1891 Encyclical of Leo XIII (*Rerum novarum*), which – besides its social messages – explicitly defended patriarchal arrangements in the family. Visions of the ideal family prevailing in the middle class and the working class were also crucial in supporting patriarchy: this family type had the providing family man at its centre, be he a small proprietor, an entrepreneur, or a respectable worker. The followers of the male breadwinner model enjoyed social prestige and recognition.[188]

The rapid changes of the mid-century can be explained primarily by political and ideological developments. The emancipation of women was one of the important traditions of the nineteenth-century labour movement and the reception of the Soviet model, and thus communist parties that gained power promoted the reform of family law. However, social and economic changes in the region also furthered these efforts. As has been pointed out above, the acceleration of industrialization and urbanization undermined paternal control. After the Second World War, the advance of wage labour played a considerably greater role in Central and Eastern Europe, when the self-employed strata were destroyed almost completely by collectivization, not only in industry and the third sector, but also in agriculture in most countries of the region. Full employment and increasingly generous welfare benefits helped women become financially independent, although the effect of several elements of the pronatalist policies was often contradictory or even adverse as far as gender roles were concerned. Moreover, the male breadwinner family rapidly disappeared from Central and Eastern Europe after the Second World War. On the one hand, female employment grew into a socially encouraged activity amidst a general labour shortage; on the other, the generally low incomes also compelled wives and mothers to work.

---

187 Angélique Janssens, 'The Rise and Decline of the Male Breadwinner Family? An Overview of the Debate', *International Review of Social History* 42 (1997): supplement, 1–23.
188 Therborn, *Between Sex and Power*, 23–4.

The second question raised earlier asked why some tendencies of Central and Eastern European family development – most notably the sentimentalization of family life and the emergence of the so-called 'child-centred family' – took place in a manner largely similar to what proceeded in Western Europe. The answer lies primarily in the relative significance of causal factors. Intimacy and the materialization of child-centredness in family were largely initiated by demographic developments – especially changes in fertility and the transformation of household structure – as well as by shifts in the functions of the family. And indeed, regarding the latter changes, one can identify considerable and increasing similarities between Central and Eastern Europe and the rest of the continent.

The influence of demographic factors on family life is quite obvious. The shrinking size of households and the change in their composition led to households transforming into domestic units, which normally took the form of nuclear families. The disappearance of servants, lodgers and kin from the households, accompanied by the decline in mortality and the shortening of the phase of childbearing, also stabilized the new family composition. Consequently, the stability of the family structure provided a firm basis all over Europe for strengthening attitudes peculiar to the modern nuclear family, such as intimacy and attention paid to the welfare of the children.[189]

The alteration of family functions also greatly contributed to family changes. The traditional peasant household was a unit of subsistence, since it provided the fundamental framework for labour organization. Although economic differentiation in pre-industrial times had already transformed the system of family production, it was the process of industrialization that made the economic functions of the traditional family obsolete all over Europe. Its dynamics and consequences have already been touched upon. With the abandonment of economic functions, family members gained greater freedom to choose their roles and to opt for their occupations, as well as their desired spouse. The separation of the home and the workplace also enabled family members to enlarge their scope of activities and to lead their own lives. Because patrilocality was exchanged for neo-locality in the case of newly married couples, they also gained greater freedom to establish privacy in their own families.

As a result of the retreat of production from households, two additional functions were able to become central to family life: securing emotional support for the adult members of the family, and the socialization of children.[190] The loss of functions also allowed the family to emerge as a place of privacy, and generally can be associated with the rise of specific social strata during the twentieth century, namely salaried employees and the new middle class. The loss of functions also explains why the modern nuclear family was eventually able to develop into a virtually universal type by the second half of the twentieth century all over Europe, and why Central and Eastern Europe participated intensively in this development.

The state and the family

Family policy is a branch of governmental social policies that targets the well-being or behaviour of families, particularly families with children. It usually aims to support them, to improve their internal cohesion and their capacity to care for dependent members, as well as to fulfil their reproductive functions. Thus, family policy may assume several forms, including legal or financial intervention, as well as provision or support of services that advance policy objectives.

---

189 Mitterauer and Sieder, *The European Family*, 70–92.
190 See, for example Talcott Parsons, *Structure and Process in Modern Societies* (Glencoe: Free Press, 1960), 302; Mitterauer and Sieder, *The European Family*, 78–90.

As legislation directly affecting family life in twentieth-century Central and Eastern Europe has already been addressed earlier in the chapter, family policy will be dealt with here in its narrower sense: cash benefits for families, maternity leave and child-care services as well as reproductive policies.

In the nineteenth century, the problems related to population and family development claimed relatively little attention from politicians all over Europe, aside from France. However, this indifference changed considerably after the First World War when a fall in fertility, accompanied by fears of family decline, led to significant state intervention in a number of European countries.[191]

In the first half of the century, Hungary stood out in the Central and Eastern European region for its pronatalist family policy. The Industrial Law introduced maternity leave in Hungary back in 1884, while Poland, for example, did so only in 1933. From 1912, Hungarian civil servants were granted a family allowance, a very early social policy measure in international comparison. Afterwards all workers in manufacturing were involved in the programme in 1938, albeit with much lower benefits.[192] In contrast, a family allowance was introduced in Poland and other countries of the region only after the Second World War.[193] The development of child-care services showed similar characteristics. Hungarian governments had initiated the development of day-care services in industrial regions back at the turn of the century. In 1930, approximately 30 per cent of children from the relevant age groups had access to this programme, and just about the same number of them attended nursery schools.[194] In the same period, Poland had hardly any form of state organized and funded day-care service. Instead, day care for children was organized by the family, and by the church and local communities. It might have been functionally equivalent to the state system, but it undoubtedly was dispersed more accidentally across the country, and subsequently far fewer children attended nursery schools in Poland in the interwar period than in Hungary.

These differences cannot be regarded as the result of a more generous state welfare activity in Hungary or a more low-profile social policy in Poland. The activity of the Polish state was quite significant in a number of other fields of welfare, including social security schemes, and Poland also pioneered the introduction of paid leave in Europe. The difference could be explained rather by the fact that demographic problems came to the foreground of public interest relatively early in Hungary. It created a particularly great stir in the 1920s and 1930s that the 'only child' system started to spread not only in cities, but also in peasant communities of certain regions.[195] Though the public discourse focused primarily on the danger of population decline, it also made the general public and the governments sensitive to the social status of children and mothers. In other words, in line with and advanced by pronatalism, various other policies related to families also developed. There is no doubt that these early interwar measures

---

191 Anne Hélène Gauthier, *The State and the Family: A Comparative Analysis of Family Policies in Industrialized Countries* (Oxford: Oxford University Press, 1996), 50–58, 73–82.
192 István Hoóz, *Népesedéspolitika és népességfejlődés Magyarországon a két világháború között* [Population policy and population change in interwar Hungary] (Budapest: Akadémiai Kiadó, 1970), 161.
193 Dorottya Szikra, 'Családtámogatások Európában történeti perspektívában' [Family benefit programmes in Europe in a historical perspective], in *Családpolitikák változóban*, ed. Ágnes Simonyi (Budapest: Szociálpolitikai és Munkaügyi Intézet, 2010), 14.
194 Szikra, 'Családtámogatások Európában történeti perspektívában', 30–33.
195 Rudolf Andorka, 'Az ormánsági születéskorlátozás története [The history of birth control in the Ormánság region]', *Valóság* 12, no. 6 (1975): 45–61.

gave life to such traditions, which influenced family policy in Central and Eastern Europe after the Second World War as well.

The following four major characteristics of family policy can be highlighted in the postwar decades of Central and Eastern Europe: first, family policy had a distinct dynamic in most countries of the region – in the beginning, it often applied repressive measures and afterwards it became more permissive. However, the development was far from linear, which generated considerable fluctuations of fertility in the region. Second, family policy became much more potent in the region from the mid-1960s. In most of the countries positive incentives were preferred, but there were examples for exceedingly repressive pronatalist measures. Growing state interventions further heightened the volatility of fertility. Third, one of the distinctive features of the region's population history during communism was that the regulation of abortion gained great significance among family policy measures. Finally, it was striking that services, primarily child day care, became pre-eminently important tools of family policy in Central and Eastern Europe, although their significance diverged in the region.

Family policy in the first half of the 1950s relied primarily on restrictions and disciplinary measures in Central and Eastern Europe. In Hungary, for example, with the fairly long pronatalist traditions referred to above, the government banned abortion in 1953 – starting in 1954 the restrictions were eased, and abortion was fully legalized in the year 1957 – and introduced what was called the 'bachelor tax' levied on single men (but not women) above a certain age. At the same time, it paid relatively little attention to other aspects of family policy: the establishment of crèches and kindergartens was left up to factories and plants, and the burden of bringing up the children remained mostly on the families.[196] The rest of Central and Eastern Europe was characterized mainly by a combination of a disciplinary approach to family life on the one hand, and relatively moderate family policy efforts on the other. However, the end of High Stalinism brought about changes in this respect as well, and the disciplinary measures were gradually eased. As a sign of the latter, between 1955 and 1960 induced abortion was liberalized in full, and divorce laws were eased in most of the region.

Unlike Western Europe, Central and Eastern Europe did not experience a baby boom; instead, the increase of fertility lasted only a short period after the Second World War. By around 1960, fertility decreased in the region, except for Poland, Albania, and Yugoslavia, providing for only simple reproduction, or even declining below this level. This is why the stimulation of births with pronatalist policy measures became part of the agenda of governments in several countries.

As suggested earlier, the increase in population policy activity prevailed in the region in the 1960s, but pronatalism assumed different forms: in some countries, incentives dominated; in other states, repressive, prohibitory steps were preferred.[197] The main followers of the former path were Hungary and Czechoslovakia.

The Hungarian governments embarked on an active family policy from the mid-1960s. In 1965, the sum of family allowance was significantly raised – for families with two children it was tripled, followed by further increases in the 1970s. In 1967, the government introduced three-year paid maternity leave (*gyes*), which was considered a ground-breaking welfare programme in the region. Besides pronatalist aims, other factors also played a role in this measure.

---

196 Éva Bicskei, 'Our Greatest Treasure, the Child: The Politics of Care in Hungary, 1945–1956', *Social Politics* 13, no. 2 (2006): 151–88.
197 Milos Macura, 'Population Policies in Socialist Countries of Europe', *Population Studies* 28, no. 3 (1974): 369–79.

The market economy reforms ('New Economic Mechanism'), which were already in planning by this time and implemented in 1968, were expected by decision makers to greatly increase economic efficiency; subsequently, they also reckoned with an upsurge in unemployment. Therefore, keeping a part of the women's workforce at home with the help of maternity leave seemed to be a logical step. Later, maternity leave was extended even further with the so-called 'maternity grant' (*gyed*) in 1985, which, instead of a lump-sum benefit, gave mothers an allowance linked to their last salaries until the child was 18 months old. Thus, it intended to provide families with higher incomes an incentive to have children.[198]

From the late 1960s in Czechoslovakia, population policy had developed in the same direction as in Hungary. After a short boom, fertility in Czechoslovakia began to fall in the early 1950s, and first hit bottom in 1962. Although thereafter fertility increased for a short period, the total fertility rate was only 2.01 in 1968, that is, it fell below the level necessary for simple reproduction in the long run. In 1968, significant cash benefits were introduced for families with children, and the level of existing benefits was also increased. The family allowance was raised considerably, which by the early 1970s became the highest compared to average industrial wages, not only in Central and Eastern Europe, but on the entire continent. In 1972, the benefit for families with two children reached 22 per cent of the average monthly industrial wage; for three children, 45.1 per cent, and for four children it amounted to an impressive 65.5 per cent.[199] The government introduced 35 weeks of paid maternity leave, during which the mother earned 90 per cent of her previous income. In addition, mothers could apply for maternity benefit for up to two years starting in 1970. In 1979, the average sum of this benefit was 19.4 per cent of the average industrial wage for one child, and 31 per cent for two children. The government also introduced a significant reduction in personal income tax in relation to the number of dependent children. Finally, starting in 1973 young married couples could acquire loans with preferential interest rates, amounting to approximately the average annual family income. When a child was born, a previously defined amount of the debt was remitted. Along with other minor family and maternity benefits, these programmes amounted to approximately seven per cent of state budgetary expenditures. If in-kind benefits – like free nurseries and subsidized meals in schools – were added to this figure, it would have amounted to more than 10 per cent of the state budget in the mid-1970s. After the population policy measures were introduced in Czechoslovakia in 1968, fertility initially increased strongly, but soon declined, and in 1982 the total fertility rate was back to only 2.2. So, in 1984 the state increased benefits again, which had considerably decreased in relative value in the meantime.[200]

Positive incentives dominated family policy in Poland as well, but Polish family policy was less vigorous than the Hungarian or the Czechoslovak programmes. The Polish government also extended maternity leave in 1968; however, this allowance was unpaid. In 1981 the state introduced paid maternity leave nonetheless, but only for families with incomes below an established threshold. In contrast, the Bulgarian government combined restrictions on induced abortion in 1967 with quite generous additional measures. As a result of reforms, the sum of

---

198 Tárkányi Ákos, 'Európai családpolitikák: A magyar családpolitika története [European family policies: the history of family policy in Hungary]', *Demográfia* 41, no. 2–3 (1998): 233–68.
199 Rudolf Andorka and György Vukovich, 'A népesedéspolitika elvi és elméleti kérdései' [Theoretical aspects of population policy], in *A népesedés és a népesedéspolitika*, ed. Kálmán Kulcsár (Budapest: Kossuth Kiadó, 1983), 184.
200 Rudolf Andorka, *Gyermekszám a fejlett országokban* [Family size in the advanced countries] (Budapest: Gondolat, 1987), 193–4.

family allowance paid after the third child increased in particular. Moreover, the sum of paid maternity leave was increased, and from 1973 it was extended to six months after the birth of the first child.[201]

One of the most repressive pronatalist policies in modern population history was introduced in Romania in 1966; all in all, it lasted until 1989. The number of births reached a somewhat higher level in Romania after the war than in Czechoslovakia and Hungary. In the second half of the 1950s, however, fertility began to decrease here as well, which was undoubtedly facilitated by the full liberalization of abortions in 1958. By 1966 the total fertility rate had already fallen to 1.90. Then the Romanian government's drastic legislation banned induced abortion for all women apart from some minor exceptions, for example, those who had already given birth to four or more children, or were older than 45 (later 40) or had serious health conditions. At the same time, the government stopped the production and import of contraceptives, and they also prohibited the sale of these products. Moreover, efforts were made for the surveillance of pregnancies to prevent their termination. Women of a fertile age were examined at their workplaces on a mass scale to determine whether they had been pregnant and to ensure they would not abort illegally. What is more, the Romanian government launched a propaganda campaign in which motherhood was depicted as a 'noble patriotic duty'. Mothers who gave birth to several children were awarded decorations including the orders of 'Heroine Mother', 'Maternal Glory' and 'Medal of Maternity'.[202] They even levied taxes on men and women over 25 who did not have a child – however, this policy was also known in other countries, although they had a more lenient system to collect them. In addition, several positive incentives were also introduced, like an increase in family allowance differentiated according to the place of residence (town/village) or the level of income.

The new population policy measures came into effect immediately in Romania, so couples had no opportunity to prepare for them. Consequently, fertility increased threefold in a couple of months. Yet this magnitude of fertility change was temporary: fertility barely exceeded the previous level in 1973, and by 1984 it had fallen right back to the 1966 level. In line with the fertility decline, the number of abortions induced for health reasons increased to a very high level. Therefore, the party leadership launched a new political campaign in 1984: it scathingly criticized overtly permissive health-care institutions and pressed party and state organizations to implement the party's directive on this matter.

These measures in themselves were not unique in the post-war history of communist countries. For example, the prohibition of abortion also existed in Hungary between 1953 and 1956. Moreover, the Hungarian government, too, rewarded mothers with orders and medals between 1951 and 1957. What made the Romanian case unique was that pronatalist measures were introduced after the period of High Stalinism, lasted for a much longer time than elsewhere in the region, comprised a complex and fairly consistent system and, finally, were often implemented with more prevalent force than elsewhere.

This is why the criminalization of abortion, as long as contraception was unavailable, had several dramatic consequences. Women resorted to illegal abortion, which entailed considerable health risks. If they suffered complications, they were often refused emergency medical assistance unless they revealed the names of those who had performed the illegal abortion.[203]

---

201 Robert J. McIntyre, 'Pronatalist Programmes in Eastern Europe', *Soviet Studies* 27, no. 3 (1975): 366–80, here 374–6.
202 Gail Klingman, 'The Politics of Reproduction in Ceausescu's Romania: A Case Study in Political Culture', *East European Politics and Societies* 6 (1992): 364–418.
203 Thomas J. Keil and Viviana Andreescu, 'Fertility Policy in Ceausescu's Romania', *Journal of Family History* 24 (1999): 478–92.

Those women who were able to acquire contraceptives on the black market were primarily better-off and more educated women who knew how to use the pill; thus, the measures affected lower-status women more extensively. Moreover, child negligence and abandonment, as well as international adoptions, were among the social outcomes that were highly publicized in the Western media after 1989.

It has already been pointed out as one of the peculiarities of population policy in the region that the regulation of induced abortion gained much greater significance than elsewhere on the continent. This characteristic can be explained by the fact that induced abortions, where allowed, became the major means of birth control throughout communist countries in the postwar era. However, the actual practice of abortion policy diverged greatly over specific countries and periods. As has been shown, the Romanian government introduced very strict, prohibitive measures on abortion in 1966. In contrast, in Poland and in the Baltic republics of the USSR, the laws concerning induced abortion – which had been accepted at the end of the 1950s and made fully available – were not changed. The possibility of choosing induced abortion was only somewhat restricted in Czechoslovakia, Hungary and Bulgaria in the 1960s and 1970s (Table 5.12).

Irrespective of whether induced abortion was regulated in a permissive way or in a more prohibitory manner, it had a fundamental impact on reproduction, as the reported levels of legally induced abortion in the region were among the highest in international comparisons between 1960 and 1990.[204] Moreover, it has been assumed that the true incidence of abortion in some states, such as Albania, Romania and Yugoslavia, was significantly higher than was officially recorded. Only a few industrial countries in the world – Japan in the early 1950s, Cuba since the mid-1960s and, most of all, the Soviet Union from the 1950s – reached this level of induced abortion. The high Central and Eastern European levels of abortion have been explained by competing interpretations in the past and in recent scholarship as well. According to the 'low-cost-of-abortion' interpretation, the high level of abortion in the region between

Table 5.12 Abortion rates in Central and Eastern European countries, 1960–1996 (induced abortions per 1,000 women aged 15–44)

Country	1960	1970	1980	1990	1996
Estonia		131.5	110.7	87.9	53.6
Latvia		123.0	107.8	87.2	46.1
Lithuania		63.4	59.3	61.7	34.0
Poland	24.2	19.9	16.7	7.0	0.06
Czech R.	35.7	34.2	32.2	49.3	20.6
Slovakia	25.1	28.2	28.7	40.9	17.2
Hungary	76.7	83.5	36.3	41.2	34.5
Romania	186.1	64.0	90.2	199.3	90.2
Yugoslavia				70.7	44.9
Bulgaria	29.0	63.2	76.7	67.8	51.3
Albania				28.4	35.8

Note: Different year for Yugoslavia, 1991/1995.

Source: Henry P. David, 'Overview', in Henry P. David, ed., *From Abortion to Contraception: A Resource to Public Policies and Reproductive Behaviour in Central and Eastern Europe from 1917 to the Present* (Westport, CT: Greenwood Press, 1999), 14.

---

204 Henry P. David, 'Abortion in Europe, 1920–91: A Public Health Perspective', *Studies in Family Planning* 23, no. 1 (1992): 1–22.

1955 and 1960, that is, before the spread of modern methods of contraception, was the result of liberalized abortion laws. These laws and the practices created in their wake institutionalized induced abortion as an important, or perhaps the most significant means of birth control.[205] Another explanation, the 'high-costs-of-contraceptives' approach, maintains that the political will to disseminate other methods of birth control was lacking in the region. This is why methods other than abortion were hardly available, or only prohibitively expensive.[206] The two explanations are not mutually exclusive and equally plausible, but they are not the only factors that played a role in the emergence of the Central and Eastern European 'abortion culture'.[207] Cultural factors include the educational level of the population, and more specifically the neglect of sex education, as well as cultural norms related to reproduction. The significance of the latter are attested by the fact that the number of births decreased dramatically in Western Europe after the mid-1960s, mostly as a result of using traditional birth control methods (and not the pill or intrauterine devices that were widely used only starting in the 1970s in Western Europe), and without resorting to abortion as much as the Central and Eastern European population. Consequently, if preferences and attitudes had been different, the Central and Eastern European population would have also been able to avoid unwanted pregnancies by applying traditional methods and thus keep the number of abortions at a lower level.

When addressing the positive incentives of family policy, primarily cash benefits have been touched upon so far. However, the relative development of in-kind benefits, that is, services given to families with children, was a further characteristic of family policies in Central and Eastern Europe. These forms of support were mostly extended from the 1960s as well.

As has already been shown, the early communist governments had greatly encouraged the employment of women: this policy was demanded by the developmental model based on extensive growth and the shortage of labour, and it meant a kind of female emancipation strategy as well. If the government wanted to ensure that women did not have to choose between the workplace and the family, then the establishment and extension of early childhood care facilities were indispensable. Most of all, it affected children who were of kindergarten age, because in the case of younger children the view prevailed that it was better for them to stay at home with their mother or with other members of the larger family. Furthermore, crèches mainly served the safekeeping of children; kindergartens, however, were also sites of indoctrination, where children were raised and socialized to become good socialist citizens. The number and capacity of crèches therefore remained limited, with coverage ranging from 5 per cent (Poland, Romania) to 12–16 per cent (Czechoslovakia, Bulgaria, and Hungary) even in the 1980s. The Baltic Soviet republics were an exception, where, for example in Latvia, crèches admitted half of the children in the appropriate age group even in the 1980s. In contrast, the enrolment of children between three and six in day care was relatively high in most of the communist countries, although significant differences also remained up to the very last years of the communist period. For instance, the percentage of children attending day-care institutions in Poland lagged far behind the respective Hungarian levels. While approximately half of Polish

---

205 Henry P. David and Robert J. McIntyre, *Reproductive Behavior: Central and Eastern European Experience* (New York: Springer, 1981), 16.
206 P. Mazur, 'Contraception and Abortion in Poland', *Family Planning Perspectives* 13 (1981): 195–8.
207 Libor Stloukal, 'Understanding the "Abortion Culture" in Central and Eastern Europe', in *From Abortion to Contraception: A Resource to Public Policies and Reproductive Behaviour in Central and Eastern Europe from 1917 to the Present*, ed. Henry P. David (Westport, CT: Greenwood Press, 1999), 23–37, here 24.

children aged between three and six attended kindergartens, 90 per cent of their Hungarian counterparts did so.[208]

When examining the results of Central and Eastern European population policy in the period after the Second World War, it can be seen that interventions were able to achieve a large-scale increase in fertility rates in the short run, either with repressive methods or with positive financial incentives. However, these changes were not lasting: fertility often boomed for only one or two years after the implementation of pronatalist measures, and then returned to the earlier trends. Consequently, these policies resulted in one of the peculiar characteristics of the post-war Central and Eastern European demographic regimes, which was the often-hectic movement of fertility levels. The impact of population policies was much more moderate in the long run. The pronatalist measures rarely led to the birth of a third child in Central and Eastern European families, where at that time the number of children typically desired was two. Instead, they resulted in the first or the second child being born earlier, and thus the average number of children born in a woman's life changed only slightly. Even in Romania, what is called 'cohort fertility' increased only slightly. Here, the average number of children born to a woman was around 2.3 in female cohorts born in the 1930s. In the cohorts born in the 1940s, which became the main target group of population policy after 1966, the fertility rate achieved was 2.4–2.5.[209] Although these measures did not bring about resounding effects, it can still be plausibly claimed that without these steps fertility would have been even lower. Even if one considers the fact that in the meantime fertility would have probably decreased in compliance with the general European trends, the most drastic Romanian pronatalist measures were able to increase cohort fertility by only 10–20 per cent.

As to the effects of specific population policy alternatives, as has been noted by Rudolf Andorka, Romanian population policy, with its draconian measures and with high social costs, ultimately achieved the same moderate fertility growth from the end of the 1960s as the Czechoslovak policy of sizeable positive incentives.[210] Thereby, the Romanian case not only serves as an example of the repressive population policy, but also shows its limitations. In addition, it demonstrates how the population was able to adapt to such policies and put forward their own preferences despite them, in other words, to evade the strong interventions of population policy.

These developments were more or less known to the Central and Eastern European population experts of the period as well as to the wider public, but the intensity and character of public discourse about population issues differed considerably in the region. Drawing conclusions by academics and publicizing them was determined by the fact that demographic research was among those social sciences most closely controlled by politics in all Central and Eastern European countries. The latter was also the case because relevant surveys were usually conducted by statistical offices, which were part of the state bureaucracy. Thus, professional discourses were differentiated in the region, depending on the extent to which governments allowed scholars to research autonomously, or the kind of population policy they pursued. Romanian demographers emphasized the fertility growth already achieved from the 1960s. Experts in Czechoslovakia, and even more so in Hungary, stressed that emergency measures raised the resistance of the population, and that the population would sooner or later find a

---

208 Dorota Szelewa and Michal Polakowski, 'Who Cares? Patterns of Care in Central and Eastern Europe', *Journal of European Social Policy* 18, no. 2 (2008): 115–31.
209 Andorka, *Gyermekszám a fejlett országokban*, 197.
210 Ibid., 197–8.

way to elude them. They also emphasized that, on the other hand, positive incentives increase the number of children planned and desired, that is, they stimulate the change in norms and values in relation to children, and therefore are more effective in the long run. As seen earlier, this proposition was only partly supported by the actual population development of post-war Central and Eastern Europe.

After the fall of communism, family policy, too, underwent transformations in Central and Eastern Europe. In this field, however, as in the case of the entire welfare system, the changes were more moderate overall than those affecting the economic and political systems. One of the important directions of early reforms was to restructure entitlement to family allowance and other family benefits, which had been based on employment in the communist systems. These reforms, executed in the aftermath of the system change, were guided by the principle of universalism. Similar remodelling was also realized in other fields of the welfare system, aiming to compensate for the loss of job security and to lower the social costs of the transformation crises.

However, by the mid-1990s fiscal problems and the policy recommendations of international agencies, most notably the IMF and the World Bank pursuing the Washington consensus, as well as internal political forces favouring neo-liberal policy solutions, drove several countries in the region to introduce means-testing for family benefits. The argument on which these policies were based was that means-testing allows the scarce resources available to be channelled to low-income families. However, the exclusion of significant parts of the middle class from these programmes gradually led to an erosion of the real value of benefits, since governments were no longer compelled by strong middle-class constituencies to raise benefits regularly in times of galloping inflation. This policy solution had a further consequence, namely that women with lower incomes stayed at home to take care of their children, so that their children were not able to participate in early childhood education. In other words, it was not only labour market segmentation that emerged, but a selective approach to day care as well. From that point on policies concerning family benefits diverged in the region. Poland, the Czech Republic, Slovakia and Bulgaria opted for targeting such schemes and applying income-testing, while a more universal approach prevailed in Estonia, Latvia, Hungary, Romania and Slovenia, where some schemes were universal, and others were based on social insurance.[211]

Besides divergence, strong volatility also emerged in several countries. Different political forces often could not arrive at a consensus about welfare policy. Therefore, successive changes of governments usually also meant rapid shifts in the direction of family policy. In Hungary, for example, it was the socialist-led government that cut back social rights including family benefits in 1995, while the government regarded as conservative restored universal entitlements, which is a textbook example of social democratic welfare principles. Romania and the Baltic states also returned to a universal family allowance after various excursions. In addition, the dramatic fall in the number of births throughout the region, which was often coupled with mass-scale emigration, made the public as well as the decision makers receptive to pronatalism. Thus, governments in Hungary, Estonia and even in Poland granted greater benefits to larger families.

In the wake of these changes, day-care coverage dropped in the region, particularly in crèches, where enrolment rates amounted to 10 per cent or less by 2010 – with the exception of some Baltic republics. Kindergarten enrolment was less affected: after the initial decline the numbers stabilized, which was greatly enhanced by the fact that fertility fell in parallel. A further

---

211 Tina Rostgaard, *Family Support Policy in Central and Eastern Europe – A Decade and a Half of Transition* (Early Childhood and Family Policy Series, No. 8) (Paris: UNESCO, 2004), 34.

reason for the initial decrease was that when unemployment boomed it was no longer vital for many parents to send their children to nursery schools, as they could take care of them themselves. This conformed to a general opinion also dominantly voiced in the media, maintaining that families could look after their children better, especially at the early ages when they would otherwise attend crèches.

The emphasis of family policies also shifted from services to cash benefits.[212] While daycare institutions lost their importance in most countries, maternity entitlements still remained relatively generous in Central and Eastern Europe, even after the system change. On the one hand, this can be regarded as the legacy of the communist system; on the other hand, it also represented the efforts of newly elected, democratic governments. Without doubt, a normative shift took place in the policies of several countries – such as Poland – which began to favour both strengthening traditional gender roles and keeping child-care in the home. More importantly, governments in the Czech Republic, Hungary and Slovenia realized that safeguarding and improving maternity benefits expanded the possibilities of families to choose among various family and employment strategies. These relatively generous programmes enabled mothers to choose between employment plus day care or raising their children at home. According to the mainstream gender approach, being a stay-at-home mother was detrimental to emancipation, as it serves to reinforce traditional gender roles. However, a great number of women in the region, often struggling with the double burden of employment and family commitments or facing the unavailability of pre-school education for their children, opted for maternity leave.

Real choice is available for parents only if the services of child-care facilities and maternity leave as well as child allowances are all provided at a relatively high level. Nevertheless, this was not the case to the same extent in all Central and Eastern European countries. As Dorota Szelewa and Michal Polakowski have already shown, child-care institutions and child-care allowances as well as maternity benefits were easily accessible and comparatively high in Hungary and Lithuania after the turn of the millennium. The policy mix in Estonia and Latvia, in contrast, served to mobilize the female labour force, because the number of families using child-care services was high, but the conditions of maternity leave were less favourable. Several countries – the Czech Republic, Slovakia, and Slovenia – were characterized by 'explicit familiarism', as child-care policies supported taking care of the children within the family, since crèches and nursery schools were only available in a restricted way, but generous paid maternity leave was granted. Finally, Poland was characterized by 'implicit familiarism', because all branches of family policy were residual, that is, at low capacity, such that the government stimulated neither the employment of women nor home child-care explicitly. In other words, they eventually put the responsibility of taking care of children onto families.[213]

---

212 Béla Tomka, 'The Politics of Institutionalized Volatility: Lessons from East Central European Welfare Reforms', in *Fighting Poverty and Reforming Social Security: What Can Post-Soviet States Learn from New Democracies in Central Europe?* ed. Tomasz Inglot (Washington, DC: Woodrow Wilson Center, 2007), 67–85.

213 Szelewa and Polakowski, 'Who Cares? Patterns of Care in Central and Eastern Europe', 115–31; see also Dorottya Szikra, 'Tradition Matters: Childcare, Preschool, and Primary Education in Modern Hungary', in *Children, Families, and States: Time Policies of Childcare, Preschool, and Primary Education in Europe*, eds Karen Hagemann, Konrad H. Jarausch and Cristina Allemann-Ghionda (New York: Berghahn, 2011), 364–84.

Conclusion

If we seek to periodize the twentieth century as analyzed in this chapter, obviously there are long-term transformations that can be interpreted mainly as a transition between premodern to modern or perhaps postmodern society. Typical examples are the reduction in fertility rates, increasing life expectancy, the nuclearization of families, increasing equality in the family, the sentimentalization of family life, the prevalence of divorce, and increasing state intervention in families and populations. However, in most European countries, and especially in Central and Eastern Europe, there are ruptures, mainly political, which divide the twentieth century into epochs with different demographic and family patterns. Those ruptures had a huge impact on family and population history. In particular, both world wars affected birth rates, and caused a fall in population due to war casualties, genocides and expulsions. They also affected marriage rates and the norms of family life.

Besides the years 1918, 1945 and 1989, we often find an important division between what we can call early and late socialism. While in the first two decades the societies experienced great progress in terms of mortality, from the late 1960s we can see various crisis phenomena, which either existed in the West as well and can therefore be called the general crisis of high modernity or emerged only in the Soviet bloc and thus can be called the crisis of state socialism. The increase in lifestyle diseases and divorce belongs to the first group. Specific Eastern crisis phenomena included the rising rates of abortion, declines in male life expectancy and rising emigration from the region to the West. In their early stages, the state-socialist regimes were progressive in these respects, but as they were unable to continue this course from the 1970s on, Western Europe became the pioneer in family policy. Examples of Eastern traits include legislation on births (abortion commissions still existed in the Eastern bloc countries during the 1970s and 1980s, and Romania banned abortions), the persistence of legislation discriminating against homosexuals, and lags in adopting liberal models of child rearing.

Along with the world wars, the changes of 1989 are considered to be the most crucial turning point of the century. This turning point can be interpreted as overcoming the crisis of socialist modernity and the start of convergence with several Western trends (postponing the age for marriage and childbirth, the disappearance of high abortion rates, public discussions on gender rights and homosexual marriages – including the right to raise children - the promotion of Western standards in parenting, abolishing barriers to migration, and from the mid-1990s on the renewed rise in life expectancy). On the other hand, post-socialism also meant the occurring of new crisis phenomena: most importantly, the fall in fertility and rising out-migration, which reached quite significant levels in certain countries.

After 2000, we see the continuation of some trends (the decline in marriage rates and the growing number of births outside marriage), while some trends reversed or slowed down (the decline in the birth rate), and in some we find conflicting tendencies (family policy). Due to the inspiration of the EU, some new legislation was enacted (e.g. on gay rights) and out-migration increased even further after accession to the EU, exacerbated by the financial crisis after 2008.

Most major monographs on the social history of the region compare it with the development of Western Europe and seek patterns of convergence and divergence between the two regions.[214] To start with the comparison of the region with the West, it must be noted that 'the

---

214 For instance, Béla Tomka, *A Social History of Twentieth-Century Europe* (London: Routledge, 2013); Hartmut Kaelble, *A Social History of Europe, 1945–2000: Recovery and Transformation after Two World Wars* (New York: Berghahn Books, 2013).

West' does not constitute a single type. For example, the family and population structure of Scandinavia is clearly different from the Mediterranean patterns. The East and West of Europe were at different stages of transition to modern societies at the beginning of the century, marked by the later arrival of demographic transition in Central and Eastern Europe. State socialism is paradoxical in its combination of divergent and convergent trends towards the West: for example, in spite of the Cold War during the 1950s, strong convergence is visible in reproductive and family patterns (marriage and divorce rates), and in the figures for life expectancy and infant mortality, in which the region was 'catching up' with the West, while the West came closer to the region in terms of decreasing ages at marriage and at first childbirth in the 1950s. The 1970s and the first half of the 1980s can be called decades of divergence, most notably in terms of the decline in marriage age, exceptionally high marriage rates, the divergence in the proportion of children born out of wedlock, and in life expectancy. Of course, there is also divergence between the migration patterns of the region and Western Europe after 1945. While both regions were sites of out-migration during the first half-century, after 1945 the West became a destination, while the Central and Eastern European region has maintained its out-migration character up until today. The post-communist period shows the region approaching the West in terms of many trends (life expectancy, marriage rate) or even overcoming it (birth rates), but also features some new specific aspects (out-migration).

A comparison of the region with Russia or the former Soviet Union[215] shows very similar demographic and family patterns in the twentieth century, particularly with countries like Bulgaria or Romania in terms of population growth and fertility rates. The territory of the future Russian Federation had 125 million inhabitants in 1897; due to the First World War and the civil war it declined to 100 million in 1926, reaching 147 million in 1989 and stagnating since. Population declines in Ukraine or Belarus between the years 1941 and 1945 are similar to the declines in Poland, the Baltic countries or Serbia during the period.[216] The Baltic republics annexed by the USSR started to resemble the demographic patterns of Russian or Ukrainian federative republics from the 1960s.[217] Declining life expectancy, the most crucial element of the population crisis in late socialism, came earlier and was graver in the USSR than in Central and Eastern Europe. The post-Soviet region seems somewhat more resistant to accepting Western models in post-socialism than Central and Eastern Europe, as seen in the persistence of a very low average age of marriage after 1989, and the moderate spread of cohabitation and births out of wedlock. Life expectancy here continued to decline after 1990, altogether for a period longer than four decades, while in Central and Eastern Europe it began to rise again soon after 1990. A detailed comparison with Western Europe is difficult, however, due to the lack of statistical data. In terms of their demographic characteristics (birth rate, age at first birth, family size, power structures within the family), the populations of ethnic Russians, Ukrainians and Belarusians are more similar to the populations of the region than the existing population enclaves within Southeastern Europe with Muslim cultural roots, which, on the contrary, have more in common with the population and family patterns of Turkey.

---

215 See more: Alexandre Avdeev and Alain Blum, 'L'Empire Russe, la Russie soviétique et la Féderation de Russie', in *La Population du Monde, Géants démographiques et défis internationaux* (Paris: Institut National d'Études Démographiques, 2002).
216 The population of Ukraine declined from 40 million in 1939 to 36 million in 1950; the population of Belarus from 8.9 million in 1939 to 7.7 million in 1950; Rothenbacher, *The Central and East European Population since 1850*, 244, 241.
217 Ibid., 66.

The comparison of population and family patterns with south-eastern neighbours in the region shows larger gaps in several respects. The closest south-eastern neighbour of the region, Turkey, exhibited extremely rapid population growth in the second half of the twentieth century, skyrocketing from 20 million in 1948 to 70 million in 2005. Despite secular reforms, a model of family with a very strong patriarchy and the subordination of women and children persisted in Turkey until the 1970s. Also, the extended family survived here longer than in Europe. This was not changed by the fact that women were already allowed to initiate divorce back in 1926, gained the right to vote in 1934 (also earlier than in most Central and Eastern European countries, see Chapter 4 for further information).[218] Since the 1960s, however, a significant convergence between the population and family patterns of Turkey and European societies has taken place. One example is the significant increase in life expectancy, which gradually overtook Russia,[219] and caught up with the life expectancy of Central and Eastern Europe in the 1990s. Other European trends also reached Turkey since the 1970s: a rise in the age of marriage, declining birth rates and infant mortality, and the withering away of households of extended families. This all occurred significantly later than in Central and Eastern Europe or in Russia: in 1978 infant mortality in Turkey was still 133 per 1,000, 82 in 1988, but only 18 in 2008.[220] The most recent trend of the 1990s was the spread of divorce, approaching Central and Eastern European levels at the beginning of the 2010s. In other characteristics, however, huge differences between Turkey and Europe still prevail, such as the low level of illegitimacy, low acceptance of premarital cohabitation, persisting patriarchy in families, and the widespread rejection of homosexuality. One fifth of Turkish women are still illiterate; especially in the east of the country, forced marriages still exist, sometimes even honour killings, and among Kurds, female circumcision.

The lessons from this chapter on family and population can be summarized as follows: first of all, analysis of demographic and family development does not reveal that Central and Eastern Europe constitutes a specific unit with its own patterns. Instead, its borders are often fluid and its internal differences strong. The internal differences in the region can be easily demonstrated by the gaps between demographic and family patterns in the Czech Republic and Albania: the former resembles Germany and the latter, Turkey. Therefore, it seems more plausible to understand the region in terms of family and demography as a continuum rather than as a unit.

Another lesson is that research on demographic and family structures in our region supports the diffusion of European modernity eastward and south-eastward. The best empirically documented example is demographic transition, but similar patterns can be found in several aspects of family life, such as the parent–child relationship. This process is nevertheless more complicated than classical theorists of modernization assumed; it develops within local traditions; it is influenced by the fields of politics, religion, and economy; and it is not linear.

The third finding concerns state socialism, which can be regarded as an alternative modernity to the Western model. With respect to its outcomes on the family and population, it is clear that in many aspects, the year 1945 marked the start of deep changes and meant strong

---

218 Zara F. Kabasakal Arat, 'Women', in *The Routledge Handbook of Modern Turkey*, eds Metin Heper and Sabri Sayari (London: Routledge 2012), 259–70, here 260–63.
219 Russia was outstripped by Turkey in the 1990s even though it trailed 18 years behind Russia in the early 1960s. Currently, the Turks live an average of five years longer than the Russians; Rothenbacher, *The Central and East European Population since 1850*, 69.
220 Ahmet İçduygu, 'Demography and Immigration/Emigration', in Heper and Sayari, *The Routledge Handbook of Modern Turkey*, 331.

convergence with the West in the 1950s and 1960s; on the other hand, this convergence did not continue later, and the overall crisis of state socialism, in combination with the general crisis of late modernity, was also manifested in the realm of family and population history. Although Central and Eastern Europe did not develop in complete isolation from Western Europe during this period, the relatively long existence of state socialism created a specific demographic and family model here, which was also influenced by older regional specificities (the Hajnal line). This model did not survive the collapse of state socialism for very long, as convergence with the West took place in many family and population patterns. This convergence is even stronger than economic convergence. After joining the EU, the inhabitants of new and old Europe were more similar in terms of demographic behaviour than in terms of their incomes.

Further reading

Achim, Viorel. *The Roma in Romanian History* (Budapest: Central European University Press, 2004).
Aldcroft, Derek H. *Europe's Third World: The European Periphery in the Interwar Years* (Farnham: Ashgate, 2006).
Andorka, Rudolf. *Determinants of Fertility in Advanced Societies* (London: Methuen, 1978).
Bade, Klaus J. *Europa in Bewegung: Migration vom späten 18. Jahrhundert bis zur Gegenwart* (München: C.H. Beck, 2000).
Bade, Klaus J., Pieter C. Emmer, Leo Lucassen, and Jochen Oltmer, eds. *Enzyklopädie Migration in Europa: Vom 17. Jahrhundert bis zur Gegenwart* (Paderborn: Schöningh, 2007).
Barany, Zoltan. *The East European Gypsies: Regime Change, Marginality and Ethnopolitics* (New York: Cambridge University Press, 2002).
Blum, Alain, and Jean-Louis Rallu, eds. *European Population, vol. 2, Demographic Dynamics* (Montrouge: John Libbey Eurotext. 1993).
Boh, Katja, Maren Bak, and Cristine Clason, eds. *Changing Patterns of European Family Life: A Comparative Analysis of 14 European Countries* (London: Routledge, 1989).
Borgetta, Edgar F., and Marie L. Borgetta, eds. *Encyclopedia of Sociology*, vol. 1 (New York: Macmillan, 1992).
Boss, Pauline G., W.J. Doherty, R. LaRossa, W.R. Schumm, and S.K. Steinmetz, eds. *Sourcebook of Family Theories and Methods: A Contextual Approach* (New York: Springer, 1993).
Braham, M. *The Untouchables: A Survey of the Roma People in Central and Eastern Europe* (Geneva: UNHCR, 1993).
Brandes, Detlef, ed. *Lexikon der Vetreibungen: Deportation, Zwangsaussiedlung und ethnische Säuberung im Europa des 20. Jahrhunderts* (Vienna: Böhlau, 2010).
Brunnbauer, Ulf, ed. *Umstrittene Identitäten: Ethnizität und Nationalität in Südosteuropa* (Frankfurt a.M.: Lang, 2002).
Brunnbauer, Ulf. *Gebirgsgesellschaften auf dem Balkan: Wirtschaft und Familienstrukturen im Rhodopengebirge – 19./20. Jahrhundert* (Vienna: Böhlau, 2004).
Brunnbauer, Ulf. *Die sozialistische Lebensweise: Ideologie, Gesellschaft, Familie und Politik in Bulgarien (1944–1989)* (Vienna: Böhlau, 2007).
Byrnes, Robert F., ed. *Communal Families in the Balkans: The Zadruga* (Notre Dame: University of Notre Dame Press, 1976).
Castles, Francis G., ed. *Families of Nations: Patterns of Public Policy in Western Democracies* (Aldershot: Dartmouth, 1993).
Castles, Stephen, and Mark J. Miller. *The Age of Migration: International Population Movements in the Modern World* (New York: The Guilford Press, 1993).
Cornia, Giovanni Andrea, and Renato Paniccia, eds. *The Mortality Crisis in Transitional Economics* (Oxford: Oxford University Press, 2000).
Cuc, Milan, Erik Lundbäck, and Edgardo Ruggiero. *Migration and Remittances in Moldova* (Washington DC: International Monetary Fund, 2005).
David, Coleman, ed. *Europe's Population in the 1990s* (Oxford: Oxford University Press, 1996).
David, Henry P., ed. *From Abortion to Contraception: A Resource to Public Policies and Reproductive Behaviour in Central and Eastern Europe from 1917 to the Present* (Westport, CT: Greenwood Press, 1999).

David, Henry P., and Robert J. McIntyre. *Reproductive Behavior: Central and Eastern European Experience* (New York: Springer, 1981).
Davies, Douglas J., and Lewis H. Mates, eds. *Encyclopedia of Cremation* (Aldershot: Ashgate, 2005).
DeMause, Lloyd, ed. *The History of Childhood* (New York: Psychohistory Press, 1974).
Eekelaar, John, and Thandabantu Nhlapo, eds. *The Changing Family: Family Forms and Family Law* (Oxford: Hart Publishing, 1998).
Eurostat, ed. *Human Resources in Europe at the Dawn of the 21st Century* (Luxembourg: European Commission, 1992).
Fassmann, Heinz, and Rainer Münz, eds. *Migration in Europa: historische Entwicklung, aktuelle Trends und politische Reaktionen* (Frankfurt a.M.: Campus Verlag, 1996).
Fischer, Wolfram, Jan A. van Houtte, Herman Kellenbenz, Ilja Mieck, and Friedrich Vittinghoff, eds. *Handbuch der europäischen Wirtschafts- und Sozialgeschichte*, vol. 6 (Stuttgart: Klett-Cotta, 1987).
Franklin, Bob, ed. *The New Handbook of Children's Rights* (London: Routledge, 2002).
Frederick, Starr S., and Karen Dawisha, eds. *The International Politics of Eurasia, vol. 5, State Building and Military Power in Russia and the New States of Eurasia* (Armonk, NY: Bruce Parrott, Sharpe, 1995).
Gauthier, Anne Hèléne. *The State and the Family: A Comparative Analysis of Family Policies in Industrialized Countries* (Oxford: Oxford University Press, 1996).
Glass, David Victor, and David Edward Charles Eversley, eds. *Population in History* (London: Edward Arnold, 1965).
Górny, Agata, and Paolo Ruspini, eds. *Migration in the New Europe: East-West Revisited* (Houndmills: Palgrave Macmillan, 2004).
Guy, Will, ed. *Between Past and Future: The Roma of Central and Eastern Europe* (Hertfordshire: University of Hertfordshire Press, 2001).
Hagemann, Karen, Konrad H. Jarausch, and Cristina Allemann-Ghionda, eds. *Children, Families, and States: Time Policies of Childcare, Preschool, and Primary Education in Europe* (New York: Berghahn, 2011).
Hahn, Eva, and Hans Henning Hahn. *Die Vertreibung im deutschen Erinnern: Legenden, Mythos, Geschichte* (Paderborn: Schöningh, 2010).
Harding, Stephen, David Philips, and Michael Fogarty. *Contrasting Values in Western Europe: Unity, Diversity and Change* (London: Macmillan, 1986).
Hawes, Joseph M., and N. Ray Hiner, eds. *Children in Historical and Comparative Perspective* (New York: Greenwood Press, 1991).
Heywood, Colin. *A History of Childhood: Children and Childhood in the West from Medieval to Modern Times* (Cambridge: Polity Press, 2006).
Holubec, Stanislav. *Sociologie světových systémů: Hegemonie, centra, periferie [The sociology of world-systems: hegemonies, cores, peripheries]* (Prague: Slon, 2010).
Hradil, Stefan, and Stefan Immerfall, eds. *Die Westeuropäischen Gesellschaften im Vergleich* (Opladen: Laske + Budrich, 1997).
Immerfall, Stefan, and Göran Therborn. *Handbook of European Societies: Social Transformations in the 21st Century* (New York: Springer, 2010).
Inglehart, Ronald, Miguel Basanez, and Alejandro Moreno, eds. *Human Values and Beliefs: A Cross-Cultural Sourcebook* (Ann Arbor, MI: University of Michigan Press, 1998).
Inglot, Tomasz, ed. *Fighting Poverty and Reforming Social Security: What Can Post-Soviet States Learn from New Democracies in Central Europe?* (Washington DC: Woodrow Wilson Center, 2007).
Kaelble, Hartmut. *A Social History of Western Europe, 1880–1980* (Dublin: Gill and Macmillan, 1990).
Kaelble, Hartmut, ed. *The European Way: European Societies during the Nineteenth and Twentieth Centuries* (New York: Berghahn, 2004).
Kaelble, Hartmut. *A Social History of Europe, 1945–2000: Recovery and Transformation after Two World Wars* (New York: Berghahn Books, 2013).
Karady, Victor. *Gewalterfahrung und Utopie, Juden in der europäischen Moderne* (Frankfurt a.M.: Fischer Taschenbuch, 1999).
Karady, Victor. *The Jews of Europe in the Modern Era: A Socio-Historical Outline* (Budapest: Central European University Press, 2004).
Kaser, Karl, ed. *Household and Family in the Balkans: Two Decades of Historical Family Research at University of Graz* (Lit Verlag: Vienna, 2012).
Kaser, Michael Charles, ed. *The Economic History of Eastern Europe 1919–1975* (Oxford: Clarendon Press, 1986).

Kocsis, Károly, ed. *South Eastern Europe in Maps* (Budapest: Geographical Research Institute of the Hungarian Academy of Sciences, 2007).
Chasteland, J.C. and J.C. Chesnais, eds. *La Population du Monde, Géants démographiques et défis internationaux* (Paris: Institut National d'Études Démographiques, 2002).
Lerner, Gerda. *The Creation of Patriarchy*, vol. 1 (Oxford: Oxford University Press, 1986).
Lutz, Wolfgang et al., eds. *The New Generations of Europeans* (London: Earthscan, 2006).
Marcus, Sharon. *Between Women: Friendship, Desire, and Marriage in Victorian England* (Princeton, NJ: Princeton University Press, 2009).
Mau, Steffen, and Roland Verwiebe. *Die Sozialstruktur Europas* (Bonn: Bundeszentrale für politische Bildung, 2009).
Mazower, Mark. *Dark Continent: Europe's Twentieth Century* (London: Penguin, 1998).
Mihaela, Robila, ed. *Families in Eastern Europe* (Amsterdam: Elsevier, 2004).
Miletcić, Aleksandar, *Journey under Surveillance: The Overseas Emigration Policy of the Kingdom of Serbs, Croats and Slovenes in Global Context, 1918–1928* (Vienna: Lit Verlag, 2012).
Mitterauer, Michael. *Historisch-anthropologische Familienforschung: Fragestellung und Zugangsweisen* (Köln: Böhlau, 1990a).
Mitterauer, Michael. *Historisch-Antropologische Familienforschung: Fragestellungen und Zugangsweisen und Zugangsweisen* (Vienna: Böhlau, 1990b).
Mitterauer, Michael, and Reinhard Sieder. *The European Family: Patriarchy to Partnership from the Middle Ages to the Present* (Chicago, IL: University of Chicago Press, 1982).
Niewyk, Donald L. *The Columbia Guide to the Holocaust* (New York: Columbia University Press, 2000).
Oddy, Derek J., Peter J. Atkins, and Virginie Amilien, eds. *The Rise of Obesity in Europe: A Twentieth Century Food History* (Farnham: Ashgate, 2009).
Oyen, Else, ed. *Comparative Methodology* (London: Sage, 1990).
Palompa, Rossella, and Hein Moors, eds. *Population, Family and Welfare: A Comparative Survey of European Attitudes*, vol. 1 (Oxford: Clarendon Press, 1995).
Parsons, Talcott. *Structure and Process in Modern Societies* (Glencoe: Free Press, 1960).
Promitzer, Christian, Sevasti Trubeta, and Marius Turda, eds. *Health, Hygiene and Eugenics in Southeastern Europe* (Budapest: Central European University Press, 2010).
Ramet, Sabrina P. *Social Currents in Eastern Europe: The Sources and Consequences of the Great Transformation* (Durham, NC: Duke University Press, 1995).
Rostgaard, Tina. *Family Support Policy in Central and Eastern Europe – A Decade and a Half of Transition* (Early Childhood and Family Policy Series, No. 8) (Paris: UNESCO, 2004).
Rothenbacher, Franz. *The European Population, 1850–1945* (Houndmills: Palgrave, 2002).
Rothenbacher, Franz. *The European Population since 1945* (Houndmills: Palgrave, 2005).
Rothenbacher, Franz. *The Central and East European Population since 1850* (Houndmills: Palgrave Macmillan, 2012).
Schwartz, Michael. *Ethnische 'Säuberungen' in der Moderne: globale Wechselwirkungen nationalistischer und rassistischer Gewaltpolitik im 19. und 20. Jahrhundert* (München: Oldenbourg, 2013).
Seewann, Gerhard, ed. *Migrationen und ihre Auswirkungen. Das Beispiel Ungarn 1918–1995* (München: Oldenbourg, 1997).
Segalen, Martine. *Historical Anthropology of the Family* (Cambridge: Cambridge University Press, 1996).
Shorter, Edward. *The Making of the Modern Family* (New York: Basic Books, 1976).
Snyder, Timothy. *Bloodlands: Europe between Hitler and Stalin* (New York: Basic Books, 2010).
Sterbling, Anton, ed. *Migrationsprozesse: Probleme von Abwanderungsregionen, Identitätsfragen* (Hamburg: Krämer, 2006).
Stone, Lawrence. *The Family, Sex, and Marriage in England, 1500–1800* (New York: Harper and Row, 1979).
Sussmann, Marvin B., and Suzanne K. Steinmetz, eds. *Handbook of Marriage and the Family* (New York: Plenum Press, 1987).
Szalai, Alexander, ed. *The Use of Time: Daily Activities of Urban and Suburban Populations in Twelve Countries* (The Hague: Mouton, 1972).
Therborn, Göran. *European Modernity and Beyond: The Trajectory of European Societies, 1945–2000* (London: Sage, 1995).
Therborn, Göran. *Between Sex and Power: Family in the World, 1900–2000* (London: Routledge, 2004).
Todd, E. *The Explanation of Ideology: Family Structures and Social Systems* (Oxford: Blackwell, 1985).

Todorova, Maria. *Myth-Making in European Family History: The Zadruga Revisited* (Washington, DC: Wilson Center, 1989).
Todorova, Maria N. *Balkan Family Structure and the European Pattern: Demographic Developments in Ottoman Bulgaria* (Budapest: CEU Press, 2006).
Tomka, Béla, *A Social History of Twentieth-Century Europe* (London: Routledge, 2013).
Vobecká, Jana. *Demographic Avant-Garde: Jews in Bohemia between the Enlightenment and the Shoah* (Budapest: Central European University Press, 2013).

6
ECONOMIC DEVELOPMENT

Jerzy Łazor and Bogdan Murgescu

Introduction

Any discussion concerning the economies of Central and Eastern Europe has to begin with the related issues of 'backwardness' and 'catching up'. At least since the first half of the nineteenth century, both Westerners and inhabitants of Central and Eastern Europe perceived the region as 'backward', meaning less developed in comparison with Western countries. It is not the aim of this chapter to discuss the implications of this perception, whether analyzed using the framework of orientalism or symbolic geography.[1] Instead, we argue that backwardness was not merely a subjective hallucination, but an insight informed by significant (and increasing) differences in economic and social structures, and levels of performance. These differences accumulated over a long span of time,[2] but during the nineteenth century they became more pronounced as a result of industrialization and more noticeable thanks to growing levels of interconnection across various parts of the world. Therefore, by 1900 backwardness had already become a major theme throughout the whole region and catching up became a core aim for a large number of members of national elites in Central and Eastern Europe, even if there was no consensus around the causes and roots of this backwardness. Joseph Love has outlined the role economists and social scientists from Central and Eastern Europe played in shaping international discussions and theories about economic development, diverging historical paths and the related economic policy implications (these theorists included, in the order in which their work was published: Mihail Manoilescu, Michał Kalecki, Paul Rosenstein-Rodan, Alexander Gerschenkron, Peter Thomas Bauer, Paul A. Baran and Irma Adelman).[3]

Several theorists have tackled the economic development of Central and Eastern Europe. Early elements of modernization theory, as outlined by Émile Durkheim and Max Weber, informed the debates in and about the region during the first half of the twentieth century. Later, the ideological divides of the Cold War limited the influence of more elaborate forms

---

1 Larry Wolff, *Inventing Eastern Europe: The Map of Civilization on the Mind of the Enlightenment* (Stanford, CA: Stanford University Press, 1994); Jerzy Jedlicki, *A Suburb of Europe: Nineteenth-Century Polish Approaches to Western Civilization* (Budapest: CEU Press, 1999); Tomasz Zarycki, *Ideologies of Eastness in Central and Eastern Europe* (London: Routledge, 2014).
2 Daniel Chirot, ed. *The Origins of Backwardness in Eastern Europe: Economics and Politics from the Middle Ages until the Early Twentieth Century* (Berkeley, CA: University of California Press, 1989).
3 Joseph L. Love, *Crafting the Third World: Theorizing Underdevelopment in Rumania and Brazil* (Stanford, CA: Stanford University Press, 1996).

of modernization theory, as developed by Talcott Parsons, Walt Rostow or Seymour Martin Lipset. At the same time, historical experiences in Central and Eastern Europe remained a subject of study. They were crucial for Alexander Gerschenkron's conceptualization of backwardness,[4] which stipulated that the timing of industrialization was essential for patterns of economic policy-making and development in various countries. Unlike early industrializing countries, where economic development was fostered by investment from private entrepreneurs, second-wave industrializers relied on banks to provide essential resources for industrial breakthroughs, while in the most backward countries, governments needed to intervene as neither entrepreneurs nor banks were able to deliver the necessary resources and leadership.

Debates about interwar Central and Eastern Europe heavily influenced the structuralist economics of Raúl Prebisch (particularly through the writings of Mihail Manoilescu and Hans Singer),[5] thus contributing to discussions on the relationship between core and periphery. These, in turn, led to dependency theory and later to world-system theory conceptualized by Immanuel Wallerstein. Wallerstein himself also acknowledges the influence of the Polish historian Marian Małowist in his analysis of unequal exchange in various geographical and historical settings.[6] Wallerstein's theoretical framework informed several analyses of the economic history of various Central and Eastern European countries that followed.[7] It also generated polemical responses. Some critics argued that the region's economic backwardness (or, expressed in a more neutral way, its 'deficit of economic performance') did not derive from the structural constraints of an inequitable capitalist world economy, but from the slow pace at which innovations were adopted, the low level of human capital, and ineffective institutions, which were sometimes even set up so as to allow local elites to drain scarce resources for their own benefit.[8] Such explanations are consistent with the institutional economics approach that also prevails in mainstream development theory, as exemplified by Daron Acemoğlu and James Robinson's bestseller, *Why Nations Fail*.[9]

Central Europe has a long and significant tradition in the discipline of economic history. Even during communist rule, Polish and Hungarian economic historians managed to combine

---

4 Alexander Gerschenkron, *Economic Backwardness in Historical Perspective: A Book of Essays* (Cambridge, MA: Belknap Press of Harvard University Press, 1962).
5 Love, *Crafting the Third World*, 101–39.
6 Immanuel Wallerstein, *The Modern World-System*, vol. 1, *Capitalist Agriculture and the Origins of the European World-Economy in the Sixteenth Century* (New York: Academic Press, 1974), xi; Carl Strikwerda, 'From World-Systems to Globalization: Theories of Transnational Change and the Place of the United States', *American Studies* 41, no. 2/3 (2000): 339.
7 A very early attempt at this type of analysis was made by Daniel Chirot about the medieval and modern history of part of Romania (Wallachia) up to the First World War. Daniel Chirot, *Social Change in a Peripheral Society: The Creation of a Balkan Colony* (New York: Academic Press, 1976). See also Iván T. Berend and György Ránki, *The European Periphery and Industrialization, 1780–1914* (Cambridge: Cambridge University Press, 1982); Florin Bonciu and Bogdan Murgescu, 'The World-Approach and Romanian Economic History', *Revue Roumaine d'Histoire* XXIX, no. 3/4 (July–December 1990): 275–89; Iván T. Berend, *Central and Eastern Europe, 1944–1993: Detour from the Periphery to the Periphery* (Cambridge: Cambridge University Press, 1996); Derek H. Aldcroft, *Europe's Third World: The European Periphery in the Interwar Years* (Aldershot: Edward Elgar, 2006); Stanislav Holubec, 'Catch Up and Overtake the West: The Czech Lands in the World-System in the Twentieth Century', *Journal of Contemporary Central and Eastern Europe* 18, no. 1 (2010): 29–51.
8 A good example of such criticism can be found in Holm Sundhaussen, 'Institutionen und institutioneller Wandel den Balkanländern aus historischer Perspektive', in *Institutionen und institutioneller Wandel in Südosteuropa*, ed. Johannes Chr. Papalekas (München: Südosteuropa-Gesellschaft, 1994), 35–54.
9 Daron Acemoğlu and James Robinson, *Why Nations Fail: The Origins of Power, Prosperity and Poverty* (London: Profile Books, 2012).

positivist traditions of serious research based on primary sources with the Marxist propensity for general theorization while they remained open to intellectual interaction with their Western counterparts. While some of the leading economic historians (like Marian Małowist, Witold Kula, Zsigmond Pál Pach and Jerzy Topolski) focused on the early modern period,[10] the Hungarians Iván T. Berend and György Ránki were less vulnerable to ideological interferences and wrote extensively about the nineteenth and twentieth centuries.[11] After the demise of communism and the early death of Ránki, Berend moved to the United States and published several books, which now constitute the main narrative for the economic history of Central and Eastern Europe in the nineteenth and twentieth centuries.[12] Besides Berend's books, the research landscape for the region's economic history is defined by several conceptualizations published before the fall of communism, which remain of value.[13] In the region itself, interest in economic history was already declining during late socialism, and declined even more extensively after the demise of the communist regimes. Historians preferred to study previously forbidden themes of political and intellectual history, while economists and social scientists focused either on post-communist transformation or microeconomic studies, which often employed anthropological methods and insights. Besides, most economic historians from the region preferred to limit themselves to the study of local or national topics, avoiding macro-analyses that encompassed larger regions or time spans. Therefore, after 1990 the most important conceptualizations concerning the economic history of twentieth-century Central and Eastern Europe were published (apart from Berend) by Western scholars, such as Derek H. Aldcroft, Steven Morewood or David Turnock.[14]

Phases and trends of economic development

General assessment

If economic backwardness was the main economic problem in Central and Eastern Europe at the end of the nineteenth century, and if it remains one today, then to assess the region's performance in the twentieth century, one needs to determine whether the development gap

---

10 Zsigmond Pál Pach, *Die ungarische Agrarentwicklung im 16. – 17. Jahrhundert: Abbiegung vom westeuropäischen Entwicklungsgang* (Budapest: Akadémiai Kiadó, 1964); Witold Kula, *An Economic Theory of the Feudal System* (London: NLB, 1976; originally published in 1962).
11 Iván T. Berend and György Ránki, *Economic Development of East-Central Europe in the 19th and 20th Centuries* (New York: Columbia University Press, 1974); Berend and Ránki, *European Periphery*; Iván T. Berend and György Ránki, *The Hungarian Economy in the Twentieth Century* (Beckenham: Croom Helm, 1985).
12 Berend, *Central and Eastern Europe*; idem, *Decades of Crisis: Central and Eastern Europe Before World War II* (Berkeley, CA: University of California Press, 1998); idem, *History Derailed: Central and Eastern Europe in the 'Long' 19th Century* (Berkeley, CA: University of California Press, 2003); idem, *From the Soviet Bloc to the European Union: The Social and Economic Transformation of Central and Eastern Europe since 1973* (Cambridge: Cambridge University Press, 2009). See also his syntheses encompassing both Western and Eastern Europe: idem, *An Economic History of Twentieth-Century Europe: Economic Regimes from Laissez-faire to Globalization* (Cambridge: Cambridge University Press, 2006); and idem, *Europe Since 1980* (Cambridge: Cambridge University Press, 2010).
13 John R. Lampe and Marvin R. Jackson, *Balkan Economic History, 1550–1950: From Imperial Borderlands to Developing Nations* (Bloomington, IN: Indiana University Press, 1982); Michael Charles Kaser and E.A. Radice, eds, *The Economic History of Eastern Europe 1919–1975*, 3 vols. (Oxford: Oxford University Press, 1985–1987).
14 Derek H. Aldcroft and Steven Morewood, *Economic Change in Eastern Europe since 1918* (Aldershot: Edward Elgar, 1995); Aldcroft, *Europe's Third World*; and David Turnock, *The Economy of East Central Europe, 1815–1989: Stages of Transformation in a Peripheral Region* (London and New York: Routledge, 2006).

increased or whether some catching up occurred. Doing so requires finding the best way to measure economic development.

The most common method would be to measure economic output, and for this purpose many would argue that Gross Domestic Product per capita (GDP/c) is the best synthetic indicator.[15] It is relatively simple to calculate or estimate, and the data is already available for much of the studied period. Moreover, the measure lends itself to spatial and temporal comparisons and seems to be highly correlated with other components of development and welfare.

Despite its popularity, GDP is not without its critics. Some criticize it on the basis of technical issues, pointing out, among other things, that it does not adequately consider non-market economic activities or the input of land (which includes various natural resources, often unaccounted for in monetary terms). Others argue that GDP merely measures current economic performance, without considering economic sustainability or social well-being.[16] As a result, a number of economists and social scientists have tried to design alternative indicators.[17] The most important attempt to achieve this, inspired by Amartya Sen's work on human capabilities, was undertaken by Mahbub ul Haq. The resulting Human Development Index (HDI) combines GDP with indices of population health (using life expectancy at birth as a proxy) and education (originally measured through a combination of literacy and gross enrolment ratios). Since 1990, the United Nations Development Programme has published annual Human Development Reports and has refined the methodology for calculating HDI by including other dimensions in a separate inequality-adjusted HDI.[18]

The financial crisis that began in 2007–8 increased the pressure to design alternative economic indicators. In 2009, the Stiglitz-Sen-Fitoussi Commission, appointed by the French president Nicolas Sarkozy, presented a thorough report containing a set of 12 recommendations to better measure economic performance and social progress. The Commission argued that the evaluation of material well-being should be based on income and consumption (preferably jointly with wealth) rather than production, as well as focus on distribution measures and more complex issues like quality of life, well-being and sustainability.[19] Taking seriously the urge to 'shift emphasis from measuring economic production to measuring people's well-being', the Organisation for Economic Co-operation and Development (OECD) set up a framework for measuring well-being and progress and in 2011 launched the publication of annual reports based on the Better Life Index, which combines 11 dimensions considered essential for human well-being (community, education, environment, civic engagement, health, housing, income, jobs, life satisfaction, safety and work-life balance).[20] Unfortunately, many of the proposed

---

15 Philipp H. Lepenies, *Macht der einen Zahl: Eine politische Geschichte des Bruttoinlandsprodukts* (Berlin: Suhrkamp, 2013).
16 National Institute for Statistics and Economic Studies (INSEE), 'Report by the Commission on the Measurement of Economic Performance and Social Progress', www.stiglitz-sen-fitoussi.fr/documents/rapport_anglais.pdf, 85–142; Emanuele Felice, 'GDP and Convergence in Modern Times', Working Paper *de l'Association Française de Cliométrie*, no. 1 (2014). This is more polemically expressed in Dirk Philipsen, *The Little Big Number: How GDP Came to Rule the World and What to Do about It* (Princeton, NJ: Princeton University Press, 2015); and some of his opinions have also been synthesized in Dirk Philipsen, 'GDP's Wicked Spell', *The Chronicle of Higher Education*, 15 June 2015, http://chronicle.com/article/GDPs-Wicked-Spell/230881.
17 Victor Anderson, *Alternative Economic Indicators* (London: Routledge, 1991).
18 United Nations Development Programme (UNDP), 'Human Development Report', http://hdr.undp.org/en.
19 INSEE, 'Report by the Commission', 12–18.
20 Better Life Initiative: Measuring Well-Being and Progress, www.oecd.org/statistics/better-life-initiative.htm

measurements are difficult to apply to the past due to insufficient statistical data. As such, they are more useful for assessing current changes rather than constructing long-term comparisons.

Economic historians tried to keep pace with debates about and shifts in the measurement of economic performance. After they were first published in 1976, most economic historians used Paul Bairoch's historical Gross National Product (GNP) data for European countries.[21] In the 1990s, they were replaced by Angus Maddison's estimates of historical GDP on a global level.[22] In spite of a variety of criticisms, the data set prevailed over alternative calculations,[23] and became the main reference point for economic historians the world over. After Maddison's death in 2010, his colleagues from the University of Groningen decided to continue and update the database with new scholarship and made it available online.[24] The estimates are given in 1990 Geary–Khamis dollars.[25]

After the first attempt to expand calculations of the HDI for years before 1980, which was undertaken by Nicholas Crafts in the late 1990s,[26] Leandro Prados de la Escosura improved the statistical methodology for producing the Historical Index of Human Development (HIHD), and managed to calculate it on a global level for the period after 1870.[27] The new index not only uses better data, but also estimates progress more accurately by using convex rather than linear transformation for creating indices.

Last but not least, in 2010 Jan Luiten van Zanden launched the Clio Infra project, which aims to collect, analyze and present online the relevant data for reconstructing global inequality since 1500.[28] In collaboration with the OECD's Better Life Initiative, the project resulted in the publication in 2014 of a preliminary analysis of global well-being since 1820. Its authors consider various dimensions and indicators (GDP per capita, the real wages of unskilled labourers, life expectancy, height, educational attainment, the quality of political institutions, personal security, environmental quality, gender and income inequality) and try to assess the chances of calculating a composite index of historical well-being.[29]

What data is available for Central and Eastern Europe, and how reliable is it? Maddison himself acknowledges that there are significant gaps in and problems with GDP estimates for this region.[30] In fact, yearly estimates only begin from the 1920s for most of these countries (but as late as 1950 for Albania or 1990 for the Baltic states), while earlier periods are covered

---

21 Paul Bairoch, 'Europe's Gross National Product, 1800–1975', *Journal of European Economic History* 5, no. 2 (1976): 273–340.
22 Angus Maddison, *Monitoring the World Economy, 1820–1992* (Paris: OECD, 1995); idem, *The World Economy: A Millennial Perspective* (Paris: OECD, 2001); idem, *The World Economy: Historical Statistics* (Paris: OECD, 2003).
23 Leandro Prados de la Escosura, 'International Comparisons of Real Product, 1820–1990: An Alternative Data Set', *Explorations in Economic History* 37, no. 1 (2000): 1–41.
24 New Maddison Project Online Database, www.ggdc.net/maddison/maddison-project/data.htm. For the current revisions, see Jutta Bolt and Jan Luiten van Zanden, 'The Maddison Project: Collaborative Research on Historical National Accounts', *The Economic History Review* 67, no. 3 (2014): 627–51. Since the submission of this chapter, a new version of these estimates has been published.
25 Also known as 'international dollars', they are an abstract unit of currency, and possess the same purchasing power as the United States dollar had in 1990. This allows for spatial and temporal comparability.
26 Nicholas Crafts, 'The Human Development Index and Changes in the Standard of Living: Some Historical Comparisons', *European Review of Economic History* 1 (1999): 299–322.
27 Leandro Prados de la Escosura, 'World Human Development: 1870-2007', *Review of Income and Wealth* 61, no. 2 (2015): 220–47.
28 The official Clio Infra website is www.clio-infra.eu.
29 Jan Luiten van Zanden et al., eds, *How Was Life? Global Well-Being Since 1820* (Paris: OECD Publishing, 2014).
30 Maddison, *The World Economy: Historical Statistics*, 91.

Table 6.1 Per capita GDP at present purchasing power (PPP) (1990 Geary–Khamis international dollars)

Year	1870	1913	1950	1973	2001	2010
Western Europe (30 countries)	1,971	3,437	4,517	11,346	19,611	20,889
Eastern Europe (7 countries)	929	1,690	2,088	5,020	6,156	8,678
Former USSR		1,414	2,841	6,059	4,747	7,733
World average	876	1,531	2,024	3,941	5,952	7,224

Notes: In Tables 6.1 and 6.2, and in subsequent tables based on Maddison's data, Western Europe includes Andorra, Austria, Belgium, Cyprus, Denmark, the Faroe Islands, Finland, France, Germany, Gibraltar, Greece, Greenland, Guernsey, Iceland, Ireland, the Isle of Man, Italy, Jersey, Liechtenstein, Luxembourg, Malta, Monaco, the Netherlands, Norway, Portugal, San Marino, Spain, Sweden, Switzerland and the United Kingdom. Eastern Europe includes Albania, Bulgaria, Czechoslovakia, Hungary, Poland, Romania, Yugoslavia and their successor states.

Source: The Maddison Project, www.ggdc.net/maddison/maddison-project/home.htm, 2013 version.

Table 6.2 Rate of growth of per capita GDP, regional averages, 1870–2001

	1870–1913	1913–1950	1950–1973	1973–2001
Western Europe (30 countries)	1.33	0.76	4.05	1.88
Eastern Europe (7 countries)	1.39	0.60	3.81	0.68
Former USSR	1.06	1.76	3.35	-0.96
World average	1.30	0.88	2.92	1.41

Source: Maddison, *The World Economy: Historical Statistics*, 263.

by estimates of varying rigidity (obviously, there are also gaps in the data for the Second World War and the immediate post-war years). While most of the yearly estimates based on national statistics have been scrutinized (especially in light of the notorious difficulty of adjusting data according to the material product approach used in the former communist countries) and are fairly reliable, some of them still need to be critically analyzed and significantly corrected.[31] As is often the case in statistics, the weaknesses of some of the national estimates have a relatively small impact on the estimates for the region as a whole. Therefore, in this chapter we prefer to refer to regional aggregates and to use national data only when we feel that none of it distorts the general picture of the region.

According to this data,[32] Central and Eastern Europe underperformed during the interwar period and after the 1970s, and then performed better than most of the world (except Western

---

31 We think that the Maddison estimates are too high for Romania between 1900 and 1913, and for Bulgaria between 1960 and 1990 (this is possibly even the case for earlier periods). At the same time, it was expected that the quality of the data would be higher after 1990, since from that point there is also extensive statistical coverage provided by specialized international organizations and Eurostat. Nevertheless, the Maddison estimates, since they use the 1990 benchmark of purchasing-power converters for a period of significant change in the structure of post-communist economies, are in some cases inconsistent with the information derived from other sources and will need to be revised (in our opinion, the Maddison estimates between 1990 and 2010 are too high for Bulgaria, Estonia, Latvia and Lithuania, and too low for Romania and perhaps also Hungary).
32 The data in Table 6.2 are based on a previous set of GDP per capita estimates, while the data in Table 6.1 are from the updated 2013 version of the Maddison database. Nevertheless, at this level of aggregation, the differences are negligible.

Economic development

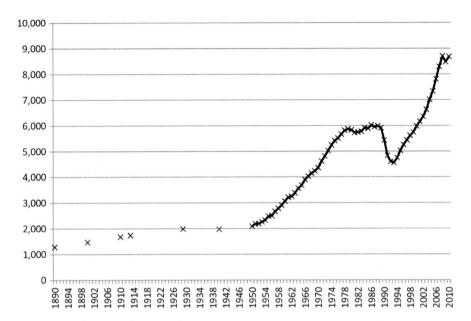

Figure 6.1 Aggregate Central and Eastern European per capita GDP at PPP, 1890–2010 (1990 Geary–Khamis international dollars)
Source: www.ggdc.net/maddison/maddison-project/data.htm (accessed 29 June 2015).

Europe) in the first few decades after the Second World War (in fact, the high growth rates continued throughout most of the 1970s and the slowdown visible in Table 6.2 for the period 1973–2001 was mainly caused by problems in the 1980s and the transformation crisis of the early 1990s).

Although the data above reflect the general evolution of Central and Eastern Europe, we consider it necessary to supplement it with additional estimates, which include Estonia, Latvia and Lithuania (Table 6.3). While the differences are rather small, due to the fact that the Baltic states represent only around six per cent of the total population of Central and Eastern Europe and about six to eight per cent of its GDP throughout the long twentieth century, we believe that these aggregate figures provide a more accurate picture of the region as a whole.

The HIHD, as provided by Leandro Prados de la Escosura,[33] shows more steady growth in Central and Eastern Europe. This confirms expectations since, as demonstrated by patterns that occur elsewhere in the world, even in times when income growth slows down, advances in education and healthcare allow significant improvement in overall human development.

The data summarized in this section provides only a very general picture of the economic performance of Central and Eastern Europe during the long twentieth century. Therefore, in the following sections we will discuss this performance more closely during different phases of economic development.

---

33 De la Escosura's original paper includes a single index for CEE countries and Russia (de la Escosura, 'World Human Development'). He kindly provided us with the underlying data, and the index we use is a recalculated population-weighted average of HIHD values for Albania, Bulgaria, Czechoslovakia, Hungary, Poland, Romania and Yugoslavia/Serbia.

Table 6.3 Central and Eastern European population and economic performance in comparison with Western Europe and the world, 1890–2010

	Population (in millions)			Gross domestic product (in billion international 1990 Geary–Khamis dollars)			Gross domestic product per capita (1990 Geary–Khamis dollars)		
	Central and Eastern Europe	Western Europe (30 countries)	World	Central and Eastern Europe	Western Europe	World	Central and Eastern Europe	Western Europe	World
1890	63	216		81	535		1,276	2,547	
1900	70	234	1,563	102	674	1,972	1,463	2,959	
1913	81	260	1,793	135	902	2,733	1,667	3,488	1,543
1929	97	275		166	1,132		1,982	4,167	
1940	101	294	2,299	185	1,337	4,503	1,969	4,551	2,181
1950		306	2,530	203	1,396	5,336	2,088	4,517	2,104
1960	105	327	3,044	335	2,251	8,433	3,058	6,806	2,764
1970	115	353	3,695	516	3,593	13,766	4,350	10,108	3,725
1980	124	369	4,444	739	4,850	20,030	5,829	13,118	4,511
1990	130	379	5,276	738	6,033	27,134	5,427	15,905	5,149
2000	126	393	6,084	778	7,538	36,688	5,980	19,298	6,029
2010	123	413	6,884	1,067	7,970	53,791	8,678	20,889	7,814

Notes: In this table, Central and Eastern Europe includes Albania, Bulgaria, Czechoslovakia, Estonia, Hungary, Latvia, Lithuania, Poland, Romania, Yugoslavia and their successor states. The population data for 1929 is from 1930. GDP includes Estonia, Latvia and Lithuania only from 1950. The average GDP for Central and Eastern Europe (CEE) includes data on Bulgaria from 1892 and 1899, and excludes Bulgaria from the 1913 result.

Sources: Franz Rothenbacher, *The Societies of Europe: The Central and East European Population since 1850* (Basingstoke: Palgrave Macmillan, 2013), 29–30, Table 2.3; F. Rothenbacher, *The Societies of Europe: The European Population since 1945* (Basingstoke: Palgrave Macmillan, 2013), 14, Table 2.2; F. Rothenbacher, *The Societies of Europe: The European Population 1845–1945* (Basingstoke: Palgrave Macmillan, 2013), 14; The Maddison Project, www.ggdc.net/maddison/maddison-project/home.htm, 2010 and 2013 versions; Population, total, World DataBank, http://data.worldbank.org/indicator/SP.POP.TOT; and League of Nations International Statistical Yearbook, 1926 and 1939–1940.

Boom of the late nineteenth century, 1890–1914

Gauging the relative development of Central and Eastern Europe before the First World War is difficult. Not only does the period encompass a 'statistical dark age',[34] with population size and foreign trade the only consistently recorded data, but imperial territories do not easily yield to the modern statistician's scrutiny in order to reveal later borders. Nonetheless, current understanding (Table 6.5) points to region-wide economic growth on a level close to the European average, with much poorer results (and starting points) in Bulgaria and Serbia. In these last two countries,

---

34 David F. Good, 'The Economic Lag of Central and Eastern Europe: Income Estimates for the Habsburg Successor States, 1870–1910', *The Journal of Economic History* 54, no. 4 (1994): 869–91, here 870.

Table 6.4 HIHD, Central and Eastern Europe, 1890–2007

	Central and Eastern Europe (seven countries)	Developed countries (OECD)	World
1890	0.122	0.220	0.095
1900	0.146	0.246	0.107
1913	0.167	0.277	0.122
1929	0.216	0.334	0.157
1938	0.253	0.366	0.185
1950	0.303	0.417	0.210
1960	0.386	0.482	0.263
1970	0.427	0.541	0.307
1980	0.473	0.593	0.334
1990	0.481	0.658	0.367
2000	0.527	0.745	0.416
2007	0.579	0.809	0.460

Source: Leandro Prados de la Escosura, 'World Human Development, 1870–2007', Review of Income and Wealth 61, no.2 (2015): 220–247 (underlying dataset); Maddison, The World Economy; F. Rothenbacher, The Societies of Europe. The Central and East European Population since 1850 (Basingstoke: Palgrave Macmillan, 2013), 29–30, Table 2.3; F. Rothenbacher, The Societies of Europe. The European Population since 1945 (Basingstoke: Palgrave Macmillan, 2013), 14; and Population, total, World Data Bank, http://data.worldbank.org/indicator/SP.POP.TOT.

Table 6.5 GDP per capita of CEE economies in 1890, 1900 and 1913 (1990 international Geary–Khamis dollars)

	Albania	Bulgaria	Czechoslovakia	Hungary	Poland	Romania	Yugoslavia	CEE countries	Western Europe (30 countries)
1890	598	1,132	1,505	1,473	1,284	1,246	776	1,276	2,547
1900	685	986	1,729	1,682	1,536	1,415	830	1,463	2,959
1913	811	1,137	2,096	2,098	1,739	1,741	973	1,726	3,488
Level of 1913 where 1890 = 100	136	100	139	142	135	140	125	135	137

Note: There are different years for Bulgaria, as follows: 1892, 1899 and 1911.

Source: The Maddison Project, www.ggdc.net/maddison/maddison-project/home.htm, 2013 version.

modern state-building rather than growth occurred.[35] In 1890, the differences between the poorest and richest countries in the region, broadly observed on a west–east gradient, were greater than those between the regional average and Western Europe. Apart from the Czech

---

35 Lampe and Jackson, Balkan Economic History, 157; Michael Palairet, The Balkan Economies c. 1800–1914: Evolution without Development (Cambridge: Cambridge University Press, 1997), 361–70; Martin Ivanov and Adam Tooze, 'Convergence or Decline on Europe's Southeastern Periphery? Agriculture, Population, and GNP in Bulgaria, 1892–1945', The Journal of Economic History 67, no. 3 (2007): 672–704; and Michael Palairet, 'Economic Retardation, Peasant Farming and the Nation-State in the Balkans: Serbia, 1815–1912 and 1991–1999', in Nation, State and the Economy in History, eds Alice Teichova and Herbert Matis (Cambridge: Cambridge University Press, 2003), 197–218, here 202–3.

lands, the only areas with noticeable levels of industry were Russian Poland and the Baltics – at the time the most developed parts of the Russian Empire – and Hungary, which profited from the flight of Austrian capital from Vienna during the Long Depression of the 1870s and 1880s.[36]

These decades witnessed the 'first globalization', which achieved unprecedented levels of foreign trade and international factor flows. It was fuelled by falling transport prices and relatively low tariffs and was aided by the spread of the gold standard.[37] As shipping costs declined, producers from other parts of the world were able to compete in the European market. Soon Europe started importing large quantities of agricultural products from the Americas, and the Long Depression saw a significant drop in prices, which hurt local producers. Both industrialized and agricultural countries reacted by protecting their markets, the latter of which did so more strongly but with smaller results.[38] Austria-Hungary was one of the first to do so by introducing a protective tariff in 1874. Germany and Russia both followed suit with policies to protect their primary producers (and waged a trade war against each other from 1893 to 1894), which limited Russian Poland's agricultural exports and allowed German Poland to evolve into the Second Reich's breadbasket.

Central and Eastern Europe participated in the first globalization, profiting to a significant degree from connections with the rest of the continent through a growing railway network initiated and financed by foreign capital. The region evolved into a provider of agricultural products and raw materials for core Western industry (part of the Great Specialization).[39] This resulted in a significant increase in exports, as shown in Table 6.6, although in per capita terms the region remained relatively closed (with the exception of Russian Poland). The highest level of exports in GDP was reached in Romania (25 per cent), achieved through its extensive agricultural production.

Table 6.6 Growth of exports in CEE economies and European average, 1870–1910; level of exports per capita in 1910

	Growth 1870–1910 (in per cent)	Level in 1910 (in current dollars)
Bulgaria	4.6	5.7
Hungary	2.7	9.0
Romania	3.5	16.2
Serbia	3.0	6.4
European average	3.0	25.0

Note: The European average per capita does not include Russia, while the Hungarian result is taken from Austria-Hungary.

Source: Thomas David, *Nationalisme économique et industrialisation: L'expérience des pays de l'Est (1789–1939)* (Geneva: Librairie Droz, 2009), 95.

---

36 Max-Stephan Schulze, 'Patterns of Growth and Stagnation in the Late Nineteenth Century Habsburg Economy', *European Review of Economic History* 4, no. 3 (2000): 311–40, here 314, 324–5.
37 Ronald Findlay and Kevin O'Rourke, *Power and Plenty: Trade, War, and the World Economy in the Second Millennium* (Princeton, NJ: Princeton University Press, 2007).
38 Stéphane Becuwe and Bertrand Blancheton, 'Politique commerciale et croissance entre 1850 et 1913: Synthèse critique des contributions', *Cahier du GREThA*, no. 2011–24 (2011); and Antonio Tena-Junguito, Marcus Lampe and Felipe Tâmega Fernandes, 'How Much Trade Liberalization Was There in the World Before and After Cobden-Chevalier?', *The Journal of Economic History* 72, no. 3 (2012): 708–40.
39 Findlay and O'Rourke, *Power and Plenty*, 411–4.

The seemingly unlimited market for agricultural products in Western Europe was a powerful incentive for increasing production. Acreage grew significantly; in the case of Serbia, it nearly doubled between 1889 and 1905, and Romania achieved one of the highest per capita amounts of acreage in the world.[40] Grains, led by wheat, comprised the main group of exports, which were supplemented by other plant and animal products, such as Bulgarian tobacco or Serbian livestock and prunes. In Hungary, a highly evolved milling industry allowed the country to export flour as well as grain.

At the same time, a belated agricultural revolution, in comparison to Western Europe, took place, although its scope was limited. In Czech lands, Hungary and German Poland, modern crop rotation, mechanization and other technical innovations were introduced. In the Balkans and less developed parts of Austria-Hungary, these changes were more modest, reflecting ownership structures, levels of available capital and the unwillingness of large owners to invest. As a result, the effectiveness of agriculture varied greatly within the region, but remained behind the success of Western European countries. In eastern Central Europe, agricultural productivity amounted to between 11 and 17 million kilocalories per male agricultural worker. In Southeastern Europe, the same metric varied between 9 and 14, while in Germany it reached 31 and in the USA 47. In the Balkans, where land was owned by masses of smallholders, there was in general terms an extensive growth in output, but in some cases, such as Bulgaria, it fell.[41]

Agriculture played a smaller role in the Czech lands and Russian Poland. They both specialized in industrial products, which were for the most part destined for the markets of their respective empires. The Czech lands, the most developed part of Central and Eastern Europe, were known for their textile, metal and engineering industries, which, together with Austrian production, dominated the Austro-Hungarian market, as well as sugar-beet refineries, which exported their products to Western Europe. Russian Poland was less industrialized and had a higher proportion of low-yield agricultural employment. Nonetheless, it possessed sizeable textile, coal mining and metal industries, which exported much of their production to the imperial Russian market. Along with the Baltics, Poland remained the industrial backbone of this largely agricultural empire, and experienced fast growth in the period, although its position began to wane after the wave of new projects in the Russian hinterland just before the turn of the century (including the 'calico war' between Polish and Russian textile producers).[42]

The first globalization also resulted in the expansion of financial flows. Foreign capital – understood broadly to include Austrian activity in other parts of Austria-Hungary – played a huge role in financing railroads and setting up modern banking sectors in the region, which significantly contributed to the modernization of local economies.[43] There was also a dominant foreign presence in industry and mining. Capital – mostly in the form of public loans and,

---

40 Lampe and Jackson, *Balkan Economic History*, 170.
41 Michael Kopsidis and Martin Ivanov, 'Was Gerschenkron Right? Bulgarian Agricultural Growth during the Interwar Period in Light of Modern Development Economics', *EHES Working Paper* 82 (2015): 9; and Juliusz Łukasiewicz, *Kryzys agrarny na ziemiach polskich w końcu XIX wieku* [Agrarian crisis in Polish lands in the late nineteenth century] (Warsaw: Państwowe Wydawnictwo Naukowe, 1968), 158.
42 Andrzej Jezierski, *Bilans Handlowy Królestwa Polskiego, 1815–1914* [Balance of trade in the Kingdom of Poland, 1815–1914] (Warsaw: Państwowe Wydawnictwo Naukowe, 1957), 147–51; and Wiesław Puś, *Statystyka przemysłu Królestwa Polskiego w latach 1879–1913: materiały źródłowe* [Industry statistics in the Kingdom of Poland in the years 1879–1913: source materials] (Lodz: Wydawnictwo Uniwersytetu Łódzkiego, 2013), 9–15. Perhaps as much as 75 per cent of textiles produced in Lodz were exported abroad.
43 Berend, *History Derailed*, 137, 154–8.

to a smaller degree, direct investment – came primarily from the great powers, in particular, Germany, France and Austria-Hungary. Within Central and Eastern Europe itself, Czech banks also contributed to investments, mostly in other parts of Austria-Hungary, but also in the Balkan countries, where they supported an import-substituting sugar-beet industry.[44] Despite limited activity, the risk aversion of investors and the insular character of investments in less-developed parts of the region,[45] the impact of foreign capital on modernization was significant.

The West not only brought capital but was also the point of reference and inspiration for the region's elites,[46] who saw the future of their countries in modernization through industrialization (the net industrial output per capita was then two to three times greater than was the case for agriculture in the region).[47] Increasing export levels could serve as an engine of growth, providing funds for technological imports and investment or export-led industrialization.[48] Some members of the elites were also under the influence of the theories of the German economist Friedrich List. He argued that, while free trade was a viable model for England, and thus also for other developed countries, latecomers to industrialization would be more likely to profit from protecting and supporting their budding industries. Such a set of policies ('proto-' or 'liberal economic nationalism') was deployed widely in Central and Eastern Europe, although its prevalence depended on the political and economic situation of each state or region. Ironically then, as the region became more integrated into the world market, it also grew more protectionist, and the state apparatus played an ever-larger role in its economies.[49]

The Czech lands, Russian Poland and the future Baltic states enjoyed tariff protection from foreign imports and were able to successfully base their growth on the large imperial markets they belonged to. Hungary found itself in a different situation. While its high-yield and modernizing agricultural producers were able to profit from Austria-Hungary's protection and successfully expanded into its market, Hungary was unable to formulate its own tariff policy and thus protect itself from industrial imports coming from Austria and the Czech lands. For the Balkan states, the situation was the reverse; after the restrictions forced on them by the great powers of the time during the Congress of Berlin in 1878 were gradually lifted in the 1890s, they were able to manage their tariffs, but had no guaranteed protected market to expand into.[50] To some extent, these different situations translated into different sets of policies.

Hungarian support for industry did not rely on tariffs. Despite this, its economic policies, dating back to 1881, were the most successful in the region. The government provided preferential rail rates, lower taxes for industrial producers and directly engaged with certain companies. Between capital formation based on successful agricultural exports and foreign investment,

---

44 Lampe and Jackson, *Balkan Economic History*, 253, 260–4.
45 Alison Fleig Frank, *Oil Empire: Visions of Prosperity in Austrian Galicia* (Cambridge, MA: Harvard University Press, 2005).
46 Diana Mishkova, 'Modernization and Political Elites in the Balkans Before the First World War', *East European Politics and Societies* 9, no. 1 (1994): 63–89, here 63.
47 E.A. Radice, 'General Characteristics of the Region between the Wars', in *The Economic History of Eastern Europe 1919–1975*, vol. 2, *Interwar Policy, The War and Reconstruction*, eds M.C. Kaser and E.A. Radice (Oxford: Clarendon Press, 1985), 23–65, here 31.
48 Iván T. Berend, 'The Failure of Economic Nationalism: Central and Eastern Europe before World War II', *Revue économique* 51, no. 2 (2000): 315–22, here 315.
49 Thomas David, *Nationalisme économique et industrialisation: L'expérience des pays de l'Est (1789–1939)* (Geneva: Librairie Droz, 2009), 93.
50 Pedro Lains, 'Southern European Economic Backwardness Revisited: The Role of Open Economy Forces in Portugal and the Balkans, 1870–1913', *Scandinavian Economic History Review* 50, no. 1 (2002): 24–43.

industry grew fast and became the main motor of growth after 1906.[51] At the same time, political considerations made the Hungarian magnates look unfavourably at the development of other nations within their domain.

Balkan countries were at first forbidden to change their tariff policies by international agreements. Bulgaria was only able to do so in 1896 which immediately led to a tariff war with Austria-Hungary. In Serbia, the reverse was true; the Pig War with Austria-Hungary over the access of Serbian hogs to the Austro-Hungarian market, which began in 1906,[52] pushed the country to pursue protectionist policies. Between falling export opportunities and home markets dominated by industrial imports, these countries pursued similar policies of economic nationalism, with Romania promulgating the first laws to this end in 1888, Bulgaria in 1894 and, finally, Serbia in 1898.[53] While these laws did bring about significant change, leading to a large number of industrial ventures, particularly in Romania, they were significantly less effective than they had proved in Hungary. The states lacked both capital and sufficient capacity for replication. As populations grew, sustained growth based on agricultural exports required increased agricultural productivity, but this did not occur.[54]

In Hungary and Romania, the strong position of both magnates and boyars allowed them to transfer the majority of the costs of these protectionist policies onto the rural population. In Romania, the state-mandated exploitative sharecropping system resulted in the outbreak of the last European mass peasant insurrection in 1907, which resulted in thousands of casualties.[55]

Despite some success in producing modernization, economic nationalism failed to significantly change the character of the region's economies before the beginning of the First World War. Even if industrial growth was impressive (such as during the Serbian 'mini-spurt' after the Pig War), the starting position was so low that expansion did not make a marked change. Table 6.8 shows the occupational structure of countries and regions within the Habsburg Empire before the outbreak of the First World War. Only the Czech lands developed into part of

Table 6.7 Per capita industrialization levels in CEE (Great Britain in 1900 = 100)

	1880	1900	1913
Austria-Hungary	15	23	32
Bulgaria	6	8	10
Romania	7	9	13
Russia	10	15	20
Serbia	7	9	12

Note: The level of industrialization is here understood, as Paul Bairoch describes, 'in the traditional sense – the per capita volume of industrial production'. 'International Industrialisation Levels from 1750 to 1980', *Journal of European Economic History* 11, no. 1/2 (1982): 281.

Source: Paul Bairoch, 'International Industrialisation Levels from 1750 to 1980', *Journal of European Economic History* 11, no. 1/2 (1982): 294, 330.

---

51 Schulze, 'Patterns of growth', 326.
52 Lampe and Jackson, *Balkan Economic History*, 175–7.
53 David, *Nationalisme économique*, 97.
54 Berend, *History Derailed*, 134; and Lampe and Jackson, *Balkan Economic History*, 70, 164.
55 Chirot, *Social Change in a Peripheral Society*, 150–4.

Table 6.8 Occupational structure in Central and Eastern European economies, 1910 (in %)

	Agriculture	Industry
Czech lands (Bohemia, Moravia and Silesia)	34	51
Poland	63	24
Hungary	64	23
Galicia and Bukovina	73	18
Romania	75	10
Bulgaria	75	10
Croatia	79	13
Serbia	82	7
Dalmatia	83	9

Source: Iván T. Berend, *History Derailed: Central and Eastern Europe in the Long Nineteenth Century* (Berkeley, CA: University of California Press, 2003), 179.

Europe's industrial centre, with Hungary and Poland occupying an intermediate position and the rest of the region remaining mostly agricultural. Ultimately, outside of the Czech lands 'the problem of securing a base for a genuine take-off' had not yet been solved.[56]

The First World War and post-war reconstruction, 1914–1929

The available data on GDP in the 1920s is paradoxically more insubstantial than that for the beginning of the century, making it difficult to gather accurate growth rates for the period. Nonetheless, sources point to a tripartite division of the years that led up to the Great Depression: a sharp decline of production during the First World War, followed by slow reconstruction in the 1920s and finally a spurt of growth in the second half of the decade. When contrasted with the performance of Western Europe, the period saw growing divergence in levels of development. Between 1913 and 1929, GDP per capita in Central and Eastern Europe grew modestly from 1726 to 1982 in 1990 international dollars, while in Western Europe the equivalent change was greater: from 3,488 to 4,167 in 1990 international dollars.[57] Considered alongside mediocre results from the next decade, this data gives little justification for the widespread idealization of the interwar period in national historiographies.[58]

The waging of war in this period – either as part of a larger empire, as in eastern Central Europe, or in alliance with them, as in the Balkans – put a significant strain on the economy, while armies inflicted direct physical damage. Problems were exacerbated by the length of the conflict in Central and Eastern Europe, where in some cases hostilities began in 1912 and lasted up to as late as 1921, resulting in a further setback to economic activity. Throughout the region, a high percentage of the male population died. Unmechanized agriculture, the primary pre-war contributor to growth, suffered greatly from the requisition and death of horses. Stocks of raw materials were depleted, and years of underinvestment resulted in a poor state of fixed capital. The transport system was in disarray, with railways and bridges

---

56 Radice, 'General Characteristics', 29–30; and David, *Nationalisme économique*, 146–50.
57 This is in reference to Albania, Bulgaria, Czechoslovakia, Hungary, Poland, Romania and Yugoslavia.
58 Bogdan Murgescu, 'The Economic Performance of Interwar Romania: Golden Age Myth and Statistical Evidence', *Jahrbücher für Geschichte und Kultur Südosteuropas* 6 (2004): 43–64.

in ruin. People needed new clothes and durable goods to replace those worn out or ruined during the war. Destruction was particularly heavy in Serbia, where almost a third of the population died, and industry was almost completely decimated.[59] In Poland, the retreating Russian army dismantled or destroyed many factories in 1915, while the occupying Germans stripped them for resources. Lithuania and Latvia suffered greatly from population movements and hostilities lasting up until 1919.[60]

When hostilities ended, severe shortages of food and fuel occurred, which were inadequately addressed by sparse international aid and exacerbated by the arrival of refugees and former prisoners of war. Unemployment was rampant. Throughout the region, the 'economic and social system was on the point of collapse'.[61] In Hungary, which lost the majority of its territory, the deteriorating situation led to an abortive communist revolution in 1919. In the short-to-medium term, governments resorted to retaining high levels of trade and exchange control from the war years and continued with deficit spending to boost the work market and aid reconstruction.[62]

Deficit spending led to inflation and – in Hungary and Poland – hyperinflation. Only Czechoslovakia was able to stabilize its currency quickly. A moderate growth in prices produced a surprising inflation-fuelled boom in the early 1920s, with rising exports and increased economic activity.[63] Hyperinflation did not provide these advantages but damaged production and destroyed savings, threatening social order. In Hungary, stabilization was achieved in 1924 under István Bethlen with help from the League of Nations, while Poland's prime minister, Władysław Grabski, was forced to draw on the country's internal resources within the same year (with a further devaluation in 1927).[64] Inflation was followed by stabilization crises along with rising unemployment. The experience of inflation resulted in a deflationary state of mind, which strengthened the economic orthodoxy at the time. The region was mostly stabilized by the time of the UK's abortive return to gold in 1925, but the cost of maintaining the new gold exchange standard proved high.

The creation of additional borders after the war erected new barriers to trade, particularly with the fall of the Habsburg customs area.[65] At the same time, revolution resulted in Russia cutting its market off from the region, leading in a sharp decline in trade which was felt particularly by the newly formed Baltic states, Romania and Poland. In Poland, per capita trade with Russia fell from

---

59 John R. Lampe, 'Belated Balkan Modernization and the Consequences of Communist Power', in *Industrialisierung und gesellschaftlicher Wandel in Südosteuropa*, ed. Roland Schönfeld (München: Südosteuropa-Gesellschaft, 1989), 23.
60 Aldcroft, *Europe's Third World*, 42–3.
61 Ibid., 43; Derek H. Aldcroft and Steven Morewood, *The European Economy since 1914*, 5th ed. (London, Routledge, 2013), 35; Rudolf Nötel, 'International Credit and Finance', in Kaser and Radice, *The Economic History of Eastern Europe 1919–1975*, vol. 2, 170–295, here 172–4.
62 Turnock, *The Economy of East Central Europe*, 159.
63 Berend, *Decades of Crisis*, 226.
64 T.J. Sargent, 'The Ends of Four Big Inflations', in *Inflation: Causes and Effects*, ed. R.E. Hall (Chicago, IL: University of Chicago Press, 1982), 41–98; Jerzy Tomaszewski, *Stabilizacja waluty w Polsce: z badań nad polityką gospodarczą rządu polskiego przed przewrotem majowym* [The stabilization of the currency in Poland: studies in the economic policy of the Polish government before the May coup] (Warsaw: Książka i Wiedza, 1961).
65 See Nikolaus Wolf, Max-Stephan Schulze and Hans Christian Heinemeyer, 'On the Economic Consequences of the Peace: Trade and Borders After Versailles', *The Journal of Economic History* 71, no. 4 (2001): 915–49; Anders E.B. Blomqvist, *Economic Nationalizing in the Ethnic Borderlands of Hungary and Romania: Inclusion, Exclusion and Annihilation in Szatmár/Satu-Mare 1867–1944* (Stockholm: Department of History, Stockholm University, 2014).

around $67 to $0.4 (from 1910 to 1938).[66] Finally, states needed to integrate new territories, often from different legal traditions, into their economies. This was particularly important for Romania and Serbia/Yugoslavia, which more than doubled in both area and population, as well as Poland, which was recreated from lands from three different empires.[67] At the same time, Bulgaria and Hungary had to lick their wounds and redefine their economies within diminished frontiers.

If regaining pre-war production levels was the initial goal, there was no going back to earlier patterns of international trade.[68] Governments were slow to let go of their wartime trade controls, and tariffs were higher than they were at the beginning of the century. The decline and slow recovery of trade was not accompanied by a comparable slowdown of output.[69] The result was a drop in prices in line with global deflationary tendencies after the return to gold. Moreover, the fall in agricultural prices was faster than that in industrial products, which resulted in deteriorating trade terms for the region (apart from Czechoslovakia, where agriculture played a smaller role in the economy). In total, trade terms for primary commodity exporters dropped by 11 per cent between 1913 and 1929.[70]

The agricultural fringes were particularly affected by the stagnation of Western European agricultural consumption, a decline that may even have been attributable to changes in dietary patterns, along with higher imports from North America, Australia and Argentina. With a worldwide rise in stocks and a fall in cereal prices, CEE economies were unable to compete. While, before 1914, half of the wheat imported by the industrial West came from Eastern Europe, by 1929 most of it came from North America. From the mid-1920s to the late 1930s, agricultural prices declined globally. The average price of a bushel of wheat dropped almost by half from $2.10 to $1.15 between just 1925 and 1929.[71] The agricultural depression, which started before and lasted beyond the Great Depression of 1929–1933, severely impacted export revenues for most countries in Central and Eastern Europe. The only growing sector in the market was alternative crops, such as vegetables, or – until the price crash in 1925–1926 – tobacco. Such diversification did indeed begin to occur in the Balkans and the Baltic states, but it was a slow process.

Agriculture in the region remained traditional and had low productivity levels. The situation was not helped by agricultural reforms that were 'not conceived primarily as a policy of modernization of agriculture',[72] which in some cases calcified negative structural characteristics of the sector. Peasant self-sufficiency (and thus low engagement with the market), small and fragmented holdings, and the overpopulation of land (except in Czechoslovakia and the Baltics)[73]

---

66 Turnock, *The Economy of East Central Europe*, 168; Radice, 'General Characteristics', 33–5.
67 Carsten Trenkler and Nikolaus Wolf, 'Economic Integration across Borders: The Polish Interwar Economy 1921–1937', *European Review of Economic History* 9 (2005): 199–231. See Lampe, 'Belated Balkan Modernization', 32.
68 Lampe and Jackson, *Balkan Economic History*, 364–75.
69 Berend, *Decades of Crisis*, 227.
70 Aldcroft, *Europe's Third World*, 49–52.
71 Berend, *Decades of Crisis*, 228.
72 Alice Teichova, 'Eastern Europe in Transition: Economic Development during the Interwar and Postwar Period', in *Central Europe in the Twentieth Century: An Economic Perspective*, ed. Alice Teichova (Aldershot: Ashgate, 1997), 5–21, here 7.
73 W.H. Meyers and N. Kazlauskiene, 'Land Reform in Estonia, Latvia and Lithuania: A Comparative Analysis', in *Land Reform in the Former Soviet Union and Eastern Europe*, ed. S.K. Wegren (London: Routledge, 1977), 87–110; Elena Dragomir, 'Development Characteristics of Interwar European Periphery: The Cases of Romania and Lithuania's Agriculture', *Revista Română pentru Studii Baltice și Nordice* 2, no. 1 (2010): 53–68, here 59.

Table 6.9 Agricultural productivity in various European countries, 1911–1936 (million calories produced yearly by a male agricultural labourer showing five-year averages around the given year)

	1911	1921	1928	1936
Austria	17.0	13.7	21.5	24.3
Bulgaria	10.7	9.3	9.0	9.8
Czechoslovakia	17.0	15.6	24.7	25.9
Germany	31.2	22.7	29.7	39.0
Hungary	17.1	12.9	15.5	16.6
Poland	11.0	9.7	11.8	13.0
Romania	14.2	8.1	11.7	11.5
United Kingdom	24.4	25.9	28.5	32.7
Yugoslavia	9.3	6.7	7.5	10.1

Source: Paul Bairoch, *L'agriculture des pays développés, 1800 à nos jours: Production – Productivité – Rendements* (Paris: Economica, 1999), 143.

led to low efficiency (Table 6.9). Apart from some larger estates, the structure and methods of production remained unchanged throughout the period.

The deteriorating situation for agriculture and problems with the current account coincided with and informed a significant change in economic policy. New states in the region 'sought to establish national identities in a form that included economic independence.'[74] The result was the more widespread prevalence of economic nationalism than had been the case in previous decades, which translated into taking over companies previously owned by foreign capital (through a process of nostrification which covered mostly German- and Austrian-owned enterprises),[75] a wide range of protective barriers and comprehensive industrial programmes that included a strong state role. On a wider level, industrialization seemed to be the only way to modernize in the post-war world. Due to the economic situation at the time, it translated into a policy of import substitution, which replaced the export-fuelled growth of previous decades. As a result, high tariffs were the order of the day, as states moved to protect their fledgling production and reduce imports. Tariffs were combined with other means of promoting local production (export bounties, import controls, subsidies). The tax burden of these policies was often placed on the already highly indebted agricultural sector.

Newly created industries experienced problems typical of this approach: they were high cost, inefficient and technologically backward. Some of these shortcomings could also be explained by the shallowness of national markets, which made long production runs impossible due to limited demand. Apart from the most industrialized country of the region, Czechoslovakia, the development of industrialization was most rapid when the starting point was low, which was particularly the case in Bulgaria (Table 6.10), while progress in Hungary and Poland was significantly worse. For a comparison of the division of labour by sector, see the data in the chapter by Zsombor Bódy and Stanislav Holubec in this volume.

---

74 Berend, *Decades of Crisis*, 234.
75 Teichova, 'Eastern Europe in Transition', 8; Bogdan Murgescu, 'Anything but Simple: The Case of the Romanian Oil Industry', in *History and Culture of Economic Nationalism in East-Central Europe*, eds H. Schultz and Eduard Kubů (Berlin: Berliner Wissenschafts-Verlag, 2006), 231–50, here 237–9.

Table 6.10 Indices of manufacturing output, 1913–1929 (1913 = 100)

	1920–21	1925	1929	Increase 1925–1929 (%)
Bulgaria	-	-	179.0	-
Czechoslovakia	69.8	136.4	171.8	26.0
Hungary	64.0	76.7	113.9	48.5
Poland	35.1	63.1	85.9	36.1
Romania	47.2	92.2	136.9	48.5
Yugoslavia	-	-	140.0	-
World	93.2	120.7	137.5	13.9

Source: Derek H. Aldcroft and Steven Morewood, *Economic Change in Eastern Europe since 1918* (Cheltenham: Edward Elgar, 1995), 44.

The Great Depression and the Second World War, 1929–1945

The period from 1929 to 1945 can again be divided into three parts. First, the Great Depression wrecked the economies of Central and Eastern Europe and was then followed by a recovery in output but without a corresponding improvement in international trade. Finally, the Second World War brought about population losses and significant damage to the economy, leaving parts of the region in ruins.

GDP per capita estimations for the 1930s (Table 6.11) are more robust than is the case for the previous decade, but little can be said about these indicators during the war. The region was 'denied an appropriate period to adjust to dramatic post-war changes',[76] and the 1930s were not kind, with GDP stagnating over the course of the decade. As a result, the distance from Western Europe grew. This growing divergence reflected both CEE's faster population growth and the larger negative impact of the Great Depression in the region.[77]

Table 6.11 GDP per capita in Central and Eastern European economies, 1929–1938

	1929	1938
Albania	926	-
Bulgaria	1,227	1,499
Czechoslovakia	3,042	2,882
Hungary	2,476	2,655
Poland	2,117	2,182
Romania	1,152	1,242
Yugoslavia	1,256	1,249
Region	1,982	1,961
Western Europe (30 countries)	4,167	4,421

Note: The Czechoslovak data for 1938 is from 1937. The CEE result in 1938 is recalculated from source data.

Source: The Maddison Project, www.ggdc.net/maddison/maddison-project/home.htm, 2013 version.

---

76 Berend, *Decades of Crisis*, 261–2.
77 David, *Nationalisme économique*, 239–40.

Table 6.12 Value of exports per ton in Bulgaria, Poland and Romania, 1929–1934 (1928 = 100)

	1929	1930	1931	1932	1933	1934
Bulgaria	126	70	47	35	41	39
Poland	109	104	82	65	59	55
Romania	89	68	48	40	35	34

Source: Rudolf Nötel, 'International Credit and Finance', in *The Economic History of Eastern Europe 1919–1975, vol. 2, Interwar Policy, The War and Reconstruction*, eds Michael Charles Kaser and E.A. Radice (Oxford: Clarendon Press, 1986), 217.

Table 6.13 Indices of GDP per capita in 1913 and the worst year of the Great Depression in each country (1929 = 100)

	1913	Year of nadir	Index of that year
Bulgaria	83	1935	85
Czechoslovakia	77	1935	79
Hungary	88	1932	87
Poland	102	1932	65
Romania	101	1932	92
Yugoslavia	81	1932	81
Europe without the USSR	94	1932	89

Source: Paul Bairoch, *Victoires and déboires: Histoire économique et sociale du monde du XVIe siècle à nos jours* (Paris: Gallimard, 1997), 54.

The Great Depression was a global economic crisis that led to an unprecedented decrease in worldwide industrial output.[78] Between 1929 and 1933, agricultural prices fell by about 60 per cent, while manufactured products experienced a corresponding decrease of 41 per cent. Trade contracted, as countries rushed to protect their markets through tariff barriers, beginning with the American Smoot-Hawley Tariff Act of 1930.[79] The financial crisis in the spring and summer of 1931 decimated the global financial market, and countries were forced to either abandon gold convertibility (most notably the United Kingdom in September 1931), or devalue their currencies. The world split into insular currency and trade blocks.

The Depression came to Central and Eastern Europe gradually, with production peaking between the first quarter of 1929 (in Poland) and the fourth quarter of 1930 (in Lithuania).[80] In agricultural countries, the value of principal export products fell dramatically (see Table 6.12). The smaller fall in industrial prices ('price scissors') significantly worsened Central and Eastern Europe's trade terms. In other words, countries in the region had to export more in order to

---

78 The literature on the Great Depression is extensive. For seminal accounts, see Charles P. Kindleberger, *The World in Depression 1929–1939* (Berkeley, CA: University of California Press, 1986); Barry Eichengreen, *Golden Fetters: The Gold Standard and the Great Depression, 1919–1939* (Oxford: Oxford University Press, 1992).
79 Barry Eichengreen and Douglas A. Irwin, 'The Slide to Protectionism in the Great Depression: Who Succumbed and Why?', *The Journal of Economic History* 70, no. 4 (2010): 871–97.
80 Thilo Albers and Martin Uebele, 'The Global Impact of the Great Depression', *LSE Economic History Working Papers* 218 (2015): 2, 30.

keep imports and debt servicing at the same levels, yet at the same time, low productivity and the global fall in demand for their products made this impossible. The Depression resulted in a significant reduction of output (see Table 6.13) and a major increase in poverty.

Agriculture was the main victim of the Depression in the region, as was the case in other global peripheral agricultural sectors. On a microeconomic level, farmers initially reacted to the fall in prices by raising supply in order to meet their obligations. Overproduction led to the accumulation of stocks and a further collapse in prices. The sector was already indebted before the crisis, but now the situation became even bleaker: 'In Hungary 60 per cent of the land of smallholders was fully mortgaged and interest paid on agricultural loans amounted to more than 25 per cent of yearly income ... [T]hroughout Eastern Europe agrarian indebtedness was a pervasive problem.'[81] As poverty spread, farmers reduced the amount they engaged with the market in the most stricken areas, buying only salt and matches. Throughout the region, the use of fertilizer almost stopped, and there was no capital for modernization. Since not all agricultural products suffered the same fall in prices, there were some attempts at structural change, particularly for labour-intensive products. This translated into an increase in the production of vegetables, wine (in Bulgaria), meat and poultry and dairy products (the latter particularly in the Baltic states); although, as was the case in the previous decade, the scale of these changes was relatively small.[82]

Industry suffered most in countries that depended on foreign markets to sell their products. While Czechoslovakia's terms of trade improved, as manufacturing prices declined more slowly than agricultural ones, the country failed to find enough buyers abroad and suffered a drop in production of 40 per cent. The traditional export industries of textiles and glass were hit particularly hard.[83] A similar drop in Poland was caused by foreign capital being pulled out of local companies. The state supported many failing enterprises, and as a result, the public sector grew. In industrialized cities, unemployment rose steeply, and partial employment became the norm. In other countries, the impact of the Depression on industry was smaller, as was the role of the industrial sector in the economy. In Bulgaria, some industrial growth was experienced even during the Depression.[84]

Financial problems worsened the crisis for the real economy. Reduced proceeds from exports, along with the necessity to service external debt, undermined gold-based monetary systems. When the financial market imploded in 1931 and capital imports ran dry, Central and Eastern Europe found itself insolvent.[85] Most countries quickly moved to protect their financial systems by introducing exchange control, which put gold and convertible currency transactions under governmental oversight. Moratoria on loans were introduced and repayment renegotiated with some lenders. Hungary began the region's shift to exchange-control regimes in 1931, with Czechoslovakia, Latvia and Estonia following suit in the same year, and Romania in 1932. Some countries (Yugoslavia, Estonia and Czechoslovakia) devalued their currencies, which was advantageous for international trade but raised the internal cost of financing external debt. Others (Hungary and Bulgaria) opted for hidden devaluation, modelled on Germany, in which multiple exchange rates were used. Some countries treated leaving the gold exchange standard with mistrust. Poland and Lithuania adhered to the rules of the game the longest, with the for-

---

81 Aldcroft, *Europe's Third World*, 57.
82 Berend, *Decades of Crisis*, 257–8.
83 Václav Průcha, 'Continuity and Discontinuity in the Economic Development of Czechoslovakia 1918–1991', in *Central Europe in the Twentieth Century: An Economic Perspective*, ed. Alice Teichova (Aldershot: Ashgate, 1997), 26.
84 Aldroft and Morewood, *Economic Change*, 61.
85 David, *Nationalisme économique*, 155.

Table 6.14 Export structure in selected countries, 1913–1937 (in %)

		Bulgaria	Hungary	Poland	Romania	Yugoslavia	European average
Agrarian and food products	1913	82.0	70.5	.	88.0	.	19.7
	1929	78.5	71.2	38.8	46.0	50.1	18.7
	1937	87.4	61.2	34.1	39.9	48.4	16.3
Raw materials	1913	7.5	11.1	.	4.5	.	14.1
	1929	12.5	7.3	18.8	15.4	32.8	13.1
	1937	8.3	8.2	19.3	17.2	35.6	14.1
Fuels	1913	0.1	1.3	.	5.9	.	5.4
	1929	1.5	0.9	16.6	35.3	0	4.8
	1937	0.6	0.7	18.9	40.7	0.2	6.4
Manufactured products	1913	10.4	17.1	.	0.9	.	59.3
	1929	7.5	20.6	25.8	2.2	17.1	62.7
	1937	3.7	29.9	27.6	1.5	15.8	62.3

Source: Thomas David, *Nationalisme économique et industrialisation: L'expérience des pays de l'Est (1789–1939)* (Geneva: Droz, 2009), 254.

mer, as a member of the gold bloc, finally introducing exchange control in April 1936.[86] This policy of prolonged deflation, which only served to further depress demand, proved disastrous for the economy and prevented a faster recovery.

After reaching its nadir, Central and Eastern Europe started to recover output but in relative isolation from the contracted world market. Since managing the balance of trade was imperative, countries followed the global trend of protectionism. At the same time, governments promoted exports through subsidies, tariff returns and dumping. Central agencies in certain sectors were created; for example, Hranoiznos in Bulgaria and Prizad in Yugoslavia managed grain exports with varied success.[87]

Despite their efforts, Central and Eastern European countries faced lower demand for their products, with major staples continuing to dominate a reduced number of exports. In agriculture, the modernization of Western European production resulted in a drop in imports,[88] further deteriorating CEE's position. Governments intervened with debt forgiveness or restructuring to assist the poverty-stricken rural population, often through newly founded state banks. In industry, the region had little to offer,[89] although Czechoslovakia achieved significant success in the armaments sector, which also had some potential in Poland.[90] The changing structure of exports is shown in Table 6.14.

---

86 Cecylia Leszczyńska, *Polska polityka pieniężna i walutowa w latach 1924–1936: W systemie Gold Exchange Standard* [Polish monetary and currency policy in the years 1924–1936: in the system of gold exchange standard] (Warsaw: Wydawnictwo Uniwersytetu Warszawskiego, 2013), 317–42. Albania kept its gold-based currency until the Italian invasion in 1939.
87 John Lampe, *Balkans into Southeastern Europe, 1914–2014: A Century of War and Transition*, 2nd ed. (Basingstoke: Palgrave Macmillan, 2014), 130–1.
88 Iván T. Berend and G. Ránki, 'L'évolution économique de l'Europe orientale entre les deux guerres mondiales', *Annales Histoire, Sciences Sociales* 33, no. 2 (1978): 389–407, here 389.
89 David, *Nationalisme économique*, 260–1. The majority of industrial production in CEE was sold on domestic markets.
90 Marek Deszczyński and Wojciech Mazur, *Na krawędzi ryzyka: eksport polskiego sprzętu wojskowego w okresie międzywojennym* [On the brink of risk: Polish exports of military equipment in the interwar period] (Warsaw: Neriton, 2004).

Exchange control and the concomitant supervision of foreign trade gave governments powerful tools to influence the economy; every import transaction required governmental consent, and exporters were required to submit their foreign-currency proceeds to a central agency. State intervention, perceived as a method to revitalize the economy, went beyond protectionism. It was possible thanks to the political monopoly of local bureaucracies, a consequence of the region-wide defeat of democratic rules. Countries reduced their dependence on imports of consumer industrial products, and at the same time, supported their home industries. Governments placed orders domestically, promoted local products and managed expanding state sectors. Raw materials and machines encroached on the share of manufactured products from imports and investment grew. The region adopted the strategy of import substitution with some preliminary forays into economic planning.[91]

Exchange control and the lack of access to capital markets, apart from a few politically motivated loans, made trade with free-currency countries difficult.[92] As a result, a growing percentage of foreign trade in CEE was conducted through bilateral clearing agreements which were much more primitive than multilateral trade. Much of it was conducted with the Third Reich. The Balkan countries in particular could count on favourable trading terms (while the reverse was true for Czechoslovakia), as Germany used commerce to cement its sphere of influence. With time, CEE countries found themselves increasingly dependent on this trade, becoming 'part of a German war economy in the making'.[93] In the Baltics, only in Lithuania was the role of trade with Germany of smaller significance, while in the south, Albania was Mussolini's rather than Hitler's satellite.

Poland took the idea of state intervention and stimulating demand further than other countries in the region. Apart from controlling foreign trade – although more in terms of protecting the balance of payments than effectively coordinating protectionism – and managing a growing syndicate of state-owned companies, the government engaged in the construction of the Central Industrial Region (*Centralny Okręg Przemysłowy*, COP) in a triangle between the Vistula and San rivers. Laid out in a four-year plan, the investment project aimed to build up industry (particularly in the military sector) and provide employment for the heavily populated region. Poland also started working on a medium-term development plan. While criticized for its bad timing and relatively small effects, it was the largest coherent modernization policy implemented in the region. Hungary also engaged in this type of state management in the Győr region, albeit on a smaller scale.[94]

Despite the relative success of state intervention in the region, the countries' economic structures remained fairly unchanging. Looking at the industrialization index (see Table 6.15), it is clear that after taking into account significant population growth, CEE's position not only failed to improve in the interwar years but even deteriorated. Moreover, while in developed countries the Great Depression led to some degree of creative destruction,[95] CEE states were unable to effectively change. As they became closed and concentrated on survival, they clung

---

91 David, *Nationalisme économique*, 156, 200; Ingvar Svennilson, *Growth and Stagnation in the European Economy* (Geneva: United Nations, Economic Commission for Europe, 1954), 307–9; Lampe, 'Belated Balkan Modernization', 32.
92 Turnock, *The Economy of East Central Europe*, 177.
93 Berend, 'The Failure', 319.
94 David, *Nationalisme économique*, 202; Jerzy Gołębiowski, *COP: Dzieje industrializacji w rejonie bezpieczeństwa 1922–1939* [COP: The history of industrialization in the security region, 1922–1939] (Cracow: Wydawnictwo Naukowe Akademii Pedagogicznej, 2000).
95 Alexander J. Field, 'The Most Technologically Progressive Decade of the Century', *American Economic Review* 93, no. 4 (2003): 1399–1413.

Table 6.15 Level of industrialization per capita in CEE countries in 1910 and 1937 within their interwar borders (UK = 100)

	Czechoslovakia	Hungary	Poland	Yugoslavia	Romania	Bulgaria
1910	52.1	29.9	30.1	7.6	6.2	5.3
1937	42.4	21.3	15.2	6.3	5.9	3.7

Source: Thomas David, *Nationalisme économique et industrialisation: L'expérience des pays de l'Est (1789–1939)* (Geneva: Droz, 2009), 253.

to inefficient economic structures, while more competitive ones were being created in Europe's hub. When new technologies, such as preliminary forays into television, came to the region, they were insular projects with no relation to the rest of the backward economies, which were plagued by 'the vicious circle of population pressure, excessive reliance on under-productive agriculture and low income'.[96]

The comparison of electricity production and car usage is telling. In 1938, the regional average per capita production of electric energy reached 117 watt-hours (Wh).[97] While this meant a 54 per cent increase compared to 1929, it put the region far behind Western Europe, with France producing 527 and Germany 807 Wh per capita. The only significant success was achieved by Czechoslovakia, which, after doubling its output, reached Western levels of production (334 Wh per capita). An even greater increase in the number of cars per 10,000 citizens allowed the country to overtake Austria and almost catch up with Italy, but with a figure of 80 cars it was still behind France and Germany, which had 544 and 242 cars per 10,000 citizens respectively.[98] In other countries, the gap was much greater, and in Poland the number decreased during the Depression as a result of strict governmental controls.[99] Moreover, the region hardly produced any of its own vehicles, with the only meaningful exception being again in Czechoslovakia. This lack underlines the region's technological backwardness, as the production of cars was the truly pioneering industry in the period.[100]

The recovery from the Great Depression came to a halt during the Second World War, which brought unprecedented levels of death and destruction to the region. Central and Eastern Europe experienced the largest relative casualties among combatant states, particularly in the northern part of the region, forming part of what Timothy Snyder calls the 'Bloodlands',[101] and in Yugoslavia where there was bitter partisan warfare. Estimates point to losses of about 15 per cent of the pre-war population in Poland, 14 per cent in Lithuania, 11 per cent in Latvia, 8 per cent in Hungary, 7 per cent in Yugoslavia, 6 per cent in Romania, 4 per cent in Estonia and smaller values for other participating states.[102] For further information, see the chapter on demography (Chapter 5, this volume).

---

96 Radice, 'General Characteristics', 31.
97 This figure covers Bulgaria, Czechoslovakia, Hungary, Poland, Romania and Yugoslavia.
98 This is calculated from data in B.R. Mitchell, ed., *International Historical Statistics: Europe 1750–2000*, 5th ed. (Basingstoke: Palgrave Macmillan, 2003), 562–3, 735–8.
99 Zbigniew Landau and Jerzy Tomaszewski, *Gospodarka Polski międzywojennej* [The interwar Polish economy], vol. 3 (Warsaw: Książka i Wiedza, 1982), 311–4, vol. 4 (Warsaw: Książka i Wiedza, 1989), 417–9.
100 David, *Nationalisme économique*, 250, 258, 278–86.
101 Timothy Snyder, *Bloodlands: Europe Between Hitler and Stalin* (London: The Bodley Head, 2010).
102 Hein Klemann and Sergei Kudryashov, *Occupied Economies: An Economic History of Nazi-Occupied Europe, 1939–1945* (London: Berg, 2012), 418; and Niall Fergusson, 'The Second World War as an Economic Disaster', in *Economic Disasters of the Twentieth Century*, eds Michael J. Oliver and Derek H. Aldcroft (Cheltenham: Edward Elgar, 2007), 119.

The region suffered material losses in agriculture, housing, mining and industry, although the degree of loss varied. In terms of GDP, Yugoslavia lost around 370 per cent of its GDP from the year 1938, while the number in Poland was over 350 per cent. For Hungary and Czechoslovakia, it was more than 200 and 100 per cent respectively, while in Bulgaria and Romania it amounted to about one third of annual GDP. The Baltic states ceased to exist and underwent a transformation towards the Soviet economic model before they were overrun by the Germans during their invasion of the USSR.[103]

Post-war reconstruction and accelerated growth, 1945–1975

Central and Eastern Europe was in disarray at the end of the Second World War. Apart from the direct human losses and the material destruction caused by military operations and German atrocities in occupied territories, the region was plagued by instability. Population displacements continued after the capitulation of the Third Reich.[104]

Besides requisitions and lootings, which included dismantling entire factories and relocating them to the Soviet Union, the Soviets organized several joint ventures, which gave them control over the basic economic resources of occupied countries.[105] Agricultural production was similarly disorganized, and in 1946–1947, parts of the region experienced the last severe famine in twentieth-century Europe.

Reconstruction was essential, but it was unclear which economic model would prevail. For a time, it seemed that the Soviet Union would be satisfied to control the region with the help of obedient coalition governments and national routes to socialism. Yet, when the United States launched the European Recovery Plan (otherwise known as the Marshall Plan), offering aid to those countries that agreed to base their reconstruction upon free-market economic policies, Stalin decided to strengthen his grip on the Central and Eastern European countries. As a result, the Soviet Union not only prevented Czechoslovakia and Poland from signing up to the Marshall Plan, but also ended the various compromise arrangements that existed with segments of the existing political elites and endorsed complete takeover by local communist parties.[106] The communist party-led states began to restructure their entire economic and social systems according to the Soviet model, purging political opponents, nationalizing industry and most of the service sector without compensation and collectivizing a large part of agriculture.

Central planning allowed close political control over resource allocation and was crucial for communist projects of economic development and societal engineering. The communists aimed to swiftly change the existing economic and social structures, foster industrial growth and bolster the number and social clout of industrial workers, thus strengthening the economic and social base of their regimes.[107] The extensive growth model was based on massive additional inputs of both capital and labour. Domestic consumption was severely restricted, and

---

103 Berend, *Decades of Crisis*, 405.
104 For more details, see the subchapter 'People on the Move: Waves of Migration' by Stanislav Holubec and Béla Tomka in this volume.
105 Florian Banu, *Asalt asupra economiei României: De la Solagra la Sovrom (1936–1956)* [Assault on the Romanian economy: from Solagra to Sovrom (1936–1956)] (Bucharest: Editura Nemira, 2004).
106 See especially the analysis of Mark Kramer, 'Stalin, Soviet Policy, and the Consolidation of a Communist Bloc in Eastern Europe, 1944–53', in *Stalinism Revisited: The Establishment of Communist Regimes in East-Central Europe*, ed. Vladimir Tismăneanu (Budapest: CEU Press, 2009), 51–101.
107 For the role values play in the design of communist economic policies, see János Kornai, *The Socialist System: The Political Economy of Communism* (Oxford: Clarendon Press, 1992), 49–61. The same author also notes that 'revolutionary fervour and self-sacrifice' were only temporary factors (ibid., 28).

resources were used for huge investments in industry and infrastructure. At the same time, the state favoured the absorption of labour reserves from agriculture into industry, as well as the mobilization of women for work outside the household.[108]

Since, with the exception of Czechoslovakia and East Germany, the countries in the region had been largely agricultural, agriculture and the rural population were supposed to provide both the labour and the food, and the raw materials needed for the development of industry. The drain on resources was engineered through a massive restructuring of both property relations and production organization. Soviet-inspired large-scale collectivization began in the late 1940s and continued through the 1950s.[109] Peasants were forced to surrender their plots and to join producers' cooperatives; the collectivization process was only abandoned in Yugoslavia and Poland due to political reasons, which occurred in 1953 and after 1956 respectively.[110]

Depriving peasant families of private land was a means to encourage their younger members to search for employment in industry and services. Therefore, the share of people employed in agriculture declined from between 50 and 75 per cent to 50 per cent in Albania, around 30 per cent in Bulgaria, Poland and Romania, and around 20 per cent in Hungary and Yugoslavia. In Czechoslovakia, where the initial share was lower, agricultural employment reached 12 per cent.[111] The ratio of relative labour and capital inputs in agriculture gradually shifted. The consolidation of plots allowed even moderate inputs of modern machinery, chemical fertilizers and better seed to achieve significant increases in productivity, especially in the cultivation of grains and other crops better suited to large farms. Modern animal husbandry contributed to an increase in meat and dairy production. For the region as a whole, net agricultural output more than doubled from the late 1940s to the 1980s. In spite of such progress, and even if we consider the productivity level per male agricultural worker, an indicator that would usually favour the countries that recorded the biggest loss of labour towards non-agricultural sectors, the socialist countries of Central and Eastern Europe continued to lag behind the fast-developing agriculture of Western Europe, and in fact the gap even increased during the post-war period.

Industry was the obvious star of economic growth in the socialist states of Central and Eastern Europe. The system favoured investments in new industrial plants, especially in heavy industry.[112] The Soviet steel complex of Magnitogorsk, along with the 'socialist city' built close to it, became a model to emulate throughout the region.[113] Nowa Huta in Poland, Eisenhüttenstadt (originally Stalinstadt) in the GDR, Kunčice in Czechoslovakia, Dunaújváros (Sztálinváros from to 1951 to 1961) in Hungary and Pernik (Dimitrovo from 1949 to 1962) in Bulgaria were all local variations on this model.[114] Production surged, as can be seen in the case of crude steel.

---

108 Ibid., 204–11. For a more theoretical analysis, see also János Kornai, *Growth, Shortage and Efficiency: A Macrodynamic Model of the Socialist Economy* (Oxford: Basil Blackwell, 1982), 102–9.

109 Constantin Iordachi and Arnd Bauerkämper, eds, *The Collectivization of Agriculture in Communist Eastern Europe: Comparison and Entanglements* (Budapest: CEU Press, 2014). See also Gail Kligman and Katherine Verdery, *Peasants under Siege: The Collectivization of Romanian Agriculture, 1949–1962* (Princeton, NJ: Princeton University Press, 2011).

110 Dariusz Jarosz, *Polityka władz komunistycznych w Polsce w latach 1948–1956 a chłopi* [The affect of communist policies on peasants in Poland, 1948–1956] (Warsaw: DiG, 1998); and Jacek Kochanowicz, 'Stato e contadini: La politica agraria polacca negli anni 1956–1970', *Studi Storici* 29 (1988): 759–85.

111 Kornai, *The Socialist System*, 6–7.

112 Ibid., 171–80.

113 Stephen Kotkin, *Magnetic Mountain: Stalinism as a Civilization* (Berkeley, CA: University of California Press, 1995).

114 See Dagmara Jajeśniak-Quast, *Stahlgiganten in der sozialistischen Transformation: Nowa Huta in Krakau, EKO in Eisenhüttenstadt und Kunčice in Ostrava* (Wiesbaden: Harrassowitz Verlag, 2010).

Table 6.16 Agricultural productivity in various European countries, 1948/52–1988/92 (in five-year averages, million calories produced yearly by a male agricultural labourer)

	1948/52	1958/62	1968/72	1978/82	1988/92
Bulgaria	12.5	22.3	49.2	89.5	117.3
Czechoslovakia	21.8	35.5	52.7	73.2	91.3
France	22.3	40.8	64.8	120.2	187.3
Germany	31.8	59.7	106.7	183.9	240.6
Hungary	12.3	21.6	35.9	71.3	90.7
Poland	19.6	28.7	35.6	40.0	45.3
Portugal	6.6	8.8	18.6	25.5	44.5
Romania	8.6	12.5	23.2	52.9	59.2
Soviet Union	21.3	38.3	55.8	58.8	63.4
Yugoslavia	18.6	33.9	40.3	75.4	88.4

Source: Paul Bairoch, *L'agriculture des pays développés, 1800 à nos jours: Production – Productivité – Rendements* (Paris: Economica, 1999), 24, 126, 148.

Table 6.17 Crude steel production (in million tons)

	1948	1960	1970	1980	1985	1989
Albania	0.00	0.00	0.00	0.19	0.65	0.20
Bulgaria	0.00	0.25	1.80	2.56	2.94	2.90
Czechoslovakia	2.62	6.77	11.48	15.22	15.04	15.46
Hungary	0.77	1.89	3.11	3.77	3.54	3.26
Poland	1.95	6.68	11.75	18.65	15.36	12.47
Romania	0.35	1.81	6.52	13.18	13.79	14.41
Yugoslavia	0.37	1.44	2.23	3.63	4.52	4.54

Source: David Turnock, *The Economy of East Central Europe, 1815–1989: Stages of Transformation in a Peripheral Region* (London: Routledge, 2006), 325.

Industrial growth was not limited to steel or other investment goods. After the death of Stalin, the uprising and protest of workers in East Germany in 1953 and Poland in 1956, and the anti-communist revolution in Hungary in 1956, the communist leadership redirected some investment towards industries producing consumer goods, and overall industrial growth became more balanced, although the propensity for heavy industry persisted. So, even if we add together all the industrial branches, the growth record is still impressive. For example, in comparison with 1950, the index of industrial production in 1980 was more than 8 times bigger in Hungary and Czechoslovakia, 10 times bigger in Yugoslavia, 15 times bigger in Poland, 24 times bigger in Bulgaria and 41 times bigger in Romania.[115] Considering that growth indices generally favour countries that started from a low initial level, we can also compare the per capita industrial output of the various countries in the region against an external benchmark.

Industry's share in the overall economy expanded significantly by 1980, reaching levels of between 50 (in the case of Yugoslavia) and 75 per cent (in the case of Czechoslovakia) of GDP.[116] These high percentages reveal the unbalanced structure of socialist economies, where

---

115 Calculations are based on Mitchell, *International Historical Statistics*, 425–6.
116 Wolfram Fischer, 'Wirtschaft, Gesellschaft und Staat in Europa 1914–1980', in *Handbuch der europäischen Wirtschafts- und Sozialgeschichte*, vol. 6, *Europäische Wirtschafts- und Sozialgeschichte vom Ersten Weltkrieg bis zur Gegenwart*, ed. Wolfram Fischer (Stuttgart: Klett-Cotta, 1987), 96.

Table 6.18 Industrial output per capita (UK in 1900 = 100)

	1938	1953	1963	1973	1980
Bulgaria	19	32	54	102	139
Czechoslovakia	60	117	193	292	344
Hungary	34	92	172	274	333
Poland	23	49	88	160	196
Romania	11	36	81	169	218
Yugoslavia	18	28	69	137	174
Soviet Union	38	73	139	222	252
Global average	31	48	66	100	103

Source: Paul Bairoch, 'International Industrialization Levels from 1750 to 1980', *The Journal of European Economic History* 11, no. 2 (1982): 302, 331.

the service sector, as well as housing and infrastructure, lag behind despite progress during the phase of rapid economic growth.

Yugoslavia embarked on a different path of development. After the Tito–Stalin split of 1948, isolated from the countries of the Soviet bloc, Yugoslav communists designed a 'third way', distinct from both the Soviet model of communism and from the capitalist model of the West. They ended collectivization and combined centralized planning with elements of worker management of socialist enterprises, also allowing a certain amount of market transactions between these enterprises.[117] At the same time, Tito asked for help from the United States and benefited from some loans and transfers of Western technology. Gradually, relations with the West became closer, and Yugoslav citizens were allowed to work in Western Europe. Exports, the development of international tourism and remittances allowed the Yugoslav economy to perform better than other socialist countries in the region.

The other countries did not dare to copy all aspects of the Yugoslav model, but some of their leaders realized that they could benefit from improving their economic relations with the West. In the early 1960s, Romania decided to avoid deepening economic integration within the Soviet-led Council for Mutual Economic Assistance (CMEA, established in 1949), and diversified its external economic relations with the West, importing Western technology and searching for new markets for its own products.[118] Some years later, Romania even applied for International Monetary Fund (IMF) and World Bank membership, which it obtained in 1972 following an admission to the General Agreement on Tariffs and Trade (GATT) in 1971.[119] The expansion of economic relations with the West was also pursued by countries like Poland and Hungary, and even the Soviet Union, to the extent that during the 1960s trade with the capitalist countries expanded faster than trade between the socialist countries. Accordingly, while in 1960 the share of imports from developed Western countries within the total imports for European CMEA countries varied in range from 13.7 per cent for Bulgaria to 27.7 per cent for Poland, in 1975 it varied in range from 23.1 per cent for Bulgaria to 49.5 per cent

---

117 Branko Horvat, *The Political Economy of Socialism: A Marxist Social Theory* (Oxford: Martin Robinson, 1982).
118 Michael Montias, *Economic Development in Communist Rumania* (Cambridge, MA: MIT Press, 1967), 193–230.
119 Ion Alexandrescu, *România între Est și Vest. Aderarea la FMI și BIRD* [Romania between East and West: joining the IMF and IBRD] (Târgoviște: Cetatea de Scaun, 2012).

for Poland, with Romania at 43.4 per cent after its peak of 48.6 per cent in 1974; the share of exports to Western countries also increased for almost all European socialist countries (with the exception of Bulgaria and probably Albania) during the 1960s and early 1970s, although this occurred at a slower pace than the shift in export levels, because it was not always easy for socialist countries to find markets in the developed West.[120]

This trend testifies to the relative failure of Soviet attempts to foster economic integration inside the socialist bloc. In 1949, the Soviet Union, along with its Central and Eastern European clients, founded the CMEA (sometimes also abbreviated as Comecon), which was later also joined by non-European socialist countries such as Mongolia and Cuba. In the first phase, Stalin did not make much use of this organization, preferring to extract resources from other socialist states through bilateral relations, and allowing smaller socialist countries to strive towards economic self-sufficiency. However, beginning in the late 1950s, the Soviet leadership realized that there were opportunities to bolster economic growth through economies of scale and specialization among the socialist countries. This policy was supported by the industrially developed GDR and Czechoslovakia, but it was blocked in 1962–1964 by Romania, which took advantage of the rule that all decisions be unanimous within the CMEA. After this setback, in 1967 the Soviets managed to forge a solution out of a compromise in the form of the 'interested party principle', which allowed reluctant countries to opt out of any agreement without having to block it completely. This allowed the adoption of the Comprehensive Programme for the Further Extension and Improvement of Cooperation and the Further Development of Socialist Economic Integration in 1971. In spite of several cooperative projects, the overall economic integration inside the Soviet bloc lagged behind the Common Market of Western Europe that was developing at the same time.

The levels of growth in Central and Eastern Europe were impressive in the 1950s and 1960s, and even during the 1970s. In three decades, the per capita GDP in each of these countries

Table 6.19 Per capita GDP at PPP (1990 international Geary–Khamis dollars)

	1946	1950	1955	1960	1965	1970	1975
Albania		1,001	1,181	1,451	1,675	2,004	2,289
Bulgaria		1,651	2,148	2,912	3,85	4,773	5,831
Czechoslovakia		3,501	3,922	5,108	5,533	6,466	7,399
Hungary	1,721	2,48	3,07	3,649	4,41	5,028	5,805
Poland		2,447	2,794	3,215	3,787	4,428	5,808
Romania		1,182	1,578	1,844	2,386	2,853	3,761
Yugoslavia		1,428	1,707	2,37	3,125	3,945	5,004
Soviet Union	1,913	2,841	3,313	3,945	4,634	5,575	6,135
Average Western Europe	3,576	4,517	5,65	6,806	8,316	10,108	11,465
Global average		2,024	2,368	2,665	3,104	3,593	3,944

Source: The Maddison Project, www.ggdc.net/maddison/maddison-project/home.htm, 2013 version.

---

120 András Köves, *The CMEA Countries in the World Economy: Turning Inwards or Turning Outwards* (Budapest: Akadémiai Kiadó, 1985), 69–70. For more about the problems the socialist countries experienced in their economic relations with Western Europe, also within the context of the integration process into the Common Market, see Suvi Kansikas, *Socialist Countries Face the European Community: Soviet-Bloc Controversies over East-West Trade* (Frankfurt a.M.: Peter Lang, 2014).

grew from 2.5 to almost 5 times its previous size, which contrasts with their modest achievements in earlier periods.

Although this performance seems impressive, several historians have pointed out its shortcomings. For example, Támás Vonyó argues that most of the growth in Hungary can be explained as the effect of post-war reconstruction and was thus unsustainable in the longer term.[121] Karl Gunnar Persson also points to the fact that

> compared to Spain and Portugal, which also suffered from authoritarian but conservative rule, the annual growth of GDP per capita was two percentage points lower in Eastern Europe from 1950 to 1973, despite the fact that the ratio of investment to GDP was 10–15 percentage points higher in Eastern Europe.[122]

Recession of the late 1970s and 1980s

According to Maddison's narrative and data, the European countries under communist rule ran into serious economic trouble after 1973:

> In the golden age, 1950–1973, East European per capita GDP growth (like that of the USSR) more or less kept pace with that in Western Europe. From 1973 to 1990, it faltered badly as the economic and political system began to crumble, with aggregate per capita growth of about 0.5 per cent per annum compared with 1.9 in Western Europe.[123]

Berend also begins his discussion of the economic factors that led to the collapse of state socialist regimes in the year 1973, but immediately acknowledges that 'this chronological division is also somewhat artificial.'[124] And, in fact, the faltering of growth only occurred gradually, and while the time lagged between the two recessions of Central and Eastern Europe, it was also more severe than those that occurred in other parts of the world economy.

There were several causes of this time lag. First of all, although almost all countries in the region were net importers of oil and gas – even Romania gradually exhausted its own oil resources and turned into a net importer in the 1970s – they were spared the effects of the first surge of oil prices, after the oil shock of 1973, by their reliance on supplies from the Soviet Union. According to CMEA agreements, prices for trade between member countries were adjusted periodically to average world-market prices for the previous five years.[125] Therefore, even if the Soviet Union succeeded in imposing an annual hike to update prices, and then also decided only to consider the average for the last three years instead of five, the actual price of Soviet oil paid by the socialist countries of Central and Eastern Europe rose only with a certain time lag.

---

121 Támás Vonyó, 'Socialist Industrialization or Post-War Reconstruction? Understanding Hungarian Economic Growth, 1949–1967', *The Journal of European Economic History* 39, no. 2 (2010): 253–300.
122 Karl Gunnar Persson, *An Economic History of Europe: Knowledge, Institutions and Growth, 600 to the Present* (Cambridge: Cambridge University Press, 2010), 197. Iván T. Berend also points to the sluggish growth of productivity in Central and Eastern Europe compared with Western and even Mediterranean Europe: Berend, *An Economic History*, 175–7.
123 Maddison, *The World Economy*, 160.
124 Berend, *From the Soviet Bloc*, 6.
125 For the price system of CMEA, see László Csaba, *Eastern Europe in the World Economy* (Cambridge: Cambridge University Press, 1990), 43–91.

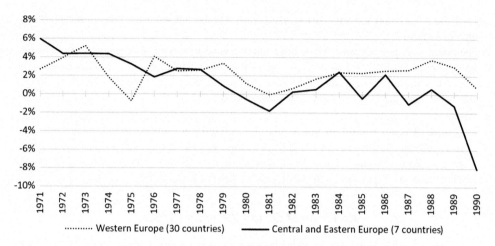

Figure 6.2 Year-to-year percentage change in per capita GDP by region (1971–1990)
Source: The Maddison Project, www.ggdc.net/maddison/maddison-project/home.htm, 2013 version.

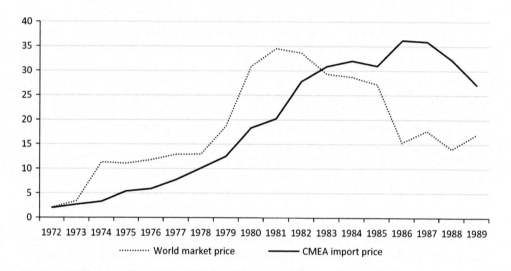

Figure 6.3 Oil import prices (1972–1989) (US dollars per barrel)
Source: Albrecht O. Ritschl, 'An Exercise in Futility: East German Economic Growth and Decline, 1945–89', in *Economic Growth in Europe Since 1945*, eds Nicholas Crafts and Gianni Toniolo (Cambridge: Cambridge University Press, 1996), 524.

While this system benefited the countries of Central and Eastern Europe as long as world prices were on the rise, when they began to decline in the mid-1980s, it was the Soviets who gained and the countries in the region that had to pay higher prices for their oil imports.

There were at least two other major implications for the rise in oil prices after 1973. One was the increased availability of financial resources for international loans, due especially to the combination of lax financial policies in developed countries and the flood of petrodollars onto international markets. Requiring hard currency in order to pay for various imports, whether consumer goods that the socialist economies were unable to supply or investment goods and

Table 6.20 Foreign debts of Central and Eastern European countries (in billion dollars)

	1971	1975	1979	1980	1981	1982	1983	1984	1985
Bulgaria	0.7	2.4	4.5	3.6	3.1	2.8	2.6	2.3	2.4
Czechoslovakia	0.5	1.5	4.0	4.9	4.5	4.1	3.7	3.4	3.0
GDR	1.4	4.9	10.1	14.1	14.9	13.0	12.7	12.9	13.1
Hungary	1.1	3.2	8.0	9.1	8.7	7.7	8.3	8.9	11.3
Poland	1.1	7.8	21.1	25.0	26.4	27.0	26.4	27.0	30.2
Romania	1.2	2.8	7.0	9.6	10.2	9.8	8.9	7.5	6.0
Soviet Union	1.8	11.4	17.2	17.8	20.9	20.0	20.5	21.6	25.2
CMEA banks	n.a.	2.8	5.2	4.7	4.3	3.8	3.6	3.6	2.5
Total	7.8	36.8	77.1	88.7	92.9	88.1	86.6	87.1	93.7

Source: Iliana Zloch-Christy, *Debt Problems of Eastern Europe* (Cambridge: Cambridge University Press, 1987), 34, 50 (rounded figures).

technology in order to improve their industrial capacities, several communist countries of Central and Eastern Europe tried to profit from the opportunity to borrow cheap money from the West. Under these circumstances, the total foreign debt of the countries in the region rose to about 13 times the size between 1970 and 1980;[126] even if we allow for the significant loss of the value of the dollar in the 1970s, the total debt still increased in real terms by about five times in just a decade.

Poland was extreme in the amount of loans it took out in the 1970s and was notorious for its inefficient use.[127] Poles bought licences to produce Fiat cars, Leyland engines, Berliet buses, Grundig electronics and many other industrial products. Yet, due to a combination of corruption, ineffective quality controls and failure to meet deadlines or adjust to foreign markets, most of these investments ended in economic disaster. For example, the Ursus factory bought the licence for Massey Ferguson Perkins tractors; the production line went into operation in 1980, but instead of 25,000 tractors, it produced only 2,000, and for each of these it used 4,000 dollars' worth of imported parts.[128] Other countries in the region were not significantly better at utilizing technological imports from Western Europe. Under these circumstances, even when foreign loans were used primarily for industrial investments, they did not in fact significantly enhance the economic capabilities of the socialist countries, so their only concrete economic significance was to indirectly subsidize domestic consumption. The situation became unsustainable when interest rates increased in the late 1970s, with the average rates paid by the CMEA countries rising from less than 7 per cent in 1978 to 11.6 per cent in 1980, and 14.3 per cent in 1981.[129] Hungary, Poland and Romania, as well as Yugoslavia, experienced serious problems and had to ask to refinance or reschedule their debts. The short-term crisis was overcome, but high interest rates and severe external conditions for rescheduling debts signalled the end of an era during which cheap foreign money was used to subsidize the economic inefficiencies of the socialist countries of Central and Eastern Europe. The communist governments of most

---

126 Berend, *An Economic History*, 184.
127 Alec Nove qualifies that the Polish 'combination of official incompetence, "illegitimacy", popular anti-Sovietism and Gierek's economic adventurism' was 'an economic policy of possibly unique unsoundness' in his *The Economics of Feasible Socialism* (London: George Allen & Unwin, 1983), 147.
128 Aldcroft and Morewood, *Economic Change in Eastern Europe*, 164.
129 Iliana Zloch-Christy, *Debt Problems of Eastern Europe* (Cambridge: Cambridge University Press, 1987), 60.

countries in the region tried to mitigate the adjustment of domestic consumption by cutting investments, but they could not avoid an economic slowdown.

Romania was an extreme case.[130] Its foreign debts had been moderate until about 1978, the money having been principally used for the technology and raw-material imports required by its expanding industry. However, the Ceaușescu regime was committed to becoming a major exporter of fuel and petrochemical products, and therefore engaged in a policy of 'reckless investment in oil refineries and the manufacturing of oil processing equipment',[131] as well as massive import of oil, although its main suppliers (first Iran in 1979, then Iraq after 1980) failed to deliver. As a result, it had to resort to short-term contracts at high prices for its imports. The gamble on the country's capacity to gain from oil processing and exports was ill thought out and, according to Western analysts, Romania lost an average of 25 US dollars per exported ton.[132] Nevertheless, as explained by Cornel Ban, Ceaușescu considered economic self-sufficiency to be a basic prerequisite for national independence, and was thus ideologically committed to advancing the pace of industrial modernization at all costs; he therefore rejected any attempts made by international creditors or Western governments to ask for economic reforms as a condition for new loans, and decided to pay off all national debts by the end of the decade with the goal of ending any dependence on Western finance for good.[133] In order to achieve this goal, Ceaușescu decided to dramatically curb imports and increase exports. Austerity hit the living conditions of the population hard, and also led to severe shortages and irrational jams in the economy,[134] which resulted in Romania realizing the worst economic performance among the countries in the region in the 1980s.

The case of Ceaușescu's Romania may have been extreme, but some patterns and constraints were common for all socialist countries in the region. After 1968, attempts to at least partially reform the mechanisms that coordinated the economy occurred less often and, in many countries, were even reversed.[135] Concomitantly, the institutional rigidities of central planning in relation to material balances became more obvious than ever, and the system was unable to cope with the growing complexity of the economy.[136] Socialist growth had been based on increasing inputs of both capital and labour. It was extensive and emphasized quantity over quality.[137] This pattern of forced growth proved less sustainable when previously cheap resources became scarce, and therefore more expensive, and the developed countries began to

---

130 When not otherwise referenced, the discussion of the Romanian case is based on Murgescu, *România și Europa: Acumularea decalajelor economice 1500–2010* [Romania and Europe: the accumulation of development lags 1500–2010] (Bucharest: Polirom, 2010) 392–401; and Cornel Ban, 'Sovereign Debt, Austerity, and Regime Change: The Case of Nicolae Ceausescu's Romania', *East European Politics and Societies and Cultures* 26, no. 4 (2012): 743–76.

131 Ban, 'Sovereign Debt', 757.

132 David Turnock, *The Romanian Economy in the Twentieth Century* (London: Croom Helm, 1986), 272.

133 Ban, 'Sovereign Debt', 763–766.

134 Constantin Ionete, *Criza de sistem a economiei de comandă și etapa sa explozivă* [System crisis of the command economy and its explosive stage] (Bucharest: Editura Expert, 1993).

135 Alec Nove, Hans-Hermann Höhmann, and Gertraud Seidenstecher, eds, *The East European Economies in the 1970s* (London: Butterworth & Co, 1982). The exceptions to this trend were Hungary and Yugoslavia.

136 Hans-Herman Höhmann, 'Economic Reform in the 1970s – Policy with no Alternative', in Nove, Höhmann and Seidenstecher, *The East European Economies in the 1970s*, 1.

137 Kornai, *The Socialist System*, 197.

shift from Fordist mass production to input-saving flexible specialization.[138] Barry Eichengreen summarizes the inability of the socialist systems to adapt as follows:

> The planned economies might be capable of producing simple goods using familiar technologies, steel being the classic example, but they were less well suited for producing the more complex products of the postindustrial era, much less for developing such products themselves. Hierarchical control was all that the planners knew how to do. And the diffusion of technologies facilitating the free flow of information was the last thing that the authoritarian regimes of Central and Eastern Europe sought to encourage. Concerned to maintain their grip on information, communist governments made access to these new technologies extraordinarily difficult.[139]

Therefore, in spite of slight attempts to modernize and diversify, communist leadership tried to continue the pattern that had worked previously, namely allocating most resources to increasing the production of basic industrial goods. Due to institutional arrangements that discouraged attempts to improve efficiency,[140] the costs of high growth became unbearable and, according to Berend, the amount of energy used to produce one unit of product was nearly eight times higher in the socialist countries of Central and Eastern Europe than in the countries of the European Union.[141] Apart from that, the problem of pollution became severe in parts of the region[142] and signalled that industrial development had reached its environmental limits. And, last but not least, because of declining birth rates, even the supply of labour became low in countries like Hungary, Czechoslovakia and Poland, as well as in the Soviet Union (including the Baltics).[143]

These constraints slowed economic growth down in the whole region, with GDP per capita in the 1980s growing at less than one per cent on average in all of its states. Several countries performed worse than others; in particular, Poland and Romania experienced negative growth at the aggregate level of the decade.[144] The general dynamic of the economy undermined one of the crucial elements that had helped to legitimize the socialist regimes after the death of Stalin and the erosion of the mobilizing capacity of ideological utopias: their ability to distribute things to the masses and to fulfil not only what were considered their basic needs but also a growing part of the consumption aspirations of large segments of the population.[145] This occurred at a moment when the West started to recover from the crisis induced by the oil shocks, and when the difference between standards of living and consumption in the socialist bloc and the developed countries of the Western world became more apparent than ever to the people in Central and Eastern Europe. As Katherine Verdery explains, the issue of consumption was politicized in ways that undermined the legitimacy of the communist regimes, and

---

138 Berend, *An Economic History*, 173–6.
139 Barry Eichengreen, *The European Economy since 1945: Coordinated Capitalism and Beyond* (Princeton, NJ: Princeton University Press, 2007), 295. See also Katherine Verdery, *What Was Socialism, and What Comes Next?* (Princeton, NJ: Princeton University Press, 1996), 33–6.
140 Kornai, *The Socialist System*, 292–301.
141 Berend, *From the Soviet Bloc*, 21.
142 Turnock, *The Economy of East Central Europe*, 404–17.
143 Berend, *An Economic History*, 176–8.
144 Maddison, *The World Economy: Historical Statistics*, 101. See also the comments in Murgescu, *România și Europa*, 397.
145 See in this volume the chapter on consumption (Ch. 7), which contains the relevant literature.

'the black markets in Western goods that sprang up everywhere enabled alienated consumers to express their contempt for their governments through the kinds of things they chose to buy.'[146]

At the same time, communist regimes failed in what had possibly been the main motive behind the Soviet drive for economic modernization: the build-up of the military.[147] Unable to sustain technological and military competition with the United States, and conscious that the Soviet Union was losing the Cold War, the new Soviet leadership around Mikhail Gorbachev realized that saving communism necessitated both an accommodation with the West and significant internal reforms. In this context, Soviet decision-makers increasingly perceived their satellites in Central and Eastern Europe as an economic burden that they were not willing to shoulder any more. Soviet reluctance to use force in order to defend the communist regimes in Central and Eastern Europe opened the way for political change in the whole region in 1989.

Transformation and EU integration, 1989 onward

Enthusiasm and high expectations accompanied the demise of communist rule in the countries of Central and Eastern Europe. The populations of the region felt they were entitled to a fresh start, which would allow them to wipe away the failures of state socialism and the stigma of underdevelopment, and to catch up quickly with the more developed West. Yet it soon became obvious that the existing economic and social structures remained cumbersome and, together with the constraints of the globalized world economy, limited options were available for post-communist transitions.

By the late 1980s, the bureaucratic coordinative mechanisms of the socialist economies were already in serious crisis, and in the turmoil of political transformation the capacity of states to keep their economies working declined dramatically. Demands for economic liberalization and increasing consumption undermined existing economic structures. Production fell, prices soared, disequilibrium increased and many enterprises experienced difficulties in adjusting to the unstable new economic landscape. The dissolution of economic relations occurred not only at the national level, but also between the socialist countries in the region and in their connections with the Soviet Union (the CMEA was dissolved in 1991, but in fact trade between its member states was already in sharp decline by 1990). In the western Balkans, the situation was worsened by the wars that accompanied the dissolution of Yugoslavia, and in the context of the demise of the Soviet Union, the Baltic countries also paid a significant economic toll for their newly acquired independence.

The 'transformation crisis' took a huge toll on the whole region. In the early 1990s, GDP declined in all countries, losing between about one-sixth to one-third of its pre-1989 levels.[148] Therefore, although many people would have liked to debate the nature, scale and pace of economic reforms, in fact most of the countries in the region had to move forward fast in order to avoid total economic implosion. There was a significant consensus that the transition should aim for a form of market economy and that the countries of the region should adopt patterns and institutions that had proven their worth in the prosperous West. Opinions diverged when

---

146 Verdery, *What Was Socialism*, 29. See also the comments in Emily S. Rosenberg, 'Consumer Capitalism and the End of the Cold War', in *The Cambridge History of the Cold War*, vol. 3, eds Melvyn P. Leffler and Odd Arne Westad (Cambridge: Cambridge University Press, 2010), 489–512.
147 Mark Harrison, 'Communism and Economic Modernization', in *The Oxford Handbook of the History of Communism*, ed. Stephen A. Smith (Oxford: Oxford University Press, 2014), 387–9.
148 Berend, *From the Soviet Bloc*, 76–8. Berend's data on Romania are wrong.

it came to defining the scope, pace and exact succession of measures that were to be implemented. Concrete economic policies varied from one country to another. Generally, analysts distinguish between the 'shock therapy' employed in Poland through the Balcerowicz Plan (named after the Polish finance minister Leszek Balcerowicz), and the more gradual and slower reforms applied in other countries, such as Romania.[149] In fact, there were not only two models, but very different policy mixes in each of the countries in the region, which were determined not only by the different options pursued by the leading politicians and political constellations that supported them, but also by the diverse initial conditions in these countries and their relations with the West. Generally, the countries in Central Europe (also known as the Visegrád group), which were already relatively prosperous, performed better and received more economic aid from the West than the Balkan countries. A special case was the newly established Baltic states, which benefited from significant investments and institutional help from the well-developed Nordic countries.

In spite of differences in economic performance, significant similarities shaped the transformation process throughout the whole region.[150] As part of liberalization, new small and medium enterprises were established, restrictions on foreign trade were removed and market prices were increasingly used. Due to the fact that in socialist systems prices had been fixed without relation to supply and demand, liberalization in contexts of increasing disequilibrium generated severe inflation shocks, which reached about 600 per cent in Poland in 1990 and more than 1,000 per cent in the Baltic states in 1993. As many enterprises were unable to adjust, privatization was soon considered to be the ultimate solution for economic recovery.[151] In agriculture, this was linked to the idea of restoring pre-communist property relations and

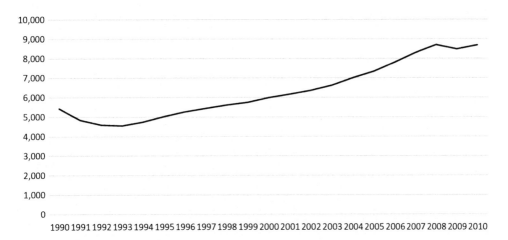

Figure 6.4 GDP per capita in Central and Eastern Europe, 1990–2010 (seven countries)
Source: The Maddison Project, www.ggdc.net/maddison/maddison-project/home.htm, 2013 version.

---

149 Leszek Balcerowicz, *Post-Communist Transition: Some Lessons* (London: The Institute of Economic Affairs, 2002).
150 Günther Heydemann and Karel Vodička, eds, *Vom Ostblock zur EU: Systemtransformationen 1990–2012 im Vergleich* (Göttingen: Vandenhoeck & Ruprecht, 2013).
151 David Stark and László Bruszt, *Postsocialist Pathways: Transforming Politics and Property in East Central Europe* (Cambridge: Cambridge University Press, 1998). See also the analysis in László Csaba, *The New Political Economy of Emerging Europe* (Budapest: Akadémiai Kiadó, 2005), 300–8.

dissolving cooperatives, a fact that led to parcelization, sharp declines in agricultural output and a temporary revival of subsistence production.[152] In industry, privatization was marred by the scarcity of available domestic capital to take over the oversized and inefficient socialist enterprises. The paradox of capitalism without capitalists[153] was for a time mitigated by various voucher privatization schemes and other mechanisms designed by ex-communist industrial technocrats to allow them to acquire as much state property as possible.[154] While instrumental in the fostering of upward social mobility, which led to the creation of a rapacious class of the nouveau riche, such schemes proved to be only moderately helpful for the majority of former employees, and did not significantly enhance the economic efficiency of the privatized enterprises. Often, the state had to step in to implement various schemes of financial aid, either by directly subsidizing inefficient enterprises or by supporting the consumers, especially in the case of public utilities. Needless to say, such measures, combined with the decline of public revenues, contributed towards producing considerable public deficits. The governments of Central and Eastern Europe had to borrow money on the international markets, and required the help of international financial institutions, particularly the IMF. In turn, the IMF and the World Bank asked for the implementation of macro-stabilization programmes, the opening up of domestic markets and fuller integration in the globalized world economy.[155] Employment in industry declined, and in several countries, rises in unemployment were prevented by schemes of early retirement, which increased the dependency rate and put social security systems under lasting pressure. While reforms continued, social tensions and structural economic problems accumulated, outlining the scarcity of local resources compared to the needs and aspirations of the people in the region.

The real solution was the takeover of large parts of Central and Eastern European economies by transnational companies.[156] As early as the beginning of the 1990s, foreign investments reached significant levels in Poland, Czechoslovakia and Hungary, and later also in the newly established Baltic states. At the same time, late reformers like Romania, Bulgaria and Albania were considered less attractive prospects, while Slovenia embarked on a policy that limited the scope of foreign direct investments.[157] These foreign direct investments allowed the recipient countries to overcome the transition crisis and resume economic growth by the mid-1990s (despite the Czech monetary crisis in 1997), while Bulgaria and Romania, after a number of years of sluggish recovery, were hit by a second massive recession in 1996–1999. The experience of the 1990s made the West acknowledge the strategic importance of providing more aid to stabilize Central and Eastern Europe and to integrate it into Western structures and organizations like NATO and the European Union. At the same time, the prospect of this integration

---

152 Katherine Verdery, *The Vanishing Hectare: Property and Value in Postsocialist Transylvania* (Ithaca, NY: Cornell University Press, 2003).
153 Gil Eyal, Iván Szelényi, and Eleanor Townsley, *Making Capitalism without Capitalists: The New Ruling Elites in Eastern Europe* (London: Verso, 1998).
154 Vladimir Pasti, *Romania in Transition* (Boulder, CO: Westview Press, 1997); and Roman Frydman, Kenneth Murphy and Andrzej Rapaczynski, *Capitalism with a Comrade's Face: Studies in the Postcommunist Transition* (Budapest: CEU Press, 2012).
155 There is a large body of literature analyzing the impact of the 'Washington Consensus' critically, which shaped the policies of international financial institutions in the 1990s.
156 Marco Neuhaus, *The Impact of FDI on Economic Growth: An Analysis of the Transition Countries of Central and Eastern Europe* (Heidelberg: Physika-Verlag, 2006).
157 For the differences between countries, see Dorothee Bohle and Béla Greskovits, *Capitalist Diversity on Europe's Periphery* (Ithaca, NY: Cornell University Press, 2012), 25–36.

was crucial in encouraging the populations and governments of these countries to continue with reforms, adjust their institutions to EU standards (the acquis communautaire) and to open their economies further to foreign direct investments. In 1999, after the first group of countries in the region had become NATO members, influenced by the Kosovo war, the European Union decided to open accession negotiations with 10 countries in the region, thus setting the framework for them becoming full members in 2004 (in the case of the Czech Republic, Estonia, Hungary, Latvia, Lithuania, Poland, Slovakia and Slovenia) and 2007 (in the case of Bulgaria and Romania). This shift was crucial in enhancing the confidence of major transnational companies to invest in these countries, so large parts of the manufacturing and service sectors were taken over and dominated by Western companies.

Direct foreign investments helped the countries in the region to catch up partially with more developed European economies in terms of the development of crucial services, such as communications and financial services. The combination of less stringent environmental and labour-market regulations, a relatively cheap labour force and proximity to the consumption markets of Western Europe also encouraged transnational companies to relocate some of their labour-intensive operations to Central and Eastern Europe, helping to halt the industrial decline in the region. Consequently, foreign investments were a major determinant of structural change in the eastern Central European economies. The share of the economy made up by agriculture continued to decline, industry stabilized – and even experienced a revival in some countries due to the impact of Western know-how, transfers of technology and better access to global markets – and the share of the economy made up by the service sector became dominant in all countries, accounting for between one half and two thirds of GDP.

If we try to sum up the economic experience of the post-communist transition, we have to distinguish between a first period, when the countries in the region seemed to diverge both in

Table 6.21 Central and Eastern European per capita GDP at PPS in 2000–2014 (EU-28 average = 100)

	2000	2004	2008	2012	2014	Difference 2000–2014
Albania	...	...	26	28	29	3
Bosnia & Herzegovina	...	...	27	28	28	1
Bulgaria	29	34	43	45	45	16
Croatia	49	57	64	61	59	10
Czech Republic	72	79	82	82	84	12
Estonia	43	55	68	71	73	30
Hungary	54	62	63	65	68	14
Latvia	36	48	60	60	64	28
Lithuania	38	50	63	69	74	36
Macedonia	27	27	33	34	36	9
Montenegro	...	...	41	39	39	-2
Poland	47	49	55	66	68	21
Romania	25	34	48	53	54	29
Serbia	...	...	36	37	35	-1
Slovakia	49	57	71	74	76	27
Slovenia	79	86	89	82	83	4

Source: Eurostat https://ec.europa.eu/eurostat/tgm/table.do?tab=table&plugin=1&language=en&pcode=tec00114

policies and performance, and a second period, when their structural differences diminished, and they converged towards the European Union average.

In spite of significant progress after 2000, the prospects for catching up were not straightforward. Some of the countries in the region experienced post-accession fatigue and slowed down the pace of economic reforms. The global crisis of 2007–2010 exposed the volatility of most of the small economies in the region to external shocks, with the Baltic countries being the most severely hit, while Poland managed to continue its economic growth even during the crisis. Most countries in the region had to enforce severe austerity policies, which caused social distress for large segments of the population. Even Slovenia, which had one of the best-performing and most stable economies in the region, had to dismantle elements of its welfare state and open itself up to transnational companies, lifting some of the previous restrictions and embarking on a programme of state asset sales to foreign investors. Under these circumstances, what has been labelled 'cocktail capitalism'[158] a decade earlier gave way to a less differentiated neoliberal pattern, which prevailed throughout the post-communist countries of Central and Eastern Europe.[159]

Although, since the crisis, the region has returned to growth and continues to catch up in terms of per capita GDP, austerity policies have eroded the social foundations of democracy, and have made the political outlook less secure than during the first decade of the twenty-first century. Or, to quote from a Polanyi-inspired analysis, 'under the pressure of an international government in which the survival of markets has once again taken precedence over the security of societies or states, the space for social compensation and democratic decision making has shrunk dramatically'.[160]

Factors determining economic performance

Natural resources

Natural resource endowment is a crucial determinant of economic output and performance. Intuitively, one can argue that an abundance of economically significant natural resources is an asset, which may be converted in various ways into economic growth. Yet, analysts have noticed that there is no strict correlation between the availability of natural resources and the economic performance of countries. Some countries with large supplies of natural resources perform rather poorly in aggregate growth, while some of the richest countries in the world have almost no significant natural resources. Based on these crude observations, economists in the 1980s began to analyze more thoroughly the complex relationship between natural resource endowment and economic performance and arrived at the conclusion that the availability of such resources can sometimes help growth, but more often proves not to be a blessing but a curse that blocks both growth and development.[161]

---

158 Lucian Cernat, *Europeanization: Varieties of Capitalism and Economic Performance in Central and Eastern Europe* (London: Palgrave Macmillan, 2006), 46, 169.
159 For the neoliberal turn in the region, see more recently, Philipp Ther, *Europe since 1989: A History* (Princeton, NJ: Princeton University Press, 2016).
160 Bohle and Greskovits, *Capitalist Diversity*, 269–70.
161 Alan H. Gelb and Associates, *Oil Windfalls: Blessing or Curse?* (New York: Oxford University Press, 1988); and Richard M. Auty, *Sustaining Development in Mineral Economies: The Resource Curse Thesis* (London: Routledge, 1993). For more recent contributions, see Nuno Torres, Óscar Afonso and Isabel Soares, 'A Survey of Literature on the Resource Curse: Critical Analysis of the Main Explanations, Empirical Tests and Resource Proxies', *CEF.UP Working Paper*, no. 2 (2013); Marc Badia-Miró, Vicente Pinilla and Henry Willebald, eds, *Natural Resources and Economic Growth: Learning from History* (London: Routledge, 2015).

There are two mechanisms that explain this negative impact. One is fuelled by the influence of rich revenues from natural resources on prices and competitiveness, and has been summarized as follows:

> Positive wealth shocks from the natural resource sector (along with consumer preferences that translate this into higher demand for non-traded goods) creates excess demand for non-traded products and drives up non-traded prices, including particularly non-traded input costs and wages. This in turn squeezes profits in traded activities such as manufacturing that use those non-traded products as inputs yet sell their products on international markets at relatively fixed international prices. The decline in manufacturing then has ramifications that grind the growth process to a halt.[162]

The other mechanism is related to the influence of windfall revenues from natural resources on institutional arrangements in the resource-rich country. Generally, such unpredictable revenues increase the incentives for establishing and/or maintaining rent-seeking behaviour, and extractive economic and political institutions, which in turn have a negative impact on long-term economic performance.[163] Besides, rich natural resources often attract political and military interference from abroad, fostering institutional instability and sometimes outright destruction.

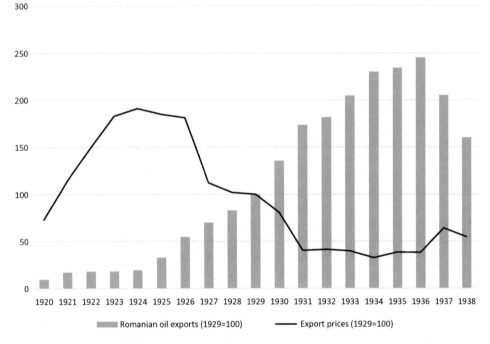

Figure 6.5 Romanian oil exports and export prices (1920–1938)
Source: Bogdan Murgescu, 'Anything but Simple: The Case of the Romanian Oil Industry', in *History and Culture of Economic Nationalism in East-Central Europe*, eds H. Schultz and Eduard Kubů (Berlin: Berliner Wissenschafts-Verlag, 2006), 243.

---

162 Jeffrey D. Sachs and Andrew M. Warner, 'Natural Resources and Economic Development: The Curse of Natural Resources', *European Economic Review* 45, no. 4 (2001): 833.
163 Acemoğlu and Robinson, *Why Nations Fail*, 212–29.

How does Central and Eastern Europe stand in terms of its endowment with natural resources? Apart from the nationalistic overtones in some of the existing literature, which praises the riches of various countries in the region, it is difficult to provide a straightforward answer to this question. For example, if we consider the quality of the soil, which is crucial for agriculture and thus for a significant component of the economy, especially in the past, it is clearly apparent that specialized institutions gather and analyze a huge number of indicators, each of which is significant for one or several different features of soil quality.[164] Combined with the internal heterogeneity of the region, this huge variety precludes an overall conclusion about the relative quality of soil across Central and Eastern Europe. Even if we were to accept that on average, soil in the region is better suited to agriculture than that in other parts of Europe and/or the world, it is striking that throughout the twentieth century the yields of the most important crops, as well as agricultural productivity in general, have been lower in this region than in Western Europe.[165] Thus, we can safely state that in agriculture, the populations of Central and Eastern Europe were unable to capitalize significantly on the relative natural quality of soil in the region.

Natural resources are not limited to soil. In fact, most of the discussions in economic literature focus on the impact of mineral resources. In his assessment of natural resource endowment in the region during the interwar period, Edward Albert Radice stated that it 'is reasonably well endowed with a number' of the raw materials required by industry, although it lacks sufficient quantities of iron ore'.[166] While the variety of minerals exploited in the region has increased throughout the twentieth century, most of them were available only in rather modest quantities. Although some of them attracted foreign investors and became significant staple exports for countries in the region, such as Yugoslav copper, lead and chrome or Hungarian bauxite,[167] none of them were able to foster major economic breakthroughs.

Oil deserves special discussion. Austrian Galicia and Romania were major producers of crude oil around 1900 and, while Galician output declined during the interwar period, Romania was able to increase its production and become one of the main exporting nations until the 1970s.[168] Nevertheless, the history of Romanian oil is also a textbook example of a waste of resources. Due to its policy of conflict with the big oil companies over ownership of the Romanian oil industry, without having the capital needed to foster output, Romania failed to increase its production during the first years after the First World War, when international prices were high, and exported larger quantities only after these prices had already fallen.

While determined by different factors, a similar situation occurred during the communist period. Romania increased its output up to the 1970s, using its resources both for exports and

---

164 See, for example, the Metadata Catalogue of the European Soil Data Centre (ESDAC), http://esdac-catalog.jrc.ec.europa.eu/; or the large collection of data and maps that have been archived at http://eusoils.jrc.ec.europa.eu/esdb_archive/eudasm/indexes/Europe.htm (accessed 31 August 2015).

165 See the data from Paul Bairoch, *L'agriculture des pays développés, 1800 à nos jours: Production – Productivité – Rendements* (Paris: Economica, 1999), 99–153; and Giovanni Federico, *Feeding the World: An Economic History of Agriculture, 1800–2000* (Princeton, NJ: Princeton University Press, 2005).

166 E.A. Radice, 'Raw Materials and Energy', in *The Economic History of Eastern Europe, 1919–1975*, vol. 1, *Economic Structure and Performance between the Two Wars*, eds M.C. Kaser and E.A. Radice (Oxford: Clarendon Press, 1985), 210.

167 Turnock, *The Economy of East Central Europe*, 328–30.

168 Frank, *Oil Empire*; Maurice Pearton, *Oil and the Romanian State, 1895–1948* (Oxford: Oxford University Press, 1971).

its growing domestic consumption. In the mid-1970s, crude oil resources reached their limit, and production began to decline. Nevertheless, the inefficient and oversized industry asked for more oil, and Romania became a net importer at the same time as international prices sky-rocketed.

Polish coal is another good example. Production increased significantly as early as the inter-war period, and growth continued until the1980s. Besides providing a crucial raw material for domestic industry, Poland was also a major net exporter of coal, both to the West and the Soviet Union. At the same time, the abundance of coal led to a waste of energy, fostered pollution and harmed the environment.

The existing information about environmental history in Central and Eastern Europe differs from country to country, but it is already reasonably reliable to reconstruct some of the basic trends.[169]

The data confirms the correlation between pollution and industrial development, as well as the poor record of socialist regimes in dealing with environmental damage.[170] David Turnock argues that 'the state was not prepared to penalise itself for pollution caused by its own enterprises in pursuit of plan targets; nor could it afford to scrap all outdated equipment in favour of the cleanest technology available on the market.'[171] Although the environment became a theme of anti-communist protests during late communism, only the decline of industrial production and EU regulations and support schemes created a significant reduction in pollution. The same factors are also crucial for the lessening of Central and Eastern Europe's dependence on imports of energy resources, particularly oil and gas, and for the recent surge in the (relatively clean) production of energy from renewable sources.

Table 6.22 Pollution in Poland compared with Western European and world averages

	SO_2 emissions per capita (metric tons of SO_2)			CO_2 emissions per capita (metric tons of CO_2)		
	Poland	Western Europe	World	Poland	Western Europe	World
1890	0.011	0.023	0.008	0.50	0.91	0.23
1900	0.015	0.029	0.012	0.70	1.13	0.32
1910	0.020	0.034	0.017	0.97	1.30	0.47
1920	0.018	0.033	0.018	0.87	1.20	0.49
1930	0.029	0.040	0.019	0.55	1.36	0.51
1940	0.045	0.041	0.020	1.68	1.35	0.58
1950	0.042	0.044	0.022	1.23	1.30	0.64
1960	0.071	0.061	0.030	2.16	1.74	0.88
1970	0.106	0.081	0.033	3.19	2.28	1.08
1980	0.156	0.072	0.028	4.74	2.43	1.19
1990	0.128	0.047	0.023	3.54	2.21	1.15
2000	0.055	0.019	0.016	3.01	2.09	1.06

Source: Kees Klein Goldewijk, 'Environmental Quality since 1820', in *How Was Life? Global Well-Being Since 1820*, eds Jan Luiten van Zanden et al. (Paris: OECD Publishing, 2014), 187–193.

---

169 For a general overview, see Kees Klein Goldewijk, 'Environmental Quality since 1820', in van Zanden, *How Was Life*, 179–98.
170 David Turnock, *The East European Economy in Context: Communism and Transition* (London: Routledge, 1997), 60–4; Berend, *From the Soviet Bloc*, 21.
171 Turnock, *The East European Economy*, 453.

Human capital

The significance of human capital for economic performance is a contested issue in economic theory. Although one can already trace discussion about the abilities, skills and talents of people as forms of economic input with a specific cost ('real expense') in Adam Smith's *Wealth of Nations*, the issue came to the forefront of economics in the early 1960s due to the seminal contributions of Theodore Schultz and Gary Becker.[172] Since then, human capital has been integrated into influential models of economic growth, and a large body of literature has developed to measure the magnitude and dynamics of human capital, as well as its impact on actual economic performance.[173] While most scholars accept that the build-up of human capital is likely to provide benefits for individuals and stimulate economic growth, there are also significant voices who point to the probability of reverse causation (i.e., the increase of human capital is determined by the increased availability of resources due to economic performance)[174] and/or to the fact that the impact of human capital is conditional on the quality of institutions, which are the main determinant of economic growth.[175]

Human capital is a metaphor, and as such, it is difficult to measure. Some scholars use various proxies, most of which relate either to the size and/or educational attainment of the labour force. Other scholars focus more on the socially recognized value of human capital, and so on the wages a society is willing to pay for people with different skills and levels of professional training. The latter argument, developed for Central and Eastern Europe by Bas van Leeuwen and Peter Földvari,[176] assumes that there is a well-functioning labour market, so that different skills and presumed levels of future productivity are rewarded accordingly. As we will try to argue in this section, this assumption is only partly applicable for Central and Eastern Europe during the long twentieth century.

Nevertheless, before discussing the issue of institutions turning labour input into economic output, it is useful to take the stock of the human resources that were and are currently available for economic purposes throughout the region. Despite several setbacks, the most important being the two world wars, the population of the region increased significantly. Demographic growth gradually slowed down in the 1960s and 1970s and finally became negative in the 1990s, but if we take the long twentieth century as a whole, population increases were nevertheless impressive (see Table 6.3 above).

The impact on the labour force was even stronger, because of the changes to the age structure of the population. Life expectancy increased from about 35 on average around 1900 to about 70 in the 1980s; most of the progress here was made in the late 1940s and 1950s.[177]

---

172 Andreas Savvides and Thanassis Stengos, *Human Capital and Economic Growth* (Stanford, CA: Stanford University Press, 2009).
173 For a recent survey of the burgeoning literature on human capital, see Marinko Škare and Sabina Lacmanović, 'Human Capital and Economic Growth: A Review Essay', *Amfiteatru Economic* 17, no. 39 (2015): 735–60.
174 Peter J. Klenow and Mark Bils, 'Does Schooling Cause Growth?', *American Economic Review* 90, no. 5 (2000): 1160–83.
175 Daron Acemoğlu, Francisco A. Gallego, and James A. Robinson, 'Institutions, Human Capital, and Development', *Annual Review of Economics* 6, no.1 (2014): 875–912. See also Daron Acemoğlu, *Introduction to Modern Economic Growth* (Princeton, NJ: Princeton University Press, 2009), especially 109–43, 359–84.
176 Bas van Leeuwen and Peter Földvari, 'Capital Accumulation and Growth in Central Europe, 1920–2006', *Eastern European Economics* 51, no. 5 (2013): 78–86.
177 For comparative global data, see Richard L. Zijdema and Filipa Ribeiro de Silva, 'Life Expectancy since 1820', in van Zanden, *How Was Life*, 107–8. For more details, see also Chapter 5 on 'Population and family' by Stanislav Holubec and Béla Tomka in this volume.

Although much of this increase was owing to the decline in infant mortality, at least a part of it was brought about by improvements in healthcare provision for adults. Under these circumstances, the amount of time people spent in economically significant activities increased, and there was a larger degree of potential for implementing technological progress through gradual learning-by-doing processes. As Jeffrey Williamson theorizes, this component of demographic transition also allowed for a windfall gain in economic performance in Central and Eastern Europe, which was reaped in Czechoslovakia as early as the interwar period and in most of the rest of the region during the post-war period.[178]

The expansion of the labour force was also due to a growth in female employment. The number of women employed in services and industry grew moderately during the interwar period and rose steeply during the communist transformation after the Second World War; growth was stimulated by both urbanization and industrialization, and the ideology of providing equal opportunities for women in education and at the workplace.[179]

Overall, the labour force increased in the region, and shifted from agriculture, industry and (particularly after the demise of communism) to services. While in Czechoslovakia the number of people employed in industry had surpassed those working in agriculture by the interwar period, in all other countries in the region, the share of agricultural workers was significantly over half of the active working-age population.[180] This situation changed drastically after the Second World War. In the context of socialist industrialization, the share of agricultural workers declined in 1989 to about 12 per cent in Czechoslovakia, 26.8 per cent in Poland and 27.9 per cent in Romania, while workers in industry (including construction) rose to levels of between 37.2 per cent in Poland, 43.5 per cent in Romania and 46–47 per cent in Bulgaria and Czechoslovakia.[181] Although the socialist economic system was slow and underperformed in tapping into the potential for growth in productivity that was opened up by this structural change, its scale was large enough to influence overall output, especially in the 1950s and 1960s.

During the early twentieth century, widespread illiteracy and low levels of education had hampered economic performance throughout Central and Eastern Europe. Progress had been considerable in the decades before the First World War with the Czech lands, Hungary and Estonia closing the gap with Western Europe, and the rest of the region also building up educational infrastructure to tackle illiteracy.[182] In the late 1920s and 1930s, due to economic difficulties that were experienced throughout the region, the advance in levels of basic education slowed down,[183] but overall progress could not be stopped, and in the first decade after the Second World War, against a backdrop of state-driven efforts, illiteracy was practically eliminated in almost the whole region. At the same time, communist regimes sought to expand secondary and tertiary education and link them to the labour requirements of the industrializing economy. Gradually, secondary education became compulsory, and the number of students continuing their studies in universities and polytechnics also increased. Nevertheless, the attitude of the communist regimes towards higher education was ambivalent. It was considered not

---

178 Jeffrey G. Williamson, 'Growth, Distribution, and Demography: Some Lessons from History', *Explorations in Economic History* 35, no. 3 (1998): 241–71.
179 For details, see Chapter 5 on 'Population and family' by Stanislav Holubec and Béla Tomka in this volume.
180 Milan Hauner, 'Human Resources', in Kaser and Radice, *The Economic History of Eastern Europe, 1919–1975*, vol. 1, 91.
181 Derek H. Aldcroft, *The European Economy 1914–2000* (New York: Routledge, 2001), 278.
182 See Chapter 2 by Zsombor Bódy and Stanislav Holubec in this volume.
183 David, *Nationalisme économique*, 341–2.

only to be a source for specialists, who were needed for the expanding economy, but also a tool for social engineering, specifically for replacing pre-communist social elites with engineers and various intellectuals from worker and peasant backgrounds. The latter aspect meant, especially in the first phase of communist rule, that there was an enforcement of various forms of exclusion and/or discrimination against youngsters of 'bourgeois origin', and there were positive initiatives to enrol students from social backgrounds that lacked economic and cultural capital. At the same time, the centralized allocation of study places favoured fields of study linked to the development of industry, especially engineering. During the first two post-war decades, this pattern put the socialist countries of Central and Eastern Europe on a par with or even ahead of many Western European countries in terms of enrolment ratios. While during the 1960s the social-engineering function of higher education was gradually downsized (so that, among other reasons, it would not backfire against the offspring of the new communist elites), beginning in the early 1970s, communist rulers became wary of the fact that graduates from higher education undermined the hegemony of the often poorly educated party activists.[184] The outcome was the introduction of centrally decided limitations in the overall allocation of study places, as well as the downsizing, or even closing, of fields of study that were considered to foster dissidence.

In some CEE states like Bulgaria, growth already resumed in the 1980s; but in most countries of the region, the number of students significantly increased only after the liberalization of access to higher education that followed the demise of state socialism. Yet, although the share of people who graduated from tertiary education trebled in the 1990s and 2000s, it is doubtful whether mass entry into higher education proportionally increased the stock of economically significant skills in the region. And, although analyses for the first two decades of the post-communist transition indicate that the returns from education slightly increased in most of the region,[185] these returns are generally lower than in Western Europe.[186] The weak connection between economic performance and the expansion of higher education has also been noted by Robert D. Reisz and Manfred Stock, who linked it to specific patterns of the socialist systems that prevailed in post-war Central and Eastern Europe.[187]

This observation raises an issue concerning the institutions that integrate human resources into economically and socially relevant activities. In this respect, Central and Eastern Europe has a long record of suboptimal social arrangements, which led to a significant waste of resources also before the enforcement of communist rule. Economic nationalism, and discrimination against Jews and various other minorities hit population groups who were educated above typical levels and had skills that were often scarce in Central and Eastern European societies. The two world wars were particularly murderous in large parts of the region, and in the 1940s, both Nazi and Soviet policies disproportionately hit the educated middle class. In the post-war period, the demise of pre-communist social elites, the emigration of Jews to Israel and that of

---

184 For this process, see the seminal analysis in György Konrád and Iván Szelényi, *The Intellectuals on the Road to Class Power: A Sociological Study of the Role of the Intelligentsia in Socialism* (New York: Harcourt, Brace and Jovanovich, 1979).
185 Mukesh Chawla, Gordon Betcherman and Arup Banerji, *From Red to Gray: The Third Transition of Aging Populations in Eastern Europe and the Former Soviet Union* (Washington, DC: The International Bank for Reconstruction and Development/The World Bank, 2007), 99–102.
186 Peer Ederer, Philipp Schuler, and Stephan Willms, *The European Human Capital Index: The Challenge of Central and Eastern Europe; The Lisbon Council Policy Brief* (Brussels: The Lisbon Council, 2007), 9–11.
187 Robert D. Reisz and Manfred Stock, *Inklusion in Hochschulen: Beteiligung an der Hochschulbildung und gesellschaftliche Entwicklung in Europa und in den USA (1950–2000)* (Bonn: Lemmens Verlag, 2007), 123–31.

Economic development

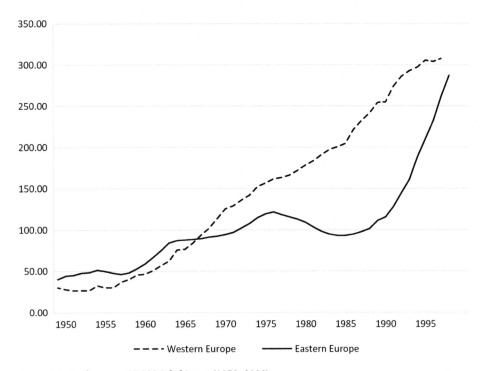

Figure 6.6 Students per 10,000 inhabitants (1950–2000)
Source: Robert D. Reisz and Manfred Stock, 'Zwischen Expansion und Kontraktion: Zur Entwicklung der Hochschulbildung in Osteuropa 1950–2000', *Berliner Journal für Soziologie* 16, no.1 (2006): 82.

many other people of different ethnicities to the West negatively affected human resources in the region, while the pattern of putting people in charge primarily on the basis of their political credentials also hampered economic performance.

One of the twists in the relationship between human resources and their value as human capital was determined by the general wage levels in Central and Eastern Europe. Largely, low wages were considered a competitive advantage for the region, and to a certain extent they still are even today. Theoretically, wage differentials are a significant driver of migration, but this depends heavily on the freedom people have to migrate. During most of the twentieth century, different regulations attempted to prevent cross-border migration, which resulted in significant social selection; people who succeeded in emigrating generally possessed more economic, social and cultural capital than the average population in their countries of origin. This tended to deprive the countries in the region of economically significant human resources and to increase the skills premium in the region, a trend which was temporarily blocked by the socialist system, but which explains to a certain degree the slightly increasing returns from education in the first phases of post-communist transition.

If we try to generalize this assessment by using the Historical Index of Human Development (HIHD), we can see that there has been significant progress in Central and Eastern Europe during the long twentieth century with sizeable differences within the region, but an overall catching up with more developed parts of the world did not occur.

The analysis, provided by Leandro Prados de la Escosura, shows the contribution of education, healthcare and income to HIHD growth in Central and Eastern Europe, and confirms

Table 6.23 Historical Index of Human Development (HIHD)

	1890	1900	1913	1929	1938	1950	1960	1970	1980	1990	2000	2007
Albania	0.103		0.068	0.076	0.111	0.212	0.276	0.347	0.366	0.381	0.473	0.528
Bulgaria	0.180	0.128	0.161	0.187	0.247	0.292	0.378	0.422	0.470	0.487	0.512	0.561
Czechoslovakia	0.145	0.208	0.241	0.298	0.340	0.383	0.470	0.479	0.522	0.530	0.561	0.636
Hungary	0.122	0.166	0.183	0.252	0.292	0.339	0.419	0.445	0.482	0.487	0.543	0.608
Poland	0.085	0.145	0.162	0.227	0.259	0.331	0.410	0.455	0.490	0.509	0.586	0.628
Romania	0.090	0.108	0.140	0.165	0.209	0.247	0.340	0.394	0.460	0.434	0.441	0.508
Yugoslavia/Serbia	0.122	0.109	0.130	0.163	0.194	0.248	0.323	0.377	0.433	0.460	0.489	0.516
CEE average	0.220	0.146	0.167	0.216	0.253	0.303	0.386	0.427	0.473	0.481	0.527	0.579
OECD average	0.095	0.246	0.277	0.334	0.366	0.417	0.482	0.541	0.593	0.658	0.745	0.809
Global average		0.107	0.122	0.157	0.185	0.210	0.263	0.307	0.334	0.367	0.416	0.460

Source: Leandro Prados de la Escosura, 'World Human Development, 1870–2007', Review of Income and Wealth 61, no. 2 (2015): 220–47 (the underlying dataset is graciously provided by the author).

Economic development

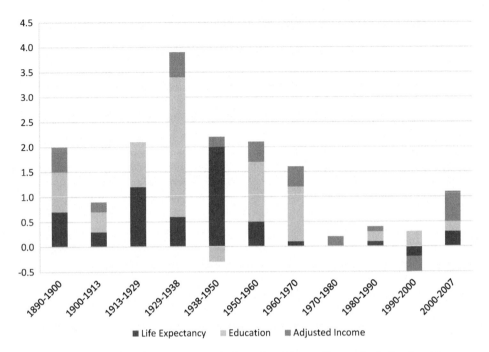

Figure 6.7 HIHD growth and its composition in Central and Eastern Europe (including Russia), 1870–2007
Source: Leandro Prados de la Escosura, 'World Human Development, 1870–2007', *Review of Income and Wealth* 61, no. 2 (2015): 60, 80.

the general picture outlined in this chapter. As Figure 6.7 shows, for most of the twentieth century, advances in education and life expectancy were crucial for human development, while economic growth only became the main driver after 2000.

Many people in the region broadly argue that its educated but still cheap labour force is a significant competitive advantage for Central and Eastern Europe in the context of its integration into the European Union. Declining birth rates, migration and ageing societies erode the share of economically active workers and put existing social systems under pressure. At the same time, educational results are worsening, especially if we consider the latest Programme for International Student Assessment results, which showed most countries in the region trailing behind in comparison with OECD countries. Whether this trend will be reversed by raising the quality of education and increasing the effectivity of lifelong learning, is still an open question for the future.[188]

The state and its policies

As Philip Hoffman states,

> Politics ... has a massive impact on economic outcomes. States redistribute wealth, make up for market failures, and enact policies ... They also provide the essential

---

188 Chawla, Betcherman and Banerji, *From Red to Gray*, 41–3.

public goods of security, the rule of law, and a means of exchange. Without these, life is brutal and trade little more than barter.[189]

With a tradition of economic nationalism, decades spent under communism and a consistent adherence to the nation state, the economy and processes of modernization of Central and Eastern Europe were particularly strongly connected with the state.

This connection was not necessarily successful, partly because the goals and schemes pursued by governments were suboptimal, and partly because there was a substantial gap between ideas and their implementation. This gap is related to the concept of state capacity – the ability of states to pursue policies to 'achieve the kinds of changes in society that their leaders sought through … planning, policies and actions'.[190] The lack of state capacity was a persistent problem in twentieth-century Central and Eastern Europe. Governments found it difficult to implement their policies and had to negotiate around existing structures and vested interests. Members of the political elites – be they in independent Balkan states before the First World War or in the Soviet-controlled Baltics – often pursued their own interests rather than those of the state. The post-Stalinist socialist state in particular was weakened, despite its declared ambitions, by its considerable inertia and the inability of its political centre to keep informal arrangements in check or to reform itself.[191]

Keeping the deficit of state capacity in mind, in this section we consider the state's three roles: as lawgiver; as the actor responsible for the politically determined transfer of resources between various economic sectors and segments of society; and as an agent directly engaged in the economy.

As Peter Evans argued in his seminal book on states and development, 'until less hierarchical ways of avoiding a Hobbesian world are discovered, the state lies at the centre of solutions to the problem of order. Without the state, markets, the other master institution of modern society, cannot function.'[192] The most basic function of the state lies in creating and fostering institutions through legislation and effective execution. At a minimum, this entails securing law and order, in particular by enforcing property rights, which are strongly correlated with growth.[193]

The foremost factor in state legislation in CEE was the significant level of instability. Since the last quarter of the nineteenth century, all countries in the region had been through a period of state formation (either before or after the First World War) and at least two dramatic regime changes (in the 1940s and 1990s). All had experienced hostilities of varying severity; in the most drastic case, the Baltic states had ceased to exist for half a century, while Yugoslavia

---

189 Philip T. Hoffman, 'What Do States Do? Politics and Economic History', *The Journal of Economic History* 75, no. 2 (2015): 303–32, here 303; Robert Hall and Charles L. Jones, 'Why Do Some Countries Produce So Much More Output per Worker than Others?', *The Quarterly Journal of Economics* 114, no. 1 (1999): 83–116; Robert H. Bates, 'The Role of the State in Development', in *The Oxford Handbook of Political Economy*, eds Barry R. Weingast and Donald A. Wittman (Oxford: University Press, 2006), 708.
190 Joel S. Migdal, *Strong Societies and Weak States: State-Society Relations and State Capabilities in the Third World* (Princeton, NJ: Princeton University Press, 1988), 4; Michael Mann, 'The Autonomous Power of the State: Its Origins, Mechanisms, and Results', *Archives européenes de sociologie* 25 (1984): 185–213. For an extensive overview of other definitions and uses of the concept, see Luciana Cignolani, *Bureaucracies for Development: Oxymoron or Reality? Studies on State Capacity in Challenging Governance Contexts* (PhD diss., Maastricht University, 2014), 23–74.
191 Verdery, *What Was Socialism*, 20.
192 Peter B. Evans, *Embedded Autonomy: States and Industrial Transformation* (Princeton, NJ: Princeton University Press, 1995), 3.
193 Robert J. Barro and Xavier Sala-i-Martin, *Economic Growth*, 2nd ed. (Cambridge, MA: The MIT Press, 2004), 541; Acemoğlu, *Introduction to Modern Economic Growth*, 120, 136.

disintegrated in a bloody civil war. This significantly affected the rule of law, both through the degree of change and through periods of state failure.[194]

While they are a significant part of the wider issue of the rule of law, in terms of economic development 'secure private property rights are central, since only those with such rights will be willing to invest and increase productivity.'[195] While their general trend followed that of the rule of law, there was interesting regional variation.[196] In the interwar period, the Baltic states were able to institute meaningful, growth-inducing agrarian reforms (where the division of land was supported by wider governmental redistributive programmes), a task which proved impossible in the rest on the region.[197] Land and property remained an issue throughout the century, and even today the region clings to both an unhealthy ownership structure and limits on trading (particularly by restricting the sale of land to foreigners).[198] On the other hand, the triad of state, collective and personal property specific to state socialism was ineffective and bad for growth, which had consequences for the state sector beyond 1989.[199]

There was another issue connected with the functioning of the communist state. The tremendous power of the secret police damaged trust and thus social capital, another important factor for growth. Recent research has shown 'a negative and long-lasting effect of spying on both social capital and economic performance' in communist Germany.[200] While the extent of Stasi operations was greater than the Eastern bloc average, a similar effect existed in all communist states within the region, which had enduring consequences for both the economy and the political sphere.

The quality of law has a significant impact on the functioning of private business, affecting both their effectiveness and investment decisions. While data for previous periods is difficult to come by, Table 6.24 shows CEE companies' declared amount of trust in the judicial system, beginning in 1999. Despite – or perhaps because of – the difficulty of achieving institutional change,[201] legal issues took a back seat to other matters during the transition, as privatization and other reforms were given greater priority. The problems were particularly difficult in the Balkans, which suffered from poor, underperforming institutions and endemic corruption.[202]

---

194 Hannes Siegrist and Dietmar Müller, 'Introduction', in *Property in East Central Europe: Notions, Institutions, and Practices of Landownership in the Twentieth Century*, eds Hannes Siegrist and Dietmar Müller (New York: Berghahn Books, 2015), 9–13.
195 Acemoğlu and Robinson, *Why Nations Fail*, 75.
196 For the role of the Austro-Hungarian cadastral system, see Dietmar Müller's contribution in the *Statehood* volume.
197 Wojciech Roszkowski, *Land Reforms in East Central Europe after World War One* (Warsaw: Instytut Studiów Politycznych, 1995).
198 Siegrist and Müller, 'Introduction', 9–21.
199 Katherine Verdery, 'The Property Regime of Socialism', *Conservation & Society* 2, no. 1 (2004): 189–98, here 194.
200 Andreas Lichter, Max Löffler and Sebastian Siegloch, 'The Economic Costs of Mass Surveillance: Insights from Stasi Spying in East Germany', in *Forschungsinstitut zur Zukunft der Arbeit*, Discussion Paper no. 9245, July 2015.
201 Douglass C. North, *Institutions, Institutional Change and Economic Performance* (Cambridge: Cambridge University Press, 1900).
202 Cynthia Clement and Peter Murrel, 'Assessing the Value of Law in Transition Economies', in *Assessing the Value of Law in Transition Economies*, ed. Peter Murrel (Ann Arbor, MI: The University of Michigan Press, 2001), 5; Karla Hoff and Joseph E. Stiglitz, 'After the Big Bang? Obstacles to the Emergence of the Rule of Law in Post-Communist Societies', *The American Economic Review* 94, no. 3 (2004): 753–63, here 755, 760; Veronica Taylor, 'The Law Reform Olympics: Measuring the Effects of Law Reform in Transition Economies', in *Law Reform in Developing and Transitional States*, ed. Tim Lindsey (London: Routledge, 2006), 94.

Table 6.24 Percentage of respondents who believe that the legal system will 'uphold [their] contract and property rights in business disputes'

	1999	2002	2005
Albania	48	48	56
Bosnia and Herzegovina	67	55	54
Bulgaria	58	48	43
Croatia	65	63	72
Czech Republic	46	47	46
Estonia	77	65	60
Hungary	73	58	48
Latvia	41	46	44
Lithuania	35	39	48
Macedonia	48	45	39
Poland	76	55	50
Romania	57	53	64
Serbia and Montenegro		62	53
Slovak Republic	64	45	52
Slovenia	73	53	64

Note: The number given is the combined percentage of the answer categories 'Fully/strongly agree', 'Agree in most cases' and 'Tend to agree'.

Source: Business Environment and Enterprise Performance Survey (BEEPS), 1999, 2002 and 2005, Questions 23a, 42 and 28 respectively, http://ebrd-beeps.com/data/.

Governments are not only legislators, but they are also important redistributors through taxes, tariffs, subsidies, government consumption, the provision of infrastructure, social transfers, education and healthcare. The redistributive actions of the state expanded enormously during the period under consideration, particularly after the Second World War. Economic theorists continue to predict the negative impact of taxes, particularly their effect of lowering productivity, and argue for a leaner state, but empirical findings fail to confirm a negative impact of tax-financed welfare on GDP. At the same time, welfare has a positive impact on other elements of development, such as education, health and social safety, which have already been partly considered in the section on human capital.[203]

Meaningful long-term comparisons of state redistribution are again difficult, as the scope of state activities changed significantly throughout the twentieth century (with the state playing a particular role in state socialism). In place of this measurement, Table 6.25 shows estimates for the degree of inequality in Central and Eastern European countries. We opt for this measurement, since state redistribution can significantly impact inequality, the high levels of which have increasingly been linked to records of poor growth in less-developed countries.[204]

---

203 Peter H. Lindert, *Growing Public: Social Spending and Economic Growth Since the Eighteenth Century*, vol. 1 (Cambridge: Cambridge University Press, 2004). For a recent review of empirical literature, see Stefan H.Thewissen,'Is it the Income Distribution or Redistribution that Affects Growth?' (Research memorandum, Department of Economics, Leiden University, January 2012).
204 Jonathan D. Ostry, Andrew Berg and Charalambos G. Tsangarides, 'Redistribution, Inequality, and Growth', IMF Staff Discussion Note 2014, SDN/14/02 2014; Era Dabla-Norris and others, 'Causes and Consequences of Income Inequality: A Global Perspective', IMF Staff Discussion Note 2015, SDN/15/13; and Amparo Castelló-Climent, 'Channels through which Human Capital Inequality Influences Economic Growth', *Journal of Human Capital* 4, no. 4 (2010): 394–450.

Table 6.25 Gross household income using Gini coefficient, 1890–2000

Country	1890	1910	1929	1960	1990	2000
Bulgaria	35			23	24	49
Croatia			48			39
Czech Republic				26	25	31
Estonia	32	37	41	45	21	38
Hungary			30	28	27	29
Latvia	35	40			24	42
Poland	30	28	26	26	31	35
Slovakia		43	48	32	22	28
Slovenia			38	43	27	27

Source: Michalis Moatsos et al., 'Gross Household Income Gini, 1820–2000', Clio Infra, www.clio-infra.eu/.

Table 6.26 The role of state expenditure in net national product directly before the First World War

Country	France	United Kingdom	Russia	Germany	Italy	Bulgaria	Serbia	Hungary
Per cent	10.80	13.70	13.70	15.60	16.8	19.90	22.00	28.50

Source: Thomas David, *Nationalisme économique et industrialisation: L'expérience des pays de l'Est (1789–1939)* (Geneva: Librairie Droz, 2009), 99.

The diversion of public funds for private benefit by elites has been an enduring issue in the region. One facet of this redistribution was the growth of government consumption through the expansion of bureaucracies and the military, leading to the inefficient use of scarce resources. As new nation states were created, they 'became instruments of revenue raising as well as of income transfer from the societies at large to the new bourgeoisie of state officials'.[205] In Hungary and the Balkans before the First World War, there were more than twice the number of public officials in relation to the total workforce than was the case in Germany.[206] Moreover, CEE states had consistently higher expenditure per capita in relation to GDP on the military, whose officers made up another part of the wealth-siphoning elite. In 1929, Albania, Romania and Yugoslavia achieved the highest military expenditure in relation to GDP in Europe, and the region as a whole spent 24 per cent more than Western Europe in relation to GDP.[207]

The mode of financing modernization projects was another way of redistributing through tariffs, tax reliefs and other methods discussed in the earlier sections on the boom of 1890–1914

---

205 Andrew C. Janos, 'The Politics of Backwardness in Continental Europe, 1780–1945', *World Politics* 41, no 3 (1989): 325–58, here 338.
206 Andrew C. Janos, *East Central Europe in the Modern World: The Politics of the Borderlands from Pre- to Post-communism* (Stanford, CA: Stanford University Press, 2000): 87; Lampe and Jackson, *Balkan Economic History*, 235.
207 CEE in this comparison encompasses Albania, Poland, Hungary, Czechoslovakia, Yugoslavia, Bulgaria and Romania, while Western Europe refers to Austria, Belgium, Denmark, Finland, France, Germany, Italy, the Netherlands, Norway, Sweden and Switzerland. The total military expenditure from the Correlates of War project (National Material Capabilities Data Documentation, 2010) was compared with the total GDP calculated from the 2013 version of the Maddison project.

and post-war reconstruction in 1914–1929. Before the First World War, the agricultural sector was forced to pay for governmental policies. While this did indeed produce a spurt of growth, the cost was heavy, leaving 'demoralized, alienated, and rebellious rural populations' behind[208] and provoking a rural uprising in Romania in 1907. In the interwar period, the record is even less positive, as poorer parts of the population were forced to finance import-substitution policies, which resulted in minimal growth at the cost of creating poverty. Arguably, the same could be said about state socialism, under which the state redistributed an unprecedented amount of funds into the industrial sector to the detriment of the rest of the economy: 'We are dealing with a grand paradox: while poverty and stagnation call for more *etatism*, this *etatism* in turn may result in still more poverty and relative backwardness'.[209]

After the Second World War, the state expanded enormously, creating what has been dubbed the premature welfare state (before 1945 this type of spending was relatively small in the region),[210] with 'full employment, price controls combined with rationing, and universal accessibility' to education and social transfers (such as pensions, sickness pay and maternity leave) as its three pillars.[211] As Donald Filtzer elaborates,

> Workers and peasants toiled in factories and fields to produce the physical wealth which the elite appropriated and redistributed between investments in industry and agriculture, public welfare, and the consumption allocated to different social groups, with itself receiving a privileged share.[212]

The system had an undeniably positive impact on the formation of human capital, as discussed earlier, although in the long term the lack of meritocratic advancement and the structure of wages had the opposite effect.[213] Moreover, socialism's bureaucratic paternalism, which treated citizens as irresponsible children,[214] generated a 'universal syndrome of "learned helplessness"',[215] which had enduring negative consequences for growth after 1989. If we use the conceptual framework designed by Amartya Sen, we see that socialist systems removed some of the deprivations that 'leave people with little choice and little opportunity of exercising their reasoned agency',[216] but, at the same time, oppressive institutions prevented people from exercising agency in a large number of areas. Because of its general pattern of blocking expressions of political or social discontent, the socialist system lacked checks on inefficiency that were ingrained in Western welfare models, which arguably contributed to drops in productivity; and by the 1960s, CEE was left behind in terms of social security as it had lower levels of expenditure and lower-quality services.[217]

---

208 Janos, 'The Politics of Backwardness', 344–5.
209 Ibid., 327.
210 Iancu Spigler, 'Public Finance', in Kaser and Radice, *The Economic History of Eastern Europe 1919–1975*, vol. 2, 167–9; and Berend, *Central and Eastern Europe, 1944–93*, 165–9.
211 Jacek Kochanowicz, 'Incomplete Demise: Reflections on the Welfare State in Poland After Communism', *Social Research* 64, no. 4 (1997): 1447.
212 Donald Filtzer, 'Privilege and Inequality in Communist Society', in Smith, *The Oxford Handbook of the History of Communism*, 505.
213 Béla Tomka, *A Social History of Twentieth-Century Europe* (London: Routledge, 2013), 103–4.
214 Verdery, *What Was Socialism*, 24–6.
215 Kochanowicz, 'Incomplete Demise', 1450.
216 Amartya Sen, *Development as Freedom* (Oxford: Oxford University Press, 1999), xii.
217 Béla Tomka, *Social History*, 160, 162.

During the transition, states had to deal with new problems as well as some old ones (such as the elites trying to siphon off public funds). The previous system left a legacy of raised expectations concerning the scale of redistribution, as well as inefficient, sprawling institutions, which, due to shrinking government income, were often left underfinanced resulting in negative consequences for education and healthcare. The transition led to a dramatic rise in poverty and a corresponding increase in welfare spending, as governments initially tried to cushion the impact of change (with a distinct regional oddity in the Baltics, which consistently spent less on support for the poorest and recorded some of the highest levels of inequality in the region).[218] The change left significant parts of the population in poverty and damaged growth.

Finally, apart from legislation and redistribution, the state directly engaged in the economy through both long-term goal setting and direct economic activity. Writing about the beginning of modernization, Alexander Gerschenkron argued[219] that due to capital scarcity in the region, the state was the only actor able to initiate the process of industrialization, since neither entrepreneurs nor banks were strong enough to do it on their own. Before the Second World War, 'the state never took over the initiative from private capital, and the methods employed were to foster, to control, or direct the economy rather than to command it directly'.[220] The approach changed markedly under state socialism. Nonetheless, there were issues that linked the two systems. In both cases, the focus on import substitution within the nation state was damaging, as all CEE countries can be considered small states, with the possible exception of Poland, and as such, they could not grow effectively based solely on their internal markets.[221] Moreover, as Peter Evans puts it, 'insofar as the international division of labour is a hierarchy, worrying about development means worrying about your place in the hierarchy.'[222] Both modernization projects occupied suboptimal positions within the hierarchy of the international division of labour.

Before the Second World War, the focus of industrialization was on consumer, import-substituting products, with leading industries from the previous century no longer playing a major role in innovation (military production was the exception, but it was hardly a significant player outside of Czechoslovakia). The exemption of capital products from strong protective tariffs was indicative of this direction. As a result, while effective at replacing imports, it did little for the long-term viability of industrialization by failing to create export products. It was 'obsolete modernization', which was not able to significantly change the character of the economies.[223]

Under state socialism, the means of production were owned by the state and central planning was managed by the party-controlled apparatus that determined production and redistribution. As such, it is warranted to attribute CEE's growth record after the Second World War to actions of the state. As Nicholas Crafts and Gianni Toniolo have shown, when 'normalizing for initial income level, East European countries' growth was less than for comparable Western European countries in 1950–73, the period of fastest growth'.[224]

---

218 H.J.M. Fenger, 'Welfare Regimes in Central and Eastern Europe: Incorporating Post-Communist Countries in a Welfare Regime Typology', *Contemporary Issues and Ideas in Social Sciences* 3, no. 2 (2007): 1–30.
219 Alexander Gerschenkron, *Economic Backwardness in Historical Perspective* (Cambridge, MA: Harvard University Press, 1962).
220 György Ránky and Jerzy Tomaszewski, 'The Role of the State in Industry, Banking and Trade', in Kaser and Radice, *The Economic History of Eastern Europe 1919–1975*, vol. 2, 40.
221 David, *Nationalisme*, 402.
222 Evans, *Embedded Autonomy*, 8.
223 Iván T. Berend, 'The Failure of Economic Nationalism: Central and Eastern Europe Before World War II', *Revue économique* 51, no 2 (2000): 315–22.
224 Nicholas Crafts and Gianni Toniolo, 'Postwar Growth: An Overview', in *Economic Growth in Europe Since 1945*, eds Nicholas Crafts and Gianni Toniolo (Cambridge: Cambridge University Press, 1996), 7.

One reason for this poor record was the economic path, as discussed in the section Post-war reconstruction and accelerated growth, 1945–1975, that was enforced by the Soviets on the region. Even when the Soviet model was created in the 1930s, indicators for heavy industrial production, which were so important for the communist regime, were poor predictors for GDP per capita in Western countries.[225] In the long term, they did not favour growth over other areas, such as flexible production, electronics or information technology, which were all brought to the fore. Vested interests made escaping from this path difficult. Periodically, social disturbances led to temporary shifts towards consumer goods, but vested interests pulled the system back onto the heavy industry investment track.[226]

Not only was the chosen path inimical to growth, but so was the nature of the command economy. With the means of production owned by the state, production quotas determined by planning and prices fixed by central authorities, the system suffered from the lack of an efficient control mechanism and the transmission of information offered by prices. Producers operated within soft budget constraints and thus overspent. Because of widespread shortages, managers hoarded both resources and labour, which created a vicious circle that led to bigger shortages. This produced a system where 'prices did not reflect opportunity costs … where "total factor productivity" failed to improve … where managers were motivated to continue with old technology, rather than risk innovation'.[227]

During the long twentieth century, Central and Eastern Europe experienced a significant variety of political regimes and state structures. Yet, in spite of the diversity of institutional arrangements and concrete policies, the overall contribution of the state to economic performance has been limited; examples of positive state intervention have been upset by recurrent failures to set adequate development priorities, and by persistent distortions in the allocation of resources. Whether this pattern will change in the twenty-first century, under the combined impact of consolidating democratic institutions and EU policies to increase state capacity, is still an open question.[228]

Institutional rigidity and historical legacies

We now turn to the subject of long-term legacies, beginning with the topic of inequality or, in a broader sense, social polarization in the region.[229] It has been argued that inequality itself, as mentioned in the previous section, affects the growth of poor countries through many channels. It can reduce access to credit markets, make markets shallower for products targeted at the middle class in relatively closed economies, inversely affect the quality of economic institutions, result in underdeveloped infrastructure, and lead to lower human and social capital. Polarization, stemming from economic, ethnic or other differences, exacerbates these problems,

---

225 Mark Harrison, 'GDPs of the USSR and Eastern Europe: Towards an Interwar Comparison', *Europe-Asia Studies* 46, no 2 (1994): 243–59; and Janos, 'The Politics of Backwardness', 355.
226 Zbigniew Landau, 'Etapy rozwoju Polski Ludowej' [Stages of development of the Polish People's Republic], *Przegląd Historyczny* 78, no 2 (1987): 211–53.
227 Nigel Swain, 'A Post-Socialist Capitalism', *Europe-Asia Studies* 63, no. 9 (2011): 1671–95, here 1672.
228 Alina Mungiu-Pippidi, *The Quest for Good Governance: How Societies Develop Control of Corruption* (Cambridge: Cambridge University Press, 2015).
229 For definitions and relations to inequality, see Jean-Yves Duclos, Joan Esteban and Debraj Ray, 'Polarization: Concepts, Measurement, Estimation', *Econometrica* 72, no. 6 (2004): 1737–72.

further reducing the effectiveness of capital usage. It severely affects trust and the formation of social capital. Sectarianism can also strengthen the role of informal arrangements.[230]

Central and Eastern Europe has a long history of social polarization, which predates the twentieth century. Before the Second World War, the biggest issue was the significant cleavage between poor, illiterate peasantry and the upper echelons of society (with different patterns in the 'incomplete' societies of the Balkans).[231] The scale of polarization was most clearly seen in Romania with the peasant rebellion of 1907, where economic, social and economic inequalities led to bloodshed. Another source of polarization was ethnic strife, which was visible in relations with Jews, but also with other minorities. This not only prevented the formation of social capital but was also a waste of human capital. It proved difficult for educated young Jews in the 1930s to find government jobs in the region, while even Romanian citizens from Transylvania felt excluded from a public administration that was dominated by officials from the 'Old Kingdom'. The same story was true for Ukrainians in interwar Poland. Today the Roma still suffer from long-term problems with integration and socialization. Under state socialism, polarization shifted, with much of the old elite deprived of their power, but, as described by Milovan Djilas, a new bureaucratic elite blossomed among party members with their own distinct privileges,[232] which were soon contested to varying degrees in all of the bloc countries. Finally, after 1989, new patterns of economic polarization emerged, as a chasm opened between those who profited from transition and those who did not, such as workers from discontinued factories or collective farms.

In other words, an important characteristic of polarization was its persistence under different guises. Indeed, it has been argued that its structure was to some extent handed down across political ruptures, shaping patterns of social trust and hierarchies. In a well-known recent argument, some elements of current Polish societal relations are believed to stem from old, feudal, manorial ones.[233] Moreover, ethnic strife was able to repeatedly re-emerge under different political systems, damaging trust and, in the most drastic example, resulting in the bloody dissolution of Yugoslavia. On the other hand, the frequent changes in patterns of polarization allowed the emergence of unsettled, 'hungry' elites, who used their position to supplement their economic situation. This was as true for Balkan officials after independence in the nineteenth century as much as for members of the nomenklatura in the 1980s and beyond. The resultant rise in informal arrangements and inefficient use of resources had negative consequences for growth.

A particular type of informal behaviour is a form of corruption that has 'the obtaining of individual or group-specific advantages by unaccepted and/or unacceptable proceedings' at its

---

230 Phillip Keefer and Stephen Knack, 'Polarization, Politics and Property Rights: Links between Inequality and Growth', *Public Choice* 111, no. 1 (2002): 127–54; Jaejoon Woo, 'Social Polarization, Fiscal Instability and Growth', *European Economic Review* 49, no. 6 (2005): 1451–77; Robert J. Barro, 'Inequality and Growth in a Panel of Countries', *Journal of Economic Growth* 5, no. 1 (2000): 5–32; Eric M. Uslaner, 'Corruption', in *Handbook of Social Capital: The Troika of Sociology, Political Science and Economics*, eds Gert Tinggaard Svendsen and Gunnar Lind Haase Svendsen (Cheltenham: Edward Elgar, 2009), 127–42.
231 Berend, *History Derailed*, 204–15.
232 Milovan Djilas, *The New Class: An Analysis of the Communist System* (London: Thames and Hudson, 1957).
233 Andrzej Leder, *Prześniona rewolucja. Ćwiczenia z logiki historycznej* [Sleepwalking through a revolution: an exercise in the logic of history] (Warsaw: Krytyka Polityczna, 2014).

core.[234] Research suggests that corruption has nuanced effects,[235] although high levels of corruption have consistent negative economic consequences, particularly by leading to reduced private investment and thus growth.[236] As Eric M. Uslaner explains, 'Corruption transfers resources from the mass public to the elites – and generally from the poor to the rich. … It acts as an extra tax on citizens, leaving less money for public expenditures'.[237] It weakens the state by potentially reducing revenue, and may adversely affect FDI.[238] Higher corruption is also correlated with higher inequality, lower levels of trust and a deterioration in the political sphere, but causation remains elusive. Corruption is a difficult phenomenon to measure, particularly in the past, for which it is often the case that no data can be reliably constructed, leaving us only with subjective assessments.

According to an anecdote describing the situation in the nineteenth century, a Jewish smuggler operating on former Polish territories preferred crossing the border between Russia and Prussia, since the situation there was clear: officials in the former country would always take bribes, whereas officials in the latter would never do so. Crossing into Austria was always hazardous, since each customs officer's corruption preferences had to be ascertained. While stereotypical, this seems to be a fairly accurate representation of the differences in the prevalence of corruption between three of the four empires in Central and Eastern Europe, with Russia (apart from the Great Duchy of Finland) plagued by endemic, systematic corruption, both petty and grand, which permeated all strata of society. Apparently, the future Baltic states were in a better position at first, but their territories converged with the rest of the empire in the years before the First World War.[239] A similarly endemic prevalence of corruption can be seen in the Balkans, carrying over patterns from the Ottoman period.[240]

Corruption is 'sticky' – it is difficult to get rid of[241]– and sources point to its persistence throughout the twentieth century, typified by endemic upsurges both in the interwar period[242] and particularly under state socialism which created 'structural incentives' for this kind of behaviour.[243] Under petty corruption, widespread small-scale payments to low-rank public officials

---

234 Hartmut Schweitzer, 'Corruption – its Spread and Decline', in *The New Institutional Economics of Corruption*, eds Johann Graf Lambsdorff, Markus Taube and Matthias Schramm (London: Routledge, 2005), 18. For a more in-depth discussion, see John Gardiner, 'Defining Corruption', in *Political Corruption: Concepts and Contexts*, eds Arnold J. Heidenheimer and Michael Johnston, 3rd ed. (New Brunswick: Transaction Publishers, 2002), 25–40.
235 Fabio Méndez and Facundo Sepúlveda, 'Corruption, Growth and Political Regimes: Cross Country Evidence', *European Journal of Political Economy* 22, no. 1 (2006): 82–98.
236 William Q. Judge, D. Brian McNatt and Weichu Xu, 'The Antecedents and Effects of National Corruption: A Meta-Analysis', *Journal of World Business* 46, no. 1 (2011): 93–103.
237 Uslaner, 'Corruption', 127.
238 Edward Glaesera, Jose Scheinkmanb and Andrei Shleifera, 'The Injustice of Inequality', *Journal of Monetary Economics* 50, no. 1 (2003): 199–222; Leslie Holmes, *Rotten States? Corruption, Post-Communism, and Neoliberalism* (Durham, NC: Duke University Press, 2006), 151–8.
239 Andrzej Chwalba, *Imperium korupcji w Rosji i Królestwie Polski w latach 1861–1917* [Empire of corruption in Russia and the Kingdom of Poland 1861–1917], 3rd ed. (Cracow: Księgarnia Akademicka, 2006), 19–53.
240 Uslaner, 'Corruption', 132; Alina Mungiu-Pippidi, 'Breaking Free at Last: Tales of Corruption in Post-communist Balkans', *East European Constitutional Review* 6, no. 4 (1997): 85–90, here 85.
241 Uslaner, 'Corruption', 128.
242 Aldcroft, *Europe's Third World*.
243 Wayne Sandholtz and Rein Taagepera, 'Corruption, Culture, and Communism', *International Review of Sociology* 15, no. 1 (2005): 109–31, here 109–10.

Table 6.27 Transparency International Corruption Perceptions Index

	1998 score	1998 position (out of 54)	2005 score	2005 position (out of 159)	2015 score	2015 position (out of 168)
Albania	-	-	2.4	126	3.6	88
Bosnia and Herzegovina	-	-	2.9	88	3.8	76
Bulgaria	2.9	66	4.0	55	4.1	69
Croatia			3.4	70	5.1	50
Czech Republic	4.8	37	4.3	47	5.6	37
Estonia	5.7	26	6.4	27	7.0	23
Hungary	5.0	33	5.0	40	5.1	50
Latvia	2.7	71	4.2	51	5.5	40
Lithuania	-	-	4.8	44	6.1	32
Macedonia	-	-	2.7	103	4.2	66
Montenegro	-	-	-	-	4.4	61
Poland	4.6	39	3.4	70	6.3	30
Romania	-		3.0	85	4.6	58
Serbia and Montenegro	-		2.8	97	-	-
Serbia	-	-	-	-	4.0	71
Slovakia	3.9	47	4.3	47	5.1	50
Slovenia	-	-	6.1	31	6.0	35

Note: The 2015 score was originally given on a 0–100 scale. Here it has been adapted to a 0–10 scale to match the 2005 score, although the two are not directly comparable.

Source: Transparency International Corruption Perceptions Index, 2005 and 2015, www.transparency.org.

were ubiquitous.[244] Likewise, economic activity (and all spheres of life) were infused with what the Russians called *blat*, 'the use of personal networks and informal contacts to obtain goods and services in short supply and to find a way around formal procedures'.[245] After the fall of communism, corruption in the region started to be perceived as an important impediment to transition and growth, and attracted a great number of publications.[246] The expansion of the private sphere offered more opportunities for corruption on a grand scale, while the low quality of many public services fuelled petty corruption.[247]

Because of the role ascribed to corruption, there are many contemporary attempts to quantify it. Table 6.27 shows one of them: The Perceived Corruption Index by Transparency

---

244 Krzysztof Madej, 'Siermiężna i dolarowa – korupcja w PRL w latach 1956–1980' [Rough trade and in dollars: corruption in the Polish People's Republic between 1956 and 1980], in *PRL. Trwanie i zmiana*, eds Dariusz Stola and Marcin Zaremba (Warsaw: Wydawnictwo Wyższej Szkoły Przedsiębiorczości i Zarządzania im. Leona Koźmińskiego, 2003), 249–80.

245 Daunis Auers, *Comparative Politics and Government of the Baltic States: Estonia, Latvia and Lithuania in the Twenty-first Century* (Basingstoke: Palgrave Macmillan, 2015), 136.

246 For extensive bibliographies, see Leslie Holmes, *Rotten States*; Rasma Karklins, *The System Made Me Do It: Corruption in Post-Communist Societies* (Armonk, NY: M.E. Sharpe, 2005).

247 For an insightful typology of post-1989 corruption, see Karklins, *The System Made Me Do It*, 20–38. See also Eric Hanley, 'Cadre Capitalism in Hungary and Poland: Property Accumulation among Communist-era Elites', *East European Politics and Societies* 14, no. 1 (1999): 143–78.

International.[248] The results confirm both the persistence of the problem in the region and, to some extent, its regional variation. Scores below 5.0 show 'serious levels of public sector corruption'. In 2005, only Slovenia and Estonia had better results, while the Balkans had particularly low scores.

After discussing issues more deeply rooted in history, we now turn to communist legacies. The notion of common legacies[249]– those traceable institutional impacts or path rigidities that extend beyond the rupture of transition – might seem spurious in light of the diversity of transition outcomes[250] or indeed the different patterns of popular dissent and development levels within the communist bloc itself. In this sense, as Valerie Bunce described, state socialism was both homogenizing and differentiating.[251] Moreover, pre-communist legacies play a significant role.[252] Nonetheless, 'invoking variations in historical structures or patterns of behaviour to explain contemporary outcomes has become a dominant paradigm in post-communist studies'.[253] After all, institutions are sticky and historical paths matter, so it is reasonable to expect persistent legacies of more than 40 years under a common, peculiar economic and social system.[254]

While in one of the founding works in this research area Ken Jowitt defined the 'Leninist legacy' as an endemic, systematic negative condition,[255] let us start by acknowledging that state socialism left a set of fairly homogeneous assets behind. CEE countries, in relation to those at similar levels of development, had better human capital, lower inequality, as well as a largely urban population. At the same time, the communist modernization project left them with diminished pressure from outdated agriculture, which had plagued the majority of the region before the Second World War. These assets largely persisted, favouring post-communist

---

248 On the measures of corruption, see Judge, McNatt, and Xu, 'The Antecedents and Effects', 95–6; Holmes, *Rotten States*, 90–123. For critique of the TI index for the region, see Stephen Knack, 'Measuring Corruption in Eastern Europe and Central Asia: A Critique of the Cross-Country Indicators', The World Bank Development Policy (research working paper 3968, 2006), 17–26.
249 As it is used in hundreds of works, the concept is a bit nebulous. For a discussion of its meaning, see Beverly Crawford and Arend Lijphart, *Liberalization and Leninist Legacies: Comparative Perspectives on Democratic Transitions* (Berkeley, CA: University of California Press, 1997); Herbert Kitschelt, 'Accounting for Postcommunist Regime Diversity: What Counts as a Good Cause?', in *Capitalism and Democracy in Central and Eastern Europe: Assessing the Legacy of Communist Rule*, eds Grzegorz Ekiert and Stephen E. Hanson (Cambridge: Cambridge University Press, 2003), 49–86; Jody LaPorte and Danielle N. Lussier, 'What Is the Leninist Legacy? Assessing Twenty Years of Scholarship', *Slavic Review* 70, no. 3 (2001): 637–54, here 637–8; Stephen Kotkin and Mark R. Beissinger, 'The Historical Legacies of Communism: An Empirical Agenda', in *Historical Legacies of Communism in Russia and Eastern Europe*, eds Mark R. Beissinger and Stephen Kotkin (New York: Cambridge University Press, 2014), 1–27.
250 Bohle and Greskovits, *Capitalist Diversity*; M. Stephen Fish, 'The Determinants of Economic Reform in the Post-Communist World', *East European Politics and Societies* 12, no. 1 (1998): 31–78; Nina Bandelja, Katelyn Finley and Bogdan Radu, 'Democracy in Central and Eastern Europe: Test of Early Impact', *East European Politics* 31, no. 2 (2015): 129–48.
251 Valerie Bunce, 'The Political Economy of Postsocialism', in 'Ten Years after 1989: What Have We Learned?', special issue, *Slavic Review* 58, no. 4 (1999): 756–93, here 785.
252 Grzegorz Ekiert and Daniel Ziblatt, 'Democracy in Central and Eastern Europe One Hundred Years On', *East European Politics and Societies and Cultures* 27, no. 1 (2013): 91–107.
253 LaPorte and Lussier, 'What Is the Leninist Legacy', 637–8.
254 Iván T. Berend, 'Social Shock in Transforming Central and Eastern Europe', *Communist and Post-Communist Studies* 40, no. 3 (2007): 269–80. For a critique of how analyses of transition did not take this properly into account, see Thomas Carothers, 'The End of the Transition Paradigm', *Journal of Democracy* 13, no. 1 (2002): 5–21.
255 Ken Jowitt, *New World Disorder: The Leninist Extinction* (Berkeley, CA: University of California Press, 1992); Vladimir Tismăneanu, Marc Morje Howard and Rudra Sil, eds, *World Order after Leninism* (Seattle, WA: University of Washington Press, 2006).

growth in relation to similarly rich economies, although econometric research suggests that this positive effect was more important for poorer socialist countries. The opposite was true for the persistence of complex manufacturing, which occurred mostly in the Visegrád states and Slovenia. While not a direct continuation of communist-era factories, which needed extensive redevelopment, this legacy was made possible through a combination of human capital and the particular timing and type of transition policies adopted by these countries.[256]

Germany proved to be a fertile ground for research on communist legacies, as its division after the Second World War had created a sort of historical experiment, in which West Germany acted as a control group. Studies often target deficiencies in social capital, showing how past forms of communism correlate with a preponderance of cheating[257] or reduced willingness to engage in spatial mobility (which has long-term consequences for the labour market).[258] Other researchers show how the communist social and economic system fostered a lack of self-reliance, which persisted through transition and continues to affect entrepreneurship and thus, arguably, growth.[259] This is provided as an argument for the entire post-communist bloc by Iván Berend.[260] These arguments are to a large degree aligned with the hotly contested concept of *homo sovieticus*: the idea that communist-period state policy created a new type of passive, non-self-reliant man.[261] Nonetheless, German findings should only be applied to the whole region with caution because of the particular nature of East German communism, its rapid transition, as well as the self-selecting process of emigration to West Germany before the creation of the Berlin Wall. Moreover, in CEE many of these features can be linked to pre-communist eras.[262] It should be noted that the existence of these legacies was arguably used in political discourse to promote neoliberal reforms.[263]

In general, while communist legacies proved to be a fertile focus for research, perhaps the single most lasting legacy of the period was the strengthening of many of the previously

---

256 Béla Greskovits, 'Legacies of Industrialisation and Paths of Transnational Integration after Socialism', in *Historical Legacies of Communism in Russia and Eastern Europe*, eds Mark R. Beissinger and Stephen Kotkin (New York: Cambridge University Press, 2014), 68–89. For an in-depth comparison of the Visegrád group, see Jan Drahokoupil, *Globalization and the State in Central and Eastern Europe: The Politics of Foreign Direct Investment* (London: Routledge, 2009).
257 Dan Ariely et al., 'The (True) Legacy of Two Really Existing Economic Systems' (discussion paper no. 2014–26, Ludwig-Maximilians-Universität, München, 2014).
258 Peter Boenisch and Lutz Schneider, 'The Social Capital Legacy of Communism: Results from the Berlin Wall Experiment', *European Journal of Political Economy* 32 (2013): 391–411.
259 Stefan Bauernschuster et al., 'The Shadows of the Socialist Past: Lack of Self-Reliance Hinders Entrepreneurship', *European Journal of Political Economy* 28, no. 4 (2012): 485–97. See also Alberto Alesina and Nicola Fuchs-Schündeln, 'Good-Bye Lenin (or Not?): The Effect of Communism on People's Preferences', *American Economic Review* 97, no. 4 (2007): 1507–28.
260 Iván T. Berend, 'Social Shock in Transforming Central and Eastern Europe', *Communist and Post-Communist Studies* 40, no. 3 (2007): 269–80.
261 Zsuzsa Ferge, 'Is There a Specific East-European Welfare Culture?', in *Culture and Welfare State: Values and Social Policy in Comparative Perspective*, eds Wim van Oorschot, Michael Opielka and Birgit Pfau-Effinger (Cheltenham: Edward Elgar, 2008), 141–61.
262 Bauernschuster et al., 'The Shadows of the Socialist Past'.
263 Krzysztof Tyszka, 'Homo sovieticus z perspektywy dwóch dekad' [Homo sovieticus from the perspective of two decades], in *Polska po 20 latach wolności*, eds M. Bucholc et al. (Warsaw: Wydawnictwo Uniwersytetu Warszawskiego, 2011), 294–311; Wojciech Woźniak, 'From Underclass to *Homo Sovieticus*: Human Constraints towards Modernization', *Praktyka Teoretyczna* 13, no. 3 (2004): 171–99; Michal Buchowski, 'The Specter of Orientalism in Europe: From Exotic Other to Stigmatized Brother', *Anthropological Quarterly* 79, no. 3 (2006): 463–82. For more on the neoliberal perspective, see Ther, *Europe since 1989*.

discussed pre-communist anti-market and socially conservative patterns, stemming from the region's relative backwardness and late modernization. Besides, the communist 'detour from periphery to periphery'[264] was a particular form of institutional instability, which prevented the gradual incremental accumulation of social capital, and thus diminished chances for economic performance. From this perspective, state socialism can itself be seen as a specific twist continuing Central and Eastern Europe's faltering advancement of a semi-peripheral mode of modernization.

Interactions with the world economy

Foreign trade can bring two broad types of gain to the economy. Through static gains, a country is able to consume more than its facilities (including technology and factor endowments) would otherwise allow, thanks to the mechanism of competitive advantage. Dynamic gains refer to international interactions that induce growth. While the former's existence is widely accepted, the latter's existence remains more ambiguous. Research points to a number of possible channels of influence. Trade may induce technological transfers and, through competition, produce stronger companies. Foreign markets may grant access to relatively cheap capital goods, increasing the efficiency of capital accumulation,[265] as well as to bigger outlets for exports, allowing greater economies of scale. Finally, trade may induce countries to specialize in high-innovation sectors, creating positive spillovers into the rest of the economy. On the other hand, international competition may destroy fledgling industries, or a country may specialize in low-innovation sectors that are inimical to growth in the long run. It has been argued that 'international markets are typically imperfectly competitive'[266] and discussion continues as to whether all trade is necessarily to the mutual benefit of trading nations. Paul Bairoch went so far as to call the positive impact of trade on growth a 'minor myth'.[267]

Access to foreign capital markets can also influence growth. Countries may use it to import more than they export or invest more than they save. Empirical research points to the positive contribution of this factor, but the effects depend on the type of capital transfers involved. Foreign Direct Investment (FDI) takes on a lasting character and an active role in the host country. It is generally assumed to have a positive effect on the economy, both as an additional input and through efficiency spillovers (technology and managerial technique transfers), although these gains may depend on the country's capacity for development.[268] On the other hand, too much FDI may not be good for growth in a similar way to investments solely in the primary sector or excessive remittance of profits.[269] Portfolio Investments lack the permanent character of FDI, and may increase growth by bolstering the amount of available capital and improving the financial market, but they may also hinder growth due to volatility. Finally,

---

264 Berend, 'Central and Eastern Europe', 1944–93.
265 Jong-Wha Lee, 'Capital Goods Imports and Long-Run Growth' (NBER working paper no. 4725, 1994).
266 P.R. Krugman, 'Is Free Trade Passé?', *Economic Perspectives* 1, no. 2 (1987): 131–44, here 134.
267 Paul Bairoch, *Economics and World History: Myths and Paradoxes* (Chicago, IL: University of Chicago Press, 1995), 136–8.
268 Neuhaus, *The Impact of FDI*, 44–6.
269 Oskar Kowalewski, 'Does Foreign Direct Investment Impact Economic Growth in Transition Economies?', in *The Role of Foreign Direct Investment in the Economy*, eds Oskar Kowalewski and Marzenna Anna Waresa (München: Rainer Hampp Verlag, 2008), 80.

private or public loans may improve access to capital and welfare but, after reaching high levels, they may start to have a negative impact on growth.[270]

The politics of countries do not function in a vacuum, and institutional arrangements relating to the economy are influenced by the outside world through coercion (power politics), dispersion and competitive imitation or simply through copying other countries' rules (demonstration effects).[271] These transfers may prove to be both positive and negative for growth by altering a country's institutional arrangements, but causality is often difficult to prove.

In the section on the boom of the late nineteenth century (1890–1914), we showed how trade at the turn of the nineteenth and twentieth centuries contributed to growth, but due to the relatively small per capita size it was unable to effect a systemic change. There was another side to CEE's integration with the world market. With the exception of Bohemia and Russian Poland, this trade reinforced the region's dependence on low-innovation staple exports, which were possibly inimical to growth in the long term.[272] Perhaps more convincingly, the danger lay in a very limited variety of staple exports, which made CEE dependent on market conditions, as demonstrated in the interwar period. On a smaller timescale, a similar reorientation effect can arguably be observed in Germany's trade policy in Central and Eastern Europe during the final years before the Second World War. While initially not a form of economic exploitation, since Germany offered very competitive prices, the leverage this arrangement provided allowed the Third Reich to influence the direction of the region's economies towards becoming its low-innovation primary product suppliers.[273]

Under state socialism the lack of convertible currencies and price mechanisms turned intrabloc relations into an 'exchange of inefficiencies'.[274] The nominal value of goods was detached from the cost of production, and trade was regulated by bilateral agreements. Exports were needed only to finance imports, which led to inefficient import substitution that strengthened the autarchic tendencies already present in the economic system. Trade with the West, which rose in importance from the late 1960s, also posed problems. To fulfil their high-growth plans, CEE countries required significant imports of technology and capital goods. To procure convertible currencies, they were forced to export increasing amounts of products (within the

---

270 Cristina Checherita and Philipp Rother, 'The Impact of High and Growing Government Debt on Economic Growth: An Empirical Investigation for the Euro Area', European Central Bank Working Paper Series, no. 1237 (2010); Stephen G. Cecchetti, Madhusudan Mohanty and Fabrizio Zampolli, 'The Real Effects of Debt', Bank of International Settlements Working Papers, no. 352 (2011).
271 A broad summary of the literature can be found in Wade Jacoby, 'Inspiration, Coalition and Substitution: External Influences on Postcommunist Transformations', World Politics 58. no. 4 (2006): 623–51.
272 Although Bairoch (Economics and World History, 140–141) mentions that the necessary relation between the export of primary goods and underdevelopment is another myth, he points out that an over dependence on primary goods is more damaging.
273 William S. Grenzebach, Germany's Informal Empire in East-Central Europe: German Economic Policy toward Yugoslavia and Rumania, 1933–1939 (Stuttgart: F. Steiner Verlag, 1988); R.M. Spaulding, Osthandel and Ostpolitik: German Foreign Trade Policies in Eastern Europe from Bismarck to Adenauer (Providence, RI: Berghahn Books, 1997); A.O. Ritschl, 'Nazi Economic Imperialism and the Exploitation of the Small: Evidence from Germany's Secret Foreign Exchange Balances, 1938–1940', new series, The Economic History Review 54, no. 2 (2001): 324–45; David, Nationalisme économique, 224; Carola Sachse, ed., 'Mitteleuropa' und 'Südosteuropa' als Planungsraum: Wirtschafts- und kulturpolitische Expertisen im Zeitalter der Weltkriege (Göttingen: Wallstein-Verlag, 2010); Carl Freytag, Deutschlands 'Drang nach Südosten': Der Mitteleuropäische Wirtschaftstag und der 'Ergänzungsraum Südosteuropa' 1931–1945 (Göttingen: V&R unipress, 2012).
274 Philip Hanson, The Rise and Fall of the Soviet Economy: An Economic History of the USSR from 1945 (London: Routledge, 2014), 120.

context of deteriorating terms of trade).[275] Eastern goods were at a disadvantage on Western markets due to lack of innovation, quality control and promotion. As a result, CEE countries had to compete with low prices, again detached from the real costs of production. Trade conducted in this manner did not assist growth, as it promoted neither innovation nor specialization.[276] Moreover, despite a relatively well-educated workforce, socialist countries could not adequately assimilate newly imported technologies due to institutional limitations. As a result, they were unable to profit from reduced research and development costs.[277]

On a more general level, CEE countries were both follower economies and largely primary product exporters, and thus seemed to profit most during periods of trade expansion, provided they possessed institutions allowing them to take advantage of these phases. Likewise, during times when state socialist countries had more open economic policies, such as Yugoslavia, they reported better results. Since Western Europe remained the primary business partner of the region, its economic stance to some extent determined trade opportunities. Tariffs (and the difficulties caused by the Common Agricultural Policy) remained a problem. From this point of view, joining the EU presented a threshold over to a new type of relationship both providing access to Western European markets and making import substitution in CEE impossible.[278]

The scarcity of local capital was a perennial problem in the region, necessitating capital imports for investment and modernization. For much of the twentieth century, their availability to the region was limited and their cost high.[279] This was partly due to the political situation, since in the interwar period the region was considered unsafe, while in the 1950s and 1960s the realities of the Cold War precluded Western lending. Through a vicious cycle, this low level of engagement also translated into low knowledge of the region on the side of capital exporters, which only raised the perceived level of risk and thus interest rates.[280]

One way of alleviating this situation could be employed by the state, that is, the state could provide foreign investors with information on the region and its business opportunities. Before the First World War, the Hungarian government considered itself a 'conveyor of foreign capital onto the home market', while after the transition in 1989, economies set up FDI agencies for prospective foreign investors.[281] Some investors were also granted preferential treatment, since governments associated FDI with positive spillovers. Signalling through the financial system was another strategy. As Michael Bordo and Hugh Rockoff argue, before the First World War, the gold standard acted as a 'good housekeeping seal of approval', allowing countries to receive

---

275 For Hungary alone, trade terms dropped by 50 per cent between 1938 and 1989. Berend, *From the Soviet Bloc*, 32.
276 Cecylia Leszczyńska, 'Socjalistyczny neomerkantylizm: System rozliczeń obrotów płatniczych między państwami socjalistycznymi w latach 1945–1970' [Socialist neo-mercantilism: account clearing between socialist countries, 1945–1970], in *W poszukiwaniu modelu gospodarki centralnie kierowanej*, ed. Piotr Jachowicz (Warsaw: Oficyna Wydawnicza Szkoły Głównej Handlowej w Warszawie, 2013), 110; Berend, *Decades of Crisis*, 271–2.
277 Berend, *From the Soviet Bloc*, 27–9.
278 N. Bandelj, *From Communists to Foreign Capitalists* (Princeton, NJ: Princeton University Press, 2007), 56.
279 For example, the American tranche of stabilization loans for Hungary after the First World War had a yield to maturity of 8.6 per cent when the US Treasury's long-term bonds were offering a yield of 3.9 per cent. J. Flores and Y. Decorzant, 'Public Borrowing in Harsh Times: The League of Nations Loans Revisited' (working paper, Series 12,091, University of Geneva, 2012), 17.
280 Aldcroft, *Europe's Third World*, 54; and Nötel, 'International Credit and Finance', 170.
281 Bandelj, *From Communists to Foreign Capitalists*, 70–2.

loans at lower interest.[282] Similar considerations continued into the 1920s, when CEE countries flocked to the gold exchange standard.[283] Another path was accepting the advice of 'money doctors' and international financial institutions (IFIs), although the conditionality of their help could be considered humiliating, and CEE countries sometimes rejected it.[284]

There were cases when the burden of (particularly public) debt overshadowed positive consequences. Taking loans presented something of a catch-22: servicing them required adequate returns on investment. If these failed – usually because the loans were used inefficiently – countries were forced to procure additional convertible currency through other means, including new, bigger loans.[285] Snowballing debt has a significant detrimental effect on growth. The story repeated itself in CEE before the First World War (in Serbia and Bulgaria), in the interwar period and again in the late 1970s.

Despite these reservations, better access to financial markets had a positive influence on growth. In an earlier section, we discussed the role of foreign investments in the nineteenth century. The interwar period inherited the pre-war state and built on it. Companies owned by Austrian and German capital were often nominally transferred to other nations in order to escape being taken over by CEE states (or by the process of nostrification). While in the nineteenth century loans played a more important role, new FDI, mostly from France, the United Kingdom, the United States, Belgium, Switzerland and Italy, was encouraged by both Western and CEE governments.[286] Foreign capital of this provenance played a tremendous role in the region's banking and, among others, in Czech, Polish and Yugoslav industry, reaching near complete monopolization in some branches (for example, in energy production). Rudolf Nötel states that while FDI 'added almost nothing to the solution of the agonizing problem of industrialization in the five industrially less advanced economies [Bulgaria, Hungary, Poland, Romania and Yugoslavia], it effectively promoted structural adaptations to changed territorial patterns and rapidly advancing industrial technologies'.[287] On the other hand, the Great Depression saw some attempts to liquidate shares in the region, which contributed to problems with the current account. Nationalization policies after 1945 resulted in a temporary disappearance of foreign owners until the post-communist transition.

After 1989, FDI was not only seen as a way to propel capital accumulation, and thus address the problems posed to privatization by limited savings (a by-product of state socialism),[288] but also as a vehicle for economic transformation. It was expected to contribute to job creation, skill upgrading and transfers of know-how. The inflow was impressive, particularly from Germany,

---

282 M. Bordo and H. Rockoff, 'The Gold Standard as a Good Housekeeping Seal of Approval', *The Journal of Economic History* 56, no. 2 (1996): 386–428; Maurice Obstfeld and Alan M. Taylor, 'Sovereign Risk, Credibility, and the Gold Standard, 1870–1913 versus 1925–1931', *Economic Journal* 113, no. 487 (2003): 1–35; see also K.J. Mitchener and M.D. Weidemier, 'Was the Classical Gold Standard Credible on the Periphery? Evidence from Currency Risk', *The Journal of Economic History* 75, no. 2 (2015): 479–511.
283 Nötel, 'International Credit and Finance', 211–12.
284 Flores and Decorzant, *Public Borrowing*, 21, 23; Ban, 'Sovereign Debt', 743–76. This was the case for Albania, Poland and Romania in the 1920s, and arguably also Romania under Ceaușescu.
285 Aldcroft, *Europe's Third World*, 52–4.
286 Alice Teichova, 'East-Central and South-East Europe, 1919–1939', in *The Cambridge Economic History of Europe*, vol. 3, *The Industrial Economies: The Development of Economic and Social Policies*, eds Peter Mathias and Sidney Pollard (Cambridge: Cambridge University Press, 1989), 915–22.
287 Nötel, 'International Credit and Finance', 287; Teichova, 'East-Central and South-East Europe', 926–7.
288 G. Swain and N. Swain, *Eastern Europe Since 1945*, 2nd ed. (Basingstoke: Macmillan Press, 1998), 236–7.

the Netherlands and other countries in Western Europe, which suddenly found themselves with a sizeable 'backyard' ready to receive capital. The low cost of labour, combined with a relatively educated workforce, played important roles in investment decisions, apart from the promise of secure profits in the telecom and financial sectors. By 2004, when EU enlargement occurred, average FDI stock amounted to 39 per cent of GDP in the region, twice as much as in developed countries and much more than in developing countries. In absolute terms, the biggest recipient was the Visegrád group, which attracted more than half of all FDI in the region by that time, with Poland heading the list (in per capita terms, Hungary's result was the highest). While FDI remained the most important form of capital inflow in the region, equity investment came in second place, particularly due to the growing role of Eurobonds in the second half of the 1990s.[289]

Empirical research points to the significant contribution of FDI inflows to growth in the period, with companies with FDI generally performing better than local ones. This was also true for financial FDI, which raised significant strategic concerns, but foreign banks provided expertise and facilitated access to international financing.[290]

Despite this overwhelmingly positive picture, the specific directions of spillovers are more nuanced. Horizontal spillovers occur when local companies benefit from the presence of FDI companies in the market, whereas vertical spillovers occur when local firms benefit from interactions with foreign firms in their supply chain (backward to suppliers and forward to local customers). As it turns out, during the post-communist transition vertical effects were much stronger than horizontal ones, with the latter even being negative in some countries (perhaps showing a crowding out of domestic firms or the process of buying out the best in progressive FDI). Vertical backward effects tended to be positive, while forward tended to be negative. In other words, it was good to be a supplier to a foreign company, but those mostly dealt with other FDI companies in turn.[291] This might point to a relatively low level of integration of FDI within host economies, which were chosen mostly for cheap labour and their convenient location, rather than any particular expertise. In the automotive industry in particular, we can see a type of insular investment, where FDI companies trade with each other almost exclusively (often across borders), while making very limited use of non-FDI suppliers and only making sales to consumers (although there are exceptions, such as the Romanian company Dacia, which has been owned by Renault since 1999).

Finally, interactions between CEE and the world occurred in less tangible form through institutional transfers. We can identify three broad waves of institution creation in the region: the first came with the emergence of new states before and after the First World War; the second, with the change to state socialism; and the third, after 1989. There are some similarities between the first and third of these waves. In both cases, a broadly defined West remained the frame of reference, providing patterns of institutional arrangements and engaging financially

---

289 Bandelj, *From Communists to Foreign Capitalists*, 1–2, 18–20; and Berend, *From the Soviet Bloc*, 111.
290 Neuhaus, *The Impact of FDI*, 132–40; Kowalewski, 'Does Foreign Direct Investment Impact Economic Growth', 83–9; S. Estrinet al., 'The Effects of Privatisation and Ownership in Transition Economies', *Journal of Economic Literature* 47, no. 3 (2009): 699–728; Timea Edelenyi, Peter Haiss and Sindhu Olimalalyil, 'Does Foreign Investment Always Foster Development? The Case of IPB and the Need for Prudence in Transition', in *Banken in Mittelosteuropa im Spannungsfeld von Transformation und Innovation*, eds H. Zschiedrich and U. Christians (München: Rainer Hampp Verlag, 2007), 337–55.
291 Adam Gersl, Ieva Rubene and Tina Zumer, 'Foreign Direct Investment and Productivity Spillovers in Central and Eastern European Countries', in Kowalewski and Waresa, *The Role of Foreign Direct Investment*, 99, 110–14.

in the region. Differences lay in detail, the method of transmission and in the extent to which market institutions had to be created.

In the first period, the difficulty lay in modernization, rather than restructuring the entire economic system. New Balkan countries adopted central banking and monetary arrangements before the First World War modelled on Western (particularly Belgian) solutions, while a significant inflow of capital from Western banks allowed the creation of modern banking systems. New bureaucracies and legal procedures were adopted, managing and facilitating economic activities. They were mostly adopted through imitation rather than forced transfers. Similarly, after the First World War, all the new nation states in the region followed the recommendations of the Genoa conference and created private-owned central banks and issued money in the gold exchange standard, thereby making their policy more internationally trustworthy.

Not all of these imported models were positive. Adhering to monetary standards in both periods was a heavy burden, as a potentially overvalued exchange rate hurt exports and facilitated imports, as was witnessed before the Second World War. Another negative import came through coercion, as the great powers forced free trade onto newly created Balkan countries. Ironically, after 1989 it was some of the CEE countries (like Czechoslovakia and Poland) that in neophyte zeal pressed for unnecessarily low import tariffs on some goods that they later had to revoke.

This last example forms part of a much greater institutional transfer after 1989, which can be roughly divided into two phases. Firstly, the region rapidly abandoned state socialism and introduced deregulation, marketization and privatization reforms; afterwards came Europeanization through the process of accession to the EU.

The Washington Consensus, a 1980s emanation of neoliberal orthodoxy, was the initial source of influence on the transition, and advocated for, among other things, financial and trade liberalization, elimination of barriers to FDI, deregulation and privatization.[292] It was espoused by international financial institutions, for which 'institutional reform in transition countries has become a core objective'.[293] Policy transfers were linked to financial assistance with conditions and, as a result, CEE countries had little room for manoeuvre in designing and following their macroeconomic restructuring plans.[294] At the same time, the anti-regulatory tenets of neoliberalism fell on fertile ground in post-communist countries with their legacy of the 'ubiquitous presence of politics (read the state) under socialism'.[295] The result was a region-wide (with the sole exception of Slovenia) adoption of reforms, which resulted in a fast transition to a market economy. Despite a drop in output that exceeded the reformers' expectations, the changes built the foundations for the region's success in the coming decade. Critics bemoaned both the speed of reforms, which extended beyond the capacity of the states that underwent them, and the lack of sufficient institution creation, as well as social inequality and the states' significant loss of autonomy to external influences and capital: 'The IMF was seen, in some cases, as overstepping its mandate and core areas of expertise, using its financial leverage to promote an extensive

---

[292] Charles Gore, 'The Rise and Fall of the Washington Consensus as a Paradigm for Developing Countries', *World Development* 28, no. 5 (2000): 789–804; John Williamson, 'A Short History of the Washington Consensus', *Law and Business Review of the Americas* 15, no. 7 (2009); and Taylor, 'The Law Reform Olympics', 83–105.

[293] Cernat, *Europeanization*, 106.

[294] Ibid., 107, 114, 142; and Witold J. Henisz, Bennet A. Zelner and Mauro F. Guillén, 'The Worldwide Diffusion of Market-Oriented Infrastructure Reform, 1977–1999', *American Sociological Review* 70, no 6. (2005): 871–97.

[295] Bohle and Greskovits, *Capitalist Diversity*, 59.

policy agenda, and thus short-circuiting national decision-making processes and overtaxing countries' implementation capacity'.[296]

The European Union was the second major force behind institutional transfers:[297] 'Domestic forces were fervently pushing for EU membership all over Eastern Central Europe, while EU actors used the accession process to lock in local commitments to a liberal-democratic order'.[298] The road to accession was based on two broad types of conditionality, supplemented by aid provided by the European Bank for Reconstruction and Development and European programmes, such as PHARE. First came the vague normative 'Copenhagen criteria' of December 1993, which were later supplemented by a more technocratic and less voluntary approach,[299] requiring candidates to implement the acquis communautaire. Constituting the accumulated legal work of the Community, the acquis amounted to over eighty-thousand pages that had to be translated, adapted and incorporated into local legal systems. This huge institutional transfer was criticized for its asymmetry, as it left little leeway for acceding states, and for concentrating on the formal aspects of adoption without putting adequate emphasis on the states' capacity to absorb the new institutions.[300] Nonetheless, it played a significant role in finalizing the region's transition and setting up a mature institutional environment, at the same time as spurring transformation laggards into action. Empirical studies have shown a positive correlation between the adoption of the acquis and growth.[301]

Conclusions

Overall, Central and Eastern Europe changed significantly during the long twentieth century. The economic landscape of the region in the early 2000s is very different from that which existed around 1900. Output grew in almost all realms, and there was also significant structural change. Yet, if we compare the economic performance of Central and Eastern Europe with that of other parts of the world, and especially with the subjective frame of reference for most people in the region (Western Europe), the picture is bleaker. The idea of catching up with the more developed West was a mirage, as during most of the twentieth century, the difference in economic development between CEE and the West consistently grew, with a major change in this trend only occurring after the fall of state socialism. In terms of human development, significant improvements in basic healthcare and education allowed some catching up until the 1970s, but afterwards, Western Europe outpaced the region as well. This fate was not unique

---

296 IMF staff paper, 'International Monetary Fund Conditionality: A Provisional Update', in *Conditionality Revisited: Concepts, Experiences, and Lessons*, ed. Stefan Koeberle et al. (Washington, DC: The International Bank for Reconstruction and Development/The World Bank, 2005), 33.
297 Cernat, *Europeanization*, 111.
298 Bohle and Greskovits, *Capitalist Diversity*, 85.
299 Cernat, *Europeanization*, 129; Berend, *From the Soviet Bloc*, 4; James Hughes, Gwendolyn Sasses and Claire Gordon, *Europeanization and Regionalization in the EU's Enlargement: The Myth of Conditionality* (Basingstoke: Palgrave Macmillan, 2005), 166; Heather Grabbe, *The EU's Transformative Power: Europeanization Through Conditionality in Central and Eastern Europe* (Basingstoke: Palgrave Macmillan, 2006), 7–31.
300 Milada Anna Vachudova, *Europe Undivided: Democracy, Leverage and Integration after Communism* (Oxford: Oxford University Press: 2005), 198–216.
301 Cernat, *Europeanization*, 123; and Karsten Staehr, 'Democratic and Market-Economic Reforms in the Postcommunist Countries: The Impact of Enlargement of the European Union', in *Eastern European Economics* 49, no. 5 (2011): 5–28.

Economic development

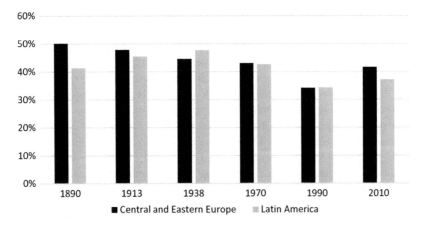

Figure 6.8 GDP per capita in Central and Eastern Europe and Latin America in relation to Western Europe, 1890–2010 (in %)

Notes: Latin America: Argentina, Brazil, Chile, Colombia, Mexico, Peru, Uruguay and Venezuela.

Source: The Maddison Project, www.ggdc.net/maddison/maddison-project/home.htm, 2013 version.

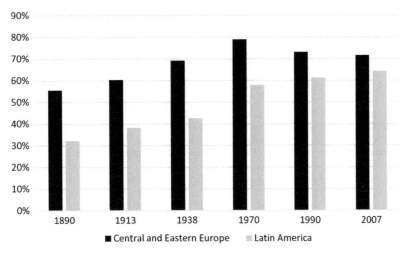

Figure 6.9 HIHD in Central and Eastern Europe and Latin America in relation to Western Europe, 1890–2007

Source: Leandro Prados de la Escosura, 'World Human Development: 1870–2007' (Working Papers in Economic History, WP 13–01, Universidad Carlos III de Madrid, underlying dataset).

to Central and Eastern Europe. In Figures 6.8 and 6.9, we compare the performance of Central and Eastern Europe with that of Latin America, which, despite taking very different political courses, achieved relatively similar outcomes.

During the long twentieth century, Central and Eastern Europe struggled both with the burden of its own rigidities and structural deficiencies – namely, its persistent premodern social structures, extractive institutions, and discrepancies between plans for development and available resources – and with challenges posed by the changing world economy. For most of the century, industry seemed to be the engine of growth, allowing for sustainable economic development and social modernization. Progress came, but the price was high. The burden of belated modernization polarized societies in the region and favoured policies that allowed extractive institutions to persist and consolidate themselves. Therefore, with few exceptions, the region failed to find an advantageous position within the international division of labour, and therefore persisted in trying to shelter itself from global agents of change. Import-substitution policies and visions of autarchic economic development marred the economic performance of various Central and Eastern European countries for a large part of the century, irrespective of the political regimes experienced by them. Only the ultimate failure of state socialism has determined the need for political elites in Central and Eastern European countries to open up and accept economic and political integration. The institutional transfers imposed by EU and NATO conditions seem to provide economic dividends, but it is still early to assess whether they will suffice to support sustainable growth and catching up, or whether the countries in the region will succumb to the middle-income trap, the resurgence of their own social conservatism and the failure of deepening and complete EU integration.

Further reading

Acemoğlu, Daron. *Introduction to Modern Economic Growth* (Princeton, NJ: Princeton University Press, 2009).
Acemoğlu, Daron, and James Robinson. *Why Nations Fail: The Origins of Power, Prosperity and Poverty* (London: Profile Books, 2012).
Aldcroft, Derek H. *The European Economy 1914–2000* (New York: Routledge, 2001).
Aldcroft, Derek H. *Europe's Third World: The European Periphery in the Interwar Years* (Aldershot: Edward Elgar, 2006).
Aldcroft, Derek H., and Steven Morewood. *Economic Change in Eastern Europe since 1918* (Aldershot: Edward Elgar, 1995).
Aldcroft, Derek H., and Steven Morewood. *The European Economy since 1914*, 5th ed. (London: Routledge, 2013).
Anderson, Victor. *Alternative Economic Indicators* (London: Routledge, 1991).
Auers, Daunis. *Comparative Politics and Government of the Baltic States: Estonia, Latvia and Lithuania in the 21st Century* (Basingstoke: Palgrave Macmillan, 2015).
Badia-Miró, Marc, Vicente Pinilla, and Henry Willebald, eds. *Natural Resources and Economic Growth: Learning from History* (London: Routledge, 2015).
Bairoch, Paul. *Economics and World History: Myths and Paradoxes* (Chicago, IL: University of Chicago Press, 1995).
Balcerowicz, Leszek. *Post-Communist Transition: Some Lessons* (London: The Institute of Economic Affairs, 2002).
Bandelj, Nina. *From Communists to Foreign Capitalists* (Princeton, NJ: Princeton University Press, 2007).
Barro, Robert J., and Sala-i-Martin, Xavier. *Economic Growth*, 2nd ed. (Cambridge, MA: The MIT Press, 2004).
Beissinger, Mark R., and Stephen Kotkin, eds. *Historical Legacies of Communism in Russia and Eastern Europe* (New York: Cambridge University Press, 2014).
Berend, Iván T. *Central and Eastern Europe, 1944–1993: Detour from the Periphery to the Periphery* (Cambridge: Cambridge University Press, 1996).
Berend, Iván T. *Decades of Crisis: Central and Eastern Europe Before World War II* (Berkeley, CA: University of California Press, 1998).
Berend, Iván T. *History Derailed: Central and Eastern Europe in the 'Long' 19th Century* (Berkeley, CA: University of California Press, 2003).
Berend, Iván T. *An Economic History of Twentieth-Century Europe: Economic Regimes from Laissez-faire to Globalization* (Cambridge: Cambridge University Press, 2006).
Berend, Iván T. *From the Soviet Bloc to the European Union: The Social and Economic Transformation of Central and Eastern Europe since 1973* (Cambridge: Cambridge University Press, 2009).
Berend, Iván T. *Europe Since 1980* (Cambridge: Cambridge University Press, 2010).
Berend, Iván T., and György Ránki. *Economic Development of East-Central Europe in the 19th and 20th Centuries* (New York: Columbia University Press, 1974).

Berend, Iván T., and György Ránki. *The Hungarian Economy in the Twentieth Century* (Beckenham: CroomHelm, 1985).

Berend, Iván T., and György Ránki. *The European Periphery and Industrialization, 1780–1914* (Cambridge: Cambridge University Press, 1982).

Blomqvist, Anders E.B. *Economic Nationalizing in the Ethnic Borderlands of Hungary and Romania: Inclusion, Exclusion and Annihilation in Szatmár/Satu-Mare 1867–1944* (Stockholm: Department of History, Stockholm University, 2014).

Bohle, Dorothee, and Béla Greskovits. *Capitalist Diversity on Europe's Periphery* (Ithaca, NY: Cornell University Press, 2012).

Cernat, Lucian. *Europeanization: Varieties of Capitalism and Economic Performance in Central and Eastern Europe* (London: Palgrave Macmillan, 2006).

Chawla, Mukesh, Gordon Betcherman, and Arup Banerji. *From Red to Gray: The Third Transition of Aging Populations in Eastern Europe and the Former Soviet Union* (Washington, DC: The International Bank for Reconstruction and Development/The World Bank, 2007).

Chirot, Daniel. *Social Change in a Peripheral Society: The Creation of a Balkan Colony* (New York: Academic Press, 1976).

Chirot, Daniel, ed. *The Origins of Backwardness in Eastern Europe: Economics and Politics from the Middle Ages until the Early Twentieth Century* (Berkeley, CA: University of California Press, 1989).

Crafts, Nicholas, and Gianni Toniolo, eds. *Economic Growth in Europe Since 1945* (Cambridge: Cambridge University Press, 1996).

Crawford, Beverly, and Arend Lijphart. *Liberalization and Leninist Legacies: Comparative Perspectives on Democratic Transitions* (Berkeley, CA: University of California Press, 1997).

Csaba, László. *Eastern Europe in the World Economy* (Cambridge: Cambridge University Press, 1990).

Csaba, László. *The New Political Economy of Emerging Europe* (Budapest: Akadémiai Kiadó, 2005).

David, Thomas. *Nationalisme économique et industrialisation: L'expérience des pays de l'Est (1789–1939)* (Geneva: Librairie Droz, 2009).

Djilas, Milovan. *The New Class: An Analysis of the Communist System* (London: Thames and Hudson, 1957).

Drahokoupil, Jan. *Globalization and the State in Central and Eastern Europe: The Politics of Foreign Direct Investment* (London: Routledge, 2009).

Ederer, Peer, Philipp Schuler, and Stephan Willms. *The European Human Capital Index: The Challenge of Central and Eastern Europe; The Lisbon Council Policy Brief* (Brussels: The Lisbon Council, 2007).

Eichengreen, Barry. *Golden Fetters: The Gold Standard and the Great Depression, 1919–1939* (Oxford: Oxford University Press, 1992).

Eichengreen, Barry. *The European Economy since 1945: Coordinated Capitalism and Beyond* (Princeton, NJ: Princeton University Press, 2007).

Ekiert, Grzegorz, and Stephen E. Hanson, eds. *Capitalism and Democracy in Central and Eastern Europe: Assessing the Legacy of Communist Rule* (Cambridge: Cambridge University Press, 2003).

Evans, Peter B. *Embedded Autonomy: States and Industrial Transformation* (Princeton, NJ: Princeton University Press, 1995).

Eyal, Gil, Iván Szelényi, and Eleanor Townsley. *Making Capitalism without Capitalists: The New Ruling Elites in Eastern Europe* (London: Verso, 1998).

Federico, Giovanni. *Feeding the World: An Economic History of Agriculture, 1800–2000* (Princeton, NJ: Princeton University Press, 2005).

Findlay, Ronald, and Kevin O'Rourke. *Power and Plenty: Trade, War, and the World Economy in the Second Millennium* (Princeton, NJ: Princeton University Press, 2007).

Frank, Alison Fleig. *Oil Empire: Visions of Prosperity in Austrian Galicia* (Cambridge, MA: Harvard University Press, 2005).

Freytag, Carl. *Deutschlands "Drang nach Südosten": Der Mitteleuropäische Wirtschaftstag und der "Ergänzungsraum Südosteuropa" 1931–1945* (Göttingen: V&R unipress, 2012).

Frydman, Roman, Kenneth Murphy, and Andrzej Rapaczynski. *Capitalism with a Comrade's Face: Studies in the Postcommunist Transition* (Budapest: CEU Press, 2012).

Gerschenkron, Alexander. *Economic Backwardness in Historical Perspective: A Book of Essays* (Cambridge, MA: Belknap Press of Harvard University Press, 1962).

Grabbe, Heather. *The EU's Transformative Power: Europeanization Through Conditionality in Central and Eastern Europe* (Basingstoke: Palgrave Macmillan, 2006).

Grenzebach, William S. *Germany's Informal Empire in East-Central Europe: German Economic Policy toward Yugoslavia and Rumania, 1933–1939* (Stuttgart: F. Steiner Verlag, 1988).
Hall, R.E., ed. *Inflation: Causes and Effects* (Chicago, IL: University of Chicago Press, 1982).
Hanson, Philip. *The Rise and Fall of the Soviet Economy: An Economic History of the USSR from 1945* (London: Routledge, 2014).
Heidenheimer, Arnold J., and Michael Johnston, eds. *Political Corruption: Concepts and Contexts*, 3rd ed. (New Brunswick: Transaction Publishers, 2002).
Heydemann, Günther, and Karel Vodička, eds. *Vom Ostblock zur EU: Systemtransformationen 1990–2012 im Vergleich* (Göttingen: Vandenhoeck & Ruprecht, 2013).
Holmes, Leslie. *Rotten States? Corruption, Post-Communism, and Neoliberalism* (Durham, NC: Duke University Press, 2006).
Hughes, James, Gwendolyn Sasses, and Claire Gordon. *Europeanization and Regionalization in the EU's Enlargement: The Myth of Conditionality* (Basingstoke: Palgrave Macmillan, 2005).
Iordachi, Constantin, and Arnd Bauerkämper, eds. *The Collectivization of Agriculture in Communist Eastern Europe: Comparison and Entanglements* (Budapest: CEU Press, 2014).
Jajeśniak-Quast, Dagmara. *Stahlgiganten in der sozialistischen Transformation: Nowa Huta in Krakau, EKO in Eisenhüttenstadt und Kunčice in Ostrava* (Wiesbaden: Harrassowitz Verlag, 2010).
Janos, Andrew C. *East Central Europe in the Modern World: The Politics of the Borderlands from Pre- to Postcommunism* (Stanford, CA: Stanford University Press, 2000).
Jedlicki, Jerzy. *A Suburb of Europe: Nineteenth-Century Polish Approaches to Western Civilization* (Budapest: CEU Press, 1999).
Jowitt, Ken. *New World Disorder: The Leninist Extinction* (Berkeley, CA: University of California Press, 1992).
Kansikas, Suvi. *Socialist Countries Face the European Community: Soviet-Bloc Controversies over East-West Trade* (Frankfurt a.M.: Peter Lang, 2014).
Karklins, Rasma. *The System Made Me Do It: Corruption in Post-Communist Societies* (Armonk, NY: M.E. Sharpe, 2005).
Kaser, Michael Charles, and Edward Albert Radice, eds. *The Economic History of Eastern Europe 1919–1975*, vol. 3. (Oxford: Oxford University Press, 1985–1987).
Kindleberger, Charles P. *The World in Depression 1929–1939* (Berkeley, CA: University of California Press, 1986).
Klemann, Hein, and Sergei Kudryashov. *Occupied Economies: An Economic History of Nazi-Occupied Europe, 1939–1945* (London: Berg, 2012).
Kligman, Gail, and Katherine Verdery. *Peasants under Siege: The Collectivization of Romanian Agriculture, 1949–1962* (Princeton, NJ: Princeton University Press, 2011).
Koeberle, Stefan, Peter Silarszky, and Gero Verheyen, eds. *Conditionality Revisited: Concepts, Experiences, and Lessons* (Washington, DC: The International Bank for Reconstruction and Development/The World Bank, 2005).
Konrád, György, and Szelényi, Iván. *The Intellectuals on the Road to Class Power: A Sociological Study of the Role of the Intelligentsia in Socialism* (New York: Harcourt, Brace and Jovanovich, 1979).
Kornai, János. *Growth, Shortage and Efficiency: A Macrodynamic Model of the Socialist Economy* (Oxford: Basil Blackwell, 1982).
Kornai, János. *The Socialist System: The Political Economy of Communism* (Oxford: Clarendon Press, 1992).
Kotkin, Stephen. *Magnetic Mountain: Stalinism as a Civilization* (Berkeley, CA: University of California Press, 1995).
Köves, András. *The CMEA Countries in the World Economy: Turning Inwards or Turning Outwards* (Budapest: Akadémiai Kiadó, 1985).
Kowalewski, Oskar, and Marzenna Anna Waresa, eds. *The Role of Foreign Direct Investment in the Economy* (München: Rainer Hampp Verlag, 2008).
Kula, Witold. *An Economic Theory of the Feudal System* (London: NLB, 1976; originally published in 1962).
Lambsdorff, Johann Graf, Markus Taube, and Matthias Schramm, eds. *The New Institutional Economics of Corruption* (London: Routledge, 2005).
Lampe, John. *Balkans into Southeastern Europe, 1914–2014: A Century of War and Transition*, 2nd ed. (Basingstoke: Palgrave Macmillan, 2014).
Lampe, John R., and Marvin R. Jackson. *Balkan Economic History, 1550–1950: From Imperial Borderlands to Developing Nations* (Bloomington, IN: Indiana University Press, 1982).

Leffler, Melvyn P., and Odd Arne Westad, eds. *The Cambridge History of the Cold War*, vol. 3. (Cambridge: Cambridge University Press, 2010).
Lepenies, Philipp H. *Macht der einen Zahl: Eine politische Geschichte des Bruttoinlandsprodukts* (Berlin: Suhrkamp, 2013).
Lindert, Peter H. *Growing Public: Social Spending and Economic Growth Since the Eighteenth Century*, vol. 1 (Cambridge: Cambridge University Press, 2004).
Lindsey, Tim, ed. *Law Reform in Developing and Transitional States* (London: Routledge, 2006).
Love, Joseph L. *Crafting the Third World: Theorizing Underdevelopment in Rumania and Brazil* (Stanford, CA: Stanford University Press, 1996).
Maddison, Angus. *Monitoring the World Economy, 1820–1992* (Paris: OECD, 1995).
Maddison, Angus. *The World Economy: A Millennial Perspective* (Paris: OECD, 2001).
Maddison, Angus. *The World Economy: Historical Statistics* (Paris: OECD, 2003).
Mathias, Peter, and Sidney Pollard, eds. *The Cambridge Economic History of Europe, vol. 3, The Industrial Economies: The Development of Economic and Social Policies* (Cambridge: Cambridge University Press, 1989).
Migdal, Joel S. *Strong Societies and Weak States: State-Society Relations and State Capabilities in the Third World* (Princeton, NJ: Princeton University Press, 1988).
Mitchell, Brian R., ed. *International Historical Statistics: Europe 1750–2000*, 5th ed. (Basingstoke: Palgrave Macmillan, 2003).
Mungiu-Pippidi, Alina. *The Quest for Good Governance: How Societies Develop Control of Corruption* (Cambridge: Cambridge University Press, 2015).
Murrel, Peter, ed. *Assessing the Value of Law in Transition Economies* (Ann Arbor, MI: The University of Michigan Press, 2001).
Neuhaus, Marco. *The Impact of FDI on Economic Growth: An Analysis of the Transition Countries of Central and Eastern Europe* (Heidelberg: Physika-Verlag, 2006).
North, Douglass C. *Institutions, Institutional Change and Economic Performance* (Cambridge: Cambridge University Press, 1900).
Oliver, Michael J., and Derek H. Aldcroft, eds. *Economic Disasters of the Twentieth Century* (Cheltenham: Edward Elgar, 2007).
Palairet, Michael. *The Balkan Economies c. 1800–1914: Evolution without Development* (Cambridge: Cambridge University Press, 1997).
Pasti, Vladimir. *Romania in Transition* (Boulder, CO: Westview Press, 1997).
Persson, Karl Gunnar. *An Economic History of Europe: Knowledge, Institutions and Growth, 600 to the Present* (Cambridge: Cambridge University Press, 2010).
Philipsen, Dirk. *The Little Big Number: How GDP Came to Rule the World and What to Do about It* (Princeton, NJ: Princeton University Press, 2015).
Reisz, Robert D., and Manfred Stock. *Inklusion in Hochschulen: Beteiligung an der Hochschulbildung und gesellschaftliche Entwicklung in Europa und in den USA (1950–2000)* (Bonn: Lemmens Verlag, 2007).
Roszkowski, Wojciech. *Land Reforms in East Central Europe after World War One* (Warsaw: Instytut Studiów Politycznych, 1995).
Sachse, Carola, ed. *"Mitteleuropa" und "Südosteuropa" als Planungsraum: Wirtschafts- und kulturpolitische Expertisen im Zeitalter der Weltkriege* (Göttingen: Wallstein-Verlag, 2010).
Savvides, Andreas, and Thanassis Stengos. *Human Capital and Economic Growth* (Stanford, CA: Stanford University Press, 2009).
Schultz, Helga, and Eduard Kubů, eds. *History and Culture of Economic Nationalism in East-Central Europe* (Berlin: Berliner Wissenschafts-Verlag, 2006).
Sen, Amartya. *Development as Freedom* (Oxford: Oxford University Press, 1999).
Siegrist, Hannes, and Dietmar Müller, eds. *Property in East Central Europe: Notions, Institutions, and Practices of Landownership in the Twentieth Century* (New York: Berghahn Books, 2015).
Smith, Stephen A., ed. *The Oxford Handbook of the History of Communism* (Oxford: Oxford University Press, 2014).
Spaulding, Robert Mark. *Osthandel and Ostpolitik: German Foreign Trade Policies in Eastern Europe from Bismarck to Adenauer* (Providence, RI: Berghahn Books, 1997).
Stark, David, and László Bruszt. *Postsocialist Pathways: Transforming Politics and Property in East Central Europe* (Cambridge: Cambridge University Press, 1998).
Svendsen, Gert Tinggaard, and Gunnar Lind Haase Svendsen, eds. *Handbook of Social Capital: The Troika of Sociology, Political Science and Economics* (Cheltenham: Edward Elgar, 2009).

Swain, Geoffrey, and Nigel Swain. *Eastern Europe Since 1945*, 2nd ed. (Basingstoke: Macmillan Press, 1998).
Teichova, Alice, ed. *Central Europe in the Twentieth Century: An Economic Perspective* (Aldershot: Ashgate, 1997).
Teichova, Alice, and Herbert Matis, eds. *Nation, State and the Economy in History* (Cambridge: Cambridge University Press, 2003).
Ther, Philipp. *Europe since 1989: A History* (Princeton, NJ: Princeton University Press, 2016).
Thewissen, Stefan H. '*Is it the Income Distribution or Redistribution that Affects Growth?*' (Research memorandum, Department of Economics, Leiden University, January 2012).
Tismăneanu, Vladimir, Marc Morje Howard, and Rudra Sil, eds. *World Order after Leninism* (Seattle, WA: University of Washington Press, 2006).
Tomka, Béla. *A Social History of Twentieth-Century Europe* (London: Routledge, 2013).
Turnock, David. *The Romanian Economy in the Twentieth Century* (London: Croom Helm, 1986).
Turnock, David. *The East European Economy in Context: Communism and Transition* (London: Routledge, 1997).
Turnock, David. *The Economy of East Central Europe, 1815–1989: Stages of Transformation in a Peripheral Region* (London and New York: Routledge, 2006).
Vachudova, Milada Anna. *Europe Undivided: Democracy, Leverage and Integration after Communism* (Oxford: Oxford University Press, 2005).
van Oorschot, Wim, Michael Opielka, and Birgit Pfau-Effinger, eds. *Culture and Welfare State: Values and Social Policy in Comparative Perspective* (Cheltenham: Edward Elgar, 2008).
van Zanden, Jan Luiten, Joerg Baten, Marco Mira d'Ercole, Auke Rijpma, Conal Smith, and Marcel Timmer, eds. *How Was Life? Global Well-Being Since 1820* (Paris: OECD Publishing, 2014).
Verdery, Katherine. *What Was Socialism, and What Comes Next?* (Princeton, NJ: Princeton University Press, 1996).
Verdery, Katherine. *The Vanishing Hectare: Property and Value in Postsocialist Transylvania* (Ithaca, NY: Cornell University Press, 2003).
Wallerstein, Immanuel. *The Modern World-System, vol. 1, Capitalist Agriculture and the Origins of the European World-Economy in the Sixteenth Century* (New York: Academic Press, 1974).
Weingast, Barry R., and Donald A. Wittman, eds. *The Oxford Handbook of Political Economy* (Oxford: University Press, 2006).
Wolff, Larry. *Inventing Eastern Europe: The Map of Civilization on the Mind of the Enlightenment* (Stanford, CA: Stanford University Press, 1994).
Wolfram, Fischer, ed. *Handbuch der europäischen Wirtschafts- und Sozialgeschichte, vol. 6, Europäische Wirtschafts- und Sozialgeschichte vom Ersten Weltkrieg bis zur Gegenwart* (Stuttgart: Klett-Cotta, 1987).
Zarycki, Tomasz. *Ideologies of Eastness in Central and Eastern Europe* (London: Routledge, 2014).
Zloch-Christy, Iliana. *Debt Problems of Eastern Europe* (Cambridge: Cambridge University Press, 1987).
Zschiedrich, Harald, and Uwe Christians, eds. *Banken in Mittelosteuropa im Spannungsfeld von Transformation und Innovation* (München: Rainer Hampp Verlag, 2007).

7

CONSUMPTION AND LEISURE IN TWENTIETH-CENTURY CENTRAL AND EASTERN EUROPE

Béla Tomka

Introduction

The main difficulty in writing a comprehensive account of the history of consumption in twentieth-century Europe – or in any other regions of the continent – is that consumption studies lack a central paradigm or set of paradigms.[1] While in the research of most areas of social life there are clearly identifiable approaches that enjoy a high acceptance among scholars, consumption research is rather diverse in terms of applied methods and current themes.[2] As suggested by Colin Campbell, a major authority in consumption history, what underlies this condition may be the fact that the field is still in a 'pre-paradigmatic stage'.[3]

---

1 The author would like to express his gratitude to Stanislav Holubec and Włodzimierz Borodziej for their enlightening comments on the first version of the text.
2 Neil McKendrick, John Brewer and J.H. Plumb, *The Birth of a Consumer Society: The Commercialization of Eighteenth-Century England* (London: Europa Publications, 1982); A.S. Deaton, 'The Structure of Demand in Europe, 1920–1970', in *The Fontana Economic History of Europe: The Twentieth Century, Part One*, ed. Carlo M. Cipolla (Glasgow: Collins/Fontana Books, 1976), 92–4; Victoria de Grazia, 'History of Consumption', in *International Encyclopedia of the Social and Behavioral Sciences*, vol. 4, eds Neil J. Smelser and Paul B. Baltes (Amsterdam: Elsevier, 2001), 2683; Victoria de Grazia and Ellen Furlough, eds, *The Sex of Things: Gender and Consumption in Historical Perspective* (Berkeley, CA: University of California Press, 1996); Hannes Siegrist, Hartmut Kaelble and Jürgen Kocka, eds, *Europäische Konsumgeschichte: Zur Gesellschafts- und Kulturgeschichte des Konsums (18. bis 20. Jahrhundert)* (Frankfurt a.M.: Campus Verlag, 1997); H. Baudet and M. Bogucka, eds, *Types of Consumption, Traditional and Modern* (Budapest: Akadémiai Kiadó, 1982); Peter N. Stearns, *Consumerism in World History: The Global Transformation of Desire* (London: Routledge, 2001); Heinz-Gerhard Haupt and Claudius Torp, eds, *Die Konsumgesellschaft in Deutschland, 1890–1990* (Frankfurt a.M.: Campus Verlag, 2009).
3 Colin Campbell, 'Consumption: The New Wave of Research in the Humanities and Social Sciences', in *To Have Possessions: A Handbook of Ownership and Property*, ed. Floyd W. Rudmin (Corte Madera, CA: Select Press, 1991), 57.

In our view, however, this high degree of diversity follows from the very nature of the subject; there are only a few social phenomena that cannot be interpreted as forms of consumption. Indeed, consumption studies, including the history of consumption, have proliferated in the last three decades, due in part to a reconceptualization of aspects of social life traditionally studied by other branches of historical and social sciences; these aspects are now increasingly interpreted as consumption. To overstate the case only slightly, we have witnessed the imperialism of consumption studies.[4]

Given its current state, any account of the field is necessarily fragmented. The problem seems to be further aggravated in the case of the consumption history of twentieth-century Central and Eastern Europe. The considerable diversity of the region and the major ruptures that took place in the last century certainly play a role here; in addition, consumption history emerged quite late in the region, in a period when this area of scholarship was dominated by cultural history. Cultural history itself can be considered a non-paradigmatic discipline, which enhances the disintegration of the narratives to an even greater degree.

Thus, we need to identify themes that allow us to include all major approaches of research in the analysis while helping us present, in the available space, a comprehensive and coherent picture of the consumption history of twentieth-century Central and Eastern Europe. In doing so we wish to explore the degree of unity that Central and Eastern Europe showed in this respect throughout the century under review, and how consumption patterns in this region related to general European trends.

For quite some time, the historical study of consumption focused on the standard of living, which, in turn, primarily implied establishing the quantity of goods and services consumed.[5] By now, research in the field of consumption history has moved beyond the mere tracking of quantitative and structural changes.[6] Further, important fields have emerged within the analysis

---

4 For reviews on recent trends in consumption research, see K. Ilmonen, 'Sociology of Consumption', in Smelser and Baltes, *International Encyclopedia of the Social and Behavioral Sciences*, vol. 4, 2687; Frank Trentmann, 'Introduction', in *The Oxford Handbook of the History of Consumption*, ed. Frank Trentmann (Oxford: Oxford University Press, 2012), 1–19; Frank Trentmann, 'Beyond Consumerism: New Historical Perspectives on Consumption', *Journal of Contemporary History* 39, no. 3 (2004): 373–401; Paul Lerner, 'An All-Consuming History? Recent Works on Consumer Culture in Modern Germany', *Central European History* 42 (2009): 509–43.

5 Cf. Norman J.G. Pounds, 'Standards of Living', in *Encyclopedia of European Social History*, vol. 5, ed. Peter N. Stearns (New York: Scribners, 2001), 451–60; Angus Maddison, 'Economic Growth and Standards of Living in the Twentieth Century: Groningen Growth and Development Centre, Research Memorandum 576 (GD-15)' (working paper, Groningen Growth and Development Centre, Groningen, 1994), 18; Richard A. Easterlin, 'The Worldwide Standard of Living Since 1800', *Journal of Economic Perspectives* 14, no. 1 (2000): 7–26; Wolfram Fischer, 'Nord und Süd – Ost und West: Wirtschaftssysteme und Lebensstandard in Europa', in *Lebensstandard und Wirtschaftssysteme*, ed. Wolfram Fischer (Frankfurt a.M.: Fritz Knapp Verlag, 1995), 213–57; Peter von der Lippe, 'Die Messung des Lebensstandards', in Fischer, *Lebensstandard und Wirtschaftssysteme*, 57–102; For the historical change of material living standards, see A.S. Deaton, 'The Structure of Demand in Europe 1920–1970', in Cipolla, *The Fontana Economic History of Europe*, 92–4; R. Floud, 'Standards of Living and Industrialization', in *New Directions in Economic and Social History*, eds Anne Digby and Charles Feinstein (Chicago, IL: Lyceum Books, 1989), 117–29; Baudet and Bogucka, *Types of Consumption*; For measuring the living standard by anthropometric methods, see John Komlos, *Nutrition and Economic Development in the Eighteenth-Century Habsburg Monarchy: An Anthropometric History* (Princeton, NJ: Princeton University Press, 1989); John Komlos and Peter Kriwy, 'The Biological Standard of Living in the Two Germanies', *German Economic Review* 4, no. 4 (2003): 459–73.

6 Siegrist, Kaelble and Kocka, *Europäische Konsumgeschichte*; recently: Stearns, *Consumerism in World History*.

of consumption, which, for lack of a better term, could be called 'qualitative aspects'. These include studying the changes in the individual's autonomy as a consumer and the shifts in the significance and function of consumption and leisure time in the life of the individual and for society as a whole.[7] The social differentiation of consumption, consumption practices and the relationship between government activity and consumption – that is, consumption policy – are further important aspects of the emergence and functioning of consumer society, and, therefore, of consumption research.

Before we outline the structure of the chapter, some conceptual issues should be addressed, most notably, the overall framework and geographical scope of enquiry, the period to which the research adheres and the limitations of the study. Consumer culture and consumer society are the main candidates for providing the conceptual frame of the research. Of the two, most recent studies on consumption history prefer consumer culture – that is, the relation of individuals to consumer goods.[8] It is a broad concept that has helped bring together different fields of research and various approaches while allowing us to analyze those societies that are not full-blown consumer societies. However, exactly for this reason it is too holistic as an analytical and explanatory concept: some forms of consumer culture existed everywhere and in every historical era. Thus, it enables us neither to properly address significant differences between post-war Central and Eastern Europe and other parts of Europe with regard to consumption, nor, consequently, to explore adequately the peculiar characteristics of the consumption regimes in post-war Central and Eastern Europe. This is a major shortcoming, since post-war consumption history is indeed an area where East–West comparisons are plausible. Such comparisons were widely practised by contemporaries throughout Europe. Since diverging consumption patterns were intensively discussed in Central and Eastern Europe by ordinary consumers as well, they contributed to the consumer experience in the region. Differences were important sources of both social dynamics and transfer processes.

It is for this reason that, in addition to the notion of consumer culture, we also use that of consumer society, which is more suitable for presenting qualitative differences between various consumer cultures. Then again, the term consumer society also entails problems of its own.[9] The question of which period saw the emergence of consumer society is already a subject of debate. Some historians regard the eighteenth century as the period of its emergence, while others cite the late nineteenth century or even the outset of the twenty-first century. Several scholars also differentiate between consumer society, which emerged in the late nineteenth century, and mass consumer society, which took shape in the late twentieth century.[10]

---

7 Heinz-Herbert Noll, 'Wohlstand, Lebensqualität und Wohlbefinden in den Ländern der Europäischen Union', in *Die westeuropäischen Gesellschaften im Vergleich*, eds Stefan Hradil and Stefan Immerfall (Opladen: Leske und Budrich, 1997), 440.

8 See Eric J. Arnould and Craig J. Thompson, 'Consumer Culture Theory (CCT): Twenty Years of Research', *Journal of Consumer Research* 31, no. 4 (2005): 868–82; Trentmann, 'Beyond Consumerism'; For examples on Central and Eastern Europe, see Ina Merkel, 'From Stigma to Cult: Changing Meanings in East German Consumer Culture', in *The Making of the Consumer: Knowledge, Power and Identity in the Modern World*, ed. Frank Trentmann (Oxford: Berg, 2006), 249–70; Ina Merkel, *Utopie und Bedürfnis: Die Geschichte der Konsumkultur in der DDR* (Köln: Böhlau, 1999); Krisztina Fehervary, 'Goods and States: The Political Logic of State-Socialist Material Culture', *Comparative Studies in Society and History* 51, no. 2 (2009): 426–59.

9 Trentmann, 'Beyond Consumerism', 374.

10 Heinz-Gerhard Haupt, *Konsum und Handel: Europa im 19. und 20. Jahrhundert* (Göttingen: Vandenhoeck, 2002), 20.

The scholarly literature on the nature and concept of consumer society is vast but somewhat inconclusive. Quite a few traits of consumer society have been proposed as distinctive features worthy of incorporation into a possible definition of the concept. The most important of these are rising affluence and ever-shorter working hours, two factors that allow individuals to dedicate more of their time to consumption instead of work. In consumer societies, not only do goods and services become commoditized, but also an increasing number of aspects of everyday life. Furthermore, consumption, as opposed to work, has become a new source of identity. While throughout the nineteenth century social class and gender were among the main sources of social division, by the end of the twentieth century distinctions in consumption patterns gained prevalence over those traditional traits. In the context of this change, consumption and lifestyle have become important indicators of social status in addition to differences in income and other social aspects.[11] In sum, there is no single chronology of consumer society, and many of the characteristic traits that the term's various definitions enlist are in fact overlapping phenomena.

Even though major changes in consumption took place in Europe from the eighteenth century onward, we stress the significance of an unprecedented rise in real wages and leisure time during the post-war decades. We also attribute special importance to qualitative factors when treating all those criteria proposed in academic debate.[12] The availability of a wide range of consumer choices can be considered one of the crucial factors in the formation of consumer societies, not only in terms of goods of vital importance but also regarding goods that fulfil 'desires' instead of rational 'needs'.[13] Consumer choice is guaranteed if goods produced all over the world are easily available, and if consumers can make their own choices among these goods. We regard these elements as major ingredients of a consumer society and will pay them proportionate attention throughout this chapter.

In line with the objectives of the volume, our research aims to provide, insofar as it is possible, a comprehensive history of consumption in the Central and Eastern European region from the early twentieth century up to the present day. In no way do we consider this period a homogeneous historical era. There are several period boundaries of great importance in the past one hundred years, both in the history of consumption and in a whole range of other aspects. At the same time, taking this long perspective is exactly what allows us to delimit and contrast various periods, and thereby better grasp the specificities of those periods. Undoubtedly, greater emphasis is placed on the period between 1945 and 1990, which is more or less the period of communist rule in the region. This is justified not only by a range of practical reasons, but also by the very nature of our topic. The end of the First World War was without a doubt an important historical milestone for both Europe and the entire world. However, in consumption history we place more of an emphasis on the middle of the century as a period boundary, while the collapse of communism emerges as another marked break in the history of Central and Eastern Europe.

---

11 Peter Kramper, 'From Economic Convergence to Convergence in Affluence?' (Working Paper, No. 56/00, LSE, London, 2000), 4.

12 Cf. United Nations Economic Commission for Europe, 'Consumption Trends and Prospects in Selected ECE Countries', Consumption Patterns in the ECE-region: Long-Term Trends and Policy Issues, *Economic Bulletin for Europe* 39, no. 2 (1987): 284.

13 John Brewer, 'Was können wir aus der Geschichte der frühen Neuzeit für die moderne Konsumgeschichte lernen?' in Siegrist, Kaelble and Kocka, *Europäische Konsumgeschichte*, 52–3.

Thus, the task of this chapter is to study the entire Central and Eastern European region – and therefore a large number of societies – across an extended period of time.[14] Consequently, we are bound to make greater methodological compromises in this research than in some less comprehensive projects. While presenting the unity and the diversity of the region and defining its place in the continent would certainly require systematic comparisons, such an exercise, if performed with due consistency, would not only breach thematic restrictions but would also take up too much space. Furthermore, the main practical difficulty lies in the fact that we have been unable to locate appropriate sources in terms of certain periods and aspects of consumption; even when they are available, the quality of the information they provide often falls far short of expectations. As compensating for such deficiencies in the available literature over the course of our research is beyond our capabilities, any shortcomings therein will inevitably be reflected in our work. A straightforward example could be the chronological imbalances characterizing this study. Even though the above reasons may justify a focus on the decades following the Second World War, our abilities to present the processes that occurred in the interwar period have been further compromised by the lack of available sources.

In line with the above considerations, the chapter will be structured as follows. First, the dynamics of the level and the structure of consumption in the region will be considered. The increase in levels of consumption in Central and Eastern European societies during the twentieth century must above all be emphasized and elaborated. Not only will we tackle the level of consumption in a narrow sense, we will also address the development of leisure time and other factors greatly affecting consumer practices. Wars, crises and political changes caused considerable ruptures in this process, which will also be a significant theme. The next section attempts to analyze the category of consumer in terms of social differences. Classes, generations and genders use consumer goods differently, and these diverging practices will be addressed here. The places and practices of consumption will then be investigated. The household remained the most important locus of consumption throughout the twentieth century; however, other new spaces related to consumption also emerged or diffused, including department stores, self-service shops, as well as school and workplace cafeterias. At this juncture, we will dedicate special attention to the effects that the shortage economy had on the everyday consumption practices of the general population. The next section concerns the role of government in shaping consumption patterns. In terms of the quality control of foodstuffs, public intervention into consumption has a long history in Europe. The First World War had already witnessed the emergence of systematic consumer politics, including such measures as rationing and price control. The post-war intensification of consumer politics created a broad, yet only partly realized agenda, including nationalization, improved planning, scientific models of consumption, standardization and the education of the populace. A further section addresses the dynamics of change and the unity of the region, regarding which, the qualitative features of consumption function as important aspects to our research: the analysis of consumer choice enables us to establish the major patterns of consumption regimes. Even though the concept of the 'shortage economy' has been recently criticized in the literature on Central and Eastern European

---

14 We use the concept of Central and Eastern Europe in the same fashion as it is used in other studies in this volume. On several occasions, Western Europe also makes an appearance as a unit of comparison. This region includes 13 countries, namely, the Scandinavian countries, Belgium, the Netherlands, Ireland, the United Kingdom, France, Germany, Austria, Switzerland and Italy.

consumption history,[15] we will argue for the analytical value of the concept and employ it when considering the qualitative characteristics of state socialist consumption regimes. The notion of a 'socialist consumer society' will also be critically examined. Furthermore, this final section summarizes the main results and suggests some peculiarities of twentieth-century Central and Eastern European consumer patterns. In Western Europe, the 'crowd pleasures' were much less self-detrimental as once assumed by many observers.[16] Mass consumption nurtured a relatively passive population – that is, consumption had a stabilizing effect on the social and political systems in the region. In contrast, in the Central and Eastern European communist systems, it had a destabilizing effect: consumption became a heavily politicized area beginning in the early 1950s and was associated with social and political unrest rather than with stability.

The structure of the chapter presents several analytical advantages. It dwells on major strands of international consumption research; it devotes as much attention to economic and social aspects as it does to cultural aspects; it maintains the significance of both shortage and abundance in the creation of consumer societies and in the lack of it; it places consumption in essential non-commercial settings such as the household; and finally, it allows us to emphasize the contribution of the state to the formation of consumption patterns in Central and Eastern Europe.

Changes in the level and structure of consumption

The first aspects addressed in this section are the level of consumption and the structure of consumption. In this context, changes in the relationship between leisure time and working time will also be tracked.

Consumption levels

Although indicators of economic output such as gross domestic product and gross national product or national income were designed to measure economic performance, the per capita values of these indicators are frequently used in literature to demonstrate levels of consumption as well.[17] There are highly practical reasons to justify the use of GDP – or GNP, for that matter[18] – as an indicator of consumption. First and foremost, data directly related to consumption – such as household final consumption expenditures – have often not been historically available. Indeed, there are several countries in Central and Eastern Europe where, at least with respect to certain time periods of varying lengths, we have barely any information at the level of the structure of consumption. GDP, on the other hand, can be considered the comprehensive economic indicator that is most readily available, even for former times. There are additional arguments in favour of using GDP, for it includes both private consumption – the most common benchmark of consumption – and collective consumption, which also contribute to the well-being of societies and individuals. In fact, these are major components of GDP. Moreover, research has come

---

15 Ina Merkel, 'Consumer Culture in the GDR, or How the Struggle for Antimodernity Was Lost on the Battleground of Consumer Culture', in *Getting and Spending: European and American Consumer Societies in the Twentieth Century*, eds Susan Strasser, Charles McGovern and Matthias Judt (Cambridge: Cambridge University Press, 1998), 283–4; Fehervary,'Goods and States', 426–59.
16 Gary C. Cross, *An All-Consuming Century: Why Commercialism Won in Modern America* (New York: Columbia University Press, 2000), 237.
17 Andrew C. Janos, *East Central Europe in the Modern World: The Politics of the Borderlands from Pre- to Postcommunism* (Stanford, CA: Stanford University Press, 2000), 344–57.
18 For all purposes relevant to our research, GDP and GNP are to be treated in the same manner.

to a much more widely supported consensus in terms of GDP calculation methodology than it has regarding any other indicator proposed for measuring consumption.

These latter considerations are especially meaningful to us considering the large number of societies involved in the research and the long period of time under review, as these two circumstances make it very difficult to compile comparable data. Therefore, it is inappropriate to rely on economic output data when studying consumption levels; however, in doing so, we must be aware of certain distorting factors.

During the twentieth century, and more specifically during the period under review, gross domestic product figures in Central and Eastern Europe have multiplied. As Chapter 6 by Łazor and Murgescu addresses these trends in detail, a brief comparative summary should suffice here.

In the economies of Western Europe, when taking the geographical term in its wider sense, per capita GDP increased, on average, by a factor of seven and a half between 1890 and 2000, and by a factor of five and a half between 1913 and the end of the millennium. Fragmented by wars, crises and revolutions, this overall tendency of growth showed significant fluctuations over time. The period of fastest growth was the two decades after 1950. Moreover, the individual regions and national economies followed their own distinct trajectories: across the entire time period, Southern Europe showed the highest growth rates, followed by Scandinavia and North-Western Europe.[19]

Central and Eastern Europe also showed remarkable growth yet lagged behind the leaders of the continent. When taking the weighted average of the seven countries of the region (Albania, Bulgaria, Czechoslovakia, Hungary, Poland, Romania and Yugoslavia), per capita GDP increased by a factor of four and a half between 1890 and 2000, while it increased by a factor of three and a half between 1913 and 2000. Between 1913 and 1989, per capita GDP increased by 227 per cent in Poland, 318 per cent in Czechoslovakia, and 229 per cent in Hungary. The south-eastern countries of the region showed similar overall performance, but even greater internal differences: per capita GDP grew by 491 per cent in Yugoslavia, 126 per cent in Romania, 305 per cent in Bulgaria, and 205 per cent in Albania.[20] The Central and Eastern European economies, again, demonstrated peculiar dynamics of growth. During the interwar period, these countries more or less maintained their distance behind Europe's most developed economies. However, the region as a whole fell behind during the decades following the Second World War – particularly as of the 1970s. The most significant outlier was Yugoslavia, which showed the best relative performance in the post-war era – granted, its internal differences were also exceptional.[21]

As outlined above, economic output, especially in the long term, can be considered the most important determining factor of consumption; accordingly, the growth path of economic output also supplies important information on changes in the level of consumption. Furthermore,

---

19 Joan R. Roses and Nikolaus Wolf, 'Aggregate Growth, 1913–1950', in *The Cambridge Economic History of Modern Europe*, vol. 2, *1870 to the Present*, eds Stephen Broadberry and Kevin H. O'Rourke (Cambridge: Cambridge University Press, 2010), 181–207; Nicholas Crafts and Gianni Toniolo, 'Aggregate Growth, 1950–2005', in Broadberry and O'Rourke, *The Cambridge Economic History of Modern Europe*, vol. 2, 296–332; Angus Maddison, *The World Economy: Historical Statistics* (Paris: OECD, 2003), 60–9.
20 Maddison, *The World Economy*, 100–1.
21 Włodzimierz Brus, '1957 to 1965: In Search for Balanced Development', in *The Economic History of Eastern Europe, 1919–1975*, vol. 3, ed. M.C. Kaser (Oxford: Clarendon, 1986), 70–138; János Kornai, *Erőltetett vagy harmonikus növekedés* [Forced or harmonious growth] (Budapest: Akadémiai Kiadó, 1972); János Kornai, *Paying the Bill for Goulash-Communism* (Boulder, CO: Atlantic Research and Publications, 2000), 58–75; Mária Barát, ed., *A magyar gazdaság vargabetűje* [Zigzags in the Hungarian economy] (Budapest: Aula, 1994).

economic output includes not only consumption, but capital formation as well. The share of capital formation has an effect on how much of the output is allocated to consumption. Moreover, international financial transfers (such as lending, borrowing and aid) can further modify the level of resources available for domestic consumption and capital accumulation. An in-depth analysis of the national accounts of the Central and Eastern European economies cannot be carried out; thus, only the effects of exports and imports will be addressed. We begin in section one by assessing changes in gross capital formation, which includes inventories in addition to investment, and follow in section two by examining whether foreign trade balances have significantly affected domestic consumption. Or, to use the language of national accounting, GDP equals consumption (private and government) plus gross capital formation (investment and inventories) and net exports.

1. Assuming a constant foreign trade balance, an increase in capital formation is bound to reduce consumption levels and vice versa. An increase in capital formation may indeed boost economic growth, thereby contributing to a future increase in consumption, but this is not necessarily the case. To be more specific, this effect is not necessarily proportionate to investment levels because the structure and efficiency of investments are also instrumental to growth rates.

Based on the highly fragmented data available to us, the rate of capital formation in Central and Eastern Europe during the years following the First World War was lower than the average rate in the Western European countries. In 1929, Poland allocated 8.1 per cent of its national income to capital formation, while in Hungary, average annual capital formation amounted to 11.2 per cent of economic output (net national product, NNP) during the second half of the 1920s.[22] However, these were years of exceptional prosperity. During the next decade, in the wake of the Great Depression, the rate of capital formation dropped by several percentage points in most Central and Eastern European countries, just as in Western Europe. Thus, during the interwar period, some opinions estimate the average rate of capital formation in Hungary in the range of five to six per cent,[23] while other calculations concluded that it had been as high as eight per cent.[24] Similar results are seen in Poland.[25] Czechoslovakia was in an exceptional situation; in 1929, the country's rate of capital formation amounted to 19.7 per cent of GNP, which was extraordinarily high not only in comparison with other countries within the region, but also in the wider European context.[26] Accordingly, the downturn Czechoslovakia experienced during the crisis was just as heavy.

During the decades following the Second World War, the ratio of capital formation increased significantly in every Central and Eastern European country. During the first half of the 1950s, it was in the range of 18 to 25 per cent of the net material product in most countries, reaching almost 30 per cent in some years. This share was similar to the average ratio of capital formation in Western Europe; however, considering the level of economic development in the region, such a percentage was considered very high.

---

22 Alexander Eckstein, 'National Income and Capital Formation in Hungary, 1900–1950', in *Income and Wealth*, ed. S. Kuznets (London: Bowes and Bowes, 1955), 219.
23 Iván T. Berend, 'Investment Strategy in East-Central Europe', in *The Rise of Managerial Capitalism*, eds Herman Daems and Herman van der Wee (Louvain: Leuven University Press, 1974), 184.
24 Eckstein, 'National Income and Capital Formation', 219.
25 United Nations Economic Commission for Europe, *Economic Survey of Europe for 1948* (Geneva: UNECE, 1949), 45; United Nations Economic Commission for Europe, *Economic Survey of Europe for 1949* (Geneva: UNECE, 1950), 23.
26 E. Lethbridge, 'National income and product', in *The Economic History of Eastern Europe, 1919–1975*, vol. 1, eds M.C. Kaser and E.A. Radice (Oxford: Clarendon Press, 1985), 550.

Throughout the years, significant disparities emerged both regionally and over time. On the one hand, Czechoslovakia was an exception – along with the German Democratic Republic, a country outside the scope of our research – because its average ratio of capital formation at this time was already much lower than the ratios seen in Bulgaria, Hungary or Poland. What is more striking, however, is the extreme fluctuation in the share of capital formation seen in every single country of Central and Eastern Europe, often from one year to the next. For example, the capital formation ratio in Czechoslovakia was 11.4 per cent in 1949 but only 5.8 per cent in 1950, only to surge to 16.4 per cent in 1953 before once again plunging to 9.2 per cent in 1954. It is no surprise that this had a significant effect on consumption levels. In most countries, the fluctuation in the ratio of capital formation in the first half of the 1950s often resulted in a decline in absolute terms in the level of consumption, a typical example being Hungary.[27] Later on, the fluctuation in the investment ratios became somewhat less extreme, yet volatility remained high. Between 1960 and 1989, the coefficient of variation of the annual average growth rate of investment was 278 per cent in Yugoslavia, 187 per cent in Poland, 171 per cent in Hungary and 131 per cent in Czechoslovakia; while the figure was 159 per cent in Ireland, 130 per cent in Sweden and 127 per cent in Austria.[28] Nonetheless, beginning at the end of the 1950s, this fluctuation resulted exclusively in consumption levels that either stagnated or rose by less than the rate of economic growth; that is, it no longer led to a fall in the absolute level of consumption.

During the following period of about two decades – until the end of the 1970s – investment activities continued to gather momentum in most centrally controlled economies, eventually reaching a plateau at the middle or end of the 1970s, with strong fluctuations remaining the norm. In Poland, the average annual ratio was 34 per cent for the period between 1971 and 1975, reaching as high as 40.4 per cent of the national income in 1975,[29] while in Romania capital formation represented, on average, 34.1 per cent of the national income during the period between 1971 and 1975. This was much higher than the roughly 25 per cent ratio often considered the standard level for Western Europe at the time.[30] Bulgaria and Hungary showed similar rates during the same period, while Czechoslovakia continued to stand out with its much lower rate. From the middle or end of the 1970s, the level of capital formation diminished across the entire region, yet still reached the Western European average.

While we do not intend to analyze changes in capital formation at any significant depth, certain conclusions can be drawn concerning the relationship between the above trends and consumption levels. The first and most important conclusion is that consumption levels were heavily influenced by levels of capital formation, which were relatively low during the first half of the century and subsequently high when compared to international averages, as well as by their strong fluctuations.

During the interwar period, most Central and Eastern European countries (again, with the exception of Czechoslovakia) showed relative consumption levels higher than those in Western Europe, more or less matching those seen in Southern Europe. Accordingly, the gap between

---

27 Tamás Bauer, *Tervgazdaság, beruházás, ciklusok* [Planned economy and investment cycles] (Budapest: KJK, 1981), 70.
28 János Kornai, *The Socialist System: The Political Economy of Communism* (Princeton, NJ: Princeton University Press, 1992), 191.
29 Bauer, *Tervgazdaság, beruházás, ciklusok*, 197.
30 For investments, see Bauer, *Tervgazdaság, beruházás, ciklusok*, 263; Bogdan Mieczkowski, *Personal and Social Consumption in Eastern Europe: Poland, Czechoslovakia, Hungary, and East Germany* (New York: Praeger, 1975), 51–71.

the region's relative consumption levels and those of the leading European economies was smaller than differences in per capita GDP levels would suggest. However, just after the Second World War, the rate of capital formation in the region increased only in certain years, and then later in a sustained manner causing a drop in the proportion of consumption in GDP; that is, in terms of consumption the gap between the western part of the continent and the region under review increased more dynamically than did the discrepancy in economic performance.

During the decades following the Second World War, the high rate of capital formation was closely linked to the priorities and possibilities of economic policy and to the characteristics of the economic system. On the one hand, in the initial period, consumption was secondary to economic growth as a political and economic objective throughout the region, and obviously, growth demanded investment efforts. Furthermore, central authorities had all the tools necessary to boost investment levels far beyond those historically found in the region as well as those considered to meet the international standard, even if such an increase was to the detriment of consumption. Later on, improving supply and meeting consumer demand were given more emphasis among other economic policy objectives in most countries; however, the poor efficiency of the economic system, especially of its investment activities, meant that maintaining an acceptable rate of economic growth demanded high rates of capital formation, which once again, was detrimental to consumption levels. Important to note is that a good proportion of the capital formation was in fact realized as increased stock levels, a phenomenon also linked to the problems of the economic system; while supply chains were unreliable, forcing companies to accumulate high stock levels in reserve, companies often manufactured products of poor quality that were difficult to sell, which also increased their inventories of finished goods.[31]

As we have seen, the high volatility of investment levels also caused fluctuations in the proportion of consumption as compared to economic output. As a result, the level of consumption was highly exposed to the decisions of the central organs of economic control that established investment levels and other economic policy objectives, one of the most important characteristics of the history of consumption in communist Central and Eastern Europe. This contributed greatly to the politicization of consumption, the effects of which will be addressed later in this chapter.

Nonetheless, the literature provides no consensus concerning the relationship between consumption and investment in terms of centrally controlled economies. Most authors are of the opinion that the objective of the planning authorities was to maximize growth, and that their primary tool was keeping investments at a high level; consumption was secondary to the drive for higher and higher investment levels, the latter crowding out the former.[32] Other authors maintain that consumption did not function as a buffer, and that its fluctuations did not depend on the will of the central authorities prioritizing investments. Instead, economic growth and, along with it, investment rates changed in a cyclical fashion, which exerted a similar cyclical effect on the share of consumption within output.[33] However, determining which mechanism was indeed at play has little relevance here; more important to us is that increasing ratios of

---

31 Mieczkowski, *Personal and Social Consumption in Eastern Europe*, 62–3.
32 János Kornai, *Economics of Shortage* (Amsterdam: North-Holland, 1979); George R. Feiwell, *Problems in Polish Economic Planning* (New York: Praeger, 1971), 280.
33 Wolfram Schrettl, 'Consumption, Effort, and Growth in Soviet-Type Economies: A Theoretical Analysis' (PhD diss., Boston University Graduate School, 1982), 160; for investment cycles, see Bauer, *Tervgazdaság, beruházás, ciklusok*; Oldřich Kýn, Wolfram Schrettl and Jiří Sláma, 'Growth Cycles in Centrally Planned Economies: An Empirical Test', in *On the Stability of Contemporary Economic Systems*, eds Oldřich Kýn and Wolfram Schrettl (Göttingen: Vandenhoeck and Ruprecht, 1979), 109–32.

investment had a negative effect on consumption levels, with the proportion between the two often changing considerably from one year to the next.

When examining the relationship between capital formation and consumption, also of note is the structure of investments in our region after the Second World War, which was very different from that of the Western European market economies. The main differences result from the fact that investments in certain sectors considered non-productive in terms of a socialist economy, such as residential construction, health care, education, etc., remained low as compared to total investment levels in the region. While in Western Europe the proportion of investments in these sectors approximated or, in some countries, constituted half of total investments as early as during the first two decades following the Second World War, and over time reached even higher levels almost everywhere, this ratio was 25.6 per cent in Czechoslovakia between 1961 and 1965, and in Hungary 25.3 per cent in 1965, and only 32.5 per cent even as late as 1980.[34] Residential construction was particularly affected. In most Central and Eastern European countries, the proportion of total investment dedicated to residential construction was far lower than typical levels seen in Western Europe – even during the 1960s and 1970s, the two decades most characterized by dynamic growth in this sector. In Czechoslovakia, 15.7 per cent of total investment was dedicated to residential construction between 1968 and 1977, while the figure was 14.9 per cent in Poland, 22.1 per cent in Yugoslavia[35] and 16.8 per cent in Hungary between 1976 and 1980; on the other hand, between 1976 and 1980, average residential construction amounted to 30.2 per cent of total investment in the Netherlands, and 29 per cent in West Germany.[36] Neglecting investment in residential construction and other sectors considered non-productive had further negative effects on the level of consumption as well as on its qualitative characteristics, which we will address later. Furthermore, over the long run, de-emphasizing infrastructure also had a detrimental effect on human capital, thereby lessening growth prospects.[37]

In most transition economies, the ratio of fixed capital formation decreased significantly during the 1990s; however, a number of countries – such as the Czech Republic and Slovakia – continued to maintain a relatively high level compared to international averages. These high levels, however, implied no significant restriction on consumption levels, especially considering the fact that FDI was already contributing considerably to investments in Hungary in the early 1990s and, in the rest of the countries, as of the mid- and late 1990s.

2. As suggested above, consumption is not only affected by capital formation, but also by net exports. A negative foreign trade balance increases a country's level of domestic use (consumption and capital formation), which then must be financed from foreign loans or other financial transfers. The opposite may also occur when exports exceed imports, meaning at least temporarily that some of the goods produced are exported rather than consumed or invested domestically.

During the interwar period, the countries of Central and Eastern Europe were also familiar with differences between domestic use and economic output. While comprehensive data is

---

34 Barát, *A magyar gazdaság vargabetűje*, 435; Teichova, 'Die Tschechoslowakei, 1918–1980', in *Handbuch der europäischen Wirtschafts- und Sozialgeschichte*, vol. 6, eds Wolfram Fischer et al. (Stuttgart: Klett-Cotta, 1987), 630.
35 Jaroslav Krejči, *National Income and Outlay in Czechoslovakia, Poland and Yugoslavia* (New York: St. Martin's Press, 1982), 38.
36 Barát, *A magyar gazdaság vargabetűje*, 194.
37 Eva Ehrlich, 'Infrastructure', in Kaser and Radice, *The Economic History of Eastern Europe, 1919–1975*, vol. 1, 323–78.

lacking in this respect, the data on capital flow and foreign trade provide some indications. Immediately after the First World War, Hungary had the highest relative level of capital import; the inflow of capital during the second half of the 1920s was as much as 7 to 8 per cent of the national income according to the calculations of the ministry of finance at the time.[38] Much of these loans were used to pay off the country's financial obligations and towards financing investment; consequently, not all of the incoming capital served as an additional source for increasing the domestic use of incomes or, more specifically, for boosting the consumption levels of the population. In other countries of the region, the relative level of capital import was lower to begin with. Czechoslovakia was also in a privileged situation in this respect; during the interwar period, with the exception of the few crisis years, the country exported significant amounts of capital.[39] Nonetheless, foreign trade balance trends clearly indicate that during the decade following the First World War the domestic use of incomes was higher than economic output in both Hungary and Poland. In Hungary, the difference between imports and exports was 2.9 per cent of the national product between 1924 and 1929.[40] During the 1930s, moderate levels of foreign trade surplus emerged not only in Czechoslovakia, but also in other countries of the region, including Hungary.[41] All in all, there are no marked interwar capital import trends to be observed in Central and Eastern Europe that would have significantly influenced consumption levels; at most, we may conclude that capital movements in Hungary during the 1920s widened the margin of manoeuvre for consumption policy, whereas in Czechoslovakia, interwar capital export somewhat curbed the domestic consumption of the national product.[42]

As of the second half of the 1950s, we can observe greater differences between the level of domestic use and the level of economic output. In some countries, these trends are persistent, while in others, they fluctuate. Based on comparative prices, domestic use in Hungary was in excess of economic output in each year between 1950 and 1983. At over 6 per cent, the difference was typically quite large, with some outstanding values in 1957 (13.8 per cent), 1971 (19.2 per cent) and 1978 (14.7 per cent).[43]

This also implies that Hungary could only maintain its levels of consumption and capital formation by increasing its external indebtedness. Changes in the structure of imports also show that the driving force behind the largest wave of indebtedness in the 1970s was the intention to increase or at least preserve the level of consumption, not any aspiration to boost investment activities.[44] As of the early 1980s, Hungary's economic policy, which relied extensively on external financing, began running into problems; the country was unable to source additional loans, partly because of its high level of indebtedness and the sudden increase in interest rates for loans. As of 1982, paying off debts required a positive foreign trade balance, which discouraged

---

38 Iván T. Berend and György Ránki, *Magyarország gazdasága az első világháború után, 1919–1929* [Hungary's economy after the First World War, 1919–1929] (Budapest: Akadémiai Kiadó, 1966), 187.
39 Rudolf Nötel, 'International Capital Movements and Finance in Eastern Europe, 1919–1949', *Vierteljahrschrift für Sozial- und Wirtschaftsgeschichte* 61, no. 1 (1974): 65–112.
40 My own computations based on Eckstein, 'National Income and Capital Formation', table 1, 165; Berend and Ránki, *Magyarország gazdasága az első világháború után*, 279.
41 Iván T. Berend and György Ránki, *Magyarország gyáripara a második világháború előtt és a háború időszakában (1933–1944)* [Hungary's manufacturing industry before the Second World War and during the War (1933–1944)] (Budapest: Akadémiai Kiadó, 1958), 36.
42 Nötel, 'International Capital Movements,' 103.
43 Based on current prices, the dynamics were somewhat different. The gap was small in the 1950s and in the 1960s but widened siginificantly in the following periods. It peaked in 1978 when internal use was 9.1 per cent higher than the GDP. Barát, *A magyar gazdaság vargabetűje*, 387, 390.
44 Ibid., 176–7.

domestic consumption and produced a very different effect on the standard of living compared to previous years and decades. Poland had similar experiences; external indebtedness provided a certain margin of manoeuvre for increasing consumption during the 1970s but having to pay off the debt during the 1980s once again caused a decrease in consumption. Romania, however, walked a different path; in the 1980s, harsh austerity measures that were enacted to pay off the external debt incurred by the state dramatically curbed consumption levels.

In several countries, the negative impact exerted on consumption by the transformation crisis following regime change was somewhat softened by sources such as the above-mentioned FDI and, especially, foreign loans. The countries already highly in debt at the time – Poland, Hungary and Bulgaria – necessarily had less opportunity to rely on foreign resources such as these; however, they remained an option for other countries such as the Czech Republic, Slovakia, Romania, Slovenia and Albania.[45] After EU accession in 2004 and 2007, the new member states from the region became eligible for significant EU subsidies that could amount to as much as four to five per cent of their GDP; this support also had an indirect yet positive effect on consumption levels.

Having examined the rate of capital formation and the domestic use of incomes, we may conclude that while during the interwar period the level of economic output is as good an indicator of changes in consumption levels in Central and Eastern Europe as it is in Western European market economies, this is decidedly not the case for the centrally controlled economies during the same period. During the decades following the Second World War, the high ratio of capital formation in the communist countries of Central and Eastern Europe reduced the number of sources available for consumption. As of the end of the 1950s, and increasingly during the 1970s, several countries in the region relied on foreign loans to make up partially for this reduction in these sources. However, this was only possible until the early 1980s when, with loans to pay back, the level of domestic consumption in these countries dropped below the level of economic output. Another important peculiarity of the region – indeed, of all centrally controlled economies – was the extreme fluctuation in the rate of consumption as a result of changing economic policy preferences, political crises and economic exigencies. However, the level and quality of consumption were influenced even more detrimentally by the peculiar composition of capital formation in the centrally planned economies, where residential construction and other infrastructural investment activities were deprioritized. After the regime change, consumption levels plummeted dramatically as a result of the transformation crisis, while the above-discussed peculiarities that had influenced consumption levels until then, for the most part, disappeared or faded significantly.

Undoubtedly, the overall picture of consumption levels in twentieth-century Central and Eastern Europe derived from economic output data seems to be painted with a rather broad brush, even after the above-described adjustments. In light of the inherent deficiencies in our understanding of the interwar period, there may emerge a need to rely on contemporary calculations of the standard of living, which are in fact available in several countries.[46] However, not only do these calculations fail to cover the entire population, they are also based on wage indices, and thus cannot be considered to reflect all households.[47] Another typical approach in

---

45 Jan Svejnar, 'Transition Economies: Performance and Challenges', *Journal of Economic Perspectives* 16, no. 1 (2002): 3–28.

46 Béla Kovrig, *Magyar társadalompolitika, 1920–1945. I. rész* [Hungarian social policy 1920–1945, part 1] (New York: Magyar Nemzeti Bizottmány, 1954), 201–6.

47 See Ágnes Pogány, 'Háztartások jövedelemszerkezete a két világháború közötti Magyarországon' [Household income structures in interwar Hungary], *Történelmi Szemle* 42, no. 1–2 (2000): 115–27.

the literature of consumption history is to present consumption levels on the basis of physical indicators. Such works offer data on a wide range of products, but most typically they illustrate changes on the basis of the consumption of foodstuffs (sugar, flour, cooking fats, milk, etc.). Various factors render these statistics unsuitable for providing a fair picture of consumption levels. For example, physical indicators – especially in the case of more complex products – blur qualitative differences; the number of cars or refrigerators per 1,000 inhabitants says little about the design or quality of the cars or refrigerators. Furthermore, the very nature of this data prevents its aggregation. Pairs of shoes and numbers of TV sets cannot be simply added up. Furthermore, they cannot be considered representative of overall consumption, as we do not know their share within overall consumption; in fact, their role within total consumption may change over time as the structure of consumption undergoes changes. For these reasons, such physical indicators can only be used later in our research, namely when we address structural changes in consumption.

Leisure

One of the major aspects of the transformation of consumption is the labour input it requires on behalf of the individual or society as a whole to achieve any given standard of living. Moreover, increasing leisure time is a fundamental factor in the emergence of consumer society. As a useful starting point for studying this latter process, it is worthwhile to define leisure as the time that remains after all other activities required for subsistence (above all, work) have been performed. Changes in working time are therefore relevant in both contexts mentioned above.

At the end of the nineteenth century, most European employees worked 10 to 12 hours a day, 6 days a week, with no paid leave. While improving productivity made it possible to decrease working time, these two processes never ran truly in parallel; more often than not, employers as well as governments declined employee demands for reductions in working time.[48] At the end of the nineteenth century and at the beginning of the twentieth century, progress was slow yet continuous; at the breakout of the First World War, the average weekly working time in Western Europe – with the exception of just a handful of countries – was already less than 60 hours.[49] After the First World War, progress gained momentum when a whole range of countries introduced an eight-hour workday and a six-day workweek.[50] During and after the Second World War, weekly working times temporarily became longer again; however, once the reconstruction process was over, working time returned to its shortening trend.

Overall, we might say that the typical workweek in Western Europe was six days long up until the First World War, five and a half days long until roughly the middle of the century, and five days long after 1960, yet with significant regional and sectoral differences.[51]

After the First World War, paid leaves gradually became available to an increasing number of employees.[52] Although the annual number of days an employee could enjoy as paid leave did

---

48 Paul Blyton, *Changes in Working Time: An International Review* (London: Croom Helm, 1985), 19.
49 Gary S. Cross, 'Work Time', in *Encyclopedia of European Social History*, vol. 4, ed. Peter N. Stearns (New York: Scribner, 2001), 504–5; Michael Huberman, 'Working Hours of the World Unite? New International Evidence of Worktime, 1870–1913', *Journal of Economic History* 64, no. 4 (2004): 964–1001.
50 Gerhard Bosch, Peter Dawkins and Francois Michon, 'Working Time in 14 Industrialized Countries: An Overview', in *Times are Changing: Working Time in 14 Industrialized Countries*, eds Gerhard Bosch, Peter Dawkins and Francois Michon (Geneva: ILO, 1993), 1–5.
51 Michael Haberman and Chris Minns, 'The Times They Are Not Changin': Days and Hours of Work in Old and New Worlds, 1870–2000', *Explorations in Economic History* 44 (2007): 538–67, here 543.
52 Cross, 'Work Time', 505.

not increase all that fast, even after the Second World War, step-by-step progress meant that by the end of the millennium employees could spend a considerable amount of time off work. Moreover, the number of paid holidays also increased. At the end of the twentieth century, paid leave and holidays amounted to an average of 36 days a year in Western European societies.[53]

Thanks to shortening daily and weekly working times, the increase in the number of holidays, and the increase in the number of days of paid leave, annual working time decreased significantly.[54] At the end of the nineteenth century, Western European employees logged an annual average of 2,600 to 3,100 working hours. At the time, Great Britain represented the lower threshold; however, most countries caught up during the decade following the First World War. This was the period when working time decreased most dynamically all over Europe. Except for during war years and post-war reconstruction periods, the trend continued throughout the following decades, although at a somewhat slower pace. Eventually, in 1990, average annual working time amounted to around 1,600 working hours.[55] The downward trend continued for the next two decades, although the rate of decrease was not as high as in the previous two decades.

In Central and Eastern Europe, working time regulation started in the industrial sector at the end of the nineteenth century, with the process gaining speed after the First World War. Legislation introduced the eight-hour workday as early as 1918 in Czechoslovakia, 1919 in Poland, 1928 in Romania and 1922 in Yugoslavia.[56] In Hungary, however, for quite some time, even during the interwar period, the length of the workday varied mostly as the function of business cycles; thus, in the second half of the 1920s, working hours increased thanks to the economic boom.[57] As a result, in 1928 only 45.4 per cent of workers in the manufacturing industry put in eight or less hours per day, with the figure increasing to 55.1 per cent during the winter.[58] However, the ratio of employees working eight or less hours per day was much higher in the mining industry, while in agriculture, which offered the bulk of all employment in the country, in catering and in commerce, those working eight or less hours per day represented an even lower proportion of all employees. In 1937, standard working time was defined as eight hours per day and 48 hours per week, except for in agriculture and catering.[59] Paid leaves were also introduced after the First World War, with Poland and Czechoslovakia acting as pioneers for the region. It must be emphasized that, with the sole exception of Czechoslovakia, the above regulation did not apply to agriculture, that is, to the largest group of all employees.

Consequently, one of the important driving forces in the reduction of working time was the structural transformation of the economy as the ratio of those working in agriculture (i.e. those working longer hours except in winter) gradually decreased. This was the case in the years between the two world wars, and even more so in the first two decades following the Second World War. Reducing working hours in industry and the service sector was not on the agenda

---

53 Huberman and Minns, 'The Times They Are Not Changin'', 546.
54 Jesse H. Ausubel and Arnulf Grübler, 'Working Less and Living Longer: Long-Term Trends in Working Time and Time Budgets', *Technological Forecasting and Social Change* 50 (1995): 205.
55 Béla Tomka, *A Social History of Twentieth-Century Europe* (London: Routledge, 2013), 212.
56 Béla Kovrig, *A munka védelme a dunai államokban* [The protection of work in the Danube states] (Kolozsvár: Universitas Francisco-Josephina, 1944), 94–108.
57 Sándor Farkasfalvi, 'Adatok a 8 órai munkaidő kérdéséhez' [Data on the question of the eight-hour workday], *Magyar Statisztikai Szemle* 8, no. 3 (1930): 193.
58 Dezső Pap, 'Munkaidő' [Working hours], in *Közgazdasági enciklopédia*, vol. 3 (Budapest: Athenaeum), 1184.
59 Kovrig, *Magyar társadalompolitika*, 91–5.

during the period of post-war reconstruction and forced industrialization; in political declarations and in official discourse, the focus was on the need to make more intensive use of the working time. As of 1956, several countries decided to shorten the 48-hour workweek; by 1967, Romania and Hungary were the only countries in the region with a six-day workweek.[60] Although the workweek was relatively long, employees could enjoy few paid holidays or paid leave days, and overtime was common. Thus, even at the beginning of the 1960s, the average number of hours worked in the region was high compared to Western European standards. In addition, unlike in Western European countries, the ratio of agricultural employees remained significantly high in the region until the regime change, with employees in this sector working longer hours than did their counterparts in most of the other sectors.

Time budget data obtained in a number of medium-sized cities shows that in the middle of the 1960s the average wage earner worked 337 minutes a day in Olomouc, Czechoslovakia; 334 minutes in Torun, Poland; 374 minutes in Győr, Hungary; 311 minutes in Maribor, Yugoslavia; and 404 minutes in Kazanlik, Bulgaria. The equivalent figure for Osnabrück, West Germany, was 234 minutes, while six French cities averaged 277 minutes.[61] The East–West gap emerged largely due to the high female employment rates in most Central and Eastern European countries which had a significant impact on the average. Moreover, from the 1960s on, several countries in the region saw the emergence of workers holding more than one job.

As a result of the withdrawal of agriculture in employment and the shortening working time in industry, the number of hours worked decreased. However, this trend unfolded rather slowly. In Yugoslavia, the average annual working time was 2,208 hours in 1970 and remained more or less the same in the following two decades.[62] In Hungary, the annual working time at the end of the 1960s was still higher than 2,000 hours, while Ireland was the only Western European country with even more hours logged annually.[63] Again in the 1980s, working time decreased quite dynamically, due to the gradual introduction of the five-day workweek beginning in 1981. Thus, by 1990 the average number of hours worked annually by Hungarian employees in their first jobs surpassed Western European standards by only about 100 working hours.[64] In the meantime, however, Hungarians – especially men – spent more and more hours in their second jobs or working overtime in order to earn additional money.[65] According to time budget statistics, this increase in the time worked in second jobs or overtime hours consumed about two thirds of the time gained by the reduction of the working time in their principal employment. In other countries of the region, second jobs were atypical; accordingly, this phenomenon had no effect on leisure time.

In most Central and Eastern European countries, the regime change did not bring along a significant reduction in working time. For the next two decades, the number of hours worked stagnated at a level significantly higher than in most Western European countries. This was

---

60 'Munkaidő és munkaidő-csökkentés az iparban, 1968' [Working hours and their reduction in industry, 1968], in *Statisztikai Időszaki Közlemények*, vol. 141 (Budapest: KSH, 1969), 22.

61 John P. Robinson, Philip E. Converse and Szalai Sándor, 'A mindennapi élet tizenkét országban' [Everyday life in twelve countries], in *Idő a mérlegen: 12 ország városi és városkörnyéki népességének napi tevékenységei a Nemzetközi Összehasonlító Időmérleg Kutatómunkálat tükrében*, ed. Sándor Szalai (Budapest: Gondolat, 1978), 139.

62 ILO: ILO Labour Statistics Database, http://laborsta.ilo.org/STP/guest#444 (accessed 26 January 2015).

63 The reduction in working time in industry was 1.5 hours per week in 1968. 'Munkaidő és munkaidő-csökkentés az iparban, 1968', 22.

64 János Timár, *Idő és munkaidő* [Time and working time] (Budapest: KJK, 1988), 194–226.

65 Ibid.

especially true in the case of women, mainly because part-time employment was much less common in Romania, the Czech Republic or Bulgaria, for instance, than in the Netherlands or the United Kingdom.[66] Accordingly, the amount of leisure time did not change in the case of those in employment; while the number of inactive persons increased significantly, we know very little in terms of their leisure-time activities.[67]

Structural peculiarities

Consumption is not only characterized by its level, but also by its structure. During the twentieth century, the ratio between private consumption and collective consumption underwent important changes in the industrialized countries, as did the composition of both of those categories of consumption. In the following passages, we will study consumption in twentieth-century Central and Eastern Europe from this point of view.[68]

We have very little data on the proportion between private consumption and collective consumption in Central and Eastern Europe during the interwar period. However, it is safe to say that collective consumption at the time was a mere fraction of private consumption, just as in Western European countries in the same era. During the subsequent period of communist rule, the ratio of collective consumption grew considerably, yet failed to reach significant levels when compared internationally. After the Second World War, and especially during Western Europe's 1960s expansion of the welfare state, the average proportion of collective consumption in Western European countries was not lower than the shares seen in Central and Eastern Europe.[69]

Where we do see the emergence of distinct differences within Central and Eastern Europe after the Second World War is in the composition of government consumption – the sum of collective consumption and social benefits in kind provided to the citizens. Within this category, the proportion of social benefits in kind (such as health care benefits, education, holidays in government or company resorts, kindergarten, etc.) was high. While these were categorized as a part of government consumption, they also constituted part of private consumption. Their significance in the context of overall consumption was particularly outstanding when compared to the Southern European countries of the region, where socio-economic development was at a similar level.[70]

---

66 Ning Tang and Christine Cousins, 'Working Time, Gender and Family: An East-West European Comparison', *Gender, Work and Organization* 12, no. 6 (2005): 534.

67 ILO: ILO Labour Statistics Database, http://laborsta.ilo.org/STP/guest#444 (accessed 26 January 2015).

68 Cf. V. Cao-Pinna and S.S. Shatalin, eds, *Consumption Patterns in Eastern and Western Europe: An Economic Comparative Approach* (Oxford: Pergamon Press, 1979). Consumption comprises two distinct items: private consumption on the one hand, and collective (or public) consumption on the other. In turn, private consumption also comprises two distinct items: personal consumption, and social benefits provided to the citizens in kind (health care, education, etc.). According to another classification, consumption comprises government consumption and personal consumption, while government consumption can be broken down into collective consumption and social benefits in kind provided to the citizens.

69 J.N. Du Pasquier and L. Solari, 'A Tentative Comparison of Consumption in Some Eastern and Western European Countries', in Cao-Pinna and Shatalin, *Consumption Patterns in Eastern and Western Europe*, 174.

70 Ilona Kovács, 'Fogyasztási szerkezetek nemzetközi összehasonlítása' [Consumption structures in international comparison], *Statisztikai Szemle* 65, no. 10 (1987): 988.

We focus our attention primarily on the structural characteristics of private consumption, as these represented the largest share of consumption throughout the entire period under review. In addition, it was mainly this area where consumer choice prevailed, a factor of fundamental importance both in the context of the birth of consumer society and in the context of studying the post-war characteristics of Central and Eastern European consumption.

When examining the entire period under review, private consumption in Central and Eastern Europe reflects the general international trends of development. Just as in Western Europe, households over the long term spent a gradually smaller portion of their budgets on food, and especially on clothing, while the proportion of transportation and communication costs, housing, heating and energy costs, and cultural and entertainment-related expenditures was generally on the rise.[71] However, this transformation was not as profound in most areas as it was in Western Europe, while certain periods showed their own peculiar trends.

Concerning the two decades following the First World War, we have only sporadic information on the composition of private consumption in Central and Eastern Europe.[72] Moreover, post-war inflation and the subsequent economic depression significantly distorted price ratios, which had an effect on the structure of consumption. We have data only on small social groups, and whether this data is representative is doubtful. According to a study carried out in 1929 on the basis of a sample of 50 working-class families and 50 bourgeois families living in Budapest, working-class families dedicated 53.3 per cent of their expenditure to food; in the case of the bourgeois families, this ratio was 33.2 per cent. Clothing constituted 10 per cent (working-class) and 8.9 per cent (bourgeois) of the family budget, rent and household costs 17.6 per cent and 23.5 per cent, respectively, while each remaining expenditure category was in the low single digits.[73] In this respect, food-related household expenses were far higher than the levels in Western Europe, and were more or less in line with the patterns in Southern Europe.[74] However, the budgetary prominence of purchasing food also showed a gradual decrease in Central and Eastern European households during the interwar period, partly thanks to falling agricultural prices brought about by the agricultural crisis. Clothing also lost some of its budgetary prominence, while the proportion of durable consumables and housing costs increased as compared to other categories of expenditure.

In the wake of the Second World War, every country in the region witnessed centralized efforts to transform income ratios across social groups as well as relative prices in a comprehensive fashion, which also exerted a marked influence on the structure of household spending.[75] This was partly related to post-war reconstruction efforts, but also reflected the social priorities of the communist regimes of the region, which, to give one example, granted special privileges to the industrial working class over the agricultural working class and the intelligentsia. Although income levels in this latter group remained high, their advantage over the working class significantly decreased. In an international comparison, the emerging new consumption

---

71 The main categories of private consumption: 1) food and excise goods; 2) clothing; 3) housing and energy; 4) furniture and household appliances; 5) health care; 6) transport and communication; 7) leisure and culture; 8) others.

72 Mátyás Matolcsy, *Az életszínvonal alakulása Magyarországon, 1924–1944* [The evolution of living standards in Hungary 1924–1944] (Budapest: Magyar Ipari Munkatudományi Intézet, 1944); Kovrig, *Magyar társadalompolitika*, 201–28.

73 Zsombor Bódy, 'Polgárok és munkások 1929-ben. Adalékok a fogyasztás történetéhez' [Citizens and workers in 1929: contributions to the history of consumption], *Korall* 3, no. 10 (2002): 187–99; Pogány, 'Háztartások jövedelemszerkezete a két világháború közötti Magyarországon', 116–7.

74 Deaton, 'The Structure of Demand in Europe', 104.

75 Mieczkowski, *Personal and Social Consumption in Eastern Europe*.

structure was marked by the high proportion of expenditure dedicated to basic food items and beverages (alcohol, coffee) as well as tobacco. One reason is that per capita food consumption significantly increased beginning in the middle of the 1950s; concerning basic food items such as flour, meat and eggs, for example, consumption in several Central and Eastern European countries, especially in Czechoslovakia but also in Hungary and Poland, soon achieved the levels seen in Western European countries. In light of the poor food supply – and, in some countries, abject poverty – of the post-war period and early 1950s, there is little doubt that the general population saw this progress as an outstanding achievement. Food provision was an important political issue and challenge in almost every country of the region, especially because the standards achieved as a result of the post-war progress mentioned above did not stabilize in every country. Yugoslavia, where the population enjoyed generally good access to all goods, was an exception in this respect. Czechoslovakia also saw the end of its food-rationing regime as early as the outset of the 1950s. From the end of the 1950s on, food provision in Hungary was also generally reliable, an important advantage over several other communist countries and thus an important factor in the legitimacy of the regime and the political elite in these countries throughout the entire period under review. We will later address the case of Poland, but it should be mentioned that food supply, especially regarding meat products in Poland, started to deteriorate again in the early 1970s, something that led to significant political consequences.

At the same time, households in the region dedicated a significant part of their budgets to purchasing food. For example, in 1960, Hungarian households still spent more than half of their budgets on food, in contrast to the 1960 Western European average of less then 40 per cent. More importantly, this difference between the eastern and western parts of the continent increased during the following decades; while in the West the proportion of food, beverages and tobacco fell considerably within the overall consumption-related spending, there was hardly any decrease in Central and Eastern Europe during the following two decades. The 1978 figures in Czechoslovakia and Poland were 40.2 per cent and 48.8 per cent, while the ratio in Yugoslavia was 42.1 per cent in 1977[76] and 44.9 per cent in Hungary even as late as 1980. While this indicator decreased a bit more dynamically in the 1980s, in 1990, the population of Central and Eastern Europe still spent an outsized proportion of its budget on food.[77]

These figures also indicate that even though Engel's law – i.e. as personal income rises, the proportion of income spent on food falls – also prevailed in Central and Eastern Europe, the income elasticity of demand for food was relatively low in the region during the decades following the Second World War. This means that the percentage of income spent on food rose nearly as fast as the share of income. A slightly different picture unfolds if we separate food from beverages and tobacco; the proportion of income spent on tobacco, coffee and alcohol was on the rise in most Central and Eastern European countries, while in Western European societies it fell. By the end of the 1970s, Hungary reached a point where its population spent more on these items in relative terms than people in Western European countries, with the sole

---

76 Jaroslav Krejčí, *National Income and Outlay in Czechoslovakia, Poland and Yugoslavia* (London: Macmillan, 1982), 49.
77 *A lakosság jövedelme és fogyasztása, 1960–1979* [Population income and consumption, 1960–1979] (Budapest: KSH, 1981), 64–5; *A lakosság jövedelme és fogyasztása, 1970–1986* [Population income and consumption 1970–1986] (Budapest: KSH, 1987), 72–3; *A lakosság fogyasztása, 1970–1990* [Population income and consumption, 1970–1990] (Budapest: KSH, 1993), 24–5; *Életszínvonal, 1960–1980* [The living standard, 1960–1980] (Budapest: KSH, 1981), 135–47; Gadó Ottó, *Az életszínvonal alakulása Magyarországon, 1950–1975* [The evolution of living standards in Hungary, 1950–1975] (Budapest: Kossuth, 1978), 62–88.

exception of Ireland. In 1983, Hungarian households dedicated 8.1 per cent of their expenditures to such articles, while this share was 6.7 per cent in Denmark and less than 4 per cent in Italy and the Netherlands.[78]

The proportion of expenditure dedicated to clothing was also very high in the region during the decade following the Second World War. This was not the result of peculiar consumption preferences, but rather a reflection of relatively high clothing prices.[79] Nevertheless, precisely this area saw the most dynamic transformation of the structure of consumption during the following decades. In 1960, households in Hungary spent 14.8 per cent of their expenditures on clothing, while in 1990 this indicator was only 6.5 per cent – a development that can be explained by a decrease in the relative cost of clothing.[80]

Taken together, food and clothing represented such a high proportion of overall spending in Central and Eastern Europe during the first decades following the war that the proportion of all other product and service categories was almost automatically low when compared internationally. This is especially true in terms of housing, heating and household energy. Of course, one of the factors contributing to this phenomenon was that rent and household energy prices were centrally regulated and kept at artificially low levels. However, the same explanation is not valid as far as household equipment and furnishings are concerned; the proportion of expenditure dedicated to these items was low despite the fact that the relative price level of these items was extraordinarily high. Peculiar patterns also emerged with health care expenditure: the proportion of health care spending more or less stagnated for a long period of time, and only started to increase at the end of the 1970s – a sharp contrast to the international trends that had begun to show an increase decades earlier.

The proportion of transportation and communication costs within overall expenditures dedicated to private consumption was especially low in Central and Eastern Europe during the decades following the Second World War. This was linked to government subsidies in public and railway transportation, which kept ticket prices at an artificially low level, as well as to the fact that communication was severely underdeveloped throughout the period under review. Access to telephone service was very poor in most countries, without any breakthrough whatsoever under the communist shortage economy. Passenger vehicle supply showed a somewhat more differentiated picture in several countries of the region. Compared to Western Europe, motorization started relatively late, gathering speed in Czechoslovakia in the 1960s, and in Hungary and Poland in the 1970s. Despite the high price yet middling quality of the available passenger vehicles, there was an especially large demand for – and therefore shortage of – cars. The motorization process was thus very slow, a fact reflected in the low proportion of expenditure it received. Yet the rate of motorization still surpassed the rate of progress in communication in the region. Furthermore, it should be noted that the proportion of expenditure dedicated to education, culture, recreation and sports was especially high and increased dynamically; once again, this was linked to the high ratio of benefits in kind offered by the government, either free of charge or at a very low cost (kindergarten education, holidays spent in company-owned resorts) as detailed above.[81]

---

78 Kovács, 'Fogyasztási szerkezetek nemzetközi összehasonlítása', 979.
79 Tibor Valuch, *A lódentől a miniszoknyáig. A XX. század második felének magyarországi öltözködéstörténete* [From loden to miniskirt: the history of Hungarian clothing in the second half of the 20th century] (Budapest: Corvina, 2004), 102–4.
80 Kovács, 'Fogyasztási szerkezetek nemzetközi összehasonlítása', 979.
81 Ilona Kovács, 'Nemzetközi tendenciák a személyes fogyasztás alakulásában' [International tendencies in the formation of personal consumption], *Statisztikai Szemle* 65 (1987): 712.

As for the structure of consumption, there was a striking divergence between the Central and Eastern European region and the western part of the continent during the roughly four-decade period following the Second World War. The peculiarities seen in the structure of consumption in Central and Eastern Europe after the Second World War and the differences in terms of the structure of consumption between the countries of Central and Eastern Europe and those of Western Europe can be only partially explained by differences in overall development levels, by national differences in consumption preferences or consumer habits, or by the lower or higher standard of overall consumption.

The differences may instead be explained mainly by peculiarities in price structures and by the high proportion of social benefits in kind.[82] For example, the high proportion of expenditure dedicated to food and clothing does not reflect the high standard of food consumption or clothing; it rather reflects the peculiarities of the price structures. Compared to Western European countries, food and especially non-basic consumables such as coffee, alcohol and tobacco were relatively expensive, as was quality clothing. In 1980, the relative price level of food, beverages and tobacco in Hungary was as much as 124.4 per cent of the relative price level of overall consumption in that country, while the same indicator for clothing was even higher at 128.6 per cent.[83]

Furthermore, it may also be established that since acquiring food, clothing, household energy and a number of other subsistence goods and services used up most of the households' purchasing power, room for consumer choice remained very limited in Central and Eastern Europe during the period after the Second World War. We will address these qualitative aspects of consumption in the following sections.

Social differentiation in consumption

Various groups within society have diverging access to consumer goods, and each uses consumer goods differently. This section aims to analyze the category of the consumer in terms of social differences. The most important dimensions of social difference studied here are class, generation, gender and the rural–urban divide.

Income and class/occupation

Although only a limited amount of information is available on the distribution of income in Central and Eastern Europe in the first decades of the twentieth century, income is certainly a major factor in determining the level of consumption. Nevertheless, several studies conclude that income inequalities, which had been increasing during the first stage of the industrial revolution, did not continue to widen in the region. This paralleled the general trends observed in industrial societies, where income inequalities gradually decreased during this period: the deviation of personal income lessened; the proportion of labour incomes to capital revenues grew; and income disparities between social classes became less striking.[84]

---

82 For these factors, see Kovács, 'Fogyasztási szerkezetek nemzetközi összehasonlítása', 986–9.
83 *A bruttó hazai termék nemzetközi összehasonlítása Európában. 1980. Nemzetközi szervezetek statisztikai tevékenységéből* [An international comparison of GDPs in Europe, 1980] (Budapest: KSH, 1985), 66; Kovács, 'Fogyasztási szerkezetek nemzetközi összehasonlítása', 987.
84 Hartmut Kaelble, 'Introduction', in *Income Distribution in Historical Perspective*, eds. Hartmut Kaelble and Mark Thomas (Cambridge: Cambridge University Press–Maison des Sciences de l'Homme, 1991), 1–56; Peter H. Lindert and Jeffrey G. Williamson, 'Growth, Equality, History', *Explorations in Economic History* 22 (1985): 341–77; Anthony B. Atkinson and Francois Bourguignon, eds, *Handbook of Income Distribution*, vol. 1 (Amsterdam: Elsevier, 2000).

As for the distribution of personal incomes, during the first decades of the twentieth century, the richest 10 per cent of the population of Western European countries disposed of an average of 35 to 40 per cent of their total income. Up until the middle of the century, income levels were quickly levelling out in almost every country, especially those in Scandinavia, where the share of the richest decile dropped from 34 to 36 per cent to 27 to 29 per cent between 1935 and 1950.[85] We have even less reliable data concerning the social groups with the lowest income; the little we have, however, indicates that their situation generally worsened during the first third of the twentieth century. Consequently, changes in this period favoured the middle strata of society.[86] During the final decades of the twentieth century, income inequalities stopped eroding and indeed started to increase again in most Western European countries as well as overseas.[87]

In communist countries, incomes levelled out quickly after the Second World War.[88] In Czechoslovakia, the top decile disposed of 14 per cent of their total personal income in 1962, which was the lowest level of income concentration in Europe and perhaps anywhere in the world.[89] Moreover, in this period ending in the early 1970s, the relative income of the poorest strata of society was on the rise in this group of countries. In the meantime, the situation for the middle strata (the 60 per cent of the population in the middle of the income scale) stayed more or less the same. However, from the 1970s onward, income inequalities once again increased in the Central and Eastern European region. The rate of growth was not the same everywhere; the trend was more pronounced in Hungary and in Poland, while Czechoslovakia witnessed only subtle changes.

By the end of the 1980s, the Gini coefficient also showed that the lowest levels of income inequality in Europe were no longer seen in communist countries but rather in Scandinavian societies, especially Finland. Indeed, net incomes were distributed more evenly in West Germany than in most communist countries.[90]

Historians are more apt to analyze the situation of various social classes or groups rather than to grapple with the abstract statistical categories addressed above. This approach reveals how belonging to different strata of society is associated with the distribution of income within the whole of society, while it makes comparisons more difficult because the available studies often work with social categories that do not quite overlap. Moreover, relatively little is known about these aspects of inequality in interwar Central and Eastern Europe, even if it is assumed that differences in income between occupational groups and social classes were much higher at that time than during the second half of the twentieth century.

Even in Western European democracies, market mechanisms were not the only forces driving change in income levels. In communist countries, however, income differences changed

---

85 Gerold Ambrosius and William H. Hubbard, *A Social and Economic History of Twentieth-Century Europe* (Cambridge, MA: Harvard University Press, 1989), 70.
86 Franz Kraus, 'The Historical Development of Income Inequality in Western Europe and the United States', in *The Development of Welfare States in Europe and America*, eds Peter Flora and Arnold J. Heidenheimer (New Brunswick, NJ: Transaction, 1981), 203–4.
87 Bennett Harrison and Barry Bluestone, *The Great U-Turn* (New York: Basic Books, 1988); Arthur S. Alderson and Francois Nielsen, 'Globalization and the Great U-Turn: Income Inequality Trends in 16 OECD Countries', *American Journal of Sociology* 107, no. 5 (2002): 1248.
88 Jens Gieske, 'Soziale Ungleichheit im Staatssozialismus: Eine Skizze', *Zeithistorische Forschungen/Studies in Contemporary History* 10, no. 2 (2013): 1–33.
89 Wolfram Fischer, 'Wirtschaft, Gesellschaft und Staat in Europa, 1914–1980', in Wolfram Fischer et al., *Handbuch der europäischen Wirtschafts- und Sozialgeschichte*, vol. 6, 61.
90 Tomka, *A Social History of Twentieth-Century Europe*, 102.

much more directly as a function of political intentions and decisions, partly because the majority of the income earners were employed by the state. Accordingly, the structure of incomes underwent fundamental changes as compared to the period between the two world wars. The salaries of teachers, physicians and other professionals were set to assure they were much closer than they had been to the wages earned by industrial workers. For example, in Czechoslovakia in 1960, professionals earned only 17 per cent more than industrial workers, while differences were higher in other countries such as Bulgaria, 42 per cent, and Hungary and Poland, 57 per cent. The differentiation within the individual groups of occupations was also smaller than in Western Europe. Highly qualified workers could expect a higher income than non-qualified workers, yet the difference was limited to a range of 5 to 20 per cent, while Poland showed no such discrepancy.[91]

The situation for industrial workers also changed dramatically as compared to other social groups. In line with the ideology adopted by communist regimes, the relative income and social status of industrial workers improved, especially when compared to the interwar period, but also relative to Western European societies. In Poland in 1937, non-manual employees earned three times more on average than manual workers; by 1960, the difference had shrunk to a mere nine per cent.[92] As compared to capitalist economies, job security was also significantly higher. However, this relative equality of incomes coexisted with other sorts of inequality that did not favour industrial workers (such as health conditions and mortality rates).

The low wages of the agricultural population clearly reflected the political priorities of the regimes. While this was designed as an incentive to attract labour to industry, it also demonstrated the ideological bias of the communist regime against the peasantry. However, after the completion of forced collectivization in agriculture in the 1960s, the income level of the peasantry rose significantly in comparison to that of industrial workers in most countries, while they were still able to produce certain foods for themselves.[93]

These trends had an obvious effect on consumption patterns, homogenizing them in general by emancipating the working class to a certain degree. The wage policies outlined above paved the way for some workers – primarily highly qualified industrial workers – to rise into the middle class, even if this meant higher income levels but not always cultural integration. In Hungary's emerging private sector in the 1980s, this process was extended beyond the workers in large-scale industrial enterprises.[94] Nevertheless, differentiation was always present during the communist period, in which over time – mainly from the 1970s onward – inequalities grew significantly in terms of consumption as well. This had a major effect on the structure of consumption. This new, compressed income scale initially curbed demand for non-basic items; subsequently, increasing income disparities gradually boosted this demand while also increasing the consumption-related aspirations and frustrations of the social strata that lagged behind.

---

91 Walter D. Connor, *Socialism, Politics, and Equality: Hierarchy and Change in Eastern Europe and the USSR* (New York: Columbia University Press, 1979), 231.
92 David Lane, 'Structural and Social Change in Poland', in *Social Groups in Polish Society*, eds David Lane and George Kolankiewicz (London: Macmillan, 1973), 24.
93 Connor, *Socialism, Politics, and Equality*, 231.
94 Eszter Bartha, *A munkások útja a szocializmusból a kapitalizmusba Kelet-Európában, 1968–1989* [The workers' road from socialism to capitalism in Eastern Europe, 1968–1989] (Budapest: L'Harmattan, 2010), 269.

In addition, it must be emphasized that, in communist countries, income distribution did not accurately reflect the inequalities that existed in material terms and thus in terms of consumption.[95] Two of these factors deserve special attention: the system of price subsidies and turnover taxes as well as inequality in the access to goods in short supply.

As János Kornai and others have pointed out, communist countries implemented extensive systems of price subsidies and turnover taxes. The declared objective of such systems was to make the most important goods and services available to even the lowest-income social strata while demanding greater material sacrifices from the consumers of luxury goods, or products considered luxurious. Price subsidies covered a wide scope of products and services such as public transportation, heating fuels, rents, bread and milk, theatre tickets and classical music records, while certain services, such as nursery schools or music classes for pupils were free of charge or available at nominal prices. On the other hand, products such as passenger cars, higher quality clothes and certain imported goods were heavily taxed.[96]

However, price subsidies did not merely serve the purposes of social policy; they fulfilled a more complex role, including helping to prop up ineffective production artificially. Price subsidies represented a major budgetary expenditure in communist Central and Eastern Europe, although at varying levels. In Hungary, they never reached the rates seen, for example, in East Germany in the 1980s, where the funds dedicated to price subsidies surpassed social security expenditure.[97] In 1988, price subsidies amounted to 5 per cent of the GDP in Hungary, and to 10 per cent in Poland.[98] In addition, the dynamics of the changes in the system of price subsidies were highly peculiar, and very different from those of any other benefit within the sphere of social policy. In Hungary, subsidies – excluding those for housing – expanded most dynamically during the 1950s, 1970s and the first half of the 1980s; after reaching a peak in 1986–87, their importance plummeted.[99] According to the conclusions of several studies, price subsidies had a rather limited effect in terms of redistribution, primarily because they disproportionately benefited the wealthier social strata.[100] They also led to highly wasteful resource management practices in some areas, such as health care.[101] For this reason, certain authors go so far as to cite 'perverted redistribution' in the context of price subsidies.[102]

---

95 David R. Henderson, Robert M. McNab and Tamás Rózsás, 'The Hidden Inequality in Socialism', *The Independent Review* 10, no. 3 (2005): 389–412.
96 Kornai, *The Socialist System*, 318.
97 Göran Therborn, *European Modernity and Beyond: The Trajectories of European Societies, 1945–2000* (London: Sage, 1995), 95.
98 John Fleming and John Micklewright, 'Income Distribution, Economic Systems and Transition', in Atkinson and Bourguignon, *Handbook of Income Distribution*, 872.
99 International Bank for Reconstruction and Development, ed., *Hungary: Reform of Social Policy and Expenditures* (Washington, DC: International Bank for Reconstruction and Development, 1992), 121; Rudolf Andorka, Anna Kondratas and István György Tóth, *A jóléti rendszer átalakulása Magyarországon: felépítése, kezdeti reformjai és javaslatok*, A Magyar-Nemzetközi Kék Szalag Bizottság 3. sz. Gazdaságpolitikai tanulmánya [The transformation of the welfare system in Hungary: structure, initial reforms and proposals] (Budapest: Kék Szalag Bizottság Alapítvány, 1994), 17.
100 Branko Milanovic, 'The Distributional Impact of Cash and In-Kind Transfers in Eastern Europe and Russia', in *Public Spending and the Poor*, eds D. van de Walle and K. Nead (Baltimore, MD: John Hopkins University Press, 1995).
101 Rudolf Andorka and István György Tóth, 'A szociális kiadások és a szociálpolitika Magyarországon' [Social expenditure and social policy in Hungary], in *Társadalmi riport, 1992*, eds Rudolf Andorka, Tamás Kolosi and György Vukovich (Budapest: Tárki, 1992), 442.
102 Kornai, *The Socialist System*, 320.

While there are several areas where it can be ascertained that the actual redistribution practices were contrary to the declared objectives, this effect is best researched in the area of housing. During the years after the Second World War, a great proportion of all flats and houses in the cities in the communist countries of Central and Eastern Europe were nationalized and used as rental real estate; however, rural homes remained almost exclusively in private ownership. This in itself created major disparities, for it was more or less true that only city dwellers had access to heavily subsidized rental homes. In villages, nearly everyone had to provide for their own housing, building and maintaining their own homes. However, there have been several studies showing that the allocation of rental flats in the cities did not reflect a certain income level of tenants; it was not only the poorest citizens who had access to rental flats at affordable rates. Indeed, those of a higher social standing were clearly overrepresented among tenants renting well-located, sizeable apartments in good condition and at very affordable rates. Thus, a greater share of the professionals, white-collar workers and highly qualified labourers received publicly built or publicly owned flats than did lower-income, semi-skilled and unskilled workers. Those who could not get an apartment through state redistribution had to build or buy their own homes.

In light of typical income levels, buying a home during this period involved an extraordinary financial burden. Iván Szelényi, a distinguished researcher in the field, concluded that the subsidy for a monthly rent of a newly built state flat was nearly as high as the monthly wage of an industrial worker in most of the region.[103] Thus, the households that had no choice but to build or buy their own homes could consume significantly less in the long run than those who were granted state-financed housing, although their income differences may not have necessarily reflected this discrepancy.[104]

Major inequalities abounded in several other services granted free of charge or for only a small fee. High-ranking party leaders and government officials, as well as a few other privileged groups such as academic or sport elites, had access to the higher-quality services of less-crowded outpatient clinics and hospitals; in fact, a number of institutions were specifically reserved for them. The lower-ranking members of the nomenklatura had less formal privileges; access to rare or quality goods and services depended on their informal ranking and connections. Other types of inequalities were a factor of one's workplace. Companies and institutions that owned their own resorts allowed their employees, especially those who were 'better connected', to enjoy their holidays there nearly free of charge. The agricultural population had many fewer opportunities to enjoy services of this type, since the standard of health care was lower in the villages and their employers rarely owned resorts.

The inequalities that emerged in distribution after the Second World War were initially secret to no one. The rationing system openly favoured social groups such as employees working in what were considered key economic sectors, workers involved in heavy manual labour and members of the armed forces. By the middle of the 1950s, the rationing system had largely run its course, yet in the case of a number of goods – such as flats or passenger cars – mechanisms of distribution on the basis of worthiness carried on.[105]

---

103 Iván Szelényi, 'Social Inequalities in State Socialist Redistributive Economies: Dilemmas for Social Policy in Contemporary Socialist Societies of Eastern Europe', *International Journal of Comparative Sociology* 19, no. 1/2 (1978): 67.
104 Szelényi, 'Social Inequalities', 63–87; Judit Bodnár and József Böröcz, 'Housing Advantages for the Better Connected? Institutional Segmentation, Settlement Type and Social Network Effects in Hungary's Late State-Socialist Housing Inequalities', *Social Forces* 76, no. 4 (1998): 1275–304.
105 For a similar account, see Kornai, *The Socialist System*, 322–3.

In addition to these more-or-less openly maintained inequalities in distribution, there existed another, arguably more significant system of hidden consumption disparities that was mostly related to the scarcity of goods.[106] Under the conditions of the shortage economy, access to quality products and articles in high demand was often restricted to individuals that had direct access to these goods or had the right informal connections, as well as to small privileged groups favoured by the political regime. Employees producing or distributing scarce goods were able to capitalize on their position. Even shop assistants could often profit from their jobs by delivering scarce goods to their relatives or friends. Higher echelons of society, such as members of party leadership and bureaucracy, top-level athletes, leading members of the academia were often eligible to enter special shops – a theme discussed later. This was one of the main reasons consumption inequalities in the communist countries of Central and Eastern Europe were greater than suggested by income distribution data alone. The following passages will address the consumption practices and consumer behaviours that emerged under the conditions of the shortage economy, and also touch upon their wider social consequences.

Income disparities skyrocketed in the region after the regime change. The turning point was highly visible in the situation for the highest income groups, in the changing income ratio of the poorest, and in the development of a comprehensive indicator – the Gini coefficient. The detailed data with respect to three Central and Eastern European countries signal that especially in Hungary and in Poland – and to a lesser extent, the Czech Republic as well – the situation for those in the highest income brackets improved while that of the lowest income groups deteriorated.[107]

Gender

Income inequalities also have a significant gender dimension. Throughout Europe, even at the turn of the millennium, whether an individual was a woman or a man, was usually still a more important indicator of that person's income level than the occupational group to which she or he belonged. While non-manual employees earned more than blue-collar workers did, the income of female non-manual employees was lower than the income of blue-collar men in all but a few countries. This cannot be explained simply by differences in their qualifications, as the income of women was always less than that of men, even in the same occupations. In this respect, there is not much difference between the various European regions; at the end of the century, the only exceptions were the Scandinavian countries and the United Kingdom, where class affiliation (belonging to the group of manual or non-manual employees) slightly overrode the significance of gender as a determinant of income levels.[108]

In addition, wages were generally lower in those sectors of the economy that relied mostly on female labour. While high female participation rates in education and the high rates of female employment reflected the achievements of female emancipation policy in the communist countries, the significant differences persisting between the income levels of men and

---

106 David H. Henderson, Robert M. McNab and Tamás Rózsa, 'The Hidden Inequality in Socialism', *Independent Review* 9, no. 3 (2005): 395–6.
107 A.B. Atkinson, *The Changing Distribution of Earnings in OECD countries* (Oxford: Oxford University Press, 2008), 48–51.
108 Rachel A. Rosenfeld and Arne L. Kalleberg, 'A Cross-national Comparison of the Gender Gap in Income', *American Journal of Sociology* 96, no. 1 (1990): 69–106; Tanja van der Lippe and Liset van Dijk, 'Comparative Research on Women's Employment', *Annual Review of Sociology* 28 (2002): 221–41.

women showed the limitations of those practices. In Czechoslovakia in 1959, women on average earned 66 per cent of what men earned, and this gap barely narrowed during the following decades. In 1988, it was still just 68 per cent.[109] In Hungary during the 1970s, women on average earned three quarters of the salary of men employed in the same occupation; while this was roughly the same level as those measured in West Germany, Finland, Great Britain and the Netherlands, it was much lower than the ratio seen in Denmark (86 per cent), Italy (85 per cent) or Sweden (92 per cent).[110]

However, the place of consumption is the household – in most cases formed by male and female partners. This is a particularly important consideration when examining the Central and Eastern European region, because marriage rates here were typically high throughout most of the century. The members of the households aggregate their incomes and expend them together; thus, it is difficult to translate gender income differences into differences in consumption. However, leisure time can be an indicator of gender inequalities in consumption, or at least a proxy for these divergences.

We have had a relatively accurate and comprehensive understanding of the distribution of leisure time from the beginning of the 1960s, which is when the first time budget surveys were launched in multiple countries using the same methodology.[111] These indicated that in the last decades of the twentieth century, household work (including production activities performed in the family setting) and leisure time were distributed unevenly among the individual family members in the Central and Eastern European region. Women performed most household chores, although the growing use of household appliances and the range of available services helped reduce their workload.[112] While the participation of men in household chores was roughly the same in the region as in a wider European comparison,[113] differences between men and women in terms of available leisure time, and especially in terms of time dedicated to entertainment, remained much higher in Central and Eastern Europe than in the rest of Europe. According to a study in 1965–66, gainfully employed urban married women in Poland had only 67 per cent of the leisure time of men in the same category, while the figure was 63 per cent in Czechoslovakia and 62 per cent in Hungary. This was similar or somewhat lower than the same indicator in Belgium, France and West Germany (69 per cent, 64 per cent and 76 per cent, respectively).[114] However, as for the time dedicated to entertainment, differences were greater between Central and Eastern European societies as well. Also, in the middle of the 1960s, the time that gainfully employed married women with children dedicated to entertainment in Poland was only 64 per cent of the time that was available to men of a similar status for similar purposes; the same indicator was 85 per cent in Czechoslovakia and 55 per cent in Hungary. However, the same ratio was 74 per cent in Belgium, 76 per cent in France and 97 per cent in

---

109 Jiří Večernik, 'Earnings Distribution in Czechoslovakia: Intertemporal Changes and International Comparison', *European Sociological Review* 7, no. 3 (1991): 245.
110 André Michel, 'The Impact of Marriage and Children on the Division of Gender Roles', in *Changing Patterns of European Family Life*, eds Katja Boh et al. (London: Routledge, 1989), 173–88, here 183.
111 Alexander Szalai, 'Women's Time: Women in the Light of Contemporary Time-Budget Research', *Futures* 7 (1975): 385–99.
112 Júlia Szalai, 'A családi munkamegosztás néhány szociológiai problémájáról' [Some sociological problems in the family division of labour], in *Család és házasság a mai magyar társadalomban*, ed. Pál Lőcsei (Budapest: Gondolat, 1971), 188.
113 Therborn, *European Modernity and Beyond*, 64.
114 Sándor Szalai, ed., *Idő a mérlegen* (Budapest: Gondolat, 1978), 474–80 [English edition: Alexander Szalai, ed., *The Use of Time* (The Hague: Mouton, 1972)].

West Germany.[115] Another series of surveys indicates that the leisure time enjoyed by women between the ages of 15 and 69 in Hungary actually dropped as compared to men between 1963 and 1976. Even though there was an increasing trend during the following decade, the ratio still only rose to 73 per cent by 1987.[116] In Western Europe, differences between men and women in this respect narrowed more dynamically. The average data of seven Western European countries indicate that in the 1980s the amount of leisure time available to women was as much as 95 per cent of the time enjoyed by men.[117]

However, there are signs of the growing symmetry between family members in post-communist Central and Eastern Europe; the difference between the leisure time of men and women also decreased somewhat after the regime change. In 2006, the free time of women between the ages of 20 and 74 amounted to 85 per cent of that of men of the same age in Poland, and 84 per cent in Estonia, Hungary and Slovenia.

Generations

Age and generation are also factors that have a significant bearing on consumption. Former research has not taken into account how generational shifts shaped the changes in consumption patterns in Central and Eastern Europe, even though these aspects are essential for the understanding of the role of consumption in state socialism and the overall dynamics of the regimes.

In the middle of the 1960s, new groups of young consumers emerged in most Central and Eastern European countries. They were much more fashion-conscious than their parents' generation and aspired to obtain products that granted them autonomy and mobility as well as expressed their new and peculiar youth culture.[118] Just like the same demographic groups in the West, these aspirations translated into the consumption of products such as motorbikes, records, transistor radios and tape recorders, as well as a new demand for specific forms of entertainment, such as rock concerts.[119] As a result, the generation that was in its twenties during the 1960s drifted much farther away than the generation of their parents from the ascetic consumption ideal of communism in terms of its consumption practices.

While such Western analogies do indeed exist, they cannot mask some of the significant differences between Eastern and Western Europe. Generational changes regarding consumption preference and practice transpired in a substantially different manner in these regions. In postwar Western Europe, a significant shift from materialist to post-materialist value orientations occurred, which originated in growing material well-being and physical security.[120] In Central and Eastern Europe, however, post-materialism never gained a significant foothold. In fact, a number of value changes can be observed that point to the opposite direction and lead to the appreciation of material values and consumption. Then again, no comprehensive empirical studies address this aspect, so our conclusions are based on whatever partial studies are available. Research indicates that consumers in the communist countries had an extra incentive to obtain

---

115 Szalai, *Idő a mérlegen*, 473–4.
116 Rudolf Andorka, Tamás Kolosi and György Vukovich, eds, *Social Report* (Budapest: Tárki, 1992), 136.
117 Therborn, *European Modernity and Beyond*, 64–5.
118 Claire Wallace and Sijka Kovacheva, 'Youth Cultures and Consumption in Eastern and Western Europe: An Overview', *Youth and Society* 28, no. 2 (1996): 189–214.
119 Ina Merkel, 'Working People and Consumption Under Really-Existing Socialism: Perspectives from the German Democratic Republic', *International Labor and Working-Class History* 55 (1999): 104.
120 Ronald Inglehart, *Culture Shift in Advanced Industrial Society* (Princeton, NJ: Princeton University Press, 1990).

material goods, since people gained more status through luxury goods than in the contemporary capitalist countries of Europe.[121]

An important reason behind this phenomenon is that, compared to their Western European counterparts, young post-war generations in Central and Eastern Europe were less capable of preserving and carrying on – and eventually establishing as the dominant social norm – their peculiar lifestyle or at least certain elements of it. On the one hand, the urban middle class, the primary vehicle of post-materialistic values, was much smaller. On the other hand, as soon as they reached their mid-twenties, almost all of them got married, which also triggered a fundamental change in their consumption behaviour. Acquiring a flat and providing for the family fully consumed their income and time. They later faced an even greater change in their financial situation when, at around the end of the millennium, they retired. Everywhere in the region, the transformation crises affected living standards, while pensions amounted to a much smaller proportion of wages and salaries than was typical in Western Europe.

In other words, improving financial security was not the key element in the long-term value changes seen in the Central and Eastern European countries. The improvement in the financial position of the population was not as pronounced and, more importantly, not nearly as predictable as in the consumer societies of the western part of Europe. As they became more and more aware of the gap separating them from the West, Central and Eastern European populations saw whatever changes in their standards of living through a very different lens, experiencing them as only a relative improvement when compared to Western standards.

Furthermore, political factors in the region played a steadily greater role in shaping value systems. Due to a series of political cataclysms – such as the aborted revolutions of 1953 and 1956 as well as the events in 1968 – the population turned away from active public life and became more focused on material objectives. Added to the shortage of supply discussed above, and to the general population's high awareness of such shortages, this feature in itself was sufficient to slow or completely block the diffusion of post-materialist value orientations. While early generations expressed their political dissatisfaction more directly, consumption eventually became the arena where people could express their opposition to, or at least detachment from and indifference towards, the regime. This was reflected in peculiar forms of conspicuous consumption, which will be discussed in the section covering consumption practices.

The village and the city

A further important dimension of consumption inequalities was the rural–urban divide, several important aspects of which have already been addressed. Throughout the region, a range of ethnographic studies documents the peculiar consumer culture of rural populations during the first decades of the century. This culture placed special emphasis on self-sufficiency, especially concerning food consumption, but also in terms of clothing as well as building and furnishing homes. During the second half of the century, the peasantry as a traditional social class gradually dissolved almost everywhere in the region; this process was significantly faster in countries where agriculture faced forced collectivization. During the 1950s, the classical period of the shortage economy, the food scarcity was less of a pressing issue in villages, while the supply of clothing and consumer durables was even less than in the cities. Old-age poverty soared in

---

121 Nan Dirk de Graaf, 'Distinction by Consumption in Czechoslovakia, Hungary, and the Netherlands', *European Sociological Review* 7, no. 3 (1991): 272.

rural areas, especially until the 1960s, as the region's system of pension entitlements was only extended to the agricultural population with a considerable delay.

As mentioned above in several contexts, collectivization induced multiple changes in the consumption patterns of the peasantry in the countries concerned. It was the beginning of the political emancipation of the peasantry, which is reflected in the fact that the authorities began paying more attention to the supply of goods in rural areas. In every country of the region, the differences between villages and cities continued to level out gradually during the 1970s and the 1980s in terms of both consumption levels and consumer habits.

The regime change unravelled these trends. On the one hand, both the supply of goods and services improved almost overnight, even in smaller settlements. Within just a few years, existing disparities in landline telephony penetration narrowed dramatically in several countries by the early 1990s, a trend that later continued with the proliferation of mobile phones. In the villages, new shops opened up, or travelling vendors compensated for the lack of existing shops. This meant that rural areas gradually began to approximate the consumption opportunities and standards typical of the cities. On the other hand, there was substantial geographical differentiation in the dynamics of the purchasing power of the population; after the initial downturn brought about by a transformation crisis – of short or long duration depending on the specific country – income levels started to increase dynamically in larger cities, while most villages either did not follow this path or followed it less dynamically. Moreover, we can observe not only a huge gap between urban and rural areas, but indeed the relative rise or fall of entire regions. Twenty years after the regime change, the populations of wide swaths of eastern Poland or eastern Hungary had half or less than half the purchasing power of the central and western populations of the same countries.[122]

Practices of consumption and leisure

As established earlier, presenting how consumption patterns evolved in Europe during the twentieth century require more than just the study of the level and structure (i.e. the quantitative features) of consumption or the standard of living. A number of other factors must also be discussed; these can be called qualitative factors. Concerning the selection of goods and other qualitative characteristics of consumption, Central and Eastern Europe differed significantly from the countries of Western Europe during the interwar period. However, these differences were not fundamental. While determined to a certain degree by cultural peculiarities, they were mostly the result of the lower purchasing power in Central and Eastern Europe, which affected the selection of the goods sold commercially as well as the forms of trade. In this context, it is highly characteristic that in the distribution of consumer durables such as radios, passenger vehicles and telephone sets – each of these became widely available during the era – Czechoslovakia more or less kept up with the societies of Western Europe. While the other countries of the region lagged significantly behind most Western European countries, this difference did not increase, but rather stabilized during the interwar period. However, it is also worthy to note that, for example, Hungary had higher radio and telephone penetration during the 1930s than some Western European countries. In other words, the countries of the region participated in the diffusion of these consumer goods according to their own level of economic development, while the autonomy of the consumers was hardly limited, as is reflected in the presence of such leading brands as Philips, Siemens and Mercedes-Benz in the markets of radios and passenger

---

122 Philipp Ther, *Europe since 1989: A History* (Princeton, NJ: Princeton University Press, 2016).

vehicles.[123] The only factors that may possibly have restricted consumer choices were certain foreign exchange restrictions introduced in the region in the wake of the Great Depression, which mostly affected consumers' ability to use foreign exchange abroad without having much of an impact on the domestic market. Limited effective demand is most likely the reason why modern commercial modalities such as department stores appeared with significant delay and why their diffusion into Central and Eastern Europe was rather slow. Czechoslovakia's first modern shopping mall, the Bílá Labut (The White Swan), opened in Prague in 1939. Other circumstances, such as the middle-class attraction to traditional consumer habits, only contributed to the effects of this main cause.[124] While the spreading of department stores sometimes appears in the literature on consumption history as an indicator of the emergence of consumer culture, the low number of classic department stores in the region does not in itself justify any doubts about whether consumer culture existed or expanded in Central and Eastern Europe during the interwar period.

In this respect, we see significantly greater differences within Europe during the decades following the Second World War. The rationing system and the shortage of goods – above all, food – during the years directly after the war were more or less a natural consequence of the war economy, wartime destruction, inflation and, in several countries, Soviet occupation and reparation payments in kind. This period also saw profound difficulties in the supply of goods in several Western European countries. In Great Britain, for example, certain foodstuffs were rationed as late as 1954. However, while supply gradually normalized in the Western countries within just a few years, the countries of the Central and Eastern European region experienced communist rule, which ushered in a social and economic system known as the shortage economy.

As is known from the work of János Kornai, who coined the very term 'shortage economy', shortages were not sporadic, but universal; that is, shortage was as equally widespread in such areas as consumer goods and services, foreign exchange, imported goods and other resources. Moreover, shortages were not occasional and temporary, but permanent. Thus, shortage had a strong effect on the behaviour of both consumers and other actors in the economy.[125]

The first half of the 1950s can be considered the age of the classic shortage economy in the region. During this period, even the most basic articles were often commercially unavailable, including bread, meat and cheese. Imported goods were hardly ever seen in shops. As a consequence of such chronic shortages, consumers could get access to important goods and services either through bureaucratic distribution mechanisms such as advance booking or special vouchers, or they had to stand in line; alternatively, they could obtain these goods on the black market. Queuing, hunting, gathering and black-marketing became major means of acquiring goods and services. Scarcity not only determined how goods were acquired, but also had an impact on the phase of consumption itself. Instead of purchasing market goods and services, people resorted to self-subsistence and repairing; in other words, a process of renaturalization unfolded in these economies. Finally, shortage also shaped the needs and aspirations of consumers; the

---

123 György Majtényi, 'Életstílus és szubkultúra: Az autózás története (1920–1960) [Lifestyles and subcultures: the history of automobility]', *Korall* 1, no. 1 (2000): 105–6; Gyáni Gábor, *Hétköznapi élet Horthy Miklós korában* [Everyday life in the Horthy era] (Budapest: Corvina, 2006), 146–7.
124 Gyáni Gábor, 'Középosztályi fogyasztási kultúra és az áruház' [The culture of middle-class consumption and the department store], *Budapesti Negyed* 16/17 (1997): 101–27; Anikó S. Nagy, *Kereskedővilág: Szemelvények a magyar kereskedelem történetéből* [The world of trading: excerpts from the history of Hungarian trade] (Budapest: Mundus, 2007), 129–45.
125 János Kornai, *A hiány* [The shortage] (Budapest: KJK, 1980).

goals of households became dominated by market materialization. People exposed to shortage goods turned to material values, and these values often outpaced life goals and aspirations associated with family, leisure and civic activities.

As early as 1953, some reforms already emerged in the centrally controlled economies in an attempt to eliminate the contradictions inherent to the system. The reforms in the region were of varying depths and were often all too transitory, which was another factor affecting the standard of the supply of goods and resulted in considerable disparities between the individual countries. Despite all these reforms, shortage remained a permanent phenomenon until the collapse of communism. In 1968, Hungary introduced the region's most consistent market-oriented reforms and therefore had the best supply of goods; yet in the 1980s, when the overall quantity of commercially available food, to cite one example, was always sufficient at the national level, difficulties in supply were still common, especially concerning non-basic items and in smaller settlements. Opportunities to obtain Western-made consumer goods were still scarce all across the country.[126] In this respect, the situation in Yugoslavia was unique, and shortage was much less typical. The country's relative openness, especially its intensive foreign trade relations with Western countries, plus the fact that massive numbers of Yugoslav guest workers found employment in Western Europe help explain why certain products that remained a dream for the consumers of other Central and Eastern European countries – blue jeans, recordings of Western performers, leading brands of alcoholic beverages – were widely available in Beograd, Zagreb and Skopje.[127]

There were only a few types of commodities or services that were relatively expensive in the western part of the continent, yet more available for citizens of the communist countries. The clearest example is the dacha. These small holiday houses of very modest architecture were typically located on the outskirts of towns and cities and were surrounded by a tiny garden used to grow fruits and vegetables for the family.[128] Other similar examples include art and music classes, which were cheap but available almost exclusively in urban settlements.

Shortage was especially great in particular markets, notably housing, telephony and passenger vehicles.[129] As mentioned above in another context, social considerations dictated that rents were set at very low levels, a practice that had grave consequences in terms of new residential construction and the maintenance of existing residential buildings. In the 1980s, those applying to the local authorities for a flat had to wait, on average, 15 to 30 years in Poland, 6 to 8 years in Czechoslovakia, and 4 to 6 years in Hungary, but the actual waiting time could indeed be much longer depending on the applicant's income, marital status, place of residence, number of children and other demographic factors.[130] Moreover, this system was primarily available only to the urban population. While public housing did exist in the villages, especially where larger industrial plants or collective farms attracted labour, it played only a secondary role in the life

---

126 Tibor Valuch, *Hétköznapi élet Kádár János korában* [Everyday life in the Kádár era] (Budapest: Corvina, 2006), 80–1.
127 Patrick Hyder Patterson, *Bought and Sold: Living and Losing the Good Life in Socialist Yugoslavia* (Ithaca, NY: Cornell University Press, 2011), 19–108.
128 Paulina Bren, 'Weekend Getaways: The Chata, the Tramp and the Politics of Private Life in Post-1968 Czechoslovakia', in *Socialist Spaces: Sites of Everyday Life in the Eastern Bloc*, eds David Crowley and Susan Emily Reid (Oxford: Berg, 2002), 123–40.
129 Luminita Gatejel, 'The Common Heritage of the Socialist Car Culture', in *The Socialist Car: Automobility in the Eastern Bloc*, ed. Lewis H. Siegelbaum (Ithaca, NY: Cornell University Press, 2011), 155.
130 Kornai, *The Socialist System*, 234; Péter Fóti, *Röpirat a lakáshelyzetről* [A leaflet on the housing situation] (Budapest: Magvető, 1988).

of the rural population; most rural residents were left with no other choice but to build their own homes. One exception was Czechoslovakia, where a significant population loss (due to the expulsion of Germans and Hungarians) and migration meant that a relatively high number of apartments were available in the villages as well. Those applying for a telephone line had to wait for up to a decade or more in several countries; however, especially in smaller settlements and in certain districts, it was often simply impossible to get one. In the early 1950s, private individuals were initially banned from purchasing passenger vehicles, and very few were allowed to use service vehicles. Purchasing a car later required a special permit. In Hungary, it was only in 1957 that a very limited number of models were first authorized for free commercial distribution. Czechoslovakia was the first communist country to follow the example of East Germany and launch a 'people's car'. In 1954, the first noteworthy pilot project was started in the Mladá Boleslav manufacturing plant in Škoda, and the first Škoda 1000MB model rolled off the assembly line in 1964.[131] Poland and Romania also launched their own automotive experiments; yet still, extreme shortage and poor product quality remained the norm not only throughout this initial stage of Central and Eastern European motorization, but also for decades to come. The waiting list – combined with the prepayment of varying sums committed by the purchaser several years in advance – emerged as the main channel of distribution. In 1989, obtaining a Soviet-made Lada, which was based on a Fiat model of the early 1960s, took five to six years of waiting in Poland, 3 to 4 years in Czechoslovakia, 4 to 6 years in Hungary, and 10 to 12 years in Bulgaria. In the case of a less popular model, the Romanian-made Dacia – also modelled after Western cars, in this case the Renault 8 and 12 – waiting lists were potentially much shorter, except for in Romania itself, where customers had to wait four to six years for delivery.[132]

Comparative literature dedicated to consumption in the era does not always take into consideration the fact that shortages and quality problems were fundamental characteristics of the supply of goods. A good example is the typology developed by the well-known Swedish sociologist Göran Therborn. Therborn cites Czechoslovakia and Hungary as two of the countries that as of the 1980s were characterized by what he calls car-driven consumption; also included were Switzerland, West Germany and Sweden. The sole basis of his classification, however, is his analysis of the number of passenger cars and television sets per 1,000 inhabitants; or, to be more precise, the relative ratio of passenger cars to television sets. In doing so, he neglects the gaping difference between the above-mentioned Western European countries and Czechoslovakia and Hungary, not only in terms of the per capita number of cars but also in the quality of the available cars; the shocking disparities between how one could obtain – and then operate – a car in Czechoslovakia and Hungary as compared to those other countries create another glaring factor.[133]

A more plausible approach is to address the peculiar socialist car culture, whose characteristics essentially reflect the overall consumer culture of the communist countries. One feature of this culture is that the authorities never succeeded in eliminating the scarcity of goods and services. In the absence of developed markets, peculiar distribution channels emerged; while these were unable to compensate fully for the lack of a free market, they managed to moderate the tensions caused by the shortage of goods. Furthermore, the highly protected status of the

---

131 Valentina Fava, 'The Elusive People's Car: Imagined Automobility and Productive Practices along the Czechoslovak Road to Socialism (1945–1968)', in Siegelbaum, *The Socialist Car*, 23–4.
132 Kornai, *The Socialist System*, 236; Ágnes Losonczi, *Az életmód az időben, a tárgyakban és az értékekben* [The way of life in time, objects and values] (Budapest: Gondolat, 1977), 430–49.
133 Therborn, *European Modernity and Beyond*, 140–6.

political elite survived throughout the entire period, albeit with significant differences within the region.[134] In addition to these factors, Western influences also determined the process of motorization in the region. Cars can plausibly be considered the Trojan horse of Western consumer culture; designers, engineers and especially consumers could hardly avoid making direct comparisons between communism and capitalism as reflected in the production and quality of their products.[135]

Shortage and quality problems were also known in the markets of other consumer durables and services.[136] It was partly because of severe shortages that, from the 1950s onward, corruption appeared and eventually became rampant in the health care systems of several countries in the region; by essentially bribing public employees, people paid doctors and nurses under the table with hopes of jumping waiting lists for treatment, securing better placement while hospitalized or simply getting better care and more attention for themselves or for their children.[137]

Certain privileged groups had special access channels to otherwise unavailable products. Members of the political nomenklatura, top athletes, leading artists and distinguished members of academia had an advantage when it came to applying for flats, telephone lines or cars.[138] More affluent individuals – such as entrepreneurs in the shadow economy – could also obtain these products through bribes. In Poland, the Office of the Council of Ministers (*Urząd Rady Ministrów*) disposed of a certain pool of cars to be distributed among private individuals. It was an open secret among leading Polish intellectuals that the prime minister's office had the possibility to assign passenger vehicles, and indeed the office received great numbers of petitions from this segment of society.[139]

There existed a number of special shops serving an exclusive circle of clients who could thus obtain otherwise unavailable goods, or purchase goods at more affordable prices. Those privileged groups of society that had access to convertible foreign currency, including those with relatives in the West, could visit these shops – e.g. the Pewex chain in Poland or Tuzex shops in Czechoslovakia, each of which only accepted payment in foreign exchange – and obtain Western products or domestic products of short supply. These commercial arrangements, however, were not equally common in the individual countries. In Hungary, the exclusive shops only serving members of the socialist aristocracy mostly disappeared by the 1970s, and the shops only accepting payment in foreign exchange had much less in terms of turnover than similar stores in, for example, Poland.[140]

While family enterprises involved in small-scale industrial activities, the services sector or commerce were allowed to operate in an official form in several countries of the region such as in Poland, Hungary and Yugoslavia, these small businesses represented a diminutive proportion of their respective sectors. Statistical reports indicate that in Poland these enterprises employed

---

134 Gatejel, 'The Common Heritage of the Socialist Car Culture', 155.
135 Fava, 'The Elusive People's Car', 18.
136 Árpád Skrabski, ed., *Mit kér a nép? Kielégítetlen szükségletek 1988-ban a magyar lakosságban, I. kötet* [What do the people want? Unmet needs of the Hungarian population in 1988, vol. 1] (Budapest: Px Informatikai és Humán Kockázatokat Kezelő Kft., 1989), 8–17.
137 György Ádám, *Az orvosi hálapénz Magyarországon* [Doctor's gratuities in Hungary] (Budapest: Magvető, 1986).
138 Mariusz Jastrząb, 'Cars as Favors in People's Poland', in Siegelbaum, *The Socialist Car*, 38–46; György Majtényi, *K-vonal* [The K-line] (Budapest: Nyitott Könyvműhely, 2009).
139 Jastrząb, 'Cars as Favors in People's Poland', 38–41.
140 David H. Henderson, Robert M. McNab and Tamás Rózsa, 'The Hidden Inequality in Socialism', *Independent Review* 9, no. 3 (2005): 389–412.

6.6 per cent of all non-agricultural workers in 1950, and only 4.9 per cent in 1980.[141] The informal economy, which appeared in a wide range of forms, made up a much larger part of the overall economy. The diverse forms in which the informal economy appeared had one common characteristic. Unlike in the case of informal activities seen in market economies, their primary incentive was not tax avoidance; rather, they can be seen as a response to rampant shortage situations and, in general, economic restrictions. Jerzy Kochanowski distinguishes between several semi-legal or illegal markets. One semi-legal 'grey market' existed for services such as letting out flats or summer houses, car repair, remedial courses, health care services provided by physicians, etc. Many of these transactions were offered outside working hours, but not infrequently in the workplace. The illegal 'brown market' offered goods that in principle were available via the state-operated commercial networks yet were in permanent short supply. These articles were often withheld within the commercial network or even at the factories that produced them, and they were sold via various channels at prices that were higher than the official ones. Finally, the black market provided the venue for selling and buying goods obtained by way of criminal activities, such as bypassing the state monopoly on the sale of alcoholic beverages.[142]

Nevertheless, what the authorities allowed or banned, and how they actually enforced rules, varied from country to country and underwent significant changes over time, as more permissive periods were often followed by campaigns of restrictive action. The authorities often turned a blind eye to certain activities that in principle were banned or subject to restrictions; on other occasions, they launched campaigns to curb these very same activities. The most tolerated and therefore most widespread forms of such activities included the unauthorized trade in food products and the letting out of privately owned or leased real estate. Moonlighting is a good example of a 'grey economy' activity that was alternately persecuted and tolerated. As the private ownership of means of production was nearly non-existent, employees often produced goods for private purposes using the machines, tools, raw materials and means of transportation found in their workplace, which was either state-owned or belonged to the cooperative sector. This type of production normally satisfied the needs of the employees and their families, and often served to fill gaps caused by shortages of certain articles. Thus, in a most peculiar way it also contributed to the massive self-subsistence that characterized these societies. Moonlighting was officially persecuted, yet workplace leadership normally turned a blind eye and only acted if it became rampant at a given location. Black market activities included more than just the sale of goods obtained by outright criminal activities, and the range of these activities also varied widely. By the 1970s, black market activities in Poland or in Hungary were much less frequent than before, partly because many of these activities were tolerated by authorities and thus shifted into the grey or even white zone. For example, in making good use of their country's relatively lenient travel authorization regime, Polish tourists created extensive networks for the legal or semi-legal exchange of goods in several countries of the region; this phenomenon was also fairly widespread in Romania.[143]

---

141 Kornai, *The Socialist System*, 84.
142 Jerzy Kochanowski, *Jenseits der Planwirtschaft: Der Schwarzmarkt in Polen, 1944–1989* (Göttingen: Wallstein Verlag, 2013), 14–16.
143 Christina Petrescu, 'Entrepreneurial Tourism in Romania: A System-Stabilizing Factor?' in *'Schleichwege': Inoffizielle Begegnungen sozialistischer Staatsbürger zwischen 1956 und 1989*, eds Włodzimierz Borodziej, Jerzy Kochanowski and Joachim von Puttkamer (Köln: Böhlau, 2010), 115–33; Kochanowski, *Jenseits der Planwirtschaft*, 414–36.

Another peculiarity in the consumption history of the communist countries was the central role the workplace played in the supply of goods and especially in the provision of certain services. Workplaces in Western European countries may have also offered welfare benefits for their employees, but this practice was much more widespread in the communist systems of Eastern Europe. Factories and other workplaces had their own welfare institutions: kindergartens, sports clubs, cultural centres, doctors' offices and resorts. Whether a company had such establishments and how well equipped they were depended on the size and resources of the company. Large industrial companies occasionally operated multiple kindergartens, while smaller plants may not have had the opportunity to finance even one. The workplace also served as a channel for distributing certain goods; using their own vehicles and staff, companies would often procure potatoes, apples and other basic food items for the use of their own employees. However, companies played the most substantial role in the distribution of flats; as mentioned above, flats were the items most in short supply. Some companies owned service apartments, but – even in the case of the rental apartments they had not built themselves – they had the right to select the tenants or to decide which employee of theirs could purchase the flat.

The shortage of goods and services also had a distinct influence on consumer demand and consumer aspirations. As a general trend, meeting material necessities was a higher priority than other demands, a fact reflected in Maslow's well-recognized hierarchy of needs. This was especially the case at the dawn of the communist regimes, when post-war reconstruction and forced industrialization consumed much of the resources, thereby decreasing consumption, and all the disadvantages of the shortage economy had already become evident. This trend was also very strong in all the austerity periods of the late communist era; examples include Poland in the 1980s, when political and economic crises besieged the country simultaneously, and Romania in the same decade, when the country decided to pay back all its external debt early, an effort that led to the further deterioration of the supply of goods, which had been rather poor to begin with.

The population of Central and Eastern Europe had therefore experienced the shortage of goods for an extended period of time, which also influenced their lives in even more complex ways than described above. From the 1960s onward, the standard of living gradually reached a level where the basic needs of the majority of the population were met, although consumption goals and materialistic values remained very much in the forefront.[144] This can be explained by the fact that while the standard of living certainly increased, the related aspirations of the population rose even faster. The most prominent factors in this regard were the ever more striking demonstrative effects of the societies of the West. After the end of High Stalinism, the Central and Eastern European countries became less and less isolated, and the population enjoyed growing access to information about the consumer societies of the West. Tourism, movies, magazines, and in particular, Western goods that made their way to Central and Eastern Europe – products ranging from cars to clothing – were all vehicles for this exchange of information. This held especially true for those countries that were closer to the West and that, from the 1960s onward, became gradually more open politically as well as economically, such as Hungary and Poland.

Consumer goals also came to the foreground as the economic failure of the communist systems became more and more obvious over time. The regimes were unable to deliver on their

---

144 Ronald Inglehart, Miguel Basanez, and Alejandro Romero, *Human Values and Beliefs: A Cross-Cultural Sourcebook* (Ann Arbor, MI: University of Michigan Press, 1998).

own promises, and any attempt to give them significant overhauls failed, as in 1953, 1956 and 1968. Materialism as a value system became more persistent only in the context of the dictatorial practices, which did not tolerate the proliferation of alternative lifestyles.

Households remained the most important places of consumption throughout the twentieth century and beyond. As described above, however, there have been notable changes in the loci of consumption in three major waves. During the interwar period, the first such shift was the spread of department stores; granted, this change was predominantly limited to larger cities in the region. The next wave of transformation swept through Central and Eastern Europe beginning in the 1960s, when self-service shops started to proliferate in the region, yet the diffusion of workplace and school cafeterias was also an important aspect of this process. The last wave of changes took place beginning in the 1990s; these were partly linked to the conversion of communist commerce into a trading system of a full-fledged market economy, and to the technological transformation processes taking place all over the world.

After the regime change, in addition to the level and structure of consumption, the qualitative characteristics of consumption also underwent fundamental transformations. Although limited purchasing power led shops to continue stocking a humbler assortment of goods than those in Western Europe, the range of products on offer changed dramatically. It was more or less the same as anywhere else in Europe, and the circumstances of sale also became rather similar. Therefore, in terms of consumer experience, Central and Eastern Europe was undeniably catching up with Western Europe, and with the Western industrial and consumer societies in general.

After the regime change, the commercial sector underwent the fastest transformation towards a market economy. Shops had formerly served primarily as a means to distribute goods, something considerably different from active engagement in commercial activities in the traditional sense. This was reflected not only in the choice of goods offered and the location of the shops, but also in their internal and external appearance, in the presentation of the goods, and in the type and quality of the services rendered to their customers. As the market economy emerged, all these aspects underwent a fundamental change. Commerce was among the first sectors to be privatized, and large numbers of small shops were established, as operating them required relatively moderate investment and expertise. While the general trend in Western European commerce was one of market concentration, decentralization was undoubtedly more typical in Central and Eastern Europe throughout the first several years of the market economy. The trend of business concentration, as had been seen earlier in Western Europe, also later appeared in the region.[145] Chains of shops and supermarkets typically owned by foreign companies followed one another. Among the first were fast food chains, especially MacDonald's and Burger King, which became symbols of the diffusion of consumer society and of Americanization. They were initially priced in the higher range; thus, they became venues of conspicuous consumption for the middle class. Over time, as the chains expanded and their pricing gradually evened out, they largely lost this symbolic role and became standard actors in the catering industry. The

---

145 Jiří Musil, 'Changing Urban Systems in Post-Communist Societies in Central Europe', *Urban Studies* 30, no. 6 (1993): 900–2; Grigoriy Kostinskiy, 'Post-Socialist Cities in Flux', in *Handbook of Urban Studies*, ed. Ronan Paddison (London: Sage, 2001), 455. Raymond J. Struyk, 'Housing Privatization in the Former Soviet Block to 1995', in *Cities after Socialism: Urban and Regional Change and Conflict in Post-Socialist Societies*, eds Gregory Andrusz, Michael Harloe and Iván Szelényi (Oxford: Blackwell, 1996), 202–03; Iván Szelényi, 'Cities under Socialism – and After', in Andrusz, Harloe and Szelényi, *Cities after Socialism*, 312–4.

mushrooming large shopping centres were not only places where one could procure necessary goods, but the mere action of visiting them soon became an element of consumption.[146]

After the regime change, motorization also gathered momentum in the region. For many, driving a modern car had long been a symbol of the desired Western lifestyle; now, all of a sudden, even the most modern cars became available for purchase in fancy automobile dealerships without any waiting time. However, for the majority of the population, a more affordable option was buying one of the used motor vehicles imported en masse from Western Europe. The consumption of consumer electronics – television sets, VCRs, DVD players and, later, mobile phones – also skyrocketed, primarily because the economy becoming ever more open allowed the population of this region to benefit from continuously decreasing relative price levels. In addition, after the turn of the millennium, just like everywhere else in the world, the electronic media and – especially in the case of the younger population – the World Wide Web also became increasingly prominent places of consumption.

However, the emergence of the consumer society did not really produce a clear improvement in the general satisfaction of the population with their standard of living, not even in the years of rapidly expanding consumption. In 2005, 35 per cent of the Polish population and only 28 per cent of the Hungarian population was satisfied with its standard of living, a rather low indicator when compared internationally, even when considering the data of both richer and poorer countries.[147] On the one hand, consumer aspirations soared with the newly experienced abundance in the supply of goods accompanied with aggressive marketing techniques. Of equal importance, however, were the increased income disparities after the regime change; large segments of society held disadvantageous positions that did not permit them to benefit from the opportunities offered by the emerging consumer society.

Leisure

When regulation caused working time in Europe to decrease slowly during the first two thirds of the twentieth century, and then later more dynamically, this not only affected the overall time dedicated to work, but also prompted a more marked separation of working time and leisure time.[148] These processes, seen in Central and Eastern Europe as well as in Western Europe, facilitated the emergence of a more abundant selection of leisure activities. As early as at the end of the nineteenth century, initially in larger cities for the most part, the traditional range of entertainment options gradually expanded to include new types of activities such as frequenting the beach, visiting spas, going to the movies, sports activities and tourism. In addition to the increasing amount of leisure time and the separation between working time and leisure time, a whole range of other social, cultural and, indeed, political processes also contributed to the

---

146 Kai-Uwe Hellmann, 'Das konsumistische Syndrom: Zum gegenwärtigen Entspreschungsverhältnis von Gesellschafts- und Identitätsform unter besonderer Berücksichtigung der Raum-Konsum-Relation', in *Räume des Konsums: Über den Funktionswandel von Räumlichkeit im Zeitalter des Konsumismus*, eds Kai-Uwe Hellmann and Guido Zurstiege (Wiesbaden:VS Verlag für Sozialwissenschaften, 2008), 39.

147 Matild Sági, 'Elégedettség az átalakuló társadalmakban' [Satisfaction in transforming societies], in *Társadalmi riport, 2006*, eds Tamás Kolosi, István György Tóth and György Vukovich (Budapest: Tárki, 2006), 157.

148 Rudolf Andorka, Béla Falussy, and István Harcsa, 'Time Strategies and Way of Life', in Andorka, Kolosi and Vukovich, *Social Report*, 129–32; Rudolf Andorka, Béla Falussy, and István Harcsa, *Időmérleg: Részletes adatok* [Time balance: detailed data] (Budapest: KSH, 1982); János Farkas and Ágnes Vajda, *Időgazdálkodás és munkatevékenységek* [Time management and working activities] (Budapest: KSH, 1989).

popularity of new forms of entertainment. These included, first and foremost, the improvement of living standards, the advance of urbanization and commercialization, yet just as important was the growth of the service sector and of the share of employees among the economically active population.

After the First World War, there was a boom in popular demand for meaningful ways to spend time off work. Sports activities designed to maintain a healthy body and mind became increasingly popular, with football leading the charts everywhere in the region. Masses started to play football for the simple reasons that it did not require complicated equipment and that it could be played practically anywhere. It also developed into a prominent competitive sport. Hungary organized its first national championship in 1901, and the first decade of the century saw the building of several football stadiums in Budapest, complete with appropriate tiered spectator seating and other facilities. National championships began in 1918 in Poland and in 1925 in Czechoslovakia. As football was seen as an exciting yet affordable spectator sport, going to a match soon became an attraction for the masses.

Some other sports also attracted a considerable number of spectators. With Hungary as an example again, these included skating, especially after the Városliget (City Park) ice rink was opened in Budapest in 1926, as well as swimming; after the turn of the century, certain Budapest schools incorporated swimming instruction into their curricula. Beaches and spas were opened, although they only functioned in summer. A national campaign was launched to build covered swimming pools. The National Swimming Stadium of Budapest was opened on Margaret Island in 1930. Hiking and rowing also became popular pastimes during the interwar period. The Association of Friends of Nature for Tourism was founded, and a network of tourist shelters established.[149] In the Slavic countries of the region, the Sokol Movement was formed to provide a unique setting for the promotion of both nationalism and athletics.[150]

Employers – especially larger companies and institutions – followed the international trends and often generously supported the sports and health activities of their employees, hoping that this would reflect in their work and loyalty. Companies opened sports stadiums, beaches and rowing houses while also establishing resorts, although this was more typical in larger industrial centres. One example is the company Bata, which promoted these new forms of recreation in the brand-new neighbourhoods of Zlin, Czechoslovakia. After the First World War, political attention also turned increasingly to exercise; this was another channel through which support was made available for the construction of sports grounds. A different early example that sheds light on the relationship between sports and politics is the 1929 launch of the annual Balkan games, a follow-up up on a Greek initiative; until the war broke out the games served to improve cooperation between the countries of the region.[151]

The commercialization of leisure-time activities, which showed a strengthening trend in the first half of the century until being pushed into the background for several decades under communism, can be well observed in how cinemas and radios gained ground.[152] In Hungary, the

---

149 Gergely Mohácsi, 'Szép, erős, egészséges. Szabadidő és testkultúra Budapesten a 20. század első felében' [Beautiful, strong, healthy: body culture and leisure in Budapest in the first half of the 20th century], *Korall* 3, no. 7/8 (2002): 40–3.

150 Diethelm Blecking, 'Zum historischen Problem des slawischen Sokolbewegung', in *Die slawische Sokolbewegung: Beiträge zur Geschichte von Sport und Nationalismus in Osteuropa*, ed. Diethelm Blecking (Dortmund: Forschungsstelle Ostmitteleuropa, 1991), 7–22.

151 Penelope Kissoudi, *The Balkan Games and Balkan Politics in the Interwar Years 1929–1939: Politicians in Pursuit of Peace* (London: Routledge, 2013).

152 Anikó Imre, ed., *A Companion to Eastern European Cinemas* (Oxford: John Wiley & Sons, 2012).

first permanent facility for regularly screening films opened in 1896, and the first proper cinemas appeared in Budapest in 1906 (Odeon, Apolló). The first cinematic distribution company was founded in 1908. In 1910, there were 114 cinemas operating in Budapest; for the sake of comparison, the same indicator was 260 in Berlin and 400 in London. Of all remaining large cities in Hungary, Miskolc was the only one that did not have a cinema prior to the First World War. After the war, the region also saw the proliferation of American films, with French, German and other European productions losing ground, while domestic film production started in every country of the region, often enjoying major state patronage.[153] In 1928, 501 cinemas operated in Hungary – 87 of them in Budapest – with a combined seating capacity of 171,717. Within just one year, films were being watched by 26 million viewers, nearly half of whom were from the capital.[154] In Hungary, the first film with sound was screened in 1929; and in 1931, Hungary was among the first countries in Europe to screen a newsreel with sound. Soon enough, legislation was passed to make the regular screening of newsreels obligatory for all cinemas. In 1939, further legislation was adopted to obligate cinemas to screen popular science and instructional films as well as productions specifically designed to 'educate the nation', as it was put at the time. Audiences were officially barred from expressing either opinions or appreciation during newsreels. Furthermore, cinemas became more and more comfortable and started to specialize; in Budapest, one of the cinemas, New York, screened only 45-minute newsreel programmes all day long. Despite the appeal of films with sound, the number of cinemas increased only very slowly in the wake of the crisis during the early 1930s, with the number of filmgoers actually dropping; in 1935, 599 cinemas sold a total of 19 million tickets. During the second half of the decade, however, audience numbers increased again dynamically.[155]

Immediately after the First World War, the changes that took place in how people spent their leisure time had the overall effect of homogenizing the habits of various social strata. A good example of this effect is cinema. People of the lower middle class rarely had the chance or intention to go to the cinema, but they nonetheless became part of the movie-going crowd. Yet films had further social effects, and one is especially worth noting: cinema promoted change in the social role of women. From the very first moment, going to the movies was an acceptable form of leisure time for each gender, which, along with the emancipated female characters who appeared on the big screen, certainly helped the dissemination of new models of female behaviour during the interwar period in Central and Eastern Europe, as it did elsewhere.

After the Second World War, the number of cinemas as well as viewers skyrocketed in the region. By 1950, as many as 1,549 cinemas operated in Hungary, selling 47 million tickets each year. Throughout Central and Eastern Europe, the popularity of this form of entertainment peaked around 1960; at that time, 140 million viewers watched nearly one million screenings in 4,558 locations in Hungary. It would be difficult, however, to speak of a heyday of moving pictures. By then the choice of shows was rather limited, as the best international films rarely made it to the cinemas of Poland, Czechoslovakia, Hungary or Bulgaria, and many of the films that did get screened openly served ideological purposes. Later on, mostly because of competition from television, the popularity of cinemas dropped dramatically; while in 1960, the average

---

153 György Vajdovich, 'Filmtörténet' [The history of film], in *Magyar Kódex. 6. kötet. Magyarok a 20. században. Magyarország művelődéstörténete, 1918–2000*, ed. József Szentpéteri (Budapest: Kossuth, 2001), 269–90.
154 Róbert Palágyi, 'Film', in *Közgazdasági enciklopédia. II. kötet*, (Budapest: Athenaeum), 230–4.
155 *Századok statisztikája* [Statistics of the centuries] (Budapest: KSH, 2001), 79–80.

Hungarian went to the movies 14 times annually, the same indicator dropped to 6 by 1980, and by the turn of the millennium Hungarians were seeing but one film per year.[156]

Public radio service started in 1923 in Czechoslovakia, 1925 in Hungary, 1926 in Poland and Yugoslavia, and in 1929 in Bulgaria.[157] Following the international trend, the number of subscribers began to increase dynamically at the end of the 1930s for two reasons: with mass production, sets became relatively cheaper, and crowds had a bigger hunger for news during the war than in peacetime.[158] The progression of new radio stations roughly reflected the rate at which radio penetration expanded in the region. Examining the two extremes of the scale, in 1937–38, Czechoslovakia had the most subscribers (72 radios per 1,000 inhabitants) and Bulgaria the fewest (8 radios per 1,000 inhabitants).[159] Even after the Second World War, the number of subscribers increased dynamically in Central and Eastern Europe, and the market reached saturation by the mid-1960s; almost every single household in the most developed countries of the region had a radio. Radio stations in Central and Eastern Europe were under government control up until the end of the century; this was fairly easy to manage, as there were only a handful of radio stations in each country, ignoring regional stations. For example, there were two national and eight regional stations in post-war Poland, but even the latter were all under the control of the central authorities. The first major change took place from the 1980s onward, when the central authority controlling radio service, the Committee for Radio and Television, was no longer capable of maintaining its former level of control in the same manner. However, the first private radio stations, such as Radio-Market in Gdansk, were set up only at the very end of the 1980s.[160]

While going to the movies and owning a radio transformed how people spent their leisure time, the influence they exerted was mostly limited to the middle decades of the century. Even then, it was weaker than the impact that television would soon have.[161] Regular television broadcasting started in 1952 in Poland, 1953 in Czechoslovakia, 1957 in Hungary and Romania, 1959 in Bulgaria, and in 1960 in Albania. In 1960, there were only 10 television subscriptions per 1,000 Hungarians; in 1965, there were 82; and in 1975, there were as many as 226. In other words, by the second half of the 1970s nearly every household owned a television set. Television airtime was initially rather limited; in Hungary, only 22 hours of television programming per week was broadcast in 1960, and it was only at the end of the 1970s that airtime exceeded 80 hours per week, including the programming of the second national channel, which was launched in 1971.[162]

Just like in Western European societies, television played an increasingly large role in the region under review, a fact best reflected in the time budget surveys that were conducted.

---

156 Barnabás Barta, ed., *Magyarország művelődési viszonyai* [Hungary's cultural relations] (Budapest: Kossuth, 1984), 227.
157 Eli Noam, *Television in Europe* (New York: Oxford University Press, 1991), 279–87.
158 László Ghimessy, 'Magyarország rádióvevő-engedélyei 1942-ben' [Hungary's radio-receiver licences in 1942], *Magyar Statisztikai Szemle* 21, no. 12 (1943): 650–60.
159 United Nations, *Statistical Yearbook 1951* (New York: United Nations Department of International Economic and Social Affairs, 1951); Therborn, *European Modernity and Beyond*, 141.
160 Noam, *Television in Europe*, 280.
161 Tibor Valuch, 'A magyar művelődés 1948 után' [Hungarian culture since 1948], in *Magyar művelődéstörténet*, ed. László Kósa (Budapest: Osiris, 2006), 616–8.
162 Barta, *Magyarország művelődési viszonyai*, 280; Rudolf Andorka and István Harcsa, 'Modernization in Hungary in the Long and Short Run Measured by Social Indicators' (working paper, Department of Sociology, University of Economics, Budapest, 1988).

These also allow us to keep track of the changing importance of other leisure-time activities. In 1963, Hungarian adult males (between the ages of 18 and 60) had 174 minutes of leisure time to dispose of each day. They spent most of this time reading and studying (54 minutes) and socializing (also 54 minutes), listening to the radio or music (24 minutes), watching television (also 24 minutes), watching cultural and sporting events (6 minutes), and walking, hiking, and sports activities (also 6 minutes). Women had somewhat less leisure time (154 minutes a day) but used it in roughly the same proportions. In the next three decades, the amount of leisure time increased significantly (281 minutes per day for men, 241 minutes a day for women). However, while leisure time increased consistently for several decades, television fully consumed the time gained for each gender; in 1993, men and women watched television for 159 and 139 minutes, respectively. Thus, watching television became by far the most prominent form of spending one's leisure time, leaving behind socialization (59 and 44 minutes), reading and studying (34 and 32 minutes), walking and sports (15 and 8 minutes), listening to the radio or music (6 and 3 minutes), and watching cultural and sports events (3 and 2 minutes).[163] After the regime change, commercial television found its way to Central and Eastern Europe; as a consequence, the time dedicated to watching the flickering screen increased even further by the turn of the millennium as television became even more dominant as a form of spending one's leisure time, with Hungary heading the charts in all-Europe comparisons. Like elsewhere in the industrialized countries, as Internet penetration reached new highs after the turn of the millennium, television's significance stopped growing; indeed, younger generations started spending continually less time watching television.

After the Second World War, the dynamic market penetration of cinemas, radios, and later television sets in the communist countries was far less commercial in nature than in Western Europe. On the contrary, these new media became vehicles of political control regularly used by governments for purposes of mass indoctrination. People listening to the radio and watching the television spent their leisure time in ways much in line with the political objectives of the regime, fitting in well with its expectations concerning the preferred structure of public communication. Easy to control centrally, these forms of media were highly fit for propaganda purposes; they offered the general population forms of entertainment typically enjoyed by individuals in isolation, and, in addition, they were affordable. During the first few decades of the television era, programming largely consisted of the same genres as with Western European public service television channels: films, sports and news. At the same time, with the sole exception of Yugoslavia, special care was taken to ensure that the programming was dominated by domestic production and programmes sourced from within the Eastern bloc, one reason being the shortage of foreign exchange. Undoubtedly, television was less of a vehicle for promoting consumer culture than in Western European societies; advertisements, for example, played a much less prominent role in the television channels of the region than in those of Western Europe. Yet, one should not underestimate the indirect influence of television and films. Western-made films and television series slowly found their way onto television screens not only in Yugoslavia, but also in Hungary and Poland, along with news reports covering events taking place in Western countries. Their images of modern cars, rich interiors, fashionable clothes and attractive streets offered the general population important information

---

163 Rudolf Andorka and Béla Falussy, 'Az időmérleg változásai, 1963–1977' [Changes in time allotment, 1963–1977], *Szociológia* 11, no. 3 (1982), 333; Béla Falussy and György Vukovich, 'Az idő mérlegén (1963–1993)' [On the allotment of time (1963–1993)], in *Társadalmi riport, 1996*, eds Rudolf Andorka, Tamás Kolosi and György Vukovich (Budapest: Tárki, 1996), 81.

about consumer societies. The interconnection between television and consumer culture only became truly strong after the regime change, once commercial television channels, as explained above, started to operate in the region. It was at this point that television became the most important medium for whetting consumer appetites and one of the primary vehicles for satisfying those appetites throughout the region.

The development of mass tourism is another major thrust of the trends seen in consumption and leisure during the twentieth century. In the nineteenth century, tourism started out in Central and Eastern Europe mostly around spas and sea resorts; some of these, such as Marienbad and especially Karlsbad, attracted many international visitors, some were less frequented yet still international (Abbazia/Opatija), while others were mainly of local significance.[164] During the interwar period, development projects were launched to put certain mountainous areas on the map as destinations for tourism, including health tourism, in the Tatra Mountains in Czechoslovakia and Poland and in the Carpathians in Romania.

Communist countries also developed their mass tourism sectors after the Second World War, albeit at a lesser scale than the countries of Western Europe, and with marked differences. Early on, propaganda placed great emphasis on the availability of holidays and resorts to those social classes – typically industrial workers and employees – that had never formerly had true access to the pleasures of tourism. Some of the peculiar features of this system included the collective nature of the scheme; while organized group holidays were meant to emphasize solidarity among the workers, they were also a means for exercising political supervision, especially when it came to trips abroad. Moreover, this type of tourism was more easily organized by larger, state-run companies, and thus compatible with the centrally planned economy. People typically spent their holidays at resort complexes owned by the state, by the company or institution they worked for, or by trade unions. These resorts offered all-inclusive services at affordable prices; however, the typical standard of those services was rather humble. Holiday rights were awarded either on the basis of workers' merits or as a bonus; often, people simply had to put themselves on a waiting list. The true expansion of the necessary resort infrastructure commenced only in the 1970s. While in 1975, a total of 1,845 company and trade union resorts operated in Czechoslovakia, just ten years later there were 3,147 such facilities with a combined accommodation capacity of 61,790 beds.[165]

Foreign tourism was much more restricted.[166] During the 1950s, for the citizens of Central and Eastern Europe's communist countries, permission to travel to even one of the other Eastern bloc countries was a special privilege. During the following decades, travel restrictions were gradually eased in most countries, but visits to the West remained under strict state control throughout the period, not only in countries with more stringent travel regimes like Czechoslovakia or Romania, but even in Hungary and Poland, the two communist countries with the most permissive travel rules from the 1970s onward.

As an example of the region's more stringent travel regimes, in Czechoslovakia, a very slow liberalization process started after 1954 in terms of eastbound trips. The new passport act and

---

164 John K. Walton, 'Preface: Some Contexts for Yugoslav Tourism History', in *Yugoslavia's Sunny Side: A History of Tourism in Socialism (1950s–1960s)*, eds Hannes Grandit and Karin Taylor (Budapest: CEU Press, 2010), xiii.
165 Allan M. Williams and Vladimir Baláž, *Tourism in Transition: Economic Change in Central Europe* (London: I.B. Tauris Publishers, 2000), 20.
166 Derek R. Hall, 'Evolutionary Pattern of Tourism Development in Eastern Europe and the Soviet Union', in *Tourism and Economic Development in Eastern Europe and the Soviet Union* (London: Belhaven Press, 1991), 104–5.

its implementation decrees were passed in 1965. Under this act, citizens still had to obtain an exit visa if they wanted to travel to the West. In 1968, the adoption of a new and more lenient passport act was underway, but the process stopped when the country became occupied and the issue was soon struck from the agenda. From 1969 onward, travelling to the West became almost impossible, except to visit relatives living legally in the West (in which case a letter of invitation was required) and for organized tourist trips. Individual trips were not formally banned, but the police rarely authorized such applications. In addition, the foreign exchange permits issued by the Czech State Bank (Státní banka československá) also limited citizens' possibilities to travel to the West. Citizens could legally purchase convertible currencies only from the state bank, no more than once a year, only right before departing, and they could only use the funds to finance their trips. After 1981, travel restrictions were introduced even for visits to Poland. From 1988 onward, exit visas for travelling to the West were usually granted without complications, but the restrictions on access to foreign exchange were maintained.

As of the mid-1960s, ordinary Hungarian citizens were allowed to visit capitalist countries with a certain regularity: initially, once in every three years, then from 1982 onward, once a year. One important stipulation was that a passport did not in itself authorize the holder to leave the country for a foreign destination; before each trip, the citizen had to obtain an exit visa from the Hungarian authorities, also when travelling to capitalist countries. In 1988, a new passport was introduced that allowed the holder to leave the country freely, yet the amount of foreign exchange that people could legally acquire was heavily restricted.[167] However, it was legal in both Hungary and Poland to open special bank accounts for foreign exchange transferred home (or obtained otherwise) and to use such funds towards foreign travel.[168]

Nonetheless, tourism between the socialist countries expanded significantly. One unique form of tourism was 'entrepreneurial' or 'trader' tourism, which also demonstrated typical consumer habits and practices. In this arrangement, travellers did not visit other countries for the purposes of traditional tourism – such as visiting historical landmarks or discovering foreign cultures – but for making an economic profit. Romanian, Polish or Hungarian travellers were eager to take advantage of the differences between the various socialist countries in terms of prices and the range of products available. They hauled hard-to-get products from one country to next, or simply purchased goods at low prices to sell them off at high prices elsewhere. The primary distinction between the activities of these individuals and those of established commercial traders was that the various restrictions on export and import usually forced these travellers to carry relatively small quantities of goods in their luggage and to prosper by circumventing customs regulations.[169]

After the collapse of communism, the tourism of the region also underwent major changes. Domestic tourism as it was known in the previous decades lost its popularity due to the fact that its traditional system – organized group trips and holidays in resort complexes owned and subsidized by the state or by companies – almost completely disappeared. In the meantime,

---

167 Péter Bencsik, 'Documents of Passage, Travel Opportunities and Border Traffic in 20th Century Hungary', *Minorities, Politics, Society* 2 (2002): 51–70.
168 Mikolaj Morzycki-Markowski, 'How People Crossed Borders in Socialism: The Polish Case', in Borodziej, Kochanowski and von Puttkamer, *'Schleichwege'*, 55–66.
169 Christina Petrescu, 'Entrepreneurial Tourism in Romania: A System-Stabilizing Factor?' in Borodziej, Kochanowski and von Puttkamer, *'Schleichwege'*, 115–33; Mark Keck-Szajbel, 'Shop Around the Bloc: Trader Tourism and Its Discontents on the East German-Polish Border', in *Communism Unwrapped: Consumption in Cold War Eastern Europe*, eds Paulina Bren and Mary Neuburger (Oxford: Oxford University Press, 2012), 374–92.

especially during the region's transformation crisis, changing real income levels meant that many citizens were unable to pay the market price of tourism-related services. In addition, as people were highly motivated to make use of their newly obtained freedom to travel, wealthier social groups travelled to Western and Southern Europe or to destinations even further away. During the years after the regime change, long rows of Czech tourist buses parked in the centre of Paris exemplified the travel fervour of Eastern European tourists, finally free of government travel restrictions and now trying to make up for decades of lost opportunities.

This loosening of the Eastern bloc also brought along major changes in the opposite direction, especially in the countries that had been selectively closed to international tourism, such as Romania or Czechoslovakia. Central and Eastern Europe started to dynamically rebuild its tourism. One of the most spectacular and earliest results of these efforts was Prague's tourist boom in the early 1990s. The city became the region's most popular destination among Western European and overseas tourists. Poland took advantage of its proximity to Germany, but also attracted masses of American tourists, largely building on the sizeable number of Polish-Americans living in the United States. As Hungary was already experienced in attracting Western tourists, the changes it underwent were not as dramatic as elsewhere.[170]

Traditional mass tourism destinations in the Southeast European region, however, stagnated after the regime change. The Yugoslav Wars kept visitors away from the beach resorts of the Adriatic – Dubrovnik, in fact, came under attack – but Romanian and Bulgarian resorts along the Black Sea also saw a downturn in visitors because of unreliable services and dwindling domestic tourism. After the turn of the century, however, these well-located destinations enjoyed a boost in their appeal.

Consumption policy

Consumption policy can be defined as the regulation of income, supply and prices by public bodies such as local or central governments.[171] Taking the form of the quality control of foodstuffs, public intervention into consumption has a long history in Europe. The First World War had already witnessed the emergence of systematic consumer politics all over the continent targeting the security of food supplies, including such measures as rationing and price control.[172]

---

170 Williams and Baláž, *Tourism in Transition*, 1–13.
171 For comprehensive accounts of consumption policy, see Martin Daunton and Matthew Hilton, eds, *The Politics of Consumption: Material Culture and Citizenship in Europe and America* (New York: Berg, 2001); Dhavan V. Shah et al., 'The Politics of Consumption/The Consumption of Politics', *The Annals of the American Academy of Political and Social Science* 611 (2007): 6–16; Jörn Lamla and Sighard Neckel, eds, *Politisierter Konsum – konsumierte Politik* (Wiesbaden: VS Verlag für Sozialwissenschaften, 2006); Sheryl Kroen, 'A political history of the consumer', *The Historical Journal* 47 (2004): 709–36; Kate Soper and Frank Trentmann, eds, *Citizenship and Consumption* (Houndmills: Palgrave-Macmillan, 2008).
172 Ina Zweininger-Bargielowska, Rachel Duffet, and Alain Droudard, eds, *Food and War in Twentieth Century Europe* (Farnham: Ashgate, 2011); Theo Balderston, 'Industrial Mobilization and War Economies', in *A Companion to World War I*, ed. John Horne (London: Routledge, 2010), 227–8; Thierry Bonzon and Belinda Davis, 'Feeding the Cities', in *Capital Cities at War: Paris, London, Berlin 1914–1919*, vol. 1, eds Jay Winter and Jean-Louis Robert (Cambridge: Cambridge University Press, 1997), 305–41; Jay Winter, 'Surviving the War: Life Expectation, Illness and Mortality Rates in Paris, London and Berlin, 1914–1919', in ibid., 487–523; Max-Stephan Schulze, 'Austria-Hungary's Economy in World War I', in *The Economics of World War I*, eds Stephen Broadberry and Mark Harrison (Cambridge: Cambridge University Press, 2005), 91–7.

During the interwar period, these types of restrictions and practices of direct state intervention were gradually phased out, only to be reintroduced again as elements of a comprehensive system constructed during the Second World War. The measures taken in German-occupied Central and Eastern European territories were, as a rule, tougher than those taken in Germany itself; for example, rations provided to the general population were smaller. The system of rationing persisted for years after the war. In Slovenia and Czechoslovakia, for example, it was abolished only in 1953.[173]

Thus, several regulative measures were already in place before the communist takeover in the region. However, with the emergence of centrally planned economies in Central and Eastern Europe during the decades after the Second World War, consumption and politics became intertwined in a manner never seen before. This created a broad, yet only partly realized agenda, including nationalization, planning, scientific models of consumption, the standardization of goods and services and the education of people.

The dominant interpretation encountered in recent literature claims that early communist regimes neglected consumption because decision makers postulated economic growth as their main goal, whereby they considered an emphasis on consumption to be an impediment to growth. There was a later shift towards consumerism, mostly modelled after the Western consumer societies, even if the countries of Central and Eastern Europe could, at most, only imitate that Western model.[174] Many authors emphasize that this shift eventually proved to be a definitive contribution to the failure of the communist regimes, as they were unable to compete successfully with Western societies in satisfying consumer desires.[175]

Although the attitudes of economic policy makers towards consumption underwent massive changes throughout the existence of the communist regimes, and a focus on the shift towards a more consumer-oriented approach does indeed identify important processes, there is still a need to fine-tune this interpretation. First and foremost, it must be emphasized that, from their earliest days, increasing the level of consumption had always been an important goal in the communist regimes of Central and Eastern Europe. This appeared in official discourse as an aspiration to improve the workers' standard of living. Official Marxist thought at the time considered the gradual increase in the standard of living as an inherent element of the reality of socialism. The idea had important ideological precursors to rely upon. As reflected in the work of the classic authors of Marxism, the original vision of communism included the idea that once a communist society is built, all needs will be satisfied on the basis of the principle known as 'from each according to his ability, to each according to his need', regardless of the individual's work performance.

However, from the very beginning, contradictions were palpable in the official economic policy; increasing the standard of living while boosting economic growth, especially by way of forced investment, remained an irresolvable conflict for the decision makers of the era.

---

173 Maja Godina Golija, 'Slovene Food Consumption in the Twentieth Century – From Self-Sufficiency to Mass Consumerism', in *The Rise of Obesity in Europe: A Twentieth Century Food History*, eds Derek J. Oddy, Peter J. Atkins and Virginie Amilien (Farnham: Ashgate, 2009), 53; Martin Franc, 'Socialism and the Overweight Nation: Questions of Ideology, Science and Obesity in Czechoslovakia, 1950–70', in ibid., 195.

174 Stephen Merl, 'Staat und Konsum in der Zentralverwaltungswirtschaft', in Siegrist, Kaelble and Kocka, *Europäische Konsumgeschichte*, 206–7.

175 Victoria de Grazia, *Irresistible Empire: America's Advance Through Twentieth-Century Europe* (Cambridge, MA: Belknap Press, 2005); Katherine Verdery, *What Was Socialism and What Comes Next?* (Princeton, NJ: Princeton University Press, 1996), 25; Merkel, *Utopie und Bedürfnis*.

Gaining prominence mostly from the 1950s onward, the concept of scientifically based consumption was highly symptomatic in this respect. While it could in fact be seen as an attempt at bridging the above-described conflict, it speaks volumes about the importance of consumption as a goal during even the earliest stages of Central and Eastern European communism. Everywhere in the region, political and economic elites shared a clear vision about organizing consumption on the basis of scientific principles, eliminating the need for consumers to make choices on the basis of their own personal preferences. Imported from the Soviet Union, this vision holds that there exists an ideal and scientifically definable model of consumption that covers both the level of consumption and its composition, and therefore can serve as a compass for central economic planning in defining the ideal supply of goods. For obvious reasons, such a centrally defined 'consumption plan' could only define consumption using some of the most important natural indicators or units of measurement such as square metres, pairs, kilograms, litres, pieces, etc. Consequently, neither the quality aspects of the products nor the selection or choice of goods and services played any role in this model. Nowhere was this vision realized in actual practice, but while efforts of this nature gradually lost ground from the 1960s onward, traces of such a 'consumption plan' continued to linger in the economic policy documents of all the countries in the region up until the regime change.[176]

The 'classic' system of the centrally planned economy, which was universally characteristic of Central and Eastern Europe in the early 1950s, underwent a considerable change in most of the countries during the later decades. From around the mid-1950s, meeting consumer needs more effectively became a recurring objective for economic planners in the region. However, the actual emphasis given to the expansion of consumption and the widening of consumer choice has varied considerably, mainly as a function of the political leadership of the individual country and the changes in its general political line. Thus, a new orientation towards consumption made its presence in Poland and in Hungary as early as after the upheavals of 1956. The comprehensive economic reforms implemented in the 1960s – the most radical being those of Czechoslovakia and Hungary – aimed partly at meeting consumer demands. For the political leaders in these countries, the Western patterns of consumption served as the point of reference, and they wanted to enable the population to adopt or to at least imitate some elements of this model. These reforms were later withdrawn either partially, as in Hungary, or completely, as in Czechoslovakia. However, this did not lead to a fall in consumption levels. On the contrary, the level of consumption continued to increase in these countries even during the 1970s. The slowing of the reform process nevertheless impeded any significant improvement in the selection and quality of the products offered.

After the close of the Stalin era, consumption was gradually rehabilitated not only as one of the goals of production, but also in public discourse. The media dedicated more and more attention to the quality of goods, new products, fashion and consumption-related topics. All the while, economic and political leadership remained ambiguous in its attitude towards consumer needs; not surprisingly, consumption itself was also portrayed ambiguously both in the press and in other forms of political communication.[177] On the one hand, improving the supply of goods was obviously key to maintaining political stability. Low provision levels and shortages of everyday necessities caused much popular dissatisfaction in the com-

---

176 Andrzej K. Kozminski, 'Consumers in Transition from the Centrally Planned Economy to the Market Economy', *Journal of Consumer Policy* 14 (1992): 352–4.
177 Tibor Valuch, 'A bőséges ínségtől az ínséges bőségig: A fogyasztás változásai Magyarországon az 1956 utáni évtizedekben' [From the poverty of richness to the richness of poverty], in Tibor Valuch, *Metszetek: Válogatott tanulmányok* (Budapest: Argumentum – 1956-os Intézet, 2006), 222–52.

munist countries. The system was forced to keep consumption objectives on its agenda, often formulating those objectives as promises for the future.[178] However, decision makers often saw the improvement of the supply of goods as a concession that the regime had to make to the politically less conscious and committed segments of society at the expense of its true objectives, particularly boosting investment and speeding up economic growth. In this mind-set, there were limits to the compatibility between consumption and the overall objectives of socialism.

Particularly in the 1950s and early 1960s, politics often labelled consumer desires as dangerous, fearing that such attitudes of the 'petite bourgeoisie' could spread to the working class as well.[179] Debates in the press echoed the asceticism of the early labour movement and its aversion to consumption, fearing that the advancement of the consumer mentality would jeopardize human activities of a higher value, such as participating in community or public life. In Hungary, the debate over 'refrigerator socialism' is a typical example in this vein. It was sparked by an article in a magazine called *Új Írás* (*New Writing*) in 1961, in which one of the regime's quasi-official poets, Mihály Váci, expressed concern about a society that places far too much emphasis on consumption.[180] Over time, opinions of this type lost ground but never completely disappeared. As late as the 1970s, publications echoing the official or semi-official position still saw a danger in certain 'distorted life ideals of the "consumer society" variety imported from the West', complaining that, as a related publication put it, 'an "upper crust" of the petite bourgeoisie – colloquially known as "the big shots" – has taken root and come to a second bloom in the pores of our socialist society, while their glitzy lifestyle is now infiltrating the working classes'.[181]

The more consumption-oriented economic policy was also designed to give people hope that in the future an ordinary socialist citizen would be able to reach or at least come close to Western levels of consumption. In several countries, the economic reform agendas of the 1960s aimed specifically at improving the quality and availability of goods and services and widening their selection. In the wake of the 1968 reform of its national economic system, Hungary was undoubtedly able to widen the range of consumer choices, albeit at the cost of giving up on certain goals traditionally considered core values of socialism, such as price stability and the equal distribution of incomes.

It is, however, doubtful that these changes can be interpreted as a gradual shift in the attitude of the political systems of the region as a whole from ignoring consumption towards better meeting consumer needs. Such a linear trajectory was arguably present in Hungary and in East Germany, a country outside the scope of our research; however, in quite a few other communist countries, such as Poland, Romania and, in fact, Yugoslavia, no such trend was palpable. In fact, the changes that took place in this latter group of countries were of a cyclical nature.

Bogdan Mieczkowski suggested that in post-war Poland the growth of consumption had been inversely related to the power of the Communist Party; the traditional policy of the communist leadership was to promote the production of capital goods, such as machinery and other industrial equipment, and investment in general. These policies, however, brought about

---

178 Stephen Merl, 'Staat und Konsum in der Zentralverwaltungswirtschaft', in Siegrist, Kaelble and Kocka, *Europäische Konsumgeschichte*, 206–13.
179 Ibid.
180 Árpád Tyekvicska, 'Fridzsider szocializmus' [Refrigerator socialism], in *Beszélő évek, 1957–1968: A Kádár-korszak története. I. rész*, ed. Sándor Révész (Budapest: Stencil Kulturális Alapítvány, 2000), 260–3.
181 Ferenc Kozma, *Jólét szocialista módon* [Prosperity in a socialist way] (Budapest: Kossuth Könyvkiadó, 1979), 99–100, 102.

consumer dissatisfaction – examples of which include the 1970 events in Gdansk, the 1976 strikes in Radom, and the workers' movement in Gdansk in 1980. In each case, the direct cause of the events was a sudden and dramatic increase in consumer prices, and especially in food prices. In 1970, for example, meat prices went up by 18 per cent and cheese prices by 25 per cent; in 1976, meat prices boomed by 69 per cent, sugar prices by 100 per cent and cheese and butter prices by 50 per cent; in 1980, meat prices once again increased, this time by 60 per cent.[182] Overall, periods of weakened communist-party power led to improvements in consumption performance, while the stabilization of communist-party rule led to the renewed onset of the traditional economic policy preferring investments and capital goods. Mieczkowski even suggests that consumption performance was at the heart of social change, and decisively contributed to the long-term transformation of the communist system.[183]

As demonstrated above, Central and Eastern European countries often followed different routes in consumption policy, yet the politicization of consumption was a common characteristic of the communist regimes. The fundamental reason for this was the fact that in each of these countries, the state, by means of nationalization, price regulation and other types of control measures, undertook an all-encompassing responsibility for providing the population with material goods. Hence, citizens widely perceived prices, the supply of goods and other aspects relevant in the context of consumption as factors easily changed by omnipotent politics.

Politics undoubtedly influenced, first and foremost, the distribution of goods. The dominant and officially declared norm was 'to each according to his work'; in other words, workplace performance was the dominant factor – in many respects a contradiction to the principles of egalitarianism. Furthermore, whether the concepts of 'to each according to his work' could actually prevail in practice was not to be taken for granted, since performance could only be measured through the labour market which necessarily had a distorting effect. In addition, as demonstrated in the previous section, certain classes and social groups enjoyed a preferential status, while a person's political merits and position in the hierarchy of power also influenced distribution. Thus, the teaching of social equality was clearly in conflict with the meritocratic doctrine of distribution illustrated above. One area where the principle of social equality did have an impact was income disparities; wide income gaps were unacceptable under the official ideology, and distribution practices served as one of the tools to curb such excesses where possible.

The close links between consumption and politics manifested themselves in other aspects as well. The fact that the communist countries failed to satisfy consumer needs did not prevent their governments from using consumption to legitimize the political aims of the party state. The interweaving of politics and consumption generated conflicts, but it also helped stabilize communist rule, since it was the communist party that would provide all the solutions to the problems concerning consumption, such as pay raises granted to certain groups and measures to improve the supply of goods in certain areas.

Viewing this setup of the system from the perspective of the general population, it is clear that consumption had become a focus for broader political grievances and criticism of the regime for the ordinary citizen in societies where the public sphere and civil society were suppressed, and traditional forms of social and political dissent were disabled. In many ways,

---

182 Piotr Wróbel, *Historical Dictionary of Poland, 1945–1996* (Westport, CT: Greenwood Press, 1998), 72.
183 Bogdan Mieczkowski, 'The Relationship between Changes in Consumption and Politics in Poland', *Soviet Studies* 40 (1978): 262–9.

consumption was a substitute for civic rights and political opposition and became a frequented and greatly politicized subject from the 1950s in Central and Eastern Europe.[184]

While sounding voices of criticism in respect to the 'system' as a whole was out of the question, rude shop assistants and poor-quality overcoats were free game. After the end of Stalinism, the press regularly ran endless commentaries, letters from readers and other articles discussing these types of consumer grievances throughout the region, with the exception of Romania and Albania. Consumption was of great importance to political practice and to the population, since the regimes were far more liable to compromise on this subject than on matters related to political life, such as freedom of the press. In 1981, even a consumer movement (*Federacija Konsumentów*) was launched in Poland, and similar efforts are also seen in Hungary, where a consumer protection magazine was published under the title *Nagyító* (*The Magnifying Glass*).[185] Impediments to higher levels of consumption arose more often from economic than from political restraints.

Consumption created a direct link between economy and politics: in particular, female workers combined their class, consumer and gender identities. Throughout the region, the dominant system was still the traditional division of labour within households – in other words, daily shopping was mostly the responsibility of women. As a result, it was mostly women who regularly had to face queuing and shortages.[186]

In most countries of the region, the fact that, from the early 1960s onward, consumption and increasing the living standard were gradually given more emphasis among the political objectives meant that while the early generations of state socialist societies expressed dissatisfaction in a direct way, later generations voiced their dissent through consumption. As demonstrated by the case of conspicuous consumption, consuming certain products, for example, blue jeans, was often interpreted as a political statement made by the wearer.

Thus, it is claimed that decision makers in these societies did not neglect consumption as much as numerous studies have suggested they did.[187] On the contrary, it emerged as a frequented and highly politicized issue in the 1960s and became visited even more frequently from the 1970s onward. Overall, it can be said that the tensions related to consumption played a definitive role in the demise of communism. However, communist regimes in Central and Eastern Europe failed not simply because of their inability to satisfy consumer needs. Problems like shortage and low levels of consumption can distress any nation state but are in themselves incapable of destroying a system. Rather, the all-encompassing role the communist state assumed in the provision of material goods, with all its inherent conflicts and inconsistencies, produced the collapse.

Conclusions: the dynamics of change and the unity of the region

This study has taken a long-term perspective of major trends in consumption and leisure in twentieth-century Central and Eastern Europe. The main interest has been how consumption in the region evolved in the wider context of the changes taking place in Europe and especially in the western half of the continent, and to what extent unity or divergence can be postulated in the consumption history of Central and Eastern European societies.

---

184 Malgorzata Mazurek and Matthew Hilton, 'Consumerism, Solidarity and Communism: Consumer Protection and the Consumer Movement in Poland,' *Journal of Contemporary History* 42, no. 2 (2007): 316.
185 Ibid., 317.
186 Padraic Kenney, 'The Gender of Resistance in Communist Poland', *American Historical Review* 104 (1999): 399–425.
187 Verdery, *What Was Socialism and What Comes Next*, 25.

Gross domestic product figures in Central and Eastern Europe have multiplied several times during the twentieth century. This undoubtedly affected the level of consumption; however, the transformation of consumption in the twentieth century cannot be adequately described by focusing only on this single factor. A range of further aspects must also be studied, such as the structure of consumption, the qualitative features of consumption and its wider social impacts.

As demonstrated, the level of consumption in Central and Eastern Europe during the interwar period was more or less in line with the relative level of the economic output of the region; in other words, consumption in the region lagged behind Western European consumption levels by just as much as the difference in economic output levels in the two parts of the continent would suggest. In fact, the actual level of consumption in Central and Eastern Europe may have been somewhat higher, in relative terms, for a number of reasons. With the exception of Czechoslovakia, the ratio of capital accumulation was lower than the Western European average; this, combined with the significant external indebtedness accumulated by some countries in the 1920s, partially helped compensate for lower economic output as far as consumption was concerned.

Increased levels of capital formation after the Second World War had exactly the opposite effect. This was a period of investment frenzy, with capital formation crowding out consumption. While in several countries foreign financing continued for a long time to widen the margin for manoeuvre in terms of consumption and investment policy, external indebtedness reached such high levels by the early 1980s that applying for additional foreign loans was no longer a possibility. In fact, increasing debt and interest payments actually started to drain resources available for consumption and, above all, investment in several countries in the region. As a result of these processes, during the decades after the Second World War, the gap between the consumption levels in the region and those in Western Europe actually widened – and by more than the disparity in the per capita gross domestic product would have suggested.

We next studied changes in the structure of consumption. Examining the changes in the ratio between collective consumption and private consumption is one aspect where we could not identify any marked tendencies in twentieth-century Central and Eastern Europe, even in international comparison. After the Second World War – and especially from the 1960s onward, after the expansion of the welfare state in Western Europe – the level of collective consumption in Central and Eastern Europe was essentially on par with the Western European average when welfare transfers are also taken into consideration. We have, however, identified a regional specificity; the share of social benefits in kind – such as access to health care and childcare facilities – was relatively high within overall consumption in Central and Eastern Europe during the post-war decades.

The prominence of various types of goods and services within the structure of household consumption underwent a continuous change in Central and Eastern Europe during the twentieth century, while the direction of transformations mostly resembled that observed in Western Europe. The specificities of the region included, first and foremost, that the portion of expenditure households budgeted for food and beverages, as well as tobacco, remained very high until the end of the century, something that clearly restricted expansion in other categories of consumption.

As important as structural changes may be, if the most significant features of consumption patterns are to be identified, special attention should also be paid to the qualitative features of consumption. Another reason that validates the study of this aspect is that it is in terms of these qualitative features that the gap between Central and Eastern Europe on the one hand, and Western Europe on the other, widens most dynamically from the middle of the century onward, and that the greatest differences between the interwar period and the post-Second

World War period of Central and Eastern Europe can be observed. In other words, the peculiarities of the history of consumption in the centrally controlled economies can best be interpreted through the qualitative features of consumption. New approaches to economic planning with more emphasis on consumer demands and, after 1953 but especially from the 1960s onward, economic reforms achieved much in this respect in several countries, where the availability of goods improved significantly. Nevertheless, shortages in important services and goods, poor product and service quality, and the generally weak position of consumers against producers and traders remained a staple throughout the economic history of the communist regime.

During this period, and especially from the 1960s onward, the most significant similarities between Central and Eastern Europe and the consumer societies of Western Europe, emerged in leisure-time patterns – that is, in the amount of leisure time and how people spent it. In the long term, the most important factor in the transformation of leisure was, in addition to shortening working hours, the more pronounced separation of working time and leisure time. Similar to the western part of the continent, this process was facilitated by the fact that the ratio of self-employed persons quickly dropped after the Second World War, while the number of employees increased mostly due to nationalization and a reduction in the number of people living from agricultural activities. The international trends also presented themselves in how people spent their leisure time; the increasing role of the television must be mentioned above all. Furthermore, the transformation of leisure time also had its unique Central and Eastern European characteristics. Much of the increase in leisure time was actually consumed by working extra hours in the informal or second economy, or overtime hours at the workplace. Another specificity in the transformation of leisure time is that commercialization was less of a driving force than either during the interwar period or in the societies of Western Europe. In contrast, inherent features of the social and economic system of communism – especially the consequences of the shortage economy – and motives of political control were more significant determinants.

Consumer society emerged in the region in the wake of the regime change. During the transformation crisis, the real income of the population decreased significantly, although less so than levels of gross domestic product. After the turn of the millennium, real incomes in most countries returned to the levels seen in the 1980s and then exceeded them. The structural changes in consumption were not limited to the recession period; in fact, they gained momentum after economic growth kicked in, and are clearly reflected in a shift towards Western European consumption patterns. While leisure time did not increase significantly, how it was spent changed substantially through a process of commoditization. The decisive change, however, affected consumer choice; the dramatic improvement seen in this field fully justifies the statement that in the 1990s, consumer society eventually arrived in the Central and Eastern European region.

This study has covered the most important areas of the twentieth-century consumption history of Central and Eastern Europe. However, such a thematic approach has necessarily pushed certain important aspects into the background. One of these is the dynamics of the changes taking place in the region. We have arrived at a number of conclusions concerning the differences and similarities between the developmental trajectories of certain societies in the region, but it seems equally justified also to address, as a topic in its own right, the internal unity of the region. Finally, another issue worthy of our attention is establishing which of the available conceptual frameworks have proven most plausible in writing the consumption history of the region.

One may observe several asynchronies in the twentieth-century history of Central and Eastern Europe, both in specific areas of consumption and among societies. As far as the whole period is concerned, the most striking trend is the radical increase in consumption. This trend, however, was interrupted on several occasions, most significantly by wars, economic shocks and political emergencies. While the First and Second World Wars and the Great Depression – the upheavals that had a particularly great impact on consumption during the first half of the century – also affected all other countries of the continent, the crises emerging during the second half of the twentieth century with a similar impact on consumption were mostly specific to the region under review. In wider Western Europe, the economic boom of the post-war era resulted in an uninterrupted upward trend in consumption levels that lasted for several decades; even when economic growth slowed down in the 1970s, it did not entail any significant drop in consumption in any of those countries. However, the societies of the Central and Eastern European region underwent more radical political transformations and even political crises during the decades following the Second World War; these events often had a negative impact on consumption for varying periods of time. Eloquent examples could be Poland in the 1980s and Yugoslavia in the 1980s and 1990s. In addition, even in the absence of any major political shocks, consumption patterns of the general population could be radically affected in most countries of the region simply by economic policy measures. Such restrictive consumption policies were common in the region during the early and mid-1950s, but in certain countries they tended to return to centre stage, such as in Romania during the 1980s. The very period of the regime change also resulted in a significant drop in consumption in almost every country, even though in the long term, the market economy led to an expansion in consumption opportunities for the vast majority of the region's population. These changes not only affected the level of consumption, but also other features such as the selection and quality of goods and services, that is, the very nature of the consumption regimes. Thus, in a wider European comparison, the dynamics of consumption, as well as the characteristics of the consumption regimes, were highly volatile throughout the region during the twentieth century.

The aforementioned wars and crises had a major impact on the transformation of consumption. The emergence of the planned economy can also be seen as a turning point, even though its significance is somewhat diminished by the mere fact that the consumption-related austerity measures often associated with the planned economy had already been present during the war and during the post-war reconstruction period. A less straightforward question to answer is whether there have been any other significant trend disruptions in the twentieth-century consumption history of the region in addition to these obvious ruptures.

Most historians emphasize a break in the region around the early 1960s, arguing that from this point on socialist countries abandoned their ideas about following a distinct 'socialist' consumption regime and began to emulate Western patterns. However, even if we accept that the emergence of the planned economy was a turning point, this study still emphasizes continuity after the end of Stalinism, a period ending between 1953 and the end of the 1950s, depending on the country. This period was when the institutional frameworks that shaped consumption policy in the countries of the region for several decades to come, first emerged. This early shift also surfaced at the discursive level; commitments to boost consumption and improve the selection of consumer goods for workers had already appeared in most of the Central and Eastern European countries at some point in the early or mid-1950s.

Nevertheless, consumer experience and behaviour greatly changed during the following decades; from spending on elementary survival-needs, to spending with the aim of realizing life-needs. In the meantime, a widening gap emerged between consumer aspirations and actual consumption possibilities, which resulted in mounting discontent. First and foremost, this was the result of growing consumer aspirations. The promises made by the Central and Eastern European regimes concerning the standard of living undoubtedly played a crucial role in this process, even though those promises may not have necessarily implied an explicit commitment to any specific increase in actual consumption. Public references to a bright future and to socialism as a superior social system became an everyday routine that was in itself sufficient in the long term to raise the working-class expectations concerning their own standards of living. From the 1960s onward, the development of mass communication and tourism made it ever clearer that the communist regimes lagged behind Western European societies in terms of meeting consumer needs. The generations entering young adulthood as of the 1960s became especially receptive to Western consumer culture.

The regime change was yet another disruption in the consumption history of the region. Market economies emerged in the region, while the political systems underwent a process of democratization and opening. The structure of consumption underwent a dynamic transformation process; the selection of goods and the range of possible consumer options widened dramatically. A change in the role played by consumption policy was also conspicuously present, as politics necessarily lost much of its power to directly shape the level and nature of consumption. However, the value orientations of the East Central European population emerging in the communist era greatly influenced the political process and social development after the regime change. First of all, growing consumer aspirations had a great impact on political life in the post-communist era. Several characteristics of post-communist societies, such as the low level of subjective well-being, low political participation and the volatility of the party systems, can be attributed to the highly materialistic and consumption-centred value preferences that emerged during the post-war decades as well as to the consequently booming consumer aspirations, which in the short term were impossible to satisfy with any policy.

The countries of the region were fairly diverse in terms of their economic and political systems during the first decades of the twentieth century. Economically, Czechoslovakia was much more advanced during the interwar period than Albania, Romania or even Poland, and these differences were also reflected in other factors having a bearing on consumption, such as the export or import of capital. During the period following the Second World War, the differences in economic development and in the implementation of reforms undoubtedly contributed to the significant disparities in consumer experience in the various Central and Eastern European countries, despite the existence of obvious similarities in their political and economic regimes. From the mid-1960s onward, Yugoslavia adopted a trade policy that was much more open than that of the other communist countries, which certainly helped improve consumer opportunities in the country. Hungary implemented deep economic reforms in 1968, as a result of which, the availability of consumer goods improved. In sharp contrast, Romania started to pay off its external debt at an unprecedented speed during the 1980s, paying back nearly everything by 1989. However, this led to massive shortages in the supply of electricity, heating, health services, food and a wide range of industrial products.

Despite the evident divergences, the similarities in the consumption history of the region still predominate. First, the economy of shortage represented insurmountable barriers to consumption all over the region. Another important commonality is that consumption and politics were closely intertwined in each of these countries. In Western Europe, mass consumption nurtured a relatively passive population, and growing consumption had a stabilizing effect on the political process. In the Central and Eastern European communist systems, as suggested earlier, consumption became a heavily politicized phenomenon from the early 1950s onward, which often contributed to social and political instability. Finally, as demonstrated, the growing gap between consumer aspirations and consumption realities has become palpable everywhere in the region. Along with the factors mentioned above, the resulting tensions created massive political potential by the 1980s.

The consumption history of the first half of the century in Central and Eastern Europe has received little attention and has scarcely generated controversy in the literature covering the period. The reason for this is that while – with the sole exception of Czechoslovakia – the level of consumption was low when compared across Europe, and the consumption patterns of the region's societies were not fundamentally different from those of the other countries. For example, regarding product range and the availability of products, the region was fairly similar to Western Europe in the interwar period. Differences were caused mainly by lower living standards, since the latter largely determined the range of the products sold.

Many more diverging interpretations are encountered concerning the period after the Second World War. The central problem is undoubtedly the relationship between the advancing consumer societies of Western Europe and the consumption regimes existing in Central and Eastern Europe. From the 1960s onward, the standard of living in the region started to grow much more dynamically than before; the range of consumer products became wider and more diverse; and consumer aspirations became more palpably manifest. Based on these and similar phenomena, Western European journalism at the time – and, somewhat later, scholarly literature – started proposing the idea that certain Central and Eastern European countries had become 'socialist consumer societies'. In this context, the most popular example was Hungary, a country often also described with the term 'goulash communism'. These ideas implied the existence of a peculiar Hungarian model that made higher levels of consumption available to the population.

Based solely on the realities of Central and Eastern Europe, it is difficult to determine whether the processes that started in the region – or in any of its countries – from the 1960s onward should be interpreted as the gradual expansion of consumer choice or, taking it one significant step further, as the emergence of 'consumer socialism'. The researcher is better positioned to judge this by relying on comparisons. As demonstrated, after the Second World War some parallel trends did indeed exist between Central and Eastern Europe on the one hand, and Western Europe on the other hand. These commonalities included, for example, the significant increase in the level of consumption and the diffusion of certain consumer durables. Although some of the quoted voices fearing overconsumption under a shortage economy may seem bizarre, it is difficult to deny that a certain 'consumption-oriented' behaviour did indeed emerge and became rather common even in Central and Eastern Europe during the decades of communism. However, the nature of this phenomenon was distinct, and so were the reasons behind it. On the one hand, because of the general shortage of supply, the population had to invest much time and mental energy in purchasing goods; as a result, the consumption of difficult-to-obtain goods undoubtedly appreciated in value. On the other hand, one's leisure time – spent consuming either alone or with family – became highly attractive, as most public activities lost their credibility and appeal as a result of being subject to strong ideological control. Finally, consumption – and especially the possession of leading brands of Western products – often demonstrated a certain detachment from official ideology, whereby it also served as a new and peculiar element of social identity.

Overall, however, Central and Eastern Europe was not only falling behind, but was actually drifting further away from the consumer societies of Western Europe in almost every respect of consumption during state socialism. These disparities manifested themselves not only in diverging levels of consumption, but also pronouncedly in the structure of consumption, not to mention the dramatic differences in the quality of consumption. Shortage in vital services and goods as well as the weak position of consumers persisted throughout the period, albeit with significant differences among the individual countries. The scarcity of goods and services was a determining factor in the behaviour of economic actors, something we have seen reflected also in consumption; for causes that cannot be discussed here, shortage combined with a change in moral standards, leading with mutual reinforcement to the emergence of certain phenomena in communist Central and Eastern Europe that were unparalleled in Western Europe. These included the emergence and strengthening of the informal sector with phenomena like the black market; bribery became rampant in the market of goods and services, although, once again, the extent and nature of corruption also varied. The prominent role assumed by the black market and institutionalized corruption in the sectors of trade and services was a specific feature of the economic and social development in Central and Eastern Europe after the Second World War, with long-term consequences. These trends were palpable in more or less every country of the region; thus, it is unjustifiable to speak about any special Hungarian or other national model, let alone to postulate a system of 'consumer socialism' to mirror the consumer societies of the West. Such a conceptual experiment only causes confusion, as it masks fundamental differences in consumption culture between the Western European societies and the countries of Central and Eastern Europe during the post-war decades.

Based on the above considerations, shortage economy is a plausible concept when approaching consumption in post-war Central and Eastern Europe, as it takes into account the wider economic context while also addressing the everyday experience of the region's population.

This concept has been strongly criticized of late in the literature on Central and Eastern European consumption history.[188] It has been argued that shortage-oriented interpretations simplify the consumption history of the communist systems. Ina Merkel argued, for example, that luxury and poverty did not exist in themselves but instead were relative concepts whose meaning depended on the historical context. The meanings of shortage and luxury depend on what is considered normal under given historical circumstances.[189]

It is true that the consumption reality of the communist systems under review cannot be described solely by using the concept of shortage. Even in these societies there existed various layers of consumption; there was luxury, and consumption carried various 'meanings'. However, shortage was never accepted as the norm in Central and Eastern Europe either by the population or by politics, except during years of post-war reconstruction. Moreover, it was primarily shortage that determined the meanings of consumption. It was shortage that turned certain forms of consumption into conspicuous consumption in this region alone, as well as into highly politicized consumption and communication about consumption. Therefore, it was shortage that offered itself as the main specificity of the region's consumption history after the Second World War and as the major component of the region's internal unity. In many respects, this internal unity had an overbearing significance beyond consumption, not only because shortage was a fundamental functional characteristic of the economy in all the countries, with further social and political consequences, but also because it was the daily experience of the entire population of the region. Besides the resemblance of the political systems – particularly the lack of civic and political rights in communist Central and Eastern Europe – the similarities in the consumption regimes and consumer experiences constituted the most significant factor of homogenization at play in the region in this era.

---

188 Fehervary, 'Goods and States', 427–8.
189 Ina Merkel, 'Luxury in Socialism: An Absurd Proposition?' in *Pleasures in Socialism: Leisure and Luxury in the Eastern Bloc*, eds David Crowley and Susan E. Reid (Evanston, IL: Northwestern University Press, 2010), 53–4; Merkel, 'Consumer Culture in the GDR', 283–4.

Further reading

Ambrosius, Gerold, and William H. Hubbard. *A Social and Economic History of Twentieth-Century Europe* (Cambridge, MA: Harvard University Press, 1989).
Andorka, Rudolf, Tamás Kolosi, and György Vukovich, eds. *Social Report* (Budapest: Tárki, 1992).
Andrusz, Gregory, Michael Harloe, and Iván Szelényi, eds. *Cities After Socialism: Urban and Regional Change and Conflict in Post-Socialist Societies* (Oxford: Blackwell, 1996).
Atkinson, Anthony B. *The Changing Distribution of Earnings in OECD countries* (Oxford: Oxford University Press, 2008).
Atkinson, Anthony B., and Francois Bourguignon, eds. *Handbook of Income Distribution*, vol. 1 (Amsterdam: Elsevier, 2000).
Baudet, H., and M. Bogucka, eds. *Types of Consumption, Traditional and Modern* (Budapest: Akadémiai Kiadó, 1982).
Blecking, Diethelm, ed. *Die slawische Sokolbewegung: Beiträge zur Geschichte von Sport und Nationalismus in Osteuropa* (Dortmund: Forschungsstelle Ostmitteleuropa, 1991).
Boh, Katja, et al., eds. *Changing Patterns of European Family Life* (London: Routledge, 1989).
Borodziej, Włodzimierz, Jerzy Kochanowski, and Joachim von Puttkamer, eds. *'Schleichwege': Inoffizielle Begegnungen sozialistischer Staatsbürger zwischen 1956 und 1989* (Köln: Böhlau, 2010).
Bosch, Gerhard, Peter Dawkins, and Francois Michon, eds. *Times are Changing: Working Time in 14 Industrialized Countries* (Geneva: ILO, 1993).
Bren, Paulina, and Mary Neuburger, eds. *Communism Unwrapped: Consumption in Cold War Eastern Europe* (Oxford: Oxford University Press, 2012).
Broadberry, Stephen, and Mark Harrison, eds. *The Economics of World War I* (Cambridge: Cambridge University Press, 2005).
Broadberry, Stephen, and Kevin H. O'Rourke, eds. *The Cambridge Economic History of Modern Europe, vol. 2, 1870 to the Present* (Cambridge: Cambridge University Press, 2010).
Cipolla, Carlo M., ed. *The Fontana Economic History of Europe: The Twentieth Century, Part One* (Glasgow: Collins/Fontana Books, 1976).
Connor, Walter D. *Socialism, Politics, and Equality: Hierarchy and Change in Eastern Europe and the USSR* (New York: Columbia University Press, 1979).
Cross, Gary C. *An All-Consuming Century: Why Commercialism Won in Modern America* (New York: Columbia University Press, 2000).
Crowley, David, and Susan E. Reid, eds. *Pleasures in Socialism: Leisure and Luxury in the Eastern Bloc* (Evanston, IL: Northwestern University Press, 2010).
Crowley, David, and Susan Emily Reid, eds. *Socialist Spaces: Sites of Everyday Life in the Eastern Bloc* (Oxford: Berg, 2002).
Daunton, Martin, and Matthew Hilton, eds. *The Politics of Consumption: Material Culture and Citizenship in Europe and America* (New York: Berg, 2001).
de Grazia, Victoria. *Irresistible Empire: America's Advance Through Twentieth-Century Europe* (Cambridge, MA: Belknap Press, 2005).
de Grazia, Victoria, and Ellen Furlough, eds. *The Sex of Things: Gender and Consumption in Historical Perspective* (Berkeley, CA: University of California Press, 1996).
Digby, Anne, and Charles Feinstein, eds. *New Directions in Economic and Social History* (Chicago, IL: Lyceum Books, 1989).
Fischer, Wolfram, and Friedrich Vittinghoff, eds. *Handbuch der europäischen Wirtschafts- und Sozialgeschichte*, vol. 6 (Stuttgart: Klett-Cotta, 1987).
Fischer, Wolfram, ed. *Lebensstandard und Wirtschaftssysteme* (Frankfurt a.M.: Fritz Knapp Verlag, 1995).
Flora, Peter, and Arnold J. Heidenheimer, eds. *The Development of Welfare States in Europe and America* (New Brunswick, NJ: Transaction, 1981).
Grandits, Hannes, and Karin Taylor, eds. *Yugoslavia's Sunny Side: A History of Tourism in Socialism (1950s–1960s)* (Budapest: CEU Press, 2010).
Hall, Derek R. *Tourism and Economic Development in Eastern Europe and the Soviet Union* (London: Belhaven Press, 1991).
Harrison, Bennett, and Barry Bluestone. *The Great U-Turn* (New York: Basic Books, 1988).
Haupt, Heinz-Gerhard. *Konsum und Handel: Europa im 19. und 20. Jahrhundert* (Göttingen: Vandenhoeck, 2002).

Haupt, Heinz-Gerhard, and Claudius Torp, eds. *Die Konsumgesellschaft in Deutschland, 1890–1990* (Frankfurt a.M.: Campus Verlag, 2009).
Hellmann, Kai-Uwe, and Guido Zurstiege, eds. *Räume des Konsums: Über den Funktionswandel von Räumlichkeit im Zeitalter des Konsumismus* (Wiesbaden: VS Verlag für Sozialwissenschaften, 2008).
Horne, John, ed. *A Companion to World War I* (London: Routledge, 2010).
Hradil, Stefan, and Stefan Immerfall, eds. *Die westeuropäischen Gesellschaften im Vergleich* (Opladen: Leske und Budrich, 1997).
Imre, Anikó, ed. *A Companion to Eastern European Cinemas* (Oxford: John Wiley & Sons, 2012).
Inglehart, Ronald. *Culture Shift in Advanced Industrial Society* (Princeton, NJ: Princeton University Press, 1990).
Inglehart, Ronald, Miguel Basanez, and Alejandro Romero. *Human Values and Beliefs: A Cross-Cultural Sourcebook* (Ann Arbor, MI: University of Michigan Press, 1998).
Janos, Andrew C. *East Central Europe in the Modern World: The Politics of the Borderlands from Pre- to Postcommunism* (Stanford, CA: Stanford University Press, 2000).
Kaelble, Hartmut, and Mark Thomas, eds. *Income Distribution in Historical Perspective* (Cambridge: Cambridge University Press–Maison des Sciences de l'Homme, 1991).
Kaser, M.C., ed. *The Economic History of Eastern Europe, 1919–1975*, vol. 3 (Oxford: Clarendon, 1986).
Kaser, M.C., and E.A. Radice, eds. *The Economic History of Eastern Europe, 1919–1975*, vol. 1 (Oxford: Clarendon Press, 1985).
Kissoudi, Penelope. *The Balkan Games and Balkan Politics in the Interwar Years 1929–39: Politicians in Pursuit of Peace* (London: Routledge, 2013).
Kochanowski, Jerzy. *Jenseits der Planwirtschaft: Der Schwarzmarkt in Polen, 1944–1989* (Göttingen: Wallstein Verlag, 2013).
Komlos, John. *Nutrition and Economic Development in the Eighteenth-Century Habsburg Monarchy: An Anthropometric History* (Princeton, NJ: Princeton University Press, 1989).
Kornai, János. *Economics of Shortage* (Amsterdam: North-Holland, 1979).
Kornai, János. *The Socialist System: The Political Economy of Communism* (Princeton, NJ: Princeton University Press, 1992).
Kornai, János. *Paying the Bill for Goulash-Communism* (Boulder, CO: Atlantic Research and Publications, 2000).
Lamla, Jörn, and Sighard Neckel, eds. *Politisierter Konsum – konsumierte Politik* (Wiesbaden: VS Verlag für Sozialwissenschaften, 2006).
Lane, David, and George Kolankiewicz, eds. *Social Groups in Polish Society* (London: Macmillan, 1973).
Maddison, Angus. *The World Economy: Historical Statistics* (Paris: OECD, 2003).
Merkel, Ina. *Utopie und Bedürfnis: Die Geschichte der Konsumkultur in der DDR* (Köln: Böhlau, 1999).
Noam, Eli. *Television in Europe* (New York: Oxford University Press, 1991).
Oddy, Derek J., Peter J. Atkins, and Virginie Amilien, eds. *The Rise of Obesity in Europe: A Twentieth Century Food History* (Farnham: Ashgate, 2009).
Paddison, Ronan, ed. *Handbook of Urban Studies* (London: Sage, 2001).
Patterson, Patrick Hyder. *Bought and Sold: Living and Losing the Good Life in Socialist Yugoslavia* (Ithaca, NY: Cornell University Press, 2011).
Rudmin, Floyd W., ed. *To Have Possessions: A Handbook of Ownership and Property* (Corte Madera, CA: Select Press, 1991).
Schrettl, Wolfram. 'Consumption, Effort, and Growth in Soviet-Type Economies: A Theoretical Analysis' (PhD diss., Boston University Graduate School, 1982).
Siegelbaum, Lewis H., ed. *The Socialist Car: Automobility in the Eastern Bloc* (Ithaca, NY: Cornell University Press, 2011).
Siegrist, Hannes, Hartmut Kaelble, and Jürgen Kocka, eds. *Europäische Konsumgeschichte: Zur Gesellschafts- und Kulturgeschichte des Konsums (18. bis 20. Jahrhundert)* (Frankfurt a.M: Campus Verlag, 1997).
Smelser, Neil J., and Paul B. Baltes, eds. *International Encyclopedia of the Social and Behavioral Sciences*, vol. 4 (Amsterdam: Elsevier, 2001).
Soper, Kate, and Frank Trentmann, eds. *Citizenship and Consumption* (Houndmills: Palgrave-Macmillan, 2008).
Stearns, Peter N. *Consumerism in World History: The Global Transformation of Desire* (London: Routledge, 2001a).
Stearns, Peter N., ed. *Encyclopedia of European Social History*, vol. 5 (New York: Scribner, 2001b).
Stearns, Peter N., ed. *Encyclopedia of European Social History*, vol. 4 (New York: Scribner, 2001c).

Strasser, Susan, Charles McGovern, and Matthias Judt, eds. *Getting and Spending: European and American Consumer Societies in the Twentieth Century* (Cambridge: Cambridge University Press, 1998).

Szalai, Alexander, ed. *The Use of Time* (The Hague: Mouton, 1972).

Ther, Philipp. *Europe since 1989: A History* (Princeton, NJ: Princeton University Press, 2016).

Therborn, Göran. *European Modernity and Beyond: The Trajectories of European Societies, 1945–2000* (London: Sage, 1995).

Tomka, Béla. *A Social History of Twentieth-Century Europe* (London: Routledge, 2013).

Trentmann, Frank, ed. *The Making of the Consumer: Knowledge, Power and Identity in the Modern World* (Oxford: Berg, 2006).

Trentmann, Frank, ed. *The Oxford Handbook of the History of Consumption* (Oxford: Oxford University Press, 2012).

Verdery, Katherine. *What Was Socialism and What Comes Next?* (Princeton, NJ: Princeton University Press, 1996).

Walle, D. van de, and K. Nead, eds. *Public Spending and the Poor* (Baltimore, MD: John Hopkins University Press, 1995).

Williams, Allan M., and Vladimir Baláž. *Tourism in Transition: Economic Change in Central Europe* (London: I.B. Tauris Publishers, 2000).

Winter, Jay, and Jean-Louis Robert, eds. *Capital Cities at War: Paris, London, Berlin 1914–1919*, vol. 1 (Cambridge: Cambridge University Press, 1997).

Zweiniger-Bargielowska, Ina, Rachel Duffet, and Alain Droudard, eds. *Food and War in Twentieth Century Europe* (Farnham: Ashgate, 2011).

INDEX

Acemoğlu, Daron 314
Adelman, Irma 313
Aldcroft, Derek H. 315
Andorka, Rudolf 69, 79, 303

Bairoch, Paul 317, **325**, 372, 373n272
Balcerowicz, Leszek 347
Baran, Paul A. 313
Bárány, Tamás 53
Barany, Zoltan 244
Baťa, Tomáš 31
Batinić, Jelena 210
Bauer, Peter Thomas 313
Becker, Gary 354
Benz, Carl 153
Berend, Ivan T. 9, 315, 341, 345, 346n148, 371
Bethlen, István 327
Bismarck, Otto von 27, 139
Blau, Eva 25
Bordo, Michael 374
Borgos, Anna 226
Brătianu, Ion 44
Bujak, Franciszek 39, 40
Bunce, Valerie 370
Burchardt, Jeremy 13

Calotescu, Virgil 51
Campbell, Colin 385
Canetti, Elias 6
Carol I, King of Romania 44
Castells, Manuel 3
Castles, Stephen 255
Ceaușescu, Elena 201, 203
Ceaușescu, Nicolae 121, 178, 185, 208, 219, 222–3, 263, 344, 375n284
Comenius, Jan Amos 116

Copernicus, Nicolaus 44
Cornwall, Mark 225
Crafts, Nicholas 317, 365
Curie, Marie Skłodowska 187

Dabčević-Kučar, Savka 200
Dąbrowski, Jan 30
Daimler, Gottlieb 153
Dalos, György 173
de Hirsch, Maurice 138
de la Escosura, Leandro Prados 317, 319, 357
Dimitrov, Georgi 57
Djilas, Milovan 67, 367
Domański, Henryk 59
Drucki-Lubecki, Prince Władysław 154
Dudová, Radka 254
Durkheim, Émile 313

Eichengreen, Barry 345
Eminescu, Mihail 6
Estreicher, Karol 50
Evans, Peter 360, 365

Fejtö, Ferenc 27
Franz Ferdinand, Archduke of Austria 154
Fidelis, Małgorzata 193–4, 197, 212
Filtzer, Donald 364
Flandrin, Jean-Louis 269
Földvari, Peter 354
Forman, Miloš 52
Freund, Kurt 226–7
Friedrich Wilhelm IV, King of Prussia 140
Fulbrook, Mary 97, 99

Galbraith, John Kenneth 55
Bibescu, Prince George III Valentin 154

Index

Gerschenkron, Alexander 313–14, 365
Gheorghiu-Dej, Gheorghe 47
Giza-Poleszcuk, Anna 197
Gorbachev, Mikhail 346
Gottwald, Klement 37, 107
Goven, Joanna 192
Grabski, Władysław 327
Gross, Jan Tomasz 32

Hajnal, John 269–70, 309
Haller, Max 70
Hammel, Eugene 285
Haney, Lynne 213
Haq, Mahbub ul 316
Haussmann, Georges-Eugène 21–2
Havel, Václav 202
Havelková, Hana 213
Henlein, Konrad 225
Herzog, Dagmar 210
Hirschfeld, Magnus 206
Hitler, Adolf 28, 334
Hlinka, Andrej 199
Honecker, Margot 201
Horváth, Sándor 97
Hugonnai, Vilma 186

Janos, Andrew C. 67, 115
Janowski, Maciej 2, 22–3
Jarosz, Dariusz 38, 107
Johnson, Janet Elise 215
Jowitt, Ken 370

Kádár, János 56
Kalecki, Michał 313
Karadžić, Vuk Stefanović 6
Kecková, Bohuslava 186
Kenney, Padraic 97
Kerbeny, Károly 224
Khrushchev, Nikita 156–7, 193
Kideckel, David 100
Klement, Václav 155
Kligman, Gail 108, 192, 218
Kogan, Irena 124
Kollontai, Alexandra 208
Kolosi, Tamás 70
Kornai, János 37, 408, 415
Kovács, Maria 198
Krumins, Juris 250
Kula, Witold 315
Kurczak, Teofil 1, 4–5, 12–13, 21, 51

Landry, Adolph 239
Laslett, Peter 269, 280, 280n136
Le Corbusier (Charles-Édouard Jeanneret-Gris) 31
Le Normand, Brigitte 159
Lebow, Katherine 52, 194
Leder, Andrzej 5

Leka, Crown Prince of Albania 264
Lenin, Vladimir 208
Leo XIII, Pope 295
Lipset, Seymour Martin 314
List, Friedrich 324
Love, Joseph 313
Łuczewski, Michał 61

Maddison, Angus **242**, 317, **318**, 318n31, 341
Małowist, Marian 314–15
Mann, Thomas 260
Manoilescu, Mihail 313–14
Márai, Sándor 23
Marinescu, Dimitrie 2
Marinetti, Filippo Tommaso 154
Marody, Mira 197
Masaryk, Tomáš Garrigue 116
Maxwell, Alexander 204
Merkel, Ina 440
Meštrović, Ivan 29, 44
Mianowski, Józef 1
Michael I, King of Romania 264
Mickiewicz, Adam 44
Mieczkowski, Bogdan 432–33
Mill, John Stuart 197
Miller, Mark 255
Mincu, Ion 25
Morazé, Charles 4
Morewood, Steven 315
Mussolini, Benito 31, 334

Nałkowski, Wacław 10, 23
Németh, László 44
Nötel, Rudolf 375

Offen, Karen 199
Olsen, Donald J. 21
Ortega y Gasset, José 32
Ossowski, Stanisław 70

Pach, Zsigmond Pál 315
Parsons, Talcott 314
Pâslaru, Margareta 173
Pauker, Ana 200
Penn, Shana 201–2
Perović, Latinka 200
Persson, Karl Gunnar 341
Pešić, Branko 45
Petrescu, Dragoş 93
Pittaway, Mark 97
Planinc, Milka 200
Polakowski, Michal 305
Pollak, Michael 21
Polonski, Antony 94
Poniatowski, Prince Józef 44
Prebisch, Raúl 314
Prunskienė, Kazimira 203

Index

Radetzky von Radetz, Josef Wenzel 28
Radice, Edward Albert 351
Ránki, György 315
Rebreanu, Liviu 28
Redfield, Robert 20n54
Reisz, Robert D. 356
Reymont, Władysław 8
Róbert, Péter 70
Robinson, James 314
Robinson, Jean C. 215
Rockoff, Hugh 374
Rosenstein-Rodan, Paul 313
Rostow, Walt 314
Rutha, Heinz 225

Sadoveanu, Mihail 36
Sarkozy, Nicolas 316
Schild, Gerhard 98
Schindler-Wisten, Petra 202
Schultz, Theodore 354
Schwartz, Michael 260
Schwarzenberg, Prince Karel 264
Schwormstädt, Felix 154
Scott, Sir Gilbert 23
Sen, Amartya 316, 364
Simeon II, Tsar of Bulgaria 264
Simionescu, Mircea H. 50
Simmel, Georg 21
Singer, Hans 314
Smetona, Antanas 199
Smith, Adam 354
Snyder, Timothy xxi, 34, 335
Spengler, Oswald 9–10, 29
Stakhanov, Alexey Grigoryevich 97
Stalin, Joseph 44, 156–7, 185, 206, 208, 210, 217, 222, 264, 336, 338–40, 345, 431
Stanoeva, Elitza 25
Stănoiu, Damian 30
Stauter-Halsted, Keely 205
Stawiński, Jerzy S. 51
Steindl, Imre 22
Stloukal, Libor 219
Stock, Manfred 356

Stolypin, Pyotr Arkadyevich 106
Strousberg, Bethel Henry 137
Suchocka, Hanna 203
Sundhaussen, Holm 65, 75, 79, 256
Surmacka, Irena 20
Švejda, Jiří 54
Szelényi, Iván 66–7, 81, 83, 409
Szelewa, Dorota 305

Teodoroiu, Ecaterina 209
Therborn, Göran 288, 292, 417
Thomson, Warren 239
Todorova, Maria 13
Toniolo, Gianni 365
Topolski, Jerzy 315
Tupolev, Andrey 168
Turnock, David 315, 353

Uniłowski, Zygmunt 30
Usackis, Uldis 250
Uslaner, Eric M. 368

Váci, Mihály 432
van de Velde, Theodoor 206
van Leeuwen, Bas 354
van Zanden, Jan Luiten 317
Verdery, Katherine 108, 178, 192, 345
Vīķe-Freiberga, Vaira 203
Vonyó, Tamás 341

Walentynowicz, Anna 201
Wallerstein, Immanuel 314
Weber, Max 66–7, 88, 313
Wicha, Władysław 45
Wierzbicki, Zbigniew T. 39–40
Wilhelm II, German Emperor 154
Williamson, Jeffrey 355
Wolicka, Stefania 186

Zagorski, Jerzy 36
Živkovova, Ludmila 201
Zubkova, Elena 36